ABORTION: LAW,
CHOICE AND MORALITY

ABORTION: LAW, CHOICE AND MORALITY

DANIEL CALLAHAN

The Macmillan Company, New York, New York

COLLIER-MACMILLAN LTD., LONDON

The Macmillan Company
866 Third Avenue, New York, N.Y. 10022
Collier-Macmillan Canada Ltd., Toronto, Ontario

Library of Congress Catalog Card Number: 78-99788

Abortion: Law, Choice and Morality is also published in a hardcover edition by The Macmillan Company.

FIRST MACMILLAN PAPERBACKS EDITION 1972

Printed in the United States of America

Daniel Berrigan & *Philip Berrigan*

WHO KNOW WHAT IT IS

TO WRESTLE IN THE ARENA

OF LAW AND CONSCIENCE

Elizabeth Bartelme

A FRIEND OF THE BERRIGANS,

MY FRIEND,

AND A SPLENDID EDITOR

Contents

Tables

Preface

I T I S M A N D A T O R Y for an author to thank those who assisted him. It is also, in the instance of this book, a great pleasure to do so. I learned as much from the letters and conversations of the many people I came in contact with during the course of my research as I did through the books and articles I read. They prodded me to think more carefully and to probe more deeply. In many cases, they read my drafts and provided me with penetrating and detailed criticism. They suggested the names of people I should talk with, of material I should read, of places I should go. When I traveled, they made contacts for me, arranged appointments and smoothed my way. I did not always take the advice I was given— and thus any errors of fact, any omissions and any mistakes of judgment are my own—but I usually did. I cannot conceive how this book could have been written without all the help I received. I shudder to think what it would have been without it.

There is a danger that I will omit names here, but I would especially like to thank the following. My research assistants usually bore the heat of the day, and, as they can testify, some of the work required for a book of this kind can only be likened to stoop labor: the seeking out and checking of obscure references (particularly of journal articles, which always seem to be "at the bindery"), the search for and verification of statistics (an aggravating business where abortion data are concerned), the ever-necessary correction of errors and corrections of the corrections of errors. But they did far more than that. They engrossed themselves in the subject, thought about it and gave me the benefit of their intelligence. Among them were Dr. Charles McGrath, Daniel Armstrong, Raymond Bronk and M.T.A. Mrs. Oona Sullivan saw me through the final year, the hardest of all. Her diligence, her mind, her thoroughness and her patience are extraordinary. Her work on the tables and her efforts to weigh and test, by lengthy research, every line in Chapter 8, "Patterns and Probabilities," were special contributions.

The librarians and staff at two libraries were particularly helpful. Those at the library of the New York Academy of Medicine, especially Miss Corcoran in the Periodicals Room, lent able assistance. The Reverend Robert O'Connor and Dr. Richard Braden of the library of St. John's Seminary, Dunwoodie, New York, provided guidance through its excellent theological holdings. Mrs. Taeko Clear proved a fine translator of Japanese material. Mrs. Midge Riggs, Mrs. Patricia Klotzman and Mrs. Rosemary Mahoney did most of the typing, and well indeed.

Frederick S. Jaffe, Vice-President of Planned Parenthood-World Population, and Dr. William V. D'Antonio, of the Department of Sociology at the University of Notre Dame, provided me with some highly useful counsel as the book was just getting under way. Two of my colleagues at the Institute of Society, Ethics and the Life Sciences, Dr. Rudolph Ehrensing and Dr. Leon Kass, read a number of the chapters and helped me to make them better. Miss Edith Adams of the United Nations Secretariat staff assisted wonderfully in making appointments with officials and staff members at the United Nations. Through a number of letters, Father Enda McDonagh gave me the benefit of his thinking. Dr. Jon Peter Wieselgren, of the Swedish Committee on International Health Relations, was a great help in arranging meetings with Swedish abortion authorities. James Colligan worked exceedingly hard in Tokyo to set up a well-coordinated schedule of interviews and conferences for me in Japan. Dr. Anna L. Southam of the Ford Foundation provided me with a fine list of suggestions about specialists to talk with in India and Latin America. Dr. Christopher Tietze did the same for Japan, Sweden, Denmark and Eastern Europe.

A number of people provided me with the benefit of their knowledge and critical intelligence by carefully reading and extensively commenting upon draft chapters or sections. In addition to Dr. Ehrensing, Mrs. Mildred Beck, Chief of the Research Support Section, Center for Epidemiologic Studies, National Institutes of Health, gave me an acute reading of the psychiatric chapter. Dr. Carl W. Tyler, together with some of his colleagues at the National Communicable Disease Center in Atlanta, Georgia, examined the chapter on fetal indications and made many helpful comments. Dr. Howard Mitchell of the Center for Health Sciences at the University of California, Los Angeles, illuminated my understanding of abortion attitudes and practices in India. Dr. Michael Zeik provided me with considerable material and insights on abortion in Far Eastern religion. Dr. Henry P. David, of the International Research Institute, Dr. Malcolm Potts, Medical Secretary of the International Planned Parenthood Federation in London, Dr. Anton Cernoch, of Prague, and Dr. Imre Hirschler, of Budapest, all read either the whole or parts of the section on Eastern Europe, supplying me with a number of useful details, corrections and interpretations. Dr. Thomas L. Hayes, of the Lawrence Radiation Laboratory at the University of California, Berkeley, Dr. Robert Francoeur of the Biology Department of Fairleigh Dickinson University, Dr. Edward Manier, of the Philosophy Department at the University of Notre Dame, and Dr. Hans Jonas, of the Philosophy Department at the New School for Social Research, forced me—by their probing remarks—to rewrite once and then rewrite again the philosophical and biological chapters. I am in Dr. Christopher Tietze's debt for a number of reasons: for the names he provided me for my trips abroad, for his careful and judicious comments on Chapter 8, "Patterns and Probabilities," for his own help and that of his staff, on countless occasions, in tracking down abortion data. He is a fount of information, which has well watered this book. Then there are the large number of people, throughout the world, who kindly gave me their time and attention when I visited their countries. I have acknowledged their help in the notes at the end of each chapter. Finally, I would like to thank Emily C. Moore of The Population Council for her discerning perusal of the manuscript; hers were the last critical comments and dead on target. Raymond Belsky of The Population Council was kind enough to read the galleys.

Writing at a moment when travel-study grants are under attack by some members of Congress, I can only testify that my own such grant from The Ford Foundation made a vast difference in what I came to know about abortion. I learned things which were simply not available in the published literature and which could not have been had by any amount of library research; there is just no real substitute for firsthand contact, especially when it is a matter of a different culture. A grant from The Population Council gave me the time and the freedom to complete this book and to have adequate research assistance.

Finally, I want to pay tribute to the patience of my wife, Sidney. Four years is a long time to carry on a household conversation, day in and day out, about abortion—not exactly the happiest topic one might think of—yet my wife endured, helped, argued, read, pushed and supported.

DANIEL CALLAHAN
Institute of Society, Ethics and the Life Sciences

ABORTION: LAW,
CHOICE AND MORALITY

CHAPTER 1

Introduction: Framing the Issues

ABORTION IS A NASTY PROBLEM, a source of social and legal discord, moral uncertainty, medical and psychiatric confusion, and personal anguish. If many individuals have worked through a position they find satisfactory, the world as a whole, and most societies, have not. There is scarcely a nation in the world which believes it has discovered the perfect solution to the legal, social and medical problems of abortion. There is scarcely any religious group in the world most of whose members are in agreement on the moral issue of abortion. The rapidity with which the laws of different nations have been changed in recent years—in either a conservative or a liberal direction—testifies to the worldwide uncertainty and flux.

On one point only is there a global consensus: the medical danger of underground abortions. Naturally, there are those who contend the moral question is also simple, and they have short, brisk arguments to show that abortion is either obviously moral or patently immoral. But, as I hope this book will show, the problem is difficult, admitting of no simple solution. The only way abortion can appear uncomplicated, capable of a decisive, lasting and satisfactory solution, is by fastening with a dedicated single-mindedness on one or another of the many facets of the question to the exclusion of all others. Catholics, for instance, have been apt to reduce the whole problem to the philosophico-theological question, "When does life begin?", while many proponents of abortion on demand see the question only in terms of feminine and civil rights: giving to women the full right to decide for themselves whether to terminate or complete a pregnancy. But the issues are not disposed of so easily. Abortion is at once a moral, medical, legal, sociological, philosophical, demographic and psychological problem, not readily amenable to one-dimensional thinking.

→It is a moral problem because it raises the question of the nature and control of incipient human life. It is a medical problem because the doctor is the person normally called upon to perform an abortion; both his conscience and his medical skills come into play. More broadly, the question is raised of the use of technological developments for the purported improvement of human life. It is a legal problem because it raises the question of the extent to which society should concern itself with unborn life, with motherhood, with family life, with public control of the medical profession. It is a sociological problem because, as Edwin M. Schur has pointed out, it touches on "woman's role in our social system, family organization and disorganization, national demographic policy, and the role of informal and formal sanctions." [1] It is a demographic problem because, at one level, it raises the question of whether abortion provides a useful, desirable and legitimate method of population limitation where such limitation is needed. At another level, there is the fact that, for good or ill, it is already being so used in many parts of the world. It is a psychological problem because, in one way or the other, the attitude of human beings toward conception, pregnancy, birth, and child-rearing touches deep-rooted drives, instincts, emotions and taboos.

A person may be convinced, from his own perspective, that all these wide-ranging, multifaceted problems admit of direct, uncomplicated solutions. But he ought at least to recognize that the great variety of differing moral and legal attitudes to abortion today suggest that it is by no means an easy problem for mankind as a whole to come to grips with. No one solution has commended itself to all men and all women. It has become a cliché to say that "men of good will" can differ on fundamental moral issues, but it is a valuable cliché in the present context. People do differ violently on the morality, legality and social implications of abortion; it is impossible to decide in advance on a man's morality or good sense simply by asking him what his "position" is on abortion. Once that is recognized, there is less reason than ever to believe that the problem could be dispatched with ease if only people would adopt the "right" moral values or take the "correct" stance toward society. Nor, apparently, has the problem ever been seen as simple or attitudes as uniform. As Devereux has pointed out in his study of abortion in primitive societies, "Contrary to our stereotype of the primitive, attitudes toward an abortion—or toward a failure to abort—may vary even within the same family. Certain individuals may even display attitudes at variance with the tribal standard." [2] In our day we are sometimes still prone to think of abortion in tribal terms: all Catholics, conservative Protestants and Orthodox Jews are purportedly opposed to liberalization of abortion laws, while liberal Protestants, reform Jews and unbelievers purportedly favor abortion law reform. It is not quite that uncomplicated, even though it may often appear easy to judge, from public statements and the like, that opinion on abortion can be thus neatly parceled out. The fact that there seem so few real options available in abortion decisions, rather than simplifying the problem, actually seems to complicate it. A woman may decide to have an abortion or not to have an abortion; there is no third way. So, too, a doctor may decide to perform an abortion or not to perform an abortion. Society can decide to allow abortion on demand or request, prohibit it altogether or allow abortion under certain specified legal conditions. It is not easy to imagine a fourth possibility. The narrow range of choices confronting both the individual and society means that, however elaborate and complex the reasoning which points to one or another solution, there are very few final options available. "On the whole," Simone de Beauvoir has written, "we may say that in this crisis [pregnancy] women give expression to their fundamental attitude toward the world in general, and toward their own maternity in particular: they may be stoical, resigned, demanding, domineering, rebellious, passive, or tense." [3] If one adds to Mme. de Beauvoir's list the possibility of women also feeling joyful, peaceful, fulfilled, one can see that the list of possible attitudes toward pregnancy far exceeds the number of options available to a woman physically: the options of having or not having a child. The simple limitation of physical, moral, legal and social possibilities, then, serves only to intensify the amount of emotion and thought which must go into choosing.

As if the intrinsic difficulty of the problem were not enough to bedevil people, the fact that it has been so polemically argued serves to obscure the values at stake. It is not so much that the "real issues" have not come out in the public debate, but that so many different candidates for the status of "real issue" have been pressed so vigorously, sometimes even fanatically. Undoubtedly the heavily legal focus of the question, which often dominates the public attention, has much to do with this. With forces on the one hand arrayed in favor of a liberalization of existing laws (or for no laws at all), and forces on the other intent on maintaining present laws (or tightening them), the issue has taken the form of various pressure groups struggling against each other for the legislative ear. This is perfectly proper in a democracy; legislators should hear the views of interested groups. But pressure groups normally argue only their side of the case, and argue it with all the passion they can muster. While this method may well serve to bring out the variety of viewpoints, it does not necessarily serve to clarify the issues. Indeed, abortion seems particularly apt to bring out the mentality of the crusader, whether of liberal, radical or conservative stripe. Crusades have their own *modus operandi*, requiring that one belittle the opposition, paint one's own position in the most attractive terms possible, muster only those facts which support one's own case and attempt as far as possible to monopolize the discussion. It is not in the tactical interest of the crusader to bring out the complexities of the problem or to provide the other side with any ammunition. Since it is true in a democratic society that the group which screams loudest and longest is liable to triumph, it is not, as tactics go, a bad one. The result, naturally enough, has been a public debate marked by acrimony, mean accusations and an attitude of utter confidence emanating from all sides. Since it is also true that those who take part in pressure movements usually feel strongly about their cause, it is a happy marriage of genuine conviction and pragmatic tactics.

The language of the debate is a clue to the level of the discussion. What are we to make of a doctor who calls a fetus "a bit of vegetating unborn matter"?[4] Or of an otherwise sensitive writer who sees the opponents of abortion as nothing but "purveyors and followers of dogma"?[5] Or the melodrama in a statement like this, supposedly describing the response of women to the work of an illegal abortionist: "The gratitude of most women is eloquent whether it be expressed in words or the look in their eyes. It is as though they are freed of a tension so terrifying there is no way out other than suicide"?[6] Whether one happens to agree with the positions expressed in these statements is not the point. They use the kind of language designed to change laws, to incite emotions, not to induce deep moral probing.

Yet the type of language used by the more zealous proponents of legalized abortion is matched by violent language on the part of many of those opposed. Prudent reflection on abortion is not much helped by the kind of statement once made by the distinguished Catholic moral theologian, Bernard Häring: "The appeal to the Christian law of brotherly love as justification for the taking of innocent life and the killing of genuine motherliness is probably the lowest depth of error attainable and the sorry fruit of the victory of the birth control campaign."[7] Nor is reasonable discussion much helped by saying, "It seems quite clear that if we are going to murder, we should call it by its name—if for no other reason than that we should know what we do. And abortion is exactly murder. . . . There are, after all, many forms of socially convenient murder."[8] In opposing a liberalized abortion law in California, Francis Cardinal McIntyre, Archbishop of Los Angeles, asked that the state "not consent to contract a responsibility in conscience for a carnage of untold numbers of the innocent and unborn in the years to come. Surely a wail from eternity will arise from those souls forbidden and denied life."[9]

Language like that throws sand in our eyes. It excites each side to escalate its own rhetoric; and it misleads just about everyone. By reducing the problem to a level of crude polemics, people are invited to emote rather than to think. Where subtlety and discrimination are called for, a bludgeon is used.

There is a still deeper hazard to reasonable discussion. Behind the language of "murder" or "vegetating unborn matter" lies the presumption that the truth about abortion is self-evident; or, if the truth is not self-evident, then the precise question at stake is. Thus there are those who believe it obvious that a zygote, an embryo or a fetus is a human being, just as there are those who think it self-evident that they are not. Each is sublimely confident that truth lies on his side—whichever side that is. And where truth is at stake, they seem to imply, no language could be too inflated or too inflammatory. Confidence about the major source of the problem is not lacking either. "It is obvious," writes Dr. Jerome Kummer, "that there is a direct derivation of attitudes concerning abortion from the prevailing attitudes toward sex in general." [10] *Time* magazine tells us that "the basic problem is unwanted pregnancy and how to treat it." [11] An equally confident editorial in the *World Medical Journal*, however, asserts that "the problem is not so much one of indications associated with physical diseases . . . or even one of psychiatric indications. . . . The problem is basically a social one, and arises from such considerations as the need to limit world population and the need for emancipated women to be masters of their reproductive life." [12] A Lutheran theologian sees the problem from still another slant: "Self-evidently, abortion raises the question about the nature of human life, and those who refuse to discuss the issue on that level are jeopardizing man's highest values for the sake of a short-range resolution of an immediate problem." [13] For a Catholic theologian, though, the basic question is something else again: "But the crucial question is: when *does* the human person begin his life?" [14] Where much of the discussion is debased, and where there is little agreement on what constitutes the basic problem, one can only expect confusion—and confusion is precisely what we now have. Put another way, when everyone is absolutely certain of his own viewpoint, and each in disagreement with the other, then we have a state of confusion, though in fact few of the individual participants in the discussion may themselves feel confused.

When one adds to this noxious brew the great discrepancies between professed attitudes and actual practice, between people's rational thinking and their emotional attitudes, and between the laws and their actual application, we descend even more deeply into the pit. What has been said of doctors could, with only a few changes in emphasis, be applied to many others concerned with abortion: "Whether we like it or not, many doctors think of abortion in one way, speak and write of it in another, and in actual practice conform neither to personally expressed beliefs nor to established legal or social codes." [15] The Lutheran theologian cited above has added some more items to this already extensive list of obstacles to rational discourse: "Five pollutants have so far spoiled the atmosphere for creative dialogue: the credibility of the Roman Catholic bishops as champions of human rights; the unfair attribution of motives to both sides; the artificial Roman Catholic versus Protestant posing of the question; the confusion of abortion with the general subject of birth control; the ambiguity about the goals of those who advocate liberalization of abortion laws." [16]

A Conflict of Values

If all these obstacles make reasoned discussion difficult, nonetheless it is hardly ever otherwise in a pluralistic society on root issues. A plurality of value systems in a society not only assures a conflict of values in that society, and thus a situation of disagreement, it also seems to assure that each group within a society will hold on all the more tenaciously to its own viewpoint (which does not preclude a sudden collapse, e.g., Roman Catholicism on contraception). Each group must constantly reiterate to itself the correctness of its own value system and continually defend itself against the attacks of other groups. In Western society, however, a further complication is often apparent. Groups may differ with each other very radically in their assessment of social and moral evils, or social and moral goals, but they also tend to share many values in common. Thus there is no group active in the abortion controversy which would not argue the need for responsible moral judgments. Whatever the viewpoint, the moral language used on all sides often tends to be much the same. The differences frequently lie in the way this common language is used to advocate or defend different values and goals, rather than in the creation of a language unique to any one group. This tends to make the accusations on all sides that much nastier. Each side claims that it represents the true embodiment of basic principles presumably accepted by all. Each side feels that it is the true defender of the common tradition. In the West, that common tradition is a respect for life and for the right of individual choice. One major task for an analyst of the abortion controversy is to attempt to discern, below the level of common discourse, the actual differences in value systems at stake, value systems which *are* different but whose divergences are often masked by the use of very similar language.

Another characteristic of contemporary Western pluralistic society is that many healthy trends have appeared on the scene more or less simultaneously, but often so as to lend themselves to uses which may seem to place them at variance with each other. A common argument of those opposed to a liberalization of abortion laws, for example, is to point out that the development of Western culture has been toward a greater protection of life, e.g., toward a heightened concern for the poor, the abolition of capital punishment, a more discriminating sense of morality concerning war, extended health services and research seeking ways to protect fetal life. It is then concluded that a liberalization of abortion laws flies in the fact of these progressive, healthy trends, all of which try to preserve, not destroy, life. But this is not the only trend one can discern. It is also true that there has been a movement toward allowing the individual in Western culture ever greater personal freedom; less and less does the culture require that the individual accept a communal moral code. It is taken for granted that, unless proven otherwise, a person has the right to determine his or her own life and establish his or her own values. This trend, of course, provides a major plank in the position of those who advocate abortion on demand: they want to allow women to decide for themselves whether or not to give birth to a child.

Both sides, then, have a point in discerning cultural trends which support their own position—trends which do represent genuine instances of cultural progress. In a situation of this kind it is misleading to argue that one side or another is the true bearer of the underlying tradition or of "progress." Each *in its own way* is being true to a different specific stream of progress. The result is simply more acrimony and a greater sense of self-righteousness on all sides. Each side is able to score effective debating points, the kind which provides fireworks at legislative hearings, but it is doubtful that this kind of confrontation is very creative or resolves many conflicts. One need only observe the various rights which have been claimed by different sides in the debate as the crucial right in question: the right of the fetus to life; the right of women to treat their body and everything in that body as their own; the right of doctors to make medical judgments without interference from the state; the right of society to judge that some matters of private morality are of concern to society as a whole; the right of one religious or ethical group to implement its own values without interference from other religious or ethical groups; the right of parents to decide the best size for their own family and to take the necessary steps to insure it. On the abstract level, there is hardly any debate about the validity of these rights. Hence any one group, seizing upon one or more of these rights, can score many telling points in an argument. Again, little is decided this way, for while all of these rights can be said to exist in free societies, there is no agreement on their relative value or on the extent to which any one of them may be implemented at the expense of any other.

An irony of the present situation is that there would not be an intense abortion debate had not society moved to a higher plateau of moral sensitivity. That some groups can seize upon "women's rights" as the basis of their advocacy of very permissive laws or no laws at all, is a tribute to the growing emancipation of women in society. That other groups can seize upon the research being done to protect fetuses as an argument for opposing liberalized laws is a tribute to the effort of scientists to seek more and better ways of enhancing human life. The encouragement of husbands and wives to plan the size of their family, taking into account the quality of their family life and not only its physical survival, is a tribute to a heightened sensitivity toward parent-child relationships and toward the requirements of a child's psychological and social development throughout his lifetime. The complaints about the medical hazards and personal degradation undergone by women who feel forced to resort to illegal abortions stem from a heightened sensitivity to personal dignity and medical safety. The drive to keep restrictive laws on abortion can be seen as a tribute to man's subtle awareness that even human life which is unseen and at present apparently valueless has to be given due weight—an awareness that stems in part from a horror about the indifference to human life displayed in many recent totalitarian regimes. In other words, there would be no abortion debate if there had not been a gradual growth of moral consciousness. To see one side or the other as representing pure progress or pure decline misses the point. The positions of all sides represent progress, though progress in different directions. To say this is not necessarily to point the way to a resolution of conflict, but it is at least to cut the ground from under those who would represent their opponents as moral barbarians.

Majorities and Minorities

Opponents of abortion reform often fail to admit that in the past highly restrictive laws on abortion were kept in force simply by the overwhelming power of majority religious or political groups. When American Catholics in the nineteenth century protested against a public school system which was *de facto* Protestant, when Jews later complained about Sunday blue laws, and when Catholics and Jews together complained about prohibition and dry laws, they were in effect saying one thing: in a pluralistic society the rights of minorities must be taken into account. The proponents of liberalized abortion laws are only claiming the same rights now. They have done so by use of the traditional means of minority pressure: the formation of pressure groups together with attempts to persuade the general public by means of articles, lectures and symposiums. Even if some do not approve of the goals of this pressure, they should recognize the need for the possibility of such pressure if there is to be full freedom in the society. Alice S. Rossi's contention (if correct) that "social reform on this particular social problem [abortion] is headed by middle-class Jews, agnostics and the less traditional Protestants such as Unitarians," [17] far from being a source of dismay to mainline Protestants and Catholics, should be seen as an occasion of satisfaction that at least now these different groups, which make up a significant segment of the population, have a recognized voice in society. That they have been able to persuade others to support their viewpoint is only an indication that pluralism is functioning as it should.

All this is said at the outset to refute the occasional claim that the desire for liberalized abortion laws represents a basic attack on Western values or, even worse, on the moral values supposedly underpinning any civilized society. On the face of it, those pressing for liberalized abortion laws are as much a part of the society as those against liberalization. Moreover, the liberalizers have undertaken their campaign in a way wholly proper. The first significant American book serving to open up the discussion was F. Taussig's *Abortion, Spontaneous and Induced: Medical and Social Aspects*.[18] That was followed a few years later by a conference held under the auspices of the National Committee on Maternal Health,[19] and then a decade later, in 1955, by an important conference sponsored by the Planned Parenthood Federation.[20] Dr. Harold Rosen's book *Therapeutic Abortion* was still another important milestone, as was the Model Penal Code of the American Law Institute in 1962.[21] In each of these instances, the pressure for liberalization came from doctors, psychiatrists, social workers and lawyers. Their method was public education and advocacy, well-established and well-sanctioned practices in Western society. Comparable statements can be made about the liberalization pressures in England and the Scandinavian countries, which saw similar processes of public argument and pressure for change. Those who would attack the advocates of abortion or complain about the increasing pressure for liberalization of the laws, must direct their criticism at the substance of the unwelcome positions, not at the character or patriotism or morality of the proponents. Neither the mere advocacy of abortion nor the use of pressure to liberalize the laws or to change public opinion, is a ground for condemnation. The use of defective or biased arguments does not provide automatic grounds for accusations of immorality. Every group advocates its own position in a one-sided way in the public arena. This is a source of public confusion, but at the same time probably a necessary polemical stance to gain a hearing for one's viewpoint.

Yet whatever one may care to say about the morality of liberalization campaigns, there can be no doubt that they have won increasing public acceptance. Between 1967 and 1969 abortion laws were liberalized in Great Britain and in the United States in the states of Delaware, Kansas,

Oregon, Florida, Colorado, North Carolina, California, Maryland, New Mexico and Arkansas. The Swedish and Danish laws will almost certainly be changed as a result of public pressure for greater permissiveness. In addition to those American states where liberalized abortion laws were passed, bills were introduced into well over half the other state legislatures, most of them based on the Model Penal Code of the American Law Institute, but some on proposals to repeal all abortion laws. While the success of liberalization bills will vary from state to state and country to country, the trend seems clear enough: present restrictive laws will shortly be liberalized in many places throughout the world, or even, in the U.S., declared unconstitutional.

This likelihood is enhanced by a number of other developments. In its first policy change on the subject since 1871, the American Medical Association's house of delegates in 1967 voted overwhelmingly in favor of liberalized abortion laws. A survey taken among some 190,000 doctors receiving the publication *Modern Medicine* found that 86 percent of those responding (40,089) favored liberalization of the law.[22] Interestingly, 49.1 percent of those who identified themselves as Roman Catholic also favored liberalization. Earlier surveys taken among doctors resulted in equally high numbers of responses in favor of liberalization.[23] There seems, then, to be strong support among doctors for liberalized laws; and their support is matched by public opinion, even a considerable body of Catholic opinion. A Louis Harris survey of American Catholics conducted in 1967 for *Newsweek* found that only 58 percent of a national sample were willing to support their church's firm stand against abortion, with some 28 percent opposing the Church's stand and 14 percent who said they were uncertain on the issue. A 1969 survey found an even greater shift of opinion, especially toward repeal.[24] A survey undertaken by the National Opinion Research Center at the University of Chicago found that a majority of the American population believes the law should be liberalized to allow abortion where a woman's health is seriously endangered, where she has become pregnant as a result of rape and where there is a serious defect likely in the baby.[25] However, it should be noted that the same survey found that far less than a majority would favor abortion in the case of families unable to afford more children, in the case of unmarried pregnant women unwilling to marry the father of the child and in the case of married women who want no more children.

When there appears, therefore, to be such a considerable body of public support in favor of some degree of liberalization, and when one adds to this the support given in the same direction by the American Jewish Congress, and by such Protestant groups as the American Baptist Convention, the General Board of the National Council of Churches of Christ, the Church Council of the American Lutheran Church, the

General Assembly of the Unitarian-Universalist Church, and such Protestant publications as *The Christian Century, Renewal,* and *Christianity and Crisis,* it becomes all the less likely that opponents of liberalization can succeed for very long. The recommendations of the American National Crime Commission in support of liberalization, the formation in Sweden in 1965 of an abortion study commission charged to develop recommendations for a more permissive law, an important movement in India to change its restrictive laws, the change in England's restrictive laws in 1967 all suggest the general direction of trends in countries with a history of restrictive laws. In the United States, moreover, the trend shows signs of rapid acceleration. In the spring of 1970, additional states changed their laws and changed them more liberally than had the states instituting changes between 1967-9; Hawaii repealed its old law altogether in 1970, and the New York law was radically changed.

While I will be concerned in the last section of this book with the direction which I believe the law should take, my major concern, so far as the legal issue is concerned, will be with trying to gauge the social, moral and cultural impact of different kinds of legal solutions rather than proposing my own (at least until the end). Nonetheless, because a general trend in favor of greater liberalization of existing laws is discernible throughout the world, the main ethical problem is shifting from the legal to the private domain, from legislatures and courts to the private conscience. It has long been possible for resourceful, determined, affluent women to procure abortions; troublesome, but possible. In the near future, and even now in many places, this possibility will be open to even more women, either because of the accessibility of illegal abortionists or because of a liberalization of laws (which may, however, *de facto* favor the affluent over the poor).

It also seems to be a consistent rule in pluralistic societies that, when restrictive laws (e.g., blue laws, dry laws, racially discriminatory laws) are removed in a few areas, they become almost impossible to maintain in others. This is not only because the attitudes ultimately responsible for a change in the law are rarely restricted to a few isolated places, but also because it soon seems to everyone patently discriminatory to deny a person in one place what she could get if she moved across the border. Needless to say, a perception of economic discrimination will be responded to in much the same way: it is not fair for the poor to be denied what the rich can get. Pluralistic societies show a tendency to accommodate the whole legal system to the views of minority groups in those cases where the minorities can effectively argue that their rights of conscience and choice are restricted. This outcome is all the more likely when those groups which sustained restrictive laws pass from majority to minority status. In the instance of abortion, restrictive laws are usually sustained by a coalition of conservative Protestants and Catholics in the United States. But this new coalition, which only doubtfully represents a majority viewpoint (public opinion surveys would suggest it does not), is open to a charge highly effective in legislatures: that it is imposing its own sectarian standards on everyone else. Thus opponents of liberalized laws are in an almost impossible position. On the one hand, they cannot effectively claim they represent a majority of public opinion (there is too much evidence to the contrary); on the other hand, they cannot effectively claim the rights of a beleaguered minority (for pluralistic societies normally favor only those minorities which want restrictions removed, not kept). For all these reasons, it is thus possible to foresee a trend toward liberalization, a trend which is already evident and likely to accelerate.

Considerations of this kind, however, have no direct bearing on the morality of abortion or even on its social desirability. A woman can have two moral problems: whether to break the law and, if the law can successfully be broken, whether to have an abortion. As the first dilemma recedes because of liberalized law, the second comes into greater prominence. To be sure, even if the laws are universally liberalized, they still will not, short of an unlikely total permissiveness, cover the case of every woman who wants an abortion. Some women will still be faced with the choice of breaking the law or heeding it, but for an increasing number it is most probable that they will have to face the question of abortion primarily at the personal moral level. At the same time, as liberalization progresses, even those groups opposed to liberalization will be forced to change the focus of their energies: from attempts to sway and deter legislatures to attempts to educate their own adherents in the light of a new social and legal permissiveness.

The Aims of This Book

The major focus of this book will be on the moral questions related to abortion. In my view, however, these questions cannot be treated in isolation from medical, social and legal questions; they form a whole. Moreover, it is my conviction that any discussion of a moral problem must blend theory and experience, principle and practice, goals and likely consequences. Hence, I have felt it important to present not only an array of theories, but also a mass of data; each seems to me vital. What is the evidence and how might it be interpreted and used in constructing an abortion ethic? The legal question raises directly the problem of the position society as a whole should take toward abortion; and this position, as reflected in state or national laws or the attempts to change those laws, will have much to do with shaping the moral attitudes of individuals on abortion. If only the legally and philosophically naïve would totally identify the regulations of the law with the moral requirements of the private conscience, it seems nonetheless true that the prohibitions and permissions of the law affect the private conscience, even if only indirectly, by way of quiet conditioning and sanctioning.

The legal question also brings into focus the effect of abortion on a society in other respects, particularly when one asks what different laws have brought about in different places and countries. What happens to values in other moral areas when abortion is easily obtainable? What happens when it is not? Since the world picture reveals a great variety of legal situations and a fair amount of data on the consequences of these different situations, there is available some data of interest to the moralist. If it can be shown empirically, for instance, that very permissive laws on abortion are followed by very permissive laws on infanticide, euthanasia and the wanton murder of adults, then the scope of moral inquiry could legitimately include such data. The lack of such data would be equally pertinent, particularly since much debate on abortion has centered upon the supposed ill consequences for the individual and society in other areas of human life if abortion is tolerated.

Yet it is also clear that a narrow focus on the legal aspects of abortion scants too many other important issues. It is the moral and social struggle which concerns me here: the struggle of individuals to come to some personally coherent, satisfactory position on the moral legitimacy of abortion; the struggle of a society as a whole to find some legal solution which preserves those rights and values which society needs preserved for its own welfare; the struggle of technological man to know how to make a moral use of the skills and talents now at his disposal (especially the talent, in this instance, of killing the fetus with very little danger to the woman); the struggle of men and women of sensitivity to take account, as part of their own moral thought, of the moralities of others—what obligations have I toward those who differ from me?

An immediate problem arises. The very diversity of values in a pluralistic society makes it difficult to come to grips with the moral question; we share no single, coherent value system. And, as suggested above, when our diversity is partially masked by use of a common vocabulary to talk about the problems, the possibility of mutual confusion and antagonism is heightened. When one group says the principle of "the sanctity of life" clearly favors the fetus, and another group says it clearly favors the woman, then it becomes questionable whether a purported agreement on the general principle of "the sanctity of life" is of any help at all. It might almost seem at that point that the air would be cleared if the opponents fashioned very different basic principles, making use of very different vocabularies. But, of course, that would have its drawbacks, too, making it all the more unlikely that any kind of effective discussion between them could take place. Even if the use of a common vocabulary and a recourse to certain common principles carry with them the seeds of confusion, they represent probably the lesser evil. More hopefully, the fact that all sides make use of certain common slogans and try to defend widely recognized "rights" as part of their argument establishes a basis for some kind of discussion—even if it is only about what the slogans mean and what the rights entail.

There is, however, an even subtler obstacle to discussion hidden beneath the battle over words and principles. If it is possible to make loose generalizations about the values held in Western pluralistic societies, most individuals probably think within the context of their own specific subcommunal value systems, at least to some degree. Hence, in one respect the obvious way to approach the moral problem of abortion is to work out of one's own value system or out of some specific value system. This has the advantage of lending coherence to one's thought, of avoiding the ambiguities which result when some other group's principles are artificially worked into an otherwise coherent system, and of enhancing the possibility that a person can at least judge his or her own case, if not necessarily that of others.

Unfortunately, to choose one from among the many competing value systems as the basis for a systematic approach of the kind aspired to by this book is to guarantee that one's efforts will have only a limited appeal and impact. If I chose, for instance, to employ a natural-law perspective, I could expect comprehension from Roman Catholics, but not from many others. If I tried to adopt a broader Christian perspective, oriented toward Biblical ethics, I might gain the hearing of both Catholics and Protestants, but I might not be speaking in a way helpful to agnostics and non-Christians. If I tried to work from a utilitarian perspective, I might gain the ear of agnostics, but I would lose convinced Christians in the process.

Now, if abortion were of concern only to individuals or only within a few isolated religious or ethical groups, these limitations would be of little importance. It would be enough if one could make sense only to one's own group or constituency; hence, there could be a "Catholic solution" for Catholics, a "Presbyterian solution" for Presbyterians, a "utilitarian solution" for utilitarians, and so on. But abortion may not be the kind of problem which should be dispatched so permissively. If abortion is actually the murder of a human being (as many would argue), then it is not sufficient to convince only oneself or one's group that this is so; the practice of other individuals and other groups must be of concern also—because murder has to be the concern of all groups. But if, at the other extreme, the permission for abortion is actually an act of necessary compassion toward women in distress or a matter of justice toward their needs and rights, then any attempt by opponents of abortion to deny women such basic rights should be a moral question for everyone. Similarly, if a highly restrictive legal system tends to multiply dangerous illegal abortions, then those who help sustain such restrictions bear some responsibility for this at times murderous consequence. Those who would bring a permissive system into public acceptance would, for their part, bear some responsibility for the abortions which would then take place. One way or the other, then, what is of concern to one faction should be of concern to other factions. Purely intramural solutions and value systems, however useful and legitimate in pluralistic societies, turn out in the instance of abortion to be less than helpful to society as a whole. They may provide an escape clause for particular groups which wish to go their own way, but they also, and more damagingly, allow society as a whole to escape its common burden.

Needed, therefore, is an approach to the problem of abortion which will cut across as many particular value systems as possible; an approach, that is, which will (a) avoid as much as possible the use of parochial assumptions; (b) draw upon the largest number of commonly accepted values; (c) make use of as many commonly recognized rules for moral discourse as possible; (d) employ moral language likely to gain the widest comprehension; (e) adopt an approach likely to win as large a hearing as possible, even if people will differ about the conclusions different groups or individuals draw. On the face of it, this may sound like either a prescription for banality or a venture in utopianism. For, if it is true that many different value systems compete with each other when abortion is discussed, and if it is true that these value systems build upon very different moral premises and make use of different modes of moral reasoning, then what hope is there for some kind of common agreement?

A Basis for Consensus

I am naïve enough to suggest there are grounds for hope. The basis of this hope is threefold. First, there are no important groups which would deny that life should be protected and enhanced; differences arise at the level of what counts as life and what counts as the protection and enhancement of life. Second, there are no groups which deny that human rights come into direct play in abortion decisions; differences arise at the level of discerning relative rights and the order of rights. Third, there are no groups which deny that people should be morally responsible for the choices they make on abortion; differences arise concerning the apportioning of responsibility, the sources, meanings and ends of responsibility. Admittedly, if these three grounds add up to a consensus, it is an exceedingly broad and vague one. It is only an agreement that life should be enhanced, that rights are involved and that responsibility is required. But we might be thankful for at least this much common basis for discussion; we are not starting with a blank slate.

Is it possible, though, to go beyond this minimal basis for agreement? If one's ultimate desire is to find a final, lasting, wholly satisfactory solution to the problem of abortion, the answer seems to be no. While individuals may and often do find their own personal answers, the likelihood that the world as a whole will in the near future do so is not great. It is just not, it seems, the kind of problem about which all people are likely to agree, not even in the same family, the same religion or the same society. If the goal, however, is to see a more fruitful discussion, one capable of making progress, of affording some illumination to all sides, of introducing self-criticism into the polemics, then that is a goal which might be achieved. The essential condition for getting at least that far is that there be an awareness of the assumptions, implications and possible consequences of different moral, legal and social courses. Latent attitudes, unrecognized forms of moral reasoning, hidden assumptions and potential implications of different positions must all be brought to the surface. None of these goals can be reached without a reasonably thorough attempt to uncover the relevant data, to dissect the moral reasoning behind the taking of different positions, and to analyze the possible or likely consequences of different legal solutions.

The difficulty in following this course is that most human beings approach a subject such as abortion with a considerable degree of ingrained bias; it may be a good bias or a bad bias, but it will still be a bias. None of us can escape our own history and our own conditioning, nor can we wholly escape our unconscious attitudes. The potential data bearing on the problem of abortion is immense. Unless it is ordered in some way, it will be useless. But as soon as one begins ordering it, decisions have to be made about the the relative importance of different facts; at that point one's bias is likely to show. The dissection of a moral position requires that one use some specific tools of dissection and employ some particular method of analysis; again, a bias will show and, more than that, will be necessary if the dissection is even to take place. To analyze the possible or likely outcomes of different legal courses raises the same kinds of dilemma. All of this is to say that objectivity, fairness and judiciousness are hard to come by, especially when it is a matter of abortion, a subject that usually elicits strong feelings. Human beings should feel strongly about those things that matter to them, and they should be free to express their feelings. At the same time, the presence of passion is not always helpful when one is trying to see the issues in some kind of balanced perspective. At that point, a corrective may be needed, and it is best that this corrective be self-applied.

The question is, how ought this to be done? What steps can a person take to insure that he has honestly investigated the different moral possibilities, that he has carefully weighed the social and legal alternatives? One obvious way is to study the alternatives, trying to see them as clearly as possible, attempting to take seriously the arguments and points made in their favor by those who commend them. It has been said that the proper appreciation of literature requires a "willing suspension of disbelief," if only temporarily. Something of the kind would seem required in evaluating the different kinds of abortion positions. There has to be, in the analytic process, some stage during which we try to appreciate why people hold positions different from our own. In the instance of abortion, this is particularly difficult. Horror stories abound: young girls who have died in great agony after a bungled criminal abortion; poor mothers whose desperation led them to try a self-induced abortion, with disastrous results; distraught women coerced or unduly influenced to have an abortion by their mothers or husbands or boyfriends; late-pregnancy fetuses, aborted alive, and left to die. At this stage in the abortion discussion most people have made up their mind. That is why most of those active in abortion debates are looking more for allies to support their own thinking than for discussions designed to help them clarify and weigh their position. The contention that everyone should make up his own mind on abortion is sensible enough; but it provides no clues as to *how* we ought to go about doing so.

I have in my mind's eye a number of images, the residue of innumerable conversations over the past few years. There is the image of the conservative Catholic doctor, whose method of argumentation is to display in a bottle a well-formed fetus (or the picture of one); his conviction is that abortion is the murder of a human being and he feels he need only show people that a fetus looks undeniably human to make his point. There is the image of the liberal social scientist, whose argument takes the form of citing overpopulation statistics, and whose conclusion at once follows: abortion is necessary to bring down a disastrously high birthrate. There is the image of the radical feminist, who cites one story after another of women being forced into illegal abortions and who come away wounded or dying; she concludes that repressive abortion laws are self-evidently wrong. There is the image of the fundamentalist Protestant who evokes a vision of infanticide, child abuse, sexual degradation and genocide following in the wake of liberal abortion laws; he foresees an apocalyptic disaster.

In trying to do research for this book, I had to take account of my own bias, my own image of the problem. Originally, I had intended to write a book defending, with some modifications, the traditional Western prohibition against abortion. As time went on, however, as I became more immersed in the problem, reading more and talking with many people, my opinion began changing. There were, I had to admit to myself, some reasonable arguments in favor of abortion under many circumstances; reading "the other side" brought me to see that not all virtue and moral insight was on the side of abortion opponents. Yet even as this was happening to me, I found myself unwilling to become a total convert. If the traditional case against abortion came to seem much weaker than I had originally believed, and the case for abortion stronger, neither side seemed to me to have a clear-cut case. I gave up my original traditional position but found I could not accept the other extreme, which comes close to holding that abortion represents no moral problem at all. Put another way, each side seemed to have valid insights, which I could not shake loose and which, increasingly, I felt should not be shaken loose. My image of the problem thus became very complex. My method of analyzing it in this book is meant to convey and give substance to this sense. If I have any one overriding and sustained conviction it is this: abortion is a serious moral problem and any solution which tries to dissolve the complexity is, for me, unacceptable.

I say all of this for two reasons. First, I think it important in a book of this kind to expose one's feelings, in order that the reader can gain some impression of the person who stands behind the writing: what motivates him, what emotions he is subject to, how he reached the position he did. Second, in trying to work out an organizational plan for this book, I had to cope with a twofold problem. On the one hand, I wanted to write a book which, as objectively, fairly and comprehensively as possible, tried to set out a good part of the known data concerning abortion. I wanted to make my own book manifest the spirit of the anthropologist Bronislaw Malinowski: "It is gratifying to a field-worker when his observations are sufficiently well presented to allow others to refute his conclusions out of his own material." [26] This is also to say that I did not want to write one more polemical book on the subject, but wanted instead to see if I could approach abortion in such a way that a potential reader could profit from the book even if he could not share the final conclusion. My aim, then, was—and now is—to write a calm book, trying to bring out the full complexity of the problem. On the other hand, the stance of pure objectivity is impossible for human beings, for reasons I have already mentioned. I do have a position on abortion and, inevitably, one's position is bound to have much to do with the way one goes about marshaling data and arguments.

Let me state, in a very general way, what that position is: (1) morally, there are no automatic "indications" for abortion; each case has to be judged individually, taking account of all circumstances; (2) there are no automatic moral lines to be drawn against abortion; again, each case must be judged individually; (3) while abortion laws ought not to be repealed, they should be free enough to place the final decision in the hands of the pregnant woman. To say that much is to stake out one set of limits: it is to affirm that abortion decisions ought not to be made in a formalistic way. This affirmation holds regardless of whether the problem is that of devising a legal code or of coming to some personal decision. Further, abortion ought to be approached as a problem involving a multiplicity of values, often in apparent and perhaps real conflict. Any solution to the problem which tries to reduce it to the maintenance or furthering of a single value—in a word, any simplistic, one-dimensional solution—is a poor one. As will be seen in Section IV, I direct my strongest moral critique at two positions: the Roman Catholic Christian position, prone to argue that the necessity of preserving all life, even potential life, is the single overriding value to be acted upon in abortion decisions; and that position, at the other extreme, which says that the invariable and overriding value at stake is a woman's right to have an abortion if she wants one. In their logical form, these two extremes seem to me very similar: each argues that the problem is not one of balancing a variety of values, but of defending and promoting one transcendent value. I thus conclude that what can be called "one-value" solutions ought to be rejected. And that is to establish another set of moral limits.

By the end of the book, therefore, I will have bracketed out a very large and very ambiguous middle ground, having tried to point out along the way that many abortion decisions could, morally, go either way with sufficient justification: in favor of a decision to abort or a decision not to abort. I will have rejected only those positions which argue (a) that abortion is always wrong; (b) that it is always right; (c) that there are automatic grounds for abortion; (d) that there are automatic grounds against abortion. Yet I will have also argued that, while one-value solutions should be rejected, a bias in favor of protecting incipient human life is legitimate, desirable and important. By a "bias" here I mean a general cast of mind, a broad stance toward the problem: it is good, so far as humanly and morally possible, to favor and promote the preservation of unborn human life.

These general conclusions on my own part presented themselves as I tried to cope with the mass of data and opinions to be found in the abortion literature; they seemed the only judicious conclusions I could reach. In the legal sphere, I was unable to discover a single country in which everyone agreed that the perfect solution had been found; every extant legal solution, from the most restrictive to the most permissive, seems to carry with it some undesirable consequences. In the moral sphere, there appears to be no solution on the horizon which will satisfy all the moral values at stake; each suffers from some liability (and, as I will try to show, my final, middle-ground position has its liabilities as well).

All of these reflections, together with the general thrust of my moral conclusions, suggested to me that abortion decisions (legal and moral) could usefully be talked about in terms of "policy" decisions. By this term I mean the following: a "policy" (regardless of the particular question at issue) represents a general direction of thought and action, providing a basic framework for making specific decisions. It is "general" insofar as it does not map out in advance the exact choice to be made in each situation; it allows for contingencies and unforeseen, complicated developments. The policy has a "direction," however, insofar as it tries to affirm and express a given cluster of values and goals; these goals and values will pervade particular choices. As part of its direction, it will specify certain lines that should not in the ordinary run of cases be crossed. In fact, it will often be clearer about what should be avoided than exactly how to achieve the positive aim of the policy. It may only know that an area of concern and aspiration has been bracketed out, that any decision taken should fall with that area and may be counted a reasonable choice insofar as it does so. An unreasonable decision will be one which oversteps the limits, unless the occasion for doing so is highly unusual.

The value of using the language of "policy" in discussing abortion decisions seems to me this: a very wide range of abortion problems admits of no simple, preconceived decisions; the choices will be complicated; it will not be easy to see how all the relevant values are to be reconciled; there will be a large hazy area. When this is the case, as it so often is, the most that one may be able to bring to the choice will be certain general attitudes and broad rules of thumb. One will, in short, bring to bear a "policy," a general direction for thinking and acting. The decision to be made will be an expression of that policy. Policies operate by means of guidelines, methods of decision-making, the presence of agreed-upon limits, and seek a balance of prudential judgment.

My major concern in this book is to discuss how both a moral policy and legal policy on abortion might judiciously be formulated. Secondarily, I will be concerned to present what seem to me wise moral and legal policies: my own solutions. To achieve these ends, I think it necessary to make clear that the moral problem is paramount, that in ways both obvious and subtle one's moral policy (latent or manifest) will and should shape one's response to all other policy questions.

As a way of bringing out the ultimately moral nature of the abortion problem and as a way of discussing particular areas which call for policy decisions, I have organized this book in the following way. The first section is entitled "Establishing an 'Indications' Policy." The second is entitled "Establishing a Legal Policy." The third is entitled "Establishing a Moral Policy." The final section, "Implementing a Moral Policy," presents my own conclusions. The aim in each of the first three sections will be to set out, with some detail and comprehensiveness, as many of the relevant considerations and as much of the relevant data as seem necessary to formulate policy options. I will be concerned to seek out the hidden assumptions behind certain possible (or recommended) choices, to explore the implications of different approaches and to lay before the reader the pertinent data now known. At the very least, I hope that the reader may come away from these three sections with some appreciation of the complexity of the problem as a whole and of particular subproblems. I will also be intent upon showing that one's moral policy inevitably comes to bear in deciding questions of subpolicy. Thus the first section, on "indications," concludes that questions concerning suitable "indications" for abortion cannot be decided on the basis of scientific data alone. They can only be decided by relating the known data to one's general moral policy on abortion. The second section, on legal systems, concludes that what one considers a desirable legal solution should, again, be a function of one's general moral policy, especially in the light of the social consequences of different kinds of legal codes. The third section, on moral policies, tries to indicate what the advantages and disadvantages of different moral policies are, and what one could or should think about in the process of trying to shape one which is coherent and consistent. In that section I lay down and try to detail what I believe the rudiments of a good moral policy would be, preparing the way for my final section. Thus the progression of the book is designed to show that the moral problems keep coming to the fore as one deals with one particular kind of abortion problem after another. This is also to say that every "indication policy" and every "legal policy" will reflect, and should reflect, a "moral policy."

NOTES

1. Edwin M. Schur, "Abortion and the Social System," in Edwin M. Schur (ed.), *The Family and the Sexual Revolution* (Bloomington: Indiana University Press, 1964), pp. 371–72.
2. George Devereux, "A Typological Study of Abortion in 350 Primitive, Ancient and Pre-Industrial Societies," in Harold Rosen (ed.), *Therapeutic Abortion* (New York: The Julian Press, 1954), p. 139.
3. Simone de Beauvoir, *The Second Sex*, trans. H. M. Parshley (New York: Bantam Books, 1961), p. 476.
4. H. B. Munson, M.D., "Abortion in Modern Times: Thoughts and Comments," *Renewal* (February 1967), p. 9.
5. Marya Mannes, "On the Casting of Stones," *New York Times* (February 28, 1967), p. 38.

6. Lucy Freeman, *The Abortionist* (Garden City, New York: Doubleday, 1962), p. 41.
7. Bernard Häring, *Marriage in the Modern World,* trans. Geoffrey Stevens (Westminster, Maryland: The Newman Press, 1965), p. 330.
8. Margot Hentoff, "Abortion: Murder as a Liberal Art," *Jubilee* (April 1967), pp. 4–5.
9. Statement of Cardinal Francis McIntyre, *The Tidings* [Los Angeles] (May 5, 1967), p. 1.
10. Jerome M. Kummer, "A Psychiatrist Views Our Abortion Enigma," in Alan F. Guttmacher (ed.), *The Case for Legalized Abortion Now* (Berkeley: The Diablo Press, 1967), p. 115.
11. "The Desperate Dilemma of Abortions," *Time* (October 13, 1967), p. 33.
12. Editorial, *World Medical News,* 13 (May-June 1966), p. 69.
13. Richard John Neuhaus, "The Dangerous Assumptions," *Commonweal,* 86 (June 30, 1967), p. 410.
14. Thomas A. Wassmer, S.J., "The Crucial Question about Abortion," *The Catholic World,* 206 (November 1967), p. 58.
15. Arthur J. Mandy, "Reflections of a Gynecologist," in *Therapeutic Abortion, op. cit.,* p. 284.
16. Neuhaus, *op. cit.,* pp. 408–09.
17. Alice S. Rossi, "Public Views on Abortion," in *The Case for Legalized Abortion Now, op. cit.,* p. 48.
18. F. Taussig, *Abortion, Spontaneous and Induced: Medical and Social Aspects* (St. Louis: C. V. Mosby Co., 1936).
19. Proceedings of a Conference of the National Committee on Maternal Health, *The Abortion Problem* (Baltimore: Wilkins and Wilkins Co., 1944).
20. Mary S. Calderone (ed.), *Abortion in the United States* (New York: Hoeber-Harper, 1958).
21. Harold Rosen (ed.), *op. cit.;* American Law Institute, *Model Penal Code,* Proposed Official Draft, Section 230 (Philadelphia: American Law Institute, 1962), pp. 187–93.
22. *Modern Medicine* (April 24, 1967), p. 216.
23. *Cf.* Robert E. Hall, "New York Abortion Law Survey," *American Journal of Obstetrics and Gynecology,* 93 (December 15, 1965), p. 1182–83; Kenneth R. Niswander, "Medical Abortion Practice in the United States," in David T. Smith (ed.), *Abortion and the Law* (Cleveland: Western Reserve University, 1967), p. 55.
24. "How U.S. Catholics View Their Church," *Newsweek* (March 20, 1967), pp. 72–73; "Changing Morality: The Two Americas," *Time* (June 6, 1969), p. 27; see also "American Attitudes on Population Policy—Recent Trends," *Studies in Family Planning,* No. 30 (May 1968), pp. 2-3.
25. Alice S. Rossi, *op. cit.,* p. 36 and *passim;* see "American Attitudes on Population Policy—Recent Trends," *op. cit.,* especially the conclusion, amply supported by the presented data, that "In no religious group is there major opposition [to more permissive laws]" (p. 6.); *cf.* Charles F. Westoff, Emily C. Moore and Norman B. Ryder, "The Structure of Attitudes Toward Abortion," *Milbank Memorial Fund Quarterly,* 47 (January 1969), No. 1, Part 1, pp. 11–37.
26. Bronislaw Malinowski, *Crime and Custom in Savage Society* (London: Routledge and Kegan Paul, 1926), p. 41.

Establishing an "Indications" Policy

Introduction

PUT IN THE simplest human terms, the problem of abortion arises for a woman when, having discovered she is pregnant, she then decides— or is inclined to decide—that she does not wish to have a child. In the simplest social terms, abortion becomes a problem when there are a significant number of women in a society who want to have an abortion (or abortions) to end unwanted pregnancies. A number of questions then arise. For the woman, there is the question of whether she has a reason to want her pregnancy ended; and one can assume that women do have such reasons (whether good or bad is beside the point here). For society, there is the question of whether to allow women to terminate those pregnancies they do not desire or, phrased alternatively, whether society should force a woman to go through with a pregnancy she does not desire.

The most common way these questions have been treated is to speak of "indications" for abortion. This is a way, in most usages, of dealing with the problem of whether, in a particular case or in a range of cases, there is a reason (or reasons) to think abortion should be permissible or desirable. To ask, What are the indications for abortion? is to ask, What reasons are there for abortion? It is not difficult to accumulate a large variety of reasons why a woman would not, under some circumstances, want to have a child: sickness or expected sickness (mental or physical); poverty; unhappy marital relationships; too many living children; the possibility of bearing a deformed child, who might be burdensome to the mother and/or the rest of her family; a housing shortage; a desire not to have any (or more) children; the social problems which arise for unwed mothers, or for women pregnant as a result of adultery, rape or incest.

The language of "indications" is used to classify all of these myriad reasons. Thus there are medical, psychiatric, socioeconomic, fetal and humanitarian indications—general categories of reasons suggestive of the need for or desirability of abortion. In this section, including Chapters 2, 3 and 4, I will be concerned with three major categories of "indications": the strictly medical, the psychiatric (which shades off into the socioeconomic), and the fetal indications (i.e., the possibility of a deformed child being born). These are by no means the only indications offered in abortion discussions, but they have been, by and large, the most important. Each of them has been the subject of considerable discussion and debate, and each brings into play a large amount of empirical data. I have reserved discussion of socioeconomic indications for Chapter 13.

My aim in this section is to ask a number of critical questions. What has been said and written about these indications? Are they valid as categories? What kind of data is available which would help one frame a moral policy for handling indications? What are some of the important problems which arise when one tries to evaluate whether, in a given case, a genuine indication exists? In the context of what other considerations might one try to approach different indications for abortion? What is the relationship between an indication policy and a moral policy? Can questions concerning indications be decided apart from moral questions?

An important point needs to be stressed about my way of discussing "indications." On the whole, the term is usually used in a legal context, specifying those conditions under which abortions may legally be performed. I am using the term, however, in the wider sense of "reasons" for abortion, reasons which can be invoked in either a legal or a personal context. My rationale for this is to avoid begging the question of whether there should be legal "indications" for abortion. If, on the one hand, there are to be legal "indications," then my discussion can be read in that light. But if, on the other, there are to be no *legal* "indications" (e.g., under a repeal of all laws on abortion), then it can be read as a discussion of the rational validity of different personal reasons for abortion. *The absence of prohibitory laws on abortion would not nullify the moral need to consider the validity of different "indications," or reasons, for abortion; that need is independent of different legal solutions to the abortion problem.*

For the most part, my conclusions are tentative, with two exceptions. I want to show that one's moral stance will, to a considerable degree, determine one's evaluation of indications. And I want to show that the literature allows one to conclude that just as there is no single indication which can be said to *necessitate* an abortion (as the *only* possible or conceivable solution), so also there is no single indication which can altogether be excluded.

CHAPTER 2

Medical Indications, Medical Sequelae

By and large, neither the nonpsychiatric medical "indications" for abortion nor the possible physical hazards of abortion have a large place in current abortion discussion. About the only time such questions arise is in the instance of the hazards of illegal abortions—whether self-induced, or performed by amateurs or by doctors working under poor medical conditions. Abortions performed by standard methods under hospital conditions are relatively simple and safe. Yet, for the sake of thoroughness and greater precision, it is worth examining the available data on the nonpsychiatric medical "indications" for abortion as well as data on the physical effects of abortion. If the available evidence does not indicate any special need to be critical of the current prevailing medical consensus that there are few, if any, medical conditions affecting a woman which any longer make pregnancy an irremediably direct hazard to physical health, the medical issues still have some life in the moral and legal discussions. More pertinent, with the prospect of increasingly permissive laws and a consequent rise in the overall number of legal hospital abortions, what is the medical safety of induced abortion? What kind of information is available on the medical effects of widespread hospital abortion and on the effects of repeated abortions? Does the number of previous pregnancies affect the margin of safety? European and Japanese data provide some useful information on those points.

The most important thing to be said about current medical indications for induced abortion is that very few are now recognized as critical. This is a direct result of the outstanding medical advances of recent decades. Illness and pathological conditions which once were menacing are now more easily controllable or open to cure. Sophisticated techniques of medical care, moreover, mean that even in the case of severe pathological conditions it is possible with intensive care to bring a woman safely through pregnancy. By the mid-1950s, Alan F. Guttmacher could write, with considerable confidence:

On the whole, the over-all frequency of therapeutic abortion is on the decline. This is due to two facts: first, cures have been discovered for a number of conditions which previously could be cured only by termination of pregnancy; and, second, there has been a change in medical philosophy. Two decades ago the accepted attitude of the physician was that, if a pregnant woman were ill, the thing to do would be to rid her of her pregnancy. Today, it is felt that, unless the pregnancy itself intensifies the illness, nothing is accomplished by abortion.[1]

Up until the late 1940s, a whole host of medical conditions was thought to warrant abortion: heart, neurologic and renal diseases, gastrointestinal disorders, pulmonary ailments, as well as a number of miscellaneous medical problems. But, as Guttmacher indicates, there has been a radical change since that time.

Kenneth R. Niswander has, more recently, surveyed the medical literature and come to a similar conclusion. In brief, he found that in (1) *cardiovascular disease,* "with improved prenatal care (including the significant advances recently provided by cardiac surgery), the number of women with cardiovascular disease whose life is actually in danger during pregnancy has decreased substantially. Certain reports state that with adequate medical attention practically every pregnancy of a cardiac patient can be completed successfully with little risk of maternal death." [2] (2) *Gastrointestinal diseases:* Niswander notes that ulcerative colitis is probably the most common gastrointestinal disease thought to merit a therapeutic abortion. He adds, "There is general agreement that emotional factors affect the medical course of the patient with ulcerative colitis. Since pregnancy regularly and sometimes severely affects the emotional stability of women, it has been felt the pregnancy may adversely affect the outcome of this hazardous disease. Fortunately, the disease is not a common one." [3] (3) *Renal disease:* Niswander mentions such conditions as chronic glomerulonephritis, hypertension of renal origin, the presence of only one functioning kidney, a history of nephrolithiasis, and chronic nephritis as possible but uncommon indications, and even then usually amenable to treatment. He makes one exception:

Since therapy in chronic nephritis is still neither definitive nor effective, there seem to be nephritis patients whose lives will actually be shortened by the effects of pregnancy. Heroic measures, such as the use of the artificial kidney, may see these women through severe life-threatening episodes; but all therapy will, in certain instances, eventually prove ineffective. Some of the renal conditions which might seem to indicate therapeutic abortion, however, do not so significantly affect the risk of maternal death.[4]

(4)*Neurologic disease:* Niswander mentions here multiple sclerosis, post-poliomyelitis paralysis, epilepsy and other conditions. He notes that, while a woman with multiple sclerosis is sometimes made sicker by pregnancy, the effect of the disease on pregnancy is unpredictable and that, in any case, there seems little evidence that the risk of death is increased in pregnancy by the disease. The same, he says, is true of an epileptic pregnant patient. Again, as with cardiovascular diseases, the major consideration will be the ability of the woman to care for a newborn baby.[5] (5) *Pulmonary disease:* At one time tuberculosis in a pregnant woman was considered a major indication for abortion. With the advent of control of the disease by means of drugs, this indication has disappeared.[6] (6) *Diabetes mellitus:* Niswander observes that diabetes can no longer be considered a major indication for abortion. He says that "the maternal mortality rate . . . is currently considered to be essentially the same among diabetic patients as with the over-all population. Fetal risk is distinctly increased in the diabetic patient, but this would seem to have little to do with the 'health' or 'life' of the mother." [7] (7) *Malignancy:* Against the opinion of some physicians who feel that pregnancy may adversely affect the medical course of a woman who has undergone treatment for a malignancy, Niswander points out that the evidence for this argument is not very solid. Only a history of cancer of the bowel seems to remain as, perhaps, an indication for abortion.[8] (8) *Other medical diseases:*

Rheumatoid arthritis, hyperthyroidism, lacerated cervix, multiple fibroids, mumps in the first trimester, and other miscellaneous diseases too numerous to mention have also indicated therapeutic abortion. It is difficult to prove that many of these diseases actually threaten the life of the pregnant patient, and social factors often seem to be a prominent consideration in the decision to abort.[9]

One must note, however, that judgments on the medical indications for induced abortion will often reflect the background and training of different physicians, as well as the practices and attitudes of different hospitals. When one says as a broad generalization that there are no longer any viable "medical indications" for abortion, this generalization must take into account the fact that many doctors will, in their medical judgment, continue to believe that indeed there are and, for that matter, will continue to perform abortions on these grounds. In addition, the fact that different women may on occasion have different combinations of illnesses means that uncommon situations can now and then arise. This possibility makes it at least necessary to qualify any flat statement about medical indications. Much depends on the state of the art of medicine, which is, as Alan Guttmacher has emphasized, "a fluid science." [10] And, of course, the actual availability of medical facilities will make a considerable difference. A study of California hospitals in the early 1960s, prior to the 1967 change in the law, indicated that abortions were still being performed for medical reasons. Forty-one percent of the abortions approved by some California hospital committees were for medical reasons: cardiovascular conditions, renal malignancies and many of the older indications.[11] Whether the doctors concerned considered these abortions *strictly* necessary on medical grounds, or whether they were influenced by other considerations is not clear.

J. J. Rovinsky *et al.*, in a study of therapeutic abortions performed at Mt. Sinai Hospital in New York during the years 1953–1964, found that the number of abortions performed on medical grounds remained stable during this period, 12 per 10,000 deliveries. The authors note, however, that "in current medical thinking the prognosis of the majority of these patients and the course of their disease would not be altered materially by pregnancy or the interruption thereof. . . . The decisions of the committee in these instances reflect a recognition of pertinent psychiatric and/or social aspects of the disease process, and of their importance in the total care of the patient." [12] M. M. Spivak, reviewing the practices of the Toronto General Hospital between 1954 and 1965, found that 10.7 percent of the therapeutic abortions were performed for cardiovascular indications, 7.6 percent for renal disease, 6.2 percent for diseases of the nervous system, 4.2 percent for malignancies, 2.3 percent for tuberculosis, 3.4 percent for hypertension, 3.1 percent for endocrine diseases (34.4 percent were performed for psychiatric reasons and 15.6 percent for rubella).[13] J. A. Cooper, surveying the London (England) Hospital from 1956–1962, found that 18.7 percent of the therapeutic abortions were performed for cardiac indications, 5.6 percent for renal, 5.6 percent for pulmonary, 8.4 percent for malignancies, 4.7 percent for hypertension, 3.7 percent for neurological indications, and 3.7 percent for pulmonary insufficiency, with 7.4 percent for miscellaneous medical reasons.[14] Robert E. Hall, surveying a number of American hospitals, found a huge variation in the number of abortions performed for medical indications, ranging from no abortions in 24,417 deliveries to one in 36 deliveries.[15] This variation has led Kenneth R. Niswander to observe that "it seems inconceivable that medical opinion could vary so widely. Socioeconomic factors must be playing a major role in the decision to abort in certain institutions." [16]

In any case, once the necessary qualifications are added, it seems increasingly difficult to disagree with the judgment of R. V. Colpitts that "whatever indications we may use, therapeutic abortion always constitutes a failure of medical science," and with Louis M. Hellman that "in the case of medical indications, it is possible almost always to give ideal care and avoid the abortion," or with Guttmacher once again: "Today it is possible for almost any patient to be brought through pregnancy alive, unless she suffers from a fatal illness such as cancer or leukemia and if so, abortion would be unlikely to prolong, much less save life." [17] Most significantly, even those who, like Dr. Guttmacher, are in favor of abortion for health reasons, rest their case more on the broad social and psychological health of patients than on the remote need for abortion for strictly medical reasons. I was able to discover in the current abortion literature only one sustained argument that medical indications for abortion, strictly taken, still constitute a major occasion for abortion (see J. A. Cooper above). But to say this is not to say that the issue is totally irrelevant. Since there always remains, as mentioned, the possibility of unusual medical situations, the issue continues to have some life in the formulating of laws and in posing difficult moral questions. Hence, while one can safely say that medical indications are increasingly nonexistent, one must also cautiously add that they are not necessarily totally nonexistent. Moreover, to be sure, the quality of medical personnel and facilities will make a difference; medical indications could well exist in underdeveloped countries where therapeutic facilities are nonexistent.

Medical Hazards of Abortion

It is necessary to place the medical indications for abortion in the context of the medical hazard. The medical object of induced abortion is to remove the fetus from the uterus as completely and safely as possible. A variety of methods is employed. The most common up to the twelfth week of pregnancy is the one-stage dilatation and curettage (D & C), the technique for which has been succinctly described by Dr. Alan F. Guttmacher:

It is ordinarily done under local anesthesia. . . . After the usual preparation and draping for a vaginal operation, the cervix is grasped with a tenaculum forceps and the uterine depth determined by a sound. The cervix is dilated up to at least a number 11 or 12 Hegar dilator, care being taken, particularly with a restroposed uterus, not to introduce the dilator too forcibly or rapidly for fear of rupturing the uterus. A sharp curette is then inserted to the top of the fundus with very little force, for it is during this phase that the uterus is most likely to be perforated. Moderate force can be safely exerted in the down stroke. The whole uterine cavity is curetted with short strokes, by visualizing a clock and making a stroke at each hour. The curette is then withdrawn several times bringing out pieces of placenta and sac. A small ovum forceps is then inserted and the cavity tonged for tissue, much like oystermen tonging for oysters. . . . When the loosened tissue has been removed, the cavity is recuretted. The alternation of curette and ovum forceps is continued until the uterus seems empty and no more gelatinous, frond-like fragments of early placenta are obtained. . . . In pregnancies beyond the seventh week, fetal parts are recognized as they are removed piecemeal.[18]

When it is not possible to stretch the cervix sufficiently, a two-stage technique is used. Strips of gauze are first packed in the uterine cavity, thus causing contractions and then dilatation of the cervix approximately 12 hours later. Dilatation thus achieved, the standard curetting procedure is then used.

For abortions performed after the twelfth week of pregnancy, a miniature Cesarean, a hysterotomy, is usually performed. However, because of the potential hazards of that procedure, as well as the hazards of a D & C after the first trimester of pregnancy, an alternative method is increasingly employed. That method, which first involves the drawing off of some amniotic fluid by the insertion of a needle into the amniotic sac (amniocentesis) and then the replacing of it with a saline or glucose solution, induces contractions and, after 20 hours or so, the beginning of labor, thus expelling the fetus. A brief mention of the history of this technique is worth recounting. In 1935, E. A. Boero proposed the injection of 40 percent formalin in the amniotic sac to interrupt pregnancy; this proposal was not widely hailed because of the possible dangers. In 1954, O. Stamm and H. DeWatteville reported success with the technique of withdrawing 100 ml. of amniotic fluid and replacing it with an equal amount of hypertonic saline solution. In 1962, Wagner, *et al.*, reported a large number of successful cases using this technique. In 1962, also, Wood, *et al.*, reported success with a 50 percent glucose solution. By 1964, J. P. Greenhill, surveying the literature, reported a widespread use of both saline and glucose solutions with apparently few serious complications. In 1966, Z. Koren, *et al.*, reported success using a variant solution in pregnancies ranging from the tenth to the twenty-fourth week of pregnancy.[19]

As for the relative safety of the introduction of these solutions, there is a fairly strong consensus that it is a safe and effective technique, although caution is required and complications, on occasion, arise. During the years 1946 to 1952 the technique was widely used in Japan, but with such serious side effects and so many deaths (25 during that period) that it was all but abandoned there. However, other investigators have suggested that the disastrous, but isolated, Japanese experience may well have been the result of inexperienced doctors working under poor conditions. Other, very frequent uses of the technique in several countries since that time indicate that, with precautions, it is a safe method (although a few deaths have been reported from England). Among the most important precautions now are a use of the method during the later stages of pregnancy rather than the earlier (at least the thirteenth or fourteenth week) and a restriction of its use to healthy women.[20] One of the reported deaths in England is related in detail in Å. D. Dayan *et al.* in the case of a twenty-three-year-old healthy woman aborted by amniocentesis and saline solution in the eighteenth week of pregnancy.[21]

While all abortions performed after the twelfth week of pregnancy carry greatly increased hazards, efforts have also been made to discover an alternative to D & C prior to that time. The main danger of D & C is perforation of the uterine wall, which increases with the length of gestation. In great part as a response to that hazard, widespread use is increasingly being made (particularly in Eastern Europe) of another method of induced abortion, that of uterine aspiration. Dorothea Kerslake and Donn Casey have provided a good description of the method:

> This basic technic is to aspirate [remove by suction] the conceptus from the uterus using a tube with a flexible connection to a suction pump. Local and/or general anesthesia is used where instrumental dilatation of the cervix is found to be necessary. Uterus-contracting drugs may be used. Aspiration of the uterine contents usually takes less than 2 mins.; the debris can readily be seen as it appears in the glass container. Occasionally after the ninth week of pregnancy, a curet or ovum forceps is used to help remove remnants.[22]

The tube mentioned in that description has a hole in the end, and it is passed over the uterine wall, sucking off the conceptus. The published reports indicate that this method has a number of advantages over the D & C. Most importantly, the danger of perforation of the uterus is apparently nil, with a number of researchers reporting no perforations at all in a very large number of such abortions.[23] While the reported incidence of perforated uteruses from D & C's has varied considerably, from .09 percent to 6 percent, the promise of a local absence of this hazard represents a major improvement in the safety of abortions performed prior to the twelfth week.[24]

Kerslake and Casey, surveying a variety of studies, found a much lower inflammation rate with aspiration, as well as minimal damage to the uterine wall, fewer general complications, less loss of blood, fewer fetal remnants, and less dilatation of the cervix required.[25] As for its drawbacks as a method, there are few untoward consequences so far reported. Vojta cites the possibility of fetal or decidual residues as the most likely hazard.[26] While Vojta reports successful use of the method past the thirteenth week of pregnancy, A. Peretz believes that it is unsatisfactory with late pregnancies.[27] Among others reporting successful use of the method are E. Vladov, who especially stresses the fact that it is frequently possible to avoid artificial dilatation altogether, a possibility offered by no other method, and Z. Dvořák et al., although the latter mention that late postoperative bleeding necessitated readmission in eight cases, that inflammation appeared in 2.4 percent, and that residue of ovum or decidua was found in 10.4 percent.[28] There seems considerable agreement, however, that a more skillful mastery of the technique will reduce such figures. P. C. Wu has reported that the method has been used in China since 1958 with great success and, because of a simple bottle employing burning alcohol to produce the suction, at less cost than in the West.[29]

Only the briefest mention is necessary of the hazards of illegal abortions. Without exception, the various methods of self-induced abortion are extremely dangerous: the insertion into the vagina of various kinds of rods and sticks, the injection of soap solutions, the application of uterine pastes, potassium permanganate tablets and any number of other dangerous substances. There exists a relatively large medical literature on the treatment of women suffering from self-induced or bungled abortions, even a cursory reading of which will remove any doubt about the dangers.[30] Of interest, but impossible to gather data on, is the danger of illegal abortions performed by qualified doctors outside of hospitals. There is reason to think, especially since the advent of antibiotics, that such abortions are comparatively safe. The real dangers are to be found in self-induced abortions and those performed by unqualified people (often paramedical personnel: nurses, midwives, technicians, etc.).

Any discussion of the "dangers" of induced abortions must be seen in the context of the relative hazards of different courses of action. The general consensus among most researchers in the field is that, under proper hospital auspices, induced abortions pose relatively few "dangers" to a woman's health. Hence one can find any number of firm statements that abortion operations are not hazardous, especially when compared with the 20 deaths per 100,000 pregnancies which occur independently of abortion.[31] So far as general trends indicate, these are correct statements. However, the normal context in which such statements are made is that of the alternatives for women who want or "need" abortions. That is, the relative hazards of abortion operations are statistically compared with the presumed or known medical hazards of carrying a child to term. Induced abortion, even very early in pregnancy, is not a wholly minor operation. There are some medical hazards connected with it. How much one should be alarmed about these hazards will be very much dependent on the extent to which one thinks an abortion would be medically or socially valuable. The agreement that hospital-performed abortions are comparatively safe is also matched by an agreement that such operations should not be undertaken lightly.

The possibility of death is not the only consideration advanced in medical evaluations of the safety of hospital abortions. The most negative evaluation of hospital abortions is to be found in an article by Carl Müller.[32] Though writing in 1966, Müller relies heavily upon the proceedings of a 1927 congress in the Soviet Union, which brought together nearly a hundred Soviet specialists.[33] Müller claims that the result of the studies "still affords us the best evidence of injury following this operation." There was found to be an operative mortality of .07–1.0 percent, a great number of inflammatory complications, including chronic inflammation of the uterus and adnexa, a high percentage of tubal pregnancies as a sequel, a 30 percent sterility rate, disturbances of the menstrual cycle, obstetric complications such as uterine inertia and subsequent habitual spontaneous abortion, and, finally, "the sudden cessation of the stimulus to uterine growth associated with pregnancy." The conclusion of the congress was that abortion is a serious biological trauma and one Russian author, Kirillov, said that "with 140,000 abortions a year we have simply changed 140,000 women into invalids." Müller goes on to say that no comparable studies have since been done and that, while improved medical techniques and the advent of better drugs have undoubtedly improved the situation, "abortion as an operation is very far from harmless" still.[34]

Müller then quotes a number of other studies, mainly from the 1940s and early 1950s which support this negative evaluation. He concludes by citing a recent statement of Dr. Hector MacLennan, president of the Royal College of Obstetricians and Gynecologists in Great Britain: "Even if the operation is to be limited to hospital practice by recognized specialists it should be stated most emphatically that therapeutic abortion, even in skilled hands, is more dangerous than the public and many doctors appreciate. This is especially so in a woman pregnant for the first time." [35]

R. R. MacDonald has stressed the potential hazards of abortions performed after the tenth week:

By that time the cervix has softened appreciably and the uterus is palpable abdominally, globular in shape, soft and vascular. Dilatation and curettage is quite likely to cause trauma to the cervix and, even with drugs to make the uterus contract, there is usually a lot of bleeding, while perforation of the uterine wall is surprisingly easy. Abdominal hysterotomy may be necessary to empty the larger uterus. This can be quite difficult and there is the extra hazard of the abdominal incision. Hypertonic glucose or saline injected into the amniotic cavity kills the fetus and induces uterine contraction quite quickly. This gives the impression of being an elegant method of inducing abortion when the uterus has reached 16 weeks' size, but in fact quite a few deaths have occurred from pelvic infection and cerebral hemorrhage. . . . A British urologist reported (February, 1967) after a visit to a kidney unit in Rumania that 300 patients had been admitted to the unit with renal failure following septic abortion.[36]

I have quoted Müller and MacDonald at length to show that it is still possible to discover an occasional article in the medical literature which heavily stresses the hazards of induced abortion even under adequate septic and professional conditions; Müller's article, in particular, is often cited in antiabortion writings. Most recent literature does not, however, present such a pessimistic outlook. Jan Lindahl conducted a careful study of 1,188 legal abortions performed in Sweden during the mid-

1950s. He points out that a number of earlier studies contended that a high degree of sterility supposedly follows in the wake of abortions. His own study did not discover any such thing. Of those studied, only one patient died and only one woman became involuntarily sterile following legal abortion. As for other pathological conditions, less than 10 percent of those aborted showed evidence of various types of inflammation. He concludes that there is little or no evidence of any significant complications as a result of legal abortions, and that the few hazards presented statistically are too small to be of great significance.[37] However, Lindhal also says that "relatively serious complications directly following the operations were recorded in 3.6 percent of the total series."[38] That last statement and his general conclusion are not necessarily incompatible, since most of the women studied had abortions performed relatively late, between nine and 24 weeks. That only 51 of the patients had D & C's performed and 989 had hysterotomies indicates that a preponderance of the abortions were performed during the later stages of pregnancy. Even under these less favorable conditions, then, a figure of 3.6 percent of serious complications could be considered relatively small.

A more recent study of over 21,000 abortion patients in Denmark from 1961–1965 found a total of 891 early complications in all.[39] The kinds of complications and their rate per thousand abortions are as follows:

TABLE 1

EARLY COMPLICATIONS WITH LEGAL ABORTION: DENMARK, 1961-65

	NUMBER	RATE PER 1,000
Bleeding *	243	11
Adnexitis **	201	9
Fever	199	9
Perforation of uterus	69	3
Rupture of wound	33	1.5
Phlebitis	33	1.5
Endometritis	27	1.2
Pneumonia	19	0.9
Pulmonary infarction	14	0.6
Injury to cervix	14	0.6
Ileus	12	0.6
Shock	8	0.4
Peritonitis	7	0.3
Sepsis	5	0.2
Other	7	0.3

* Including 91 cases of repeat evacuation presumably because of bleeding.
** Including oophoritis, salpingitis and parametritis.

As for mortality connected with legal abortions, Christopher Tietze points out that both the number of deaths and their rate per 100,000 abortions have shown a marked decline in Sweden and Denmark over a 20-year period. For example, there were 27 deaths out of a total of 10,500 abortions in Sweden during the period, 1946–1948 (a rate of 257 per 100,000), while in the longer period 1960–1966 there were only 12 deaths out of 30,600 abortions (a rate of 39 per 100,000). In Denmark, deaths declined from 38 out of 19,500 abortions during 1940–1950 (a rate of 195 per 100,000) to 9 out of 21,700 abortions from 1961–1965 (a rate of 41 per 100,000).[40] It will be noted that there were more abortions in the first five years of the 1960s than in the whole decade of the 1940s, but less than a quarter of the number of deaths.

Probably the most thorough recent studies are those which have been conducted in East Europe. The overall data show a rapid reduction in the death rate following the legalization of abortion, as well as a reduction of other hazards.[41] In a careful survey of the East European countries, K.-H. Mehlan found that severe complications and death after legal abortions are increasingly rare. He points out that during the years 1963 and 1964 there were no deaths among 140,000 cases of legal abortion in Czechoslovakia and none among 67,000 in Bulgaria. In Hungary in 1963 and 1964, there were only two deaths in 358,200 abortions, and in Yugoslavia in 1961 five in 104,700 operations.[42] Imre Hirschler disagrees slightly with Mehlan's figures for Hungary, citing four deaths in 1963 and two in 1964 (for a total of six for the period). Hirschler's figures for subsequent years are as follows: three deaths in 1965 (out of 180,300 abortions), four in 1966 (out of 186,800) and none in 1967 (out of 187,-500). Anton Cernoch has showed the mortality rate associated with abortion in Czechoslovakia decreased from 3.1 deaths per 100,000 abortions in the period 1958–1962 to 2.5 per 100,000 in 1963–1967. Hirschler finds an even more radical decline in Hungary, from 5.6 per 100,000 in 1961 to 1.2 per 100,000 for 1964–1967. Slovenia (in Yugoslavia), according to Franc Novak, continues to have higher mortality rate than the other two nations, averaging 5.7 deaths per 100,000 abortions in the period 1961–1967.[43] András Klinger concludes that the overall death rate from abortion in East Europe has dropped considerably in recent years and that an average of only one or two women a year die in each of the East European nations where legal abortions are readily available.[44]

As for other complications, Mehlan's data indicate that they increase with the lateness of the abortion, and that they are significantly higher in those having their first pregnancy, and especially so for those under seventeen years of age. He also notes that the literature shows that repeated abortions double the normally low rate of subsequent spontaneous abortions, premature births, stillbirths and various other complications.[45] Imre Hirschler's figures for the incidence of complications following induced abortions in Hungary follow: [46]

TABLE 2

COMPLICATIONS PER 1,000 REGISTERED INDUCED ABORTIONS: HUNGARY

	1960	1964	1967
Perforation of the uterus	1.41	1.23	0.93
Fever of gynecological origin	5.72	3.75	4.81
Hemorrhage after the abortion	6.27	6.19	7.27
Readmission within 4 weeks for fever due to the abortion	5.29	4.73	4.56
Readmission within 4 weeks for hemorrhage due to the abortion	11.16	10.19	10.72

Both the early complications and hospital readmissions due to complications that developed later, then, show a gradual decline in Hungary during the 1960s, as they have elsewhere in East Europe. And Malcolm Potts speculates that "with the wider use of the vacuum technique the complication rates may fall even lower." [47]

The fact that the death rate from legal abortions has been higher in northern European, particularly Scandinavian, countries than in a country like Japan is generally attributed to the fact that abortions are normally performed later in the former countries, primarily because of the more complicated and time-consuming legal requirements. Tietze estimates that there are about 40 deaths per 100,000 legal abortions in northern Europe (where laws are relatively stringent) and fewer than five in East Europe and Japan (where the laws are relatively permissive).[48] After discussing the East European death rates, Malcolm Potts concludes: "Legal abortion is many times safer than leaving the woman the risk of obtaining a criminal abortion and in the early months is safer than carrying a pregnancy to term." [49]

That much said by way of generalization, some nuances must be added. The general agreement on the relative safety of legal abortions performed under hospital conditions is matched, it appears, by an equally strong consensus in East Europe and Japan that abortion is by no means the ideal method of conception control. After noting the low mortality rate in East Europe, Tietze and Lehfeldt observed that, nonetheless, "in none of the countries in eastern Europe where interruption of pregnancy has recently been legalized is it considered a desirable method of fertility control by responsible leaders of the medical profession." [50] The reason for this conclusion appears to be some continuing uncertainty (among specialists) about the physical effects of abortion, particularly on those having their first pregnancy, those who are in their teens and those who have had repeated abortions.

In a study of abortion in Czechoslovakia, Anton Cernoch concludes that legal abortion is a feasible way to control criminal abortions and that the medical aftermath of legal abortions is far less severe than after criminal abortions. He also observes, however, that

after the interruption the subsequent pregnancy must necessarily be considered to be twice or three times more threatened by [spontaneous] abortion, premature labor, disturbances of uterine activity, separation of the placenta, placenta praevia, any premature abruptio placentae and any intrapartem or postpartem hemorrhage. . . . In these groups the number of premature labors has increased, according to the available analyses, as much as three times. Surgical intervention for complications in subsequent labors is twice as frequent and so are deaths of fetuses in gravidity and during labor. . . . Although the execution of the intervention has become relatively safe, it is clear that the consequences accompanying interruptions of pregnancies cannot be without significance for the biological fertility of women.[51]

András Klinger reaches a similar conclusion after analyzing the Hungarian experience with permissive laws:

Although the legalization of induced abortion now insures its performance under proper medical auspices, this still remains an undesirable method of birth limitation. Repeated induced abortion endangers the health of the woman and children born subsequently. There is a correlation, for example, between the frequency of induced abortion and the proportion of premature births.[52]

Tietze takes note of this phenomenon, too, but adds that, nevertheless, infant mortality, usually associated with prematurity, has dropped in Hungary from 58.8 per 1,000 live births in 1956 to 38.4 per 1,000 in 1966.[53] K.-H. Mehlan reports a similar concern in Rumania during its period of very permissive abortion laws, a concern leading to a desire to increase the use of contraceptives.[54] F. Novak cites an increase in ectopic pregnancy in Rumania and reports that various Polish gynecologists have found similar increases. Ectopic pregnancies as an aftermath have also been suspected to increase in Yugoslavia.[55]

A Soviet demographer, E. A. Sadvokasova, has stated:

Many studies carried out on the problem both in the Soviet Union and abroad have been shown that the artificial termination of pregnancy, even when carried out in proper medical conditions, is not without effect on women's health and may be followed by various immediate or later adverse effects, up to and including secondary sterility. The reason for this is that pregnancy is not a function of the female reproductive organs alone, so that any sudden violent termination of pregnancy upsets the natural harmony of the maternal organism as a whole. Abortion is particularly harmful to the health of a primapara; but later abortions are undesirable also, particularly when carried out at short intervals (less than six months). . . . In the Soviet Union, the problem of artificial termination of pregnancy is discussed in many regional and republic meetings, conferences and symposia of obstetricians and gynaecologists. They are all agreed that abortion has harmful effects on women's health and should therefore be replaced by contraceptive methods.[56]

One of the most useful studies done anywhere in the world was a series of surveys undertaken by the Family Planning Federation of Japan, *Harmful Effects of Induced Abortion.*[57] While the authors of the different studies point out that there are limitations in their surveys, nonetheless it is clear that the studies were carried out with considerable care. That they were for the most part conducted in university hospitals, the best in Japan, should be borne in mind. Since this book is not readily available in English-speaking countries, I will summarize the main findings. In one study of 821 cases of legal abortion performed in 41 hospitals in Tokyo and adjacent areas, the authors summed up their findings as follows: Comparing the patients studied with a control group, they say that

in the follow-up apparent abnormal bleeding, fever, lower abdominal pain and lumbago were more frequent than control subjects up to the one and two postoperative month. With the course of the postoperative period these complaints or abnormalities became less frequent and approximate in rate those in control subjects and became statistically insignificant. . . . Together with the effect to reduce injury due to artificial abortion it is more important to prevent artificial abortion, or in further step to prevent pregnancy which might end in artificial abortion.[58]

A study of menstrual abnormalities following abortions concluded that an "artificial abortion operation is not likely to promote the development of menstrual abnormality, although there may be a prolonged menstrual interval or prolonged menstrual bleeding at the first menstrual cycle." [59] On the question of postabortion sterility, one study concluded that "of subjects complaining of secondary sterility, 46.7 percent of them had history of previous artificial abortion. The percent is similar with the 49.4 percent in the full-term delivery patients who had history of pregnancy more than 2 times . . . of sterile females, 41.4 percent of them terminated their first pregnancy artificially, whereas this was 32.6 percent in the control group." [60] The authors of this study are cautious about their findings: "It is too rash to conclude that artificial abortion is not significantly related [to] sterility, but the incidence is not so high [as contended in earlier Japanese studies]." [61]

On the subject of abortion and ecotopic pregnancies, the study concludes that

only a slight relationship was established between the artificial abortion and the interstitial type ectopic pregnancy. At any rate, the artificial abortion could not be recognized as the major factor [in] the increase of ectopic pregnancy. Finally, we think that there is no significant correlation between the artificial abortion and the ectopic pregnancy, at least not as much as the general belief goes.[62]

Again, though, as in a number of other studies, the authors stressed that their research was based on a limited number of cases and that the issue could not be considered closed. On the problem of the relationship between subsequent spontaneous miscarriages and premature births, another study concluded that there was a significant correlation:

The results of our investigation . . . showed that the experience rate of preceding artificial abortion to the present pregnancy was significantly higher in both spontaneous or habitual abortion and premature birth than the fullterm delivery. . . . the artificial abortion was surely the cause of spontaneous or habitual abortion and premature birth.[63]

On the effect of artificial abortion on subsequent deliveries, a study concluded that a history of artificial abortion shows no ill effects on deliveries in the future.[64]

One of the organizers of the study, in analyzing the overall findings, stated that extreme caution is necessary in interpreting the survey results. Stressing repeatedly that the survey was limited in scope, primarily restricted to the Tokyo area, and by no means complete there, he states "the conclusion that induced abortion does not have any harmful effect on the following pregnancy and delivery cannot be made." [65] Another Japanese book, also published by the Family Planning Federation of Japan and taking into account the above summarized book as well as other studies, concluded:

It may be said that induced abortion performed by a designated physician in Japan in these days is not particularly hazardous in so far as serious complications are concerned. But this does not mean that induced abortion is always perfectly safe; there are observed a small number of cases for which major treatment is necessary because of perforation, massive hemorrhage, severe infection and other medical sequelae. This possibility of serious consequences has to be taken into consideration especially in the case of induced abortion performed on the first pregnancy, which appears to be increasing nowadays in Japan.[66]

Genichi Nozue, correlating various Japanese studies, found that by 1954 the mortality rate from abortion was .0007 percent and the direct injury rate was 3.8 percent (perforation of the uterus, cervical lacerations, etc.).[67]

Finally, one should mention studies undertaken in Seoul, Korea, and in Israel. In Seoul, it is reported that out of 1,484 women studied who had induced abortion, 8 percent were judged to have very severe complications, another 8 percent severe, 20 percent not severe and for the remaining 64 percent no complications at all. The author cautions, however, that the severity of the complications was determined only by a questionnaire, thus depending upon the subjective response of the women questioned.[68] In Israel, R. Bachi has reported the conclusions of "a subcommittee formed by four leading Israeli gynecologists charged to express their opinion on the consequences of abortion":

Research performed by us on the clinical material at our disposal has shown that induced abortion is an important cause and even a leading cause of different gynecological and obstetrical situations and complications, the more important of which are the following: chronic inflammation of the internal genital organs, secondary sterility, insufficiency of the os uteri, intrauterine adhesions, amenorrhea or hypomenorrhea, repeated miscarriages, premature births, disturbances of implantation of placenta, extrauterine pregnancy, and various types of neuro-vegetative disturbances.[69]

There are many questions these surveys do not enable one to answer. One cannot easily determine, for instance, the training of the doctors performing the abortion, the nature and quality of the medical facilities and other technical questions. Some speculations seem in order, however. While almost all of the studies conclude that the extent of severe disturbances after an abortion is relatively slight, there is a general caution, suggested by many of the passages I quoted, about concluding that abortion, even under ideal circumstances, ought to be fully accepted as a safe operation (even though it may be safer, statistically, than carrying a pregnancy to term). There is also a general agreement both in East Europe and Japan that there are enough undesirable medical aftermaths to make abortion less acceptable than contraception as a method of fertility control. The reservations, so far as I can observe, seem to be all the greater in those countries which now have or have had very permissive abortion laws: the Soviet Union, Rumania, Hungary and Japan.

The most confident statements, by contrast, come from specialists in those Western nations which have been fairly restrictive in allowing legal abortions. This would suggest two things. On the one hand, induced abortion, when viewed as an unusual and infrequent medical operation resorted to only for serious reasons, can be looked upon as relatively safe—no doubt because the doctors involved will be relatively careful. On the other hand, in countries where legal abortions are easy to obtain and thus widespread, and where many physicians perform many abortions, the possibility of human error increases. Then, too, permissive legal systems mean an increase in repeated abortions, thus introducing a new factor. This would help explain why so many East European and Japanese observers can say, on the one hand, that abortion is relatively safe, and yet, on the other hand, also state that it would be much better if abortions were not so common. The East European and Japanese specialists appear fearful of proclaiming abortion procedures to be trivial and routine. There appears to be a general consensus that abortion operations, of all sorts, should be taken with utmost seriousness and avoided if possible. At the same time, though, both the data and the testimony would seem to indicate that arguments based upon the "danger" of abortion procedures cannot legitimately be counted as a real objection to the liberalization of laws. There is some danger involved, but if the presumption is that abortion is desirable (because of the hazards of the alternatives), these dangers are not unacceptable. That appears to be the general consensus of the Eastern European and Japanese commentators, as well as those in the West.

NOTES

1. Alan F. Guttmacher, "The Shrinking Non-Psychiatric Indications for Therapeutic Abortion," in Harold Rosen (ed.), *Therapeutic Abortion* (New York: The Julian Press, 1954), p. 13; see E. Quay, "Justifiable Abortion," *Georgetown Law Journal*, 34 (1960–1961), Part 1, pp. 181ff., for a comprehensive review of the medical literature through the late 1950s, the net import of which is to support the contention of Guttmacher; *cf.* J. G. Moore and J. H. Randall, "Trends in Therapeutic Abortion: A Review of 137 Cases," *American Journal of Obstetrics and Gynecology*, 63 (January 1952), pp. 28–40, which reaches a similar conclusion.
2. Kenneth R. Niswander, "Medical Abortion Practices in the United States," in David T. Smith (ed.), *Abortion and the Law* (Cleveland: Western Reserve University, 1967), p. 42. Niswander adds that decisions concerning pregnant cardiac patients are frequently influenced by the possible difficulty which a patient could have in caring for a newborn baby.
3. *Ibid.,* p. 42.
4. *Ibid.,* pp. 42–43.
5. *Ibid.,* pp. 43–44.
6. *Ibid.,* p. 44.
7. *Ibid.*
8. *Ibid.,* p. 45.
9. *Ibid.*
10. Guttmacher, *op. cit.,* p. 13.
11. Keith P. Russell and George F. Moore, "Maternal Medical Indications for Therapeutic Abortion," *Clinical Obstetrics and Gynecology*, 7 (March 1964), pp. 43–53; *cf.* M. F. Loth and H. C. Hesseltine, "Therapeutic Abortion at the Chicago Lying-In Hospital," *American Journal of Obstetrics and Gynecology*, 72 (August 1956), pp. 304–11; A. S. Majury, "Therapeutic Abortion in the Winnipeg General Hospital," *American Journal of Obstetrics and Gynecology*, 82 (July 1961), pp. 10–15; Keith P. Russell, "Therapeutic Abortions in California in 1950," *Western Journal of Surgery*, 60 (October 1952), pp. 497–502, for an earlier study.
12. J. J. Rovinsky, *et al.*, "Current Trends in Therapeutic Termination of Pregnancy," *American Journal of Obstetrics and Gynecology*," 98 (May 1, 1967), p. 1117.
13. M. M. Spivak, "Therapeutic Abortions, A 12-Year Review at the Toronto General Hospital, 1954–1965," *American Journal of Obstetrics and Gynecology*, 97 (February 1, 1967), pp. 316–23.
14. J. A. Cooper, "Therapeutic Abortion: A Survey with a Series from the London Hospital," *The British Journal of Clinical Practice*, 22 (February 1968), pp. 49–57. The author of this article believes that "therapeutic abortions should be considered on patients who have a sure history of heart failure during or between previous pregnancies, clinical evidence of severe pulmonary or septic hypertension, cardiac enlargement or atrial fibrillation" (p. 49).
15. Robert E. Hall, "Therapeutic Abortion, Sterilization, and Contraception," *American Journal of Obstetrics and Gynecology*, 91 (February 15, 1965), p. 518.
16. Kenneth R. Niswander, *op. cit.,* p. 54.

17. R. V. Colpitts, "Trends in Therapeutic Abortion," *American Journal of Obstetrics and Gynecology,* 68 (October 1954); Hellman makes his statement in Mary S. Calderone (ed.), *Abortion in the United States* (New York: Hoeber-Harper, 1958), p. 95; Alan F. Guttmacher, "Abortion—Yesterday, Today, and Tomorrow," in Alan F. Guttmacher (ed.), *The Case for Legalized Abortion Now* (Berkeley: Diablo Press, 1967), p. 9.

18. Alan F. Guttmacher, "Techniques of Therapeutic Abortion," *Clinical Obstetrics and Gynecology,* 7 (March 1964), p. 103; see also John Rock and Armand Maillot, "Abortion," in *Gynecology and Obstetrics,* Vol. 1, Chapter 10 (Hagerstown, Maryland: W. F. Prior Co., 1963). For a more literary account, see Lael T. Wertenbaker, *The Afternoon Women* (New York: Bantam Books, 1967), pp. 250ff. Unless otherwise specified I will use the word "abortion" to mean, following the usage of Glanville Williams, "Any untimely delivery procured with intent to destroy the fetus" (Glanville Williams, *The Sanctity of Life and the Criminal Law* [London: Faber and Faber, 1958], p. 139). While it is common in medical literature to distinguish among "ovum," "embryo" and "fetus," I will generally use the word "conceptus" to cover all the stages of gestation, except where greater precision of phrasing is necessary. My intent here is one of convenience and to avoid begging any questions.

19. E. A. Boero, "Interruption de la Grossesse Incompatible Avant La Viabilité Foetale," *Gynécologie et Obstétrique* (Paris), 32 (December 1935), pp. 502–04; O. Stamm and H. DeWatteville, "Étude Expérimentale sur le Mécanisme d'avortement par hydramnios Artificiel," *Gynécologie et Obstétrique,* 53 (1954), p. 171; G. Wagner *et al.,* "Induction of Abortion by Intraovular Instillation of Hypertonic Saline," *Danish Medical Bulletin,* 9 (August 1962), p. 137; C. Wood *et al.,* "Induction of Labour by Intra-Amniotic Injection of Hypertonic Glucose Solution," *British Medical Journal,* 2 (September 15, 1962), p. 706; J. P. Greenhill (ed.), *Yearbook of Obstetrics and Gynecology, 1963–1964,* p. 137; Z. Koren *et al.,* "Induction of Legal Abortion by Intra-Uterine Instillation of Pargyline Hydrochloride (Eutonyl)," *Journal of Reproduction and Fertility,* 12 (August 1966), pp. 75 ff.; see also Bela Ruttner, "Termination of Midtrimester Pregnancy by Transvaginal Intra-Amniotic Injection of Hypertonic Solution," *Obstetrics and Gynecology,* 28 (November 1966), pp. 601ff.

20. For a study of the Japanese experience, see Takashi Wagatsuma, "Intra-Amniotic Injection of Saline for Therapeutic Abortion," *American Journal of Obstetrics and Gynecology,* 93 (November 1, 1965), pp. 743fl. See also D. N. Menzies *et al.,* "Therapeutic Abortion Using Intra-Amniotic Hyertonic Solutions," *The Journal of Obstetrics and Gynaecology of the British Commonwealth,* 75 (February 1968), pp. 215ff.; Melville G. Kerr *et al.,* "Studies of the Mode of Action of Intra-Amniotic Injection of Hypertonic Solutions in the Induction of Labor," *American Journal of Obstetrics and Gynecology,* 94 (January 15, 1966), pp. 214ff.; John W. C. Johnson *et al.,* "Hazards of Using Hypertonic Saline for Therapeutic Abortion," *ibid.,* pp. 225ff.; V. N. Pathak, "Intra-Amniotic Saline Induction for Termination of Early Pregnancy," *The West Indian Medical Journal,* 15 (June 1966), pp. 89ff.; Gorm Wagner, "Induction of Abortion or Labor by Intra-Amniotic Injection of Hypertonic Solutions," *Clinical Obstetrics and Gynecology,* 9 (June 1966), pp. 520ff.; W. M. Alpern *et al.,* "Hypertonic Solutions for Termination of Pregnancy," *American Journal of Obstetrics and Gynecology,* 100 (January 15, 1968), pp. 250ff.

21. A. D. Dayan *et al.,* "Fatal Brain Damage Associated with Therapeutic Abortion Induced by Amniocentesis: Report of One Case," *Medicine, Science and the Law,* 7 (April 1967), pp. 70–72.

22. Dorothea Kerslake and Donn Casey, "Abortion Induced by Means of the Uterine Aspirator," *Obstetrics and Gynecology,* 30 (July 1967), p. 35.

23. *Ibid.,* p. 38; M. Vojta, "A Critical View of Vacuum Aspiration: A New Method

for the Termination of Pregnancy," *Obstetrics and Gynecology*, 30 (July 1967), pp. 28ff.

24. The following incidences of perforated uteruses from the D & C have been reported: .09 percent, by N. Chitu *et al.*, "Major Traumatic Lesions Following Lawfully Induced Abortions," *Obstetrica si Ginecologia* (Bucharest), 3 (1963), p. 237; .17 percent, by K.-H. Mehlan, "The Effects of Legalization of Abortion on the Health of Mothers in Eastern Europe," *Proceedings of the Seventh Conference of the International Planned Parenthood Federation, Singapore, February 1963, Excerpta Medica:* International Congress Series, No. 72 (1964), p. 214; .7 percent by E. Vladov *et al.*, "Schwangerschaftsunterbrechung mit Vakuumaspiration," *Gynaecologia* (Basel), 159 (1965), p. 54; 6 percent, by K.-H. Mehlan, "Legaliserung der Schwangerschaftsunterbrechungen: Ja oder Nein," *Das Deutsche Gesundheitswesen*, 15 (June 9, 1960), p. 1206.

25. Kerslake and Casey, *op. cit.*, pp. 38–39, 41.

26. Vojta, *op. cit.*, p. 32.

27. A. Peretz *et al.*, "Evacuation of the Gravid Uterus by Negative Pressure," *American Journal of Obstetrics and Gynecology*, 98 (May 1, 1967), p. 18–22.

28. E. Vladov, "The Vacuum Aspiration Method for Interruption of Early Pregnancy," *American Journal of Obstetrics and Gynecology*, 99 (September 15, 1967), pp. 202–07; Z. Dvorák *et al.*, "Termination of Pregnancy by Vacuum Aspiration," *Lancet*, 2 (November 11, 1967), pp. 997–98 (Dvořák, incidentally, believes the method is unsuitable after the 10th week of pregnancy); *cf. Uterine Aspiration Procedures* (Wilmington, Delaware: The Lalor Foundation, January 1968), for a number of further articles on the method, including discussions of various machines and parts.

29. P. C. Wu, "The Use of Vacuum Bottle in Therapeutic Abortion: A Collective Survey," *Chinese Medical Journal* (Peking), 85 (April 1966), pp. 245–48.

30. D. E. Reid, "Assessment and Management of the Seriously Ill Patient Following Abortion," *Journal of the American Medical Association*, 199 (March 13, 1967), pp. 805–12; M. D. Silver *et al.*, "Air Embolism: A Discussion of Maternal Mortality with a Report of 1 Survivor," *Obstetrics and Gynecology*, 31 (March 1968), pp. 403–05; C. R. Oberst, "Septic Shock in Abortion," *Journal of the Kentucky Medical Association*, 65 (September 1967), pp. 857–62; L. Speroff *et al.*, "The Management of Bacterial Shock and Septic Abortion," *Connecticut Medicine*, 30 (October 1966), pp. 722–24; T. H. Freilich *et al.*, "Complete Obstruction of the Vagina After Use of Potassium Permanganate," *Journal of the American Osteopath Association*, 67 (September 1967), pp. 31–33. For some detailed studies on the cause of death in illegal abortions, see: L. B. Stevenson, "Maternal Death and Abortion, Michigan 1955–1964," *Michigan Medicine*, 66 (March 1967), pp. 287–91; G. Cimbura, "Studies of Criminal Abortion Cases in Ontario," *Journal of Forensic Sciences*, 12 (April 1967), pp. 223–29; L. P. Fox, "Abortion Deaths in California," *American Journal of Obstetrics and Gynecology*, 90 (July 1, 1967), pp. 645ff.

31. C. Tietze, "Mortality with Contraception and Induced Abortion," *Studies in Family Planning*, No. 45 (September 1969), pp. 6–8; see, for instance, the following statement: "There is little scientific evidence that in the United States today, in the year 1953, any marked deterioration in the physical condition of women, aborted for therapeutic reasons in a hospitalized setting, will take place" (Alan F. Guttmacher, in *Therapeutic Abortion, op. cit.*, p. 12). A similar claim is made by Garrett Hardin in *The Case for Legalized Abortion Now, op. cit.*, p. 72; and by Kenneth R. Niswander, *op. cit.*, p. 57.

32. Carl Müller, "The Dangers of Abortion," *World Medical Journal*, 13 (May-June 1966), pp. 78–80.

33. Müller cites the published proceedings of that congress as: A. Mayer, *Erfahrungen mit der Schwangerschaftungsunterbrechung in der Sowjetrepublik* (Stuttgart: Enke-Verlag, 1933).

34. Müller, *op. cit.*, p. 79.
35. *The Times* (London), January 21, 1966, cited by Müller, *ibid.*, p. 80.
36. R. R. MacDonald, "Complications of Abortion," *Nursing Times*, 63 (March 10, 1967), pp. 305–07.
37. Jan Lindahl, *Somatic Complications Following Legal Abortion* (Stockholm: University of Stockholm, 1958), pp. 166–70.
38. *Ibid.*, p. 168.
39. C. E. Olsen, H. B. Nielsen, E. Østergaard, "Abortus Provocatus Legalis: En Analyse af 21,730 Anmeldelser Til Sundhedsstyrelsen 1961–1965," *Ugeskrift for Laeger*, 129 (October 12, 1967), pp. 1341–51.
40. Tietze, *ibid.*, p. 29.
41. A summary of some of these studies can be found in Franc Novak, "Abortion in Europe," *Proceedings of the Eighth International Conference of the International Planned Parenthood Federation, Santiago, Chile, April, 1967* (London: International Planned Parenthood Federation, 1967), pp. 135–38.
42. K.-H. Mehlan, "The Socialist Countries of Europe," in Bernard Berelson *et al.*, (eds.), *Family Planning and Population Programs* (Chicago: University of Chicago Press, 1966), pp. 211–12.
43. Imre Hirschler, "Abortion in Hungary," paper presented at the International Conference on Abortion, Hot Springs, Virginia, November 17–20, 1968; Anton Cernoch, material presented at the International Conference on Abortion; Franc Novak, material presented at the International Conference on Abortion. The papers given at this conference are scheduled for publication in early 1970 in a book entitled *Abortion in a Changing World* (New York: Columbia University Press).
44. András Klinger, "Demographic Effects of Abortion Legislation in Some European Socialist Countries," in *Proceedings of the World Population Conference, Belgrade, 1965*, Vol. II (New York: United Nations, 1967), p. 89.
45. Mehlan, "The Socialist Countries of Europe," *op. cit.*, p. 212.
46. Hirschler, *op. cit.*
47. Malcolm Potts, "Legal Abortion in Eastern Europe," *The Eugenics Review*, 59 (December 1967), p. 235.
48. Tietze, *op. cit.*, p. 25.
49. Potts, *op. cit.*, p. 235.
50. Christopher Tietze and Hans Lehfeldt, "Legal Abortion in Eastern Europe," *Journal of the American Medical Association*, 175 (April 1, 1961), p. 1153.
51. Anton Cernoch, "Experiences in Czechoslovakia with the Effects and Consequences of Legalized Artificial Termination of Pregnancy," unpublished paper delivered at the United Nations World Population Conference, Belgrade, August 30–September 10, 1965, pp. 4–5; a summary of this paper may be found in *World Population Conference, Belgrade, 1965, op. cit.*, p. 314; *cf.* Anton Cernoch, "Authorizations for Interruption of Pregnancy in Czechoslovakia: Study of Their Effects and Consequences," *Gynaecologia* (Basel), 160 (1965), pp. 293–99.
52. András Klinger, "Abortion Programs," in *Family Planning and Population Programs, op. cit.*, p. 474.
53. Tietze, "Legal Abortion in Industrialized Countries," *op. cit.*, p. 27.
54. K.-H. Mehlan, "Legal Abortions in Roumania," *The Journal of Sex Research*, 1 (March 1965), p. 37.
55. Franc Novak, "Abortion in Europe," *op. cit.*, p. 138.
56. E. A. Sadvokasova, "Birth Control Measures and Their Influence on Population Replacement," in *World Population Conference, Belgrade, 1965, op. cit.*, p. 114.
57. *Harmful Effects of Induced Abortion* (Tokyo: Family Planning Federation of Japan, 1966); a preliminary report on this study was published by Y. Koya, "The Harmful Effects of Induced Abortion," *World Medical Journal*, 13 (November-December 1966), pp. 170–71.

58. Hidebumi Kubo and Hiroshi Ogino, "Current Aspect and Postoperative Follow-up Study," in *Harmful Effects of Induced Abortion, op. cit.,* p. 26.
59. Seuchi Matsumoto and Matsuo Ozawa, "Artificial Termination of Pregnancy and Menstrual Abnormality," *ibid.,* p. 35.
60. Motoyuki Hayashi and Kazuo Momose, "Statistical Observations on Artificial Abortion and Secondary Sterility," *ibid.,* p. 43.
61. *Ibid.,* p. 42.
62. Chiaki Sawazaki and Shinobu Tanaka, "The Relationship Between Artificial Abortion and Extra-Uterine Pregnancy," *ibid.,* p. 63.
63. Yutaka Mariyama and Osamu Hirokawa, "The Relationship Between Artificial Termination of Pregnancy and Abortion of Premature Birth," *ibid.,* p. 72.
64. Yoshio Furusawa and Tomohiko Koya, "The Influence of Artificial Abortion on Delivery," *ibid.,* p. 83.
65. Yutaka Mariyama, "In Closing," *ibid.,* pp. 94–95.
66. M. Muramatsu, "Medical Aspects of the Practice of Fertility Regulation," in M. Muramatsu (ed.), *Japan's Experience in Family Planning—Past and Present* (Tokyo: Family Planning Federation of Japan, 1967), pp. 77–78.
67. Genichi Nozue, "Abortion in the Far East," *Proceedings of the Eighth International Conference of the International Planned Parenthood Federation, Santiago, Chile, op. cit.,* p. 132.
68. Sung Bong Hong, *Induced Abortion in Seoul, Korea* (Seoul: Dong-A Publishing Co., 1966), p. 60.
69. "Report of the Committee on Natality Problems," submitted to the Head of Government, Jerusalem, 1966 (in Herbrew). Cited in R. Bachi, "Induced Abortions in Israel," paper delivered at the International Conference on Abortion, Hot Springs, Virginia, November 17–20, 1968.

CHAPTER 3

Psychiatric Indications,
Psychiatric Consequences

THE COMPILATION OF DATA and reliable judgments on the psychiatric aspect of abortion is immensely frustrating. The literature on the subject is large, but marked on the whole by vagueness, an excessive reliance on the personal impressions of psychiatrists, a lack of empirical studies, and the absence of any systematic worldwide attempts to bring some methodological order into the whole area. Part of the problem is the result of the illegality of abortion in many places, as well as the controversial nature of the subject; this has hindered research, as has an absence of research funds in general. Part of the difficulty is undoubtedly attributable to the fact that, as many hardheaded empiricists claim, there are few empirical studies which have attempted to evaluate different psychiatric theories, judgments and practices. [1] Thus one finds again and again in the literature the use of interesting hypotheses, imaginative speculations and suggestive insights, but very little in the way of controlled tests to determine the validity of these probings. To say this is hardly to imply that psychiatry as a discipline ought to be rejected; on the contrary, it is extremely valuable. But for the sake of a book of this sort, one would prefer to have genuine data which could be said to represent a consensus on the part of working psychiatrists. This we do not have at present, but a growing interest in the problems should stimulate it in the near future, aided by the availability of more private and government research money. Abortion as a subject of careful, systematic study has been of specialized interest only to relatively few psychiatrists and clinical psychologists. The same names continually leap out at one in the literature. The same data, usually old, keep reappearing. Not only is this frustrating to the researcher, but it means the possible perpetuation of myths and fads. One just doesn't know. In any case, it is necessary to work with the material which exists, however inadequate.

One thing seems clear. Psychiatric indications as a basis for induced abortion are more and more accepted in principle and in practice, at least among those who have not precluded abortion altogether on moral grounds. Those nations which have liberalized their abortion laws in recent decades always take account of possible psychiatric grounds for abortion, under the broad rubric of "health," and this trend is present in the United States as well, particularly where changing state laws are based on the draft code of the American Law Institute. What is less clear, however, is whether abortions granted on the basis of psychiatric indications are actually on the increase (excluding those states which have changed their law and now allow that as an indication). The available evidence points at least to a rise in the *ratio* of abortions performed on psychiatric grounds, if not necessarily a rise of significance in the actual *rate* of such abortions. Harold Rosen, though citing only one article, and that written in 1953, asserts that recommendations for interruption on psychiatric grounds are now on the increase, an assertion supported by Kenneth R. Niswander. [2] J. J. Rovinsky et al. found a rise in the ratio of psychiatric indications at Mt. Sinai Hospital in New York from 24 per 10,000 deliveries in 1953 to 56 per 10,000 in 1964.[3] M. M. Spivak found a rise in the ratio at the Toronto General Hospital from 15 percent in 1954–1597 to 33 percent in 1958–1961 to 58 percent in 1962–1965.[4] Keith P. Russell noted, however, that in the early 1950s there was evidence of a decline in the total number of hospital abortions performed on all grounds, medical and psychiatric, and André Hellegers believes this trend still holds (while conceding a rise in the *ratio* of psychiatric indications).[5] J. A. Routledge discerned a similar trend in Canada by the early 1960s.[6] In New York City the annual number of therapeutic abortions dropped from around 700 in 1943–1947 to about 300 in 1960–1962.[7] Christopher Tietze, citing the above and other studies, also believes a downward trend is discernible, although he mentions that there is an "irregular upward trend" for abortions performed on psychiatric grounds.[8] Not fully known as yet is the effect of the changes in the law in a few states, though the early data from the states of Colorado and California show that psychiatric indications accounted for two-thirds of the legally performed abortions under the new laws.[9]

More germane to this chapter is the rationale behind the use of a "psychiatric indication." *My concern transcends its use as a legal indication for abortion; it will be discussed here as a "reason" for abortion, pertinent to women, doctors and counsellors even in the absence of restrictive laws.* The first point to be observed is that it is in line with current medical practice and ideology to consider the mental and emotional well-being of a person as an appropriate concern of the medical profession. Any number of doctors writing on "psychiatric indications" are fond of citing the definition of "health" formulated by the World Health Organization: a state of physical, mental, and emotional well-being. Their point is a valid one. A doctor has the responsibility, as does the medical profession, to see medicine in a wide context. In line with this responsibility, it is increasingly common for doctors to be concerned with preventive medicine, the psychological and environmental conditions necessary for health, and many other social and physical conditions which have a bearing on a person's "well-being." [10] While a distinction can be made between a woman's physical and mental health, enough is known about psychosomatic medicine to realize that the two are often inseparably related. A physician concerned only with a person's body, interested in curing only her manifest physical ills, would be inadequate, perhaps at times even irresponsible. Naturally, different areas of specialization will take account of different aspects of a person's overall well-being, but in the medical profession as a whole, taking account of psychiatry as part of the medical profession, it should be considered an advance in medicine that the net of concern is being spread ever more widely. Objections can, of course, be raised when there is a genuine trespassing by a doctor or a psychiatrist into areas beyond his competency; but having said this, one should still acknowledge that the trend signaled by the World Health Organization's definition of health is a good one.

To argue, as has André E. Hellegers, that a term like "mental health" is so relative as to be open to any interpretation is to miss the point.[11] All broad concepts are vague, but that is no reason for not employing them and attempting to work with them—assuming all the while that some honest attempt is made to specify their meaning. That it is difficult to define the words "justice" or "peace" or "truth" does not make these words any the less useful as pointing to a domain of concern to human beings. "Health," even restricted to bodily "health," is a vague concept, and it is doubtful that any doctor could give a perfect definition. The phrase "mental health" is no less vague, and psychiatrists wrangle incessantly about what constitutes mental health—as well as what constitutes "sanity" or "normalcy." General phrases can be used to obfuscate issues, and no doubt this is what Hellegers is concerned about, but they also serve the purpose of delineating general areas of human concern. In the absence of better words and in the context of the human necessity to use language, I see no reason why the vagueness of the phrase "mental health" should rule it out as worthy of use, attention and clarification. Equally important, it is vital to take into account the fact that psychological handicaps can be as harmful to human beings as physical handicaps. A visit to any mental institution or a recollection of the effects of psychological disturbances on one's friends and acquaintances underscores this. Psychological illness, in both its extreme and benign forms, is indeed a form of illness and dysfunction, of consequence not only to the individual but to those around him. The long struggle in Western society to take seriously psychiatric disturbances as a form of illness should not be set aside in the abortion discussion. Those who contend, then, that a woman's psychological state in the face of pregnancy should be of major interest are on firm ground, not only in terms of developments in medical thinking, but also, I would add, in terms of broad sensitivity. Moreover, the potentially disastrous impact of maternal mental illness on a child, especially in the first year, cannot be ignored.

To say this, though, is not to deny the need for criteria. There are many degrees of psychological maladjustment and illness, and many real difficulties in establishing meaningful standards. This applies as much in contexts of private counselling as in those of legal indications. How ought one to go about establishing standards, and what ought to count as meaningful norms? One might well agree with those who hold that there are many situations in pregnancy which, if not life-threatening, are "life-devastating." But what are we to count as irreversibly "life-devastating" and what are we to count as open to therapy and amelioration? Moreover, one cannot even begin to grapple with the question of psychiatric indications for abortion unless one also simultaneously grapples with the alternatives provided by the possibility of psychotherapy and drug therapy. This is only to say that psychiatric thinking, so far as it concerns the pregnant woman, must be broad enough to encompass various alternatives. What is humanly possible and what is humanly reasonable? These are very real questions which should be ever present when the mental health of a pregnant woman is considered.

Psychological Effects of Pregnancy

A sensible place to begin is with the psychological effects of pregnancy itself, whether under ideal or poor circumstances. Pregnancy is a major event in the life of a woman. It is a biological event of the first order, since important changes take place in her body both at the hidden level of hormonal and uterine change and at the visible level of a change in weight and appearance. Pregnancy is a psychological event of the first order as well. It will affect a woman's attitude toward herself, toward her body, toward her husband and toward her other children. The attitude of a woman's friends and relatives will influence her response to the event. It can also be called a cultural event, since by producing a child or by the possibility of producing a child a woman is placed in the position of contributing to the procreation of the species and thus relating herself to the broadest biological current in society. Pregnancy, then, raises for a woman the question of her nature as a woman, her potential role as a mother, her relationship to those close to her, including the father and her relatives, her relationship to the whole of society and, most importantly perhaps, her situation as a person in the world. For all these reasons, it is not extreme to say, with Joseph C. Rheingold, that "pregnancy is a crisis." [12]

Precisely what kind of a crisis it is and how the various ingredients should be understood, is less clear. It is still possible, though much less so than in the past, for a woman to die as a result of pregnancy or childbirth. It is also possible for a woman to undergo a very painful childbirth. Possibilities like this, often abetted by misinformed folklore concerning pregnancy, mean that fear will frequently be present, even under the best of circumstances. No woman can automatically assume that she will pass through pregnancy and childbirth in safety; an element of uncertainty remains, especially in areas of poor medical facilities and inadequate prenatal care. Few women, however well off financially and however confident their doctors, can be totally indifferent to the fact that something very important is happening to their bodies. Like the onset of puberty and the advent of menopause, pregnancy represents one of the most important biological incidents in a woman's life. L. H. Biskind, A. A. Robin, N. Pleshette *et al.*, S. M. Tobin and B. Jansson have all stressed, with accompanying evidence, the prevalence in normal women of anxiety, ambivalence and strain when faced with pregnancy.[13]

That such biological changes and crises should evoke a wide variety of psychological responses is hardly surprising. As in puberty and menopause, a woman is forced to make adjustments to the changed state of her body. "All three states," Joseph C. Rheingold writes, "seem to revive and unsettle psychologic conflicts of earlier developmental periods, requiring new and different solutions; all three are significant turning points in the life of the individual, and the mastery of the thus initiated phase depends on the outcome of this crisis, namely, on the solution and maturational reorganization of this disequilibrium." [14] To say that pregnancy is a maturational crisis does not imply that it is not a normal kind of crisis; it is only to say that it is one capable of bringing to the surface a great variety of emotional and mental responses and reactions.

Possibly the best way of putting this is to say that pregnancy represents a personal crisis for a woman, bringing about a special interaction of mind and body, self and society. It is possible to probe this personal crisis at many levels. Rheingold has been suggestive in trying to substantiate his hypothesis that "both the complications of pregnancy and childbirth and the deleterious elements in the rearing process are related to the mother's rejections of herself as a woman." [15] The particular details of his hypothesis need not concern us here, but it is important to see that a woman's evaluation of herself as a person and of herself as a woman will be vitally affected by pregnancy. M. B. Clyne, in fact, has argued that habitual spontaneous abortions in a woman often indicate an ambivalence toward childbearing, uncertainty of feminine role and faulty identification processes in childhood.[16] A woman who has been raised or conditioned to believe that childbirth is normally a joyful event will respond differently from a woman conditioned to believe that pregnancy and childbirth are usually dirty or repugnant states. Where pregnancy is accepted and desired in a society, or in a family setting, the reaction will be different from those circumstances in which pregnancy is socially frowned upon, or families are critical. Erik H. Erikson and G. L. Bibring see pregnancy as a developmental crisis for the personality of the woman.[17] How a woman passes through this crisis will be dependent upon the biological conditions of her pregnancy, which vary from woman to woman, and upon the whole social, psychological and cultural context of her past, present and projected future life.

The social setting of her personal crisis has been stressed by Helene Deutsch:

> The treatment of the pregnant woman by society depends chiefly upon the value that society ascribes to the blessing of children; this value varies at different periods and in different countries. National, political and economic interests as well as ethics and constitutional law play their part here. . . . The psychological experience of pregnancy to a large extent depends upon the condition under which the woman has conceived and in which the expectant child is born. . . . The social fear of the unmarried woman accompanies the psychologically determined normal or neurotic fears. Economic difficulties and illnesses and death in the family may play their part. In brief, environmental factors, direct and indirect, certainly have an effect on the course of the reproductive process.[18]

The extreme steps some women take to avoid pregnancy, documented by the horrendous array of instruments and drugs women have used to abort themselves under the most hazardous conditions, is matched by the extreme dangers some women will risk in order to achieve a birth. A host of investigators of pregnancy have found that fear is a constant element in almost all pregnancies.[19] There may be the fear of not giving birth, or the fear of giving birth; the fear of physical deterioration, of being overburdened, of changing the attitude of those around her; there are any number of possible directions fear can take and any number of possible real or imagined causes. Frequently, fear may be attended with great ambivalence: a desire both to have and not to have a child at the same time, for different reasons and in different degrees. Sheer indifference, absolute calm and perfect certainty of a safe delivery would be most remarkable in any woman. And if this is true of the physical problems of pregnancy, it is no less true of the psychological problems. Considering the physical, psychological and social implications of pregnancy, it is hardly surprising that a woman could have many different and conflicting feelings simultaneously. Given the great variety of life situations and backgrounds of different women, it is not surprising that there are so many different possible reactions.

Moreover, the feelings of a woman at one stage of pregnancy may be very different from those at another stage.[20] A woman's initial reaction to her pregnancy, whether that of depression or elation, is no necessary index of what her attitude might be some weeks or months later. "Morning sickness," the frequent unexpectedness of a pregnancy, the immediate response of those around her may all have a great initial impact on a woman, but may, as the pregnancy progresses, give way to different responses. There appears to be no fixed course. Morning sickness may, for instance, soon disappear, to be succeeded by a feeling of normal health; but toward the end of the pregnancy the additional physical weight a woman will usually bear, which varies from person to person, may introduce a new discomfort. So, too, a family which responds casually to the advent of pregnancy may become more nervous as the actual birth approaches; contrariwise, many women who initially panic in the face of pregnancy are able to pass beyond this to relaxed acceptance. The life situation of the particular woman will obviously make a considerable difference in the way she responds. The psychological impact of pregnancy on an unmarried girl, which in most societies could induce fear and uncertainty because of social disapproval, can easily be matched in power in a married woman already overburdened with a number of small children and a precarious financial situation: the reactions may be different because of these different situations, but may be equally strong and equally fearful.

What induces fear and hostility in one woman may be a source of pleasure and expectation in another—there seem to be no fixed rules for gauging psychological responses in advance. To assert dogmatically that a woman ought not to fear pregnancy or that she should indeed fear pregnancy would be unwise. Women respond differently, and very often the external conditions of their lives—those aspects which might strike a casual observer—have very little to do with the subjective response of the women. How a woman will respond subjectively is not easily predictable, making it almost impossible to lay down external norms about how a woman *ought* to respond to pregnancy. Moreover, how a woman *ought* to respond and how she does in fact respond are two different things. The moralists and the theoreticians of marriage and pregnancy may be able to set forth all sorts of reasons why a woman should react happily to pregnancy. It will be the duty of the psychiatrist, however, or the doctor to take account of the actual psychological situation of the woman and not just how, in the best of all possible worlds, any given woman should react to pregnancy.

Pregnancy: Mental Illness and the Mother-Child Relationship

There is, though, a need to be more specific here and to go beyond the perhaps banal observation that the reaction of women to pregnancy can vary to a considerable degree. Two questions may be raised. First, what is the effect of pregnancy and childbirth on preexisting mental illness? Second, what difference is a woman's attitude toward pregnancy likely to make in her later relationship with her child? On the first question, no common agreement seems to exist. On the one hand, L. Linn and P. Polatin hold that childbirth plays an important role in the development of mental disease.[21] With Gregory Zilboorg, they would agree that "childbirth appears to be the nodal point of the conflict and the casuative agent of the psychosis."[22] The general reasoning in both cases is that, because pregnancy and childbirth are critical events, a woman predisposed to mental illness is likely to have this illness triggered by the trauma of pregnancy. It is not the pregnancy per se which is the cause of mental illness so much as the possibility that pregnancy can incite latent illness or exacerbate already existing neuroses and psychoses. Rheingold has also pointed to a number of circumstances under which pregnancy can trigger a severe neurotic or psychotic reaction.[23] On the other hand, however, T. Harder noted in a Norwegian study that women who had shown symptoms of mental disability or illness prior to pregnancy had about the same features afterwards, while women who had previously been mentally well were for the most part still well afterwards.[24] Noyes and Kolb have written that "experience does not show that pregnancy and the birth of the child influence adversely the course of the schizophrenias, manic-depressive illnesses or the majority of the psychoses. . . . Even women who have a postpartum psychosis often go through later pregnancies without ego disorganization."[25] Alan F. Guttmacher takes much the same position: "There is little evidence that pregnancy in itself worsens a psychosis, either intensifying it or rendering prognosis for full recovery less likely."[26] Indeed, the possibility of birth may in some cases help a woman's psychological condition, but of course there is again not enough evidence thoroughly to substantiate this hypothesis.[27] C. Tetlow has aptly observed that one finds, in fact, two schools of thought, one seeing pregnancy as causative of mental disease in those already predisposed, and the other holding that pregnancy is at most a precipitating occasion.[28]

The second question is more critical. While it may be perfectly pos-

sible to bring a woman through pregnancy and childbirth without exacerbating latent neurotic or psychotic tendencies or without worsening
already overt states, this is not the same as saying that her relationship
with her child once born, or even before birth, will not be affected.
Robert Seidenberg and Mary F. Brew, in a study of 103 cases of psychotic reactions associated with pregnancy, report that "rejection of the
newborn was a universal finding, symbolically or in fact, i.e., neglect of
the infant and in some cases actual attempts at infanticide." [29] That kind
of situation is undoubtedly extreme, but any strong form of infant rejection, with all of the havoc such rejection can wreak in the formative
years of a child's life, is of more than ordinary concern. As Harry M.
Murdock has suggested: "So far as the mother goes, it is our belief that
the existence of psychosis per se is not a valid reason for abortion: the
children of psychotic mothers run no greater risk of becoming psychotic . . . than do the children of non-psychotic parents. The danger lies in
the prolonged, close influence of such exceedingly sick people on the
child, particularly during its formative years." [30] Murdock, however, is
here touching upon a disputed area. Three researchers at the National
Institute of Mental Health, for instance, found that the rate of schizophrenia in children of schizophrenic mothers, but raised before their first
year of age by normal parents, was twice that of a control group of children from normal mothers adopted similarly by normal parents.[31]

Apart from the extreme hazards of psychosis, there seems little doubt
that a mother hostile to her child can psychologically harm the child in
many terrible ways. What the child comes to be will in great part be dependent upon the earliest responses of his mother toward him. There are
few psychiatrists who would disagree with the flat assertion of Richard
Jenkins: "There is no emotional deprivation more severe than the rejection of the young child by the mother or mother person who takes care
of him." [32] At the same time, as Jenkins stresses, and as Rheingold brings
out with even greater force, ambivalence on the part of a mother toward
her child is common, even in those who would by all standards be adjudged perfectly "sane" and "normal." Precisely because a child makes so
many demands on a mother, calling her out of herself in ways which are
often pressing and aggravating, the presence of a newborn child can
pose a serious crisis for a woman, particularly a woman who is immature or suffering from physical disabilities. Rheingold goes so far as to
hypothesize the existence of a maternal filicidal impulse. As he puts it:
"The maternal filicidal impulse is both a fact and a hypothesis; that it
exists is a fact, that it exists in every mother is a hypothesis." Citing Helene Deutsch and J. C. Flugel, as well as others to support his theory, he
also suggests that "in some cases of self-abortion one has the impression
that the woman was intent on murdering the fetus, not just trying to rid
herself of an unwanted child." [33] While the existence of such an impulse

is a matter of speculation, it is hardly speculative to say that many women, for good reasons and bad, do not want to have the child they carry within them, much less to raise the child afterwards. N. M. Simon *et al.*, evaluating the psychiatric illnesses in a group of 32 women after abortion in St. Louis, 30 of whom had illnesses predating their abortions, found a high rate of rejection of the female biological role and the presence of sadomasochistic impulses. "Therapeutic abortion," they wrote, "offers an optimal circumstance for acting out sadomasochistic fantasies and impulses. . . . Pregnancy in many cases fulfills the role of gratifying the woman's unconscious masochistic wish, while the abortion gratifies the sadistic impulse (directed against the fetus) as well as the masochistic wish (assault on the self)." [34]

Yet a rejection reponse is frequently matched by an equally strong response to have the child; that is why ambivalence, stemming from simultaneous but contradictory impulses, seems so characteristic of pregnancy. The relationship of a newly born child to its mother will be very much determined by which of these contrasting impulses gets the upper hand. Therese Benedek has put the matter very nicely: "The physiologic and mental apparatus of the infant represents a system which communicates broadly and fluently with the system of the mother—with all aspects of the mother's personality: with her id, her ego, and her superego. Through the processes of identification with the mother, the infant develops from the undifferentiated state of the newborn to an individual with structuralized mental apparatus which is in control of psychic and somatic processes."[35] Of relevance also here is the increasing, though still inadequate, data suggesting that the attitude of a woman toward her pregnancy can have an affect on the fetus itself. A study conducted by D. H. Stott discovered that, in a group of mentally defective children, a large proportion were born after periods of marked emotional stress during pregnancy, either because of psychological conflicts within the mother or family conflicts.[36] W. R. Thompson found that prenatal maternal anxiety has a significant affect on the emotional characteristics of newborn rats.[37] A 1961 study of 48 pregnant women showed that women who were later to experience complications during delivery or to give birth to children with mental or physical abnormalities, had displayed high scores on anxiety tests during their pregnancies; the anxieties stemmed mainly from fear of pregnancy and childbirth.[38]

Rheingold summarizes a number of further studies and speculations which make it seem increasingly likely that there is indeed a prenatal influence possible on the fetus.[39] Premature births, congenital malformations, emotional disturbances, behavioral disorders, delinquency, schizophrenia, epilepsy and mental subnormality may all have a relationship to the emotional attitude of the mother toward the fetus or to the emotional circumstances of her pregnancy. It is not necessary to take these possibilities as proven facts. It is only necessary, for our purposes, to keep an open mind about the possibilities. If it is at all possible that the attitude of a mother toward her fetus may significantly affect the future life of that fetus, then the course of responsibility would seem to require taking into account, so far as possible, the evidence there is and making use of the evidence accordingly. There is still much that is not known about the relationship between a woman and her fetus, and not much more is known about the relationship of a mother to her newborn child. Both are areas of considerable controversy and speculation. That some relationship of importance exists in both cases seems a reasonable hypothesis; just exactly what the relationship is and what, apart from the most extreme circumstances, is crucial to this relationship is much less clear than one would wish.

There is, however, a considerable difference between noting the possibility of damage being done to a fetus by a disturbed woman and damage done to a newborn infant (both physical and psychological). and concluding, therefore, that an abortion is warranted by the data. If, as suggested, it is the case that a very large proportion of women, possibly the majority, may have feelings of hostility toward their potential children or at least sufficient fears to make them ambivalent about giving birth to a child, one would then seem forced to conclude that the mere existence of hostility toward a fetus, or fear of childbirth, would not in itself be a significant indication that an abortion was required for mental health. If even women who are relatively mentally healthy and women who would in most circumstances be quite capable of raising and enjoying a child, can at at times be hostile toward their fetus or child, or anxious about pregnancy, childbirth and childbearing, then the mere existence of these reactions would seem to indicate, by themselves, only one safe conclusion: a subjective report from a woman that she is hostile, fearful or anxious provides no presumption for or against abortion. So, too, the fact that attitudes can vary considerably from one period during pregnancy to another and that the attitude after birth can either improve or deteriorate—usually in an unpredictable way—gives one even less solid ground to stand on in trying to specify genuinely disabling and significantly dangerous psychological conditions which might be used to indicate the need for an abortion. At the same time, since dangerous conditions may be possible and will in fact exist in some cases, the vagueness and uncertainty of the whole area provides no excuse to dodge it entirely. Bengt Jansson, at the conclusion of a lengthy, careful study in Sweden, a study not directly related to the problem of abortion, found that the following factors are, in general, likely to increase the risk of mental illness in pregnant women: "age over 30 years, illegitimacy, previous psychiatric hospital care—especially if this care was related to a previous delivery, vulnerable personality equipment—especially asthenic attitude." [40] While useful to know, it is clear that the general rise in risk for women in these categories is *too* general to serve as adequate criteria for abortion.

Formulating Psychiatric Criteria

The corrective for vagueness is the formulation of workable criteria, criteria which can be given a *reasonably* clear meaning and which could be applied in particular situations. Jerome M. Kummer is certainly correct in saying that "no hard and fast criteria have been established (and they never will be!) for the indication of therapeutic abortion in connection with psychiatric illness. Considerable diversity of opinion exists among psychiatrists." [41] Kummer is, however, quite wrong in saying that, apart from his own attempts to spell out criteria, "no others have been written." [42] On the contrary, there have been a number of attempts to fashion criteria. Perhaps the first and still most systematic attempt was made by H. Binder, in two articles, appearing in 1943 and 1951. [43] Binder contended that abortion was indicated if it was found that pregnancy had given rise to a state of grave and chronic mental disease or if a woman displayed little power of resistance to psychological stress. He spelled out two general standards: (1) evidence of an abnormal psychological constitution prior to pregnancy and (2) social stress of such a kind and degree that the situation could not be relieved by ordinary social measures. Binder emphasized that *both* these conditions should be fulfilled before termination of pregnancy could be justified on psychiatric grounds.

J. D. W. Pearce points to three other attempts in the literature, all relatively early, to formulate criteria: [44] A. Lewis, for instance, stated in 1950 that abortion could be psychiatrically justified when there exist symptoms of organic psychoses which are likely to get worse, a history of suicidal attempts or infanticidal attempts in connection with previous pregnancies, and evidence of severe depression in present pregnancy. Tredgold and Tredgold in 1953 distinguished between mental disorders appearing before quickening, which they felt to be capable of amelioration, and disorders appearing after quickening, which they felt to be more serious and not so open to therapeutic help. Hart in 1929 succinctly stated his own norms (as quoted by Pearce): "for preexisting psychosis terminate only very rarely; for schizophrenia arising in pregnancy and for recurrent psychosis not related to former pregnancy, no termination; for recurrent psychosis of pregnancy and puerperium, terminate; for severe active anxiety and depressions stemming from pregnancy, termination depends on a question of degree." During the debate leading to the change in the English law in 1967, the British Royal

Medico-Psychological Association issued a statement on criteria which, among other things, proposed that if a "severely subnormal woman, or one who is suffering from severe chronic mental illness, becomes pregnant, there is a *prima facie* case for therapeutic abortion." [45]

More recently, Alexander Simon has suggested, not strict criteria, but elements which should enter into any decision to abort on psychiatric grounds:

(1) the danger of the exacerbation of an existing psychosis or the precipitation of one, including postpartum psychosis; (2) the exacerbation or precipitation of a serious neurosis; (3) the number of children the patient already has (two or three or more children) and her serious wish regarding the pregnancy; (4) the question of depression and suicide; (5) the family situation and the relationships, e.g., if the husband suffers from alcoholism or other mental and emotional disturbances which interfere with his role as father and household head; (6) mental retardation; (7) the patient's socioeconomic state; and (8) fetal indications. [46]

This is, of course, a very comprehensive list and just as obviously subject to varying interpretations. But it is a list which covers well all of the considerations suggested in the literature dealing with the psychiatric indications for abortion.

What is lacking here, and what someone like Binder would emphasize, is a mention of the problem of a *severe* versus a *relatively mild* indication. Each of the "considerations" mentioned by Simon could obviously be the occasion of a psychological crisis. However, the main emphasis in the literature places the stress on a *severe* crisis: a psychiatric indication would exist, following Binder, only if one could honestly say the crisis was *very severe*. This is the emphasis of E. W. Anderson, who holds that abortion would practically never be indicated in the case of an affective illness unless it could be shown that this illness was directly associated with a personality disorder likely to be intensified by the arrival of a child. With most others, Anderson argues that, while there is a divergence of opinion on the advisability of termination in the case of a schizophrenic woman, there does not seem to be much evidence that pregnancy will have an intensifying effect on the psychosis. In the instance of women with obsessional disorders and anankastic personalities, Anderson believes that abortion in such instances is usually risky because this personality type is likely to suffer guilt reactions. The only instance in which Anderson would readily advise abortion is in the case of a "worn-out" mother, one whose total life situation clearly suggests that she would not be able to tolerate the stress of another child, an important "indication" in the Scandinavian countries. Even here, though, Anderson points out that no rigid lines can be drawn, since a woman may, with the help of social workers and other supportive agencies and individuals, be able psychologically to survive another birth. Throughout, he stresses that each case must be judged individually.[47]

Jerome M. Kummer's own criteria are not very different from those of Binder, Simon and Anderson:

> In general it can be said that the therapeutic interruption of pregnancy should be considered when the history of pregnancy and psychiatric examination provides strong reason to believe that the pregnancy, if permitted to continue, or the delivery, would result in a mental illness of a serious nature (or would gravely impede the recovery of an already ill woman). As to what constitutes a *serious* illness, some of the criteria are: (1) the possibility of the patient injuring or killing herself and others, particularly the newborn; (2) the problems related to management (hospitalization, restraint, care of the newborn, etc.); (3) extremes in anguish such as seen in some obsession-compulsion neuroses; (4) the length of the illness and its reversibility either spontaneously or with treatment; (5) the effect on the child through heredity and environment.[48]

Harold Rosen has usefully distinguished among a variety of different types of women who are referred to psychiatrists. One group "can be carried to term with relatively superficial, primarily supportive, infrequent psychotherapy." Another group are "those who are determined to have an abortion, legally or otherwise, and who, if they do have it, show no untoward emotional after effect." A third group

> is composed of those patients who, once they do have the interruption which they so desire, either develop severe neurotic or psychotic symptoms or separate from their previous sexual partners, sometimes even by divorce. In most such patients, the undesired pregnancy merely highlights their already existent, and usually pronounced maladjustment. These patients as a result concentrate their hostility, but for the moment only, on the still unborn child.[49]

Judging the Criteria

What are we to make of this welter of possible criteria and indications? On the face of it, none of the criteria and considerations put forward by the different writers cited is irrational; they are, indeed, quite reasonable if one is going to be at all concerned with psychiatric considerations in making a determination about abortion. The distinction between severely crippling psychological illnesses and mild disabilities is some help, but naturally even words like "severe" and "mild" are vague, open to divergent readings. Two questions may help to focus the issues more sharply. The first is, what likelihood is there that the potentially extreme psychological dangers will materialize and breakdowns actually take place? This question can be answered only in the context of the possibility of therapeutic success during the potentially dangerous times. The second question is, when we speak of psychiatric indications and criteria, is it legitimate to bring in the total life situation of a woman, encompassing such things as her social and economic state?

On the first point, the possibility of suicide and the most extreme kind of psychotic breakdown would surely count, if anything would count, as a severe indication. While a number of psychiatrists stress the *possibility* of suicide, on the basis of some threats and some genuine attempts, the evidence of the actual incidence of suicide suggests that it is in fact very rare. Kerstin Höök's study of refused abortions in Sweden points out that, between 1938 and 1958, there were only three cases of suicide following rejection of an application for legal abortion.[50] So far as I can judge from the literature, there are no data to support a view that suicide for refused abortion, or as the result of pregnancy, is significant anywhere. Harold Rosen, while citing the possibility of suicide as a psychiatric indication, is prone to be very skeptical of threats of suicide, pointing out that such threats are often used to blackmail psychiatrists.[51] Howard C. Taylor makes substantially the same point.[52] S. Leon Israel, Kenneth R. Niswander, Rosenberg and Silver, Myre Sim and William B. Spry are all skeptical of the real likelihood of suicide.[53] The source of this widespread skepticism rests on one simple point—the absence of any significant evidence showing the likelihood of suicide if an abortion is denied. Indeed, there is some evidence that the incidence of suicide during pregnancy is actually lower than at other times in women's lives.[54] On the other hand, this generalization does not necessarily apply to suicide *attempts* in pregnant women, which two Australians, Whitlock and Edwards, found to be comparable to that in nonpregnant women of the same age. The authors also found, however, that pregnancy itself was the main cause of the attempt in only 7 percent of the cases, the vast majority (76.5 percent) having tried to kill themselves on an impulse, because of an "interpersonal dispute" (after a fight with their husbands or boyfriends); that was also the main cause among the nonpregnant women studied. None of the pregnant women in the study succeeded in taking her life (whereas some of the nonpregnant patients did), and the authors add that a search of the records in Brisbane "failed to discover a pregnant woman who had taken her life." [55] This study was not directly concerned with the possibility of abortion, but the authors noted that, in their opinion, "for the majority of patients making suicidal threats, termination of pregnancy will not necessarily deter the patient from putting her threat into action, as the pregnancy is not the most important cause of her emotional distress." [56] Harold Marcus has made the interesting suggestion that, when a woman knowingly undergoes the risk of an illegal abortion, she may unwittingly be desirous of suicide. It may be the desire for an abortion (at least an illegal abortion) which represents a real suicidal threat.[57] Nonetheless, even the most remote possiblity of suicide (especially when a threat has been made) cannot be put aside; no physician can simply ignore a threat of suicide.

As for the likelihood of a severe neurosis or psychosis as a result of a pregnancy carried to term, the general opinion seems to be that only in the rarest cases would supportive therapy be totally useless. As early as 1934, long before the advent of new techniques and drugs, Clarence O. Cheney argued that there seem to be no psychiatric disorders which would be a total contraindication to pregnancy. He also pointed out that abortion does not necessarily guarantee that a woman's psychotic condition will be helped.[58] John L. McKelvey has noted that the Sloane Hospital for Women shut off all psychiatric indications out of a belief that there are no "psychiatric indications which will involve the interruption of a pregnancy which will cure the patient's psychiatric difficulty and which cannot be handled in some other way." [59] Myre Sim, E. W. Anderson and G. F. Abercrombie are all skeptical of the general category of "psychiatric indications for abortion," not on the grounds that severe psychiatric difficulties cannot exist in pregnancy, but that there exist alternative ways of handling these difficulties other than by abortion.[60] The point of these citations is not to suggest that the whole category of "severe" indications is a fiction—for that would be unreasonable—but only to point out that no one, so far as I can discover, is willing to claim that there exist cases which are absolutely hopeless, so hopeless that, even with psychotherapy, intensive care, and social and family support, a woman could not carry through a pregnancy. This is only to say that the "severity" of psychological danger as an indication cannot be determined independently of a related judgment on the possibility of treatment and amelioration of the psychiatric condition.

That this kind of contextual judgment is necessary would seem indirectly indicated by the generally admitted trend on the part of psychiatrists to take into account not only specific psychiatric illnesses—of the kind which can be labeled for textbook or legal purposes—but also a woman's psychiatric situation in light of the social and economic setting of her life. As Harold Rosen has put it: "The medical, including the psychiatric, indications must be utilized if the abortion is to have legal justification. However, in most cases, the socioeconomic factors are pronounced and whether the interruption of the pregnancy is legal or extra-legal, the actual indications, are, for the most part, economic." [61] Kenneth R. Niswander, in surveying the psychiatric literature, points out that most authors are now prone to align themselves with "progressive social change," and they thereby consider the "socioeconomic factors rather than the psychiatric indications." [62] Some investigators complain very loudly about this trend, arguing that the psychiatrist is called on when no other legal tactic seems feasible.[63] Sidney Bolter observes that psychiatrists are often under great pressure to give specific psychiatric appraisals on the basis of few and very rushed visits, and then urged to state in an unequivocal fashion that suicide or severe breakdown is probable, something they are likely to be in no position really to know. [64] And A. Peck notes that, after a psychiatrist has been consulted by a gynecologist on behalf of a woman wanting an abortion, "it is unusual for the psychiatrist to remain in contact with the patient. Follow-up interviews are infrequent and treatment is rarely begun as a result of consultations sought to obtain an abortion." [65] Whether this shows, in general, an inability to pay for long-term treatment, or that the psychiatric condition was temporary, is unclear.

Jacob H. Friedman, while envisioning the possibility of defining reasonably exact criteria, also observes that a decision on the part of a psychiatrist is likely to be influenced by his own personality, his particular psychiatric training and his overall approach to humanitarian, social, economic and religious problems.[66] Richard Fox has stressed the difficulty in practice of drawing a sharp line between "social" and "psychiatric" indications:

A woman with an alcoholic husband, seven children, no friends, and arrears in rent has social problems which cannot fail to influence her mental state, and hence the justification for therapeutic abortion: If there is one lesson to be learned from fifty years' research it is that social and mental health are inseparable.[67]

If, then, there are many signs that psychiatrists will in fact make their judgments in the light of very broad considerations of "health," ought one to conclude that psychiatrists are overstepping the limits of their competence? Should they restrict themselves solely to the most narrowly definable cases of extreme, proven threats to a woman's psychological health? I do not believe that this need be demanded of a psychiatrist. As suggested earlier, the general trend in medicine is to see health in the broadest possible terms. In the field of psychiatry as a whole, it is surely considered acceptable today for a psychiatrist to take into account the entire life setting of a person. Very few psychiatrists are any longer content to see their role as simply that of labeling this condition or that, or making predictions about the outcome of illnesses. On the contrary, their usual concern, prescinding from the abortion controversy, is to help a person function adequately in his or her social and cultural environment. The judgment, for instance, whether a person should be committed to a mental institution, whether he should be given certain drugs, whether he should be given intensive or relatively relaxed treatment, will be very much determined by a psychiatrist's consideration of the broadest context of a person's life.

If this breadth of concern is considered legitimate in most other psychiatric situations—where a person's family may be consulted and brought into treatment, where biographical details are solicited, where a person's education and income are at times considered relevant—there seem no good grounds for excluding it from consideration where abortion is concerned. The laws of different states or nations may, of course, not allow such breadth, which poses a separate legal problem. But, in general, psychiatrists should not be blamed for approaching the problem of abortion much as they approach other problems which come before them: taking into consideration all the different influences and situations which bear upon a patient's life. This is not to imply that a psychiatrist who personally favored abortion on demand, even request, should arbitrarily tailor his reading of the evidence to support a recommendation for abortion. That would surely be unprofessional conduct. Yet it would be equally unprofessional for a psychiatrist opposed to abortion on moral grounds systematically to minimize a woman's psychiatric difficulties. In the same vein, to expect that a physician could free himself from the influence of his own training and experiences, rendering Olympian judgments, is to expect too much of any human being. Like everyone else, a psychiatrist must make his professional judgments out of the background of his personal history, training and professional experience, and these elements will differ from person to person. That this is so, however, is no basis for arguing that psychiatrists should be kept entirely out of the area of abortion. What one can do is to attempt to get a number of psychiatric judgments and see if something of a professional consensus can be achieved. Beyond that, human resources come to an end.

One further argument should be considered here, put forward so far as I know only by Jerome M. Kummer. Kummer has contended that the universal prevalence of abortion, legal and illegal, and the extraordinary trouble women will go to achieve an abortion point to the existence of an "instinctive" drive for abortion once the internal and external stresses on a woman's life reach a critical point.[68] He implies, but does not say, that the existence of this "instinct" points to the reasonableness of allowing women to fulfill such an instinctive drive. It is hard to know what to make of an argument like this. In situations of stress, people have all kinds of "instincts": lovers may be said to have an instinct to kill their rivals; mothers driven to distraction by existing children are sometimes given to homicidal drives toward these children; husbands often feel compelled to kill their wives in unhappy marriages, just as wives feel impelled to kill husbands. In other words, all situations of stress are likely to induce feelings of hostility, aggression, escape and so on. If there is an "instinct" to abortion under certain conditions of high stress, it should be subsumed under the generic head of the reaction of all individuals to situations of extreme stress. The mere presence of an impulse to escape stress, therefore, proves nothing and entails nothing. More to the point is what means are effective and what means are ineffective in coping with the stress? In the case of abortion, that question throws us back into the whole host of other considerations which should come into play in making a judgment on abortion. Even if one could agree with Dr. Kummer that there is an "instinct" to abortion in certain situations, even he would probably agree that this hardly provides us with an answer as to whether an abortion is thereby made desirable or morally correct. In any case, caution is needed because, as Joseph C. Rheingold has suggested, the apparent drive for an abortion can possibly be masking very different unconscious drives: a drive to self-destruction, in the instance of women who repeatedly use dangerous means to abort themselves, or perhaps a drive not just to be free from abortion but positively to commit feticide. These are only speculations, though very interesting ones, but of a sort to make considerable caution necessary in arriving at any judgment concerning the true nature of a woman's expressed desire to have an abortion.[69]

Has anything been achieved in the above discussion of criteria? Perhaps not, for in the absence of systematic empirical studies and in the presence of a vast difference of opinion among psychiatrists themselves, it is unlikely that anything approaching consistency of practice, necessary clarity and definition can be at present achieved. This is not, however, to say that consistency and clarity cannot be achieved in some local areas and hospitals, primarily as the fruit of experience and the cumulative development of a working local consensus among psychiatrists and medical men who have learned how to correct and complement each other's judgment. J. M. Ingram *et al.* discuss the great effectiveness of periodic retrospective reviews of past judgments in facilitating consistency and consensus.[70]

My own conclusions at this point from the literature are as follows. First, the category of "psychiatric indications" is legitimate, as much in the absence of any abortion laws—where the "indications" would be "reasons" rather than legal standards—as where there are laws. Moreover, the raising of psychiatric indications to a status equal to that of purely medical indications is both reasonable and desirable in the light of general trends in medicine. Second, although almost any woman *could*, with intensive care and support, be brought through a pregnancy in no worse a state than she began, it seems reasonably clear that pregnancy and childbirth can precipitate or intensify psychological illness. Third, it is professionally legitimate for a psychiatrist to make his professional judgments not only on the narrow basis of specifiable mental or emotional conditions but also on the broader grounds of these conditions as they are likely to interact with the social, economic and cultural environment of a patient's life. The full significance of psychological illness can be seen only in the full setting of a woman's life.

Fourth, the fact of considerable, and perhaps intractable, vagueness in this whole area, while it calls for considerable caution in making any judgments at all, provides no good basis for ignoring the whole problem or ruling it out of consideration in making moral decisions; the danger of arbitrariness, though, is of course heightened.

Psychological Reactions to Abortion

Just how complicated and slippery the whole psychiatric problem is may be indicated by an analysis of the psychological reactions to abortion. As noted above, a number of psychiatrists believe that the possibility of a guilt response or of psychological depression is a consideration of some importance in making psychological judgments. Thus even those who would argue vehemently that psychological indications are a valid ground for abortion would also concede the necessity of taking into account a woman's possible psychological reaction in the aftermath of an abortion. Would the abortion worsen her psychological condition in the instance of a woman already afflicted prior to pregnancy with some degree of maladjustment, or, in the case of psychologically normal women, would an abortion be likely to bring on feelings of guilt or perhaps instigate other adverse psychological reactions?

Let us survey this literature and see what we find. One could do no better than to begin with Martin Ekblad's follow-up study of 479 Swedish women who had undergone legal abortion.[71] Ekblad's study is one of the few reasonably thorough ones in the whole of the literature and for that reason has a special importance. The study was begun in 1949 and finished in the early 1950s, and all of the women studied had their legal abortions in a Stockholm hospital. Sixty-five percent of the women were married, 8 percent divorcees or widows, and 27 percent unmarried. All of these women had legal abortions, thus passing through a number of examinations to be granted the abortion in the first place. They were not a "typical" group of women in terms of their psychological adjustment; 58 percent had manifested symptoms of chronic neurosis of abnormal personality even before the pregnancy in question. There were also among this group a very large number of disturbed marriages or, in the case of the unmarried women, disturbed relationships with the father of the child. The full breakdowns would be too lengthy to present here, but the upshot was as follows: 65 percent of the women stated that they were satisfied with their abortion and had no self-reproaches; 10 percent had no self-reproaches, but felt the operation itself was unpleasant; 14 percent had mild degree of self-reproach; and 11 percent said they had a serious degree of self-reproach or regretted having had the operation. Ekblad also found that the guilt was greatest in women influenced by others toward abortion and least in those women who wanted an abortion themselves. Of the group of 11 percent with severe self-reproach, Ekblad notes that, even though the women themselves reported a severe reaction, from a psychiatric point of view the reactions were considered mild; that is, only 1 percent actually had their further ability to work impaired. Ekblad also adds that there was a correlation between the degree of felt self-reproach and the severity of the woman's psychological condition prior to pregnancy: "The greater the psychiatric indications for a legal abortion are, the greater is also the risk of unfavorable psychic sequelae after the operation." [72]

This last point of Ekblad's seems worthy of note. Ekblad himself clearly accepts a psychiatric indication for abortion, but he also makes clear that the stronger the grounds for such an indication, the greater the likelihood that the person involved will suffer at least some degree of self-reproach. He also concludes from his study that the strongest indications should be required in the case of married women in stable marriages, that is, the group most likely to be able to profit from psychiatric aid and support as an alternative to abortion. However, since many women applying for abortion do not fall in this category, he also states that the abortion seems the only answer in many other, less favorable situations.

Bengt Jansson, in another Swedish study, found evidence confirming Ekblad's conclusion. Studying a group of women who had legal abortions in Goteborg between 1952 and 1956, he found:

> Mental insufficiencies are, to judge by the writer's investigation, strikingly more common after legal abortions than after other abortions (1.92 percent and 0.27 percent respectively), and also distinctively more common than after delivery (1.92 percent and 0.68 percent respectively). In itself this is not particularly surprising, since among women granted a legal abortion there are reasonably bound to be a good many with a high degree of psychic vulnerability, which may also manifest itself in the form of insufficiency *after* abortion. . . . We thus have the paradoxical situation that it is in the cases in which legal abortion can best be justified from the psychiatric standpoint that the risk of a mental insufficiency during the post-course is greatest. . . . It may be said, perhaps, that legal abortion stands out as a fairly ineffective therapeutic means.[73]

N. M. Simon *et al.* in St. Louis, came to a conclusion consistent with that of Ekblad and Jansson, without, however, drawing Jansson's specific conclusion about the ineffectiveness of abortion for therapeutic reasons: "Certainly the unrelieved pessimism expressed by some authors about the outcome of therapeutic abortion is not borne out in our study. Psychiatric illness does occur after therapeutic abortion, but is not primarily related to abortion itself." [74] They also found that the greater the psychological health of a woman prior to abortion, the greater the likelihood of mild and transient reaction after the abortion, another finding which receives wide support in the psychiatric literature. For his part, Jansson, while holding that abortion was ineffective as therapy, also observed that it does often have the practical, short-term value of reducing a source of immediate, extra stress; its value is thus temporarily ameliorative. Pertinent also is the common suggestion that an abortion will help to stave off later, secondary problems, or avoid exacerbating an ongoing psychological deterioration.

What is ironic about the general interpretation of the Ekblad study is that it has been used to support both sides in the debate over guilt. Anderson, for instance, says that "this unfavorable sequel to abortion is worthy of emphasis," citing the 25 percent of those women who had some degree of guilt reaction (either mild or serious).[75] Other authors, though, come to just the opposite conclusion: a 25 percent guilt reaction, with only an 11 percent severe guilt reaction, seems to them to indicate that the possibility of guilt is not a very serious one. In a sense, there is no way of resolving a difference of this kind. Whether one wants to call a 25 percent guilt reaction a serious reason to be hesitant about abortion or a good reason not to be very hesitant seems to depend very much on the overall attitude of the author toward abortion in general. Those favorable to abortion feel that the figure indicates only a slight hazard; those unfavorable feel it indicates a significant hazard. If one wants to argue that abortion is just a routine operation, hardly worth any special worry, then Ekblad's study would indicate otherwise: any operation with a 25 percent possibility of observable psychological sequelae would hardly be treated as a routine matter by any doctor. However, if one wants to argue that abortion is a serious operation but necessary on some occasions, then the 25 percent figure appears in a very different light; the risk then becomes relatively low in the context of the purported good to be achieved by it. In other words, almost everything depends upon one's general stance toward abortion.

But let me cite some other studies as well. Malmfors, in his less extensive study of guilt feelings among Swedish women who had abortions, found that 37 percent of those he studied reported guilt feelings.[76] Anderson cites a small study he conducted of 24 women who had undergone legal abortion. Seven of the 24 showed signs of significant self-reproach.[77] Per Aren, in a 1958 study of 100 unselected women who had had an abortion and then became pregnant, reported that 34 of these 100 now showed signs of guilt. He concludes "that guilt feelings cannot be regarded as trivialities, but rather as serious complications." [78] Per Kolstad in a study of 968 cases from a Norwegian hospital during the years 1940–1953 found that 82.8 percent were glad without any reservation that they had an abortion, 9.8 percent were satisfied but somewhat doubtful about it, 3.7 percent were not happy that they had had the abortion but still believed it was necessary, and 3.7 percent were positively repentant.[79] Franc Novak, surveying the European literature, takes seriously the possibility of psychiatric consequences after an abortion, deploring the fact that so little attention is paid to this possibility. He does not, however, present any figures, but points out that much will depend upon the circumstances of the woman's abortion, especially that circumstance where a woman has been persuaded by a husband to undergo an abortion against her wishes; in that case, disturbances are more apt to occur.[80] Carl Müller, citing early Soviet and other European sources, argues that disturbances are very common after induced abortion, usually involving a considerable degree of guilt and self-reproach.[81]

Possibly the most surprising data come from Japan. A 1965 survey conducted by the Mainichi Newspapers found that only 18 percent of those who had abortions felt no guilt feelings at all while more than 60 percent admitted to some degree of regret or remorse.[82] This finding was also consistent with earlier surveys. The only available Korean study, by contrast, showed 90 percent reporting no guilt, and the rest some degree of guilt or adverse psychological reaction.[83] A study of 85 women conducted by Arthur Peck and Harold Marcus under the auspices of Mt. Sinai Hospital in New York found 92 percent of the women to have been improved or unchanged after abortion, and only one case of an acute adverse reaction.[84] K. R. Niswander *et al.* found from a questionaire survey that 95 percent of those granted an abortion at a Buffalo, New York, hospital felt that abortion had been the best answer for them, though they also found that three of those granted abortion on severe psychiatric grounds made the poorest adjustment.[85] D. W. K. Kay and Kurt Schapira, in surveying the psychiatric-sequelae literature, come to the following conclusion: "The outcome after legal abortion is good (considering the very adverse conditions that often exist) in 85 percent; some 10–15 percent experience little actual disability; about 1–2 percent suffer definite psychiatric illness not necessarily directly connected with the abortion; and finally, when abortion is refused, the personality disorders and other unfavorable factors present in many cases render the outlook for future adjustment precarious both for mother and child." [86] The conclusion of the authors of this survey is that the risk of a bad psychological aftermath of abortion is relatively slight and should pose no serious obstacle to abortion. M. D. Enoch, however, in a subsequent letter to the editor, contends that the very figures presented by Kay and Schapira could be used to support an opposite view.[87]

Exchanges such as the last mentioned typify the whole discussion of the aftermath of abortion. One discovers there is a group of psychiatrists who firmly believe, to use the word of Jerome M. Kummer, that postabortion psychiatric illness and guilt is rare and amounts to a "myth." [88] "No attempt has been made," Arthur J. Mandy has written, "to gather data on the thousands of women who have had one or more induced abortions without suffering any ill effects. In an obstetrical practice, one sees little evidence to justify the alarm created by psychiatrists in this regard." [89] The Gebhard study found no significant evidence of a traumatic aftereffect.[90] R. F. Tredgold comes to the same judgment.[91] By contrast, David C. Wilson concludes from his studies that in every case there is danger of a severe depressive reaction.[92] Flanders Dunbar states quite flatly that "whatever the differences in conscious or unconscious motivations for abortion, the experience of abortion inevitably arouses an unconscious sense of guilt." [93] Carl H. Jonas, contending that an abortion "is almost always a regression to . . . primitive destructive forces" and a violation of woman's nature as "giver, nurturer and protector of life" concludes, therefore, that a woman will suffer "severe self-reproach, loss of identity and irresolvable guilt as a result of an abortion." [94] R. R. MacDonald comes to a similar conclusion.[95] Myre Sim uses Ekblad's study to support his judgment that psychiatric indications are usually meaningless and abortion a definite hazard to mental health.[96] Of Ekblad's study, he says, "A conservative figure of 25 percent is a very big error and reinforces what many of us have stressed: that 'not wanting' is a temporary state of mind." He calls the 25 percent figure "conservative" because "a woman who has persuaded a tribunal to abort her is unlikely to round on them later and say she regretted it, if only not to prejudice her chances of a second abortion." [97]

Some Missing Distinctions

In the light of such contradictory professional judgments, the inadequacy of the data and a lack of anything approaching methodological refinement, one might almost feel justified in concluding that the surveys and the professional opinions are of little help. Some of the professional psychiatric judgments may be quite sound and others quite biased; but it is just about impossible in most cases to know which is which. One searches the literature in vain for the guiding hand of a sociologist in the preparation of the surveys or in interpreting their results; even Ekblad's study, more thorough than any, is devoid of this kind of necessary methodological sophistication. Nor has anyone attempted to study the (poor) data in terms of a comparison of different cultures and what effect that would have on the meaning of the evidence. Studies based on whole populations, those granted and those denied an abortion, are scanty; more are badly needed. Worst of all, there is hardly any attempt to clarify the meaning of the concepts employed. "Guilt" is usually lumped with "depression," for instance, or joined together by an exasperatingly vague "or": "guilt or depression." What is the difference between a woman who is severely depressed in the aftermath of an abortion and one who reports that she feels self-reproachful? Can one be guilty, but not be depressed? Or depressed, but not guilty? The literature hardly provides any illumination on basic distinctions of that kind. And what does it mean for a woman to feel "guilty"? Does it mean she feels guilty in the light of some specific moral code or cultural mores —which one might term a "rational" guilt if she says she accepts that code? Or does it mean that she feels guilty in spite of her moral judgment that there is nothing immoral about an abortion in her situation— which one might want to term "neurotic" guilt?

In short, what is meant by the word "guilt" and what kinds of guilt come into play here? More basically, is there such a thing as instinctual guilt, common to all women who undergo abortions regardless of cultural values, or is all guilt conditioned by the cultural values? Can a woman be conditioned to feel that abortion is evil or be conditioned to feel that abortion is a moral good? How does one take account of conditoning and social context when making a judgment about the existence of guilt? Is it true, as some argue, that women who undergo legal abortions in hospitals feel less guilt than those who resort to illegal abortions (because the law and her doctors provide her with psychological sanctions)? If so, what does this tell us about the social significance of guilt? Are there any clear behavioral indications of the presence of unconscious guilt? When a woman claims she does not feel guilty, how can one test the truth of this claim? If she claims she does feel guilty, how could one determine whether, in fact, she is perhaps only depressed, with the moral element of guilt only negligible in her depression?

The list of questions that could be raised about the meaning and significance of "guilt" is, as one can see, a very long one. Yet there is hardly an article in the whole of the literature which attempts either to raise such questions for the sake of clarity or attempts something in the way of a coherent answer. If I may put it so, the psychiatric literature is a conceptual desert, employing all sorts of common terms, but practically never telling us what they mean or ought to mean. Lacking such needed clarification, the survey results in turn tell us too little of any value. No wonder, then, that the same data are read in contradictory ways and are easily used to justify the most divergent moral evaluations.

The discussions of the psychological dynamics of guilt or the lack of guilt are not much more enlightening. This is particularly unfortunate, for even if one is convinced that abortion is morally justifiable under some or many circumstances, one still has to deal with the problem of culturally induced guilt, which could well work to a woman's psychological disadvantage. From the other extreme, the problem of educating people to see the immorality of abortion (should that seem desirable) would be immensely complicated in a culture which had conditioned people to take for granted the moral indifference of abortion. In either case, one would need to know what specific psychological problems, if any, abortion poses for women. Can anything, though, be said here with some hope of reflecting the trend of the literature? Very little, but nonetheless it is worth a try.

A passage on abortion by Simone de Beauvoir in *The Second Sex* catches well the ambivalences and subtleties noted in the psychiatric literature:

[The] moral aspect of the [abortion] drama is more or less intensely felt according to circumstances. It hardly comes in question for women who are highly "emancipated," thanks to their means, their social position, and the liberal circles to which they belong, or for those schooled by poverty and misery to disdain bourgeois morality. There is a more or less disagreeable moment to live through, and it must be lived through, that is all. But many women are intimidated by a morality that for them retains its prestige even though they are unable to conform to it in their behavior; they inwardly respect the law they transgress, and they suffer from this transgression. . . . In her heart she often repudiates the interruption of pregnancy which she is seeking to obtain. She is divided against herself. Her natural tendency can well be to have the baby whose birth she is undertaking to prevent; even if she has no positive desire for maternity, she still feels uneasy about the dubious act she is engaged in. For if it is not true that abortion is murder, it still cannot be considered in the same light as a mere contraceptive technique; an event has taken place that is a definite beginning, the progress of which is to be stopped.[98]

The virtue of this passage is that it underscores the ambivalence of most women about abortion, a point stressed by almost all of those psychiatrists who have written at any length on the problem. It also helps explain why psychiatrists can have such divergent views on the guilt or lack of guilt following an abortion: much will depend upon the type of women a psychiatrist sees (and vice versa). As Mme. de Beauvoir stresses, attitudes toward abortion appear very much influenced by the subculture of which a woman is a part. Both the ambivalence and the cultural conditioning are no doubt closely related, and no doubt also together influenced by deeper psychological currents from the woman's relationship to her body.

Just why a woman should feel an aversion to abortion seems easier to understand than why she might be attracted to it. Jerome M. Kummer has hypothesized, plausibly enough, that the aversion to abortion stems from an identification of a woman with the fetus, a culturally induced equation of abortion and murder, a psychoanalytical equation of castration, multilation and self-destruction, as well as the instinctive satisfactions of pregnancy and childbirth.[99] At the same time, unless we are totally to discount the testimony of those numerous psychiatrists who state that they have not seen any desperate instances of postabortion guilt—and there seems no special reason to do so—we have to take account of the fact that many women are apparently able to overcome a natural aversion to abortion without suffering a traumatic aftermath. The very real possibility that pregnancy can pose some extremely difficult problems for a woman—if she is unmarried, or if she already has too many children, or if her previous pregnancies have been harrowing —should lead one to doubt any psychiatric speculation which would explain away the desire to avoid pregnancy as inevitably and always a case of an immature or a disturbed personality. An instance of this kind of speculation, which appears based on *a priori* assumptions rather than empirical evidence, is the earlier quoted passage of Carl Jonas and the following lines written by May E. Romm: "The very fact that a woman cannot tolerate pregnancy, or is in intense conflict about it or about giving birth to a child, is an indication that the pre-pregnant personality of this woman was immature and in that sense can be labeled as psychopathological. . . . The problem centers around unresolved oedipal situations. Exaggerated narcissism is present in all cases." [100]

Even if adjudged morally wrong, or socially and psychologically unnecessary for a woman to have an abortion even in the most extreme circumstances, surely, as most of the literature indicates, extreme circumstances can exist, and a desire to flee from or ameliorate them can be seen as a perfectly normal, human kind of response. It does not seem necessary to hypothesize a psychopathological state to explain why a poor woman with more children than she can care for would seek an abortion, especially if she lived in a subculture which did not condemn abortion. A more cautious and thus wiser statement, far closer to the mainstream of psychiatric testimony, is that of Theodore Lidz: "Despite the frequency of voluntary abortion and the decrease in danger to life since antibiotics have become available, the willful loss of the fetus remains a potential major trauma to a woman because of its emotional significance. The question that concerns psychiatrists is how to judge when this trauma will be less than the burden of the pregnancy or of having the child." [101] As long as the stress is put on the word "potential" in that passage, Lidz's judgment seems compatible with most of the literature. At the same time, there is little data to support a conclusion that "a potential major trauma" will *inevitably* develop into an *actual* major trauma. Bearing in mind that different women may well react in different ways because of the great number of different possible contexts of their pregnancy (personal, familial and social), it seems most prudent to say this: since a major trauma is a possibility, with a varying probability from one patient to the next, this possibility should be taken into serious account by any psychiatrist trying to calculate the possible effect of an abortion on a woman.[102] This is a cautious statement, and deliberately so; but it is all the literature would justify. Moreover, a further caution is necessary, put beautifully by Theodore Lidz:

Childbirth is a critical juncture in the life of a woman, and procreation is essential to the vitality of a society. The linkage between the urgent, pleasurable motivating force of sexuality and the responsibility of parenthood is not fortuitous. A matter so central to the mainsprings of human behavior cannot but be enmeshed in complexities of religion, law, tradition, and superstition. The psychiatrist, concerned with the effects of the termination of pregnancy upon the integrity of the woman's personality structure, cannot remove the patient or himself from the operational setting. One may yearn to discuss the influence of an abortion upon a "psychic economy" abstracted from mores and attitudes, but the abstraction would be devoid of practical meaning.[103]

It seems to me, therefore, that however vague and unsatisfactory the psychiatric knowledge of the effect of abortion, a sensitive psychiatrist might well conclude, concerning a given patient, that she will be able to undergo abortion with little or no serious guilt. Concerning another patient, he might conclude that her background and situation make a serious guilt reaction likely. As long as he was continually sensitive to his own values concerning abortion, and not unduly influenced by them, and sensitive to the personal and cultural setting of his relationship to both types of women, he could well be correct in both instances. If the psychiatric material now available tells us anything, it at least tells us that much.

The Effect of Refused Abortions

A discussion of the problem of postabortion guilt and of various kinds of psychological trauma would not be complete without an examination of the effect of a refused abortion on women. Since, obviously enough, one alternative to the granting of an abortion on psychiatric grounds is a refusal of abortion, what happens to woman who are refused? The data on this point are exceedingly scant, restricted to a few Scandinavian studies; and even then, as Henrik Hoffmeyer has pointed out, "the results are difficult to interpret. Groups of women who had legal abortions are barely comparable to the groups whose applications were turned down. Furthermore, the pregnancy of many years ago becomes blurred with later happenings and later pregnancies in the memories of the studied women, making it often very difficult to isolate the effect of the topical pregnancy." [104]

With that caution in mind, a number of studies can be cited. Hoffmeyer himself mentions the results of a follow-up study conducted by the Mothers Aid Institution in Denmark, of 180 women, whose applications for abortion were refused: 31 women reported themselves as happy; 40 said they were only moderately happy because of serious troubles in managing their children; another 40 reported themselves as only moderately happy because of difficulties during pregnancy; 29 said they could not make up their minds because their children had been placed elsewhere after their pregnancy; finally, "The number of mothers who affirmatively stated that they did not care for their babies and did not feel anything for them was only 13. Most of these women were psychopathic or mentally defective." [105] Hoffmeyer also reports that the same study included 126 women who had had a legal abortion. After five years, 112 reported they were absolutely happy, five reported they regretted the action and nine had mixed feelings. Hoffmeyer's conclusion from both studies is worth quoting: "The conclusion was that about 80 percent are satisfied in all groups [abortions refused and granted], and around 20 percent are dissatisfied. Those who were turned down, however, seemed to [have] certain reservations. It must be remembered also that the natural attachment to the child, even though unwanted originally, may overshadow later complications." [106]

P. Aren and C. Åmark examined 195 women who, between 1950 and 1952, were granted permission in Sweden for a legal abortion but then did not go through with the operation.[107] They found that 63 percent of these women were, after three to five years, caring for the child themselves and well adjusted to their situation. Of the 142 women who kept their babies, 21 percent developed adverse psychological problems (though only 11 percent of this group were worse because they did not have an abortion), while 37 percent showed an improvement in their mental health after the birth of the child. Some 89 percent reported they felt justified in not having the abortion. Bengt Jansson, commenting on this study, said that "the post-course seems, if anything, to have been more favorable for these women than is generally the case after a legal abortion." [108] Hoffmeyer notes that, when this study came out, it was considered to be a strong argument against the Swedish abortion policy, but he adds that this particular group of women, who did not go through with an approved abortion, must have been particularly ambivalent about their requested abortion in the first place.

A Swedish survey made by Bengt F. Lindberg during the period 1940–1946, comprising 344 women whose request for legal abortion had been disapproved, found that 294 of the women gave birth while 50 women (14.5 percent) had an abortion anyway (mainly illegally).[109] Lindberg also found that esthenic personality traits predominated among those who gave birth after refusal, while hysterical traits were the dominating feature among those who finally aborted. Among those who threatened to have an illegal abortion if legal permission was refused, 30 percent carried out their threat. Some 18 percent threatened suicide if turned down, but none carried through on that threat. G. Hultgren, in a study conducted in Norway during the mid-1950s, found that the illegal abortion rate for women refused legal abortion was well over 10 percent.[110] Hans Forssman and Inge Thuwe, in another Swedish study, examined 120 children born after their mothers had applied for induced abortion on psychiatric grounds but had been refused.[111] From a study of the life histories of these children through the age of twenty-one, they found that the children had a statistically higher rate than the average of psychiatric disturbances, criminal and other antisocial behavior. Forssman and Thuwe concluded from the study that the very fact a woman applies for abortion means that her subsequent child, if she is refused, will have to surmount greater social and mental handicaps than children who had been wanted, "even when the grounds for the application are so slight that it is refused." [112]

Unfortunately, the Forssman and Thuwe study was not deep enough or wide-ranging enough to come to any clear judgment which might enable one to answer a question posed by Julian Pleasants: what does the knowledge that a woman aborted an earlier pregnancy do to the mother-child relationship in later pregnancies carried to term? [113] Pleasants suggests such knowledge may well be harmful to the mother-child relationship, but the Forssman and Thuwe study would indicate that the mother-child relationship of a child born of a refused abortion is not likely to be altogether healthy either. Little imagination is required to guess that a woman who wants an abortion which she cannot get has a poorer prognosis as a mother than a woman who accepts her pregnancy, But then, too, if we are to believe the speculations of Joseph C. Rheingold, maternal rejection of a fetus, usually on the unconscious level, is already pervasively common even among well-adjusted women; the difference between the latter latent rejection and the more overt rejection of a woman who seeks an abortion may not be all that great. In theory, it seems sensible to suppose that the outlook for an unwanted child is dimmer than that of a wanted child. In practice, though, the available literature would indicate that there is as yet no proved correlation between a desire for abortion and subsequent failure in the demands of motherhood; nor, for that matter, is there a clearly established correlation between an apparent overt acceptance of motherhood and subsequent success. If nothing else, many things can happen to a woman during the many years of motherhood, nullifying the advantage of an initially positive acceptance. The data do not enable one to make clear predictions in any but the most extreme cases of fetal rejection, and then such predictions must be made hesitantly.

In cases which are less extreme, the data would suggest that so many imponderables exist, at the conscious and unconscious, the personal and the sociofamilial levels, that any prediction is risky and any dogmatic conclusion worthy of doubt. Much can depend here on the general stance one takes toward those conditions thought broadly necessary for the development of psychologically healthy children. As Henriette R. Klein has remarked:

The preservation of life no longer connotes merely organic survival; such considerations are now based on considerations of emotional adaptation. Under the circumstances it is not surprising that the incidence of therapeutic abortion on the grounds of psychiatric illness has risen so it is now the most common single precipitating factor. This trend, which reflects current opinion that severely disturbed women should not bear children, also indicates an increasing awareness of the importance of early environmental and psychological factors for future development.[114]

In this passage one sees exemplified a point made in the introductory chapter; that it is otherwise valuable and important cultural and medical advances which often incline psychiatrists toward abortion, by no means justly reducible to a purported disrespect for human life. The rapid rise of concern about the "battered child" surely reflects a heightened emphasis on the conditions of childhood development.[115] Whether psychiatrists (and pregnant women themselves) should allow these valuable insights to lead them to give a priority to them over considerations of the protection of fetal life is a different matter, as is the question of achieving a morally viable balance of values, and these problems will be dealt with more extensively in later chapters.

The final study I will cite is Kerstin Höök's follow-up survey of 249 women refused abortion in Sweden.[116] Though dealing with relatively few women, this is the most complete survey in the psychiatric literature. Of this group, 60 percent were classified as psychologically normal, with the remaining 40 percent displaying a variety of deviation symptoms; this distribution of abnormality was judged to be far higher than in the rest of the Swedish population. Some 48 percent of the women were married at the time of application, 8 percent were widows or divorcees and 44 percent were unmarried. After the requested abortion was refused, 86 percent of the women continued their pregnancy, 3 percent had spontaneous abortions and 11 percent procured an illegal abortion. Concerning those who had illegal abortions after legal refusal, Höök found that the rate was twice as high among women who had been deserted by the father or who were in conflict with the father as compared with those whose relationship with the father was good. Twenty-three percent of the women adjusted to their situation almost immediately; 53 percent achieved adjustment after an initial period of disturbance; and 24 percent were still showing significant signs of disturbance after 18 months. Moreover, 81 percent of those classified as mentally normal were satisfied with their situation, while 40 percent of those showing signs of deviation expressed dissatisfaction. Finally, "when the women's opinion regarding their situation—their attitude—was considered in association with their adjustment at the follow-up, it was found that among those who gave birth to the child 69 percent had adjusted themselves and were satisfied with their situation. Thirty-one percent were dissatisfied with their situation in spite of adjustment at the follow-up, or were poorly adjusted. In these cases it may be presumed that the environment for the child would be unfavorable."[117] Some 7 percent were certified unfit for work within 18 months of the rejected application, and at a later date, 13 percent. Höök concluded that the mental health of women denied abortion was worse than those granted an abortion.

What the Höök study does not speculate upon, nor do the other studies, is what effect intensive psychiatric care and family help might have had in helping those women who remained disturbed and maladjusted. In the nature of the case, comparisons in particular cases are impossible; there is no direct way of telling what would have happened to a woman denied an abortion if she had had an abortion, and vice versa. As suggested before, there seem to be few cases of psychological maladjustment or illness so severe as to render psychiatric care worthless in enabling a woman to bear and raise a child. As Theodore Lidz has pointed out, "The question of the need for abortion is often broached without ample consideration of psychotherapy as an alternative. If the pregnancy is considered as an unalterable fact, the prospective mother, or, occasionally, the prospective father, may be amenable to modification by psychotherapy that leads to acceptance of this fact. At other times, adequate ventilation of concern and discussion may alter the perspective." [118] In short, it would seem that, if it is possible to deter a woman from seeking either a legal or illegal abortion by psychotherapy, it should also be possible for a woman refused legal abortion to be helped to surmount the refusal. Naturally, the second situation is different, for presumably the woman would have had an abortion if allowed to do so; while in the first case, she would presumably be diverted from wanting the abortion. A related option, of course, is to help a woman to have an abortion and then deal with any adverse reactions by psychiatric means. This, in fact, appears to be the reasoning implicit in the above-cited article by Peck and Marcus, who speak of a few women being helped to overcome depression or guilt after an abortion by short periods of therapy.[119]

The critical problem, I would suggest, is whether there could exist any situations involving either psychological indications or the likelihood of a dangerous psychological aftermath which would make abortion appear the *only* course. There is nothing in the literature to impel this kind of conclusion. But a distinction must be made here. It is one thing to say that any woman could be brought safely through pregnancy by intensive care where the presumption (or plan) is that the child is immediately to be put in the hands of others once born; it is quite another thing to say that any woman could be brought through pregnancy safely and then be given enough care to insure that she would be an adequate mother. The first proposition receives plentiful support in the literature, but the second receives considerably less. And, on the second, there is the practical point not only whether a woman could, in principle, be cared for after the birth of her child, but also whether her financial and social situation is such as to make this care likely or realistically feasible. On this last point, a psychiatrist would be forced to take account of a whole host of socioeconomic considerations: could she pay for private care? are adequate government facilities or government care available for poorer patients? what would intensive care, particularly if it involved an extended stay in an institution, do to her relationship with her husband and any other children?

"The techniques of psychiatry, clinical psychology and social casework are adequate to meet a great many of the problems resulting from a lack of maternal response adequate to the needs of the child," Dr. Richard L. Jenkins has written.[120] But this leaves unanswered the problem of what is to be done about cases where these techniques are not likely to be adequate or available; and that is the hard question, the answer to which will vary from person to person and place to place. In this regard, I would like to quote the words of a New York psychiatrist, Dr. Rudolph Ehrensing, who brings out well some of the considerations which may influence psychiatric judgments. Speaking of the problem of a woman who has shown suicidal tendencies, he points out:

> Often a woman is depressed but is not very suicidal as long as she has hope she can get an abortion, i.e., she does not need to be hospitalized. If abortion is refused, the risk of suicide may increase, requiring long-term hospitalization for 6–9 months through pregnancy, which may mean a state hospital. This seems to be an influence on the psychiatrist to decide in favor of abortion. He has a middle-class patient who is an outpatient and who will not have to be hospitalized (or so he hopes) if she gets an abortion, but who will have to be hospitalized for the duration of her pregnancy to be on the safe side to avoid possible suicide. The psychiatrist knows she cannot afford 6–8 months at a private mental hospital and is reluctant then to send her to an undesirable state hospital.[121]

And one can readily imagine how such additional complications as the fact of other children whom she needs to care for, or an even lower income, would further incline a psychiatrist to favor abortion. Even if the doctor knows that it is rare for pregnant women actually to commit suicide, his problem is to know in this case at this time that she will not; understandably, he may, as Ehrensing notes, want to be "on the safe side" so that his patient does not prove to be an unhappy exception to the general rule. "The psychiatrist," Ehrensing comments, often feels "overwhelmed with mental illness and the great difficulty in obtaining 'cures.' He often sees abortion as a means of preventing hospitalization for a lengthy time."

Are we to say that, when facilities to help the mother through pregnancy and ensuing motherhood are not available, abortion becomes psychologically *required*? Not necessarily, so long as it remains possible to put a child up for adoption or to place it in the care of foster parents. The latter option, though, raises another difficulty. Harold Rosen argues vehemently: "No one in the technical literature has stressed the heartlessness, the cruelty, and the sadism that the pregnant woman so frequently senses—perhaps correctly, perhaps mistakenly—when physician, minister, or lawyer suggests to her that she carry the child to term and then hand it over, never to see it again, to someone else to rear." [122] Dr. Rosen states that in his professional experience the overwhelming reaction of women toward pressure to carry the child to term and then put it up for adoption was a total rejection of this option. He further states:

During the past eighteen years [he] has seen only three patients for whom "farming out" of a child for adoption would not have been emotionally exceedingly traumatic and psychiatrically contra-indicated. For some twenty-nine patients who came into psychiatric treatment within one to four years after they had accepted this kind of recommendation, what they considered to be the abandoning of their infants required careful, cautious, and (in all but seven) extensive therapeutic considerations. [123]

Dr. Rosen's argument is not wholly persuasive. Not only does it lack any support in the rest of the literature (where I have been unable to discover any studies of the effect on women of putting their children up for adoption after being refused abortion or dissuaded from it), but it seems to neglect taking seriously the possibility that the "extensive therapeutic considerations" he mentions could be preferable to an abortion. Surely some criteria, backed by some hard data, are needed here before speaking confidently. More importantly, perhaps, the kind of situation Dr. Rosen describes would seem to involve, more than any other psychiatric situation, the value one attributes to an unwanted fetus; here, the inextricable relationship of professional judgment and moral evaluation comes into especially prominent play (though it is hardly anywhere absent).

One can only finish a survey and discussion of the psychiatric literature on abortion with a feeling of frustration and inadequacy. As mentioned, there are innumerable questions one wants to ask which the literature either does not ask or does not answer, and usually both. Perhaps because of increased public concern, in the near future extensive research will be undertaken; for all the seriousness of the abortion problem, it has not so far inspired the expenditure of great amounts of research money anywhere in the world. There can be no doubt that a full-scale, worldwide study of the psychiatric problems of abortion (which would entail lengthy personal interviews and testing by a host of carefully trained personnel) would be a tremendously expensive project, requiring many years for completion. That means that those interested in clarifying the psychological indications for abortion, as well as the likely psychological effect of legal abortion, refused abortion and different alternatives to abortion, will have to make do for the time being with the grossly inadequate material at hand. It also means, as R. F. Tredgold cogently pointed out in an exchange with Myre Sim, that even if one in general accepted, say, that data which indicated that abortion on psychiatric grounds was rarely required, "it would still be possible for doctors to disagree in good faith on a given case." [124]

To expect anything approaching a consensus, then, among psychiatrists on fixed and clear norms for psychiatric indications for abortion or on the psychological effect of abortion is to expect what is most unlikely to be forthcoming. If one considers also the general state of flux in the whole field of psychiatry, where many traditional pathological labels are being questioned or abandoned and many new techniques of treatment are coming into play because of the advent of new drugs and new theories of treatment, the likelihood of clear norms is all the more problematical. At most, one will probably be in a position only to reject or be resolutely suspicious of far-ranging, undocumented generalizations based on the personal impressions of psychiatrists. Beyond that, much will be gray. By the time the psychiatrist has considered all the scanty data and then applied that data to such diverse cases as young, unmarried girls, older, married women with few children and older, married women with many children, widows and divorcees, working into their deliberation the previous mental health of the girl or woman, her social and economic situation, her personal value system and their personal values—by that time, any given case could be very difficult to decide. Comparable problems could arise under a legalized abortion system, if and when women asked psychiatrists for advice. With the exception of Jonas, Sim and Müller, almost every psychiatrist cited in this chapter seems to support, in principle, induced abortion on the basis of psychiatric indications. This support, given the possible complexity—theoretical and practical—of individual cases, is compatible with an equally salient trend in the literature: that therapeutic help can enable all but the rarest and most extreme cases psychologically to survive pregnancy, even under very unfavorable conditions. To throw out all psychiatric indications because of the difficulty of formulating exact criteria, or of making decisions in complex cases, or uncritically to assume that a great number of women are necessarily candidates for abortion on psychiatric grounds would be equally irresponsible.

My own conclusion is that the category of "psychiatric indications" is as valid, *qua* category, as that of "medical indications." At the same time, in the light of the wide consensus that, in principle and under ideal circumstances, a woman could be brought safely through even the gravest psychiatric difficulties while pregnant, there should be a presumption against an automatic invocation of this category in the generality of distressed-pregnancy cases. However, because of the variations in the cases of particular women and the variations in the feasibility and availability of therapeutic facilities, there remains a large area of ambiguity. Consequently, it is inevitable that some psychiatric judgments will have to be uncertain and prudential, with the final judgment (or advice) reasonably (though not apodictically) going in either direction. Whether and to what extent a psychiatrist should be placed or forced into the position of making judgments of this kind in the first place is itself a serious moral and legal problem. A psychiatrist might well complain that he is being asked to make final judgments when, at most, his role, for both moral and professional reasons, should be limited to giving advice when that is requested of him. Even in the latter role, however, the problem of "indications" will remain important; that will make a difference in the kind of advice he gives and the range of considerations he puts before a woman.

Of obvious importance also is the moral stance taken by a physician toward abortion in general and fetal life in particular. The discrepant evidence cited in this chapter, the extreme divergence of opinion on many aspects of the psychiatric problem, and the apparently wide variation in professional experience all open the way to different judgments on "psychiatric indications." A physician morally opposed, under most circumstances, to the taking of fetal life can easily cite those studies showing that almost any woman can, psychiatrically, be brought through a pregnancy safely. Even fully conceding all the possible practical difficulties in some circumstances, he could still opt to risk (or recommend to a woman that she risk) these difficulties; for in his moral view the protection of fetal life as a prime obligation would incline him to run or commend special risks and recommend even admittedly difficult solutions. This is important to see and why, invariably, a psychiatrist's moral perspective is bound, overtly or latently, to influence his judgment one way or the other. A doctor, by contrast, who takes a different view toward fetal life, may well decide that the difficulties of therapy are too great to be borne and recommend an abortion; and he also will find considerable professional support for such a decision.

In neither case would it be fair to accuse the psychiatrist of "unprofessional" conduct. In a professional area of much dispute, it is not unreasonable or unethical for a doctor to be drawn to and more impressed by that school of opinion and that body of data consonant with his own moral perspective. Only if he willfully or negligently ignores the opinion and data put forward by those holding different positions could he be accused of failing in his human and medical responsibilities. To say this is not to evade the question of which moral perspective a psychiatrist or doctor ought to adopt in the making of choices; that is a problem to be taken up later. It is only to say at this point, on the matter of "psychiatric indications," that, once a moral stance has been adopted, the variations in the data and opinions are such as to open the way for professional support for a wide range of moral stances. It should go without saying, naturally, that the process of adopting a moral stance should be undertaken in the light of available evidence; it is a two-way street.

NOTES

1. For a strong empiricist's critique of psychoanalytic categories, see Sidney Hook, "Science and Mythology in Psychoanalysis," in Sidney Hook (ed.), *Psychoanalysis, Scientific Method and Philosophy* (New York: New York University Press, 1959), pp. 212–24. Hook's critique, to be sure, is directed specifically at psychoanalysis but it also raises a number of pertinent empirical problems in general for the broader field of psychiatry, as does the whole book.
2. Harold Rosen, "Psychiatric Implications of Abortion: A Case Study in Social Hypocrisy," in David T. Smith (ed.), *Abortion and the Law* (Cleveland: Western Reserve University Press, 1967), p. 82; Kenneth R. Niswander, "Medical Abortion Practices in the United States," *ibid.*, p. 52. See also W. E. Copeland *et al.*, "Therapeutic Abortion," *Journal of the American Medical Association*, 207 (January 27, 1969), pp. 713–15, a review of therapeutic abortions in Ohio State University Hospital from January 1, 1949 to January 1, 1966. The authors say generally that in recent years medical indications for abortion have not been cited so frequently as psychiatric or fetal indications.
3. J. J. Rovinsky *et al.*, "Current Trends in Therapeutic Termination of Pregnancy," *American Journal of Obstetrics and Gynecology*, 98 (May 1, 1967), pp. 11–17.
4. M. M. Spivak, "Therapeutic Abortion: A 12-Year Review at the Toronto General Hospital 1954–1965, " *American Journal of Obstetrics and Gynecology*, 97 (February 1, 1967), pp. 316–23.
5. Keith P. Russell, "Changing Indications for Therapeutic Abortion," *Journal of the American Medical Association*, 151 (January 10, 1953), pp. 108–11; André E. Hellegers, "Law and the Common Good," *Commonweal*, 86 (June 30, 1967), p. 420; *cf.* Irving Siegel and A. E. Kanter, "Therapeutic Abortion," *Chicago Medical School Quarterly*, 21 (March 1960), pp. 14–19, which comes to a similar conclusion.
6. J. A. Routledge *et al.*, "The Present Status of Therapeutic Abortion," *Obstetrics and Gynecology*, 17 (February 1961), pp. 168–74.
7. E. M. Gold *et al.*, "Therapeutic Abortions in New York City: A 20-Year Review," *American Journal of Public Health*, 55 (July 1965), pp. 964–72.
8. C. Tietze, "Therapeutic Abortion in the United States," *American Journal of Obstetrics and Gynecology*, 101 (July 15, 1968), p. 786.
9. A. Heller and H. G. Whittington, "The Colorado Story: Denver General Hospital Experience with the Change in the Law on Therapeutic Abortion," *American Journal of Psychiatry*, 125 (December 1968), pp. 809–16; W. Droegemueller, E. S. Taylor and V. E. Drose, "The First Year of Experience in Colorado with the New Abortion Law," *American Journal of Obstetrics and Gynecology*, 103 (March 1, 1969), p. 694; John C. Cobb, "Abortion in

Colorado, 1967–1969," paper delivered to the American Association of Planned Parenthood Physicians, San Francisco, April 10, 1969; H. C. Pulley, "Abortions—First Annual Report," *California Medicine*, 108 (May 1968), p. 403.

10. Among the many discussions (favorable) of the validity of a person's general well-being as a legitimate concern of the psychiatrist are Kenneth J. Ryan, "Humane Abortion Laws and the Health Needs of Society," in *Abortion and the Law, op. cit.*, p. 68; Harriet F. Pilpel, in a symposium on "The Social Problem of Abortion," *Bulletin of the Sloane Hospital for Women*, 11 (Fall 1965), p. 66; *Abortion: An Ethical Discussion* (London: Church Information Office, 1965), p. 34; *cf.* M. F. Loth and H. C. Hesseltine, "Therapeutic Abortion at the Chicago Lying-In Hospital," *American Journal of Obstetrics and Gynecology*, 72 (August 1956), pp. 304–11.

11. Hellegers, "Law and the Common Good," *op cit.*, p. 420.

12. Joseph C. Rheingold, *The Fear of Being a Woman* (New York: Grune & Stratton, 1964), p. 518.

13. L. H. Biskind, "Emotional Aspects of Prenatal Care," *Postgraduate Medicine*, 24 (December 1958), pp. 633–37; A. A. Robin, "The Psychological Changes of Normal Parturition," *Psychiatric Quarterly*, 36 (1962), p. 129; N. Pleshette *et al.*, "A Study of Anxieties During Pregnancy, Labor, the Early and Late Puerperium," *Bulletin of the New York Academy of Medicine*, 32 (June 1956), p. 436; S. M. Tobin, "Emotional Depression During Pregnancy," *Obstetrics and Gynecology*, 10 (December 1957), pp. 677–81; Bengt Jansson, "Psychic Insufficiencies Associated with Childbearing," *Acta Psychiatrica Scandinavica*, Supplementum 172, 40 (1964), p. 21.

14. Rheingold, *op. cit.*, p. 516.

15. Joseph C. Rheingold, *The Mother, Anxiety and Death* (Boston: Little, Brown, 1966), p. 71.

16. M. B. Clyne, "General Practitioners Forum. Habitual Abortion: A Psychosomatic Disorder," *Practitioner*, 199 (July 1967), pp. 83–90.

17. Erik H. Erikson, "Growth and Crisis of the Healthy Personality," in C. Kluckhohn, H. A. Murray and D. Schneider (eds.), *Personality in Nature, Society and Culture* (New York: Alfred Knopf, 1953); G. L. Bibring, "Some Considerations of the Psychological Processes in Pregnancy," *The Psychoanalytical Study of the Child*, No. 14 (New York: International Universities Presses, 1959); Erikson's and Bibring's developmental theory is discussed by Rheingold, *The Fear of Being a Woman, op. cit.*, p. 518.

18. Helene Deutsch, "An Introduction to the Discussion of the Psychological Problems of Pregnancy," in M. J. E. Senn (ed.), *Transactions of the Second Conference [on] Problems of Early Infancy*, 2 (New York: Josiah Macy, Jr., Foundation, 1948), pp. 11–17.

19. Rheingold, *The Fear of Being a Woman, op. cit.*, p. 527.

20. See James L. Mathis, "Psychiatric Complications of Obstetrical Practice," *Journal of the Oklahoma Medical Association*, 58 (November 1965), pp. 494–98; and Henriette R. Klein *et al.*, *Anxiety in Pregnancy and Childbirth* (New York: Hoeber-Harper, 1950), especially pp. 67–68.

21. L. Linn and P. Polatin, "Psychiatric Problems of the Puerperium from the Standpoint of Prophylaxis," *Psychiatric Quarterly*, 24 (April 1950), p. 383.

22. Gregory Zilboorg, "Post-Partum Schizophrenias," *Journal of Nervous and Mental Disease*, 68 (October 1928), p. 383.

23. Rheingold, *The Fear of Being a Woman, op. cit.*, p. 549.

24. T. Harder, "Efterundersogelse af en gruppe Patienter der ka vaeret nidlagt til Observation for Abortus provocatus," *Nordisk Medicin*, 64 (1960), p. 921. Cited in Kerstin Höök, "Refused Abortion: A Follow-Up Study of 249 Women Whose Applications Were Refused by the National Board of Health in Sweden," *Acta Psychiatrica Scandinavica*, Supplementum 168, 39 (1963), p. 17.

25. A. P. Noyes and L. C. Kolb, *Modern Clinical Psychiatry* (Philadelphia: Saunders, 1963), p. 407.
26. Alan F. Guttmacher, "Therapeutic Abortion: The Doctor's Dilemma," *Journal of the Mt. Sinai Hospital*, 21 (1954–1955), p. 121.
27. See Harry M. Murdock, "Experiences in a Psychiatric Hospital," in Harold Rosen (ed.), *Therapeutic Abortion* (New York: The Julian Press, 1954), p. 203; and R. S. Paffenbarger *et al.*, "The Picture Puzzle of the Postpartum Psychoses," *Journal of Chronic Diseases*, 13 (February 1961), pp. 161–73.
28. C. Tetlow, "Psychoses of Childbearing," *Journal of Mental Science*, 101 (July 1955), p. 629.
29. Mary F. Brew and Robert Seidenberg, "Psychotic Reactions Associated with Pregnancy and Childbirth," *Journal of Nervous and Mental Diseases*, 111 (May 1950), p. 422.
30. Murdock, in *Therapeutic Abortion, op. cit.*, p. 199.
31. Reported to author by Rudolph Ehrensing, M.D. (personal communication).
32. Richard Jenkins, "The Significance of Maternal Rejection," in *Therapeutic Abortion, op. cit.*, p. 271.
33. Rheingold, *The Fear of Being a Woman, op. cit.*, p. 126.
34. N. M. Simon *et al.*, "Psychiatric Illness Following Therapeutic Abortion," *American Journal of Psychiatry*, 124 (July 1967), p. 64.
35. Therese Benedek, "The Psychosomatic Implications of Mother-Child Relationships," *American Journal of Orthopsychiatry*, 19 (October 1949), p. 652.
36. D. H. Stott, "Physical and Mental Handicaps Following a Disturbed Pregnancy,' *Lancet*, 1 (May 18, 1957), pp. 1006–12.
37. W. R. Thompson, "Influence of Prenatal Maternal Anxiety on Emotionality in Young Rats," *Science*, 125 (April 12, 1957), pp. 698–99.
38. Anthony Davids, Spencer DeVault and Max Talmadge, "Anxiety, Pregnancy, and Childbirth Abnormalities," *Journal of Consulting Psychology*, 25 (February 1961), pp. 74–77.
39. Rheingold, *The Fear of Being a Woman, op. cit.*, p. 635.
40. Jansson, "Psychic Insufficiencies Associated with Childbearing," *op. cit.*, p. 163.
41. Jerome M. Kummer, "A Psychiatrist Views Our Abortion Enigma," in Alan F. Guttmacher (ed.), *The Case for Legalized Abortion Now* (Berkeley: Diablo Press, 1967), p. 117.
42. *Ibid.*
43. H. Binder, "Die psychiatrische Abortindikation," *Schweizerische Medizinische Wochenschrift*, 24 (April 17, 1943), pp. 489–92; and "Die psychiatrischen Indikationen zur Unterbrechung der Schwangerschaft," *Schweizer Archiv Fuer Neurologie, Neurochirurgie und Pychiatre*, 67 (1951), pp. 245–63. A good background on the early European debates, as well as a generally comprehensive discussion of psychiatric indications can be found in Herbert Heiss, *Die Künstliche Schwangerschaftesunterbrechung und der Kriminelle Abort* (Stuttgart: Ferdinand Enke Verlag, 1967), pp. 597–637.
44. A. Lewis in Frederick William Price (ed.), *A Textbook of the Practice of Medicine* (8th edit.; London: Oxford University Press, 1950); A. F. Tredgold and R. F. Tredgold, *Manual of Psychological Medicine* (3rd edit.; London: Baillière, Tindall and Cox, 1953); and B. Hart, "Induction of Abortion from a Psychiatric Standpoint," *Lancet*, 1 (March 30, 1929), p. 658, cited by J. D. W. Pearce in "The Psychiatric Indications for the Termination of Pregnancy," *Proceedings of the Royal Society of Medicine*, 50 (May 1957), p. 321.
45. "Royal Medico-Psychological Memorandum on Therapeutic Abortion, June 1966," *Archives of General Psychiatry*, 16 (January 1967), p. 129.
46. Alexander Simon, "Psychiatric Indications for Therapeutic Abortion and Sterilization," *Clinical Obstetrics and Gynecology*, 7 (March 1964), p. 71.
47. E. W. Anderson, "Psychiatric Indications for the Termination of Pregnancy," *World Medical Journal*, 13 (May-June 1966), p. 83; and _____, "Psychiatric Indications for the Termination of Pregnancy," *Journal of Psychosomatic*

Research, 10 (July 1966), p. 129; see also S. B. Cohen, "Abortion for the Emotionally Disturbed?," *Journal of the Medical Association of Georgia*, 57 (November 1968), pp. 489–94. Cohen remarks that, although "virtually all women experience some fantasies of rejection and some desires to rid themselves of the products of conception, albeit generally in a fleeting and guilty manner" (p. 490), nevertheless the emotional state of many women improves markedly during pregnancy, including some schizophrenics, whose symptoms seem ameliorated while they are pregnant. Thus, the psychiatrist consulted in a request for abortion has to consider not only the woman's present emotional state but also possible changes in it. In the end, the psychiatrist must decide, against the background of the woman's whole life circumstances, whether she has the capacity for warmth necessary in a mother and whether she can take care of the child; in short, what kind of mothering relationship the expected child is likely to experience. Such criteria are extremely vague, but in many instances they are the only ones a psychiatrist has to go on.

48. Jerome M. Kummer, in *The Case for Legalized Abortion Now, op. cit.*, p. 117; *cf.* Jerome M. Kummer, "Psychiatric Contraindications to Pregnancy," *California Medicine*, 79 (July 1953), p. 31.

49. Harold Rosen, "The Emotionally Sick Pregnant Patient: Psychiatric Indications and Contraindications to the Interruption of Pregnancy," in *Therapeutic Abortion, op. cit.*, p. 221; Richard L. Jenkins has provided an equally helpful list of the different kinds of women who seek abortion, ranging all the way from those who do not really want one but are responding to the pressures of others, to those who could not, even with psychotherapy, accept a child ("The Significance of Maternal Rejection," *op. cit.*, p. 270).

50. *Statens Offentliga Utredningar*, 1953, no. 29; "Abortfragan," 1950 ars Abortutredning (Stockholm: National Board of Health, 1953).

51. Harold Rosen, in *Therapeutic Abortion, op. cit.*, p. 220.

52. In Mary S. Calderone (ed.), *Abortion in the United States* (New York; Hoeber-Harper, 1953), p. 108.

53. S. Leon Israel, "Therapeutic Abortion," *Postgraduate Medicine*, 33 (June 1963), p. 620; Kenneth R. Niswander, in *Abortion and the Law, op. cit.*, pp. 52–53; A. J. Rosenberg *et. al.*, "Suicide, Psychiatrists and Therapeutic Abortion," *California Medicine*, 102 (June 1965), pp. 407–11; Myre Sim, "Abortion and the Psychiatrist," *British Medical Journal*, 2 (July 20, 1963), pp. 145–48; William B. Spry, "Abortion and the Psychiatrist," *British Medical Journal*, 2 (August 10, 1963), p. 385.

54. See Natalie Shainess, "Psychological Problems Associated with Motherhood," Chapter 4 of *American Handbook of Psychiatry* (New York: Basic Books, 1966), Vol. III, pp. 53–59; *cf.* an article by the same author, highly permissive toward abortion: Natalie Shainess, "Abortion: Social, Psychiatric and Psychoanalytic Perspectives," *New York Journal of Medicine*, 68 (December 1968), pp. 3070–3073.

55. F. A. Whitlock and J. E. Edwards, "Pregnancy and Attempted Suicide," *Comprehensive Psychiatry*, 9 (January 1968), p. 11.

56. *Ibid.*

57. Harold Marcus, Symposium on "The Social Problem of Abortion," *Bulletin of the Sloane Hospital for Women, op. cit.*, p. 79.

58. Clarence O. Cheney, "Indications for Therapeutic Abortion from the Standpoint of the Neurologist and the Psychiatrist," *Journal of the American Medical Association*, 103 (December 22, 1934), pp. 1914–18.

59. John L. McKelvey, Symposium on "The Social Problem of Abortion," *Bulletin of the Sloane Hospital for Women, op. cit.*, p. 76.

60. E. W. Anderson, "The Psychiatric Indications for the Termination of Pregnancy," *Proceedings of the Royal Society of Medicine*, 50 (May 1957), p. 325; G. F. Abercrombie, "The Psychiatric Indications for the Termination of Pregnancy," *ibid.*, p. 327; Myre Sim, "Abortion and the Psychiatrist," *op. cit.*

61. Harold Rosen, in *Abortion and the Law, op. cit.*, p. 87.

62. Niswander, *ibid.*, p. 50.
63. Edmund W. Overstreet, "Foreword—Symposium on Therapeutic Abortion and Sterilization," *Clinical Obstetrics and Gynecology*, 7 (March 1964), p. 11. One psychiatrist, Willard Gaylin, has observed that the very vagueness of psychiatric criteria is precisely what makes a "psychiatric indication" attractive for those intent on abortion (personal communication).
64. Sidney Bolter, "The Psychiatrist's Role in Therapeutic Abortion: The Unwitting Accomplice," *American Journal of Psychiatry*, 119 (October 1962), pp. 312–16.
65. A. Peck, "Therapeutic Abortion: Patients, Doctors, and Society," *American Journal of Psychiatry*, 125 (December 1968), pp. 802–03.
66. Jacob H. Friedman, "The Vagarity of Psychiatric Indications for Therapeutic Abortion," *American Journal of Psychotherapy*, 16 (April 1962), pp. 251–54. M. P. Joyston-Bechal has discussed some of the possible influences, often at the unconscious level, which affect the psychiatrist's judgment in: "The Problem of Pregnancy Termination on Psychiatric Grounds," *Journal of the College of General Practitioners*, 12 (November 1966), pp. 304–12.
67. Richard Fox, "The Law on Abortion," *Lancet*, 1 (March 5, 1966), p. 542.
68. Kummer, in *The Case for Legalized Abortion Now*, *op. cit.*, p. 116.
69. Rheingold, *The Fear of Being a Woman*, *op. cit.*, pp. 551–52.
70. J. M. Ingram *et al.*, "Interruption of Pregnancy for Psychiatric Indication—A Suggested Method of Control," *Obstetrics and Gynecology*, 29 (February 1967), pp. 251–55.
71. Martin Ekblad, "Induced Abortion on Psychiatric Grounds: A Follow-Up Study of 479 Women," *Acta Psychiatrica et Neurologica Scandinavica*, Supplementum 99–102 (Stockholm, 1955), pp. 3–238.
72. *Ibid.*, p. 234.
73. Bengt Jansson, "Mental Disorders After Abortion," *Acta Psychiatrica Scandinavica*, 41 (1965), pp. 108, 110.
74. N. M. Simon *et al.*, "Psychiatric Illness Following Therapeutic Abortion," *op. cit.*, p. 64.
75. E. W. Anderson, "Psychiatric Indications for the Termination of Pregnancy," *World Medical Journal*, *op. cit.*, p. 82.
76. Malmfors, cited by Anderson, *ibid.*, p. 82.
77. Anderson, "Psychiatric Indications . . . ," *op. cit.*, p. 82.
78. Per Aren, cited by Anderson, *ibid.*
79. Per Kolstad, "Therapeutic Abortion: A Clinical Study Based Upon 968 Cases from a Norwegian Hospital, 1940–1953," *Acta Obstetrica et Gynecologica Scandinavica* (Oslo), 36, Supplement 6 (1957), 72 pp.
80. Franc Novak, "Abortion in Europe," *Proceedings of the Eighth International Conference of the International Planned Parenthood Federation, Santiago, Chile, April 9–15, 1967* (London: International Planned Parenthood Federation, 1967), pp. 135–39.
81. Carl Müller, "The Dangers of Abortion," *World Medical Journal*, 13 (May-June 1966), p. 80.
82. Minoru Muramatsu (ed.), *Japan's Experience in Family Planning—Past and Present* (Tokyo: Family Planning Federation of Japan, Inc., 1967), p. 78. This is a particularly intriguing figure in light of the supposed Oriental "indifference to life" and the apparently general acceptance of abortion. For a further comment on these data, see Chapter 7, pp. 260–62.
83. Sung Bong Hong, *Induced Abortion in Seoul, Korea* (Seoul: Dong-A Publishing Co., 1966), pp. 50ff.
84. Arthur Peck and Harold Marcus, "Psychiatric Sequelae of Therapeutic Interruption of Pregnancy," *The Journal of Nervous and Mental Diseases*, 143 (November 1966), p. 425.
85. K. R. Niswander *et al.*, "Psychologic Reaction to Abortion: Subjective Patient Response," *Obstetrics and Gynecology*, 29 (May 1967), pp. 702–06.
86. D. W. K. Kay and Kurt Schapira, "Psychiatric Sequelae of Termination of

Pregnancy," *British Medical Journal*, 1 (February 4, 1967), p. 299; R. B. White, in his survey of the literature, comes to a similarly optimistic conclusion: "Induced Abortions: A Survey of Their Psychiatric Implications, Complications, and Indications," *Texas Reports on Biology and Medicine*, 24 (Winter 1966), pp. 531–38.

87. M. D. Enoch, *British Medical Journal*, 1 (March 4, 1967), p. 563.
88. Jerome M. Kummer, "Post-Abortion Psychiatric Illness—A Myth?," *American Journal of Psychiatry*, 119 (April 1963), p. 982.
89. Arthur J. Mandy, "Reflections of a Gynecologist," in *Therapeutic Abortion, op. cit.*, p. 292.
90. Paul H. Gebhard, W. B. Pomeroy, C. E. Martin and C. V. Christenson, *Pregnancy, Birth and Abortion* (New York: Hoeber-Harper, 1958), p. 209.
91. R. F. Tredgold, "Psychiatric Indications for Termination of Pregnancy," *Lancet*, 2B (December 12, 1964), pp. 1251–54.
92. David C. Wilson, "Psychiatric Implications in Abortions," *Virginia Medical Monthly*, 79 (August 1952), pp. 448–51.
93. Flanders Dunbar, "Psychosomatic Approach to Abortion and the Abortion Habit," in *Therapeutic Abortion, op. cit.*, p. 31.
94. Carl H. Jonas, "More Victims Than One," *Way*, 23 (July-August 1967), p. 40.
95. R. R. MacDonald, "Complications of Abortion," *Nursing Times*, 63 (March 10, 1967), pp. 305–07.
96. Myre Sim, "Psychiatric Sequelae of Termination of Pregnancy," *British Medical Journal*, 1 (March 4, 1967), pp. 563–64.
97. *Ibid.* Sim may be right in this last speculation, but there is nothing in Ekblad's study to lend it any special credence.
98. Simone de Beauvoir, *The Second Sex*, trans. H. M. Parshley (New York: Bantam Books, 1961), pp. 461–62.
99. Kummer, in *The Case for Legalized Abortion Now, op. cit.*, p. 118.
100. May E. Romm, "Psychoanalytic Considerations," in *Therapeutic Abortion, op. cit.*, p. 210.
101. Theodore Lidz, "Reflections of a Psychiatrist," in *Therapeutic Abortion, op. cit.*, p. 279.
102. Cf. David C. Wilson, "The Abortion Problem in the General Hospital," in *Therapeutic Abortion, op. cit.*, pp. 196–97.
103. Lidz, *op. cit.*, p. 276.
104. Henrik Hoffmeyer, "Medical Aspects of the Danish Legislation on Abortion," in *Abortion and the Law, op. cit.*, p. 201.
105. *Ibid.*
106. *Ibid.*, p. 202.
107. P. Aren and C. Amark, "The Prognosis of Granted But Not Performed Legal Abortion," *Svenska Läkartidningen*, 54 (1957), p. 3709.
108. Jansson, "Mental Disorders After Abortion," *op. cit.*, p. 87.
109. Bengt F. Lindberg, "Vad gor den abortsokande kvinnan nar psykiatern sagt nej?"[What does the woman do when the psychiatrist says no to her application for abortion?], *Svenska Läkartidningen* (Stockholm), 45 (1948), pp. 1381–91.
110. G. Hultgren, "Avslag pa ansokan om legal abort.," *Nordisk Medicin*, 62 (1959), p. 1182. Cited in Kerstin Höök, "Refused Abortion . . . ," *op. cit.*, p. 16.
111. Hans Forssman and Inga Thuwe, "One Hundred and Twenty Children Born After Application for Therapeutic Abortion Refused," *Acta Psychiatrica Scandinavica*, 42 (1966), pp. 71–88.
112. *Ibid.*, p. 87.
113. Julian Pleasants, "A Morality of Consequences," *Commonweal*, 86 (June 30, 1967), p. 416.
114. Henriette R. Klein, "Obstetrical and Gynecological Disorders," in A. M. Freedman and Harold Kaplan (eds.), *Comprehensive Textbook of Psychiatry* (Baltimore: Williams and Wilkins Co., 1967), p. 1084.
115. See Ray E. Helfer and C. Henry Kempe (eds.), *The Battered Child* (Chicago:

University of Chicago Press, 1968). Unfortunately this book makes no attempt to analyze the relationship between being "a battered child" and being an "unwanted child."

116. Kerstin Höök, "Refused Abortion . . . ," *op. cit.*, pp. 1–156.

117. *Ibid.*, p. 131.

118. Lidz, in *Therapeutic Abortion, op. cit.*, p. 280.

119. Peck and Marcus, "Psychiatric Sequelae of Therapeutic Interruption of Pregnancy," *op. cit.*, p. 423. The *moral* legitimacy of such a procedure will, to be sure, be a function of one's moral perspective on abortion. Peck and Marcus seem unaware of some important moral problems implicit in their psychiatric strategy. Speaking of a group of women aborted on nonpsychiatric grounds and who had ensuing mild, brief depressive reactions, they state: "All of them wanted the baby but *consented* to the abortion on medical advice. . . . They recognized that the medical reason for the abortion was valid but regretted that the abortion had been *necessary* and keenly missed having the baby" (*ibid.*, p. 420). The words *"consented"* and *"necessary"* (my italics) suggest (*a*) that the woman herself had not initiated the request for an abortion—an impression clearly borne out in their detailed descriptions of some of the cases; and (*b*) that the judgment that an abortion was *"necessary"* was the doctors' judgment, not the women's. The line between reasonable persuasion on the part of a doctor and the quiet coercion of a patient unequipped to dispute a doctor's "medical" judgment is exceedingly fine (and particulary so in this instance since 50 percent of these nonpsychiatric cases were women who had contracted rubella, some of whom were persuaded to "consent" to an abortion on the ground that it was "necessary"). In discussing the problem of women with strong religious scruples against abortion, Jan-Otto Ottoson says that "they should not be operated on, or, if this is the only thing to be done, she should be helped with psychotherapy. *It is important to give her the impression that she did not make the decision herself, but that it has been made on medical grounds"* ("Experience Under Law in Sweden," Harvard Divinity School–Kennedy Foundation International Conference on Abortion, Washington, D.C., September 1967, p. 14, my italics). I will return to the general problem of coercion in later chapters. (See also the chapter of fetal indications for a discussion of what is and is not "necessary" so far as that indication is concerned.)

120. Richard L. Jenkins, "The Significance of Maternal Rejection . . . ," *op. cit.*, p. 274; *cf.* Mary S. Calderone, "Illegal Abortion as a Public Health Problem," *American Journal of Public Health,* 50 (July 1960), p. 951: "When a woman seeking an abortion is given the chance of talking over her problem with a properly trained and oriented person, she will in the process very often allay many of her qualms and will spontaneously decide to see the pregnancy through, particularly if she is assured that supportive help will continue to be available to her"; and Vladimir Eliasberg, "Psychiatry in Prenatal Care and the Problem of Abortion," *Medical Woman's Journal,* 58 (January-February 1951), p. 30: "I want to point out that modern psychiatry and psychoanalysis should be called upon much more often to help the mother solve her many mental problems during gestation. Many conflicts which seem insurmountable will yield to treatment and it is very important to have such treatment offered to the pregnant woman whenever necessary."

121. Rudolph Ehrensing, M.D. (personal communication).

122. Rosen, in *Abortion and the Law, op. cit.*, p. 94.

123. *Ibid.*

124. R. F. Tredgold, "Psychiatric Indication for Termination of Pregnancy," *op. cit.*, p. 1253.

CHAPTER 4

Fetal Indications

A TREMENDOUS NUMBER of things can go wrong in the development of a conceptus. Perhaps 30 percent of all fertilized eggs are spontaneously aborted at some stage in their developmental process. Those that survive run the risk of a wide variety of defects, from the most minor to those which will ultimately result either in severe crippling or in early death. Part of the fear of pregnancy in many women is undoubtedly the fear of having a defective child—a child which could be a burden to itself and to its family. Some of the fear is undoubtedly a residue of centuries of superstition and misinformation, but part of it is not without foundation. Defective children are born who are, in fact, doomed from birth to a great range of serious defects, some correctable only by means of expensive and difficult therapy and others barely correctable at all. Since this is a possibility, it is understandable that there has been pressure to allow abortion on the grounds of what have been called "fetal indications." By this phrase is normally meant the possible birth of a child whose mental or physical handicaps or a combination of both would be such as to render the child's life insupportably unhappy, or would impose heavy burdens on the family or on the society which must support the life of this child. The problems to be dealt with in this chapter are: (a) the likelihood of a defective child's being born under certain conditions, with an emphasis on congenital rubella (German measles); and (b) the pertinent criteria for determining the presence of a "fetal indication." As in the previous chapters, I am using the term "indications" to mean "reasons," to avoid begging the question whether such "indications" should be written into the law.

What congenital defects may afflict a child? What sort of criteria, and alternatives, should be considered in dealing with "fetal indications" for abortion? As with other indications, the picture is far less clear than one would wish. An advantage of the fetal data, however, is that much of it has been collected and analyzed in a context where the problem of abortion was not being considered; that is, when information is being given to the physician or researcher for the care and treatment of patients, rather than being put forward as part of the abortion debate.

Some congenital defects are quite common and others are comparatively rare. Among the more common are mongolism, congenital syphilis, the Rh factor, Tay-Sachs disease, congenital rubella, and sickle-cell anemia (which particularly affects Negroes). In addition, there is some evidence to indicate that the rate of congenital defects after cases of Asian influenza is considerably higher than normal, and also after cases of poliomyelitis and hepatitis.[1] Complete data on the rate of likely defects from the latter are not available, but it is generally known that mongolism occurs in about one in every 700 births; less frequent but also well known is the "cat-cry syndrome," which also leads to serious defects and usually to an early death. In the instance of mongolism, the risk rises to about one percent in women bearing a child after forty years of age; it can also run as high as 50 percent (or even 100 percent) for some younger women because of chromosomal translocation.

It is not my intention here, though, to survey the wide range of congenital defects and their respective risks. Rather, my concern is with those situations most frequenty invoked as fetal indications for abortion. These situations appear to be five: where there is a sensitization to the Rh factor; where the fetus has been exposed to a dangerous amount of radiation; where serious hereditary defects are likely to be present and cause genetic abnormalities; where harmful drugs (such as thalidomide) which have a high likelihood of producing fetal defects have been taken during pregnancy; and finally, where the mother has contracted viral infections, particularly rubella.[2]

To consider these situations, or indications, one by one: The danger to the fetus of the Rh factor is likely to diminish given the development of exchange transfusion techniques and the advent of a gamma-globulin injection which forestalls Rh complications from the outset. In the case of radiation hazards, particularly when radiation has been used for the treatment of cancer of the cervix, but also when X rays have been heavily used for diagnostic purposes, defective children may also be born. The data on the dangers here are, once again, incomplete, but some specialists believe they are significant enough to count as grounds for abortion. (However, women with cancer of the cervix often abort spontaneously.) While the likelihood of genetic abnormalities is an indication for abortion in some countries (especially those with generally permissive laws), it is not anywhere a commonly employed ground even when legally available (see Chapter 7). However, the rapidly developing art of amniocentesis—involving removal of some of the amniotic fluid anytime from the fourteenth week of pregnancy on, together with more sophisticated techniques of karyotyping (which requires another two to six weeks to grow cultures of cells in the amniotic fluid)—is making it increasingly more possible to determine whether a fetus has gross chromosomal defects. Already mongolism can be thus detected, as can some other congenital abnormalities (deviations in sex chromosome number, and structural rearrangements, including deletions and breaks).[3] Undoubtedly as the techniques are refined, they will enable the detection of a far wider range of congenital abnormalities and gene defects. This means that the problem of a fetal indication could well become more acute in the future, particularly if it becomes possible early in pregnancy to predict a defect with 100 percent accuracy—much earlier than the amniocentesis-karyotyping method, which is not initiated until a woman is 14 or more weeks pregnant and may not be completed until she is 20 or more weeks advanced in pregnancy. Any abortion at that stage (in the fifth or sixth month), besides being more dangerous than in the first trimester, would occur after quickening (fourth or fifth month) and thereby be less acceptable morally to many. The likelihood that detection methods for abnormalities will be developed before corrective techniques will only exacerbate the moral dilemmas.

The thalidomide tragedy, which came to light in the early 1960s, is perhaps the best example in the harmful-drug category. It turned out that pregnant women who had taken thalidomide (designed as a tranquilizer) stood a considerable danger of bearing defective children. The International Pediatric Conference of 1962 estimated that there were some 5,000 defective children born of women who had taken the drug; the main defect was the absence of various limbs.[4] The efforts of Sheri Finkbine to have an abortion after having taken the drug were given considerable publicity and no doubt helped bring to public attention the whole question of fetal indications for abortion. Other drugs, however, are also suspected of being able to cause defects in fetuses, and it seems likely that, with the increasing use of a variety of drugs, this situation will reappear from time to time.[5]

At present, however, rubella is the most frequently invoked fetal indication for therapeutic abortion. For that reason, and also because the data are plentiful if not altogether adequate, I want to concentrate my attention in this chapter on rubella. That there now exists an effective vaccine against rubella means that its incidence is likely to drop sharply in the years ahead, with a strong possibility that the epidemic expected in 1970–1971 can be averted.[6] Even so, there are bound to be many cases throughout the world for some years to come.[7] Rubella provides as good a test case as any of the technical problems, as well as questions of norms and criteria, that arise with the whole category of fetal indications. If some norms can be developed here, then the way will be open for the development of norms which could probably apply in other cases of potential or actually known (by amniocentesis) fetal defects.

To place the problem of rubella in a meaningful context, it is useful at the outset to mention briefly the overall likelihood of defective children's being born in all pregnancies. The most common estimate is that in the United States, of the three and one-half to four million babies being born alive each year, approximately 120,000 are mentally retarded and physical defects are present in another 250,000. The gross figure takes into account both severe retardation and physical defects as well as minor retardation and defects. This means that about one in ten children will, from a wide variety of causes, have some degree of mental or physical defectiveness or both. Yet a figure like this is inherently unilluminating, precisely because of the great variety of malformations and the great range in severity. Moreover, as Kalter and Warkany have pointed out, "it is . . . obvious that incidence figures will vary according to the definition and method used and that such figures will be of limited value unless their derivation is explicitly stated." [8] Surveying the literature, Kalter and Warkany state that it appears that from 2 to 3 percent of all live-born infants show one or more major and significant congenital malformations at the time of birth and that this figure is probably doubled at the end of one year after initially inapparent defects begin to show themselves. These figures refer to what the authors call "gross structural defects," so that, if one adds minor defects, an overall defect rate of 10 percent appears plausible, neither too radical nor too conservative.

One of the most unique and valuable studies of defect rates was done on the island of Kauai in Hawaii, a study which had the advantage of covering an entire population and all the pregnancies which occurred in the community. Moreover, the island is one whose health and living standards and facilities are comparable to those existing in the best mainland American situations.[9] Of a total of 1,922 live births out of 3,000 pregnancies, it was found that 14.7 percent of the children (283) had some degree of defect. Of this number, 130 had very minor handicaps requiring little or no specialized care; 106 had handicaps which were amenable to short-term, specialized care; 3.7 percent of the total live-born children (47) had defects which required long-term, specialized care.[10] Of further relevance here is data indicating that a threatened spontaneous abortion during pregnancy does not significantly increase the likelihood of defective birth, and data indicating that there is a relatively high correlation between physical stress during pregnancy and retardation.[11] Taken together, these data—which are incomplete—would indicate that physical stress during pregnancy is not very likely to produce defects, but that when later defects are found, one should not be surprised if there had been some stress present during pregnancy. I do

not intend to draw any immediate conclusion from the overall defect
rate in all live births. The main point is that probably 3 to 5 percent of
all children suffer from some serious congenital defect, of a reasonably
crippling nature. This figure helps provide a background for comparison
in a discussion of rubella.

The Significance of Rubella

It is not difficult to understand why rubella should loom so large in
the abortion discussion. It is well known that maternal rubella is a
significant cause of defects in children. Rubella epidemics have appeared periodically every seven to eight years, and the extent of the
disease, its highly contagious nature, and the number of children estimated to suffer from congenital rubella (10,000–20,000 estimated in the
1963–1964 epidemic) all make the problem widespread and recognizable.[12] In addition, the absence of a vaccine until very recently meant
that control of the disease had not been achieved. There were also great
problems in early detection of maternal rubella.[13] Some decades ago,
rubella was thought to be simply a mild childhood disease, the main
symptom of which was a slight rash. The presence of the disease in
children was first noted early in the nineteenth century, and epidemics
were observed in Germany prior to the middle of that century. Though
noted, the disease was not taken seriously by medical investigators,
mainly because there seemed no reason to do so.[14]

The problem was first brought to serious medical attention by the
observation of an Australian ophthalmologist, Norman M. Gregg, that a
number of children born in the aftermath of a 1940 Australian rubella
epidemic had congenital cataracts. In an important paper delivered before the Ophthalmological Society of Australia in 1941, he pointed out
that, in 67 out of 78 infants born with congenital cataracts, the mothers
had contracted rubella during the first three months of pregnancy or just
before conception.[15] The cataracts in many of the infants affected both
eyes and, in addition, 44 of the infants also had congenital heart lesions.
Moreover, the infants were difficult to feed, often smaller than average
and underweight. Gregg's paper was also important because, for the first
time, a clearly specified teratogen—an external agent causing developmental anomalies—had been discovered. Up to that time, phrases such
as "faulty germ plasm" were still being used in talking about congenital
defects.[16] Alerted by Gregg, other Australian investigators shortly thereafter confirmed his findings and, in addition, enlarged the list of defects
associated with rubella: cataracts, heart disease, deafness, mental deficiency, and a higher than average mortality rate. Microcephaly was
discovered in 62 percent of the studied rubella cases, heart disease in

52 percent, deaf-mutism and deafness in 43 percent, cataracts in 18 percent and mental deficiencies in 5 percent.[17] Further studies during the
1940s in other parts of the world put the suspected hazards of maternal
rubella beyond all doubt. For some time, though, there was much that
was not known about the disease. That rubella was a virus disease was
not confirmed until 1938, and it was not until the 1950s that the patho-
genesis of rubella was understood. Not until 1962 was the rubella virus
actually isolated.[18] Shortly thereafter diagnostic tests for rubella were
developed which are still in the process of refinement. One of the most
important discoveries during these years was that infection could be
present without any visible symptoms at all, specifically without the
manifestation of a rash. This finding was particularly disturbing since it
meant that a woman could contract rubella and, apart from special diagnostic tests, be totally unaware of the presence of the disease.

Galvanizing the research efforts even more was a major rubella epidemic which began in Great Britain in 1962 and soon appeared in the
United States in 1964.[19] This was probably the largest of all rubella
epidemics, with possibly as many as 20,000 children born with one degree
or another of defects. One important study calculated a frequency of 22
cases of clinical rubella per thousand pregnancies during the 1964 American epidemic, against a rate of one per thousand in nonepidemic years.[20]
Prior to this epidemic, the main cluster of defects associated with the
rubella syndrome were heart defects, cataracts and deafness, occurring
alone or in combination.[21] The 1962–1964 epidemic, however, brought to
light a whole host of abnormalities, recognizable at birth or at some time
thereafter. These included jaundice, hepatitis, anemia, bone lesions, myocardial damage and damage to the central nervous system, among other
things. These new manifestations, usually referred to as the "expanded
rubella syndrome," raised the question of whether a new viral strain was
manifesting itself or whether better diagnostic techniques, plus the large
number of cases, had simply uncovered data which had been overlooked
earlier. It is generally believed that the latter is the case.

At present, under the expanded rubella syndrome, the following defects are most common in cases of congenital rubella: low birth weight,
cataracts, microphthalmia, retinopathy, deafness, congenital heart disease, bone lesions and psychomotor retardations. Less common, or rare,
are jaundice, glaucoma, cloudy corneas, myocardial damage, hepatitis,
and various forms of anemia.[22] The very extent of this list gives a further
indication of why this disease has proved so worrisome. Congenital
rubella can be the cause of eye, ear, blood, heart, nervous system, liver
and circulatory abnormalities. Thus there is hardly a single important
part of the body system which is not liable to be affected by congenital
rubella.[23] Moreover, the fact that infants can continue to secrete the
virus well after birth means that they can not only spread the disease

further (not only to other infants, but also to adults, hospital staff for example, some of whom may be young pregnant women), but are also subject to postnatal defects from the continued presence of the virus.[24] M. Siegel and his colleagues, for instance, carefully studied 1,526 infants, half infected, half control, born in New York City between 1957 and 1964. While they found no increase in the fetal death rate during the epidemic year of 1964, they found that low birth weights increased about 50 percent in 1964, as well as a fourfold increase in the risk of congenital cataract and a twofold increase in heart disease.[25]

From a number of different studies, the following seems to be the breakdown on the incidence of defects. *Multiple defects:* The Manson study found that 24 percent of the deformed children they studied had more than one defect.[26] A study at the London Hospital for Sick Children found 21 percent with single defects, the most common of which was either deafness or heart lesion, and 79 percent with more than one defect.[27] The 1965 American Rubella Symposium also discovered a large number of multiple defects. A common finding is that the rate of multiple defects is greatest when fetal infection occurs in the first two months of pregnancy.[28] *Low birth weight and retarded growth:* Gregg was the first to notice this symptom, and it was further documented by others. Lundström, in a follow-up study of children ages one to three, found that 27 percent were below average in height and weight and had a small head circumference.[29] The 1965 Rubella Symposium found that 50 percent to 80 percent of the children had a lower than average birth weight.[30] A study by Cooper and his colleagues found that 90 percent were below the mean birth weight.[31] *Heart defects:* These are generally judged to be the most common of all rubella deformities and very often associated with cataracts and deafness.[32] As R. C. Way has written: "Based on several reports since the 1964 epidemic the incidence of heart defects in infants with congenital rubella was found to be 59 percent. Patent ductus arteriosus continues to be the most frequent lesion (32 percent) but multiple lesions in the pulmonary and systemic arteries have been observed with increasing frequency." [33] *Myocardial damage:* The Korones study found that 7 of 22 infants had myocardial damage.[34] Ainger, Lawyer and Fitch found 10 out of 47 infants with congenital rubella and significant electrocardiographic evidence of myocardial damage.[35] *Eye defects:* After heart defects, cataracts appear to be the most common kind of abnormalities. About 70 percent of the cataracts affect both eyes and, again, are commonly associated with multiple defects. Microphthalmia is also frequent, as are glaucoma and pigmentary retinopathy.[36] *Hearing defects:* Barr and Lundström found evidence to suggest that deafness may be as high as 25 percent in children born of mothers who contracted rubella during the first trimester.[37] The Barr and Lundström study showed, moreover, that the deafness may not

manifest itself clearly until after five years of age. Jackson, Fisch and
Sheridan found a deafness rate of 6 percent in their studies of two-year-
olds.[38] Plotkin and his associates found that some of the earlier symptoms, for instance pupura and bone lesions, tend to recede and other
symptoms, for instance deafness, microcephaly and mental retardation,
become more common as the child grows older.[39] *Bone defects:* The Rudolph study reported in 1965 the discovery of numerous cases of bone
defects in newborn infants,[40] a finding which was confirmed in the
Rubella Symposium of 1965.[41] Other investigators, specifically Singleton
et al. and W. C. Marshall *et al.*, have detailed some of the leading characteristics of these defects.[42] *Central nervous system abnormalities:* Rudolph *et al.*, Singleton *et al.*, and Desmond *et al.* have traced the development of microcephaly, mental retardation, neurosensory impairment, and
electroencephalographic abnormalities.[43]

J. A. Dudgeon has helpfully surveyed a considerable part of the
literature and charted the main statistical results. In the category of
major defects, he arrived at the following summary data: low birth
weight: over 80 percent; major heart defects: between 50 percent to 60
percent; cataracts: slightly over 50 percent; deafness: 50 percent; defect
of the central nervous system, particularly full fontanelle: about 40 percent; major blood defects: about 55 percent; major liver defects: 60 percent; bone lesions: 40 percent.[44]

Distinguishing Among "Defects"

I have presented these findings fairly explicitly because it is important,
in order to grasp the full range of the rubella syndrome, to descend into
the details. Too much of the literature on abortion is content simply with
citing gross figures, providing no particulars. When one begins to ask
more specific questions about the data, it is possible to see the problem
in a more revealing light. It is not enough to speak of "defects" caused
by congenital rubella. Everything depends on the severity of the defects,
the possibility and practicability of treatment, and the possibility of
making reasonably reliable predictions. It is now recognized, for instance,
that early estimates on the extent of rubella-connected defects were
much too high. One of the early researchers, C. Swan, used a figure of 80
percent to 90 percent, and it was widely accepted.[45] But his investigations, like most of the early ones, were marred by a number of methodological inadequacies, most notably by a heavy dependence on retrospective studies of children known to have been born with congenital rubella.
(Later studies, based on prospective data, showed the risk to be much
lower than that posited by Swan.)[46]

The trouble with retrospective studies is obvious: they study only those children who have manifested defects. That means there is no possibility of comparing them with children of mothers who had contracted rubella and yet who were born without any abnormalities. If one wants to know only the various symptoms and defects of a child who is in fact born with rubella, then retrospective studies are adequate. If one wants to know, however, what the chance of an abnormal child is in the case of a woman who has contracted rubella during pregnancy, only prospective studies are adequate for a balanced perspective. Since it is this latter question which has been most prominent in abortion decisions —whether a woman who has contracted rubella should have an abortion—the results of the prospective studies are particularly critical.[47]

For the purpose of this discussion I will use the definition of major and minor defects employed in the Manson study, which reflects the general usage. Major defects are "those which might affect the life of the fetus or seriously handicap the living child." Minor defects are those "conditions which in a mild form cause some inconvenience, but if severe would be a serious handicap—when there was no indication of their severity." [48] With these definitions in mind, it may be said that comparatively few studies confirm a *major defect* rate anywhere near the 50 percent rate often cited in abortion arguments. Invariably, that high a rate, when reported, only occurs in the case of women contracting rubella during the first month of pregnancy. A few studies, though, did find a very high defect rate. Louis Z. Cooper cites a prospective study conducted in 1960 by Richard H. Michaels and Gilbert W. Mellin of the Columbia University College of Physicians and Surgeons reporting a fetal hazard of 47 percent for rubella in the first month, 22 percent in the second and 7 percent in the third. Cooper himself believes that these figures may in fact be conservative.[49] Another study, conducted in France by Lamy and Sérer, found a 50 percent major-defect rate, although this study comprised only 48 cases.[50] Samuel J. Salomi, in a review of a number of small-scale prospective studies, concluded that, from a total of 222 live births, the risk of major deformities was 61 percent in women who had contracted rubella during weeks 1–4, 26 percent in weeks 5–8, and 8 percent in weeks 9–12. Of 109 pregnancies complicated by rubella in week 1–8, only 39 (35.8 percent) ended in normal live births; 43 percent ended in spontaneous abortions or stillbirths, and 27 percent in gross fetal anomalies.[51]

The figures from most other prospective studies are considerably lower. Morris Greenberg et al., in a study of 104 women who had rubella during the first trimester, reported that 27 percent gave birth to normal infants, 3 percent had congenitally malformed infants, 3 percent ended in stillbirths and 12 percent had other nonviable fetuses. Therapeutic abortions were performed on 46 percent and 10 percent were lost from the study. Taking into account other elements, the authors concluded that the incidence of serious deformities was 9.7 percent.[52] They also cite in their study an article by R. MacIntosh *et al.* which found an incidence of 7 percent congenital malformation in the children of women who did not have rubella.[53] Rendle-Short states that the risk of fetal abnormality is about 20 percent during the first trimester, but then goes on to say: "This figure is approximately true, but gives little idea of the probable outcome of the pregnancy in any particular case, because the risk varies greatly with the fetal age." [54] In summarizing a number of scattered, small prospective studies adding up to 200 cases altogether, he calculated that "if the mother contracts rubella 1–4 weeks after the onset of the last menstrual period, the chance of her having a deformed baby is nearly 60 percent; at 5–8 weeks the chance is about 35 percent; at 9–12 weeks it is 15 percent; and at 13–16 weeks 7 percent. The overall risk up to 16 weeks is 21 percent." [55]

A prospective study carried out in England by Margaret Manson *et al.*, covering the period 1951–1952, shows a much lower figure.[56] Of 578 cases of rubella in pregnancy, there were 547 live-born infants and 37 with major malformations. The result, then, was a 6.4 percent major-defect incidence. Of the infants who died, major malformations were observed in 46 percent, compared with 34 percent in the control group (of 5,717). Manson also found that the percentage of malformations during the period up to the fourth week of pregnancy was 15.6 percent; 5–8 weeks 19.7 percent; 9–12 weeks 13 percent; 13–16 weeks 4.2 percent; 17 weeks or later 2.2 percent. And 15.8 percent of the infants born with major malformations had mothers who had contracted mild cases of rubella; 17 percent were born of mothers who had moderate cases, and 22.2 percent whose mothers had severe cases.[57] These last figures would suggest that the severity of the infection in the mother is not a particularly significant factor.

The Manson study seems to me particularly important, not only because it was sponsored by the British Ministry of Health with the cooperation of all the regional health authorities in England, but also because it had the advantage of comparison with a large control group (i.e., women who had not contracted rubella in pregnancy). Manson *et al.* conclude:

> The risk of defective children following rubella in the first three months of pregnancy is relatively high but it should be remembered that by no means all of the defective children were severely handicapped. Operative treatment had been successfully carried out on some of the children with heart and eye defects; about two-thirds of the deaf children were able to attend ordinary schools. Only a few children had multiple defects of heart, eye, hearing or intelligence. Mental defects . . . were not common.[58]

It should be noted, however, that this study was conducted prior to a knowledge of the "expanded rubella syndrome." Whether this further knowledge, not available until after 1964, would have significantly altered the findings cannot, of course, be known.

A later follow-up study of the same group was reported by Mary D. Sheridan and covered examinations at the age of two years for one group, three to six years for another group and eight to eleven years for still another group. There it was found that congenital abnormalities in infants were significantly higher if the mother had been infected with rubella during the first 16 weeks, but that after 16 weeks the abnormality rate was no higher than in the control group. Of the rubella children, major abnormalities (primarily of eye, ear and heart) occurred in 15 percent of the children, with 8 percent having multiple abnormalities. Minor abnormalities were found to be present in another 16 percent with 4 percent having more than one minor abnormality. Noteworthy is the rise from a 6.4 percent major-defect rate in the Manson study to 15 percent in the Sheridan study. The author stresses, however, that "these are outside estimates, as it is possible that some of the abnormalities discovered were due to causes other than maternal rubella." [59]

On other points, Sheridan reported that the intelligence level of the rubella children was normal, and she had an interesting comment on the problem of social adjustment: "It has been suggested that rubella children often show emotional instability and difficult behavior, but although the information was specifically requested there was little supportive evidence in the reports. . . . Only one, a blind child, was reported as psychologically difficult." [60] At the time of the third follow-up, covering children in the age group of eight to eleven, 92 percent of the children were attending ordinary schools.[61] Also of interest with respect to long-term prognosis is a report of M. A. Menser et al. that a satisfactory socioeconomic adjustment was achieved by "many" of those in a group of 50 who had been born with rubella during the 1940 Australian epidemic. Twenty-five years later, five of the group were mentally defective, one severely so; the remaining 45 were within the normal range of mental ability. Ten had cataracts, all of which had been treated surgically, but three with poor results; 11 had congenital cardiovascular defects; 48 were deaf to some significant degree, with severe bilateral deafness in 43. All in all, a mixed picture, although the authors point out that many had adjusted much better than had been predicted of them.[62]

Another important study, by John L. Sever and associates, also presents a relatively low incidence of serious abnormality.[63] This report was based on a prospective study of 6,161 pregnant women, 10 percent of whom reported exposure to rubella during the first trimester. Of the exposed women, 2 percent developed clinical rubella, with 40 percent of the cases occurring during the first trimester. Ten percent of the women with rubella infection during the first trimester had a child with a congenital rubella syndrome recognizable during the first month after birth. Of those who were exposed to rubella during the first trimester, but showed no clinical illness, 0.6 percent had a child with congenital rubella.[64] Gilbert M. Schiff, in a study of infants born following the 1964 rubella epidemic, found that out of 300 of 1,549 infants who were tested for the presence of virus, virus was recovered in 43 (14 percent). Of this 43, 33 had no detectable abnormalities, meaning an abnormality rate (major and minor) of 23 percent.[65] Lundström, summarizing 15 prospective studies conducted between the years 1946 and 1951, found a total of 96 infants with major defects out of 1,231 live-born infants, for an overall major-defect rate of 8 percent. Of this number 33 percent of the defective children were born to mothers who had contracted rubella up to the fourth week; 25 percent, 5–8 weeks; 9 percent, 9–12 weeks; 4 percent, 13–16 weeks; and 1 percent thereafter.[66] Another prospective study carried out by Lundström himself (in Sweden) in 1951 found 51 infants with major defects out of 1,121 live-born births, for a total major-defect rate of 6.6 percent.[67] Bradford-Hill *et al.*, summarizing four prospective studies between 1949 and 1954 (and included in Lundström's survey), found a 16.4 percent rate of major defects.[68]

In assessing these last-mentioned studies, Dudgeon points out that there are ample statistics supporting a higher infant mortality rate in the case of congenital rubella. Cooper *et al.* found a rate of 29 percent in one series of studies, and Horstmann, a figure of 14 percent mortality rate.[69] Another study, by Pitt and Keir, showed that of 107 live-born children of 145 pregnancies, major rubella defects were discovered in 20 of the children. The incidence of major defects for infection during the first month was 60 percent, for the second month 33 percent, for the third 33.4 percent and for the fourth 5.7 percent, with an overall average of 23.8 percent for the first 16 weeks.[70] Robert H. Green and his colleagues surveyed the literature and posited a 15 percent to 20 percent figure, with 50 percent for infection during the first month.[71]

Dudgeon observes that there can be considerable variation in the reported incidence of malformation even using the prospective method. A difference in survey methods, the different ages at which children are examined in different studies, the possibility of different strains of the virus in different epidemics and other factors which are not understood, could give very discrepant results from one survey to another. Nonetheless, he seems quite correct in concluding from the large number of studies he summarized that the greatest danger in the aftermath of maternal rubella comes in the first 12 weeks of pregnancy, with some risk through the sixteenth week, and a sharply declining risk thereafter.[72] As we will see, the first four weeks are the most dangerous and the curve of the risk declines perceptibly after that point.

The somewhat bewildering variation in defect rate reported from one

study to the next, however, raises the question of whether some outstanding general patterns can be found. There is only one relatively
recent study which points to a very high rate of major defects for infection during the first trimester: the (1) *Lamy and Sérer* study, with
its 50 percent rate. Then there is a cluster which comes up with a much
lower rate: (2) *Michaels-Mellin:* 25 percent (47 percent first month, 22
percent second month, and 7 percent third month); (3) *Salomi:* 31 percent (61 percent first month, 26 percent second month, 8 percent third
month); (4) *Rendle-Short:* 21 percent (60 percent first month); (5)
Sheridan: 15 percent; (6) *Pitt and Keir:* 23.8 percent (60 percent first
month, 33 percent second month, 33.4 percent third month, 5.7 percent
fourth month); (7) *Bradford-Hill:* 16.4 percent (50 percent first month);
(8) *Green:* about 15 percent to 20 percent (50 percent first month).
Thirdly there is a cluster considerably lower still: (9) *Manson:* 6.4 percent (raised, though, to 15 percent in Sheridan's follow-up); (10) *Lundström summary* of 15 studies: 8 percent; (11) *Lundström's own study:*
6.6 percent; (12) *Greenberg:* 9.7 percent; (13) *Sever:* 10 percent.

Which of these three groups of figures should be given the greatest
credence? This is a question which cannot be answered in any decisive
way, partially because the studies, on the whole, are not detailed enough
in spelling out their methodology to allow one to make strict comparisons; some were done with the advantage of control groups for comparison, others were not, to take only one important methodological difference. Also, most were done prior to the 1962–1964 epidemic. How
does one judge the relative validity of these former studies in comparison with the latter? Again, no clear answer is available.

One cannot help, though, being impressed particularly with the
Manson study and the Sheridan follow-up to that study: the very size,
care and presence of a control group make these two studies stand out
in the literature. Of the three different groups categorized above, the
third, with its very low major-defect rate, seems the most impressive,
mainly because it covers a far larger number of cases and involves more
different studies than either of the other two; hence, one cannot help
being struck by its average of a major defect incidence of under 10
percent. However, because (with the exception of the Sever study) all of
the studies were done prior to the 1962–1964 epidemic and thus prior
to a knowledge of the "expanded rubella syndrome," and because the
Sheridan follow-up raised the low Manson figure from 6.4 percent to
15 percent, there is good reason to be hesitant about accepting any
overall major-defect rate which is below 10 percent. There is, though,
equally good reason to be hesitant about accepting as definitive the
figure of the first group, one study only, which would suggest a rate

of 50 percent or higher for the first trimester. We are, therefore, left with the second group as the least assailable, if not necessarily the most definitive.

On the whole, on the basis of the above reasoning, I am inclined to agree with the judicious conclusion of Dudgeon, that the "over-all effect of rubella infection in the first 16 weeks of pregnancy with fetal damage by (spontaneous) abortion and stillbirths, major and minor defects, is approximately 30–35 percent." [73] A figure of 15 percent to 20 percent chance of major defects for live-born infants of mothers who are infected during the first trimester seems to me a reasonable kind of figure to work with, granting that the expedient of averaging out a number of studies produces an unstable kind of figure. At the same time, though, the different studies do point up the significantly greater danger if the infection is contracted during the first month of pregnancy. A figure of 40 percent to 60 percent chance of major defects for infection during weeks 1–4 seems another reasonable figure to work with.

One point at any rate should now be clear. There are few data to bear out the loose proclamation of a 50 percent danger of major defects for rubella contracted during the first trimester. As suggested, if one is going to talk in a general way about major defects, 15 percent to 20 percent would be a much more judicious figure to use, stipulating that 40 percent to 60 percent would be more precise if the infection was contracted during the first month. Put another way, there would be about an 80 percent to 85 percent chance that a pregnant woman who contracted rubella during the first trimester would bear a child whose defects, if any, would be minor and easily correctable. There would be a 65 percent to 70 percent chance that her child would be born without any defects at all. If she contracted rubella during the first month, there would be a 40 percent to 60 percent chance that she would bear a child with a major defect; and that figure might be high, since the Manson-Sheridan studies would bring it down under 25 percent. Also, since the likelihood of *contracting* the infection is no more likely during the first month than any other month, there would be no special warrant for assuming that one had to use the most-hazardous first-month figures rather than the trimester figure if the infection was discovered after the second or third month. Add to that the current estimate that fewer than 15 percent of women in the reproductive age group are susceptible to rubella in the first place and the chances of defective births are put in somewhat less dramatic perspective. [74]

The Possibility of Treatment

Any attempt to refine the figures reported in different studies and to arrive at some kind of sensible working average for the sake of making predictions and charting relative hazards will not, of course, be complete until account has been taken of the possibility of treatment. It is not enough to point out that a baby with a major defect or a combination of major defects may be born to a woman who has contracted rubella. One also needs to know whether even major defects can be corrected or alleviated. To say a baby may be born with a major defect is not to say that the baby, as it matures into an adult, is necessarily doomed to a crippled life as a result of the initial defect or defects. This point is too frequently scanted in the abortion literature. Louis Z. Cooper has helped to put the problem of treating major defects in a clearer perspective:

> The outlook for rubella-damaged infants varies with the specific defect. One heart defect, patent ductus arteriosus, can be repaired quite readily. Septal defects—openings between the left and right chambers of the heart— can be closed by more complicated open-heart surgery. The rubella cataract is more difficult to repair than adult cataracts, and children with cataracts in both eyes may have little vision. There is no specific treatment for the deafness caused by rubella, but the nerve damage is usually not complete, so that hearing aids and auditory training can be quite helpful. The outlook for infants with severe brain damage is very poor. Since brain damage seems to accompany prolonged persistence of the virus, it is these infants who provide the greatest stimulus to current efforts to find ways of combatting the chronic post-natal infection.[75]

If we recall Dudgeon's breakdown of the percentage incidence of major and minor defects in established cases, Cooper's statement takes on a special significance. Dudgeon, for instance, points out that patent ductus arteriosus is the most common major heart defect; according to Cooper this defect is readily repairable. Dudgeon also found that perceptive deafness is another major defect; and Cooper says (as does Dudgeon) that hearing aids and other training can ameliorate this condition considerably.[76] This leaves, then, only those infants with severe brain damage and those children with bilateral cataracts as the most difficult remaining problem. We are left with somewhere between 40 percent to 50 percent of the major defects, cataracts and damage to the central nervous system, as the most difficult to treat.

Yet, while comparisons of this kind—between the defect and the possible treatment of it—leave some room for optimism, it must not be forgotten that the high frequency of multiple defects complicates this picture considerably. Dr. Cooper and his colleagues have detailed the difficulties, expense and therapeutic requirements involved in caring for infected infants; needed are medical specialists, public-health nurses, special educators, audiologists, social workers, physical and educational therapists.[77] The most common grouping seems to be that of heart malformations, eye and ear defects. This might suggest that, even if the heart defects can be surgically corrected and the hearing improved with hearing aids, a child might still be left with cataracts. If one recalls the Manson and Sheridan studies, though, one cannot ignore the fact that the overwhelming majority—92 percent—of the defective children surveyed there were found in later years to be attending ordinary schools and to have an average social adjustment and intellectual level. The Menser study, to be sure, leaves less room for optimism, but it was a considerably smaller group than that studied by Manson and Sheridan.

In any case, all the studies cited here and taken together indicate how extremely difficult it is to predict the long-term outcome of any given pregnancy in the case of women who contract rubella. One would have to know the time at which the rubella was contracted; calculate the possible defect rate for rubella infections at that period; project the possible range of conceivable defects resulting from the infection; estimate the available therapies for the different likely defects (which may well vary from region to region); and, finally, make some judgment about the practical possibility of medical corrections when theoretically possible (which would involve financial, social and psychological considerations).

One can easily see that this could be a most difficult kind of calculation, subject to a huge number of variables and complicated by the different results of the available surveys of defect rates. While the need for such a calculation would not necessarily tell against the theoretical desirability of abortion on the basis of a rubella indication, it would suggest that the mere presence of rubella infection in a pregnant woman does not, in itself, *necessitate* an abortion. Since there are so many variables to be taken into account, one could be taking a major risk whatever course one chose: the risk of giving birth to a child with multiple defects, and the risk of killing a perfectly normal fetus. The preponderance of the evidence, however, would indicate that the latter is far more likely than the former. More than that, if one takes into account the possibility of corrective therapy even for major defects, the possibility of killing a defective fetus which could well make an all but normal adjustment after birth and development is considerably increased. If the risk of a major defect in a child is 15 percent to 20 percent for infection of the mother during the first trimester, and if half of the most likely major defects can be corrected, then one is left with approximately a 10 percent chance of bearing a child whose defects may genuinely cripple that child.[78] Naturally, a different calculation comes into play for rubella infections during the first month of pregnancy; and still another if it came in the third month. The point is simply that, one way or another, the calculation of probabilities will have to be relatively complicated.

Should one be willing to make such calculations in the first place?

That is an ethical question which no amount of perusal of the rubella literature can answer. As matters now stand, there may be another rubella epidemic about 1970–1971, if the normal seven- to eight-year cycle of such epidemics continues to hold and if the just recently available vaccine has not come into worldwide use. Thus, if there are grounds for hope that substantial progress in prevention and control will be made in the years ahead, the fact is that at present this remains only a hope. Moreover, if one has ethically decided that one should take into account the possibility of a fetal indication for abortion, and if one is willing to include in one's calculation a consideration of the therapeutic potentialities for a deformed child, then it is necessary to consider the availability and practical feasibility of therapy.

Generally speaking, the therapeutic possibilties in the United States as a whole are mixed, with much dependent upon the locality. They are probably better in Eastern Europe and the Scandinavian countries and considerably worse in the underdeveloped countries. In addition, facilities will sometimes be available for the wealthy, who can afford to seek them out wherever they might be located in the country (or abroad), which will not be available for the poor. Open-heart surgery, for instance, which will correct some congenital heart defects, is by no means routinely available to every American regardless of where he lives or what his income is. The care and treatment of the mentally defective, the blind and the deaf is good in some areas, poor in others, and scandalous in still others. While one can find in the rubella literature articles describing new operative techniques to alleviate various eye, ear and heart defects, there is often a long lapse between the time of such a discovery by one specialist and its routine employment by others. Again, while the techniques for therapy may be known, a general shortage of trained therapists may make the therapy generally unavailable; and this is the situation in most of the United States.

During the past few years, any number of federal and state projects have been initiated or extended for the care and training of the handicapped, but by and large the efforts made nowhere meet the full needs of the situation. Under the terms of the 1967 Vocational Rehabilitation Act, the National Center for Deaf-Blind Youths and Adults was established. Public Law 90-31, the Mental Health Amendments of 1967, extended federal authority for grants and staffing of community health centers through 1970. Since the 1963 Mental Retardation and Community Health Centers Construction Act nearly 300 community health centers, serving over 40 million people, have been established. This is an impressive figure, but since there are now over 200 million Americans, it is obviously insufficient and will remain so for the forseeable future. An article by Leston L. Havens and Gerald Cubelli has called attention to the "almost unlimited" number of psychiatric services available to patients through state vocational and rehabilitation agencies; but they also point out that considerable knowledge on the part of the psychiatrist is necessary to take advantage of these possibilities.[79] And, of course, those familiar with the facilities and personnel of many state agencies will realize that the quality of the help available is often exceedingly low. The Bureau of Education for the Handicapped, established by the U.S. Office of Education in 1967, is another promising start; but, again, it is only a start. Educational facilities for the handicapped are nowhere near a level of adequacy in the United States and they vary considerably in other parts of the world. Other examples of promising new programs and extensions of old ones could be mentioned. But the gap between all the existing programs and the actual needs is still great and will undoubtedly remain so for some years to come.

Two conclusions can be drawn here. First, so long as the general therapeutic and rehabilitation facilities remain below standard, the argument for the whole category of "fetal indications" retains some force. One cannot, at any rate, glibly invoke the theoretical possibility of care and correction of defects as a decisive negation of fetal indications for abortion. The question here is not only whether therapy is in principle available (somewhere), but whether it is in fact available (here) to those who need it or are likely to need it. Naturally, any attempt to project the possibility of care would have to take account of a future improvement in local or accessible facilities and the availability of specialists; and this could be most difficult, adding still another complication to any decision. Second, however, the fact that in principle care and treatment could be had (somewhere), and the possibility that it could be had locally in many situations, means that any decision on fetal indications would have to repudiate the element of a presumptive *necessity* which pervades much of the discussion of fetal indications. As long as there are in principle therapeutic options available, there are no fetal indications which per se and in complete isolation from the therapeutic possibilities necessarily point to an abortion (so far as rubella is concerned). The therapeutic possibilities should always be considered, because they often exist and can often be effective, and the introduction of these possibilities further removes any element of necessity or inexorability in the making of medical judgments. Only if it can be shown that the practical possibility of therapy is out of the question, or that for a variety of social or psychological reasons a defective child would pose a major, devastating problem would it be possible to offer a strong case for abortion. And even here, I am assuming that the earlier-mentioned prudential calculations have already been made: the likelihood that an infected mother will bear a child with a major defect or defects; the likelihood that these defects will be the kind which are amenable to treatment; the likelihood, finally, that therapy could be had.

Considering the data discussed in this chapter, it should be un-
mistakably clear that there are no grounds for an automatic medical
judgment that the mere contraction of rubella in pregnancy (even during
the first month) ineluctably points to a hopeless situation for the child
born of that pregnancy. On the contrary, the general probabilities point
in the opposite direction. The preponderant data would support the
rational hope that the child will be born without major or minor defects
and that, if the the defects are major, perhaps half of them most likely
would be correctable in principle and that, if correctable in principle,
there would be a good chance that they could be correctable in fact.
The odds that any given mother who contracts rubella during pregnancy will bear a child which will have an uncorrectable, insupportable
major defect turn out to be relatively low.

Calculating Odds

But is it enough simply to calculate the odds? The trouble with such
a calculus is its impersonality. What about the mental anguish of a
pregnant woman who fears that she might be one of the unlucky mothers
(which, statistically speaking, she could be)? Should we not take into
account this anguish? Is it enough only to say that the odds that a
seriously defective child will be born are relatively low? Do we not
have an obligation to spare such a child from being born at all? These
are all relevant questions, if only because it is apparently the practice
of some doctors and certainly many pregnant women to judge the
problem of fetal indications in a context broader than that of the strictly
medical odds of major defects. Not that this is necessarily an objectionable practice, particularly if one sees the obligation of the doctor
as extending to the general well-being of a person, whether of a pregnant woman or the child she will bear, or both together.

Kenneth R. Niswander has pointed out a common practice where
rubella is concerned:

> Some hospitals . . . are willing to abort a pregnant woman when there is a
> strong possibility that the baby will be abnormal. For example, the consultant
> who recommends an abortion may simply state that the danger of fetal
> malformation due to maternal rubella in the first trimester of pregnancy
> makes an abortion advisable. On other occasions, however, a psychiatric
> opinion may be sought, and the specialist may suggest that the patient's mental
> condition, influenced by the fear of fetal malformation from the rubella, may
> become suicidal if the pregnancy is not interrupted. Her life is thus endangered.
> There is little practical difference in these two approaches since the result
> is the same: interruption of the pregnancy.[80]

This passage helps to focus part of the issue. Two questions can be
asked. First, is it actually the case that there is danger of suicide in a

woman who is abnormally fearful of bearing a deformed child? Second, if there is such a danger, could it be said that the mentally disturbed woman who contracts rubella during pregnancy stands in a kind of double jeopardy? On the one hand, she stands in jeopardy of bearing a deformed child; on the other hand, she also stands in jeopardy of a serious breakdown, possibly to the point of suicide. She would thus have a claim to abortion twice over.

The answer to the first question will determine the answer to the second. On the first question there is one major point to be made: there does not exist any empirical evidence to support the claim that suicide is a real, much less likely possibility. As pointed out in the chapter on psychiatric data, the likelihood of suicide among women wanting abortions is all but nil; if it is a possibility, it appears from most data to be very remote. On the specific point of a suicidal possibility among women threatened with the birth of a deformed child, there exist—so far as I could discover—no specific studies at all. In the absence of such studies, it would appear that there exists no scientific basis for claiming the likelihood of suicide.[81] At best, one can only make a guess from the general evidence on suicidal threats and possibilities in distressed pregnancies, and that evidence points to the exceedingly high improbability of suicide. But even if it could be shown from existing data—which no one has done—that there is a strong possibility of suicide, it would also have to be shown that such a disturbed woman could not be protected from her suicidal impulse by means of psychotherapy. That could be very difficult to show, needless to say. In this light, the purported double jeopardy begins to dissolve: the danger of suicide is slight and the danger of bearing a seriously deformed child is relatively low.

Of course, much will depend here upon one's evaluation of an acceptable and nonacceptable risk. Since there is some possibility (even if remote) of a double jeopardy, to what extent should the possibility be accepted? Kenneth J. Ryan has pointed out that, during the 1964 rubella epidemic, the great number of requests for abortions on the basis of rubella indicated that "most physicians and patients wanted to take no chances." [82] If, indeed, one has decided to "take no chances," then it is perfectly easy to find a reason for abortion in rubella cases: it is well known that *some* children will in fact be born with major defects. Within the framework of taking no chances, few data are required; very poor data will, in fact, be sufficient, even the personal "impression" of a doctor or psychiatrist. The problem of whether one should be willing to take a chance seems to me a directly moral question. It is sufficient to point out here that, if there is a willingness to run some degree of risk, it is a relatively safe risk, both on medical and (until proven otherwise) psychiatric grounds.

Socioeconomic Considerations

Yet further problems remain. If we broaden the category of fetal indications to include socioeconomic considerations as well as considerations of family stability, more complications set in. Among the socio-economic considerations would be the feasibility of a family's providing the probably expensive and lengthy therapy necessary to correct major defects or the therapy and custodial care necessary to sustain the life of a child whose defects could not be corrected. As suggested above, federal and state facilities are not uniformly good; many, in fact, are very poor. Private agencies exist, but not everywhere. A parent could well be reluctant to see a child doomed to spend his or her life in a poor state institution. Moreover, for those in the lower-income stratum a reliance upon state or federal help might be the only alternative open to them; indeed, a middle-income family could be hard-pressed to pay for private treatment and care. Problems of this kind should not be dismissed; they have a place in any moral discussion of fetal indications. But if they should not be dismissed, they are exceedingly difficult to come to grips with.

We are forced back to the question of acceptable and unacceptable chance-taking. What are the chances that a child will be born with a major rubella defect or combination of defects, and that this child will be born into a family unable to pay for a correction or amelioration of these defects, and that this child will also live in an area where state facilities are grossly inadequate, and that, therefore, the deformed child's prospects of anything approaching a minimally satisfactory life will be remote? Clearly, to introduce these many variables into a discussion of advising an abortion for a woman who has contracted rubella during pregnancy is to enter a very uncertain domain of calculation. Reasonable guesses rather than clearly ascertainable odds will inevitably come into play. Naturally, since a doctor or an abortion committee may know at the outset of the decision-making process the socioeconomic situation of a woman and know also something about local facilities, the guess will not have to be sheerly arbitrary. But even under these conditions there could rarely be any certain prognosis. The most critical factor in making the prognosis is likely to be the degree of risk a mother, a doctor or an abortion committee judges acceptable; and that judgment, as in psychiatric judgments, is likely to reflect the training, experience, knowledge and moral values of those who make the judgments.

The question of family stability poses similar difficulties. To what extent would the introduction of a deformed child into a family threaten the welfare of that family? Little imagination is necessary to envision the different kinds of threats: a hazard to the mother's physical and emotional energy; a hazard to the family's economic life; a hazard to the welfare of the other children, who may be deprived of the full care and attention they require because of the excessive demands made on the parents by the deformed child. All of these possibilities represent important imponderables, especially when it is a case of making a projection about the future life of a family. As the Church Assembly Board in England has concisely put it:

> Once again we face questions of degree—the degree of handicap in the child, the degree to which family resources can be stretched to accommodate him, the degree to which the contemplation of these uncertainties impairs with anxiety the health and well-being of the mother. The introduction of a defective child may well—indeed does—produce very considerable emotional difficulties, particularly when, over a long term, there is heavy pressure upon everyone to give way to the supposed needs of the defective child. There are situations in which such a child can strain family relationships to an intolerable degree. . . . On the other hand, while acknowledging these undoubted facts, we must be sure that we are not acquiescing in a reduced estimate of man and his capacity to respond to human demands.[83]

It is very tempting at this point to throw up one's hands in despair, opting for some simple decision-making process. There are just too many elements of uncertaintly, except in the most obvious circumstances of a family already passing into disintegration even prior to the arrival of a deformed child. But despair because of the uncertainties is a useless if understandable response. Difficult or not, an estimate and a prognosis will be required, however much it may come down to little more than a guess. The importance of the moral perspective brought to bear in making the guess and, even more importantly, in deciding the degree of risk that should be taken, is evident.

The final problem of relevance here is that of the welfare of the child. It has been argued that a pregnant woman owes it to the child not to bring it into the world if it is likely to suffer from major life-destructive or life-crippling defects. Obviously this line of argument is based on a fundamental kind of moral judgment; but that will not concern me for the moment. More germane to my immediate purposes is the factual question of whether certain defects are such as to make a minimally meaningful and satisfactory life impossible or unlikely. It is extraordinarily difficult to know how to begin getting at this kind of a question. Part of the difficulty stems from the great variation among human personalities; some people manage to surmount very serious handicaps, and others do not. There is no way we could conceivably predict in advance what type of personality a rubella-infected fetus is likely to have once developed. Another part of the difficulty stems from the kind of reception a handicapped or deformed child is likely to receive. A child who is welcomed and cherished, accepted as part of a family and society, will have a far greater chance of adapting to his or her deformities than a child who is unwanted and unloved. But there is no simple way one could predict with any certainty what the reception will be. Some mothers will come to love children they did not want and who were initially repugnant to them, while others may find their initial distaste increased by actual exposure to the deformed child. Even in the latter case, though, what would happen if the mother were given extensive counseling (presuming it were available)? Perhaps that would make a significant difference in her attitude. Perhaps it would just be a waste of time. Who could possibly say in advance?

Another approach is to ask whether, of those deformed people now living, the majority would prefer never to have been born at all. If one could come up with some solid testimony from the handicapped on this point, one might be in a better position to judge the validity of the argument that one has an obligation to a possibly deformed fetus not to bring it into the world. L. A. M. Stolte and André Hellegers report a study of the records of 222 successive suicides in Baltimore in 1964 and 1965. "We found not a single case of suicide," Dr. Hellegers writes, "among anyone who has any congenital anomalies or where there was evidence of a history of deafness or blindness." [84] This is an interesting but inconclusive bit of data; it does not answer the question of whether the seriously handicapped are actually sorry they were born, even if they don't commit suicide. Thus, if it could be decisively shown that their suicide rate is no higher than other, nondeformed people, we would still not have a full answer to our question. Or would we? Is the burden of proof on those who claim that a handicapped life is a life not worth living, or on those who claim that, for the handicapped, it may well be worth living and that they, not us, should in any case be the ones to decide? I think the burden of proof must be on the former group. Unless it can be shown from some decisive evidence that most handicapped people would prefer not to have been born, there is no special reason to assume that their instinctual desire for life is less than that of the nonhandicapped.

Actually, the whole problem is insoluble in principle. There is no possibility of pointing out to a fetus what his prospects are and then asking him whether he desires to live or die. Nor is there any possibility of anticipating how a fetus would feel if he could know his future. To ask a deformed person whether he would prefer not to have been born begs the important question, which is not whether he would prefer now, in retrospect, never to have been born, but what he would have preferred then had he known of the various possibilities open to him. If one asked a person whether, at the outset of an automobile trip, he would prefer to take the trip or not take the trip and he answered that he would, we would not fault him for inconsistency if, after an accident on that trip, he decided in retrospect that he was sorry he made the choice in the first place. The point is that we cannot logically assume from the testimony of a person whose life has turned out badly and who wishes he hadn't been born that he would have had the same wish had we put the question to him before he had actually been born.

In any case, were a survey taken of all seriously handicapped persons, we would probably get a variety of answers on their satisfaction with life; some people adapt well, others, poorly and others, not at all. It is not clear that we would, with such information in hand, be in any special position to make a judgment whether any given fetus would be better off alive or dead. Human beings differ considerably in their desire to live, and the presence of a handicap is no predictor of the strength of that desire; no one has produced data showing that it is a predictor. For all these reasons, it must be said that any argument for abortion for the sake of the child lacks any confirming or indicative medical or psychiatric confirmation.

Two Larger Questions

Two larger questions are raised by this lengthy discussion of rubella. I have concentrated on rubella because it is a real problem (though hopefully on the way to solution because of the vaccine) and because it serves well as a model in handling similar problems in the future. The first question is this: How ought judgments be made when there is a known though imprecise probability of fetal deformity if a woman takes certain dangerous drugs, is exposed to dangerous radiation, or contracts rubella, and so on? As we have seen, this is preeminently the situation with rubella and forms one category of fetal indications. The second question is this: How ought judgments to be made when there is a known, certain, 100 percent probability of deformity? This situation is likely to become increasingly common as the technique of amniocentesis is refined; it will be possible to know, from an examination of the amniotic fluid, whether a woman carries an abnormal fetus. This is already possible in the case of some gross abnormalities (e.g., mongolism) and will undoubtedly be extended to others. Already, abortions are being performed in some places on the basis of amniocentesis evidence. As difficult as the first question is, the second is hardly less complex.

On the first question, it is possible to extrapolate a model from my treatment of rubella. As a model, the following elements emerge as critical to the decision-making process. A decision should be made in the light of (*a*) knowledge of probabilities of abnormality, major and minor; (*b*) knowledge of the theoretical probability of correcting major and minor defects in a handicapped infant or child; (c) knowledge of actual likelihood or possibility or feasibility of corrective therapy; this estimation, in turn, will have to take account of the quality and availability of specialists and facilities as well as the general effect upon a family of trying to care for and correct the abnormalities of one child in that family. As noted, the moral perspective of those making the judgment, particularly their evaluation of what counts as an acceptable risk ("chance-taking"), will inevitably color their judgment. Naturally, one who believes that the protection of life, even abnormal life, is a primary consideration may come to a very different judgment than one who believes that the expected quality of a life or the effects upon a woman or family in caring for an abnormal child are the primary considerations. Some will believe that one ought to "take no chances" that life will be destroyed, others that one ought to "take no chances" that a deformed child will be born. As in the psychiatric situation (see end of previous chapter), each side will be able to find data to support its judgment that an abortive or nonabortive course will involve some degree of serious risk to someone. This is a point to be kept clearly in mind, since it is evident that the different perspectives will see the data—the same data very often—in a very different way, leading to very different judgments.

On the second question, judgments concerning known deformities, the extrapolated rubella model ceases to be wholly useful. Where it retains its utility is under categories (b) and (c) above, for the question does arise whether even a fetus known with certainty to be abnormal is a fetus that *ought* to be aborted. There is no automatic answer to this question; one will have to know what the specific abnormality syndrome is, what the possibilities of amelioration of the syndrome are—category (b)—and what the actual feasibility of amelioration is—category (c). While mental retardation is, for instance, one characteristic of mongolism, the retardation is not in all cases severe; some mongoloids can be taught some primitive skills. In the case of trisomy 13, however, a chromosomal defect, affected children do not live more than a few weeks. In between are a whole host of chromosomal defects, some giving rise to comparatively mild defects (e.g., infecundity, as in Klinefelter's syndrome, or sterility, as in Turner's syndrome), and others to severe defects (e.g., autosomal trisomies, or trisomy 21, in which the No. 21 chromosome is triple rather than double, and which gives rise to mongolism). The point is that even with known gross abnormalities, the questions inherent in (b) and (c) are still pertinent. And, needless to stress, they would still remain pertinent as amniocentesis is developed and more and more abnormalities are capable of being discovered during the fetal stage.

More difficult, in principle, is the question of whether an abortion is indicated in those detectable cases of gross abnormality where the prognosis is known—having taken account of (*b*) and (*c*)—to be consistently bad.[85] One common argument here is that, since nature itself manifests a 25 percent or more rate of spontaneous abortion as a result of severe genetic abnormalities (with a likelihood that the remaining 75 percent of spontaneous abortions are also the result, in large part, of genetic defects), it would not be unnatural or immoral to supplement the correctives of nature by inducing abortion in those fetuses known to be (hopelessly) abnormal.[86] Moreover, to abort in those situations could, many would argue, be to do a service both to the species and to the particular families involved. The fact that the involved mother could most likely conceive a normal child shortly after such a "genetic abortion," replacing the lost fetus, would, by this reasoning, remove the final grounds of objection, i.e., the loss of "human life."

I do not want, at this point, to deal with the particular argument directly, but only to suggest some of the elements relevant to an adequate consideration of it. One element is, of course, what we decide to call "human life" (see Chapters 10 and 11) and then to see whether even a severely abnormal fetus would count as such life. Another element will involve our moral stance toward the protection of nascent life, normal and abnormal (see Chapter 9). Still another element will be what we take our duties to be in preserving and improving the human species, particularly when it comes to intervening actively in the outcome of pregnancies. Our moral bias (in the good sense of the word) on all of these points will make a difference in inclining us to make a judgment one way or the other. The important perception, initially, is to see the latent implications of these different elements, to see the way in which they will influence moral judgment.

Once we have sifted the scientific evidence, it is our moral policy which must come into play. The scientific data on the incidence of abnormalities provide no answers to the fundamental moral question of whether abnormal fetuses should be aborted. That will be a result of our moral policy. This is only to say that there are no purely scientific determinants for the category of "fetal indications"; there is data available, but how this data ought to be read for legal, social or moral purposes is a different question, involving nonscientific perspectives and policies. The decision to "take a chance" (and not abort) or to "take no chances" and abort is, ineluctably, a moral decision. The data ought to illuminate our decision, but they cannot make that decision.

NOTES

1. "Hazards of the First Trimester," *Journal of the American Medical Association*, 175 (April 1, 1961), pp. 1174–75; V. P. Coffey and W. J. E. Jessop: "Ma-

ternal Influenza and Congenital Deformities: Prospective Study," *Lancet*, 2 (November 28, 1959), p. 935; Harry T. Wright, Jr., "Congenital Anomalies and Viral Infections in Infants," *California Medicine*, 105 (November 1966), pp. 345–51; J. B. Hardy, "Viruses and the Fetus," *Postgraduate Medicine*, 43 (January 1968), pp. 156–65.

2. Kenneth R. Niswander, "Medical Abortion Practices in the United States," in David T. Smith (ed.), *Abortion and the Law* (Cleveland: Western Reserve University, 1967), p. 46; see also Charles P. Kindregan, *Abortion, The Law, and Defective Children* (Washington, D.C.: Corpus Books, 1969).

3. "A Way to Sidestep Mongoloid Birth?" *Medical World News*, 7 (September 30, 1966), pp. 32–33; H. A. Thiede, "Obstetricians Should Learn the Technic of Amniocentesis," *Obstetrics and Gynecology*, 31 (January 1968), pp. 146–48; C. B. Jacobson *et al.*, "Intrauterine Diagnosis and Management of Genetic Defects," *American Journal of Obstetrics and Gynecology*, 99 (November 15, 1967), pp. 796–807.

4. For a good summary of the thalidomide disaster, see Norman St. John-Stevas, *The Right to Life* (New York: Holt, Rinehart and Winston, 1964), pp. 19ff.; Helen B. Taussig, "The Thalidomide Syndrome," *Scientific American*, 207 (August 1962), pp. 29–35; Lawrence Lader, *Abortion* (Indianapolis: Bobbs-Merrill, 1966), pp. 10–16.

5. Niswander, *op. cit.*, p. 46.

6. Recent advances in the development of a rubella vaccine were reported at the "International Conference on Rubella Immunization," held at the National Institutes of Health, Bethesda, Maryland, in February 1969, the proceedings of which are published in the *American Journal of Diseases of Children*, 118 (July 1969).

7. For cautionary articles warning against premature expectations from the new vaccine, see S. Krugman, "Prospects for Vaccination Against Rubella," *Archives of Environmental Health*, 15 (October 1967), pp. 495–501, and J. L. Sever, "Rubella Epidemiology and Vaccines," *The Sight-Saving Review*, 37 (Summer 1967), pp. 68–72.

8. Josef Warkany and Harold Kalter, "Congenital Malformations," *New England Journal of Medicine*, 265 (November 16, 1961), p. 994.

9. Jessie M. Bierman *et al.*, "Analysis of the Outcome of All Pregnancies in a Community," *American Journal of Obstetrics and Gynecology*, 91 (January 1, 1965), pp. 37–45.

10. *Ibid.*, p. 40.

11. See, for instance, E. S. Burge, "The Relationship of Threatened Abortion to Fatal Abnormalities," *American Journal of Obstetrics and Gynecology*, 61 (March 1951), pp. 615–21; D. H. Stott, "Physical and Mental Handicaps Following a Disturbed Pregnancy," *Lancet*, I (May 18, 1957), pp. 1006–12.

12. "Epidemic's Aftermath Bares Rubella Peril," *Medical World News*, 6 (December 10, 1965), pp. 92–98; W. E. Rawls *et al.*, "WHO Collaborative Study on the Sero-Epidemiology of Rubella," *Bulletin of the World Health Organization*, 37 (1967), pp. 79–88.

13. W. E. Rawls *et al.*, "Serologic Diagnosis and Fetal Involvement in Maternal Rubella," *Journal of the American Medical Association*, 203 (February 26, 1968), pp. 627–31.

14. See John A. Forbes, "Rubella: Historical Aspects," *American Journal of Diseases of Children*, 118 (July 1969), pp. 5–11.

15. Norman M. Gregg, "Congenital Cataract Following German Measles in the Mother," *Transactions of the Opthalmological Society of Australia*, 3 (1941), pp. 35–46; ——, "Further Observations on Congenital Defects in Infants Following Maternal Rubella," *ibid.*, 4 (1944), p. 119–31.

16. Louis Z. Cooper, "German Measles," *Scientific American*, 215 (July 1966), p. 31.

17. See, for instance, C. Swan, B. Moore, H. Mayo and G. H. B. Black, "Congenital Defects in Infants Following Infectious Diseases During Pregnancy," *Medical Journal of Australia*, 2 (September 11, 1943), p. 201; C. Swan, A. L.

Tostevin and G. H. B. Black, "Final Observations on Congenital Defects in Infants Following Infectious Diseases During Pregnancy, with Special Reference to Rubella," *ibid.*, 2 (December 28, 1946), p. 889.

18. J. A. Dudgeon, "Maternal Rubella and Its Effect on the Foetus," *Archives of Diseases of Childhood*, 42 (April 1967), p. 110.
19. See "Rubella," *Morbidity and Mortality Weekly Report*, 13 (March 27, 1964), pp. 93–100.
20. J. L. Sever *et al.*, "Rubella in the Collaborative Perinatal Research Study," *American Journal of Diseases of Children*, 118 (July 1969), pp. 123–132.
21. Dudgeon, *op. cit.*, p. 111.
22. L. Z. Cooper and S. Krugman, "Diagnosis and Management: Congenital Rubella," *Pediatrics*, 37 (February 1966), p. 336; D. B. Singer *et al.*, "Congenital Rubella Syndrome," *American Journal of Diseases of Children*, 118 (July 1969), pp. 54–61; see also M. Siegel *et al.*, "Comparative Fetal Mortality in Maternal Virus Diseases," *New England Journal of Medicine*, 274 (April 7, 1966), pp. 768–71.
23. S. A. Plotkin *et al.*, "The Congenital Rubella Syndrome in Late Infancy," *Journal of the American Medical Association*, 200 (May 8, 1967), pp. 435–41. S. A. Plotkin *et al.*, "Some Recently Recognized Manifestations of the Rubella Syndrome," *Journal of Pediatrics*, 67 (August 1965), p. 182; H. P. Lambert *et al.*, "Congenital Rubella Syndrome," *Lancet*, 2 (October 23, 1965), p. 826.
24. Saul Krugman, "Rubella: New Light on an Old Disease," *Journal of Pediatrics*, 67 (August 1965), pp. 159–61; Gordon B. Avery *et al.*, "Rubella Syndrome After Inapparent Maternal Illness," *American Journal of Diseases of Children*, 110 (October 1965), pp. 444–46; S. B. Korones *et al.*, "Congenital Rubella Syndrome: Study of 22 Infants," *ibid.*, p. 434.
25. M. Siegel *et al.*, "Rubella in Mother and Congenital Cataracts in Child—Comparative Data in Periods With and Without Epidemics from 1957 to 1964," *Journal of the American Medical Association*, 203 (February 26, 1968), pp. 632–36.
26. Margaret M. Manson, W. P. D. Logan and R. M. Loy, "Rubella and Other Virus Infections During Pregnancy," *Report on Public Health and Medical Subjects:* Document 101 (London: Ministry of Health, 1960).
27. Dudgeon, *op. cit.*, p. 112.
28. "Rubella Symposium," *American Journal of Diseases of Children*, 110 (October 1965), p. 345.
29. R. Lundström, "Rubella During Pregnancy: A Follow-Up Study of Children Born After an Epidemic of Rubella in Sweden in 1951," *Acta Paediatrica* (Uppsala), 51 (May 1962), Supplement 133.
30. "Rubella Symposium," *op. cit.*, p. 345.
31. L. Cooper and S. Krugman, "Diagnosis and Management: Congenital Rubella," *op. cit.*, p. 336.
32. Dudgeon, *op. cit.*, p. 112; G. M. Folger, "Congenital Rubella Syndrome: Cardiovascular Defects," *Journal of the Medical Association of Georgia*, 57 (February 1968), pp. 86–87.
33. R. C. Way, "Cardiovascular Defects and the Rubella Syndrome," *Canadian Medical Association Journal*, 97 (November 25, 1967), p. 1334.
34. Korones *et al*, *op. cit.*, p. 434.
35. L. E. Ainger, N. G. Lawyer and C. W. Fitch, "Neonatal Rubella Myocarditis," *British Heart Journal*, 28 (September 1966), p. 691.
36. Dudgeon, *op. cit.*; M. L. Sears, "Congenital Glaucoma in Neonatal Rubella," *British Journal of Ophthalmology*, 51 (November 1967), pp. 744–48; A. M. Murphy *et al.*, "Rubella Cataracts: Further Clinical and Virologic Observations," *American Journal of Ophthalmology*, 64 (December 1967), pp. 1109–19.
37. B. Barr and R. Lundström, "Deafness Following Maternal Rubella," *Acta Otolaryngologica* (Stockholm), 53 (May-June 1961), p. 413.

38. A. D. M. Jackson and L. Fisch, "Deafness Following Maternal Rubella: Results of a Prospective Investigation," *Lancet*, 2 (December 13, 1958), p. 1241; Mary D. Sheridan, "Final Report of a Prospective Study of Children Whose Mothers Had Rubella in Early Pregnancy," *British Medical Journal*, 2 (August 29, 1964), pp. 536–39.
39. Plotkin *et al.*, "The Congenital Rubella Syndrome in Late Infancy," *op. cit.*, p. 440; *cf.* P. H. Ward *et al.*, "Inner Ear Pathology in Deafness Due to Maternal Rubella," *Archives of Otolaryngology*, 87 (January 1968), pp. 22–28.
40. A. J. Rudolph *et al.*, "Osseous Manifestations of the Congenital Rubella Syndrome," *American Journal of Diseases of Children*, 110 (October 1965), p. 428.
41. "Rubella Symposium," *op. cit.*, p. 345.
42. E. B. Singleton *et al.*, "The Roentgenographic Manifestations of the Rubella Syndrome in Newborn Infants," *American Journal of Roentgenology*, 97 (May 1966), p. 82; W. C. Marshall *et al.*, personal observations reported by J. A. Dudgeon, *op. cit.*, p. 114.
43. Rudolph *et al.*, *op. cit.*, p. 428; Singleton *et al.*, *op. cit.*, p. 82; M. M. Desmond *et al.*, "Congenital Rubella Encephalitis: Effects on Growth and Early Development," *American Journal of Diseases of Children*, 118 (July 1969), pp. 30–31.
44. Dudgeon, *op. cit.*, p. 113.
45. C. Swan, "Rubella in Pregnancy as an Aeteological Agent in Congenital Malformations, Stillbirths, Miscarriage and Abortion," *Journal of Obstetrics and Gynaecology, British Empire*, 56 (1949), p. 341; cited in Dudgeon, *op. cit.*, p. 112.
46. Dudgeon, *op. cit.*, p. 110.
47. Morris Greenberg *et al.*, "Frequency of Defects in Infants Whose Mothers Had Rubella During Pregnancy," *Journal of the American Medical Association*, 165 (October 12, 1957), p. 678; *cf.* Morris Siegel *et al.*, "Fetal Mortality in Maternal Rubella," *American Journal of Obstetrics and Gynecology*, 96 (September 15, 1966), pp. 247–53.
48. Manson *et al.*, *op. cit.*, p. 33.
49. Cooper, "German Measles," *op. cit.*, p. 31.
50. Cited in Dudgeon, *op. cit.*, but with no reference, p. 115.
51. Samuel J. Salomi, "Rubella in Pregnancy: A Review of Prospective Studies from the Literature," *Obstetrics and Gynecology*, 27 (February 1966), pp. 252–56.
52. Morris Greenberg *et al.*, *op. cit.*, p. 678.
53. R. McIntosh *et al.*, "Incidence of Congenital Malformations: Study of 5,964 Pregnancies," *Pediatrics*, 14 (November 1954), pp. 505–21.
54. John Rendle-Short, "Maternal Rubella: The Practical Management of a Case," *Lancet*, 2 (August 22, 1964), pp. 373–76.
55. *Ibid.*, p. 373.
56. Manson *et al.*, *op. cit.*, p. 33.
57. *Ibid.*, p. 40.
58. *Ibid.*, p. 67.
59. Mary D. Sheridan, *op. cit.*, p. 539.
60. *Ibid.*, p. 538.
61. *Ibid.*, p. 539.
62. M. A. Menser *et al.*, "A Twenty-five-Year Follow-Up of Congenital Rubella," *Lancet*, 2 (December 23, 1967), pp. 1347–50.
63. John L. Sever *et al.*, "Rubella Epidemic, 1964: Effect on 6,000 Pregnancies," *American Journal of Diseases of Children*, 110 (October 1965), pp. 406–07.
64. *Ibid.*, p. 407.
65. Gilbert M. Schiff *et al.*, "Studies on Congenital Rubella," *American Journal of Diseases of Children*, 110 (October 1965), pp. 441–43.
66. R. Lundström, *op. cit.*, p. 58.

67. R. Lundström, "Rubella During Pregnancy: Its Effects Upon Perinatal Mortality, the Incidence of Congenital Abnormalities and Immaturity, A Preliminary Report," *Acta Paediatrica* (Stockholm), 41 (1952), p. 583.

68. A. Bradford-Hill *et al.*, "Virus Diseases in Pregnancy and Congenital Defects," *British Journal Preventive and Social Medicine*, 12 (January 1958), p. 1.

69. L. Z. Cooper *et al.*, "Neonatal Thrombocytopenic Purpura and Other Manifestations of Rubella Contracted in Utero," *American Journal of Diseases of Children*, 110 (October 1965), p. 416; C. M. Horstmann *et al.*, "Maternal Rubella and the Rubella Syndrome in Infants," *American Journal of Diseases of Children*, 110 (October 1965), p. 415.

70. D. Pitt and E. H. Keir, "Results of Rubella in Pregnancy," *Medical Journal of Australia*, 52 (October 16, 1965), p. 647.

71. Robert H. Green *et al.*, "Studies of the Natural History and Prevention of Rubella," *American Journal of Diseases of Children*, 110 (October 1965), p. 348.

72. Dudgeon, *op. cit.*, p. 116.

73. *Ibid.*

74. David J. Sencer *et al.*, "The Epidemiology of Rubella in the United States," paper presented at the International Association of Microbiologic Societies, 23rd Symposium on Microbiologic Standardization, Rubella Vaccine, London, England, November 18, 1968.

75. L. Z. Cooper, "German Measles," *op. cit.*, p. 36.

76. N. D. Matkin *et al.*, "Maternal Rubella and Hearing Loss: A Preliminary Report on Findings from the 1964 Epidemic," *Connecticut Medicine*, 31 (December 1967), pp. 850–54; they concluded that most of the rubella children should be classified as partially hearing rather than deaf.

77. L. Z. Cooper *et al.*, "Congenital Rubella: Clinical Manifestations and Management," *American Journal of Diseases of Children*, 118 (July 1969), pp. 18–29.

78. This figure turns out, coincidentally, to be the same as that arrived at by Lundström, "A Follow-Up Study . . . ," *op. cit.*, p. 86, who was working with a smaller range of studies. Also coincidentally, and as a conclusion from the figure of 10 percent, Lundström writes "that—ethical considerations aside—abortions should be induced after maternal rubella only when other factors constitute an indication for interruption of pregnancy" (*ibid.*).

79. Leston L. Havens and Gerald E. Cubelli, "The Psychiatrist and the State Vocational Rehabilitation Agency," *American Journal of Psychiatry*, 123 (March 1967), pp. 1094–99.

80. Niswander, *op. cit.*, pp. 45–46.

81. *Cf.* Note 41, Chapter 3, for a study which considers this problem.

82. Ryan, *op. cit.*, p. 66.

83. Lader, *op. cit.*, p. 40.

84. André E. Hellegers, "A Doctor Looks at Abortion," Edward Douglas White Lecture, Georgetown University Law Center, March 16, 1966, p. 13 (unpublished); *cf.* T. F. Rodger, "Attitudes Toward Abortion," *American Journal of Psychiatry*, 125 (December 1968), pp. 806–08. Rodger speculates about the future possibility of a deformed adult's suing the state or his doctor or hospital because he had been allowed to be born with one or more major defects, because he had not been aborted. Rodger interprets this possibility as an extension of the contemporary view of the "gift of life," which, he believes, is gradually coming to assume the right of the unborn to be born without deformity.

85. A good description of such cases is to be found in Carlo Valenti, "His Right to Be Normal," *Saturday Review* (December 7, 1968), pp. 75–78.

86. D. H. Carr, "Chromosomal Anomalies as a Cause of Spontaneous Abortion," *American Journal of Obstetrics and Gynecology*, 97 (February 1, 1967), pp. 283–93.

SECTION II

Establishing a
Legal Policy

Introduction

IT IS OFTEN CONTENDED by those opposed to permissive abortion laws that, in addition to the death of countless fetuses, a widespread recourse by women to legal abortion would have many deleterious side effects on the whole of the culture. Among these, supposedly, would be a lessened respect for the sanctity of life, a consequence which could pose a threat to the born as well as unborn, the old, the sick, the weak, the undesirables. The image of Nazi Germany is frequently evoked in antiabortion polemics to dramatize the danger of a lessened respect for life—even though, in fact, Nazi Germany had stringent antiabortion laws. In the light of these worries, it is worth inquiring into the discernible effect of different kinds of abortion laws. Another argument is the mirror image of the first. Those who favor permissive abortion laws (or the repeal of all abortion laws) imply that society will appreciably benefit from such laws: the dignity of existing human life will be enhanced, greater freedom of personal choice will exist, the laws (or lack of them) will take better account of the actual desires and values of people, legal and medical hypocrisy will be avoided, and so on.

One ought to ask, though, what actually happens when laws are very restrictive, when they are very permissive. What happens to birthrates, to the dissemination and use of contraceptive devices, to attitudes toward the dignity of life, toward children, the old and the weak? If, as I am assuming throughout this book, a responsible moral approach to abortion requires looking at the problem in the broadest possible context, then these questions become relevant.

Yet they cannot be answered with any certainty. Even under the best research and data-collecting circumstances, it is not at all clear just how one could determine the moral effect upon society of different kinds of abortion laws. Too many other variables come into play to discern easily the specific cultural consequences of abortion laws in distinction from all the other moral influences at work in a society. Nor is it at all evident how one could determine whether different abortion laws are a consequence of prior moral attitudes which these laws simply reflect, or a source of subsequent moral attitudes which these laws have directly or indirectly engendered. The possibility, perhaps likelihood, that the relationship between abortion laws and the general moral ethos of a society is reciprocal, a case of mutual interaction (with many other variables also entering in), further increases the difficulty of coming to any kind of decisive judgment. For all these reasons, a more modest goal will be set in this section of the book: discussing the data available on *some* of the effects on society of different abortion laws—effects which can be said to be "known" rather than those which are only "speculative." As in the previous chapters, my concern will be to sort out the data, to relate what is known and to discuss in a tentative way the critical problems posed by the data.

For the sake of convenience, I will present and discuss in the next three chapters the legal and social data in a schematic form: restrictive, moderate and permissive legal codes. As it turns out, the different legal solutions throughout the world lend themselves fairly well to this kind of schematization. Some legal codes on abortion are highly restrictive; others are highly permissive; and still others are moderate and "mixed," i.e., they allow a wide range of indications for legal abortions (and in that sense are permissive), but also require the meeting of established standards for approval of an abortion (and in that sense are restrictive). In some instances this tripartite division of legal codes must be qualified (often because of very recent law changes), and I will indicate where and how when appropriate. In dealing with each of the legal systems, I will be concerned with three general questions: (1) What problems are the different types of abortion laws meant to solve and what social concerns are they trying to embody? (2) How well are these problems met and the social concerns embodied? (3) What social consequences, foreseen or unforeseen, result from the laws? My intent is to remain as close as possible to the actual data, but I will also cite heavily the expressed judgments and opinions of those interested in or affected by the laws. Such a procedure, it should be clear, prescinds from the moral problems strictly taken; that is, it does not confront directly the moral rectitude of the opinions expressed and the judgments reached (which would be the function of a given, specific moral perspective), but is only interested in the fact that different judgments are reached and what those judgments are.

For my examples of countries which have had experience with restrictive laws (Chapter 5), I will use the United States, India, some Latin-American countries and Great Britain (prior to the 1967 change in its abortion laws). Since some of the states in the United States have now liberalized their laws, as has England, it will be possible to examine some of the consequences of these changes from restrictive to moderate laws. For my examples of countries with moderate laws, I will use the Scandinavian countries (Chapter 6). For my examples of countries with permissive laws, I will use a number of Eastern European countries and Japan (Chapter 7). Naturally, this limited range does not take into account all those countries about which something could be said on the basis of available (mostly inadequate) data. Finally, in Chapter 8, an attempt will be made to discern worldwide patterns and probabilities.

CHAPTER 5

Restrictive Legal Codes

THERE APPEARS TO BE A TWOFOLD REASON why most of the
states in the United States and why Great Britain prior to 1967 had
highly restrictive abortion laws on the statute books. Their implicit
cultural purpose was primarily that of embodying the Judeo-Christian
belief in the right to life and the necessity of preserving human life even
when the existence of "human life" was problematic to some degree.
Legislatively, restrictive laws, which came into explicit existence during
the nineteenth century for the most part, were also meant to protect the
health and life of pregnant women by keeping them out of the hands of
incompetent abortionists and by restraining them from attempting
dangerous self-induced abortions. If it was often the second reason which
actually led to the passage of restrictive laws, the moral context of their
passage was the much broader Judeo-Christian value system. Some, however, argue that restrictive laws reflect a puritanical attitude toward
sex or are, latently, designed to punish and subjugate women.

The moral purpose of the restrictive laws is at present the prime
motive of those who want to keep them on the books. The heart of
their argument is that the restrictive laws reflect the deepest and most
abiding affirmations and values of the Anglo-American legal system. It
was this affirmation which led to the restrictive laws in the first place
and the reasons for adhering to such laws, it is said, remain as morally
and legally solid today as in the past. These laws, it is argued, embody
the highest values of Western civilization; to rescind or dilute them
would, therefore, amount to a moral capitulation and a regression from
a noble legal code. "The integrity, the untouchableness, the inviolability
of every human life by any other human being has been the cardinal
principle and the centerpiece of the legal institutions of the English-
speaking world and, to a large extent, of every system of law devised by

man," Father Robert F. Drinan, S.J., has written.[1] The specific legal implication of this general line of reasoning is clear: "Any change of a substantial kind in America's abortion laws would be a notable departure from that body of Anglo-American law which regulates conduct deemed to constitute a crime against society." [2] Another Roman Catholic, the English lawyer Norman St. John-Stevas, has stated the issue as follows: "The principle which the Western world has accepted in theory, although it has certainly not always lived up to it in practice, is that, apart from self-defense against aggressors, human life may not be taken. Innocent human life is sacred." [3] The legal implications immediately follow: "The gain to the community from an extension of legal abortion seems dubious and would be heavily outweighed by its undermining of the principle of respect for the sanctity of life." [4]

It is not necessary to multiply quotations of that kind; the argument they embody is familiar, can draw upon some Protestant and Jewish support, and provides the basis of the traditional contentions against liberalized abortion laws with which advocates of liberalization have had to cope.[5] Ralph Potter, Jr., has characterized what he calls the "right-wing argument":

> The nub of the right-wing argument . . . is simple and stark: the condoning of widespread resort to abortion would undermine civilization. The argument is couched in theological terms; it leads, however, to conclusions in the realm of cultural anthropology. . . . The destination is a flat prediction concerning consequences for all human relationships if a significant number of people come to accept abortion in good conscience. . . . The constant goal is to convince hearers . . . that the practice of abortion is incompatible with the attainment of man's true humanity.[6]

The legal corollary is that a liberalization of restrictive laws would do direct harm to man's humanity; restrictive laws help protect man against his own tendencies to inhumanity.

A number of specific assumptions lie behind resistance to liberalized laws. One of them is that the fetus is either a human being or at least a potential human being; in any case, it is entitled to the protection of the law. Another is that the sanctity of life in this as in other areas is abetted by laws which penalize attempts to hinder or destroy life. Still another is that the protection of life in one area (e.g., the life of the fetus) is indirectly a protection of life in all other areas (e.g., the life of the old, the sick, the unwanted); hence, restrictive laws on abortion benefit everyone and not just fetuses.

Since, therefore, it is claimed that restrictive laws have all these benefits for society, one may ask if there is any evidence which would support the claim. In the nature of the case, this question is hard to answer; and it is hard to see how it could be answered. It is utterly impossible to judge how effective restrictive laws against abortion have been in enhancing a general respect for the sanctity of life. Such a judgment would depend in great part upon knowing how much general respect for life there would have been had there not been any restrictive abortion laws on the books. But since there have been such laws, a controlled comparison (within the confines of Anglo-Saxon culture) cannot be made. It is exceedingly hard even to make a sensible imaginative guess. Violence and murder, for instance, have been much more common in the United States in recent decades than in Great Britain, and yet both nations have had restrictive laws on abortion; similar laws on abortion, therefore, provide no simple index of a nation's actual attitude toward the sanctity of life. Further bafflement is provided by the fact that in both the United States and Great Britain the movement to abolish capital punishment has roughly coincided with the movement to liberalize abortion laws. A major argument in favor of abolishing capital punishment has been precisely that capital punishment is an affront to the sanctity of life (even the life of the criminal). Similarly, the campaign in America for Negro civil rights and a greater recognition of the human dignity of minority racial groups has roughly paralleled the campaign for more permissive abortion laws. The struggle against poverty, urban slums and poor health facilities has been stronger in recent years than at any time in American history (just those years when there was the greatest pressure to repeal restrictive abortion laws).

These are only random correlations, from which it would be hazardous to draw any firm conclusions. One could also point to the other side of the ledger, a rise in the actual level of violence and poverty and urban blight—offensive to man's dignity—at just that historical moment when pressure is increasing to liberalize restrictive abortion laws. It is sufficient only to observe the practical impossibility of measuring the impact of restrictive abortion laws on the general ethos of the United States and Great Britain. If someone could show, through a carefully designed sociological and psychological survey, that those favoring restrictive abortion laws were in general more respectful of all forms of human life than those who favored liberal laws, an empirical point might be scored in favor of restriction. But no such survey has been made and, even if made, would have to be uncommonly persuasive as surveys go to show a direct, causal relationship between attitudes toward abortion and attitudes toward the sanctity of life in general. None of this is to say, by any means, that it is wrong or silly for someone to affirm that restrictive abortion laws enhance society's respect for life. *It is only to say that it is an affirmation which has not been supported with any carefully marshaled data.* This means also that there is no empirical basis whatever for a prediction that a liberalization of abortion laws will necessarily have a harmful effect on general attitudes toward the sanctity of life; it is an a priori assumption. Similarly, of course, there is no obvious empirical basis for a prediction that a liberalization of laws will have *no* effect on society's general respect for the sanctity of life.

Is there any point, then, at which empirical data provide some illumination? There is such a point, though it, too, is shot through with uncertainties and ambiguities. It is hardly unreasonable to say that restrictive abortion laws have kept the number of legal abortions down. There would not exist pressures to liberalize the laws if there did not exist substantial numbers of women who would have abortions if it were legally possible for them to do so. Even if one assumes a high rate of illegal abortions, it is reasonable to guess that some undetermined additional number of women do not get the abortions they would like to have, either because they cannot meet the legal requirements or because they cannot or will not resort to illegal abortions. There is considerable agreement on the estimate that the number of legal abortions in the United States, under laws for the most part still highly restrictive, averages about 8,000 a year.[7] Christopher Tietze, working with this estimate, has arrived at a ratio of two legal abortions per 1,000 live births.[8] This figure is very low when compared with Tietze's figure for Northern Europe (with its moderate legal codes) of 30–70 legal abortions per 1,000 births, and even lower when compared with his figure of 300–1,400 legal abortions per 1,000 live births for Eastern Europe and Japan. If the aim, therefore, of a restrictive legal system is to keep the number of legal abortions very low, then the evidence is solid enough that this aim was achieved by restrictive American and English laws. This has also been true of other countries which have had restrictive laws, even though their motives were different in some cases from those in England and the United States.

A further conclusion beckons. If restrictive laws keep down the number of legal abortions, as they seem to, it could also be argued that they help affirm society's formal recognition of the sanctity of life. On the level of society's proclaimed traditional values, the value of fetal life and the value of all forms of human life, restrictive laws may retain a symbolic as well as a functional importance. To say this is not to attempt to utter a profundity or even to say something which might appear contentious. It is only to say that, if restrictive laws remain on the books and if the intent of these laws is to embody a traditional cultural evaluation of the sanctity of life, there is no special reason to assume that the general public motive which keeps them there is significantly different from the motives of a historically earlier public which put them there in the first place. In this sense, the success of those who are able to keep the laws restrictive might be called a victory for an ongoing affirmation of the sanctity and inviolability of life.

Unfortunately, the issue cannot be dealt with so easily. For it is the contention of those who would liberalize the laws that (*a*) the symbolic victory is very shaky because of the widespread recourse to illegal abortion—restrictive laws keep down the number of legal abortions but by no means the number of *all* abortions; (*b*) the sanctity of life is actually violated by a legal code which drives so many women to dangerous illegal abortions; and (*c*) a liberalization of abortion laws would in no way detract from the sanctity of life but would, because of the greater respect accorded women who wanted or needed abortion, actually enhance it. The main argument, in brief, against restrictive laws is that they accomplish neither their symbolic nor their functional purpose. Indeed, they are said to be counterproductive, bringing in their train as many evils, or more, as they are supposed to cure or preclude.

The arguments between those who would keep the laws highly restrictive and those who would introduce liberalization help to bring some of the issues into better focus. Examined independently, highly restrictive codes are not directly amenable to any kind of empirical testing for their total effectiveness in sustaining respect for life; as pointed out, there is just no way of knowing whether they actually achieve this particular aim. Only by comparing the consequences of restrictive and other kinds of codes in terms of other indices than the directly moral can one even begin to establish the relevance of empirical data. Practically speaking, this comparison has been forced on Western society by the existence of groups desirous of liberalizing restrictive laws and who have empirically oriented arguments. It should be stressed, of course, that these are not the only arguments which have been put forward in favor of liberalized laws; they are simply those arguments where empirical data is either evidently relevant or said to be relevant.

The two major propositions I want to examine in this chapter are these: (1) *Restrictive abortion laws give rise to a major health problem, encouraging hazardous illegal abortions and degrading those women forced to resort to illegal abortions. A liberalization of such laws would alleviate this problem.* (2) *Restrictive abortion laws are* de facto *discriminatory. The affluent woman can much more easily and safely get an illegal abortion than a poor woman.* Part of the first assertion can be dealt with quickly. There is no special reason to deny that a woman intent upon abortion, convinced it is the right course, could find the process of procuring an illegal abortion degrading. In a restrictive system she is forced to go outside the law, to act in clandestine ways, to deal with doctors or unskilled abortionists themselves operating outside the law, and very often to undergo the abortion under medical conditions which are unsanitary, unsafe and unappealing. An illegal abortion places her in legal and medical danger. Any number of popular articles have been published in recent years detailing the harrowing experiences of women intent on gaining an illegal abortion, and, leaving aside the question of the moral rectitude of resorting to illegal abortions, the claim of degradation can be sustained.

Far more difficult to deal with is the argument that restrictive abortion laws lead to a major public-health problem because of their encouragement of illegal abortions. K.-H. Mehlan has presented data from the 1950s showing that the stricter the laws of a country, the greater the number of illegal abortions.[9] The same point has been pressed vehemently by a variety of commentators. "Criminal abortion," Kenneth R. Niswander claims, "remains the major health problem which cannot be ignored. . . . Legal abortion in a well-equipped hospital is not hazardous, but criminal abortion currently accounts for thousands of deaths annually in the United States. If a realistic relaxation of state laws on abortion will decrease this total of needless deaths, society owes this protection to desperate women." [10] Using a figure of a million to a million and a half illegal abortions per year in the United States, Harriet F. Pilpel has written:

It is one of the most tragic aspects of the situation that only one-third of those out-of-hospital abortions are performed by doctors, so that in, let's say, 650,000 or more cases every year, an operation which would be relatively safe and simple if properly performed under proper conditions, becomes a fantastic health hazard. . . . It seems fair to say that any other health problems of these dimensions would be the concern, not only of substantial private groups . . . but also of the government itself. . . . The "disease" of abortion is man's own creation in the sense that it is the government itself which has created, and which perpetuates, the problem.[11]

Lawrence Lader underscores the point: "When so great a number of women each year are forced into the hands of private abortionists, the result is a shocking toll in injuries and fatalities." [12]

The essence of the "public health" argument is threefold: women who cannot get legal abortions are "forced" to procure illegal abortions; there is a very large number of illegal abortions performed each year; illegal abortions, as usually performed outside of hospitals, are dangerous and the source of many deaths and injuries each year. The first point is almost self-evident. If a woman has decided that one way or the other she will procure an abortion when a legal one is not available, then she is "forced" to get an illegal abortion. Logically taken, there are only two courses open to a woman intent on abortion, legal or illegal abortion —if the one is not available, the other must be employed. This is, of course, very different from saying that a woman is "forced" to have an abortion in the first place; it is her intention to have an abortion which "forces" her into the choice of illegality where legality is denied.

The actual number of illegal abortions and the medical disasters which follow such abortions pose more complicated problems. That there are illegal abortions in countries with highly restrictive laws is undeniable, just as it is undeniable that some women are seriously injured or die from these abortions. But how many illegal abortions and how many injuries and deaths? In the nature of the case, the available data from all over the world are poor. Rarely are illegal abortions reported to public-health authorities, much less to the police. This poses obvious difficulties for the data collector, who is forced to make estimates of the general incidence of illegal abortions from indirect clues. Among these clues are surveys based on questionnaires, normally involving a sample of the female population and presupposing (what cannot necessarily be presupposed) honest responses; extrapolations from hospital admissions of women suspected of having had an illegal abortion; fluctuations in cases reported as "spontaneous abortion"; and, simply, educated guesses on the part of public-health experts, social workers and doctors. The results of such methods are bound to be inadequate, and inadequate they have been. Those strongly favoring liberalized laws are prone to cite very high estimates, and those opposed, to cite very low estimates. Most often, some very broad estimate is cited (e.g., 200,000–1,200,000 illegal abortions every year in the United States), so broad as to be all but useless in determining how extensive the problem of illegal abortions actually is.

United States

The estimates of illegal abortions each year in the United States have been exceedingly broad, even wildly so (both very high and very low). A useful place to start looking at the various estimates is in the literature of the 1930s, when the first efforts to change the laws were made. M. E. Kopp, in a 1934 study of 10,000 women who had attended the Margaret Sanger Birth Control Clinic in New York between 1925 and 1929, found that out of 38,985 pregnancies there had been 27,813 live births and 11,172 abortions, two-thirds of them illegal. This amounted to one abortion per 2.44 live births. Among the 10,000 women studied, 5,010 admitted having had at least one induced abortion, with 2.23 abortions the average.[13] D. Wiehl and K. Berry, in studying a sample of women from New York City in 1937, found an illegal abortion rate of 4 percent, which would project to a national figure of 200,000 (the U.S. population at that time, it should be kept in mind, was under 140,000,000).[14] A study of 22,657 women in the late 1930s by a demographer, Raymond Pearl, calculated that 1.4 percent of all pregnancies among white women ended in illegal abortion, and .5 percent of the pregnancies of Negro women (which would work out to something under a total of 50,000 illegal abortions a year for both races for that period).[15] The most oft-cited and influential figure, though, was that calculated by F. Taussig in his 1936 book, *Abortion, Spontaneous and Induced*.[16] He estimated 681,600 induced abortions a year, of which 60 percent to 65 percent were assumed to be illegal. He based this total figure on an estimate of one abortion per approximately 2.5 live births in cities, and one abortion per five live births in rural areas.

The 1940s did not see any significant attempts to refine the above figures. P. K. Whelpton and C. V. Kiser, in a 1941–1942 study of 1,080 couples, calculated 1 to 1.9 illegal abortions per 100 pregnancies, which would put the national rate well under 100,000.[17] By the late 1940s and the early 1950s, however, the figures tended to be revised sharply upward. John McPartland, in a 1947 book, vaguely estimated nearly two million abortions a year, a substantial number of them illegal.[18] Russell S. Fisher in 1951 said that a minimum figure would be 330,000 illegal abortions a year,[19] and Glanville Williams thought that a rate of 1,000 per day would be a reasonable estimate.[20] The Kinsey studies at the University of Indiana found that, of the married women they surveyed, 22 percent had had at least one abortion (with two abortions the average) by the time they reached forty-five years of age.[21] An extrapolation from this figure would yield about 600,000 illegal abortions a year. A statistics committee commissioned by the 1955 Planned Parenthood conference on abortion summarized its findings:

> Taking into account the probable trend of the abortion ratio since the interwar period, a plausible estimate of the frequency of induced abortion in the United States could be as low as 200,000 and as high as 1,200,000 a year, depending upon the assumptions made as to the incidence of abortion in the total population as compared with the restricted groups for which statistical data are available, and upon the assessment of the direction and magnitude of bias inherent in each series of data. There is no objective basis for the selection of a particular figure between these two estimates as an approximation of the actual frequency.[22]

Despite the cautionary emphasis of the last sentence in the preceding conclusion, recent years have seen the constant use of very high figures by proponents of legal reform, though practically nothing has been educed as new data to support the high figures. Alan F. Guttmacher estimates 800,000 illegal abortions a year, Harold Rosen's figure is over one million per year, and Alice S. Rossi calculates the number to be one million a year, as do Jerome M. Kummer and Zad Leavy.[23]

Before attempting to report various criticisms of these figures, the question of the death and injury rate from illegal abortions must be considered. That is usually taken to be the crux of the argument against a restrictive legal code said to encourage dangerous illegal abortions. By Taussig's 1935 calculation, there were 8,179 deaths each year from abortions, the preponderance from illegal abortions, amounting to a death rate of 1.2 percent per 100 abortions (spontaneous and induced).[24] By the 1950s, however, Fisher believed that the advent of improved antibiotics had probably reduced the rate to .5 percent which he estimated would yield a figure of 5,000 to 6,000 deaths from illegal abortions each year.[25] Kummer and Leavy estimate the number at 5,000 per annum.[26] Other scattered studies, while not attempting to project national figures, have pointed to the high ratio of illegal abortions as a cause of maternal death. Montgomery and Lewis, in a study of maternal deaths between 1957 and 1962 in California concluded that illegal abortion accounted for one-third of all such deaths.[27] Gold and his colleagues, in a 20-year review of maternal deaths in New York City, decided that one in four puerperal deaths among whites were due to abortion and one in two among nonwhites and Puerto Ricans.[28] Guttmacher places the New York death rate even higher, arguing that the overall rate of maternal deaths associated with illegal abortion has been 50 percent in recent years.[29] Niswander contends that the comparative death rate from illegal abortion has been increasing and is still a major cause of maternal death.[30]

The very high figures, for both illegal abortions and resultant deaths, have been called into question from a variety of sources. Even as early as the 1955 Planned Parenthood Conference, Milton Helpern, chief medical examiner for New York City, pointed to a decline in the number of abortion deaths, both legal and illegal, beginning as early as the mid-1930s. By 1940, the known abortion death figures in New York City were half what they had been in 1921 (declining from 144 to 70), and by 1951, they had dropped to 15 deaths for that year.[31] In 1948, Christopher Tietze noted that "the general picture of mortality from abortion in all countries studied is one of steady decline over the past 30 years. In the U.S. the rate per million women of reproductive age has decreased by about ⅘ from 1927 to 1945." [32] More recently, Dr. Tietze has estimated that about 500 deaths a year from all abortions, legal and illegal, would be nearly accurate, the majority being caused by illegal procedures. Pointing out that only 45,000 women of child-bearing age die from all causes, he notes, "It is inconceivable that of 45,000 deaths so large a number as 5,000 are from one source." [33] The number of registered abortion deaths in 1964 was 247, and in 1965 the total was 235.[34] Even allowing, as does Dr. Tietze, for a large number of unrecorded or disguised deaths due to abortion, it becomes difficult to project a figure up into the thousands. Dr. Tietze's figure of 500 per year, both because of his stature as a demographic statistician and his known advocacy of abortion on request, takes on a special significance.

A more aggressive attack on the high death figures both of the present and the past has been waged by four defenders of restrictive laws: André Hellegers, Robert M. Byrn, Norbert J. Mietus and Herbert Ratner.

Hellegers believes that the use of a very high figure like 10,000 deaths a year can be traced back to the 1936 Taussig study, which, in turn, depended upon the figures given in the 1934 Kopp book (drawn from the Margaret Sanger Clinic). Since the beginning of this statistical chain was an estimate of 681,600 abortions a year (which, magnified by the population rise since then, would give a present-day figure of 1.2 million illegal abortions a year), and an estimated death rate of 1.2 percent, Taussig arrived at a figure of 8,179 deaths each year, and then added an extra 2,000 (roughly) to be on the cautious side: 10,000. But the trouble with these statistics, Hellegers argues, is that the Sanger Clinic sample from which the projections originated was hardly representative of the population (41.7 percent of the women were Jewish, and 26.1 percent Catholic). They thus suffer from the same weakness which marked the later Kinsey studies, that is, dubious projections from an unrepresentative sample of the American female population (82.4 percent of Kinsey's sample, for instance, had a college education, as against a 13.2 percent national average for urban white females).[35] Hellegers also notes that, if the recorded number of present-day deaths from abortion is doubled, as was Taussig's procedure, it would still be well under 1,000 per year. Norbert J. Mietus argues much the way Hellegers does, but especially centers his attack on the figures cited by Jerome E. Bates and Edward S. Zawadzki in their book *Criminal Abortion: A Study in Medical Sociology*.[36] Their figure is one million criminal abortions per year, drawn from studies of Gebhard, Taussig, Kopp and Stix. But each of these studies is open to serious objections: Gebhard's because of the poor sample used by the Kinsey Institute, Taussig and Kopp because of their dependence upon the Sanger Clinic data, and Stix [37] because her sample was two-thirds Jewish. Mietus concludes that their figure for the number of illegal abortions is highly inflated and, correspondingly, their figure for the number of resultant deaths.[38] Herbert Ratner, working with a recorded figure of about 50,000 deaths yearly among women in the reproductive-age period, observes that it is almost impossible to get a figure anywhere near 10,000 illegal abortion deaths a year when one takes account of the 25,000 or so known deaths a year from cancer, heart and kidney diseases, the 7,000 deaths from automobile accidents, not to mention all the other assorted causes of death.[39] Alex Barno has observed that Minnesota, with a birthrate of approximately 80,000 per year, should have about 100–200 deaths each year from illegal abortion if a national figure of 5,000–10,000 such deaths is plausible. However, he points out that only 20 deaths from illegal abortion were recorded in 1950–1964.[40]

The force of these considerations, along with those of Tietze, would seem to rob the very high death-rate figures of much of their plausibility. And the plausibility of the very high estimates of the number of illegal abortions each year does not appear very strong either. Kinsey, Gebhard,

Taussig, Kopp and Stix, as noted, did not have representative population samples, and yet their figures were used to provide the basis for the high estimates. However, unlike the death statistics, there is just no final way of telling whether the figure should be high or low. The increased use of contraceptives, especially the anovulant pill, could well be reducing the illegal abortion rate just as it seems to be reducing the overall birthrate; on the other hand, the declining number of legal abortions performed each year, primarily by a drop in those done on medical grounds, might be driving more women to illegal abortions. The data just do not exist to test these speculations. In any event, since it is the death rate which has often been put forward as the crucial consideration, the statistical grounds for that argument seem considerably weakened. Lacking any real accuracy, the data on illegal abortions can be used either way, by choosing to stress the high or the low estimates; but neither side can make a solid case. Significantly, however, even those who have complained about the constant citation of high, but unverified, figures on the number of illegal abortions have not tried to contend that illegal abortion does not constitute a problem. Even if the lowest cited figure, 200,000, is closest to the truth, it is a figure worthy of considerable concern. Similarly, even the low figure of 500 deaths each year from illegal abortion means that illegal abortions constitute a significant health hazard.

Discrimination

If the number of illegal abortions, and attendant deaths and injuries, has constituted the main argument of those unhappy with restrictive American law, the apparent discrimination which has accompanied the application of these laws takes a very close second place. The discrimination argument has a number of related aspects. First, it is held that educated, affluent women find it much easier to purchase a safe illegal abortion than do poorer women. Second, it is contended that it is much easier for a woman on the private services of a hospital to get an abortion than a woman on the ward services. Third, it is argued that there is a tremendous variation among hospitals in the performance of abortions, meaning that a woman's chance of getting a safe hospital abortion depends in great part upon which hospital she happens to chance upon or live near. On the first point, Dr. Harold Rosen has said that "the difference between having an abortion or a child (so the cynical and frequently heard non-medical aphorism has it) is the difference between having one to three hundred dollars and knowing the right person or being without funds and the right contacts." [41] There is no reason to dispute this argument. It is well known, in many areas of

American life, that the affluent find it safer to break the law than do the poor. In addition, one of the advantages of an education is that a woman will sometimes (but not always) be more resourceful in finding a safe abortion, whether by taking a trip abroad or by locating those qualified doctors who perform illegal abortions, either in their offices or in hospitals.

On the second point, more hard data are available. Dr. Alan F. Guttmacher has summed up the evidence: "Both in regard to incidence and indications between patients on private and clinic services and voluntary and municipal hospitals . . . it has long been apparent to physicians, district attorneys and laymen that municipal hospitals follow the letter of the law of the abortion statute much more exactly than voluntary hospitals, and also that private patients are generally treated by a more lenient interpretation of the law than service patients." [42] Robert E. Hall, in particular, has been assiduous in collecting data which bear out this assertion:

National surveys bear testimony to the fact that hospital abortions are performed four times as often on the private services as on the ward services. In New York City, between 1960 and 1962 the ratio of therapeutic abortions to live births in the proprietary hospitals was 1:250; on the private services of the voluntary hospitals, 1 : 400; on the ward services of the same voluntary hospitals, 1 : 1,400; and in the municipal hospitals, 1 : 10,000. The same inequity pertains to ethnic origin. The rate of therapeutic abortions per live births among white women in New York is 1 per 380, among nonwhites 1 per 2,000, and among Puerto Ricans 1 per 10,000. Approximately half of the puerperal deaths among New York's Negroes and Puerto Ricans are due to criminal abortions, as opposed to only a quarter of the puerperal deaths among white women. [43]

In a survey undertaken by Dr. Hall of 65 randomly selected major American hospitals, he found that, of 60 which returned usable information, the rate of therapeutic abortions was 3.6 times higher on their private than on their ward services. [44] Kenneth R. Niswander has substantiated similar data from a study of Buffalo, New York, hospitals. [45]

While complaints about inequality are thus common among those favoring a change in the laws, a complaint apparently borne out by available studies, some important qualifications have been noted. Robert E. Hall has observed that the reason for a discrepancy between the availability of abortion to private and ward patients cannot be entirely traced to rank discrimination:

Part of the explanation lies in the dual tendency of the ward patients to register for antepartum care later in their pregnancies and to be less aware of their need to be aborted. That even this obstacle to ward-private equality can be overcome has been shown at Mount Sinai Hospital in New York, where the abortion rates for the two services between 1952 and 1955 were virtually identical. Another part of this discrepancy may be attributed to the higher incidence of abortions for psychiatric indications among private patients.[46]

J. G. Moore and K. P. Russell have further qualified the inequality argument:

Close study of the various factors, however, would indicate that such differences are due to the nature of the groups, rather than to the standards applied. The ward patients tend to seek care late, or not at all, and are much less apt to follow specific medical recommendations. Their care usually is thus compromised and far from optimal. Such factors have a direct effect on the application of therapeutic modalities, such as interruption of pregnancy.[47]

These qualifications, to be sure, are not meant to deny the existence of what amounts to *de facto* discrimination, solidly enough established, but only to note that it is not necessarily deliberate on the part of hospitals.

On the third point, the variation among hospitals in the number of abortions performed, Kenneth R. Niswander has written:

Hospitals vary greatly in their abortion practices. At the Los Angeles County Hospital, which treats only clinic patients, Russell reports that from 1946 to 1951 there was an incidence of one therapeutic abortion per two thousand eight hundred sixty-four (2,864) deliveries. At the opposite extreme, one finds reputable hospitals permitting abortion for one out of every 35–40 deliveries. The variation in the hospitals survey by [Robert E.] Hall extended from no abortions in 24,417 deliveries to one in 36 deliveries. It seems inconceivable that medical opinion could vary so widely. Socioeconomic factors must be playing a major role in the decision to abort in certain institutions.[48]

Hall himself has written:

Abortion practices vary not only from hospital to hospital but also from service to service within the same hospital. They also vary widely from doctor to doctor on the same service of the same hospital. In one of the largest teaching hospitals in the East, for example, the individual abortion-to-delivery ratio of its staff members ranges from 1 : 140 to 1 : 11. The victim of all this confusion is, of course, the American female. Even if she has a legitimate reason for therapeutic abortion she must find Doctor X in hospital Y with policy Z in order to have it done.[49]

Herbert L. Packer and Ralph J. Gampell, in a study of California hospitals during the period 1952–1956 (before the change in California laws), found that "the five-year TA [therapeutic abortion] rates for each respondent hospital varied from a low of 7,616 : 0 to a high of 126 : 1. In other words, there was one hospital which performed 7,616 deliveries without performing any TA's, while another performed one TA for every 126 live births." [50]

Beyond the three specific complaints against restrictive American laws related above is a more general charge of hypocrisy. There is the hypocrisy, it is said, which sees the law openly violated in numerous hospitals, a violation which goes unpunished by the law. Johan Eliot, for instance, in a 1967 survey of non-Catholic hospitals under private and public control, found that, of the private hospitals responding, 79.4 percent permitted abortion on the indication of German measles; 88.9 percent permitted psychiatric indications for abortion. Of the hospitals under public control which responded, 66 percent permitted a German-measles (rubella) indication and 80.6 percent a psychiatric indication. It goes without saying that these particular indications are not countenanced in the laws of most of the states; but that did not stop the hospitals from accepting them.[51] Again, it has often been pointed out that it is extraordinarily rare for a woman to be prosecuted for having an abortion, just as it is rare for a doctor who has performed an illegal abortion in a hospital to be prosecuted. No doubt the difficulty of successful prosecution is a major deterrent to district attorneys but, at the same time, it seems evident that there exists comparatively little desire to press the prosecution either of women or of doctors performing abortions in hospitals.

It is not my intent at this point to deal with the question of what would constitute a good law (see Chapter 14). It is sufficient simply to note that the charge of hypocrisy and discrimination has been leveled against a legal system which encompasses strict laws coupled with a widespread disregard of those laws. As we shall see, it is a standard complaint against restrictive legal codes, in other countries as well as in the United States. Most importantly, perhaps, no genuinely effective legal rebuttal has been offered. The response that many laws are frequently violated (e.g., the laws concerning theft and murder), without the conclusion being drawn that the laws should be abandoned, is inadequate. Unlike abortion laws, there exist no significant pressure groups which propose that the murder and theft laws be abandoned, and no significant groups which argue that murder and theft are morally acceptable; quite the contrary is the case with restrictive abortion laws. As for the rebuttal that a law should not be changed simply because it accidentally and *de facto* discriminates against some groups, this might make sense if the discrimination involved a very tiny minority. But in the case of abortion, there is reason to believe that the poorer groups in our society suffer more from the laws than the affluent. If a poor woman is determined to have an abortion, she is much less likely to have a safe abortion. Moreover, it has been part of American public policy to seek to reduce the inequities between groups; the fact that an affluent woman can more easily obtain a safe abortion does amount to an inequity. That a sizable proportion of people want the laws changed indicates that the discrimination in question falls within the scope of legitimate public concern.

Results of Changes in American Laws

By mid-1969, ten states had liberalized their abortion laws: Colorado, North Carolina and California in 1967, Georgia and Maryland in 1968 and Arkansas, Kansas, Delaware, Oregon and New Mexico in 1969. Generally they have changed their laws according to the recommendations of the Model Penal Code of the American Law Institute and now allow a medical, psychiatric, fetal and humanitarian (i.e., rape and/or incest) indication. Despite their similarities, the states differ in some respects. For example, Georgia and Maryland do not recognize incest as grounds for abortion, and in California the fetal indication was removed from the original bill upon the insistence of Governor Ronald Reagan, who threatened to veto the whole bill if the fetal clause were not eliminated. In the psychiatric indication, California, Maryland and North Carolina require a substantial risk that continuation of the pregnancy will gravely impair the woman's health, and Colorado and Georgia stipulate serious and permanent impairment or injury. In the fetal indication, Colorado and Maryland insist that the defect be grave and permanent, Georgia, that it be irremediable and North Carolina, simply that the defect be grave. In early 1970, Hawaii repealed its abortion law.

It probably will be several years before the overall effects of these changes can be estimated, but some early information is available from California, Colorado and Baltimore, Maryland. According to the California State Department of Public Health, 3,775 abortions were performed in the 435 hospitals which reported abortion statistics during the first 11 months after liberalization of the law. (Forty-two other hospitals gave no statistics.) Based on this figure, plus an estimate of the number of abortions performed in the 42 hospitals which did not report statistics, it is calculated that there were approximately 4,800 legal abortions in California during the first year, or eight times the number performed under the old law (estimated to have been about 600 a year). Sixty-three percent of the abortions were performed in the San Francisco Bay area, although only 23 percent of the state's births occur there. By contrast, only 19 percent of the abortions were performed in the Los Angeles metropolitan area, which accounts for 44 percent of the state's births.[52] Critics who feel that the law is not liberal enough say that this discrepancy is just one reflection of the timidity, conservatism and, in some places, outright discrimination which has dominated application of the new law. The critics are dissatisfied because of the red tape a woman must go through before her application for abortion is approved (the written consent of the majority of the hospital abortion committee, preceded by examinations and written recommendations by her physician, another doctor and in many cases a psychiatrist); because of the continuing high cost of abortions (ranging from 500 dollars to 1,800 dollars, with an average of 600 dollars to 700 dollars for doctors' and hospital fees, including a separate fee for the recommending psychiatrist, some of whom charge as much as 100 dollars for a single consultation); and because application of the law depends too much on the personal attitudes of physicians, many of whom are opposed to abortion, or on the fear of hospital administrators that they will be harassed by medical examiners or private groups if their institutions allow too many abortions.

The vast majority of abortions in California (upwards of 80 percent) have been performed on psychiatric indications, although it is admitted that this is a way of getting around the lack of a fetal indication and other strictures of the law. Finally, it is asserted, and not disputed, that the increase in legal abortions has scarcely put a dent in the large number of illegal abortions performed in California each year.[53] For many critics, including those who once supported reform of the old California abortion law, the only remedy now is repeal of the abortion law—to have no law at all and to leave abortion decisions to the women concerned and their doctors. Advocates of this course believe that only the courts, not the state legislature, will provide the remedy by declaring even the reformed law an unconstitutional invasion of privacy. (In the fall of 1969, the California Supreme Court, in *People* v. *Belous,* declared the old law unconstitutional on the grounds of the vagueness of the law and a violation of due process. A short time later, in *United States* v. *Vuitch,* District Court Judge Gerhard A. Gesell declared the District of Columbia law invalid for essentially the same reasons.)

In the first year after the new law went into effect in Colorado, 407 legal abortions were reported, compared with 51 the previous year. They were performed in 21 of the state's 52 accredited hospitals, but the majority were done in the Denver area. A survey conducted by the University of Colorado Medical Center showed that, of the 407, 71 percent were done for psychiatric reasons, 12 percent for fetal reasons, 11 percent for rape and 6 percent for the physical health of the mother. Sixty-eight percent of the women were Colorado residents, 55 percent were single, 34 percent married and 11 percent divorced; 56 percent had had no previous births and 13 percent had had four or more deliveries. Nineteen percent of the women reported incomes under 3,000 dollars a year, similar to the percentage in the general population, but 31 percent reported over 10,000 dollars, much higher than the 16 percent in that bracket in the state's population as a whole, according to the 1960 census.[54] There are no residency requirements for abortion in Colorado, but some hospitals, fearful of the "abortion mill" label, hesitate or refuse to perform abortions on women from out of state. Denver General, for example, finally declared that it would permit abortions on nonresidents only for fetal indications. Similarly, three major hospitals in

Baltimore, Maryland (Sinai, Johns Hopkins and the Greater Baltimore
Medical Center), have ceased performing abortions on women from
out of state, partly because of the demand from within the state (as in
Colorado many smaller hospitals hesitate to perform any abortions, leaving the large city hospitals to carry the major burden) and because they
are unable to handle the large number of requests from nonresidents,
and partly because hospital officials are loath to have their institutions
become known as "abortion mills." Like California, Maryland also has
its liberal critics of the new law, mainly on the grounds that it has not
helped the poor as much as was originally intended. One doctor observed that 90 percent of the abortions at Johns Hopkins Hospital are
performed on private patients, for whom the cost is from 450 dollars to
650 dollars. The price is 250 dollars for a ward patient, but even that is
too much unless she has some kind of insurance, and most of the poor
do not.[55]

Great Britain: Before and After 1967

In 1967, as a result of many years of pressure and agitation, the
English and Welsh law governing abortion was substantially changed,
widely extending the permissible indications; it went into effect in 1968.
Before discussing the results of this change, however, it is worth looking
at the earlier, restrictive law and its consequences. Precisely these consequences, as they were interpreted by those pressing for reform, led to
the 1967 reform law. Before 1803, the rule of the common law was that
abortion was a crime only if it took place after quickening. In that year
the law was put on a statutory basis and was also changed to make
abortion a crime before quickening as well. For the purpose of the
present discussion, however, the important law was that of the Offenses
Against the Person Act of 1861, which established a maximum penalty of
life imprisonment for an abortion performed before or after quickening.
On the face of it, this law was exceedingly severe, admitting of no
"indications" and punishing both the woman herself and the person who
performed the abortion. Unsuccessful attempts at abortion were severely
punishable as well.[56] In practice, the women themselves were rarely
prosecuted, and even when they were, they hardly ever received the
maximum penalties. Most of the prosecutions under the law were directed
at illegal abortionists, the "back-street surgeons" as they were called. In
1939, after many years of uncertainty about whether the law could
countenance an induced abortion for the purpose of preserving the
woman's life, the famous case of *Rex* v. *Bourne* established by implication an important precedent not only for a medical indication but for a
psychiatric indication as well. After the rape of a girl of fourteen by

several soldiers, with resulting pregnancy, Dr. Alex Bourne, a prominent gynecologist, performed an abortion and promptly notified the police that he had done so. He was then charged with a felony. Adopting as his line of defense the claim that an abortion was legally justifiable for purposes of saving a life, he also argued that no distinction could be drawn between that purpose and the preservation of a mother's mental health (which was the specific purpose of the abortion in question). In his instructions to the jury, the judge said that, if the Crown had not been able to prove that Dr. Bourne had not acted in good faith, he should be acquitted and that the jury was to take a prudent view of what the preservation of life included.[57] He was acquitted.

After this decision, it was possible to say with some certainty that a clear threat to a mother's health was a legally justifiable ground for abortion, though it was still uncertain just how far and in what ways this exception could be interpreted. As a result of the considerable confusion and also because of a growing desire for a more liberal law, the Abortion Law Reform Association was established in 1936 and, beginning in the early 1950s, repeated attempts were made in Parliament to change the law. Finally, on July 14, 1967, a reform bill introduced by a Liberal M.P., David Steel, passed by a vote of 167 to 83. The bill became law on October 27, 1967, and went into force in April 1968.[58] It applies to England and Wales, but not to Northern Ireland.

A primary consideration, used with great effect by the proponents of a reform law during the many years before it was actually passed, was the hazard of illegal abortion. Estimates of its frequency during the period of restrictiveness ranged anywhere from 10,000 to 250,000 cases a year. The estimate made in a book published by the Abortion Law Reform Association, *Back-Street Surgery,* was 100,000 per year, and this became a commonly cited figure in favor of liberalization of the law.[59] The working assumption of the Anglican Church Assembly Board's study of abortion in England, while not committing itself to a specific figure, was that the incidence of illegal abortion in England was sufficiently serious to warrant some change in the law.[60] Moreover, indirectly alluding to the great demand for induced abortions, the Board noted that "all *a priori* considerations of religion and philosophy apart, there are social reasons, connected with the continuance and well-being of the nation, which have induced States to legislate on abortion, not only to forbid the unskilled and physically dangerous practice of it, but also to limit and control the conditions in which it may be done, even in the best possible way, by skilled and authorized medical practitioners."[61] Glanville Williams, citing a number of English estimates during the 1940s and 1950s, said that the number must run into the "tens of thousands each year." [62] Professor D. V. Glass, in *Population Policies and Movements,* estimated a figure of 100,000 per year in the late 1930s, and the Interdepartmental Committee on Abortion (a prewar government committee which was working toward reform) accepted, in 1939, a figure of 110,000–150,000 abortions per year, two-fifths of them criminal abortions. The committee also estimated that there were, at that time, between 411 and 605 deaths per year associated with abortion, legal and illegal.[63] Eustace Chesser, in 1950, placed the figure as high as 250,000 illegal abortions each year.[64] Marie Stopes claimed that 10,000 women had written to her asking for an illegal abortion.[65] A more recent study by C. B. Goodhart placed the actual figure during the early 1960s at 10,000 illegal abortions each year, conceding, however, that this figure could well be too low.[66] That the high figures were usually used by known advocates of a liberalization of the law must, of course, be taken into account (just as it should be taken into account that they may have been advocates because they accepted the figures). Yet in any event it is notable that the debate over abortion-law reform in England did not bring forth (so far as I can determine) any efforts on the part of the opposition to discount the seriousness and frequency of illegal abortions (nor was that Goodhart's intention). Even Goodhart's minimal figure of 10,000 was taken as a sufficient indication that a serious problem existed.

In a paper delivered at the University of Chicago Conference on Abortion in 1968, Malcom Potts estimated the number of illegal abortions in Great Britain on the basis of replies to a 1966 National Opinion Poll (N.O.P.) questionnaire. An annual rate of 40,000 induced abortions was computed for the years 1946–1968; of this number 31,000 a year were admitted to be criminal. Another 88,000 women a year apparently admitted to attempting to induce an abortion. But, on the assumption that many women would suppress such information, Potts believes that "the N.O.P. figures probably need to be doubled to at least 80,000 a year," and on that reckoning the number of illegal abortions would be at least 62,000 per year.[67] Keith Simpson, going considerably beyond Potts' estimate, says the number of illegal abortions in England may be as high as 300 to 400 per day (which would amount to 109,500 to 146,000 per year), but he does not say how he arrived at that figure.[68]

As for legal therapeutic abortions, Christopher Tietze, in a survey of abortion practices in several European countries, noted that about 1,600 abortions were performed in National Health Service hospitals in 1958, rising to 3,300 in 1964.[69] Madeleine Simms, of the Abortion Law Reform Association, says that by 1966 the number of therapeutic abortions performed in NHS hospitals in England and Wales had increased to 6,380.[70] Tietze also cites the estimate made by Paul Ferris that 10,000 so-called West-End legal abortions were performed annually in private nursing homes or in the offices of gynecologists and surgeons in private practice, most of them in London.[71] These are the "Harley Street" physicians who, according to Ferris, may charge a woman as much as 150 pounds for an abortion. Often a gynecologist would work with a psychiatrist willing to certify that the abortion was justifiable on psychiatric grounds, so that technically these abortions were legal. Peter Diggory, using data provided by the Minister of Health, has given figures for therapeutic abortions performed in NHS hospitals: 1958: 1,570; 1960: 2,040; 1962: 2,830; 1964: 3,300; 1966: 6,380; 1967: 10,000 (estimated). In addition, he estimated that, in 1958, 12,000 private therapeutic abortions were performed, a figure which had risen to 17,500 by 1967.[72]

The Harley Street abortion is for the rich or the middle-class woman who can manage to scrape together the necessary cash. The poor depend on the nonphysician, often a neighborhood abortionist recommended by a friend or relative. Ferris says there is more risk in this kind of abortion (chronic ill health and sterility may result from a botched operation), but he insists that not all suffer from it and in fact quite a few women have *not* been ill from illegal abortions. For one thing, he says, "antibiotics have reduced the risks from sepsis, and the necessary drugs may be given by an abortionist or by the woman's G.P. without her having to go to hospital."[73] Madeleine Simms holds that three out of four illegal abortions require no subsequent treatment.[74]

Despite these observations, few English commentators discount the possible effects of criminal abortions. Glanville Williams, in his introduction to A. Jenkins' book *Law for the Rich*, a strong brief on behalf of abortion-law reform in England, remarks that "cases have been known where she [the aborted woman] has been made a complete cripple."[75] Williams gives no specifics of such cases, but he is able to cite another effect of such abortions—widespread absenteeism from work. According to statistics supplied by the Minister of Pensions in 1958, 76,000 working days were lost by 6,000 insured women in one year on account of criminal abortions.

The ultimate risk, of course, is death. Keith Simpson cites the main mortality risks of illegal abortion to be (a) sudden death from vagal shock, air or chemical embolism; (b) delayed death from hemorrhage; (c) later death from infection; and (d) indirect deaths from renal or hepatic failure.[76] Estimates of the actual numbers of deaths, however, are considerably reduced for recent years. The Abortion Law Reform Association cites 28 deaths from induced abortions in 1964 (four from legal abortions performed in private nursing home and NHS hospitals and 24 from illegal abortions); 27 deaths in 1965 (six from legal and 21 from illegal) and 34 deaths in 1966 (four from legal and 30 from illegal).[77] Again, the use of antibiotics may have helped reduce the death rate as well as the medical complications following criminal abortions.

The man or woman who performs illegal abortions is universally deplored in the literature, but Moya Woodside, who studied 44 "back street" women abortionists in Holloway Prison, contends that in their own working-class milieu they were not looked upon with any particular scorn; on the contrary, in some places they were regarded as public benefactors. For the most part, their prices were moderate and financial gain did not seem to be their main motive. In any case, their clients could not afford to pay too much. Since there is still great ignorance about contraceptives in poorer districts, where the woman abortionist draws most of her clientele, she is for them the court of last resort in keeping down family size.[78] But whether the criminal abortionist is an avaracious, clumsy butcher or a kindly neighborhood practitioner of folk medicine, few believe that the new liberalized British abortion law will quickly eliminate criminal abortions. Philip Rhodes, in the symposium *Abortion in Britain*, insisted that, even with a change in the law, illegal abortion would still have a future and that the numbers might even rise.[79]

Whatever the new law's effect on criminal abortions, the demand for the legal variety has increased markedly. It is hard to disagree with Madeleine Simms of the Abortion Law Reform Association, who says that the full extent of the abortion problem is finally beginning to come into public view.[80] In a survey of the first eight months under the new law, from April 27, 1968, to December 31, 1968, T. L. T. Lewis reported that there were 22,256 induced abortions in England and Wales. The numbers have increased steadily each quarter, leading to an estimate of 35,000 for the first full year. In a breakdown of the second and third quarters, Lewis reports 12,351 for the whole country, of which 7,657 were in National Health Service hospitals and 4,667 in "approved places," mostly nursing homes and private hospitals. Sixty-two percent of the abortions occurred in London: 4,378 were performed in "approved places" in one wealthy section of London alone, the North West Metropolitan Region. In that area there were only 768 NHS abortions. In all the Metropolitan regions there were 2,267 NHS and 4,514 "approved places" abortions. The remaining NHS abortions (5,390) were distributed among 11 hospital boards throughout the country: Newcastle had the most, with 705, Manchester was second, with 642, Birmingham third, with 516, and Liverpool had the fewest, 194. Lewis further reports that in the second and third quarters 45 percent of the women having abortions were married, 47 percent were single and 8 percent were widowed, divorced or separated. Combining the latter category and the single women, the total "unmarried" came to 55 percent. Also in the second and third quarters, 14 percent were between the ages of sixteen and nineteen, 2 percent were under sixteen, and the majority, 62 percent, were between twenty and thirty-four years old. Lewis concludes that since the new law has been in force, the whole character of the gynecologist's outpatient work has altered. He now must deal with two, three or four requests for termination at almost every session, and it often takes longer to reject a case than accept one.[81]

Peter Diggory, however, believes that it is a mistake to think that the new law represents a sharp break with earlier trends. Pointing to the steady rise in legal abortions performed prior to the new law, he contends that it has only had the effect of continuing a trend already present. Moreover, he adds that while the English situation has improved this is due as much if not more to the debate which preceded the new law as to the effect of the law itself.[82] And the debate is still going on. As the demand for legal abortions has risen, so have complaints about inadequate facilities, the hostility of some gynecologists and the long delays even after two doctors have approved abortion applications.[83] In some areas waiting lists for NHS hospitals are so long that many women run the risk of going beyond the twelfth week of pregnancy, when the abortion would be a simple procedure, and reach a stage where it becomes a serious operation. As a result, poorer women may revert to the back street, richer women to a private nursing home or the private wing of a hospital.[84]

As Madeleine Simms sums up the situation in the ALRA *Newsletter:* "It is no longer the law that is preventing women obtaining NHS abortions, it is the attitude of some of the doctors and the shortage of NHS facilities. A further reform of the law will not alter these factors in the slightest." [85] The solution, it is said, is not, then, abortion on request, but a reorganization of existing staff and facilities and pressure on the Ministry of Health to bring that about. The ALRA thinks this is possible because the birthrate has fallen steadily in Great Britain since 1964 (50,000 fewer babies were born in 1967 than in 1964), from 18.5 live births per 1,000 in England and Wales and 20 in Scotland to 17.2 and 18.6 respectively in 1967.[86] Therefore there is less of a demand for maternity beds. Also, ALRA contends, if legal abortions are available, there should be fewer septic complications from illegal abortions which take up emergency space.[87] Finally, the ALRA says, the immediate solution to increased demand is to create special abortion units attached to hospitals. These, too, however, will require strong pressure to bring about. In Birmingham, long a center of opposition to abortion-law reform, the Pregnancy Advisory Service has registered as a charity, which enables it to establish abortion clinics if it can raise enough money.[88] There are now several Pregnancy Advisory Services, including one in London.

The British medical establishment, by and large, is not altogether happy with recent developments and with the continuing pressure being put upon physicians to provide more abortions. H. A. Robinson, for instance, has complained bitterly about the new law, pointing out that it seems actually to open the way for abortions on very flimsy grounds, thus making it difficult for doctors to turn women down.[89] It is one of the ironies of the new law that a phrase inserted into the act by opponents of liberalization, specifying that an abortion would be permitted if continuing the pregnancy involved greater risk than terminating—greater not only to the physical or mental health of the woman but also to that of "any existing children"—has made possible a very free interpretation of the law. Generally, any pregnancy carried to term is riskier than an early abortion, and taking into account the effect of another child on the existing family borders on a purely social indication. N. M. Cogan, a medical social worker, asserts that the new law "represents a foot in the door of abortion on demand," one effect of which may be to put pressure on women in some circumstances to have abortions they don't really want.[90] Complaints have also come from Catholic quarters, which see the new law as, in fact, tantamount to abortion on demand. Indeed, one article argues, the permissive wording of the law makes it "unlikely . . . that any prosecution will in future be brought against a doctor who observes the ostensible requirements of the Abortion Act. The danger now lies in those cases where a doctor refuses a demand to perform an abortion." [91] The author also argues that the so-called conscience clause of the new act, which would supposedly exempt a doctor with conscientious objections to abortion from performing one, is all but nullified by another part of the same clause (Section 4), which says that conscientious objections cannot be pleaded where an "abortion is necessary to save the life or prevent grave permanent injury to the physical or mental health of the pregnant woman."

Further cause for concern in some quarters has been the influx of foreign women seeking abortions. They come from Western Europe, the United States and Canada, for the most part, and account for an estimated 7 percent to 10 percent of abortions in Great Britain. The vast majority of the foreign women go to a private hospital or clinic (about 60 new ones were opened in the first year of the new law, more than half in the North West Metropolitan Region of London) and pay 500 dollars or more, as compared with fees of 150 dollars to 400 dollars which British women are charged for private abortions, and no fee for an NHS abortion. Critics of the foreign abortion trade are apprehensive that it may lower international opinion of the ethics of the British medical profession, branding it as primarily interested in the money these abortions bring. Others focus criticism on the health standards and quality of care offered in the private abortion centers, whether the patients are British or foreign. Some would like the law amended to stipulate a six-month residency requirement in order to prevent foreign women from visiting England expressly for an abortion. Others would be content with a more precise specification of the medical facilities required for licensing the private abortion clinics—such as equipment for resuscitation in the operating rooms, blood for transfusions and elevators to transport patients. These critics contend that the public needs protection from the unskilled and the unscrupulous and that this is not presently insured under that part of the law covering registration of places where abortions may be carried out.[92]

In sum, a number of points seem to be emerging from the British experience with the new law. First, it has raised the number of legal abortions, but it is too early to know what effect it will have on the illegal abortion rate—assuming that could ever be determined, which is doubtful; for the time being, it would appear that this rate is not likely to decline very rapidly. Second, resistance by many members of the medical profession, bureaucratic difficulties and inadequate facilities are likely to mean an erratic and inconsistent practice for some time to come. Third, those who opposed a change in the law in the first place are not likely to find anything in the application of the new law to lessen their criticisms. Finally, it is too early as yet to determine whether the new law will eventually lead to a decline in overall abortions (legal and illegal) or a general rise.

India

India is a demographer's nightmare, embodying as painfully as any country in the world all the problems of overpopulation, poverty, undernourishment, a shortage of housing, educational and medical facilities. With a population which has gone well over the 500 million mark, approximately one out of every seven persons in the world is an Indian; 55,000 children are born every day and 21 million a year; about 13 million people are added to the Indian population each year (with 21 million births and eight million deaths per annum). The population growth rate is slightly over 2.5 percent. India's birthrate per 1,000 population declined only slightly from 1950 to the present—from 39.9 to 38.4— but its death rate dropped radically in the same period—from 27.4 to 12.9.

At the present rate of population growth (about 2.5 percent), the Indian population could reach one billion within 25 years; between 1951 and 1966 the population increased by 140 million. While food production increased from 55 million tons per year in 1951 to 72 million tons in 1966, the food per capita per day dropped from 12.8 ounces in 1951 to 12.3 ounces in 1966; unemployment rose from three million in 1951 to ten million in 1965–1966.[93] Not surprisingly, India has been making intensive efforts to develop family-planning programs, relying primarily upon contraceptives and sterilization. So far, only slight success, varying from one state to the next, has been achieved overall. According to figures supplied by the Minister of Health in early 1968, effective contraception is practiced by only 8 percent of the population in the reproductive-age group. By March 1968, about 3.8 million (mostly men) had been sterilized. Aside from a traditional resistance to change, the main obstacles to family planning in India have been the shortage of trained personnel to educate the people in the techniques of and need for birth control, the low national literacy rate (25 percent) and the communication barrier caused by the multiplicity of languages.[94] (There are over 1,500; English is spoken by the tiny minority of educated people; Hindi, the official language, is spoken by only 30 percent of the population.) At the same time, India is the focal point of a great variety of religious and cultural traditions. Hinduism (the religion of 83 percent of the Indian people), Islam, Christianity and Buddhism all have a place in Indian life; Eastern and Western cultures find there a point of confluence. As a society, however, India has a traditional, highly structured social system, with a Western-oriented, educated élite at one extreme, and millions of village-bound, illiterate peasants at the other.

All of these elements have a place, although usually ambiguously, in any discussion of abortion in India. As of early 1969, the provisions of the Indian Penal Code placed India in the category of those countries with highly restrictive abortion laws. Code 312 of the Indian Penal Code provides:

> Whoever voluntarily causes a woman with child to miscarry, shall, if miscarriage be not caused in good faith for the purpose of saving the life of the woman, be punished with imprisonment of either description for a term which may extend to three years, or with fine or with both, and if the woman be quick with child, shall be punished with imprisonment of either description for a term which may extend to seven years, and shall also be liable to fine.[95]

Further provisions of the Penal Code provide severe penalties for abortions performed without the woman's consent, and for infanticide. As the wording of Code 312 makes evident, only strictly "medical indications" are acceptable and this has been the way the law has in practice been construed. The origin of this code was the British law of the nineteenth century; thus its presence on the books bespeaks, in the first instance, a Western influence. From all reports, and despite a possible aversion to abortion on the part of the traditionally religious, poor Indians have long resorted to abortion to limit births.

At present, there is a movement to liberalize the law, and it represents, in considerable part, the impact of Western, technological and secular thought. As the *Report of the Committee to Study the Question of Legalisation of Abortion* puts it:

> The whole process of "development," with its stress on industrialization and technological achievement for achieving better living standards, has entailed a

new way of life affecting not only the economic or political sphere but the social sphere as well. It is not possible to try to utilize modern science and technology for the betterment of economic conditions for the masses and at the same time to preserve unchanged traditional ways of family organization and life. The changed position of the women and the child in the new society that is being built up, is also a very relevant factor, for they cannot be regarded any longer as subordinate with lesser rights.[96]

This statement represents better than anything else in the report the philosophical rationale behind the movement to change the laws. It bespeaks a perspective more characteristically secular and technological than traditionally Indian.

More concretely, the movement dates from August 25, 1964, when the Central Family Planning Board recommended to the Ministry of Health that a committee be constituted to study the question of the legalization of abortion. The recommendation was adopted late in 1964, and a committee was formed, with representatives from a variety of Indian public and private agencies. The committee issued its report on December 30, 1966, and it has since formed the basis for a public discussion, not yet very extensive, of the abortion question. As a result of the report, a bill encompassing its recommendations was to have been drawn up in 1968 and debated in parliament sometime in 1969. By late 1969, however, the bill had still not been debated and its outcome was uncertain.

The procedure of the committee involved sending a questionnaire to a large number of private and public agencies, studying abortion laws in other countries, and interviewing people in varied fields in Delhi, Calcutta and Bombay. According to the report, the major concern of the committee was the hazards of illegal abortion. Some 92.3 percent of the respondents to the questionnaire reported their belief that the incidence of illegal abortion was rising. The committee itself estimated that there may be as many as 3.9 million illegal abortions a year, citing a variety of studies (mainly scattered and regional).[97] The estimate was thus only a very uncertain extrapolation from sketchy data, buttressed, though, by the opinion of the questionnaire respondents. Various figures for 1960–1961 are cited in the report to lend credence to the belief that illegal abortions account for a significant number of deaths and injuries each year. "Abortions accounted for 5–10 percent of the group deaths of which two-thirds to three-fourths were with mention of sepsis," was the way one government report summarized data from a number of cities and areas in 1961.[98] After surveying the available data and estimates, the committee stated its major rationale for a change in the law:

It is this sheer, futile wastage—of the mother's health, strength and perhaps life, and of medical skill and resources—that has made some doctors and lay people demand that the question of illegal abortion be reviewed as a whole. Deep compassion at the suffering involved and exasperation at the wastage that occurs have both played their part in such a demand.[99]

The committee specifically denied that any part of its intention is to press for the legalization of abortion for the sake of population control. Even if that were felt desirable, the committee notes, there do not exist now and will not exist in the forseeable future either the doctors or the medical facilities to support an extensive abortion program. Comparing its own situation with that of Japan, where permissive abortion did contribute to a sharp drop in the birthrate, the committee report observes that behind the Japanese success was a solid and widespread desire for small families, a situation, the report implies, which does not yet pertain in India. Finally, the report says, "it is felt, therefore, that the legalising of abortions with a view to obtaining demographic results is unpractical and may even defeat the constructive and positive practice of family planning through contraception." [100] Despite some skepticism about the actual intentions of the committee with respect to this question—especially among opponents of a liberalized law—the well-known scarcity of doctors and medical facilities lends some credence to the committee's protestations (there are approximately 6,000 people per doctor in India, most of the doctors are concentrated in cities and most are not gynecologists). Nonetheless, it is easy to find observers in India, even among those favorable to a liberal law, who believe the real aim is population control. It is worth citing, in this regard, what seems to me an ambiguous passage in the report itself:

> It must be made quite clear . . . that the words "family planning" connote the control of conception which does not include abortion which takes place after conception. However, abortion also can be used as a means to control family size, as is being done currently in several countries, in which case, family planning or contraception and abortion, are in two parallel categories, both of which can lead to population control.[101]

As for the proposed wording of the revised law, the committee would extend the present medical indication to include a possible grave injury to the physical or mental health of the woman (before, at or after the birth) and would add a fetal and a humanitarian (e.g., rape) indication. Under medical indications, a paragraph was added in October 1967 which would allow termination of pregnancy "provided the woman or her husband undergo voluntary sterilization to ward off the danger of repeated abortions and further pregnancies" (except in exceptional circumstances where sterilization would be considered unnecessary).

Most notably, the proposed law would require only the approval of the operating doctor within the first trimester and would not require the consent of husbands in the case of married women (or the father in the case of unmarried women). On the face of it, the proposed law would appear to open the way for considerable permissiveness (judging at least by the one-doctor permission). However, the present plan, as called for in the proposed law, would be to restrict legal abortions to government hospitals "for the time being," thus keeping down the number of legal abortions—a figure unlikely, in any case, to reach large proportions in the near future because of the shortage of doctors mentioned above.[102]

As of late 1969, the fate of the proposed new legislation was uncertain. Both the Central Family Planning Institute and the Ministry of Health and Family Planning are, however, reasonably confident that the law will be changed in line with the recommendations of the committee. Their reasons for optimism are that the committee itself had representatives of some of the most important medical and social groups in India, that its recommendations were made with an eye to likely parliamentary reaction, and that the widespread acceptance of the existing family-planning programs (contraception and sterilization) has prepared the way for an acceptance of a liberalized law. Also thought to be preparing the way for a change is a comparatively new development, the willingness, particularly on the part of upper-class Hindu women, to resort to abortion, as well as a change of attitude on the part of gynecologists, many of whom until recently were strongly opposed to any change.[103] Nonetheless, there is the distinct possibility of opposition, some of it from Catholic sources (which constitute a tiny minority of the Indian population), some from Hindu, Muslim or Jain sources, and some from within the medical profession. The widespread recourse to abortion at the rural-village level, however, suggests that a liberalized law could find considerable popular support. Yet it is nonetheless the case that the proposed new law has been slow in its passage, suggesting some degree of wariness about public reaction.

It is a matter of dispute and interpretation whether classical Hinduism (the religion of the vast majority of Indians) contains clear, specific prohibitions against abortion. Indeed, so many streams of thought enter into the Hindu tradition that it is hazardous to begin a sentence on any subject with the words, "The Hindu position is . . ." With regard to abortion, it is possible only to cite certain classical principles, historical laws and long-standing customs, which suggest a general bias against the practice. For example, the principle of *ahimsa* (literally, "no-harming") would run counter to abortion. According to Gandhi: "A votary of *ahimsa* therefore remains true to his faith . . . if he shuns to the best of his ability the destruction of the tiniest creature, tries to save it, and thus incessantly strives to be free from the deadly coil of *ahimsa*." [104] Gandhi observed this principle to the extent that he would not allow anyone to kill the poisonous snakes which infested his Sabarmati Ashram. Even the practice of artificial birth control—seemingly less of a violation of *ahimsa* than abortion—seemed to Gandhi morally reprehensible. On the other hand, the *Bhagavad Gita,* the great devotional classic that appears in the *Mahabharata* epic, allows a warrior to take life when it is done not for gain or glory, but out of duty.[105] Although not directly applicable to the question of abortion, the *Gita* does show that exceptions to *ahimsa* were sanctioned within the Hindu tradition.

A specific reference to abortion can be found in the code of Manu, the earliest of the *Dharma Sastras* (Instructions in the Sacred Law), which may have been written as early as the first century B.C., although it appears in its final form in the second or third century A.D. The Laws of Manu had binding power for many centuries. In Section XI, Verse 88 of these laws, we read: "One should also practice these observances [penances] on having slain an embryo not distinctly known [whose sex is not known]—or [on having slain] a woman while in her courses [pregnancy]." [106] In the context, it is clear that the penance is prescribed for a Brahman, a member of the priestly caste. Sins were held to differ in degree according to whether they were committed on or by high- or low-caste persons. In the case of untouchables (casteless persons), it would seem that little attention was paid to their behavior, so long as it did not injure members of higher castes. The apparent ruling against abortion, therefore, cannot be generalized to apply to Indian society as a whole. It does indicate, however, a norm for Brahmans, which the other "twice-born" castes would tend to emulate.

In many other respects, the customs, traditions, and even religious sacraments of the Indian people also appear to run counter to the practice of abortion. There are as many as 40 sacraments in traditional Hinduism—more than in any other religion. These 40 *samskaras* (ceremonies) were designed to sacralize all the major events in the life of the Hindu. The three that are relevant here took place *before* the birth of the child. First came the *garbhādhāna,* the sacred rite to promote conception; then came the *pumsavana,* designed to enhance the chances of the birth of a male; and, finally, to ensure the embryo's safety in the womb, the *sīmatonnayana* ceremony was performed.[107] The last mentioned, in particular, suggests an attitude toward the unborn child that would make abortion distasteful, at least as a common practice. Taken together, all these ceremonies indicate how important the child was to the expectant parents—a son, especially. (Sons were looked upon as one of the greatest blessings that could be bestowed upon an Aryan family. In fact, the father's fortune in the next world depended a good deal upon the exact execution of the funeral rites by his son. Not to have a son was to endanger one's whole future security.)

The principle of *ahimsa* is even stronger in the Jain tradition than in Hinduism. Since they conceived of the whole universe as composed of mixtures of *jiva* (life particles) and *ajiva* (lifeless, material particles), the Jains not only avoided the taking of animal life, but trod gently on the earth, lest they crush the *jiva* particles in the earth. It is said of Mahavira, greatest of the Jain saints, and, to some degree, the founder of the sect:

Thoroughly knowing the earth-bodies and water-bodies and fire-bodies and wind-bodies, the lichens, seeds, and sprouts, he comprehended that they are, if narrowly inspected, imbued with life, and avoided to injure them. Walking, he meditated with his eyes fixed on a square space before him of the length of a man. . . . Looking a little sideward, looking a little behind, attentively looking on his path, he walked so as not to step on any living thing. Many sorts of living beings gathered on his body, crawled about it and caused pain there. But he exercised self-control so as not to scratch himself.[108]

The Jain monk does not eat meat, strains both his drinking water and the air he breathes through a cloth (lest small organisms be consumed), and he refuses to eat anything except the leftovers from another's meal. He will not even eat what has specially been saved for him; for in that way, he would bring down upon himself the bad *karma* attached to the taking of life. If it can be said flatly of any Eastern religion that for it the practice of abortion is impossible, it can be said of Jainism. But Jains constitute less than one percent of the Indian population, and Jainism is considered a heresy in the eyes of the Hindus.

Within the Hindu tradition itself, to sum up, one may argue that there is a bias against abortion based on the three sacraments relevant to the gestation period, as well as on the laws of Manu (keeping in mind that the laws' sanctions against abortion applied only to Brahmans) and on the principle of *ahimsa*. On the other hand, laws are not usually framed without some necessity for their existence, including laws against abortion. Therefore, while acknowledging some bias against the taking of life, and for the continuity of the family, in the Hindu tradition, we would still have to conclude that with regard to abortion there has been as much divergence between thought and practice in India as there has been in the West. In any case, the classical principles and traditions of Hinduism do not seem to have generated a strong cultural basis for contemporary opposition to more permissive abortion laws.

In the present debate, the most consistent opposition has come from Catholics. For example, a special issue of the New Delhi Catholic weekly *Orbit* was given over to a wide range of articles and statements against the proposed change in the law. Among other things, the issue contained lengthy extracts from the *Rig-Veda* and other parts of the Vedic sacred literature which were interpreted to argue for a condemnation of abortion as murder. It also contained a sharp critique of the committee report, particularly on the following points: (*a*) that its data, particularly on illegal abortions, were scanty, and most of its conclusions based on "opinions, hearsay, intuitive and inspired guesses," and (*b*) that the questionnaires were printed only in English and "were sent almost exclusively to educated professional people. . . . No women from the slums, from industrial townships, from the lower middle or working classes, only the educated élite." [109] Nonetheless, few seem willing to deny that illegal abortion is a major problem, both in the cities and in the rural areas, suggesting that in India, as elsewhere in underdeveloped countries (e.g., Latin America), desperation and poverty are able to overcome many possible scruples.

The debate leading up to the change in the English laws in 1967 as well as the fact of widespread changes to more permissive laws in recent decades throughout the world all appear to be playing a role in influencing Indian attitudes, at least those of the professional classes and those associated with Indian family-planning programs. In short, the movement in India from a restrictive to a more permissive law (assuming passage of such a law) would seem to represent many of the same forces operative in other countries which have moved in the same direction, with the problem of poverty and overpopulation a contributing factor.

Latin America

Without exception, the laws of the Latin American countries on therapeutic abortion are stringent, normally admitting only strictly medical indications.[110] Nonetheless, there is widespread agreement, even among those resolutely opposed to any liberalization of the laws, that illegal abortion is a major health problem, with comparatively few of the illegal abortions performed by trained doctors. "*La sonda*" (the probe) is a common nickname in many of the countries of Latin America for any kind of rod capable of rupturing a placenta; the use of such a rod (or, almost as often, a rubber tube) is a major method of self-induced abortion, exceedingly crude and dangerous. An important reason behind a growing receptivity of the Catholic Church in many parts of Latin America to family-planning programs is a tacit recognition of the extent and hazards of illegal abortion. As an area of the world marked by an exceedingly high birthrate, extensive poverty and underdeveloped resources, it is hardly surprising that illegal abortion should be a major—if not *the* major—method of birth limitation. That the ethos of the area is overwhelmingly Roman Catholic seems to make comparatively little difference, serving mainly to deter governments from passing more liberal abortion laws and possibly explaining the absence of any extensive campaigns among medical men and family planning experts to press for a change in the laws. At the same time, as will be noted more extensively below, attitudes toward abortion and the incidence of abortion vary from country to country in Latin America. It is thus hazardous to speak generally of "abortion in Latin America," considering the regional and national variations, and the absence of systematic, hemispheric data. A corrective, though, is available in some comparatively extensive studies in a few of the countries, which suggest the scope of the illegal abortion problem.

A 1964 study of 1,721 female patients (age twenty-five to forty-nine) who had attended clinics in Buenos Aires, found that 532 married women admitted to having 1,356 children and 658 abortions, 510 of them induced; thus 25.3 percent of their pregnancies had ended in induced abortions.[111] A 1963 sample of 1,734 married women in urban Rio de Janeiro, Brazil, showed that 9.2 percent (159) had had at least one induced abortion, with the rate of induced abortions higher among the blacks and the poor and those in irregular marital relationships than in other groups.[112] Octávio Rodrígues Lima estimated in the mid-1960s that there were well over one million illegally induced abortions annually in Brazil. He also reports that in a study of 55 maternity hospitals over an eighteen-year period, a total of 29,541 women were treated for abortion complications, of which 63 percent (18,610) were provoked abortions.[113] A survey conducted in Lima, Peru, by M. Françoise Hall found that induced abortions are a common means of fertility control among all social classes, but especially resorted to by the middle and upper classes. The same study found Peru to have the lowest reported abortion rate of any Latin-American country, with fewer than 5 percent of women aged twenty to thirty-nine admitting induced abortion. However, the fact of a high overall abortion rate (spontaneous and induced) led the author to conclude that there were far more induced abortions than admitted.[114] Hall also notes that the "high rate of provoked abortions, especially in the upper and middle socioeconomic groups, shows that at these levels the need for family limitations is very strong, indeed, and does not go unsatisfied, even at the risk of high social, health, and legal costs. If values and motivations of the lower socioeconomic levels are modeled on those of the higher socioeconomic levels, the findings would suggest that the provoked abortion rate may well increase in the years to come." [115]

A sketchy survey undertaken at the General Hospital, Port of Spain, Trinidad, found an overall incidence of 34.6 percent of all pregnancies ending in induced abortion.[116] A 1962–1963 study in Honduras of 602 abortion cases admitted to a general hospital found that these women had a total of 667 abortions among them and accounted for 17.5 percent of admissions to the obstetrical ward and 47 percent of the blood dispensed by the blood bank.[117] In 1964, Costa Rica had 42,964 hospital discharges for abortion, 12 percent of the total of all obstetrical discharges; abortion accounted for 14 percent of the intrahospital maternal deaths and 40 percent of the blood dispensed in the hospital.[118]

COLOMBIA

Somewhat more extensive data is available on abortion in Colombia. Intensive studies of Candelaria, a town of 5,300 in 1966 with a 10 percent annual growth rate and a birthrate of over 60 live births per thousand population, revealed that 20 percent of the most recent pregnancies of women taking part in a birth-control program had ended in abortion (spontaneous and induced) or stillbirth, and that, next to delivery, women suffering from the side effects of induced abortion comprised the largest number of admissions to the Candelaria Health Center.[119] A 1964 study estimated that there were, nationwide, 136.1 abortions per 1,000 births, or about one abortion for every six live births. Of the total number of abortions (117,401), induced abortions were estimated to account for 56 percent, resulting in a figure of 76 induced abortions per 1,000 live births.[120] A 1964 survey of the city of Cali found that there were 8,981 births and 1,303 abortions (spontaneous and induced), an abortion rate of 14.5 percent.[121] A Bogotá study carried out in the mid-1960s of 100 cases of provoked abortion found that the women involved had had an average of 2.1 previous induced abortions, that 43 of the 100 had required hospitalization, that the *sonda* was used in 79 percent of cases, that 30 percent of the women had had three or more previous abortions, and that the average number of living children among the 100 women was 5.3.[122]

For the year 1965 in Bogotá, there were 280,671 recorded births and 56,438 hospitalized abortion cases (spontaneous and induced), a ratio of one abortion for every five live births. A national study of available data for a period of one year (1965–1966) showed 117,401 hospitalized abortion cases, or one abortion for every 6.4 live births (a rate of 135.6 abortions for every 1,000 pregnancies).[123] The same study presented a more detailed survey of 123 women treated for abortion at the San Ignacio Hospital in Bogotá. Of this number, 102 had spontaneous abortions and 21, provoked abortions. Of those admitting provoked abortion, only 14.3 percent had been performed by doctors, with 19 percent being performed by nurses or midwives and 66.7 percent by "others"; the *sonda* was the main instrument employed to effect the abortion.

The social reality behind these figures has been graphically summarized in the Candelaria study, which begins with a description of Colombia as a whole:

low per capita income which is ten to fifteen times less than in many other countries; a constant increase in the cost of living, amounting to 190% in the last ten years; rising unemployment, with, at present, 190,000 men being added annually to the labor force, of whom 75% are illiterate or have had only one or two years of primary school; a housing deficit (estimated at 800,000) which is mounting by 50,000 dwellings each year. The repercussions on the social structure are equally grave; inadequate educational facilities (only 20% of Colombians finish primary school and only 3% finish secondary school); a national ratio of one doctor per 2,400 inhabitants and one nurse for every 16,000.[124]

One is hardly surprised, then, to find that in Candelaria, a town which epitomizes the more general Colombian problems, 79 percent of the women surveyed reported that the having of one additional child "would present an insuperable economic problem." Nor can one be surprised by the frequency of a resort to illegal abortion (cited above) or to "masked infanticide":

> The other solution to the mother's problems is the death of the child ("masked infanticide") in which children between six months and four years of age are often allowed to die when attacked by any disease, particularly diarrhea. We have even seen mothers who objected to their children being treated and, in the same vein, were upset when curative measures were successful.[125]

MEXICO

While the socioeconomic situation of Mexico presents a somewhat less desperate picture than that of Colombia, it is nevertheless a nation with serious economic, educational and demographic problems. As of 1968, the Mexican birthrate was 44.1 per 1,000 (over twice that of the United States), the illiteracy rate for those over fifteen years of age was about 30 percent to 35 percent, the rate of population growth was 3.5 percent per year and the infant mortality rate was 60.7 per 1,000 live births.[126] While there are no solid, nationwide figures on the annual number of illegal abortions, the most common estimates place the figure at 300,000–600,000 (out of a population of 48 million). Unlike a number of Latin American countries, it is reportedly not easy even for a wealthy woman to procure a safe abortion, i.e., one performed by a trained gynecologist, although comparatively unsafe illegal abortions are more readily available, usually performed by midwives. Juarez and Tijuana for a time enjoyed a reputation as places where American women could, by just stepping across the Mexican-American border, procure illegal abortions.[127]

As for the extent to which Mexican women resort to illegal abortions, the data are scant, though strengthened by a number of studies in the Mexico City area. One random sample of 1,000 Mexican women during the early 1960s found that 307 admitted having at least one abortion

(30.7 percent) and a total, among them all, of 797 admitted induced abortions.[128] Generally speaking, other abortion surveys in Mexico, particularly in Mexico City, have resulted in much lower figures. A careful survey of 500 women in one quasi-suburban area of Mexico City, who, among them, had given birth to 2,552 living children, found that of the admitted abortions 245 had been spontaneous (95.7 percent) while only 11 (4.3 percent) reported provoked abortions. The authors of the study, however, believe that some reservations are in order about the low rate of provoked abortions since they discovered a general fear among those surveyed to admit illegal abortions.[129] A 1967 survey of 1,734 women in Mexico City covered by the Mexican Social Security Program revealed a total of 6,200 pregnancies. Of this number, 492 women declared abortions, mainly spontaneous, with 5 percent of the women admitting provoked abortions. Of those who did admit a history of provoked abortions, they averaged 1.3 provoked abortions each. Of the total of 6,200 reported pregnancies, 1.5 percent had ended in provoked abortion (again, a figure which may have been lower than the actual number).[130] From May 1961 to May 1968, the Social Security Hospital #2 in Mexico City treated a total of 120,710 pregnant women, an average of 17,244 a year. During this seven-year period a total of 19,544 abortion cases were treated, with an annual average of 2,792. Of this number, about 13.4 percent were treated for septic abortion (believed to be mainly criminal abortions).[131] A study by Dr. José Luis Pérez de Salazar covering the period of June 1964 through May 1966, conducted at the Social Security Hospital #3 in Mexico City, recorded 31,745 live births and 7,231 abortions (spontaneous and induced, with an estimated 10 percent to 15 percent induced) for a ratio of one abortion for every four live births. Abortion cases accounted for a significant number of recorded maternal deaths in the hospital. Deaths from induced abortion are the leading cause of maternal deaths in the three Social Security hospitals.[132]

In 1965, Dr. Manuel Mateos Fournier studied 596 women hospitalized for abortion in both Social Security hospitals and public-welfare hospitals. Of this number, 53 percent were hospitalized for spontaneous abortions (316) and 47 percent for provoked abortions (280). Of the latter group, the largest number were found in the thirty to thirty-nine age group (124), with the second largest number in the twenty to twenty-nine age group; only ten of the entire group were age nineteen or younger. Moreover, the overwhelming majority of the women were married (238 out of 280) and were occupied as housewives (56 percent); nearly 40 percent of the women had five or more children, though those with three or fewer children accounted for 42 percent of the total.[133] The same study reported the results of a 1965 survey conducted among doctors working in private practice. Among their patients there had been 5,901 births and 2,086 abortions. Of the abortions, 1,110 were provoked and 976 were spontaneous. Among those women who had provoked abortions, 34 percent reported their main reason to be an excessive number of children, 27 percent gave their reason as a bad economic situation, and 23 percent attributed their resorting to abortion to living alone. Of the group of women reporting provoked abortions, 17.39 percent of the abortions had been performed by doctors, 13.06 percent, by nurses and midwives, and 69.55 percent had been caused by the use of *sondas*, caustics and other kinds of amateurish methods.[134] Of the women admitting to induced abortion, 84 percent stated they were Catholic and 16 percent "other."

One of the most thorough Mexican studies of women resorting to induced abortion has been provided by an analysis of 1,059 women taking part in an abortion-prevention program being conducted by the Department of Preventive Medicine of the Mexican Institute of Social Security. This program, working through the three large gynecological hospitals of the Social Security system in Mexico City, aims at the reduction of induced abortion by a systematic program of contraception information and free contraceptive material. At present it is limited to women who have had at least three children or two induced abortions. Relying primarily on the anovulatory pill and a system of monthly consultations, the program has been, so far, remarkably successful. Of approximately 1,000 women taking part in the program from February 1967 to September 1968 (the latest date for which figures are available) there were only 42 pregnancies and three induced abortions (out of 10,000 menstrual cycles).

These figures are all the more impressive when one considers the medical history of the 1,059 women who have taken part in the program.[135] Of the 1,059 women, 516 (48.7 percent) had two previous abortions, 222 (21.0 percent) had three and 102 (19.5 percent) had four or more. Among the 1,059 women there was a total of 2,841 induced abortions, for an average of 2.7 abortions per woman; 29.5 percent of all their pregnancies had ended in induced abortion. As for the education of the women: 1–2 years of primary school: 31.0 percent; 3–5 years of primary school: 20.6 percent; complete primary education: 20.5 percent. The remainder of the women were either totally uneducated (10.6 percent) or had a few years of secondary education; 71 percent of the women were housewives, while the remainder worked outside of the home in some capacity. Together, the 1,059 women had a total of 9,654 pregnancies, an average of 9.1 per woman. (In the Salazar study, abortion was found to be much more common among women having five or six children than in a comparison group of women with fewer children, all of whose pregnancies had gone to term.) [136] In their religious affiliation, 98 percent of the women identified themselves as Catholics, with 30 percent attending Mass at least once a month (the remainder only occasionally). Of the reasons given for procuring an abortion, 53.9 percent of the women gave reduced income as their motive; 20 percent, an excessive number of children; with the remainder, a variety of different reasons. Of the methods used to induce the abortions 50.9 percent were performed by doctors or paramedical personnel (primarily the latter) using standard techniques, 25.6 percent were induced by "popular remedies," 17.2 percent by use of a *sonda,* and the rest by other methods. Unfortunately, no information is provided on attempts at contraception by this group of women prior to their participation in the abortion-prevention program.

A widespread lack of knowledge of effective contraceptive methods is believed, by many Mexican observers, to lie behind the frequent employment of induced abortion as a method of birth control. Though the pill can be bought without prescription in Mexico, knowledge of its correct use is apparently limited even among those who know of its existence (and many do not). In the Cándano study, 71 percent of the 500 women surveyed had no knowledge at all of contraception techniques; of the remainder of the women, 24 percent knew of the pill, 0.8 percent had knowledge of diaphragms and 0.4 percent knew of intrauterine devices. Despite this lack of knowledge, 88.2 percent of the women accepted the idea of controlling fecundity and 84.2 wanted, in fact, no more children.[137] The discrepancy between their desires and their knowledge is obvious here, the kind of discrepancy which leads Mexican observers to place such a strong stress on the importance of contraception as the most likely method of reducing the illegal abortion rate. Luis L. Otero, in his study of 5,000 Mexican couples, found that 71 percent of the husbands had given no thought prior to marriage to the ideal number of children their marriages might produce; only 14 percent thought it would be a good idea to begin birth limitation from the outset of marriage. Otero believes that these figures give a good picture of the lack of foresight and family planning, and he hypothesizes that induced abortion is most likely to be employed later in a marriage when birth limitation is desired but not planned for and contraceptively implemented.[138]

At present, there exist no important movements to liberalize the Mexican abortion laws; at most, scattered individuals would like to see this happen sometime in the future. For the present, the main emphasis is in the direction of contraception programs. Yet, while the present law itself is strict, prosecutions for illegal abortion are rare. As for public attitudes toward abortion, little information is available. While induced abortions are obviously resorted to on a significant scale, there seems to be no public clamor for a liberalization of the present law. Otero, who in his survey asked his respondents under what conditions they would find abortion acceptable, found that these conditions would be few: 35.8

percent would find abortion acceptable in cases of danger to the life of the mother (while 63.4 percent would not), and 30.1 percent in cases of a possibly deformed child (while 68.7 percent would not). The acceptability of abortion in instances of rape, poverty and a desire for no more children was negligible, ranging between 2 percent and 5 percent of the respondents.[139]

CHILE

Of all the Latin American countries, the best information comes from Chile, a country notable in our context for its nascent government-sponsored family-planning program and for the quality of its abortion studies. In comparison with Mexico, for instance, it has a much smaller population (about nine million), a considerably more liberal Catholic hierarchy, a significantly lower birthrate (29.2 per 1,000 as contrasted with Mexico's 44 per 1,000), a higher per capita income, a lower illiteracy rate; at the same time, it has a higher infant mortality rate (107.1 per 1,000 live births).[140] It also has, undeniably, a very serious and recognized illegal abortion problem. A 1959 survey of 2,000 women, undertaken by the National Association of Family Protection, found that the ratio of abortions to live births was one to three for married women and slightly over two to three for estranged or common-law wives. In addition, in one out of five pregnancies which went to term, abortion had been contemplated.[141] "We also know," Hernán Romero wrote, "that cases of complicated and incomplete abortion which come to the hospital for treatment make up 8.1% of all admissions and add up to 67 for every 100 deliveries. . . . Those admissions increased from 12,963 in 1937 to 57,368 in 1960 (they multiplied 4.4 times as against 1.8 for deliveries). . . . In 1963 abortions were responsible for 39% of maternal mortality."[142] Romero also pointed out that "abortion is now the most popular method of fertility control for people who are ignorant of other methods or who have no other means at their disposal or whose motivations are weak."[143] Mariano B. Requeña, in an early 1960s study of Santiago, found that 23.2 percent of all pregnancies ended in induced abortions. He also found a direct correlation between abortion and female employment, unemployed fathers and prolonged residence in large cities. The rate of induced abortion was significantly higher for practicing Catholics than for other groups (e.g., nominal Catholics and Protestants).[144]

A carefully drawn urban sample of 1,890 Santiago women, surveyed in 1962 by Armijo and Monreal, discovered a total of 496 women with an admitted history of provoked abortion, 29.2 percent of all the women surveyed. This group had, among them, a total of 1,394 admitted provoked abortions, with an average of 2.8 each. The highest number were found in the twenty-five to twenty-nine age group, with the twenty to twenty-four age group the next highest. Significantly, the authors noted, "seventy-seven percent of the provoked abortions were concentrated in women who had three or fewer children alive, including five percent who had no children. There is a common trend among obstetricians to stress education and help, even sterilization, for women who have a large number of children. Meantime, very little or no attention is paid to women who have fewer than four children, precisely those who, according to these findings, are contributing the bulk of provoked abortions."[145] Only 11.5 percent of the abortions had been induced by doctors, with 50.3 percent induced by graduate midwives, 27.3 percent by amateur midwives, and 11 percent by the women themselves. The insertion of a rubber tube into the cervix was the most popular method of inducing abortion (46 percent). Of the reasons given for the abortions, 56.5 percent gave an economic motive, while the rest were distributed among such motives as marital problems, unmarried motherhood, large family, health and some (5 percent) because they did not want any children at all. While some 74 percent of the women favored family planning, fewer than two-fifths were using some method of contraception, and then, mainly, an unreliable method at that. A direct relationship was found between social bracket and use of contraceptives; the higher the social class, the greater the use of contraceptives. Extrapolating from their sample of 1,890 women, the authors arrived at a figure of 17,483 provoked abortions in Santiago for 1962.[146]

The hazards of illegal abortion are underscored by another Armijo and Monreal study. Analyzing 1,322 cases of provoked abortion, they found that 31.6 percent of them required hospitalization.[147] The strain upon hospital facilities in Santiago as a result of women injured from illegal abortions provides a concrete instance of the seriousness of the problem. In 1937 there were 153,354 births in these hospitals and 12,963 women hospitalized for abortion complications, 60 percent to 70 percent the result of illegal abortions. By 1964 these figures had risen to 275,323 live births and 56,391 abortions (60 percent to 70 percent induced) or 20.4 abortions per 100 live births.[148] Onofre Avendaño, Chief of the Maternity Section of the Baros Luco Hospital in Santiago, estimates that in 1968 there was a total of 140,000 abortions in Chile, with about two-thirds of these induced, i.e., about 95,000 illegal abortions in that year. Between 1961 and 1967 there were an average of 21,000 cases per year treated in the hospitals of Santiago (spontaneous and induced).[149] In San Salvador Hospital, the largest in Santiago, abortion accounts for 50 percent of the maternal mortality rate; 50 beds in the maternity section of the hospital are reserved solely for abortion cases.[150] The statistical division of the San Salvador Hospital has recorded the following figures on hospitalized abortion cases there: 1964: 3,484 abortions (septic, 1,747; nonseptic, 1,737), and 13,871 live births; 1965: 4,855 abortions (septic, 2,759; nonseptic, 2,096), and 14,058 live births; 1966: 5,304 abortions (septic, 2,971; nonseptic, 2,333) and 13,213 live births; 1967: 5,409 abortions (septic, 3,595; nonseptic, 1,814) and 12,495 total births. The mortality figures for the same year in this hospital are as follows: 1964: 14 deaths (perfringens, 9; sepsis, 4; septic shock, 1; other, 1); 1965: 17 deaths (perfringens, 7: uterine gangrene, 1; anemia, 1; sepsis, 7); 1966: 18 deaths (perfringens, 11; sepsis, 1; peritonitis, 2; uterine gangrene, 1; septic shock, 1; other, 2); 1967: 15 deaths (perfringens, 6; sepsis, 2; septic shock, 4; peritonitis, 3). A good number of these mortal injuries are attributed to the *sonda*, while the high incidence of perfringens is believed to be caused in particular by a vegetable compound, *perejil*, which is inserted into the uterus as an abortifacient.[151]

A considerable number of women who resort to induced abortion in Chile are repeaters. Mariano Requena, analyzing 2,617 pregnancies in a group of women who had employed induced abortion, found that the greater the number of previous abortions, the greater the chances for another one:

TABLE 3

PROBABILITY OF ABORTION IN RELATIONSHIP TO PREVIOUS ABORTIONS

Previous abortions	No. of pregnancies	% of induced abortion
0	1,817	11.5
1	336	39.0
2	183	45.5
3	93	49.5
4	43	55.8
5	26	69.2
6 or more	119	86.6
	2,617	23.1

Thus a woman who has had one induced abortion has a 39.0 percent chance of having another, and a woman with four previous abortions has a 55.8 percent chance of having still another.[152] As discovered in other parts of the world, when a woman has successfully turned to induced abortion as a method of birth control and lacks knowledge about or is not motivated to use contraception, a pattern of induced abortion is frequently established.

The extent of the Chilean illegal-abortion problem requires no further elaboration here. Of great importance, however, are the steps being taken in Chile to reduce it. As in Mexico, one can find scattered individuals who would like to see the Chilean abortion laws liberalized, but there is nothing approaching an organized movement toward this end. The entire emphasis of the government family-planning program, the most advanced of its kind in Latin America, is on the reduction of illegal abortions by the promotion of contraception as an alternative. Though the program is relatively new and still reaches only a small proportion of the population, the early results help to throw some light on a question which has arisen elsewhere in ths book: can an educational and contraception program succeed in reducing the incidence of provoked abortions?

The Chilean program began informally in the early 1960s, spurred by a number of studies which made clear the extent of the illegal abortion problem. A 1962 meeting called by the Director General of the National Health Service and involving professors of obstetrics, gynecology, public health and preventive medicine, led eventually to the initiation, in 1963, of a prevention program under the auspices of the Chilean Association for the Protection of the Family. The general objectives of the program at that time were the prevention of induced abortion, the reduction of maternal mortality and the establishment of the right of women to plan their families. In 1965 the Chilean government began to take a more direct part in the program and, by 1967, the activities of the Association for the Protection of the Family were formally incorporated into the maternal-infant activities of the National Health Service. Culturally and politically, there were a number of background ingredients which made the development of a government program possible: a long tradition of separation between church and state, a liberal Catholic hierarchy which posed no religious obstacles, a strong tradition of democratic freedom of choice and conscience, a recent history of informal family-planning programs and a strong impetus among the Chilean population toward family planning.

In 1968, the official goals of the government program were stated: (1) a diminution of the maternal mortality, particularly that mortality resulting from provoked abortion; (2) reduction of the cases of infant mortality, an important determinant of the level of well-being of a significant part of the population; (3) promotion of the well-being of the family, a goal which is assisted by responsible parenthood and the establishment of the right of conscientious parenthood.[153] In 1968 the aim of the program was to reach 15 percent of the fertile female population, with priority being given to women treated for abortion in the National Health Service hospitals, women with a large number of children, women in poor health and women with severe socioeconomic problems. Women eligible for the program receive free contraceptive devices and take part in an educational program.[154] In the government program intrauterine devices and the anovulatory pill are the primary methods used. By the end of 1967, a total of 99,345 women were taking part in the program; of this number, 76,551 were using intrauterine devices and 22,794 were taking the anovulatory pill; a total of 242,513 consultations were recorded.[155]

How successful has the program been? In general, it is widely believed in Chile that the program helps account for a steady decline in the birthrate. In 1962, there were 289,758 births, a birthrate of 36.1 per 1,000 population. In 1964, live births rose to an all-time high, with 298,980 birth recorded, a birthrate of 35.4 per 1,000. Beginning in 1965, however, both the number of live births and the birthrate began to decline; in that year there were 294,397 live births and a birthrate of 34.1. In 1966 there were 283,619 births and a 31.9 birthrate. By 1967 the births and birthrates had dipped even lower: 265,637 births and a 29.2 birthrate.[156] Figures like these are often cited as an index of the success of the program in reducing the birthrate. It is also pointed out that the relative stability of the abortion admissions to Santiago National Health Service Hospitals in recent years (a persistent 21,000 or so), despite an annual growth in the Santiago population of 2½ percent per year, provides another index of the likely success of the program in reducing provoked abortions in proportion to pregnancies.

However, while the belief that the program has been helpful in reducing the birthrate has not been challenged, Tequalda Monreal and Rolando Armijo have, in an important study,[157] argued persuasively that the abortion rate has actually risen (at least in Santiago) since the inauguration of the program. Using the year 1962 as a base, they show that there has been an important drop in the Santiago fertility rate, with a decline of 19.7 percent between 1962 and 1967; they calculate that, since the beginning of the program (through 1967), a total of 16,097 births had been prevented, a figure which takes account both of the effect of the program itself as well as concurrent private action. Thus, insofar as the government program was intended to reduce fertility, they judge that it has been successful. However, in light of the intention of the program to reduce the abortion rate, they come to a different judgment. In their earlier (1962) survey of Santiago women, a total of 1,890 women were interviewed. In 1967, making some methodological changes in light of the population increases, 2,425 women were interviewed, the aim being again to achieve a comparable representative sample. With this latter sample in hand, they discovered that, while there had been only a 4.9 percent drop in the fecundity rate (number of pregnancies), there had been a 13.8 percent drop in the fertility rate (the number of births). But they also discovered that there had been a 15.1 percent increase for all abortions and 25.8 percent increase for induced abortions. From these figures they conclude that "it is obvious that the observed fall in fertility must be due not only to prevention of pregnancies but to an increase in abortions, a very significant fact if it is remembered that one of the most important objectives of the family planning program is the prevention of induced abortion."[158] Significantly, it was found that, while the greatest drop in the fertility rate appeared in women from the lowest socioeconomic groups (from 276.8 per 1,000 to 185.5 per 1,000), that same group showed the greatest increase in the induced-abortion rate (from 48.8 per 1,000 to 75.3 per 1,000). They also found that there was a notable increase in the frequency of induced abortion among widows, divorcees and the unmarried (up to 80 percent), leading the authors to observe, "It is probable that in these groups, more than in the others, the failure of contraceptives leads to abortion and this may be the reason for this increase."[159] The general increase in the abortion rate took place despite the fact that 19.6 percent more women were employing contraceptives in the 1967 sample than in the 1962 sample. Moreover, while only 10 percent of the 1962 group were using an effective method of contraception (the IUD and sterilization at that time), 75 percent of the 1967 group were using effective methods (oral pills, IUDs and sterilization). Significantly also, they discovered, from the same 1967 sample, that of the evolution of 474 pregnancies of 1,502 women making use of contraception, 46.10 percent of these pregnancies had ended in a birth while 39.87 percent had ended in induced abortion. Finally, they note that, of the births prevented by the family-planning program, only about 50 percent could be attributed to the prevention of conception; the other 50 percent reduction is attributable to induced abortion.

From these figures, and others in the study, Monreal and Armijo conclude that the government program has not succeeded in reducing the incidence of abortion; instead, it has increased it. However, far from judging the program a failure because of this increase, they argue that it shows, particularly among the poorer classes, "an awakening to the necessity for limiting the family."[160] It is this "awakening" (as instanced by an increase, for instance, in the use of contraceptives by the poorer women) which accounts for the increasing resort to induced abortion when contraception fails. Thus, while the increased abortion rate can be taken to indicate a failure to achieve the government's intention to reduce the abortion rate, that very failure can be taken as a sign that it is succeeding in its aim of alerting women to the need for family planning. Monreal and Armijo speak here of a "first" and "second" stage in the development of a family-planning awareness. During the first stage, abortion will take an important place in the reduction of fertility, especially because of contraceptive failures among marginal social groups making use of contraceptives for the first time. In the second stage, apparent in the higher classes, contraceptives will be used more effectively, with a corresponding drop in the abortion rate (a theory substantiated by their finding of a significant decline in the abortion rate for the highest socioeconomic group). At the end, the authors say "that the increase of abortion registered should not be considered as a failure of the program. This increase shows that what has been done with the program is still insufficient and that the desired useful levels have not been reached. When these levels are reached, it will mean that abortion as a method of control has been replaced in a high proportion by contraceptives." [161] They also add that, since a high proportion of women experiencing contraceptive failure turn to illegal abortion, induced abortion should be included in the birth-prevention programs, especially for those women experiencing a contraceptive failure.[162]

Considerably more success in reducing the induced-abortion rate by means of education and contraception has, however, been reported in one section of Santiago as the result of a special, experimental program. The section is called San Gregorio and it has a stable population of about 32,000 people, primarily laborers. Beginning in 1964 an intensive contraception program was pressed there, aiming both at a reduction of fertility and of induced abortion. At the outset of the program it was found that the birthrate in this group was 46 per 1,000, with an abortion rate of 20 per 1,000. Though 90 percent of the women declared themselves to be Catholic, 88 percent stated, at the outset, that they would be willing to use contraceptives. By the end of 1967, when a survey was taken of 20 percent of the dwellings to discern the female pregnancy history of the San Gregorio population, it was found that there had been a reduction in the fertility rate of 19.4 percent and a reduction in the abortion rate (spontaneous and induced) of 39.4 percent.[163] Thus the success in reducing the abortion rate was even greater than the success in reducing the fertility rate. In 1964 it was estimated that one-third of all pregnancies in the San Gregorio area ended in an abortion; by 1966 a little over one-fourth of the pregnancies were thus ended. In particular it is believed that the 39.4 percent reduction in all abortions actually represents a significantly greater reduction in the illegal abortion rate than in the spontaneous abortion rate (which, in 1964, was estimated to represent 47 percent of all abortions in the area). Particularly striking success was found in reducing the fertility rate of those women with five or more children, an important element since the children of those women accounted for a disproportionate share of the infant-mortality rate. It has been an expensive program, however, aided by money from American foundations; whether its success can be duplicated, less expensively, on a larger scale is not certain.

While there exists no formal movement to legalize abortion in Chile or to modify the present laws, and only scattered individuals seem publicly to support such a development (e.g., Armijo and Monreal), it is nonetheless clear from the high Chilean abortion rates that resistance to illegal abortion is not intense; obviously, many women make use of illegal abortion to control birth. The available studies on Chilean attitudes toward abortion, however, present a somewhat confusing picture. Armijo and Monreal found in their 1962 survey in Santiago that 71.3

percent of their sample of 1,890 women were "openly in favor of legaliza-tion of abortion." [164] A survey conducted among obstetricians and gyne-cologists in five Santiago hospitals found considerably less acceptance of abortion. When asked their opinion on what political methods they would recommend for the control of illegal abortion, 65 percent of the 203 doctors questioned favored a massive contraceptive program but only 14 percent favored the legalization of abortion.[165] Significant differ-ences, however, were found among those who identified themselves as Catholics and those who described themselves as nonreligious. Only 18 percent of the Catholics favored legalization of abortion while 48 percent of the nonreligious expressed a favorable attitude.[166]

Another study, involving a sample of lay Catholics and lay Catholic leaders throughout Chile, found that 24.1 percent of the surveyed lay leaders would approve abortion in cases of danger to the life of the mother, while another 17.6 percent would do so with some reservations. Only 19.9 percent of the laymen sample would approve abortion under those circumstances, though another 26.4 percent would do so with reservations. However, in the case of abortion on the grounds of poverty, 25.0 percent of the lay leaders expressed a favorable attitude, while an-other 71.4 percent were favorable with reservations. Abortion on these grounds was also favorably viewed by 31 percent of the laymen sample and by another 41.1 percent with reservations. On the grounds of abor-tion in case of illness or weakness, 26.2 percent of the lay leaders would accept such abortions, with another 29.4 percent favorable with reserva-tions. Among the laymen sampled, 25.9 percent would accept abortion on these grounds, with another 23.3 percent willing to accept it with reservations.[167] Taken together, these three surveys, though inconclusive, would suggest that lay Catholics and lay Catholic leaders are consider-ably more willing to entertain the possibility of legal abortions under some circumstances than the Catholic doctors of Santiago. In comparison with identical surveys undertaken in Brazil, Colombia, Mexico and Vene-zuela, the FERES study showed Chilean laymen and lay leaders to be consistently more favorable toward abortion than their peers in the other countries (though, oddly enough, they were less favorable toward the idea of family planning than almost any other country).

Some General Patterns

As mentioned at the outset of this section, it is hazardous to make gen-eralizations about "abortion in Latin America." There exist too little data on many of the countries, the available studies of individual coun-tries often vary in character and scope, and, in any event, there are enough differences, cultural and economic, among the countries to make

generalizations suspect. However, there does exist at least one sophisticated attempt to compare abortion patterns in a number of different
Latin-American countries. Mariano Requena, utilizing standardized data
from the Urban Comparative Fertility Survey undertaken in 1964 in
several Latin-American cities by the Latin American Demographic Centre (CELADE), achieved some noteworthy results. The cities dealt with
were Mexico City, Bogotá, San José, Caracas, Panama City, Rio de
Janeiro and Buenos Aires.[168] In what follows I will summarize some of
his major findings.

PREVALENCE OF ABORTION [169]

The proportion of women using both contraception and abortion
was approximately the same in each city, but the proportion of women
who used neither abortion nor contraception, and the proportion of
women using abortion only, directly correlated with the average
number of live births; the proportion of women using contraceptives,
however, showed an inverse correlation. Thus Mexico City with an
average of 3.3 live births per woman (the highest of all the cities),
had the highest proportion of women who did not use contraceptives or abortion as well as the highest proportion of women who had
employed abortion. At the other extreme, Buenos Aires, with an average
of 1.5 births per woman, had the lowest proportion of women who did
not use either contraceptives or abortion; it also had the lowest proportion of women with abortions. At the same time, Mexico City had the
lowest proportion of contraceptors and Buenos Aires, the highest. Requena also points out that use of abortion continued even in areas of
high contraception usage. Moreover, he shows that there is an inverse
relationship between pregnancy rates and the incidence of abortion: the
greater the probability of getting pregnant (e.g., in Mexico City), the
lower the abortion rate per 1,000 pregnant women. Hence, in those
cities with a larger number of pregnancies per woman, a smaller proportion of these pregnancies end in abortion than in cities where contraception is more widely used.

From his data, though, Requena also notes that the use of contraception directly correlates with an increased incidence of abortion, attributing the determining factor here to the motivation to control fertility.
While there is, for instance, a considerably higher abortion rate per 1,000
woman-years (the product of the abortion rate per 1,000 pregnant women
and the pregnancy rate) in Mexico City than in Buenos Aires, the
abortion rate per 1,000 pregnant women is considerably higher in Buenos
Aires. In short, while the percentage of all (nonsingle) women using
induced abortion only is higher in Mexico City than in Buenos Aires, the

abortion rate per 1,000 pregnant women is considerably higher in Buenos Aires. One of Requena's tables is particularly helpful in making these relationships clear:

TABLE 4

ABORTION IN LATIN AMERICAN CITIES

CITY	Children per woman*	Abortion rate per 1,000 woman-years	Abortion rate per 1,000 pregnant women	Pregnancy rate per 1,000 woman-years	Live births per 1,000 woman-years
Mexico City	3.3	37	155	237	201
Bogotá	3.2	26	117	226	200
San José	3.0	33	161	207	173
Caracas	3.0	34	163	207	173
Panama	2.7	24	211	186	162
Rio de Janeiro	2.3	21	141	147	126
Buenos Aires	1.5	21	246	84	63

* Married or in consensual unions

Thus Requena sums up this section by saying that "the higher the fertility the higher is the rate of abortions (per 1,000 woman-years). . . . This phenomenon is largely the result of the higher fertility, and not of an increase in the abortion rate per 1,000 pregnant women which, in fact, declines with increases in the number of pregnancies per woman." [170]

SOCIOECONOMIC LEVELS

From the CELADE data Requena found that the incidence of abortion was highest among women at the medium socioeconomic level. As for the relationship between live births, use of effective contraception and use of induced abortion, Requena found:

Women in the lowest socioeconomic-cultural stratum have a high birthrate, have few abortions, and make practically no use of contraception. The medium stratum has an intermediate birthrate, uses abortion more frequently, and begins to intensify the use of contraception. Finally, the highest stratum has the lowest birthrate and has fewer abortions, with contraception becoming the most important factor. [171]

Requena here cites in particular one Colombian study which found exactly this kind of correlation, and he adds that the relationship between educational level and abortions in a number of the cities substantiates further the correlation. [172] Significantly, Requena found that the incidence of abortion is related to the duration of residence in rural and urban areas, with the higher incidence in the urban areas. He gives Santiago as an example, pointing out that those women who had lived in the city for more than ten years had a higher risk of induced abortion than those who had lived there for a shorter period.[173]

ADDITIONAL FINDINGS

Going beyond the CELADE data, Requena notes (from his own experience and the Latin American literature): (*a*) the incidence of abortion is greatest in the middle age groups, twenty to thirty-nine; (*b*) since the risk of pregnancy is greater among married than single women, and when the criterion of measurement is the number of pregnancies, single women have as many abortions as married women; (*c*) that, so far as abortion is concerned, "formal adherence to the Catholic Church is not the decisive factor, but the degree of religiosity must be ascertained." [174] Requena adds that cautionary note about "religiosity" because he is aware of some studies which show that, in some places, the incidence of induced-abortion rate is somewhat lower among Catholic women than among nonreligious women (though not so low as that among women adhering to a non-Catholic religion).[175] He also speculates, as do Armijo and Monreal, that while the maximum incidence of abortion is now found in the middle socioeconomic groups, it will probably shift to the lower classes:

> Once the lower stratum is made aware of a need for and possibility of family planning, it will resort first to induced abortion. The desire for abortion does not imply the automatic adoption of contraception. . . . Furthermore, the practice of contraception among inexperienced people is likely to be irregular or unskilled, and it is likely that they will abandon their contraceptive practices more frequently in the early stage of its adoption (thus turning to abortion as a "curative" for unwanted pregnancy). Although the middle classes may increase the use of contraception and reduce the use of induced abortions, the total number of induced abortions will probably increase because the lowest socioeconomic group is larger than the middle group.[176]

What remains unexplained is the variation among the different countries in Latin America in both the incidence of abortion and the use of contraceptives. Certain salient pieces of data, however, strike the eye. Argentina, for instance, has a reputation in Latin America for the ease with which illegal abortions may be obtained, abortions performed by doctors.[177] This information is, of course, consistent with Mariano Requena's finding of a low birthrate and a high rate of abortion (per 1,000 pregnant women) in Buenos Aires. Also striking is that the illiteracy rate (5 percent to 8 percent of those fifteen and over) and the birth rate (21.5) are among the lowest in Latin America, and the per capita income one of the highest. In short, as a literate, comparatively prosperous country, the pattern of birth limitation in Argentina is closer to the North American–European pattern than it is to the Latin-American pattern: prosperity, literacy, a strong motivation toward family limitation, an availability of abortion and contraception (despite restrictive laws) and, most critically, the successful use of these means in limiting births. Uruguay presents a similar, if slightly less pronounced pattern. Its birth-rate is comparatively low (23–25 per 1,000), as is its illiteracy rate (8 percent to 10 percent of those fifteen and over); again, like Argentina, it has a reputation for the availability of safe illegal abortions. According to one recent report, there are three abortions for each live birth in Uruguay and the overall abortion rate is six times greater today than in 1956.[178] In both Argentina and Uruguay, unlike Latin America generally, doctors are reported to perform a high proportion of the illegal abortions.[179] The data are inadequate here to formulate iron-clad laws. However, it seems safe to speculate that, as economic development progresses in Latin America, other countries are likely to begin displaying the pattern of Argentina and Uruguay; hence one may expect not only more abortions, but perhaps also a greater participation on the part of the medical profession in illegal abortions and more openness in ignoring the laws.

NOTES

1. Robert F. Drinan, S.J., "The Inviolability of the Right to Be Born," in David T. Smith (ed.), *Abortion and the Law* (Cleveland: Western Reserve University, 1967), p. 123.
2. *Ibid.*, p. 122.
3. Norman St. John-Stevas, *The Right to Life* (New York: Holt, Rinehart and Winston, 1964), p. 10.
4. *Ibid.*, p. 35.
5. See, for instance, the survey of Robert F. Drinan, S.J., "Contemporary Protestant Thinking," *America*, 117 (December 9, 1967), pp. 713ff.; and Immanuel Jakobovits, "Jewish Views on Abortion," in *Abortion and the Law, op. cit.*, pp. 124ff.
6. Ralph B. Potter, Jr., "The Abortion Debate," in *The Religious Situation 1968* (Boston: Beacon Press, 1968), p. 123.
7. Alan F. Guttmacher, "Abortion—Yesterday, Today and Tomorrow," in Alan F. Guttmacher (ed.), *The Case for Legalized Abortion Now* (Berkeley: Diablo Press, 1967), p. 8; Alice S. Rossi, "Public Views on Abortion," *ibid.*, p. 27; André Hellegers, "Law and the Common Good," *Commonweal*, 86 (June 30, 1967), p. 421; Robert E. Cooke *et al.* (eds.), *The Terrible Choice: The Abortion Dilemma* (New York: Bantam Books, 1968), p. 41.
8. Christopher Tietze, "Therapeutic Abortions in the United States," *American Journal of Obstetrics and Gynecology*, 101 (July 15, 1968), p. 787.
9. K.-H. Mehlan (ed.), *Internationale Abortsituation Abortbekämpfung Antikonzeption* (Leipzig: George Thieme, 1961), pp. 5ff.
10. Kenneth R. Niswander, "Medical Abortion Practices in the United States," in *Abortion and the Law, op. cit.*, p. 59.

11. Harriet F. Pilpel, "The Abortion Crisis," in *The Case for Legalized Abortion Now, op. cit.,* pp. 101–02.
12. Lawrence Lader, *Abortion* (Indianapolis: Bobbs-Merrill, 1966), p. 3.
13. Marie E. Kopp, *Birth Control in Practice* (New York: R. M. McBride Co., 1934), Part II, pp. 47–78.
14. D. G. Wiehl and K. Berry, "Pregnancy Wastage in New York City," *Milbank Memorial Fund Quarterly,* 15 (July 1937), pp. 229–47.
15. Raymond Pearl, *The Natural History of Population* (London, 1939), pp. 222, 237; cited in Glanville Williams, *The Sanctity of Life and the Criminal Law* (London: Faber and Faber, 1958), p. 190.
16. F. J. Taussig, *Abortion, Spontaneous and Induced* (St. Louis: C. V. Mosby, 1936), pp. 387–88.
17. P. K. Whelpton and C. V. Kiser, "Social and Psychological Factors Affecting Fertility," *Milbank Memorial Fund Quarterly,* 22 (January 1944), pp. 72–105.
18. John McPartland, *Sex in Our Changing World* (London: Torchstream Books, 1947), p. 175.
19. Russell S. Fisher, "Criminal Abortion," in Harold Rosen (ed.), *Therapeutic Abortion* (New York: Julian Press, 1954), p. 6.
20. Williams, *op. cit.,* p. 191.
21. Alfred C. Kinsey, in Mary S. Calderone (ed.), *Abortion in the United States* (New York: Hoeber-Harper, 1958), pp. 54–55; see also P. H. Gebhard *et al., Pregnancy, Birth and Abortion* (New York: Hoeber-Harper, 1958).
22. In *Abortion in the United States, op. cit.,* p. 180.
23. Guttmacher, *op. cit.,* p. 8; Harold Rosen, "Psychiatric Implications of Abortion: A Case Study in Social Hypocrisy," in *Abortion and the Law, op. cit.,* pp. 90–91; Alice S. Rossi, in *The Case for Legalized Abortion Now, op. cit.,* p. 27; Jerome M. Kummer and Zad Leavy, "Criminal Abortion—A Consideration of Ways to Reduce Incidence," *California Medicine,* 95 (September 1961), p. 170.
24. Taussig, *op. cit.,* pp. 27–28, 361.
25. Fisher, *op. cit.,* pp. 8–9.
26. Kummer and Leavy, *op. cit.,* p. 170.
27. Theodore A. Montgomery, Arline Lewis, Marjorie Hammersly, "Maternal Deaths in California, 1957–1962," *California Medicine,* 100 (June 1964), p. 415.
28. Edwin M. Gold, Carl L. Erhardt, Harold Jacobziner, Frieda Nelson, "Therapeutic Abortions in New York City: A 20-Year Review," *American Journal of Public Health,* 55 (July 1965), p. 965.
29. Guttmacher, *op. cit.,* p. 9.
30. Niswander, *op. cit.,* pp. 37–38. Niswander's figures, however, do not include the total number of puerperal deaths, which has been declining; he shows only that the proportion of abortion deaths in the total number is increasing. Milton Helpern's figures (see note 31) would seem to take away even more of the force of this argument.
31. Milton Helpern, in *Abortion in the United States, op. cit.,* p. 68.
32. Christopher Tietze, "Abortion as a Cause of Death," *American Journal of Public Health,* 38 (October 1948), p. 1441; see also Christopher Tietze, "Some Facts About Legal Abortion," in Roy O. Greep (ed.), *Human Fertility and Population Problems* (Cambridge, Massachusetts: Schenkman, 1963), pp. 222–36.
33. Statement made at Harvard Divinity School–Kennedy Foundation International Conference on Abortion, Washington, D.C., September 1967.
34. Robert E. Cooke *et al.,* (eds.), *op. cit.,* p. 43.
35. André Hellegers, "A Doctor Looks at Abortion," Edward W. White Lecture, Georgetown University, March 16, 1966 (unpublished); a brief but incisive critique of the figures of Whelpton and Kiser, Wiehl and Berry and the findings of Kinsey's Institute for Sex Research can be found in the "Report of the Statistics Committee," in *Abortion in the United States, op. cit.,* pp. 179–80.

36. Jerome E. Bates and Edward S. Zawadzki, *Criminal Abortion: A Study in Medical Sociology* (Springfield, Illinois: Charles C. Thomas, 1964), p. 3.
37. Regine K. Stix, "A Study of Pregnancy Wastage," *Milbank Memorial Fund Quarterly*, 13 (October 1935), pp. 347–65.
38. Norbert J. Mietus, "The Therapeutic Abortion Act," privately printed paper, April 1967, pp. 4–5.
39. Herbert Ratner, "A Public Health Physician Views Abortion" *Child and Family*, 7 (Winter 1968), p. 39.
40. Alex Barno, "Criminal Abortion—Deaths and Suicides in Pregnancy in Minnesota, 1950–1964," *Minnesota Medicine*, 50 (January 1967), pp. 11–16.
41. Rosen, in *Abortion and the Law*, *op. cit.*, p. 89; see also Nancy Howell Lee, *The Search for an Abortionist* (Chicago: University of Chicago Press, 1969), especially pp. 59–77.
42. Guttmacher, *op. cit.*, p. 11.
43. Robert E. Hall, "Abortion in American Hospitals," *American Journal of Public Health*, 57 (November 1967), p. 1934.
44. Robert E. Hall, "Therapeutic Abortion, Sterilization, and Contraception," *American Journal of Obstetrics and Gynecology*," 91 (February 15, 1965), p. 519.
45. Niswander, *op. cit.*, p. 53.
46. Hall, "Therapeutic Abortion, Sterilization, and Contraception," *op. cit.*, p. 519.
47. K. P. Russell and J. G. Moore, "Maternal Medical Indications for Therapeutic Abortion," *Clinical Obstetrics and Gynecology*, 7 (March 1964), pp. 52–53.
48. Niswander, *op. cit.*, pp. 54–55.
49. Hall, "Abortion in American Hospitals," *op. cit.*, p. 1935.
50. Herbert L. Packer and Ralph J. Gampell, "Therapeutic Abortion: A Problem in Law and Medicine," in *The Case for Legalized Abortion Now*, *op. cit.*, p. 148.
51. Johan Eliot *et al.*, "Therapeutic Abortions in Teaching Hospitals in the United States and Canada," paper delivered at the International Conference on Abortion, Hot Springs, Virginia, November 17–20, 1968.
52. "California Abortions under the New Law," ASA [Association for the Study of Abortion] *Newsletter*, 4 (Spring 1969), p. 4.
53. Keith Monroe, "How California's Abortion Law Isn't Working," *The New York Times Magazine* (December 29, 1968), pp. 18–19. See also Edmund W. Overstreet, "Experience with California's New Therapeutic Abortion Law," paper delivered at the International Conference on Abortion, Hot Springs, Virginia, November 17–20, 1968; and H. C. Pulley, "Abortions—First Annual Report," *California Medicine*, 108 (May 1968), pp. 312–20.
54. W. Droegemueller, E. S. Taylor and V. E. Drose, "The First Year of Experience in Colorado with the New Abortion Law," *American Journal of Obstetrics and Gynecology*, 103 (March 1, 1969), p. 694. See also A. Heller and H. G. Whittington, "The Colorado Story: Denver General Hospital Experience with the Change in the Law on Therapeutic Abortion," *American Journal of Psychiatry*, 125 (December 1968), pp. 809–16.
55. "3 Baltimore Hospitals Curb Abortions," *The New York Times* (March 2, 1969).
56. Williams, *op. cit.*, pp. 144ff.
57. *Ibid.*, pp. 151ff; see also St. John-Stevas, *op. cit.*, p. 27.
58. The following sections, 1 and 4, of the British Abortion Act of 1967 are especially pertinent:
    "1. (1) Subject to the provisions of this section, a person shall not be guilty of an offense under the law relating to abortion when a pregnancy is terminated by a registered medical practitioner if two registered medical practitioners are of the opinion, formed in good faith—
        (a) That the continuance of the pregnancy would involve risk to the life of the pregnant woman, or of injury to the physical or mental health of the pregnant woman or any existing children of her family, greater than if the pregnancy were terminated; or

(*b*) that there is a substantial risk that if the child were born it would suffer from such physical or mental abnormalities as to be seriously handicapped.

"(2) In determining whether the continuance of a pregnancy would involve such risk of injury to health as is mentioned in paragraph (*a*) of subsection (1) of this section, account may be taken of the pregnant woman's actual or reasonably foreseeable environment.

"(3) Except as provided by subsection (4) of this section, any treatment for the termination of pregnancy must be carried out in a hospital vested in the Minister of Health or the Secretary of State under the National Health Service Acts, or in a place for the time being approved for the purposes of this section by the said Minister or the Secretary of State. . . ."

"4. (1) Subject to subsection (2) of this section, no person shall be under any duty, whether by contract or by any statutory or other legal requirement, to participate in any treatment authorized by this Act to which he has a conscientious objection:

"Provided that in any legal proceedings the burden of proof of conscientious objection shall rest on the person claiming to rely on it.

"(2) Nothing in subsection (1) of this section shall affect any duty to participate in treatment which is necessary to save the life or to prevent grave permanent injury to the physical or mental health of a pregnant woman."

59. Editorial, "Abortion, 1929–1952," *Journal of Sex Education,* 5 (September–October 1952), p. 34.
60. *Abortion: An Ethical Discussion* (London: Church Assembly Board for Social Responsibility, 1965), p. 7.
61. *Ibid.,* p. 19.
62. Williams, *op. cit.,* p. 192.
63. *Ibid.,* pp. 192, 194.
64. Eustace Chesser, "The Law of Abortion," *Medical World,* 72 (June 16, 1950), p. 495.
65. Cited in Williams, *op. cit.,* p. 192.
66. C. B. Goodhart, "The Frequency of Illegal Abortion," *The Eugenics Review,* 55 (January 1964), pp. 197–200.
67. Malcolm Potts, "Induced Abortion in the United Kingdom," unpublished paper, University of Chicago Conference on Abortion, Spring 1968, p. 1.
68. Keith Simpson, "Abortion Risks," in *Abortion in Britain,* Proceedings of the Conference on Abortion in Britain (London: Pitman, 1966), pp. 51–53.
69. Christopher Tietze, "Abortion in Europe," *American Journal of Public Health,* 57 (November 1967), p. 1925.
70. Editorial, *Newsletter,* Abortion Law Reform Association (ALRA), 22 (Autumn 1968).
71. Paul Ferris, *The Nameless: Abortion in Britain Today* (London: Hutchinson, 1966), pp. 42–46.
72. Peter L. C. Diggory, "Some Experiences with the New British Abortion Law," paper delivered at the International Conference on Abortion, Hot Springs, Virginia, November 17–20, 1968.
73. Ferris, *op. cit.,* p. 77.
74. Editorial, *Newsletter,* ALRA, 21 (Summer 1968).
75. A. Jenkins, *Law for the Rich* (London: Gollancz, 1960), p. 13.
76. Simpson, *op. cit.,* p. 52.
77. *A Guide to the Abortion Act 1967* (London: Abortion Law Reform Association, 1968).
78. Moya Woodside, "The Woman Abortionist," in *Abortion in Britain, op. cit.,* pp. 35–38.
79. Philip Rhodes, "A Gynaecologist's View," in *Abortion in Britain, op. cit.,* p. 31.
80. Editorial, *Newsletter,* ALRA, 21 (Summer 1968).
81. T. L. T. Lewis, "The Abortion Act," *British Medical Journal,* 1 (January 25,

1969), pp. 241–42; the final figures for the first year of the Act came to 40,202 for England, Wales and Scotland. (Malcolm Potts, personal communication.)

82. Diggory, *op. cit.*

83. See, for instance, "Abortion, 1968," *New Society*, 12 (July 18, 1968), pp. 88–89.

84. Editorial, *Newsletter*, ALRA, 22 (Autumn 1968).

85. *Ibid.*, p. 3.

86. *Ibid.*

87. Editorial, *Newsletter*, ALRA, 21 (Summer 1968).

88. Editorial, *Newsletter*, ALRA, 22 (Autumn 1968).

89. H. A. Robinson, "Implementing the Abortion Act," *British Medical Journal*, 2 (April 20, 1968), pp. 173–74.

90. N. M. Cogan, "Account of the Environment: A Medical Social Worker Looks at the New Abortion Law," *British Medical Journal*, 2 (April 27, 1968), pp. 235–36.

91. R. A. G. O'Brien, "Abortion: Conscience and the Law," *The Tablet*, 222 (April 27, 1968), p. 411.

92. Muriel Bowen, "London's Newest Role: Abortion Capital," *New York Post* (also *Los Angeles Times* and *Washington Post*), (April 28, 1969); Gloria Emerson, "British Abortion Debate Still Rages . . . ," *The New York Times* (May 8, 1969); "Demand for Abortion," *British Medical Journal*, 1 (January 25, 1969), pp. 199–200; "Abortion," *Lancet*, 1 (February 15, 1969), pp. 355–56.

93. *Population Problem of India* (New Delhi: Ministry of Health, Family Planning and Urban Development, 1967).

94. See, for instance, D. V. R. Murty, *Studies in Family Planning in India* (New Delhi: Central Family Planning Institute, 1967); *Director's Report, 1966–67* (New Delhi: Central Family Planning Institute, 1968); B. L. Raina, "India," in Bernard Berelson (ed.), *Family Planning and Population Programs* (Chicago: University of Chicago Press, 1966), pp. 111–21; and "India," *Situation Report* (London: International Planned Parenthood Federation, March 1968), pp. 1, 4–5; S. Chandrasekhar, "How India Is Tackling Her Population Problem," *Demography*, 5:2 (1968), pp. 642–50.

95. *Report of the Committee to Study the Question of Legalisation of Abortion* (New Delhi: Ministry of Health and Family Planning, 1966), p. 35.

96. *Ibid.*, p. 48.

97. *Ibid.*, pp. 16 ff, citing especially D. Anand, "Clinico-Epidemological Study of Abortions," *Licentiate*, 15 (1965), p. 7; and S. N. Agarwale, *Fertility Control Through Contraception* (New Delhi: Directorate General of Health Services, 1960). With the exception of a Madras study, mentioned but with no citation, the cited studies were all from the New Delhi area. See also N. Biswas, "The Trend of Fertility and Vital Loss of Pregnancy in an Urban Community," *Journal of the Indian Medical Association*, 51 (July 1, 1968), pp. 10–16. This small study, of 239 lower-income women who attended a prenatal clinic in the Urban Health Centre of the Chetta district in Calcutta, revealed an abortion rate of 46.7 per 1,000 pregnancies and 50.8 per 1,000 live births. Nor is abortion a problem of recent origin only; frequent illegal abortions were reported as early as the middle of the nineteenth century. See Nirad C. Chaudhuri, "Legalized Abortion," *Now* (February 25, 1966). The author quotes, in particular, an English report of 1854 complaining of almost daily abortions in Bengal.

98. *Vital Statistics of India for 1961* (New Delhi: Registrar General of India), p. LX, cited in *Report of the Committee to Study the Legalisation of Abortion, op. cit.*, p. 22.

99. *Report of the Committee . . . , op. cit.*, p. 39.

100. *Ibid.*, p. 47. *Cf.* T. J. Samuel, "Population Control in Japan: Lessons for India," *The Eugenics Review*, 58 (March 1966), pp. 15–22; S. Chandrasekhar,

"Should We Legalize Abortion in India?" *Population Review*, 10 (July 1966), pp. 17–22.
101. *Report of the Committee* . . . , *op. cit.*, p. 40; the Indian Health Minister, S. Chandrasekhar, has noted that a liberal law would help reduce the birthrate and the argument about inadequate facilities is not wholly persuasive. ("How India Is Tackling Her Population Problem," *op. cit.*, p. 649.)
102. *Ibid.*, pp. 51ff., with appended Resolution No. 9 of October 6, 1967. Also, the author's interviews with Lt. Col. B. L. Raina, Director, Central Family Planning Institute, and Dr. Leila Mehra, Deputy Assistant Commissioner, Ministry of Health and Family Planning.
103. The author's interviews with Lt. Col. Raina and Dr. Mehra, and with Dr. V. N. Purandare, Secretary, Bombay Obstetric and Gynecological Society, Dr. B. N. Purandare, Secretary of the Federation of Obsterical and Gynecological Societies of India, and Drs. Usha Krishna and Parviz Battiwalla of the Obstetrical Department, K. E. M. Hospital, Parel, Bombay. For two fairly recent examples of medical opposition to a more liberal Indian law, see: Amir Chand, "Legalizing Abortion for Birth Control," *Journal of the Indian Medical Association*, 45 (July 16, 1965), pp. 95–97; and B. Krishna Rao, "The Impact of Legalisation of Induced Abortion: International Experience," *ibid.*, pp. 97–100.
104. Mohandas K. Gandhi, *An Autobiography* (Boston: Beacon Press, 1957), p. 349.
105. Franklin Edgerton (trans.), *The Bhagavad Gita* (New York: Harper & Row, 1964), pp. 12–13.
106. Edward Hopkins (ed.), Arthur C. Burnell (trans.), *Ordinances of Manu* (London: Kegan Paul, Trench, Trubner & Co., Ltd., 1891), p. 336.
107. A. L. Basham, *The Wonder That Was India* (New York: Grove Press, 1959), pp. 159–60. *Cf.* S. V. Venkateswara, *Indian Culture Through the Ages* (London: Longmans Green & Co., 1928), Vol. I, p. 300.
108. Hemann Jacobi (trans.), *The Gaina Sutras, The Sacred Books of the East*, Vol. 22 (Oxford: Clarendon Press, 1884), pp. 79–80.
109. *Orbit*, 11 (July 2, 1967).
110. R. Armijo, "Abortion in Latin America," *Proceedings of the Eighth International Conference of the International Planned Parenthood Federation*, Santiago, Chile, April 1967 (London: International Planned Parenthood Federation, 1967), p. 144. However, Honduras and Peru allow abortion to preserve the health of the woman, while Mexico allows it in cases of rape. See Ruth Roemer, "Abortion Laws: the Approaches of Different Nations," *American Journal of Public Health*, 57 (November 1967), p. 1917.
111. N. Gomez and C. Garcia, "Investigación sobre aborto ilegal Planificación de Familia en el Centro Municipal de Saxologia (Hospital Rawson, Buenos Aires). Paper No. 2, 4th Conference IPPF Western Hemisphere Region, San Juan, Puerto Rico, April 1964. Cited in R. Armijo, *op. cit.*, p. 143.
112. Bertram Hutchinson, "Induced Abortion in Brazilian Married Women," *América Latina*, 7 (October–December 1964), pp. 21–33.
113. Octávio Rodrígues Lima, "Abôrto Provocado" (Rio de Janeiro: privately printed, 1965).
114. M. Françoise Hall, "Birth Control in Lima, Peru: Attitudes and Practices," *Milbank Memorial Fund Quarterly*, 43 (October 1965), Part II, p. 426.
115. *Ibid.*, p. 433; see also R. Delgado, "Perspective on Family Planning Programs in Latin America," in Joseph Stycos (ed.), *Population Dilemma in Latin America* (Washington, D.C.: Potomac Books, 1966), pp. 215–16, for a discussion of some discrepancies in Latin-American statistics.
116. Ralph Alan Hoyte, "An Analysis of Abortion at the General Hospital, Port of Spain," Paper No. 58, Fourth Conference of the IPPF Western Hemisphere Region, San Juan, Puerto Rico, April 1964.
117. E. Faraj and R. Carranza, "Aborto: Factores Médico Sociales." See also *Family Planning in Five Continents* (London: International Planned Parenthood Federation, 1968), p. 14, which states that there is approximately one abortion to four live births in Honduras. No source is cited for this figure, however.

118. J. A. Guevara *et al.*, *Nuestro Problema Demográfico* (Costa Rica: Ministerio de Salud Pública, 1966). Cited in R. Armijo, *op. cit.*, p. 144.

119. "Colombia: The Family in Candelaria," *Studies in Family Planning*, No. 11 (New York: The Population Council, April 1966), p. 4.

120. "Estudio de Recursos Humanos Para la Salud y Educación Médica en Colombia: Investigación Nacional de Morbilidad," *Hechos Demográficos* (Bogotá), (January 1968).

121. "Datos Preliminares de Las Encuestas Sobre Aborto," unpublished paper, Asociación Colombiana de Facultades de Medicina, Division de Estudios de Población, September 23, 1968.

122. German Riaño Gamboa, "Analisis de 100 Casos de Aborto Provocado," unpublished paper presented at the VIIth Congreso Colombiana de Ginecología y Obstetricia en Cúcuta, [Colombia], December 1967.

123. Francisco Pardo Vargas *et al.*, "Aspectos Medico-Sociales del Aborto," unpublished paper presented at the VIIth Congreso Colombiano de Ginecología y Obstetricia en Cúcuta, [Colombia], December 1967.

124. "Colombia: The Family in Candelaria," *op. cit.*, p. 2.

125. *Ibid.*, p. 2.

126. "World Population Data Sheet—1968," (Washington, D.C.: Population Reference Bureau, 1968).

127. For a graphic account of an American woman's experience with an illegal Mexican abortion, see Patricia Wetherby, "The Mexican Abortion Trip," *Cheetah*, 8 (May 1968), pp. 61ff.

128. A. Aldama, "El Aborto provocado, problema de salud pública," *Higiene*, 14 (November-December 1962), p. 214; see also Henry Giniger, "Birth Curb Gains in Mexican Study," *New York Times* (August 12, 1967), p. 26.

129. Manuel Mateos Cándano, Rosalba Bueno Lázaro, and Luiz Fernando Chávez Muruetta, *Actitud Y Anticoncepción* (Mexico City: Centro Estudios Reproducción Ac. Cerac, 1968), pp. 50–51.

130. Figures provided by Dra. Blanca Raquel Ordóñez, Departamento de Medicina Preventiva, Instituto Mexicano del Seguro Social, December 1968.

131. Figures provided by staff members of the hospital. The services of the Social Security hospitals are available only to those taking part in the Mexican Social Security Program, a joint industrial-government program covering about eight million Mexicans.

132. Dr. José Luis Pérez de Salazar, "Aborto Provocado en México y Problemas de Población," *Planeación Familiar*, 1 (November-December 1967), pp. 4–6.

133. Manuel Mateos Fournier, "El Aborto Criminal Como Problema Social, Su Prevención," *Planeación Familiar*, 1 (May-June 1967), pp. 4–5.

134. *Ibid.*, p. 5.

135. This information and the data following it were supplied by Dra. Blanca Raquel Ordóñez and are contained in an unpublished paper, "Programas de Investigación Epidemiológica y de Prevención del Aborto Inducido del Instituto Mexicano del Seguro Social, 1968." Some earlier information from the first two months of the program is provided in a published article: Blanca R. Ordóñez de la Mora, "Programa del I.M.S.S. para la prevención del aborto inducido," *Salud Pública de México*, 9 (September-October 1967), pp. 755–59.

136. José Luis Pérez de Salazar, *op. cit.*, p. 5.

137. Manuel Mateos Cándano *et al.*, *op. cit.*, pp. 70, 101.

138. Luis Leñero Otero, *Investigación de la familia en México* (Mexico City: Instituto Mexicano de Estudios Sociales, A.C., 1968), p. 160.

139. *Ibid.*, p. 336.

140. "World Population Data Sheet—1968," *op. cit.*

141. Hernán H. Romero, "Chile," in *Family Planning and Population Programs*," *op. cit.*, p. 245.

142. *Ibid.*

143. *Ibid.*, p. 246.

144. Mariano B. Requena, "Social and Economic Correlates of Induced Abortion in Santiago, Chile," *Demography*, 2 (1965), pp. 37, 41.

145. Rolando Armijo and Tequalda Monreal, "Epidemiology of Provoked Abortion in Santiago, Chile," *The Journal of Sex Research*, 1 (July 1965), p. 151.

146. *Ibid.*, p. 150. See also, Rolando Armijo and Tequalda Monreal, "Epidemiología del Aborto Provocado en Santiago," *Revue Chilena Obstet. y Ginec.*, 29 (1964), pp. 33–42; ———, "El Problema del Aborto Provocado en Chile," *Boletín de la Oficina Sanitaria Panamericana*, 60 (January 1966), pp. 39–45 (this involved a national study of 3,926 women with results very similar to those discovered in the authors' Santiago studies); ———, "Epidemiology of Provoked Abortion in Santiago, Chile," in Minoru Muramatsu and Paul A. Harper (eds.), *Population Dynamics* (Baltimore: The Johns Hopkins Press, 1965), pp. 137–60.

147. R. Armijo and T. Monreal, "Factores asociados a las complicaciones del Aborto Provocado," *Rev. Chil. Obstet. Ginec.*, 29 (1964), pp. 175–78. Cited in Armijo, "Abortion in Latin America," *op. cit.*, p. 146.

148. Rolando Armijo and Mariano Requena, "Epidemiologic Aspects of Abortion in Chile," *Public Health Reports*, 83 (January 1968), pp. 41–48, provide yearly admission figures from 1937 to 1964.

149. Interview with Dr. Onofre Avendaño.

150. Interview with Dr. Anibal Rodriguez, Chief, Gynecological Section, San Salvador Hospital, Santiago.

151. Data provided by the Statistical Section, San Salvador Hospital, Santiago. The steady rise in the number of abortion cases at San Salvador Hospital is not there taken necessarily to mean a rise in the frequency of abortion. In recent years the hospital has added more beds and more abortion patients are being sent there from other sections of the city and by other hospitals. The number of hospitalized abortion cases in Santiago has remained stable for the past seven years, i.e., as mentionad above, at about 21,000 cases a year.

152. Mariano Requena, "Condiciones Determinantes del Aborto Inducido," *Revista Médica de Chile*, 94 (November 1966), pp. 714–22.

153. "Resumen Normas Básicas sobre Regulación de la Natalidad en el Servicio Nacional de Salud," Circular A.2.1, No. 3, Servicio Nacional de Salud, Dirección General No. 227, Santiago, October 8, 1968.

154. *Ibid.*

155. "Acciones de Regulación de Natalidad por Establecimientos—S.N.S. [National Health Service]—Chile, 1967." I am grateful to Dr. Fernando Rodriguez, of the Dirección General Servicio Nacional de Salud, for making these statistics available to me.

156. "Cuadro Bioestadístico de Chile: 1958–1967," *Boletín de la Asociación Chilena de Protección de la Familia*. 4 (June 1968), p. 8.

157. Tequalda Monreal and Rolando Armijo, "Evaluation of the Program for the Prevention of Induced Abortion and for Family Planning in the City of Santiago," unpublished paper, 1968.

158. *Ibid.*, p. 11.

159. *Ibid.*, p. 12.

160. *Ibid.*, p. 20.

161. *Ibid.*, p. 21.

162. I am indebted to Dr. Tequalda Monreal for making their paper available to me and for discussing it with me.

163. This information and that which follows was provided to me in an interview with Dr. Onofre Avendaño; see also two published reports on the program: Anibal Faúndes-Latham, Germán Rodríguez Galant, Onofre Avendaño, "Effects of a Family Planning Program on the Fertility of a Marginal Working Class Community in Santiago," *Demography*, 5:1 (1968), pp. 122–37; and "The San Gregorio Experimental Family Planning Program: Changes Observed in Fertility and Abortion Rates," *Demography*, 5:2 (1968), pp. 836–45.

164. R. Armijo and Tequalda Monreal, "Epidemiology of Provoked Abortion in Santiago, Chile," *op. cit.*, p. 153.
165. Guido Solari Canessa and Gerardo González Cortés, "Actitudes de Obstetras y Ginecologos sobre la Regulación de la Natalidad," unpublished preliminary study (Santiago: Centro Latinoamericano de Poblacion y Familia (CELAP), 1967), p. 104.
166. *Ibid.*, p. 112.
167. These figures were made available to me by Luis Leñero Otero of the Mexican Institute of Social Studies, Mexico City, and are part of an unpublished study being conducted by the International Federation of Social and Socio-Religious Studies (FERES), entitled "Church and Demographic Change," dated July 6, 1968.
168. Mariano B. Requena, "Induced Abortion in Latin America," unpublished paper delivered at the International Conference on Abortion, Hot Springs, Virginia, November 17–20, 1968. I am grateful to Dr. Requena for making this paper available to me as well as for his hospitality in allowing me to make use of his extensive files on Latin America during a visit to Santiago. Dr. Requena notes at the outset of his paper that he decided to use the total number of abortions (spontaneous and induced) in each place for his comparisons. He based his decision on an established variation in the number of spontaneous abortions, ranging from 80 to 100 per 1,000 pregnancies, and on the assumption "that the amount of the total of abortions will be altered only by a change in the induced abortion proportion, since the spontaneous remains almost unaltered" (*ibid.*, p. 2).
169. By "prevalence," Requena here means "the number of women, existing at a given moment in a population, who have undergone one or more induced abortions in their lives" (*ibid.*).
170. *Ibid.*, p. 5.
171. *Ibid.*, p. 6.
172. *Cf.* C. Agualimpia, A. Mejía, R. Paredes *et al.*, "Investigación Nacional de Morbilidad: los Hechos Demográficos," monograph (Bogotá; Public Health Ministry and the Colombian Association of Faculties of Medicine, 1968). Cited by Requena, "Induced Abortion in Latin America," *op. cit.*, p. 6.
173. *Cf.* Requena, "Social and Economic Correlates of Induced Abortion in Santiago, Chile," *op cit.*, pp. 33–49.
174. Requena, "Induced Abortion in Latin America," *op. cit.*, p. 9.
175. *Cf.* Mariano B. Requena, "Studies in Family Planning in the Quinta Normal District of Santiago," *The Milbank Memorial Fund Quarterly*, 43 (October 1965), pp. 66–93; ———, "Social and Economic Correlates of Induced Abortion in Santiago, Chile," *op. cit.*; A. Alpana, "El Aborto Provocado como Problema de Salud Pública," unpublished paper XVIth Annual Meeting of the Mexican Association of Hygiene, Mexico City, 1962 (cited by Requena, "Induced Abortion in Latin America, *op. cit.*, p. 9); Hutchinson, "Induced Abortion in Brazilian Married Women," *op. cit.*, p. 24. In this context, the remarks of a priest with long pastoral experience in Latin America can be quoted. Though they specifically bear on the problem of contraception, they can apply, to a considerable extent, to abortion as well: "Among the urban middle classes—and here I refer particularly to traditional Catholics, the sort that sometimes describes itself as 'Catholic but not fanatic'—the attitude toward the traditional prohibition of contraception fits in fairly well with the general context of the encyclical [*Humanae Vitae*]. Arguments from natural law are quite meaningless; the traditional prohibition of contraception is placed more or less on the same level as the equally traditional laws concerning the Eucharistic fast. If one did not fast, one did not go to Communion. Abstention from contraceptive practices became another ritual requirement for frequenting the sacraments. Legalism is curiously mixed with a traditionally anti-legal Latin attitude which prevails both in religious and secular matters. Law is a

terribly important factor in life; authority is unquestioned. But once the point is established, a working distinction is introduced between *acatamiento*—acceptance of the law and recognition of its authority—and *cumplimiento*—compliance with the thing prescribed. Rebellion against authority would be regarded as scandalous and impious, but compliance with the law is a gringo hangup" (Jordan Bishop, O.P., "Imperialism and the Pill," *Commonweal*, 89 [January 10, 1969], p. 466). Others have observed the seemingly odd phenomenon of Catholic women who resort to abortion but resist contraception. The most plausible explanation, as these women themselves sometimes explain, is that contraception and abortion are both regarded by the Church as "mortal"—grave—sins. But the use of contraceptives would involve frequent mortal sins, while a recourse to abortion would be much less frequent; hence, one who used abortion would commit fewer "mortal" sins than one who regularly employed contraceptives. A similar kind of logic has been expressed by Catholic women in other parts of the world.

176. Requena, "Induced Abortion in Latin America, *op. cit.*, p. 12.

177. Information supplied by Dr. Onofre Avendaño.

178. *Family Planning in Five Continents*, *op. cit.*, p. 16; again, no source is cited for these figures.

179. For an analysis of some important variables in Latin-American fertility patterns, see Carmen A. Miró and Walter Mertens, "Influence of Some Intermediate Variables in the Level and Differentials of Urban and Rural Fertility in Latin America," provisional edition (Santiago: Centro Latinoamericano de Demográfia [CELADE], Series A, no. 80, April 1968). Valuable also, for a more theoretical discussion, is Ismael Silva Fuenzalida, "El Condicionamiento Cultural de la Fecundidad en América Latina," preliminary study (Santiago: Centro Para el Desarrollo Económico y Social de América Latina [DESAL], 1965).

CHAPTER 6

Moderate Legal Codes:
The Scandinavian Countries

FOR A NUMBER OF YEARS, the abortion laws of the Scandinavian countries, particularly Sweden and Denmark, have been a source of considerable interest to other countries. As liberal but not permissive laws, they have been looked upon as a possible "middle way" for other nations to emulate, broad in their range of permitted indications, but restrictive in their requirements that a strict legal procedure be followed. For countries with restrictive codes, the Scandinavian laws and practice have exerted a special attraction: they have seemed to provide a way of allowing more legal abortions when reasonable grounds exist but also of stopping short of abortion on request.

An analysis of the Scandinavian laws and experience is useful for two reasons. First, it will provide some test cases of the effectiveness of moderate or "mixed" codes in reducing the public-health hazards of illegal abortions and in meeting public demand for a wider range of permitted indications. Second, it will point up some of the social consequences of moderate codes.

As with restrictive codes, however, moderate codes cannot with full profit be examined by themselves; they need to be compared with other kinds of codes in order to provide some illumination for those considering different legal and moral alternatives. So far we have seen that one consequence of highly restrictive laws is a serious illegal-abortion problem. In all of the countries considered in the previous chapter—sharing restrictive laws—complaints about the difficulty of getting safe abortions, with a consequent public-health problem, have been widespread. The question which can now be asked is whether a moderate code, as in the Scandinavian countries, meets the public-health problem, reduces complaints about the law, and does these things without deleterious effects.

As in England and the United States, however, public attitudes toward abortion have undergone considerable change in the past few years. Since 1965, each of the Scandinavian countries, with the possible exception of Finland, has shown a significant rise in the number of granted legal abortions, concomitant with a change in attitude on the part of legal boards and the general public.[1] In order to help bring out the sharpness of this shift, and some of its consequences, the first part of this chapter will be concerned primarily with the situation prior to 1965, and the second, with the years since then. As it turns out, the Scandinavian experience since 1965 helps answer some of the most common questions raised about the success of its laws and provides considerable insight into the validity of the criticisms directed at those laws from a variety of quarters.

The Situation Prior to 1965

SWEDEN

A helpful summary of the background for the present Swedish law has been provided in a brochure published by the Swedish Institute:

> The law on abortion in Sweden goes back to the 13th century, to the old Vastergotland law, which forbade any form of induced abortion. During the 15th century severe penalties were introduced for breaking this law, and during the 17th century violation was made punishable by death. The legal code drawn up in 1734 preserved the death penalty. Not until 1864 was the law liberalized, the penalty being then reduced to penal servitude for a maximum of six years. The law was further liberalized in 1890 and still more in 1921. The act of 1921 still did not sanction abortion under any circumstances, but by this year abortion for indisputable medical reasons had been unofficially sanctioned for some time. During the 1920s the number of criminal abortions performed in Sweden began to rise rapidly, and during the first half of the 1930s about 70 women a year died from the sequels of abortion. This caused great alarm among responsible citizens and, as it was assumed that fewer criminal abortions would be done if doctors were given legal sanction to perform abortion under certain circumstances, in 1931 a proposal was made in Parliament that the law be changed to provide for legal abortion. The proposal also emphasized that the new law should distinguish clearly between lawful and unlawful abortion, to prevent what might lead to a greater laxity in morals. In 1934 a commission was appointed to work out a plan for new legislation on abortion. The commission submitted their bill in 1935, and the present law on abortion (passed in 1938) took effect on January 1, 1939.[2]

Since the law took effect in 1939, it has been amended a number of times and now allows legal abortion on medical, eugenic, psychiatric, fetal, and socioeconomic grounds.[3] At the same time as the 1938 Basic Act was passed, provisions were also made for various preventive measures against abortion. Birth control and pregnancy counseling centers were established, laws were passed prohibiting dismissal from employment because of pregnancy and entitling women to a maximum six-month leave of absence. The dual aim of the law was to make legal abortion possible under carefully controlled circumstances while, at the same time, creating a medical and social climate which would make pregnant women feel less compelled to resort to abortion.

Prior to 1946, when sociomedical indications were added to the purely medical reasons for allowing abortion, decisions to abort were made in the applicant's own region, by the operating physician in combination with one other doctor (this is the "two-doctor authorization"), both of whom submitted a written statement to the Royal Medical Board after the operation, describing the reason for it. But with the broadened indications, extensive social investigations of abortion applicants were introduced, and gradually the Royal Medical Board began to handle most abortion applications. The usual procedure is as follows: A woman considering abortion goes to one of the special advisory centers on abortion where she receives a thorough gynecological examination and, as a rule, a psychiatric evaluation as well. Her application is then forwarded to the board, accompanied by her birth certificate, a biography, usually compiled by social workers and including detailed descriptions of the applicant's personal life (family history, childhood environment, education, sexual life, finances, housing, number of children, etc.)—all verified by social workers in home visits and interviews—and, finally, a medical certificate from a licensed doctor, based on his personal examination of the woman and including a description of her physical and mental condition plus a statement of his opinion as to whether the pregnancy ought to be interrupted, and why. (All of these documents are confidential.)

Usually within a week of receiving an application, the board turns it over to its Social-Psychiatric Committee, which meets once a week. The committee consists of the head of the Bureau for Social and Forensic Psychiatry (who is assisted by two part-time psychiatrists), a woman experienced in social welfare and politics, and a gynecologist, who serves as chairman. (Four women and four gynecologists take turns serving on the committee.) The committee may ask medical specialists for an opinion on a case or they may arrange to have the applicant examined at a special institution. Applicants may not appeal the committee's decisions, but they may ask it to reconsider if they feel they have further evidence. Finally, a woman may have her application reviewed by the Royal Medical Board. If permission is granted, the abortion must be performed in a public hospital by a staff surgeon, except in special cases when the board may allow the operation in another hospital by a board-appointed surgeon.[4]

Until the mid-1960s, 80 percent of all abortion cases were decided by the board, with the remaining 20 percent granted on the basis of "two-doctor" reports. The twentieth week of pregnancy is the normal limit, except where there are severe medical indications; in exceptional circumstances, however, the board is empowered to grant abortions up to the twenty-fourth week. Since the 1938 act, the two most important amendments have been the establishment of a sociomedical indication in 1946 and a fetal indication in 1963, thus taking account of all the commonly proposed therapeutic-abortion indications. In 1938 and thereafter, abortion on demand or on purely social indications was rejected, partly out of ethical considerations and partly out of a fear that abortion on demand in particular would increase the incidence of abortion.[5]

DENMARK

In Denmark, legislation relating to abortion has paralleled that in Sweden. Prior to 1937, abortion was totally outlawed, although it had long been accepted, *de facto*, that doctors could perform abortions on strictly medical indications. In 1937, with the first Pregnancy Act, abortion was made the subject of special legislation and three indications were specified: *medical and sociomedical* (threat to the life or health—mental or physical—of a woman); *ethical* (impregnation through criminal acts); *eugenic* (danger that child will suffer from hereditary illness).[6] The first Pregnancy Act did not, however, take effect until 1939, in order to allow time for the establishment of Mothers' Aid Centers. Their purpose, in part, was to help women with unwanted pregnancies solve the personal, social, economic and familial difficulties leading them to seek abortion. As time went on it fell increasingly to the Mothers' Aid Centers to make the final determination whether an abortion was to be permitted, in cooperation with two doctors. Thus the function of the Mothers' Aid Centers is twofold: to deter women from abortion by counseling and assistance and to facilitate abortions where the problems seem insuperable. In 1956 the Pregnancy Act was further clarified, and as of early 1969 four general indications were accepted: (1) a serious hazard to the life or health of the woman; (2) cases where the woman has been impregnated through a criminal act; (3) instances in which the child is likely to be born with serious mental or physical deficiencies or abnormalties; (4) cases where the woman's mental or physical condition is such that she is deemed unfit to provide proper care for her child.[7] The legal limit on abortions is 16 weeks.

In Denmark, decisions to interrupt pregnancy are made by a joint council set up in connection with the 11 Mothers' Aid Centers in the country. There are 21 such councils, each with three members: the director of the local Mothers' Aid Center, or some other equally qualified center employee (e.g., a lawyer or trained social worker), a psychiatrist and a gynecologist, if possible the senior gynecologist at the local hospital. Each application is thoroughly investigated by social workers, lawyers and doctors in an effort to arrive at a composite picture of the woman's physical and social situation. As for the sequence of the application process, the woman is first examined by a gynecologist, especially to determine the length of gestation. Then she is referred to a psychiatrist, and in some cases is placed under observation either in a hospital or in one of the special homes for pregnant women run by the state. If her problem is social, economic or both, a social worker may try to devise a program of help for her on the chance that an abortion may thereby be avoided. If she persists in her desire for an abortion, the investigation continues. When all the reports are completed, they are studied by the members of the joint council, who meet once or twice a week. They try to measure each case against the provisions of the Pregnancy Act; the decision to abort must be unanimous. If an application is rejected by the council or if the woman changes her mind about wanting an abortion, the Mothers' Aid Center tries to help her in every way possible to carry through her pregnancy. A mother's helper is often provided and, in some cases, economic assistance is offered. The center also helps women whose requests for abortion have been granted, providing follow-up medical or social assistance, contraceptive instruction and family counseling.

FINLAND AND NORWAY

Finland's abortion law dates from July 1950. Prior to that time there was no legal regulation of induced abortion, but the number of "criminal" abortions (self-induced or performed by untrained, nonmedical personnel) had increased so markedly in the 1940s that the present law was passed with the express purpose of preventing them.[8] The Finnish law is largely patterned on the Swedish abortion law, although the allowable indications are less comprehensive in Finland. Purely social indications are not recognized as sufficient grounds, in themselves, to terminate a pregnancy. According to Rouhunkoski and Olki, the framers of the law wished to make establishment of medical grounds necessary for termination; they wanted not only to curb criminal abortions but also to prevent the development of an "abortion mentality."[9]

In Finland, pregnancy may be terminated if the mother's ill health, infirmity or physical weakness is such that pregnancy or childbirth would cause serious physical or mental danger. In determining whether this is the case, the conditions of the woman's life and other circumstances affecting her health are taken into account. (Thus, social indications are viewed as an influence but not as a sole determinant.) Pregnancy may also be interrupted if it is the result of rape, or occurs in a girl under sixteen, or if there is good reason to believe that either of the parents has hereditary predispositions likely to lead to mental disease or deficiency, a serious physical illness or other serious infirmity in descendants. The time limit for an abortion is the fourth month, except in special cases where it may be authorized for a later date, but in any case, not after the fifth month.

The Finnish law requires that an application for abortion be approved by two doctors, one the person who is to perform the operation, the other appointed by the State Medical Board. If an application is not approved, the woman may appeal the doctors' decision to the board. The law also specifies that abortions be performed in approved hospitals by affiliated physicians, that all abortions be registered and that records be carefully kept. If all of these preliminary requirements are found impossible to fulfill, however, because of the need for immediate action or some other good reason, the law says that "the pregnancy may be interrupted by a qualified physician irrespective of the above-mentioned provisions." [10]

In the first ten years of the law's existence, the number of legal abortions in Finland doubled (Table 6), from 3,007 in 1951 to a high of 6,188 in 1960.[11] In subsequent years the number fluctuated, but showed a 1963–1965 decline and a 1966 rise (the last year for which official figures are available). One early result of the marked increase in abortions in Finland was, reportedly, to put a strain on hospital facilities. Rauramo and Grönroos report that of 9,645 days of gynecological treatment at the Women's Clinic of Turku University Hospital in 1958, 1,119 days (or 11.6 percent) were taken up by legal abortions.[12] Sterilization is often recommended to abortion applicants who have four or more children. The more children a woman has, the more likely her application for an abortion will be approved; the younger a woman, married or unmarried, the less likely the approval. (An abortion is not approved solely on the grounds that the applicant is unmarried.)[13] As in Denmark, Finland has developed a system of social aid and guidance centers to provide relief and support for families generally and for young, unmarried mothers in particular. The Population League, under the State Medical Board, also runs marriage counseling clinics and gives instruction in the use of contraceptives, encouraging resort to them, not abortion, to limit family size.[14]

In Norway, the present law was introduced in 1960 and took effect in 1964.[15] The permitted indications are similar to those in the other Scandinavian countries: medical and mental health, fetal, humanitarian;

there is also a separate indication for maternal deficiency. In taking account of a woman's "health," the intent of the Norwegian law is to be sensitive to the general living conditions of the applicant. Speaking of a danger to health, one passage in the law says that "in determining the extent of the danger, account shall be taken of whether the woman concerned is particularly disposed to organic or mental disease, and likewise of living conditions and other circumstances which may make her ill or lead to a breakdown in her physical or mental health." Under the category of "maternal deficiency," the Norwegian law has as its intent more the benefit of the expected child and of society than the protection or cure of the woman herself. In this category, abortion may thus be permitted when a woman is insane or a low-grade mental defective (a person with an IQ below 55).

The time limit for legal abortions in Norway (12 weeks) is the shortest of all the Scandinavian countries (except for Iceland, where it is 8 weeks), although exceptions are allowable. Decisions on legal abortions are fairly decentralized, being made by two-doctor boards in different regions of the country; one doctor is the operating surgeon and the other is a member of the public-health service or the National Board of Health.[16] As for the incidence of legal abortion, prior to 1965 the ratio per 1,000 live births ranged between 40 and 50. It began rising in 1965 (Table 6), as did the rate of permissions granted (78 percent in 1966). Since the present law is comparatively new, there are apparently at present no immediate plans to change it. Andenaes reports, however, that the 1960 law simply codified practices which had already existed prior to that time (so far as indications are concerned) and mainly had the effect of providing more formal rules concerning the legal procedure.

In all of the Scandinavian countries, the motives behind the laws were multiple: reduction of dangerous illegal abortions, closer reflection of public opinion, government supervision of abortion, and the general relief of difficult pregnancy situations. All the countries have made their abortion laws part of a general effort to assist pregnant women, those who want their child and those who do not. Abortions are thus discouraged when felt to be unnecessary or avoidable and facilitated when no other course appears open.

What were the results up to 1965? In Sweden, the passage of the 1938 Abortion Act did not immediately provoke any great rise in the number of legal abortions (in 1938 there were fewer than 1,000). By 1945 the number began to increase, reaching 6,328 in 1951 (57 per 1,000 live deliveries), dropping to 2,000 to 3,000 a year between 1958 and 1961 (Table 6). This drop was attributed to a more restrictive attitude on the part of the Royal Medical Board during that period, an increased knowledge of contraceptive methods, and the effect of various preventive measures.[17] During these years, the rate of legal abortion in relation to live deliveries was less than 1 percent in 1938, about 6 percent during the peak year 1951, less thereafter and rising again over 5 percent by 1965 (Table 6).[18] During the years from 1938 forward, the Swedish birthrate rose during World War II, dropped sharply during the 1950s and then began rising again during the 1960s (Table 5). With the exception of the 1930s and 1940s, before the new abortion law had a chance to take hold, there seems to have been some correlation between birthrate and legal abortion—high birthrate, high legal-abortion rate—suggestive, perhaps, of a correlation between the total number of pregnancies and the total number of legal abortions (Tables 5 and 6). Of those women granted an abortion during the years 1960–1963, the majority were married and between the ages of thirty and thirty-four; from 1964 on there was a shift to younger women, with the majority of those having abortions being between twenty and twenty-four years of age (Table 9). The main grounds for permission were medical and sociomedical (Table 8).

Of some importance is the fact that the number of Swedish women hospitalized for cases of infected abortions (legal and illegal) dropped considerably during the past decade. The reasons for this are not altogether clear; it could mean a drop in the number of illegal abortions or the advent of improved antibiotics or both.[19] Since, as we shall see, it is generally believed that the illegal-abortion rate did not immediately decline with the initiation of the 1938 law and its later amendments, the latter reason seems more plausible.

In Denmark, prior to 1965, between 7,000 and 8,000 women a year applied to the Mothers' Aid Centers for abortions, increasing to slightly over 8,000 in 1964.[20] During these years (1951–1963), live births in Denmark increased from 76,600 to 82,400. As in Sweden, married women formed the preponderance of the applicants, with some 66 percent married (during 1963–1964), 24 percent unmarried, and 10 percent divorced, separated or widowed. The highest number of applicants were between twenty and twenty-four, the second highest between twenty-five and twenty-nine, a switch from two years earlier, when the highest number were in the twenty-five to twenty-nine age group, the second highest twenty to twenty-four (Table 11). The decline in age was not so dramatic as in Sweden, however. Approximately half the applicants had their requests granted, with an increase in recent years.[21] Approximately 81 percent of the permissions were on the basis of sociomedical indications (life and health of mother threatened, understanding "health" in heavily social and psychological terms).

TABLE 5

POPULATION, BIRTHRATES

Sweden, Denmark, Finland, Norway, 1951–1968

	Population in Millions				Birthrate per 1,000 pop.			
	SWEDEN	DENMARK	FINLAND	NORWAY	SWEDEN	DENMARK	FINLAND	NORWAY
1951	7.0	4.3	4.0	3.2	15.6	17.8	23.0	18.4
1952	7.1	4.3	4.0	3.3	15.5	17.8	23.1	18.8
1953	7.1	4.3	4.1	3.3	15.4	17.9	22.0	18.7
1954	7.2	4.4	4.1	3.3	14.6	17.3	21.5	18.5
1955	7.2	4.4	4.2	3.4	14.8	17.3	21.2	18.5
1956	7.3	4.4	4.2	3.4	14.8	17.2	20.8	18.5
1957	7.3	4.4	4.3	3.4	14.6	16.8	20.1	18.1
1958	7.4	4.5	4.4	3.5	14.2	16.5	18.6	17.9
1959	7.4	4.5	4.4	3.6	14.1	16.3	18.9	17.7
1960	7.5	4.5	4.4	3.6	13.7	16.6	18.5	17.3
1961	7.5	4.6	4.5	3.6	13.9	16.6	18.4	17.3
1962	7.6	4.6	4.5	3.6	14.2	16.7	18.1	17.1
1963	7.6	4.7	4.5	3.7	14.8	17.6	18.1	17.3
1964	7.7	4.7	4.6	3.7	16.0	17.7	17.6	17.7
1965	7.7	4.8	4.6	3.7	15.9	18.0	16.9	17.8
1966	7.8	4.8	4.6	3.8	15.8	18.4	16.8	17.9
1967	7.9	4.8	4.7	3.8	15.4	16.8	16.5	18.0
1968	7.9	4.9	4.7	3.8	14.3	–	16.0	17.7

Sources: *Demographic Yearbook, 1965,* 17th issue (New York: United Nations, 1966) and *Demographic Yearbook, 1967,* 19th issue (New York: United Nations, 1968); for 1968: *Monthly Bulletin of Statistics,* 22 (May, 1969) (New York: United Nations, 1969); and *Population and Vital Statistics Report* (New York: United Nations, various issues).

There are at least three critical questions arising out of the Scandinavian experience prior to 1965. Did the liberalized laws of its mixed system lead to a reduction in respect for the sanctity of life? Did the laws lead to a reduction in the illegal-abortion rate? Did the laws lead to a reduction in the death and injury rate resulting from abortion?

On the first question, no answer whatever can be given. As pointed out earlier, there is just no clear way of measuring the degree of respect for the sanctity of life in a society. On the face of it, though, there are no special reasons for assuming that the Scandinavian laws led to a lessened respect for life. On the contrary, the genesis of the Scandinavian laws indicates that they were part and parcel of an attempt to improve the overall welfare of pregnant women, and, of course, the advanced social welfare policies of the Scandinavian countries would suggest a greater concern with the quality of life than in many countries with restrictive abortion laws and *laissez-faire* medicine. This kind of point

TABLE 6

LIVE BIRTHS AND ABORTIONS: SWEDEN, DENMARK, FINLAND, NORWAY, 1951–1967

	Number of Live Births				Number of Legal Abortions				Ratio per 1,000 Live Births			
	SWEDEN	DENMARK	FINLAND	NORWAY	SWEDEN	DENMARK	FINLAND	NORWAY	SWEDEN	DENMARK	FINLAND	NORWAY
1951	110,200	76,600	93,100	60,600	6,300	4,700	3,000		57	62	32	
1952	110,200	76,900	94,300	62,500	5,300	5,000	3,300		48	65	35	
1953	110,100	78,300	90,900	63,000	5,000	4,800	3,800		45	61	42	
1954	105,100	76,400	89,900	62,800	5,100	5,100	3,700	3,200	48	67	41	50
1955	107,300	76,800	89,700	63,600	4,600	5,400	3,700		43	70	41	
1956	108,000	76,700	88,900	64,200	3,900	4,500	4,100		36	59	46	
1957	107,200	75,300	87,000	63,100	3,400	4,000	4,600		32	53	52	
1958	105,500	74,700	81,100	63,000	2,800	3,900	5,300		27	52	65	
1959	104,700	73,900	83,300	63,000	3,100	3,600	5,800		29	48	69	
1960	102,200	76,100	82,100	61,900	2,800	3,900	6,200		27	51	75	
1961	104,500	76,400	82,000	62,600	2,900	4,100	5,900		28	54	72	
1962	107,300	77,800	81,500	62,300	3,200	4,000	6,000		30	51	74	
1963	112,900	82,400	82,300	63,300	3,500	4,000	5,600		31	48	68	
1964	122,700	83,400	80,400	65,600	4,700	4,500	4,900	2,900*	38	54	61	44
1965	122,800	85,800	77,900	66,300	6,200	5,200	4,800	3,500	51	60	61	53
1966	123,400	88,300	77,700	67,100**	7,300	5,700	5,200	4,500	59	67	67	66
1967	122,100	79,200	77,000**	68,000**	9,600	6,400	—	—	79	80	—	—

Sources: Births: *Demographic Yearbook*, 1965, 17th issue (New York: United Nations, 1966) and *Demographic Yearbook*, 1967, 19th issue (New York: United Nations, 1968). Abortion data: *Sweden*—Medicinalstyrelsen, Allmän Hälso-och Sjukvård. Various years. *Denmark* —Sundhedsstyrelsen. *Medicinalberetning for kongeriget Danmark*. Various years. For 1967—Mothers' Aid Center of Copenhagen. *Finland*— Lääkintöhallitus. *Yleinen terveyden-ja sairaanhoito* (Suomen Virallinen Tilasto, XI; 67), pp. 154–56 (Helsinki, 1966). *Norway*—Justisde-partementet. *Innstilling fra straffelovrådet om adgangen til a avbryte svangerskap*, p. 74 (Trondheim, 1956); for 1964–1966—Directorate of Health.

* Number for February–December projected to a full year.
** Preliminary Estimate.

TABLE 7

ABORTION IN SWEDEN, 1951–1967

	TOTAL BIRTHS	APPLICATIONS TO MEDICAL BOARD	NUMBER GRANTED	PERCENT GRANTED	NO. ABORTIONS AFTER BOARD APPROVAL	NO. ABORTIONS AFTER 2-DR. APPROVAL	NO. EMERGENCY ABORTIONS	TOTAL ABORTIONS PERFORMED
1951	112,331	6,884	5,751	84%	5,324	997	7	6,328
1952	112,244	6,023	4,790	80%	4,509	811	2	5,322
1953	112,151	5,908	4,758	81%	4,275	634	6	4,915
1954	106,907	6,079	4,792	79%	4,488	599	2	5,089
1955	109,124	5,694	4,060	71%	3,922	638	2	4,562
1956	109,796	5,229	3,583	69%	3,265	582	4	3,851
1957	108,868	4,853	2,994	62%	2,882	501	3	3,386
1958	107,203	4,366	2,830	65%	2,376	445	2	2,823
1959	106,397	4,346	2,821	65%	2,628	440	3	3,071
1960	103,255	4,085	2,552	62%	2,377	414	1	2,792
1961	105,913	4,094	2,664	65%	2,474	434	1	2,909
1962	108,179	4,257	2,957	69%	2,772	431	2	3,205
1963	114,158	4,532	3,313	73%	3,100	426	2	3,528
1964	123,425	5,469	4,314	79%	4,073	596	2	4,671
1965	121,037	6,669	5,745	86%	5,346	860	2	6,208
1966	123,354	6,499	5,782	89%	5,375	1,876	3	7,254
1967	122,100	7,380*		92%*		3,318*	3	9,593

* Preliminary estimate

Source: Medicinalstyrelsen, *Allmän Hälso-och Sjukvård*. Various years. 1967: *Betaekning om Adgang Til Svangerskabsafbrydelse* (Copenhagen: Statens Trykingskontor, 522, 1969), p. 27.

TABLE 8

ABORTION IN SWEDEN 1951–1966

SOCIOMEDICAL GROUNDS FOR ABORTION

	DISEASE (MEDICAL)	"WEAKNESS"	"ANTICIPATED WEAKNESS"	HUMANITARIAN (E.G., RAPE)	EUGENIC	FETAL RISK (in effect from June 1963)
1951		2,913	736	29	486	—
1952		2,503	373	28	329	—
1953		2,280	522	26	235	—
1954		2,533	542	47	110	—
1955		1,147	376	44	74	—
1956		1,690	268	39	96	—
1957		1,498	169	54	72	—
1958		1,432	188	60	67	—
1959		1,507	182	87	58	—
1960		1,479	139	63	21	—
1961	1,172	1,482	175	64	18	—
1962	1,267	1,675	162	89	12	—
1963	1,119	2,060	133	83	17	36
1964	1,395	2,840	207	99	14	116
1965	1,463	3,988	597	98	6	57
1966	1,470	4,443	1,205	78	9	59

Source: Medicinalstyrelsen, *Allmän Hälso-och Sjukvård.* Various years.

TABLE 9

ABORTION IN SWEDEN: BY AGE OF WOMAN AND
NUMBER OF EARLIER DELIVERIES
1960–1966

AGE	1960	1961	1962	1963	1964	1965	1966
−14	46	59	75	73	63	57	34
15–19	243	291	320	424	669	1,005	1,080
20–24	328	364	436	557	843	1,217	1,300
25–29	496	523	595	633	794	1,044	1,008
30–34	582	550	606	648	831	945	975
35–39	539	541	525	586	663	908	862
40–44	287	290	346	351	422	525	472
45–	31	46	54	41	29	44	51
EARLIER DELIVERIES							
0	431	478	600	697	1,016	1,463	1,642
1	320	350	435	520	681	1,029	1,009
2	492	544	560	638	848	1,135	1,045
3	522	519	564	593	766	991	939
4	374	398	395	461	496	615	588
5	230	217	220	219	287	299	263
6	105	84	108	103	139	132	122
7	40	46	46	47	43	43	42
8	20	16	12	18	21	21	21
9 or more	18	12	17	17	17	17	11

Source: Socialstyrelsen–P.B. 3 March 7, 1968 / DS.

TABLE 10

DENMARK: ABORTIONS APPLIED FOR, APPROVED, AND
TYPE OF APPROVAL—SELECTED YEARS

	1958–59*	1960–61	1962–63	1963–64	1964–65	1965–66	1966–67	1967–68
Total applicants	7,656	7,566	7,121	7,260	8,092	8,759		
Total approved	3,697	3,719	3,659	3,936	4,597	5,341	5,726	6,362**
Percent approved	48	49	52	54	57	61		
by Board	43	46	49	51	54	58		
by Hospital	5	3	3	3	3	2		

* Figures are for the fiscal year.
** Provisional.
Sources: 1958–59, 1960–61 based on a table in Henrik Hoffmeyer, Magna Nørgaard, Vera Skalts, "Abortion, Sterlization, and Contraception: Experiences with the Mothers' Aid Centers in Denmark," The Journal of Sex Research, 3 (February 1967), p. 9. 1962–63 through 1965–66: Beretning om Modrehjaelpsinsgitutionernes Virksomhed; IX 1 April 1962–31 Marts 1966 (Copenhagen, 1967), p. 34. 1966–67 and 1967–68: Magna Nørgaard (personal communication).

TABLE 11

DENMARK: APPLICANTS FOR ABORTION TO MOTHERS' AID CENTERS
FOR WHOLE COUNTRY—SELECTED YEARS

By Age °

	1951–52		1956–57		1961–62		1963–64		1966–67	
	NO.	%	NO.	%	NO.	%	NO.	%	NO.	%
UNDER 20	778	9.6	1,262	13.2	1,304	15.8	1,248	16.7	1,682	17.9
20–24	1,731	21.3	2,079	21.7	1,814	22.0	1,739	23.3	2,337	24.9
25–29	1,973	24.3	4,061	42.4	1,845	22.4	1,629	21.8	1,820	19.3
30–34	1,772	21.8			1,482	17.9	1,308	17.5	1,546	16.4
35–39	1,246	15.4	1,397	14.6	1,157	14.0	959	12.9	1,262	13.4
40–44	617	7.6	770	8.1	652	7.9	518	7.0	677	7.2
45–49							61	0.8	87	0.9
TOTAL	8,117		9,569		8,254		7,462		9,411	

° Figures are for the fiscal year.
Source: Information provided by Magna Nørgaard, Head of Department of Information and Statistics, Mothers' Aid Center of Copenhagen.

TABLE 12

DENMARK: APPLICANTS FOR ABORTION TO MOTHERS' AID CENTERS
SELECTED YEARS

By Marital Status °

	1951–52		1956–57		1961–62		1963–64		1966–67	
	NO.	%	NO.	%	NO.	%	NO.	%	NO.	%
UNMARRIED	1,590	20	1,992	21	1,905	23	1,789	24	2,694	29
MARRIED	5,799	71	6,783	71	5,601	68	4,905	66	5,768	61
PREVIOUSLY MARRIED°°	728	9	794	8	748	9	768	10	949	10
TOTAL	8,117		9,569		8,254		7,462		9,411	

° Fiscal year figures.
°° Separated, divorced, widowed.
Source: Information provided by Magna Nørgaard, Head of Department of Information and Statistics, Mothers' Aid Center of Copenhagen.

should not be pressed too far, given the absence of clarifying studies and data, but if one assumes that the burden of proof rests on those who claim that the general respect due life will be lessened by a liberalization of abortion laws, then the Scandinavian experience provides no data to support their case. The melioration of the Scandinavian laws has not led to light penalties for murder, infanticide or euthanasia; by these criteria, respect for life remains high despite liberalization of abortion laws. In this context, it is worth bearing in mind a valuable point made in *The Terrible Choice*. Commenting on the problem of whether liberalized abortion laws are harmful to a society's respect for life, it notes:

> If there is an answer, it may well lie in the meaning that society attaches to abortion: if it is defined as killing of a defenseless being, as many people believe it is, then it is possible that there might be negative effects; if it is said that up to a certain point—quickening, viability, or what have you— abortion does not represent taking of life, as many believe it does not, then there might not be any ill effects.[22]

Since it appears to be the case that most Scandinavians do not believe that abortion is equivalent to the taking of a human life, it is not surprising, therefore, that one is hard-pressed to discover any general lessening of respect for life in those areas where it is believed that life and death decisions are at stake.

On the question of the effectiveness of the Scandinavian laws in reducing illegal abortions there has been considerable dispute. On the cautious side, Lawrence Lader holds that the data are insufficient to allow any clear conclusion, and Christopher Tietze believes that the effect of legalization in this respect remains "undetermined." [23] Most other observers are not so cautious. Indeed, the most common charge leveled at the Scandinavian solution is that illegal abortions have not been reduced and that the laws are thereby a failure in that respect. This conclusion has been strongly urged by Byrn, Hellegers, Mietus and Harrison (all opposed to liberalization), but also by some seeking a repeal of all laws (on the ground that moderate reform is insufficient).[24] There is some evidence and Scandinavian testimony to support the belief that moderate laws do not reduce illegal abortions. Kerstin Höök, in the Swedish "refused abortion" study, cites a number of Swedish studies from the 1930s through the 1950s, all indicating a steady rise in the number of illegal abortions, unabated by the newer laws.[25] Several authors, it is noted, "consider that people have become more abortion-minded since the Abortion Act came into force." [26]

Skalts and Nørgaard point to a Danish study which found "that the number of illegal abortions amounted to nearly 15,000 a year—three or four times the number of legal abortions. Even though it was found in this study that the last ten years seemed to have brought a slight decrease (10 to 14 percent) in the number of illegal abortions, the figure is still far too high." [27] L. Huldt, in a study of the city and county of Stockholm in 1950–1965, found that "the criminal abortion rate remained unchanged except for the past four years, when it tended to decline. Apparently, the abortion law in its present form has not reduced criminal abortions." [28] A number of other analysts, English and American, have decided that the Scandinavian laws did not reduce the illegal abortion rates. This is the conclusion of the Anglican abortion study, of Robert E. Hall, of Gebhard and his associates, the Council of the Royal College of Obstetricians and Gynaecologists, of S. A. Cosgrove, as well as of Hellegers, Mietus, Byrn and Harrison.[29] It should be noted of course that these negative conclusions are usually drawn from the comparatively few Scandinavian studies cited above, but it is equally important to note that no one, not even Scandinavian authorities, has pressed a claim that the liberalized laws reduced the illegal-abortion rate.[30]

For that matter, a number of those in the United States pressing for abortion on demand point to the Scandinavian results to support their case that mixed laws, with their halfway solution, are futile in eliminating illegal abortions and that only wholly permissive laws will suffice to achieve that goal. At the same time, however, the same critics argue that some liberalization, if not ideal, is better than none at all. Thus, Jerome M. Kummer wrote:

> We are not under the delusion that modifying our existing laws will eliminate criminal abortion. As long as there are any restrictions at all, women with unwanted pregnancies who are determined to abort will seek out and find illegal abortionists. This is no reason, however, for abandoning all attempts to prevent widespread termination of pregnancy by unskilled hands and to relieve the extreme hardship cases.[31]

Glanville Williams, arguing for a more permissive English law (prior to the 1967 changes), has written:

> How is it, then, that in Sweden with its liberal laws there are still illegal abortions? The answer is obvious: their law is not sufficiently liberal. We are told that in Sweden the special hospital boards which hear applications for abortion allow only 40 percent of the applications. In addition to the 60 percent who are turned down, there is the unknown number of women who do not apply for legal abortions, either because they realize that their case does not fall within the rules, or because they cannot tolerate the formality and even humiliation of applying to a hospital board in a matter they regard as being uniquely their own affair. These are the women who go to illegal abortionists.[32]

Lawrence Lader observes that "although the Scandinavian 'middle way' has made impressive gains in granting medical, humanitarian, and social abortions, the very fact that the system is tightly controlled, and many cases rejected, makes it almost impossible to cut deeply into underworld abortion." [33]

What all of these authors point to, as do many others, is the fact that the legal requirements in the Scandinavian countries inevitably mean that many women who want abortions will not be able to get them legally for lack of sufficient grounds or will not be willing in the first place to go through the lengthy, probing investigatory process. Moderate systems, therefore, cannot take care of all the desired abortions, and illegal abortions will thereby continue to be a problem. It is hard to fault this judgment. As we shall see below, considerations of this kind are partially responsible for the recent trend toward more permissive laws in Denmark and Sweden. Both those opposed to any liberalization of the laws and those who want very permissive laws are agreed on the drawbacks of moderate codes as a means of cutting down illegal abortions. But they diverge totally on what conclusion should be drawn from these drawbacks, and their divergence seems traceable mainly to their different moral evaluations of abortion.

Before passing to the effect of legalized abortion in moderate systems on the death and injury rate, three other considerations have some relevance here. One of these is well expressd in a quotation from Glanville Williams: "There is now convincing evidence [from Sweden] that it is to a large extent an entirely new clientele that is now granted legal abortion, that is to say women who could not have had an illegal abortion if they had been refused the legal one." [34] Whether the "evidence" is all that "convincing" may be doubted, but it is suggestive. Williams cites only a passage in Martin Ekblad's psychiatric study of Swedish abortion as part of this "evidence," but it is worth repeating here. Speaking of married women living in harmonious marriages, Ekblad observes: "Previously, and as a rule thanks to their personal disposition, these women had taken an unwelcome pregnancy with resignation, submissively accepting it without protest. The Abortion Act now gives possibilities of helping them." [35]

Ekblad himself found that from 15 percent to 33 percent of those women refused legal abortion had their pregnancy ended either by a spontaneous or illegal abortion, mainly the latter. This suggests that, had the Swedish laws been totally permissive, the number of women having abortions might have been much higher (assuming that many of those denied abortions under the present system would have gotten them if no obstacles had been put in their way). It also suggests that, if denied an abortion under a moderate code, a portion of women will find a way to get an illegal abortion if they are really intent upon ending their pregnancy. The second consideration is that, despite the failure of the liberalized laws to reduce the illegal-abortion rate, the Scandinavian countries held on to them through the 1960s, resisting until after 1965 both greater strictness and greater permissiveness in interpreting them. In Denmark, for instance, pressure for a less restrictive law was resisted primarily out of a belief that the main answer to both legal and illegal abortions lies in the direction of improved assistance to women: "(1) an expansion of the Mothers' Aid, (2) an expansion of the contraceptive clinics, and (3) an increase in general sexual guidance." [36]

Yet the failure of the moderate laws to stem illegal abortions was not taken as a fatal weakness in the laws since that aim was only one of many motives which led to them in the first place. In terms of providing for a regulated system of legal abortions, of providing coherent procedures for doctors and pregnant women to follow, of providing a compromise response on the part of the government between those wanting highly restrictive and those wanting permissive laws, and of providing an approach combining prevention and permission, the Scandinavian laws were until recently felt to be moderately successful.

The third consideration is the issue of a "changing clientele" which Glanville Williams mentions. This is interesting, not only from the aspect he mentions (married women in stable marriages), but also from the aspect of the age of women seeking abortions and the number of previous children these women have. There seems to be mounting evidence throughout the world that a larger number of young women and a larger number of women with no or few children are seeking abortions, and this holds in restrictive, moderate and permissive systems. Not long ago, it was generally assumed that the main group of women seeking abortions were married women with three to four children, most of whom could in fact probably bear another pregnancy and raise another child if they had to. Thus it was often held that mixed systems did not in fact cover the large proportion of women who resorted to illegal abortionists anyway, a fact which once again was used by opponents of liberalized laws to point to their uselessness, and by proponents to point out the need for "realistic" laws which cover the bulk of women desirous of an abortion but who could not normally qualify under moderate codes.

Yet if it is true, as some recent data suggest, that the age of women seeking abortions is dropping and the number with no or few children seeking abortions is rising, then some different conclusions may suggest themselves. The trends I have in mind here have been reported by M. McDermott of the New York City District Attorney's Office at the Sloane Hospital Symposium on "The Social Problem of Abortion," by Kenneth R. Niswander, by Armijo and Monreal for Latin America, by Hong for Seoul, Korea, and by Japanese and Eastern European observers. [37] Since the social situations of the countries and areas mentioned are quite different, but the hint of an emergent pattern seemingly consistent, one can only make some guesses about the causes at work. The most likely reason is that the pattern reflects a worldwide aspect of the general movement for female equality, increased female employment, the increasing time needed to complete the educational process, changing family patterns and the impact of the birth-control movement, with its stress on planned parenthood and voluntary pregnancies.

On the question of whether the laws in a moderate system help to reduce the death and injury rate from illegal abortions, comparatively little data can be brought to bear. As noted earlier, Christopher Tietze has observed that there has been a sharp downward trend all over the world in recent years in the number of deaths attributable to abortion, legal and illegal. The most likely reason is obvious: the increased use of modern antibiotics, certainly in hospitals and, most likely, also in developed countries, even in the illegal-abortion trade (where a large percentage of abortionists are doctors operating illegally). Yet because of the widespread use of these drugs, it becomes impossible to know how much of the decreasing death rate is due to the drugs and how much due to changes in the law; comparing mortality data from the preantibiotic era with the present era tells one nothing about the effectiveness of moderate laws as a public-health measure. Suffice it to say—for what it is worth—that both Sweden and East Germany provide instances of countries where a drop in the abortion-death rate took place at the same time as liberalized laws took effect (though during periods when new antibiotics were also coming into widespread use). In East Germany, which temporarily enlarged the scope of indications for abortion in 1947, there was a sharp rise in the number of legal abortions performed through 1950. It was generally agreed that the greatly increased number of these legal abortions did not reduce the number of illegal abortions, however, and at the end of 1950 the law was again tightened. But during this short period of 1947–1950 the number of deaths attributable to abortion declined by two-thirds.[38] In this case, at least, it would not be too hazardous to suppose that the change in the law was at least as important a factor in the remarkable drop in the death rate as the use of drugs. Unfortunately, data on the East German death rate after the retightening of the law in 1950 are not available. But it was after 1950 that the general decline in abortion deaths around the world began to become apparent, so even if the facts were available, they might not tell us very much about the pertinent causal relationships.

As we shall see in the next chapter, however, there is a considerable body of evidence to show that very permissive legal systems are effective in reducing illegal-abortion death and injury rates. An awareness of the data is behind the claims of Glanville Williams, Jerome Kummer and others that the only fully effective way to cut down on illegal abortions and the injuries resulting from them is a system of legalized abortion on demand. That the death rate from legal abortions in the Scandinavian countries is considerably higher than in Eastern Europe and Japan (with permissive systems)—Tietze's figures show a death rate of about 40 per 100,000 legal abortions in Northern Europe versus fewer than 5 per 100,000 in Eastern Europe and Japan—indicates that there is a certain health price to be paid even for a moderate code.[39] This price stems from the fact that in countries with moderate codes the bureaucratic and investigatory procedures delay the performance of abortions, pushing them into the later and medically more dangerous months. Very permissive codes, by contrast, make possible quick and early legal abortions. Naturally, these facts can be and have been used in very different ways: conservative opponents of moderate laws can use them to argue that they only show the futility of trying to help women medically by means of liberalized laws; and proponents of abortion on demand can use them to show that the only way to help women fully is to remove all legal impediments to abortion. Again, though, such arguments usually seem to reflect a prior moral evaluation of abortion.

The Situation After 1965

So far I have restricted my remarks to the Scandinavian situation prior to 1965. I have chosen that year as a dividing line because after 1965 some important changes began appearing in public attitudes and, correspondingly, in the practice and thinking of some of the Scandinavian governments. More than anything else, these shifts reflect a judgment on the success of the Scandinavian "middle way" and thus provide some important clues for other countries tempted to emulate it.

SWEDEN

A turning point in Swedish thinking came in 1965 with the prosecution of a Swedish newspaperman who had organized trips to Poland for Swedish women wanting abortions.[40] Not only was he breaking Swedish law, but so also were those women who had gone to Poland for purposes of obtaining an abortion. The result of this revelation was an immediate outcry in the press, so much so that the government dropped the prosecution of the newspaperman. The press debate, however, marked the opening round in a fresh wave of public agitation to have the Swedish law liberalized. Youth and women's groups in particular pressed the campaign vigorously in the press and elsewhere. The essence of the reform argument was that the law by no means took care of all those women wanting abortions, that it was overweighted with bureaucratic red tape, and that, in the end, the decision to abort should be left to the woman herself. Behind these specific complaints were some broader social pressures: a heightened female emancipation movement with a heavy stress on freedom of choice and self-determination for women; a housing shortage which made it difficult for young married couples or prospective married couples to find adequate accommodations; the increasingly extended period of female higher education, which means that many young women continue their education well into their twenties; and, finally, the general impact of a vigorously pressed family-planning campaign.

One direct consequence of the 1965 public debate was a decision by the government to form an abortion study commission. In his directives to this commission, the Swedish Minister of Justice suggested that the time was ripe for a consideration of the possibility of a more liberal law. He also suggested that one possible way to effect this liberalization would be to give women the full right during the early stages of pregnancy to make their own decision, provided some procedure was established to insure her freedom from the pressure of others. These were, however, only suggestions and the commission was left free to explore different possible solutions.[41] The commission was scheduled to make its recommendations in the fall of 1969. Thus, at the outset, the Swedish abortion commission was given a strong mandate to propose a more liberal law if it saw fit.

In part as a consequence of the formation of the study commission, and in part as an expression of a changing public attitude, some important changes began appearing in the statistics on legal abortions after 1965. First, a significant rise is discernible in the percentage of abortion applications granted by the Royal Medical Board, rising from 79 percent in 1964 to over 90 percent in 1967, with the trend continuing upward. By 1968, very few applications were being denied by the Medical Board (Table 7). At the same time, there has been a gradual increase in the number of applications to the Medical Board; thus, more applications are being made and a much higher proportion are being granted. Second, there has been a sharp rise in the number of abortions granted on the basis of the two-doctor permission. Between 1965 and 1967, that figure quadrupled (Table 7). Third, there has been a sharp rise in the overall number of legal abortions, with twice as many in 1967 as in 1964 (Table 6). Fourth, there has been a steep rise in the ratio of legal abortions per 1,000 live births, going from 38 in 1964 to 79 in 1967 (Table 6). The number of women receiving legal abortions in the fifteen to nineteen age group has more than quadrupled since 1960 and has almost doubled since 1964 (Table 9). The corresponding change in the data for women over thirty is much less. Moreover, as Table 9 shows, there has been a rise in legal abortions granted to those women who have had no previous pregnancies and a very significant increase (nearly double) in the number of unmarried women granted legal abortions. Sixth, there has been a huge change in the number of women granted an abortion on the basis of the "anticipated weakness" category (Table 8).

What do these shifts signify? Primarily, they indicate that both the Royal Medical Board and those physicians involved in the two-doctor decisions have become, since 1965, increasingly permissive in interpreting the law. This permissiveness is said to reflect four influences: 1) the very existence of the study commission, which portends a change in the law in the near future in a more liberal direction; 2) a change in attitude on the part of doctors, many of whom are more tolerant toward legal abortion than was the case some years ago; 3) the absence of any effective opposition from religious, medical or social groups to further liberalization of abortion law and practice; 4) and a great increase in the number of women applying for abortion. The sharp rise in abortions performed on the basis of the two-doctor decisions is thought to signal the beginning of a trend away from recourse to the Royal Medical Board (which the board, reportedly, would welcome). At present, the rise in the total number of legal abortions is heavily traceable to the rise since 1965 in the two-doctor form of legal authorization (Table 7). And the rise there is thought to be due to a greater permissiveness on the part of doctors. As Table 8 indicates, much more frequent resort is made to the category of "anticipated weakness," a category particularly used to justify the granting of abortions to young and unmarried women. The rise in the number of abortions granted to young and unmarried women is one of the major elements in the overall rise in legal abortions since 1965. More and more doctors responsible for the two-doctor decisions, as well as the Royal Medical Board, are now willing to take account of the future prospects of unmarried women, and therefore make use of the category of "anticipated weakness"—which can be interpreted to mean anticipated psychological, economic and social difficulties attendant upon unmarried motherhood. Similarly, the fact of earlier marriages, particularly among women students, has increasingly disposed doctors to be sympathetic to abortions among women who have no immediate prospects of setting up self-sustaining households. It also seems likely that there is a heightened responsiveness to the demands of many women for greater sexual freedom and freedom of procreative choice.

There is widespread agreement that, at present, it has become relatively easy for a woman to get a legal abortion. As the law is now being interpreted, no woman with any reasonable grounds for an abortion is likely to be denied. One consequence of this trend is that illegal abortions are now thought to be declining. Estimates during the late 1960s (particularly by members of the Ministry of Justice) are that there are

anywhere from 2,500 to 5,000 illegal abortions annually, with 5,000 as
the highest estimate. There has also, reportedly, been a sharp drop in
the price of illegal abortions (now thought to be only about 100 dollars),
a drop traceable, in effect, to a declining "market" for such abortions.
At any rate, there is a wide consensus that the number of illegal abortions now runs well below the number of legal abortions. Thus, while
it may no longer be possible to say, as was said prior to 1965, that the
Swedish laws have not succeeded in reducing the illegal-abortion rate,
it has, of course, to be taken into account that the more permissive
attitude in interpreting the law is a major explanation of the change.

Despite the greater permissiveness in interpreting the present law,
there appears to be little inclination on the part of Swedish authorities,
legal and medical, either to remove all abortion laws from the books or
to so rewrite the law as to institute an unregulated abortion on request.
For one thing, it is pointed out that the present law as presently
interpreted (rather loosely) now makes abortion available to most of
those women who have any reasonable grounds for wanting an abortion.
Many believe that the introduction of any further indications into the
law—particularly a purely "social" indication—would make the law all
but meaningless; at that point the criteria would become even more vague
and subjective. For another thing, there remains a persistent conviction
among Swedish authorities that some kind of regulation of abortion is
necessary. The main reason for this conviction is twofold. First, it is
widely felt among doctors that late abortions should be avoided,
particularly after the twelfth week; hence it is felt that any change in
the law should have the effect of putting pressure upon women to have
early abortions. Many Swedish doctors already believe that too many
abortions are now performed too late in pregnancy, increasing the
possibility of complications for the women involved and the difficulty
of the operation for the doctors. Second, it is felt that, for the sake of
greater freedom of choice for women, there has to be some consultative
process. If a woman is to be genuinely free, particularly free from the
coercion or undue pressure of family, friends or consorts, then it is
necessary that she have an independent source of counsel and assistance.
Also, and in conjunction with improved programs of social assistance to
pregnant women in difficult straits, it is felt that it remains important
that women be offered real alternatives to abortion. To have a law
which allowed a total abortion on request would, therefore, open the
way to a persistence of late abortions and also, in effect, not give a
woman full freedom of choice.

Just how these goals will be effected is not yet clear, but the elements
of a consensus exist. Thus, it is believed that either by changing the
wording of the law itself or by instituting procedural changes (e.g.,
having the bulk of the decisions made by the two-doctor method), abor-

tion decisions ought to be placed almost entirely in the hands of pregnant women up until the twelfth week. The only condition would be
a required consultative process, but a process which would, in the end,
leave the final decision up to the woman. After twelve weeks, however,
the process would remain as it presently is and perhaps be made even
more difficult. The end result of this strategy would be (1) to eliminate
the lengthy social investigation required by the present law (thus responding to the objection that the present law imposes bureaucratic
indignities on women as well as delaying their legitimate abortions);
(2) to give women full freedom of choice up until the twelfth week
(thus responding to those who think women should be free to make the
final decision themselves); (3) to put some degree of pressure on
women to make rapid decisions about whether they want an abortion
(thus cutting down on the number of medically hazardous late abortions); (4) to insure, by the consultation requirement and improved
social-welfare help, that women, in making their own decisions, are
free from undue outside pressure and presented with some viable and
strengthened alternatives to abortion.

DENMARK

Though less dramatically, events and public attitudes in Denmark in
the past few years have been similar to those in Sweden.[42] As Table 10
indicates, there has been a steady rise in the number of applications
and in the percentage of the applications approved. By 1968, nearly
75 percent of the applications made in Copenhagen were granted. There
has also been a steady rise in the rate of abortions per 1,000 live births
(Table 6). Of those applications granted in 1965, about 80 percent were
approved under the category of mental and physical health, with a heavy
proportion of these on the grounds of mental health, normally construed
to include a social indication. About 2 percent were granted on the
grounds that a woman would be an unfit mother, for either physical or
psychiatric reasons. The rest were divided among ethical (e.g., rape)
and eugenic indications. There also has been an increase in the number
of applicants from fifteen to nineteen years old and in unmarried applicants (Tables 11 and 12).

While there is a widespread belief that the Mothers' Aid Centers have
become more permissive over the years in granting abortions, a point
conceded by the centers themselves, the centers also insist that the
women being granted abortions now tend to have more serious problems
than those some years ago; hence the shift does not entirely reflect a
change in the philosophy of the centers. While it is true that the percentage of applications granted in Denmark has not risen so sharply as
in Sweden in the past few years, a comparison of the population of

Denmark with that of Sweden (Table 5) and a comparison of the number of abortions performed in the two countries (Table 6) show that Denmark has, comparatively speaking, had a much greater proportion of legal abortions for the size of its population than has Sweden. Moreover, the ratio of abortions to 1,000 live births has been consistently higher over the years in Denmark, although the Swedish figure, because of a sharp rise after 1965, is beginning to close the gap. The reasons for the higher rate of legal abortions in Denmark is not clear, but some Swedish observers have suggested that contraceptives have always been more readily available in Sweden than in Denmark.

Within the past few years, the Danish Mothers' Aid Centers have come under increasing criticism for not granting more abortions. This was not the case in earlier years. During the early 1950s, the centers were criticized for being too liberal in their interpretation of the law. The new criticisms appear to reflect the same constellation of changing public attitudes noted in Sweden: increased pressure from women's and youth groups for abortion on request; the pressures of female-emancipation movements; longer educational requirements for women; a more permissive general attitude toward sexual freedom; and the pressures of rising costs and housing shortages. Unlike Sweden, there has apparently been comparatively little diminution in the illegal-abortion rate over the years. M. Ingerslev has concluded that the number of illegal abortions may actually be rising.[43] Henrik Hoffmeyer and his colleagues have written, concerning illegal abortions:

> The maximum number for 1961 was estimated at about 15,400, the minimum number at about 5,800. There is reason to believe, however, that the maximum number is closer to the actual occurrence. Corresponding calculations for the years back to the commencement of the Pregnancy Act show that the number of illegal abortions (like that of legal abortions) rose sharply until 1950, while after that time there has been a fall of 10 to 14 percent. The number of illegal abortions, however, is still far too big and presents a very serious problem to the national economy as well as to the individual.[44]

According to a 1967 estimate, the number ranged from 10,000 to 12,000 a year.[45] These estimates are particularly significant in the light of similar calculations from Sweden (5,000 maximum) with its much larger population, again indicating that abortion in Denmark presents a different picture in many regards from Sweden. As Henrik Hoffmeyer has suggested, nothing short of abortion on request would bring the illegal-abortion rate down very sharply, simply because many of those women who now get illegal abortions do so because they have decided they want no more children; they have no "indication" they could claim.[46]

In 1967 the Danish government appointed a committee under the Ministry of Justice to reevaluate the abortion law of 1956.[47] In the spring of 1969, the committee offered a series of proposals which will be acted upon by Parliament. Four new indications were recommended. The first two are "automatic," that is, women citing one or both may have an abortion performed without the permission of one of the joint councils, thus eliminating an investigation. The third and fourth indications require council permission. The two automatic indications are *Advanced Age*: if the woman has completed her thirty-eighth year prior to the end of the twelfth week of pregnancy, and *Multiparity*: if the woman has given birth to at least four children who live at home and are under eighteen years old. Since 90 percent of the applicants citing these conditions under the medical and sociomedical indications of the old law were granted permission by a council, it was concluded that they had become established as grounds for abortion in themselves and therefore investigation and permission should be no longer necessary. The committee also recommended that an abortion be allowed without special permission when it is necessary to avoid danger to the woman's life or deterioration of her physical or mental health. Under the old law the danger to life and health had to be "serious"; the committee recommended that this qualification be dropped but that the character of the danger be exclusively or mainly medical.

The other new indications, which require council permission, are *Immaturity*: if the woman cannot for the time being take care of a child in a responsible manner because of her youth or immaturity, taking into account possible help from the woman's family, the child's father or other sources, and *Social Stress*: if pregnancy, childbirth, or care for a child or another child may be assumed to result in severe stress on the woman, which may not be averted in any other way except by the termination of the pregnancy. The woman's age, workload, care of other children in the family and other personal factors, as well as the family's housing, economic situation and health should be taken into account.

The immaturity proposal is worded rather vaguely as to age partly because the committee did not wish to weaken motivation for contraception among the young by offering the possibility of abortion for all women under a particular age—under twenty, say, or under eighteen. (As in the old law, however, a girl who becomes pregnant before the age of fifteen may always obtain a legal abortion, if the pregnancy is not too far advanced.) However broad the social-stress indication, the committee stopped short of allowing abortion for personal reasons, that is, if a woman simply did not want a child, or another child, or did not wish to give up her job or studies. Many consider it a sufficiently liberal reform that "social stress" has been recommended as an indication in itself instead of being lumped under the broad medical, medicosocial indication. Others reason that any woman living under very stressful social circumstances could easily develop medical symptoms which would permit her an abortion and that this new indication merely anticipates that possibility.

Among other committee recommendations were that the time limit for abortions be shortened from 16 to 12 weeks of gestation, that legal abortion be restricted to residents of Denmark (except for strictly medical reasons), that women not be punished for self-induced abortion or resort to other kinds of illegal abortion (such cases have not been prosecuted in recent years anyway), and that in cases of rape it no longer be considered necessary to involve the police before accepting the application under the "ethical" indication.

Only one member of the committee, Dr. Henrik Hoffmeyer, recommended abortion on request. He contended that, with the recommended new indications and a generally broader interpretation of the new law, even more applications will be granted in the future than in the past (60 percent to 70 percent in recent years). The few cases that will be refused would not justify the huge sociomedical bureaucracy now required to process and judge applications. Dr. Hoffmeyer also criticized the willingness to recognize social indications but not personal reasons for abortion, especially since women who claim the latter frequently resort to illegal abortion, which remains a fairly sizable problem in Denmark. Finally, according to Dr. Hoffmeyer, contraception is so widely used in Denmark that even abortion on demand would not raise the total number of abortions by much, if at all. In any case, he argued, some of the modern contraceptive methods reveal little or no difference between abortion and contraception.

In the last two years there has been a sharp decline in the number of live births in Denmark. Part of the decline may be due to the widespread contraception Dr. Hoffmeyer refers to. But, according to the Mothers' Aid Center in Copenhagen, there has also been a rise in the number of legal abortions, which, along with continuing illegal abortions, also contributed to the drop in the number of births. Whether the committee's recommendation, if accepted by the Parliament, will substantially increase legal abortions and reduce illegal abortions remains to be seen. It may be that, as Dr. Hoffmeyer has said, only abortion on demand will radically cut the incidence of illegal abortion, but even then, as in Eastern Europe, there is liable to be a residue. If nothing else, however, the committee's proposal to shorten the time limit for abortion, it is believed, should help lower Denmark's comparatively high abortion-mortality rate by reducing the risks attendant upon late abortion and encouraging wider use of the vacuum aspiration method for the majority of abortions (best used in the earlier stages of pregnancy).

While there is a considerable likelihood that, as a result of public pressure for liberalization, plus the recommendations of the committee, the Danish law will be changed to some extent in the near future, the thinking of Danish specialists on the nature of a possible liberalization is very similar to that found in Sweden. Many staff workers at the Mothers' Aid Centers, for instance, while favoring some change in the law or its application, nevertheless are doubtful about the wisdom of a purely "social" indication, one which would altogether prescind from some connection with mental or physical health. One objection to such an indication is the likely impossibility of establishing meaningful norms; better, many feel, that there be abortion on request than have norms so loose and open to different judgments as to be all but useless in making decisions. Another objection rests on a widespread conviction that either a much looser law or abortion on request would have the effect of slowing the growing acceptance of contraception. Despite this acceptance, in great part due to the systematic program of education conducted by the Mothers' Aid Centers but also as a result of the June 1966 act entitled the "Prophylactic Care of Pregnant Women"—which entitles pregnant women to see a doctor without cost five times and obliges doctors at the six-week postnatal visit to provide contraceptive information—the abortion rate has not declined.

The most common explanation of this phenomenon is that some groups in the female population are still using contraceptives very ineffectively. Moreover, it is believed that the creation of the concept of an "unwanted pregnancy" is a direct result of the abortion liberalization and contraception drive. That concept, once socially established, leads women to take whatever steps are necessary to terminate a pregnancy. In general, abortion is now seen as a method of family planning, and the fear is that a much greater liberalization of the law, or abortion on demand, would make abortion the method of choice for what is considered already too large a group of women: those who are indifferent about or overly casual in the use of contraceptives. One important aim of the contraception drive is to reduce the abortion rate: hence, it is felt, too liberal an abortion law could thwart the purposes of that drive. At the same time, however, there is some agreement that a tightening of the abortion law—which few, in any case, desire—would be a bad way of pressing the contraception program. Instead, something in the way of a compromise solution is likely to emerge from any change in the law: some further degree of liberalization in the wording of the law or some change in the procedure to be followed under the law. But any change would stop short of abortion on request, which seems desired neither by the public at large nor by most specialists concerned with abortion.

Although it is true, as noted, that Sweden and Denmark do not present identical abortion pictures, there are some important common patterns. Both countries have seen a steady rise in the number of legal abortions, primarily because of public pressure toward greater permissiveness, which has resulted in greater permissiveness on the part of those authorities charged with making abortion decisions. Both countries have also seen a steady rise in the number of applications for abortions, despite a great increase in the use of contraceptives, including a growing use of the pill. Further, there is a widespread belief in both countries that the Scandinavian "middle way," or the employment of what I have called a "moderate code," is inherently unstable. As the present laws are worded, they provide the basis for granting most women with a genuine problem a legal abortion. Yet, especially in Denmark, illegal abortions remain a problem; a significant number of women want abortions who would not, even under the loosest possible "indications," have a case for legal abortion. Short of abortion on demand, no further liberalization of the law would be likely to meet the demands of this group of women. Thus, many conclude, it is impossible for any genuine "middle way" to cope entirely with the problem of illegal abortions. The real dilemma, as many see it, is that while a "middle way" does not entirely work (at least if one of its purposes is to reduce illegal abortions significantly), a system of abortion on demand would, despite what many women think, actually lead to a lessened freedom of choice, particularly by leaving women vulnerable to outside pressures.[48] Thus, while there is a strong drive for easier abortions in the Scandinavian countries and a rise in the number being granted in Sweden, Denmark and possibly Norway, there is still a considerable reluctance about abortion on request, even though it is fully recognized that the present "middle way"— even a "middle way" which has become increasingly liberal in its direction—has many drawbacks. Though demands for a repeal of all abortion laws are becoming more common in the United States, the Scandinavians, on the whole, have not found that their experience suggests this resolution; they continue to believe some government control of induced abortion is necessary.

NOTES

1. Gunnar af Geijerstam, "Abortion in Scandinavia," paper presented at the International Conference on Abortion, Hot Springs, Virginia, November 17–20, 1968.
2. *Therapeutic Abortion and the Law in Sweden* (Stockholm: The Swedish Institute, n.d.), pp. 3–4.
3. U. Borell and L. Engstrom, "Legal Abortions in Sweden," *World Medical Journal*, 13 (May-June 1966), pp. 72–75; C. Tietze, "Legal Abortion in Scandinavia," *Quarterly Review of Surgery, Obstetrics and Gynecology*, 16 (October-December 1959), pp. 227–30; Jans Otto Ottoson, "Abstract," Harvard Divinity School–Kennedy Foundation International Conference on Abortion, Washington, D.C., September 1967; Lawrence Lader, *Abortion* (Indianapolis: Bobbs-Merrill, 1966), pp. 117–20; and *Swedish Laws on Sterilization, Abor-*

tion, and Castration (Summary) (Stockholm: National Board of Health, October 1963), which states:

"The law on abortion of 1938 was amended in 1941, 1942, 1946, and 1963. Under the law as it now stands, abortion is permitted

1) if due to a woman's illness, physical defects or weakness (medical-social reasons) childbirth would entail serious danger to her life or health, i.e. on medical reasons;

2) if with regard to a woman's condition of life and other circumstances there is reason to assume that her physical or psychic strength would be seriously reduced through child birth and child care, i.e. on social-medical reasons [1946 Amendment];

3) if a woman has become pregnant as the result of rape, other criminal coercion or incestuous sexual intercourse, if she is insane or an imbecile, or under 15 years of age at the time of the fertilizing coition, i.e. on humanitarian reasons;

4) if there is reason to assume that the woman or the father of the expected child would transmit to their offspring hereditary insanity, imbecility, a serious disease or a serious physical handicap; i.e. on eugenic reasons. An abortion for the reason of any hereditary defect in the mother is contingent on sterilization simultaneously with the abortion, unless sterilization appears risky or unnecessary (e.g. with regard to the woman's advanced age or because she is to be permanently committeed to an institution). In other words, sterilization is laid down as a condition of abortion, the subject being under the necessity of taking both or foregoing the abortion.

5) if there is reason to presume that the expected child will suffer from severe illness or a serious defect due to injury during the embryonal stage [1963 Amendment].

"An abortion for other reasons than disease or a physical defect in the woman (i.e. the most cogent medical reasons) may not be performed after the twentieth week of pregnancy. The National Board of Health may make exceptions and authorize the performance of the operation before the end of the twenty-fourth week of pregnancy."

4. *Therapeutic Abortion and the Law in Sweden, op. cit.,* pp. 6–9.
5. Borell and Engstrom, *op. cit.,* p. 72.
6. Vera Skalts and Magna Nørgaard, "Abortion Legislation in Denmark," in David T. Smith (ed.), *Abortion and the Law* (Cleveland: Western Reserve University, 1967), p. 149.
7. *Ibid.,* p. 155.
8. K. Niemineva and O. Ylinen, "The New Law Concerning Therapeutic Abortion in Finland," *International Journal of Sexology,* 6 (August 1952), pp. 43–46.
9. M. Rouhunkoski and M. Olki, "Therapeutic Abortion in Finland," *Fourth International Conference on Planned Parenthood* (London: International Planned Parenthood Federation, 1953), pp. 76–82. Condensed in *International Journal of Sexology,* 7 (November 1953), pp. 81–82.
10. Finland: Laws, Statutes, Etc., "Interruption of Pregnancy," *International Digest of Health Legislation,* 2 (1951), pp. 559–61.
11. "Public Health and Medical Care, 1964" *The Official Statistics of Finland,* 11 (1967), p. 155.
12. L. Rauramo and M. Grönroos, "On Subjective and Objective Motivation for Legal Abortion in a Social Advice Centre's Material," *Annales Chirurgiae et Gynaecologiae Fenniae,* 49 (1960), pp. 1–14.
13. *Ibid.*
14. Rouhunkoski and Olki, *op. cit.,* p. 82.
15. Unless otherwise indicated, the information on Norway is taken from Johannes Andenaes, "A Presentation of Data Concerning Abortion from Other Nations," unpublished paper, University of Chicago Conference on Abortion, Spring 1958. The following quotation from the Norwegian law on abortion is from

Norway: Laws, Statutes, etc., "Interruption of Pregnancy," *International Digest of Health Legislation,* 16 (1965), p. 148:

"1) Any pregnant woman shall be authorized to apply for interruption of her pregnancy:

    (1) when this operation is necessary to avoid serious danger to her life or health. In estimating how serious such danger is, any special tendency to physical or mental diseases shown by the woman must be considered, and also living conditions and other circumstances liable to affect her health or to give rise to physical or mental exhaustion;

    (2) when there is a serious risk because of:

        (*a*) a hereditary defect in one of the parents;

        (*b*) the woman becoming ill during pregnancy;

        (*c*) a lesion in the embryo *in utero*

which might lead to grave illness or a serious physical or mental defect in the child;

    (3) when there are reasons for believing that the pregnancy is the result of a criminal act committed under the conditions defined in Sections 192 to 199 of the Penal Code, or of circumstances specified in Sections 207 and 208 of the code, or if the woman is obviously mentally ill or mentally retarded."

16. C. Tietze, "Abortion in Europe," *American Journal of Public Health,* 57 (November 1967), p. 1927.

17. Borell and Engstrom, *op. cit.,* p. 74.

18. *Ibid.,* p. 75.

19. *Ibid.,* p. 74.

20. Skalts and Nørgaard, *op. cit.,* p. 161.

21. *Ibid.,* pp. 161–62, from which the following quotation is taken: "The last few years have shown an increasing incidence of recommendation for abortion. This is probably due to the fact that the women and their doctors are becoming increasingly familiar with the practice of the Mothers' Aid Centers, so that only those women who have some chance of getting a favorable recommendation from the Centers apply to Mothers' Aid."

22. Robert E. Cooke *et al.* (eds.), *The Terrible Choice* (New York: Bantam Books, 1968), p. 66.

23. Lader, *op. cit.,* p. 120; C. Tietze, "Tables with Basic Statistics," mimeographed sheet distributed at the Harvard Divinity School–Kennedy Foundation International Conference on Abortion, Washington, D.C., September 1967.

24. See particularly C. P. Harrison, "The Futility of Legalizing Abortion," *Canadian Medical Association Journal,* 95 (August 20, 1966), pp. 360–66.

25. Kerstin Höök, "Refused Abortion: A Follow-Up Study of 249 Women Whose Applications Were Refused by the National Board of Health in Sweden," *Acta Psychiatrica Scandinavica,* Supplementum 168, 39 (1963), p. 12.

26. *Ibid.,* citing Åren and Simon; Kerstin Uhrus, "Some Aspects of the Swedish Law Governing Termination of Pregnancy," *Lancet,* 2 (December 12, 1964), p. 1292.

27. Skalts and Nørgaard, *op. cit.,* p. 167; *cf.* Mary S. Calderone (ed.), *Abortion in the United States* (New York: Hoeber-Harper, 1958), pp. 173–74.

28. L. Huldt, "Outcome of Pregnancy When Legal Abortion Is Readily Available," *Lancet,* 1 (March 2, 1968), p. 467.

29. *Abortion: An Ethical Discussion* (Church Assembly Board for Social Responsibility, London: Church Information Office, 1965), p. 54; Robert E. Hall, "Thalidomide and Our Abortion Laws," *Columbia University Forum,* 6 (Winter 1963), p. 10; P. H. Gebhard *et al., Pregnancy, Birth and Abortion* (New York: Hoeber-Harper, 1958), p. 224; "Legalized Abortion: Report by the Council of the Royal College of Obstetricians and Gynaecologists," *British Medical Journal,* 1 (April 2, 1966), pp. 851ff; S. A. Cosgrove, "Lack of Relation Between Therapeutic and Criminal Abortion," *Quarterly Review of Sur-*

gery, Obstetrics and Gynecology, 16 (October-December 1959), pp. 223–26.
30. *Cf.* L. Freundt, "Surveys in Induced and Spontaneous Abortions in the Copenhagen Area," *Acta Psychiatrica Scandinavica,* 40 (1964), Supplementum 180, pp. 235–37.
31. Jerome M. Kummer and Zad Leavy, "Therapeutic Abortion Law Confusion," *Journal of the American Medical Association,* 195 (January 10, 1966), p. 99.
32. Glanville Williams, "The Legalization of Medical Abortion," *The Eugenics Review,* 56 (April 1964), p. 24.
33. Lader, *op. cit.,* p. 120.
34. Glanville Williams, *The Sanctity of Life and the Criminal Law* (London: Faber and Faber, 1958), p. 242.
35. Martin Ekblad, "Induced Abortion on Psychiatric Grounds," *Acta Psychiatrica et Neurologica Scandinavica,* Supplementum 99–102 (Stockholm, 1955), p. 19; discussed in Williams, *The Sanctity of Life, op. cit.,* p. 219.
36. Skalts and Nørgaard, *op. cit.,* p. 168.
37. M. McDermott, in the Sloane Hospital for Women's Symposium on "The Social Problem of Abortion," *Bulletin of the Sloane Hospital for Women,* 11 (Fall 1965), p. 74; K.-H. Mehlan, "Reducing Abortion Rate and Increasing Fertility by Social Policy in the German Democratic Republic," in *Proceedings of the World Population Conference, Belgrade, 1965,* Vol. 2 (New York: United Nations, 1967), especially section 11, p. 226: "There is a marked increase in the proportion of women without a previous birth or with only one child. . . . Abortion is shifting to younger and childless women"; Kenneth R. Niswander, "Medical Abortion Practices in the United States," in *Abortion and the Law, op. cit.,* p. 54; András Klinger, "Abortion Programs," in Bernard Berelson, *et al.* (eds.), *Family Planning and Population Programs* (Chicago: University of Chicago, 1966), especially the following: "[East European data] indicate the insistence of women still in their prime reproductive years to limit their families to one or two children. The increasing trend of induced abortions among young unmarried women is especially noteworthy" (p. 473); and Minoru Muramatsu (ed.), *Japan's Experience in Family Planning—Past and Present* (Tokyo: Family Planning Federation of Japan, 1967), pp. 71, 78.
38. Mehlan, *op. cit.,* p. 226.
39. Tietze, *op. cit.*
40. Except where indicated, much of the following information was gathered by the author on a trip to Sweden and Denmark in the fall of 1968. I am indebted to the Swedish officials and doctors I interviewed, in particular to: Dr. Karl-Inge Öster, Head of the Division of Social and Forensic Psychiatry of the National Board of Health and Welfare; Dr. Nils Wiqvist, Associate Professor, Department of Women's Diseases, Karolinska Hospital, Stockholm; Dr. Kjell Ohrberg, Bureau of Mental Care, Stockholm; and Kansliradet Gunvor Bergstrom, of the *1965 års abort-kommitteé; cf.* Birgitta Linnér, *Sex and Society in Sweden* (New York: Pantheon, 1967), pp. 74ff.; an important recent survey on Swedish sexual attitudes and practices in Hans L. Zetterberg, *Om Sexuallivet; Svevige* (Stockholm: Statens offentliga utredningar, 1969).
41. *Cf.* Andenaes, *op. cit.*
42. I am particularly indebted, in the remarks which follow, to information and opinions provided me by Dr. Henrik Hoffmeyer, formerly head of the psychiatric staff of the Mothers' Aid Center in Copenhagen and at present Assistant Superintendent of the State Psychiatric Hospital in Copenhagen; to Magna Nørgaard, Chief of the Department of Information and Statistics, Mothers' Aid Center, Copenhagen; and to Dr. Erik Rosen, Chief Gynecologist of the Mother's Aid Center, Copenhagen.
43. M. Ingerslev, "The Danish Abortion Laws," *Medicine, Science and the Law,* 7 (April 1967), p. 79.
44. Henrik Hoffmeyer, Magna Nørgaard and Vera Skalts, "Abortion, Sterilization, and Contraception," *The Journal of Sex Research,* 3 (February 1967), p. 14.
45. Mogens Landgreen, *Ugeskrift for Laeger* (1967), p. 434.

46. Author's interview with Dr. Hoffmeyer, September 1968; see also Sidney Gold-
    stein, "Premarital Pregnancies and Out-of-Wedlock Births in Denmark, 1950–
    1965," *Demography*, 4 (1967), pp. 925–936, in which a steady rise in out-
    of-wedlock births is discussed.

47. I am indebted to Dr. Henrik Hoffmeyer for a free translation of the main
    recommendations of the committee and his comments about them, and to
    Dr. Christopher Tietze of the Bio-Medical Division of the Population Council
    of New York for an abstract (in translation) of the committee's report,
    Betaenkning om adgang til svangerskabsafbrydelse [Report on access to termi-
    nation of pregnancy], Betaenkning nr. 522 (Denmark: Justitsministeriet.
    Copenhagen Statens Trykningskontor, 1969), pp. 188.

48. Freundt, *op. cit.*, p. 236. Freundt found that 11 of the 74 women he studied
    who had been legally aborted had been pressured by their mothers into hav-
    ing an abortion; 17 out of 63 who had illegal abortions had been similarly
    pressured.

CHAPTER 7

Permissive Legal Systems

IN A DISCUSSION OF the social consequences of different legal codes, those that put few if any obstacles in the way of women desiring abortions take a special place. On the one hand, they bring to pass the situation those opposed to abortion most fear: the existence of a permissive legal code verging upon or actualizing abortion on request. Yet precisely because they do so, they afford one an opportunity to see whether very permissive legal systems do in fact bring about some or any of the disastrous consequences envisioned or imagined by those vehemently opposed to abortion. On the other hand, very permissive systems represent what many reluctant advocates of limited liberalization, on political-pragmatic grounds only, would see as the ideal solution if it were politically possible. From the latter vantage point, one is able to see whether a very permissive system does in fact have the social benefits attributed to it.

As noted in the previous chapter, my interest lies in the social consequences of different kinds of legal codes, as a way of assembling further data to illuminate the moral problem. For if one should be concerned with the consequences of different ethical choices, and the embodiment on occasion of these choices in law, then it becomes important to see precisely what happens when one legal line or another is pursued. Naturally, the same caveat must be entered here as in the previous chapter: cultures differ, and any extrapolation from the social consequences of a legal system in one culture to the likely consequences in quite another culture must be approached warily. At the same time, as we shall see in Chapter 8, there are enough patterns which cross cultural lines—for instance, patterns common to Eastern Europe and Japan, whose cultures are quite different—that some cross-cultural comparisons can be made and used. The basis for such comparison is the existence of similar types of behavior under similar, or related, circumstances. One reason for the parallels is obvious. Abortion is performed on a woman's body, thus involving very basic psychological and physiological responses and reactions. Cultures differ, but the bodies of women are the same from one culture to another. Similarly, a desperate shortage of food or housing or employment, or the advent of technology, all seem to have roughly similar effects on very different cultures. Thus it is not surprising that certain similarities appear between one culture and another and that certain relationships will seem to hold from one culture to another.

My concerns here will continue those of the previous chapters, in which restrictive and mixed codes were investigated. What are the social consequences of permissive legal systems? What are the motives behind permissive legal systems, and to what extent are the goals of these systems, in the terms of those who framed them, realized? To what extent, in empirical terms, can one determine whether permissive systems do in fact bring about the harmful social consequence projected by those supporting the retention of restrictive laws? To what extent do permissive systems obviate some of the weaknesses of mixed systems? In general, what happens when a country puts into effect a very permissive abortion law?

One question can, once again, be dealt with briefly. What is the effect on the ethos of a culture when abortion laws are permissive? The same answer must be given here as was given when the question was raised about restrictive and mixed systems. There is just no way of knowing. There exist no data for measuring the general ethos of an entire culture, nor any clear criteria which would apply even if such data were available. It must suffice to say, at least on empirical grounds, that there is no significant evidence which would prove that the introduction of permissive laws has a disastrous general effect on the attitudes toward human life expressed in other areas of the culture. If one believes that permissive laws on abortion will inevitably produce harmful attitudes toward the whole of human life, one is under some obligation to show empirically where and how this has happened in some existing culture. For my part, at any rate, I can find no such evidence from the countries I am going to examine here—Japan and the East European nations. On the contrary, it is much more realistic to say that if there is any correlation, it is most likely that abortion law and practice will reflect the ethos of a culture, rather than be its cause. But again, of course, that kind of statement is equally unverifiable, at least in terms of existing data. What one can do, alternatively, is simply to try and chart some of the different social effects of abortion in permissive legal systems. The result will be a much more complex body of data, but it might be possible at least to ask the question, when inquiring into the value of restrictive and mixed systems, whether one wants to achieve or to avoid some of the consequences of permissive systems.

If the United States, Great Britain (until 1967), India and the Latin American countries have provided the prime examples of countries with restrictive systems, and the Scandinavian countries examples of nations with moderate systems, the East European countries and Japan provide the main examples of countries with permissive legal systems. I will deal first with the Eastern European countries and then move on to Japan.

A Point of Departure: 1955

In 1955 the Soviet Union, after nearly twenty years of restrictive laws, introduced a considerable liberalization. This change set the pattern for other East European countries. Poland introduced a permissive system in 1956, as did Bulgaria and Hungary; Czechoslovakia did the same in 1958; and Yugoslavia followed in 1960. The purpose behind this general move has been described by András Klinger:

> Each of these measures started from the fact that it is the right of the woman (mother) to determine the size of the family, and that it is the woman who is entitled to interrupt a desired pregnancy by means of induced abortion. Besides, the basic goal of the measures taken was also the protection of the health of the women, since in the preceding years a great number of women had undergone illegal abortions, which have often jeopardized not only the health, but in many cases also the life of the woman. On the basis of the new legal measures, abortions may be carried out, in general, only in hospitals and health institutions.[1]

The key motives thus were broadly two: freedom of choice on the part of the woman, and the protection of the health of women. As we shall see, however, other factors, such as the lack of effective contraceptives, also had a part to play in some of the East European countries. But in general the public-health argument and the desire to accord women social equality (taken to mean a free choice on the part of women to have only those children they desire) were the major considerations behind the permissiveness of the laws.

During the years after 1955, the East European countries (with the exception of East Germany until 1965) permitted legal abortion on easy and flexible grounds unless there were specific medical contraindications. Abortion was not anywhere exempted from legal control, but the control was loose; hence, the legitimacy of labeling (with the noted exception) the East European laws and practice "permissive."[2] Czechoslovakia required that a woman present specific indications, but the criteria were not difficult to meet; in Czechoslovakia, East Germany, Yugoslavia and Hungary abortions had to be authorized by medical commissions; in

Rumania and the Soviet Union women could go directly to outpatient clinics. Hungary and Bulgaria required that women go to hospitals, and in Poland a woman was permitted to go to her family doctor. In all these countries, according to K.-H. Mehlan, the ultimate decision rested with the surgeon who was to perform the operation.[3] In each, the acceptable indications for abortion were very broad: medical, social, socioeconomic, eugenic, fetal and psychiatric. In short, all the common indications were acceptable in principle and the practical conditions easy to meet. Poland, Yugoslavia and the Soviet Union required instruction in contraception when abortions were authorized, and the other countries also made some attempts in the same direction.[4]

Soviet Union

With these generalities as a background, it will be useful to take a look at the East European countries one by one (updating the history when necessary), beginning with the Soviet Union. M. G. Field and Lawrence Lader have provided excellent accounts of abortion there, and H. Kent Geiger treats the subject in the context of the social and cultural changes that have rocked the Soviet family since the Revolution. It is from these three works that much of the following sketch is taken.[5] The Soviet laws on abortion fall into four distinct periods: 1917 to 1920, during which abortions were totally illegal, even on medical grounds; 1920 to 1936, during which abortions were legal, providing that certain indications were present; 1936 to 1955, during which abortions were once again made illegal, except on strictly medical grounds; and 1955 to the present, during which abortions on the request of the woman and in the absence of medical contraindications have been permitted. The primary reasons behind the liberalization of the laws from 1920 to 1936 were a desire to avoid the physical harm believed to have been caused by illegal abortions during the earlier restrictive period, and the goal of granting women social freedom and equality. Lenin, in particular, had insisted that women should have the right "of deciding for themselves a fundamental issue of their lives."[6] Since women were being exhorted to enter the work force, it was felt to be only logical to provide them with the means of controlling their fertility.[7]

Originally, the liberalization beginning in 1920 was intended to be temporary. The reigning theory was that, as social conditions improved and as the state took over the burdens of childrearing, abortions would become increasingly unnecessary and the problem of unwanted pregnancies would cease to exist. Concurrently, attempts were made to keep the rate of abortions down by means of government dissemination of birth-control information and contraceptives (at that time, of course,

neither the IUD nor anovulatory pills existed), and by the development
of institutions and facilities to help mothers take care of their children.
Just how concerted this campaign was may be doubted; a number of
American visitors at the time believed the effort was very slight.[8] In any
case, the government was unable to make good on its promise to re-
lieve women of the major responsibilities of child care. As for contraception, Lenin thought it "defeatist," and he also worried that it might
encourage libertinism, especially among the peasants.[9]

Along with the new liberal laws, an educational campaign was put
into effect after 1920 warning women that, although abortions were
much safer when carried out under hospital safeguards, they still carried a degree of risk to a woman's health and should be avoided if at all
possible. Doctors, while given wide latitude on the performance of abortions, were subject to severe penalties if their abortion practice was
carried out for strictly monetary gain (though how this could have been
proved is hard to guess). Doctors also were urged to discourage abortions, particularly in the case of a first pregnancy. By the end of the
1920s, it was generally felt that the permissive laws had in fact led to a
significant drop in the number of illegal abortions and a corresponding
decline in the number of injuries and deaths due to these abortions.
Nevertheless, according to Geiger, the problem of abortion in Moscow
and Leningrad during the 1920s was called "massive" and "horrifying"
by older party members. Women resorted to abortions so they could
stay at work—and work outside the home was strongly urged upon them
as a revoluntionary ideal. In effect, Geiger says, they were forced to
choose then, as today, between motherhood and social equality.[10]

By the early 1930s, the Soviet government had begun to show alarm
at the large number of abortions, and particularly at what they took to
be an increasing indifference on the part of many women to family responsibilities.[11] There had been for at least a decade a disturbing number of abandoned and otherwise homeless children (estimates for 1922
ranged as high as nine million), and the state institutions to provide for
them were too few and generally inferior.[12] The civil strife, the poverty
and the general disorganization attendant upon the wholesale recon-
struction of society after the Revolution were particularly hard on
family stability. The regime's early hands-off policy toward the family,
the encouragement of individual freedom in sexual matters and the easy
divorce laws promulgated in the 1920s (not to mention the political ar-
rests and purges) resulted in countless broken homes and widespread
social disruption, with women and children the chief victims. (Even
some party members refused to support their children after divorce.)
Before his death Lenin was urging more discipline, less personal freedom as a proper revolutionary attitude. "The Revolution," he said, "cannot tolerate orgiastic conditions."[13]

Gradually the government reversed its early permissiveness and began to move toward a conservative support of the family. In 1934 a campaign was mounted against adultery, bigamy and sexual promiscuity; marriage was approved, divorce frowned upon and the stable family held up as an ideal. To make clear its seriousness about the latter, the government decreed that parents would be liable for the delinquent acts of their children.[14] Two years later, in 1936, abortions were again made illegal except on the basis of carefully specified, wholly medical indications. The prohibition was unpopular despite the promise of material help for mothers of large families and pressure on divorced men to keep up alimony payments and child support. But the regime was adamant in proclaiming it, partly because of concern about family stability and partly because of the anxiety felt by many doctors about the medical dangers of abortion on a massive scale. There was also worry about the country's rate of population growth and specifically Stalin's fear of the military threat of Nazi Germany. Stalin wanted the insurance of a higher birthrate: more people would mean more workers and more soldiers.[15]

The new restrictiveness is generally believed to have immediately raised the rate of illegal abortion, with a corresponding higher maternal-mortality rate. Many doctors, it seems, continued to perform abortions even after the restrictive laws had gone into effect, and many saw them as morally desirable as well as economically advantageous. During this restrictive period, the Soviet government took steps to provide aid to mothers, particularly by the establishment of child-care centers, and in general attempted to encourage family cohesion. For example, a few years later, in 1944, common-law marriages, which had been allowed under the 1926 code, were no longer recognized as legal.[16]

In 1955 the law was again liberalized, essentially out of concern for what was felt to be the great harm done by illegal abortions and the desire to stop the profiteering of criminal abortionists. There was also a realization that "the legal prohibition of abortion could neither eradicate the practice nor raise the birthrate,"[17] a greater responsiveness to the raising demand for smaller families, and a renewed emphasis on the ideal which had led to the 1920 liberalization: the granting of greater social freedom to women, in this case the freedom to decide whether or not to bear a child. K.-H. Mehlan has pointed to some additional reasons for the 1955 change: the absence of effective contraceptives that were acceptable to all classes of people, and a desire to bring all women under closer medical supervision. Yet as András Klinger has pointed out, the intention of the 1955 liberalization was only to effect a temporary, emergency measure; it was not intended that the liberalization should remain permanent.[18] Also, as in 1920, the liberalization of the abortion laws was accompanied by added special provisions for the care of pregnant women and mothers.

Some of the details of these associated methods of controlling abortion and encouraging motherhood are of interest. Working pregnant women are given 18-week vacations with full pay; all medical care and hospitalization connected with delivery are free; families with more than two children receive birth subsidies and children's allowances; and, after 1970, 75 percent of the expenses involved in the maintenance of education of children will be paid by the government.[19] Throughout the Soviet Union there is a network of maternity centers, and attached to each center is a special unit whose function is to reduce the number of legal abortions and to encourage the use of contraceptives.

What has been the extent and the effect of the 1955 abortion laws? There appears to be a general agreement on the part of Soviet medical experts that widespread abortion, even legal abortion, still remains a sufficient hazard to a woman's health to warrant being discouraged. Women are therefore encouraged to make a greater use of contraception. Between 1955 and 1963 there was reportedly a threefold increase in the number of legal abortions, the greatest increase coming just after relegalization, with a slight decline since 1965.[20] The total number of legal abortions per year, as of 1968, is estimated to be six million, with more abortions than live births. According to Mehlan, "nearly 3 of 4 pregnancies are terminated by abortion."[21]

As for general patterns, there is reported to be a considerable variation from one part of the Soviet Union to another, with abortion far more common in the European sector than in the Asian. In 1959, for instance, there reportedly were 61 births and 165 abortions per 1,000 fertile women in the Moscow area of the Russian Socialist Federal Soviet Republic (RSFSR).[22] Also, a greater number of abortions, proportionally, are performed in large towns and cities than in rural areas.[23] Unfortunately, Soviet authorities have not made available exact figures on the number of legal abortions during the years since 1920, that is, under the alternating liberal, strict, liberal laws. At any rate, it was the conviction of the Soviet authorities in 1955 that the illegal-abortion problem was sufficiently serious to justify the reintroduction of permissive laws. Since these laws are still in effect (although, as noted, a source of concern to Soviet physicians), one can only assume that the Soviet Union believes that the permissive laws are preferable to a return to restrictive laws.

It is difficult to discern precisely how different changes in the laws on abortion, contraception, divorce and family life have influenced the Soviet birthrate. Within the past 50 years, the birthrate in the Soviet Union has declined by more than half. In 1913 the rate was 45.5 births per 1,000 population. By 1927, despite seven years of a permissive law, the birthrate had dropped only to 44.8. By 1937, however, a steeper decline became apparent; in that year the birthrate was 38.7. By 1940 it had dropped to 31.2, by 1950 to 26.7, by 1960 to 24.9, by 1963 to 21.2, and by 1966 to 18.2. Unfortunately, sufficient data on the use of contraceptives (and the types presently used) do not exist and one cannot therefore calculate the relation between abortion and contraception in reducing the birthrate.

It is also impossible to correlate the birthrate figures with the shifts in the abortion laws.[24] During all these years the Soviet Union was experiencing a rapidly expanding industrialization, a great increase in the number of women in the work force, and a rise in the general prosperity level of the country. The only real constant which can be discerned is that evident everywhere in industrialized countries: the greater the industrialization, the greater the likelihood of a declining birthrate, some of it undoubtedly due to abortion. Similarly, the greater the number of working women, the greater the decline in the birthrate.[25] This appears to be the case in the Soviet Union, where the proportion of working wives and mothers is nearly twice as high as in the United States. This pattern has been constant since the 1920s, and the percentage of women in the work force has been close to 50 percent for a similarly long time.[26]

Mehlan reports that the abortion rate for working women is three times greater than for housewives.[27] He also notes that 58 percent of the scientific staff in the Soviet Union are women, and that, for many, pregnancy and birth can hinder their careers. Preschool child-care centers have a capacity of only one-fourth the total number of children. All of these things have doubtless contributed to the fact that the small family of one or two children has become a strongly entrenched cultural ideal in the Soviet cities and is on its way to acceptance in rural areas as well.[28] Malcolm Potts, citing Ovsienko, came to a similar conclusion in 1967: "In 50 percent of the families of salaried employees in Russia there is one child under the age of sixteen and in only 9 percent are there three or more children. Although families are a little larger in lower social groups, 72 percent of farm workers have one or two children under sixteen." [29]

In the large cities, with a higher concentration of working women, there are more abortions than births: 1 : 1.5; in industrial districts the ratio is 1 : 1.8; rural areas 1 : .5; in the Asiatic part of the Soviet Union 1 : .3, except for large towns.[30] K.-H. Mehlan, using the only available Soviet survey, has reported that in a study of 26,000 legal abortions in an urban population during the period 1958–1959, 35 percent were judged by Soviet investigators to have been absolutely avoidable, 17 percent possibly avoidable, 10 percent unavoidable; 38 percent were considered too unclear to make any judgment at all. On the basis of this study, then, somewhat over half of all abortions which were granted probably could have been avoided had there been sufficient motive to do so. However, it must be kept in mind that this apparently was the judgment of specialists and not a reflection of the woman's own judgment; the fact that she applied for and got a legal abortion indicates that, in her eyes at least, abortion was justifiable. Whether these women considered their abortions avoidable cannot be determined.[31] In any case, a continuing housing shortage, particularly acute in the cities, is often cited as an important reason for the large number of abortions. Also, Soviet women marry later now than in earlier decades; the average age is twenty-seven, and abortion is apparently a common practice among women university students determined to finish their education.[32] The Soviet attitude toward contraception should also be taken into account; it seems less than enthusiastic and, as in the 1920s, birth-control programs are pushed fitfully and erratically, probably expressing a continued uncertainty about whether and to what extent Soviet population growth should be strictly controlled.[33]

Finally, it is generally believed that the liberalization of the Soviet law since 1955 has greatly reduced the deaths and injuries associated with illegal abortion (which, incidentally, has apparently not vanished entirely and is, reportedly, particularly resorted to by unmarried women).[34] At the same time, the great number of legal abortions has placed strains on Soviet public-health services. Mehlan states that 16 percent of the Soviet women have had more than one abortion a year, and that in a Leningrad study of 1,350 women who had had legal abortions 70 percent were found to have had two or more, and 12 percent six or more. Figures like these make plausible his statement that "nearly each fifth woman treated in a hospital during 1965 in the Soviet Union had a legal abortion. . . . Abortion caused 18.5% of all admissions." [35]

Yugoslavia

Permissive abortion laws went into effect in Yugoslavia in 1960, and were further liberalized in April 1969 to allow abortion on request in a number of circumstances. Legal abortions may be performed on a variety of grounds (mental health, fetal abnormalities, rape), but perhaps most distinctively "when it can be reasonably expected that the pregnant woman will find herself placed, as the result of the birth of the child, in difficult personal, family, or material conditions, which cannot be remedied by any other means." [36] Applications for abortion are reviewed by a committee, and approximately 10 percent to 15 percent of all applications are rejected.[37] Potts reports that one Yugoslavia study discovered that, among 700 women who had been refused abortions, some 40 percent to 50 percent subsequently had criminal abortions.[38] While this comparatively small denial rate indicates the general permissiveness of the Yugoslav system, it is noteworthy that there is also, in principle and apparently in practice, considerable pressure against a recourse to abortion. The code of Yugoslav health workers states:

A health worker should regard abortion as biologically, medically, psychologically, and sociologically harmful. Corresponding to the principle of socialist humanism and medical knowledge human life must be respected from its beginning. Therefore, the health worker should conscientiously endeavor to see that the true humanist privilege of maternity be valued above the privilege of abortion.[39]

Doctors are obliged to provide contraception information prior to performing an abortion.

Despite intensive efforts to encourage the use of contraceptives, by the early 1960s some 30 percent of all women indicated that abortion was the only method of birth control acceptable to them.[40] Since that time, however, there apparently has been considerable improvement in the use of contraception. The anovulatory pill, for one thing, is now being produced and distributed. Whatever the cause, and despite efforts against abortion and in favor of more effective contraception, the Yugoslav legal-abortion rates have remained stable in the most recently reported years, running at about 150,000 a year (Table 15A) with a persistent ratio of 360 to 370 abortions per 1,000 live births (Table 15B). The birthrate has also remained relatively stable, decreasing only very slightly in recent years (Table 13). Potts believes (on the basis of information supplied to him during a trip to Yugoslavia) that the birth differential between rural and urban parts of Yugoslavia is traceable to a more frequent recourse to abortion in the urban areas; he adds that some observed differences in the incidence of abortion between generations can be correlated with the increased urbanization and economic development of a region.[41]

Hungary

The highest ratio of abortions to live births is to be found in Hungary —though Rumania had a higher ratio prior to its change in regulations—where the number of abortions has for some years exceeded the number of live births. The main reason for this high ratio, which reached 1,400 induced abortions per 1,000 live births in 1964 (Table 15B), is not difficult to locate. When the Hungarian laws were liberalized in June of 1956, the result was a formal specification of abortion on request: "[The] authorization . . . depends exclusively on the request of the pregnant woman, not requiring any special social or sanitary indication." [42] Nevertheless, even in Hungary, which requires that a woman make her request to a regional board, efforts are made to dissuade women from resorting to abortion; the interviewing board itself is specifically required to warn her of the possible hazards of abortion. The final choice, though, is up to the woman, and the restraining power of the committees can be exercised only on abortions requested after the twelfth week of pregnancy; they are authorized, on occasion, to grant abortions up to 18 weeks.[43] In two studies reported by Károly Miltényi, undertaken in 1960 and 1964, the first involving 26,100 women and the second 27,900, it was found that only 10 percent in 1960 and 5 percent in 1965 had requested abortion for medical reasons. Ninety and 95 percent, respectively, wanted abortions for primarily personal and social reasons. "According to the personal opinion of the concerned persons too, over ⅔ of total cases had a subjective nature. In ⅓ of the cases the aborting females stated that they considered their actual number of children as being sufficient."[44]

Significantly also, at that time, legalized abortion was believed to have a negative impact on the use of contraceptives: 48 percent of the women in 1960 and 46 percent in 1964 did not practice contraception in any systematic way.[45] "The legalization of abortion in Hungary," Mehlan has written, "was followed by a continuous increase in the number of legal abortions, which reached its maximum in 1964. . . . Changing attitudes towards family size, the ease of obtaining legal abortion, and the limited use of contraception combined with its lack of effectiveness count for the unfavorable development."[46] Miltényi has estimated that the number of induced abortions for each married woman probably exceeds three by the end of her reproductive life.[47] Despite the liberality of the law, illegal abortions (subject to severe penalties) continue, though their exact number is not known. Imre Hirschler states that some women, particularly unmarried girls, divorced, widowed and separated women, are apt to avoid abortion committees and hospitals in order to keep their pregnancy secret; others think their application might be rejected or that a private gynecologist will perform the operation less painfully.[48]

The absence until recently (after 1967) of an effective contraception program has also contributed to the high Hungarian abortion figures. The Ministry of Public Health has promoted birth control since 1956, but its campaign was conducted mainly through gynecologists' advice to women patients; that it failed to extend to the public at large and to the whole medical profession, probably accounts for its general ineffectiveness.[49] There had been heavy reliance on coitus interruptus, but efforts are currently being intensified to make modern contraceptives available and the Hungarian government strongly urges their use; condoms are on sale, and in 1967, a Hungarian-produced pill was put on the market.[50] Yet this is a late development compared with efforts made in other East European countries and, even now, contraceptives are not free, which may be a deterrent to their use. Potts believes, in fact, that the high abortion rate in Hungary (and in Rumania as well, before the law was changed) may have more to do with the absence of an effective contraception program than with the permissiveness of the law.

In many respects the relation between legal abortion, contraception and the birthrate remains obscure in Hungary, but the relation between legal abortion and the Hungarian birthrate seems to be direct: Hungary has one of the lowest birthrates and has had the highest abortion rate (Tables 13 and 15B). Mehlan, for one, believes this to be the case.[51] Potts, however, cautions against this kind of deduction:

> The number of legal abortions registered each year gives no indication how many babies might have been born if the law had been otherwise. In 1952 there were 185,800 live births in Hungary and 1,700 legal abortions. Twelve years later, after the alteration of the law in 1956, there were 184,400 abortions but the number of live births had not fallen correspondingly but in fact stood at 132,100. Therefore, criminal abortion must have been common in 1952 and a proportion of the legal abortions in 1964 would have occurred as illegal abortions if the law had not been changed.[52]

A different conclusion, though, might be reached by examining the birthrate per 1,000 population, which reached its lowest point (Table 13) in 1964, the same year in which the greatest number of legal abortions was recorded through 1964 (Table 15A). Whether this would have happened anyway, if the law had not been changed—that is, as a result of illegal abortions—is, of course, indeterminable; but Potts' conclusion, intended more as a caution than a hard deduction, remains worth bearing in mind.

Another point on the relation between legal abortion and the birthrate has been pressed by Hirschler, who notes that the birthrate began to climb after 1966 even though the legal abortion rate also continued to rise (see Table 15A). He believes this proves that the decrease in the birthrate is not the result of legalizing abortion.[53] Whether these figures can be said to constitute proof, however, is less than clear. The rise in the number of abortions between 1966 and 1967 is, after all, very slight compared with the variations observable among other years (Table 15A). They could just as well be taken as a sign of a stabilization of the abortion rate, so slight is the difference between 1966 and 1967, and thus as a further sign that such a stabilization could also signal a rise in the birthrate—which, in fact, there has been. Neither Potts nor Hirschler argues that the overall abortion rate (legal and illegal) has no connection with the birthrate; the point in question is the connection between *legal* abortions and the birthrate. As we shall see shortly, the decline in the Japanese birthrate correlates well with the legalization of the Japanese abortion law in 1948; among the countries of the world, Japan and Hungary have the highest rate of legal abortions and the lowest birthrates.

In both countries, correspondingly, an increase in the probability of abortion in relationship to parity has been a problem. "In Hungary while each 6th woman among the childless married women terminated her first pregnancy by abortion (in most cases to postpone childbirth), the number of interruptions for those having one child is more than one half, and for those [with] two children, more than three-fourths of the total number of pregnancies." [54] Figures of this magnitude are suggestive of the extent to which, in the absence of effective contraception, abortion is relied upon as the main method of birth control, at least by a significant minority. An extensive Hungarian survey, covering 0.5 percent of all Hungarian women between the ages of fifteen and forty-nine, found that in 1958–1960 an average of 2.4 children was desired by each couple, while in 1965–1966 the average dropped to 2.1.[55] With this kind of desired family size, in the absence of effective contraception and with legal abortion available, it is not hard to understand the high Hungarian abortion rate. As we will see also with Japan, it is not legal abortion as such which leads to a desire for small families; rather, legal abortion makes it possible to realize this desire. Put another way, the Hungarian abortion rate is an index of the strength of the desire to limit family size; legal abortion makes this desire efficacious.

The Hungarian government as well as those concerned with family planning are apparently not happy with this high abortion rate. András Klinger has noted:

> The fact that our official interruption of pregnancy is permitted does not mean that our health policy regards induced abortion as the only or best means of birth control. Its only purpose is to make it possible for women who conceive through ignorance or unsatisfactory knowledge of prevention to terminate an unwanted pregnancy.[56]

Efforts have been made to reduce their number of abortions by extending maternity leaves from 12 to 20 weeks and by allowing mothers to take unpaid leaves for up to two years without any loss of social-security rights. Intensive contraceptive education and increased family allowances are also being used in an attempt to reduce the number of legal abortions. As Miltényi puts it, "The urgently desired decrease in the high number of induced abortions requires, therefore, partly the propagation, on a larger scale, of both the practice of contraception and its application, partly, however, the enhancement of the effectiveness of the preventive methods and devices." [57]

The difficulty of persuading Hungarian women to shift from abortion to contraception has been stressed by Tietze and Lehfeldt: "Legalization, by increasing the total number of abortions, has resulted in an increased number of conceptions. . . . Any early termination of pregnancy makes it possible for a woman to conceive again nine months to one year earlier than if the pregnancy had been permitted to go to term." [58] Two Hungarian demographers have further emphasized the obstacles, pointing out that a concerted effort by the Ministry of Health to promote the use of contraceptives, "has not proved efficacious. It has not yielded a satisfactory result; no change occurred in the frequency of pregnancies. The conclusion can be drawn that, in certain cases, the availability of legal abortion can lead to a casual attitude towards birth control, which hinders the propagation of contraception." [59] In any case, despite both official and unofficial unhappiness with the high abortion rates which have come in the wake of the liberal Hungarian law, there is little inclination to make the law or its application stricter: "Although the number of legal abortions is increasing there is no tendency to alter the present law because of the danger of possible increase of illegal abortions." [60] A rise in family allowances, and a liberal maternity-leave policy have as their ends both a raising of the birthrate and a reduction of abortions.

Czechoslovakia

The Czechoslovakian liberalized laws went into effect in January of 1958. Abortion is permitted on medical and a wide variety of other grounds, spelled out in great detail in the law's regulations. The normal limit for legal abortions is the twelfth week of pregnancy, though exceptions (which amount to 0.4 percent) may be made on medical grounds. Each application is subject to the approval of three-person regional commissions (there are some 200 commissions in all), composed of a gynecologist and two laymen. Applications are processed within one to two weeks. At present, a fee is charged for all abortions except those performed on medical grounds and except to women in dire financial straits. The purpose of the fee (which can amount to as much as a week's salary for a blue-collar worker) is to place some obstacle in the way of those desiring abortions as well as to help defray hospital costs. At least six months is required between legal abortions.

Though the law was, in general, liberalized in 1957, it has been subject to fluctuating interpretations and modifications, mirrored in the Czechoslovakian abortion statistics. In 1956, prior to the passage of the new law, there were some 3,100 legal abortions; from 1957 to 1962, the number rose from 7,300 to 89,800 (Table 15A). While the law was from the first liberal in its wording, a fee was required and a woman had to have the abortion performed in the area in which she lived. After considerable agitation against the fee and domicile requirements, they were both dropped in 1960. Despite this concession, the birthrate between 1960 and 1962 remained virtually stationary (Table 13), even though the number of legal abortions rose in 1961. Malcolm Potts believes that the combination of increased legal abortions and a stationary birthrate most likely indicated "a large transfer from the criminal to the hospital sector." [61]

In 1962, as a result of alarm at the low, and stagnant, birthrate as well as at the large number of legal abortions, stricter requirements were once again introduced. In particular, women having their first pregnancy were treated less permissively, as were married women with fewer than three children. A fee was again required and the regulation limiting abortions to the first trimester was more rigorously adhered to. The result of these stricter conditions was to reduce the number of legal abortions in 1963 to 70,500 (Table 15A); even so, the denial rate (for that time) was only 13 percent of the requested abortions. [62] During 1963–1964, a rise in the number of live births and in the birthrate was discernible (Tables 13 and 14). [63] At the same time extensive efforts were made to make maternity easier for women, with extended maternity leaves and provision of better housing.

In 1965, there was again a shift, which now remains in effect. While the stricter requirements and the fees were retained, the regional commissions began to act more permissively in approving applications. In 1965, about 90 percent of all applications were granted, and the figure has remained at that level since then. The result has been a steady rise in the number of legal abortions, reaching an all-time high in 1968 (Table 15A), with a drop in the number of live births and in the birthrate (Tables 13 and 14). There is at present no expectation that the law will be changed in the immediate future. As in Hungary, wariness about an increase in illegal abortions remains a strong motive for not returning to a restrictive code or to a stricter interpretation of the present law. In this respect, it is generally believed that the liberalized laws, even after the modifications of 1962, led to a sharp drop in the number of illegal abortions and in the consequent death rate from them. But when the stricter requirements took effect in 1962, there was, briefly, an increase in the number of deaths and injuries from illegal abortions. Before World War II there were an estimated 100,000 illegal abortions a year, and perhaps several hundred abortion deaths annually. [64] Cernoch reports that during the years 1958–1964 there was a drop of 68 percent to 80 percent in the number of illegal abortions. [65] As of 1968, Cernoch estimates about 5,000 illegal abortions a year.

As in other East European countries, an erratic and small-scale use of effective contraceptives is taken to be a factor in Czechoslovakia's abortion rate. With an average desired family size of approximately two children, induced abortion remains a major method of birth control. [66] While efforts are being undertaken to promote the use of contraceptives, and while Czechoslovakia now produces its own anovulatory pill and

IUD, a comparatively small proportion of the female population is being reached. As of 1967, M. Vojta estimated that there were about three million women of fecund age, but with only one-third of this number covered by all methods of contraception (modern and traditional).[67] Vojta also believes that, by the end of 1967, probably only 100,000 women were being covered by the very best modern methods (IUDs and pills). He has further pointed out that the IUD can be prescribed and inserted only in hospitals, by a gynecologist, and that the pill can be prescribed only by a gynecologist. Even then, women must pay for them, which poses still another hindrance to their dissemination.[68] As a consequence, inadequate methods such as coitus interruptus remain common, with many resultant failures and subsequent applications for legal abortion. In Cernoch's opinion, the availability of legal abortion has made the promotion of contraception all the more difficult, especially among the lower classes; they would rather run the risk of an abortion than chance the use of contraceptives.[69] The combination of available abortion and inadequate contraception also helps account for a high percentage of women having repeated abortions (Table 17). As in Chile, there is a correlation between a stepped-up contraception program and an increase in the number of legal abortions.[70]

Table 18 presents a picture of the reasons women give for resorting to legal abortion in Czechoslovakia. Behind these figures lie some important social considerations. Housing generally remains in short supply in Czechoslovakia, especially in the cities. Some 43 percent to 46 percent of all women work, an economic necessity for most since the salary of the average blue-collar worker, for instance, is only sufficient to support three persons. Family planning is thus seen by large numbers as an economic necessity. In recent years there has been an upward trend in the number of women aged fifteen to nineteen obtaining abortions (Table 16), a figure thought to reflect the greater permissiveness of the commissions and the larger number of women attending universities. Correspondingly, those who have legal abortions now tend to have fewer living children than in previous years (Table 19). Even though the present Czechoslovakian policy is to make abortions comparatively difficult for those who have had no previous children, the proportion of women in this category who do receive abortions is rising (Table 19).

Poland

In the East European context, Poland is interesting for a number of reasons. It is the most intensely Catholic country despite (or perhaps because of) the severe conflicts between the Church and the government; it has the most advanced family-planning services; and it is the one country where contraception seems to have significantly reduced the abortion rate. In 1954, induced abortion was authorized to protect the health of the women but a continuingly high illegal-abortion rate (with some 80,000 hospital admissions a year from the results of illegal abortions) led to a permissive law on April 27, 1956.[71] This law, vague in its wording on acceptable indications (perhaps deliberately so), but emphasizing the protection of maternal health and difficult living conditions, allows a single doctor to issue the permission for an abortion (though he himself cannot perform it). The idea of granting permissions through a commission was rejected on the grounds of attendant delays, which it was believed would increase illegal abortions.[72] The only significant modification in the law came in 1959, when contraceptive advice was made obligatory, and in 1961, when an earlier requirement that a woman's social circumstance be reviewed by an independent observer was dropped.[73] An oral declaration, made to the pregnant woman's family doctor, that hers is a "difficult social situation," is sufficient to meet the provisions of the present laws.[74] Although the woman may apply to her family doctor, the abortions are performed, often on an ambulatory basis, at the outpatient departments of hospitals. No fee is charged for these abortions (only in East Germany and the Soviet Union is this also the case), but private physicians charge a fee for those they perform.

Despite Poland's strongly Catholic character (conservative, with high rates of observance), and repeated condemnations of abortion by the Polish hierarchy, the legal abortion rate and ratio are high (Tables 15A and 15B), and the birthrate low (Table 13). It is also the only country in East Europe, however, where a distinct decline in the number of annual abortions is observable without the assistance (as in Bulgaria and Rumania) of a change in the law. The reason for this seems, on most accounts, attributable to the success of the government's efforts to integrate family-planning programs into the public-health services of the country. A family-planning program has existed since 1957, with birth-control advice and material available in the country's 1,400 outpatient departments, in addition to all the gynecological and obstetrical wards in Polish hospitals. There are also over 3,000 consultation centers throughout the nation. Buttressing the services is a requirement that every new mother be instructed in family planning and the exemption of 70 percent of the price of contraceptives under the social-insurance system.[75]

The net result of these contraception efforts—as the only clearly discernible variable—has been a reduction in the number of abortions (Table 15A), a reduction in the birthrate (Table 13) and in the number of births (Table 14). It should be noted, however, that the ratio of abortions to live births has remained high (Table 15B). It is also clear from the tables that the proportionate drop in the number of live births has been less than the proportionate drop in the number of abortions. These figures tend to confirm the thesis that the drop both in birthrate and in the number of abortions is due to the contraception program. However, one must here add a caution. There has been a reported drop in the number of women in the fertile age group; obviously, that could help account also for the decline in the number of live births.[76]

Rumania

The final countries to be surveyed, Rumania, Bulgaria and East Germany, have a special place in Eastern Europe: each has significantly changed its laws within the past few years. Rumania and Bulgaria were, until the change, notable for the exceptional permissiveness of their laws and their very high number of legal abortions. Rumania is now notable for the strictness of its laws and procedures. Bulgaria's change, not so drastic as Rumania's, is still important because of a shift to stricter standards. East Germany, by contrast, had the most restrictive laws on abortion and was the one East European country with a very low number of abortions; now, after the 1965 liberalization of the law (by administrative decree) the figures are high. Other East European countries, as we have seen, have modified sections of their law and have sometimes varied its application. But none of them displays the abrupt changes obvious in Rumania, Bulgaria and East Germany.

In September 1956, following the lead of the Soviet Union, a law was decreed in Rumania which enabled every woman to make her own decision on whether or not she wanted an abortion, regardless of whether any indications existed. The intent of the law was to reduce the number of illegal abortions as well as to give women totally free choice in their pregnancies. As K.-H. Mehlan has noted (writing of the years preceding the 1966 restrictions):

In Rumania, the ideal of responsible maternity is almost entirely implemented by legal abortion. Contraception plays an unimportant role. Stations equipped to handle abortions exist all over the country. There are no commissions to review applications, or to grant or deny requests. Women may go directly to the abortion ward of a hospital or the out-patient clinic of a factory. If there are no medical contra-indications and the pregnancy is not more than twelve weeks old, the operation is performed on the same day, and the patient may go home in two hours. Physicians, who work in shifts, are not allowed to perform more than 10 abortions in one day.[77]

The passage of the 1956 law led to a sharp increase in the number of legal abortions—from 112,000 in 1958 to 219,000 in 1959 (Table 15A). There is a gap in the statistics for the next few years, but in October 1967 the Rumanian government informed a visiting Danish mission (which was investigating Rumania's experience with a permissive abortion law as part of Denmark's reevaluation of its own law) that there had been more than a million abortions in Rumania in 1965.[78] The estimate given, 1,115,000, has been supported since that time by other official Rumanian agencies. In a country with under 20 million population (see Table 13), the number seems enormous. The rise in abortions over the years was accompanied by a rapid decline in births. In 1956 the birthrate was 24.2 per 1,000 inhabitants, but had dropped to 14.3 by 1966, one of the lowest birthrates in the world (Table 13).

"The one-child family," K.-H. Mehlan writes, "is considered ideal in Rumania—1.3 children per family in Bucharest and 0.7 children for educated mothers," and he adds that, significantly, by the late 1950s 96 percent of the women did not have any knowledge of contraceptives; abortion was almost the sole method of birth control.[79] As in the other East European countries, however, the 1956 liberalized law in Rumania was accompanied by a variety of devices to reduce the number of abortions, including attempts at dissuading women from abortion, sick leave for pregnant women and free medical care. But effective contraceptives remained unavailable and the evidence seems clearly to point to the liberalized law as the single most important cause of the sharp drop in the birthrate. As in Hungary, the liberal law made it possible to realize the desire for small families. Again, however, Potts has cautioned that the liberal law per se may not be the most important factor behind the high figures, but rather the absence of contraceptives.[80]

In October 1966, apparently as a result of government unhappiness over the rapid decline in the birthrate, the law was radically changed.[81] The opening words of the 1966 decree speak of the "great prejudice to the birthrate and the rate of natural increase" in addition to "severe consequences to the health of the woman." Under the new decree, abortion on request is permitted only for women forty-five years of age or older. Otherwise, abortion is possible only where there is a risk to life, the possibility of deformity, after rape, or when the woman is "physically, psychologically or emotionally incapacitated."[82] (Although certainly stricter than the previous law, the new decree is much more liberal than restrictive laws in the West.) At about the same time as these changes were made, a bonus system for babies was established, maternity leaves were lengthened, added taxes were levied on single people and childless couples over twenty-six years of age, and divorce was made more difficult and expensive.

The initial results of the change were dramatic. "Predictably," Christopher Tietze has written, "the birthrate began to rise in the seventh month after the promulgation of the decree. By the third quarter of 1967, the birthrate had jumped to 38.4 per 1,000 population, compared with 14.3 in 1966." [83] Rumania would therefore seem to provide as perfect an instance as one can find of the impact of abortion laws on birthrates. At the same time, though, the scarcity of contraceptives in Rumania makes the country a special case, hardly suitable for many international generalizations about the relation of abortion, contraception and birthrates. Furthermore, the rapid rise in the birthrate for nearly two years after the law was changed (it reached nearly 40 per 1,000 in some months) proved to be only a temporary phenomenon. By mid-1969, the birthrate had dipped into the middle 20s and was still falling, which suggests the difficulty of enforcing a restrictive law among people who had previously revealed a strong motivation to limit births. Evidently the Rumanians eventually found ways of getting around the new law and subverting the sternly pronatalist policies of the government—by use of traditional contraceptive methods, by obtaining modern contraceptives on the black market (the law forbids their manufacture or import) and by resorting to illegal abortion.[84]

Bulgaria

The permissive Bulgarian law came into being in 1956 when the Ministry of Health and Social Welfare issued instructions that any woman who expressed a desire for an induced abortion could have it. As Section 4 of the legislation stated: "Any woman wishing to have an abortion induced shall notify the women's consultation centre for the area in which she resides." Nevertheless, the following precautions were to be observed: "The staff of the consultation centre shall inform the woman of the harmful nature and danger of abortion, of the necessity of carrying the pregnancy to term, etc., and, in short, do everything in their power to dissuade all women who express a wish for the interruption of pregnancy." [85] Abortions must be performed in hospitals, and a fee is charged except for those performed on medical indications.

The main result of the 1956 instruction was a sharp increase in the number of legal abortions, which gradually continued up through 1966 (Table 15A). By the early 1960s, the ratio of abortions to live births had become one of the highest in East Europe. During the same period there was a gradual drop in the number of live births (Table 14) and in the birthrate (Table 13). Bulgaria's fertility rate was low before the liberalization of the abortion laws, however, indicating that contraception was being practiced, however traditional the methods used. Since 1966, IUDs have been available at a number of Bulgarian clinics, and a variety of oral contraceptives are now being imported.[86] But, given the recent advent of these more efficient contraceptives, and the high abortion rate before they became available, it seems reasonable to conclude that the permissiveness of the Bulgarian law encouraged women to rely on abortion as the principal method of birth control and therefore was a major reason for the declining births.

This, in any case, seemed to be the belief of the Bulgarian government, which, on December 22, 1967, introduced major changes in its instructions. Abortion on request is now available, without committee approval, only for women forty-five or older and for women with three children. Childless women are prohibited from having induced abortions except for serious medical indications. Women with one or two children, however, may still receive abortions if they persist in their desire after vigorous attempts at dissuasion fail.[87] In a word, legal abortions have been made more difficult but by no means impossible. Unfortunately, recent data on the number of abortions and live births have not been made available by the Bulgarian government so it is impossible to specify what effects the new regulations have had.

East Germany

The German Democratic Republic (East Germany) presents a very different picture from that of any of the other East European countries. Along with Albania, it did not follow the trend of its East European neighbors in the late 1950s and early 1960s toward liberalized abortion laws. Just why is not clear, but perhaps the fact that the East German birthrate during that period was already the lowest in East Europe (Table 13), together with opposition from a conservative medical profession (as some say in East Europe), suggest a possible explanation. Still another factor may have been its own earlier experience with liberal abortion laws. Historically speaking, East Germany was the first East European country after World War II to introduce relatively liberal abortion laws. In 1946, the live-birth rate reached the phenomenally low figure of 10.4 per 1,000 population. In that year over 500 women are reported to have died as the result of illegal abortion, with a figure of 400 in 1947.[88] These conditions led to a temporary extension of allowable abortion indications in 1947. In 1950, 26,400 legal abortions were performed, with a legal abortion rate of 15.6 per 10,000 population.[89]

However, Mehlan reports, the desired decrease in illegal abortions did not take place; in fact, they increased. At the end of 1950, the temporary extensions of indications were rescinded—henceforth only strictly medical and eugenic indications would be acceptable—with a consequent drop in the number of legal abortions (Table 15A). Thereafter, the number of legal abortions in East Germany was the lowest known in all of East Europe (no information is available on Albania). One can only surmise that the East German authorities decided that their venture into liberalized laws in 1947–1950 was an unhappy one, failing to produce the intended results (i.e., decreasing illegal abortions).[90] Efforts to reduce illegal abortion were then shifted in the direction of added assistance to mothers and support of large families. This policy was believed to be moderately successful and there was a steady decline in the estimated number of illegal abortions. In 1946 there were an estimated 54,000 illegal abortions, from 60,000 to 70,000 between 1948 and 1950, and by 1962 there were an estimated 20,000–41,000 such abortions (minimum and maximum estimates).[91] Thus it may well have been the combination of a bad experience with liberal laws in 1947–1950 and a moderate success with alternative methods of diverting women from illegal abortion, plus a low birthrate, which disinclined East Germany to join the liberalizing trend after the mid-1950s. Both during that period and after (as well as at present) abortion applications were decided upon by commissions.

It is evident from Tables 13 and 14 that the number of live births and the birthrate remained relatively static over the years. Part of the reason was a decline in the number of fertile women by some 25 percent, but part must also be due to the continuance of a high number of illegal abortions.[92] In recent years, East Germany has been producing its own anovulatory pills, and IUDs have also become available. But these effective contraceptive methods were not available during the 1950s, when the birthrate was, nevertheless, very low.

In March of 1965, a number of changes were made by decree in the East German regulations; they particularly took account of a woman's environment, of women under sixteen and over forty, of women with five or more children and those with closely spaced pregnancies.[93] The consequence of the change was a sharp jump in the number of legal abortions (Table 15A) and in the ratio of abortions to live births (Table 15B). There was also, correspondingly, a decrease in the birthrate discernible after the year 1965, though it is not evident that it is entirely traceable to the change in the abortion law. About this time effective contraceptives were also coming into greater supply and use. By 1968 Mehlan could say that 6 percent to 8 percent of all fertile women were using the pill.[94]

TABLE 13
EASTERN EUROPE
Population and Birthrates
1954–1968

	Population (in millions)							Birthrate per 1,000 Population						
	BUL-GARIA	CZECHO-SLOVAKIA	E. GER-MANY*	HUN-GARY	POLAND	RUMANIA	YUGO-SLAVIA	BUL-GARIA	CZECHO-SLOVAKIA	E. GER-MANY*	HUN-GARY	POLAND	RUMANIA	YUGO-SLAVIA
1954	7.4	12.9	16.8	9.7	26.7	17.0	17.2	20.2	20.6	16.6	23.0	29.1	24.8	28.5
1955	7.4	13.0	16.7	9.8	27.2	17.3	17.5	20.1	20.3	16.7	21.4	29.1	25.6	26.8
1956	7.5	13.2	16.5	9.9	27.8	17.5	17.6	19.5	19.8	16.2	19.5	28.0	24.2	25.9
1957	7.6	13.3	16.4	9.3	28.3	17.8	17.8	18.4	18.9	15.9	17.0	27.6	22.9	23.7
1958	7.7	13.4	16.2	9.8	28.7	18.0	18.0	17.9	17.4	15.6	16.0	26.3	21.6	24.0
1959	7.8	13.6	17.3	9.9	29.2	18.2	18.2	17.6	16.0	16.9	15.2	24.7	20.2	23.3
1960	7.9	13.7	17.2	9.9	29.7	18.4	18.4	17.8	15.9	17.0	14.7	22.6	19.1	23.5
1961	7.9	13.8	17.1	10.0	30.0	18.6	18.6	17.4	15.8	17.0	14.0	20.9	17.5	22.7
1962	8.0	13.9	17.1	10.1	30.3	18.7	18.8	16.7	15.7	17.4	12.9	19.6	16.2	21.9
1963	8.1	14.0	17.2	10.1	30.7	18.8	19.0	16.4	16.9	17.4	13.1	19.2	15.7	21.4
1964	8.1	14.1	17.0	10.1	31.1	18.9	19.2	16.1	17.2	16.9	13.0	18.1	15.2	20.8
1965	8.2	14.2	17.0	10.1	31.5	19.0	19.5	15.3	16.4	16.5	13.1	17.3	14.6	20.9
1966	8.3	14.2	17.1	10.2	31.7	19.1	19.7	14.9	15.6	15.8	13.6	16.7	14.3	20.2
1967	8.3	14.3	17.1	10.2	31.9	19.3	19.9	15.0	15.1	14.8	14.6	16.3	27.4	19.5
1968	8.4	14.4	17.1	10.3	32.2	19.4	20.1	16.9**	14.9	14.3	15.1	16.3	26.3**	18.9

Sources: Demographic Yearbook, 1965, 17th issue (New York: United Nations, 1966) and *Demographic Yearbook, 1967,* 19th issue (New York: United Nations, 1968); for 1967–1968—*Monthly Bulletin of Statistics,* 22 (May 1969) (New York: United Nations, 1969); *Population and Vital Statistics Report,* xxi, No. 4, (New York: United Nations, Oct. 1969).
* Figures include data for East Berlin 1959–1968.
** Provisional.

TABLE 14

EASTERN EUROPE

Number of Live Births

1954–1967

	BULGARIA	CZECHOSLOVAKIA	EAST GERMANY	HUNGARY	POLAND	RUMANIA	YUGOSLAVIA
1954	149,900	266,700	280,500	223,300	778,100	422,300	493,600
1955	151,000	265,200	280,000	210,400	793,900	442,800	471,400
1956	147,900	262,000	268,200	192,800	779,800	425,700	460,200
1957	141,000	252,700	260,200	167,200	782,300	407,800	426,700
1958	138,300	235,000	258,000	158,400	755,500	390,500	432,400
1959	136,900	217,000	277,000	151,200	722,900	368,000	424,300
1960	140,100	217,300	277,400	146,500	660,900	352,200	432,600
1961	137,900	218,400	284,300	140,400	627,600	324,900	422,200
1962	134,100	217,500	280,400	130,100	599,500	302,000	413,100
1963	132,100	236,000	301,500	132,300	588,200	294,900	407,400
1964	131,000	241,300	291,900	132,100	562,900	287,400	401,100
1965	125,800	231,700	281,100	133,000	546,300	278,400	408,200
1966	123,000	222,500	268,900	138,500	530,300	273,700	398,900
1967	124,700	215,800	252,900	148,300	521,600	522,900	388,200

Sources: *Demographic Yearbook 1965*, 17th Issue (New York: United Nations, 1966) and *Demographic Yearbook, 1967*, 19th Issue (New York: United Nations, 1968); for 1967: *Monthly Bulletin of Statistics*, 22 (May 1969) (New York: United Nations, 1969).

TABLE 15
EASTERN EUROPE

TABLE A: NUMBER OF ABORTIONS, 1954–1968

A	BULGARIA	CZECHOSLOVAKIA	EAST GERMANY	HUNGARY	POLAND†	RUMANIA	YUGOSLAVIA‡
1954	1,100	2,800	1,700*	16,300	—	—	—
1955	—	2,100	1,200	35,400	1,400	—	—
1956	—	3,100	1,000	82,500	18,900	—	—
1957	30,900	7,300	900	123,300	36,400	—	—
1958	37,500	61,400	900	145,600	44,200	112,100	—
1959	45,600	79,100	700	152,400	79,000	219,600	54,500
1960	54,800	88,300	800	162,600	158,000		76,700
1961	68,800	94,300	800	170,000	155,300		104,000
1962	76,700	89,800	700	163,700	199,400		150,000
1963	83,300	70,500		173,800	190,000		150,000
1964	91,500	70,700		184,400	177,500		150,000
1965	96,500	79,600		180,300	168,100	1,115,000	
1966	101,400	90,300	16,000**	186,700	156,700		
1967	98,200	96,400	20,000**	187,500			
1968	85,200	99,700		201,100	121,700		

TABLE B: RATIO OF ABORTIONS PER 1,000 LIVE BIRTHS

B	BULGARIA	CZECHOSLOVAKIA	EAST GERMANY	HUNGARY	POLAND†	RUMANIA	YUGOSLAVIA‡
1954	10	10	6.0	70			
1955		10	4.4	170			
1956		10	3.6	430	20		
1957	220	30	3.5	740	50		

B	BULGARIA	CZECHOSLOVAKIA	EAST GERMANY	HUNGARY	POLAND†	RUMANIA	YUGOSLAVIA‡
1959	330	360	2.7	1,010	110	510	130
1960	390	410	2.7	1,110	240		180
1961	500	430	2.9	1,210	250		250
1962	570	410	2.6	1,260	330		360
1963	630	300		1,310	330		370
1964	690	290		1,400	320	4,000	370
1965	750	350	61**	1,360	420		
1966	760	400	80**	1,350	420		
1967	790	440		1,260			
1968	600	465		1,300			

Sources: For Bulgaria, Czechoslovakia, Hungary, Poland, 1954–1959: András Klinger, "Demographic Effects of Abortion Legislation in Some European Socialist Countries," in *World Population Conference, Belgrade, 1965,* Vol. II (New York: United Nations, 1967), p. 91. For those countries 1960–1966, for Yugoslavia 1959–1964 and for Rumania 1958–1959: K.-H. Mehlan, "Changing Patterns of Abortion in the Socialist Countries of Europe," unpublished paper delivered at the International Conference on Abortion, Hot Springs, Virginia, November 17–20, 1968. For Czechoslovakia in 1967: Jiri Prokopec, "Rok 1967–Kriva Potratu Stoupa" in *Zprávy Statni Populacni Komise, No. 3:* Prague, 1968.

For Hungary in 1967: Imre Hirschler, "Abortion in Hungary," paper presented at the International Conference on Abortion, Hot Springs, Virginia, November 17–18, 1968.

For East Germany, 1954–1962: K.-H. Mehlan and S. Falkenthal "Der legale Abort in der Deutschen Demokratischen Republik: Statistik der Jahre 1953–1962," *Das Deutsche Gesundheitswesen,* 20 (June 24, 1965), pp. 1163–67.

For 1968: Henry P. David, *Family Planning and Abortion in the Socialist Countries of Eastern Europe* (New York: McGraw-Hill, forthcoming, 1970).

For Rumania in 1965: Rumanian Communist Party: Central Committee, "Analiza starii de sanatate a populatiei si masurile privind perfectionarea organizarii retelei si imbunatatirea asistentei medicale in Republica Socialista Romania," *Scienteia* 27 Oct. 1968.

* Note: These figures are for applications for abortions which were approved.

** Estimated.

† Potts and Tietze have both noted that some doubt is prudent when citing official Polish figures, primarily because many women have their abortions performed by private doctors, who, though required to report them, may often be remiss in doing so.

‡ Potts has observed that compulsory registration of legal abortions did not take effect until 1960, thus possibly leading to an inflation of the 1960 figures. In general, also, Yugoslavian figures are collected regionally and may not be fully reliable in underdeveloped areas.

TABLE 16

CZECHOSLOVAKIA: INDUCED ABORTIONS PER 100 LIVE BIRTHS
BY AGE OF WOMAN: 1958–1966

	15–19	20–24	25–29	30–34	35–39	40–44	45–49	TOTAL
1958	10.8	10.6	24.0	42.7	63.8	80.3	82.8	25.2
1959	16.7	15.5	33.4	64.8	98.9	139.2	115.4	35.6
1960	20.0	16.7	37.3	72.7	115.8	157.9	123.8	39.9
1961	23.3	17.2	39.1	78.0	127.4	190.2	194.7	42.8
1962	22.4	16.5	36.9	77.8	132.1	192.0	171.6	40.9
1963	13.1	11.1	25.4	56.2	105.5	175.1	102.6	29.4
1964	15.1	12.7	25.1	52.0	97.1	152.1	207.8	28.9
1965	19.4	16.7	31.6	61.0	108.2	163.3	188.6	34.2
1966	23.3	21.4	31.9	75.0	123.7	177.4	169.4	40.0

TABLE 17

CZECHOSLOVAKIA: FREQUENCY OF ABORTION
WOMEN HAVING FIRST, SECOND, ETC., INDUCED ABORTIONS
1960–1967 (IN PERCENTS)

	FIRST	SECOND	THIRD	FOURTH OR MORE	UNKNOWN
1960	63.3	26.2	7.2	3.0	0.3
1961	54.7	28.2	8.6	3.8	4.7
1962	51.8	29.4	9.8	4.5	4.5
1963	52.4	30.5	11.4	5.7	—
1964	52.7	29.3	11.4	6.6	—
1965	54.5	28.6	11.1	5.7	0.1
1966	55.0	28.5	10.6	5.8	0.1
1967	55.0	28.0	10.6	5.8	0.1

Source: For Tables 16 and 17: Tomáš Frejka and Josef Koubek, "Les Avortements en Tchécoslovaquie," *Population et Famille,* 16 (December 1968), pp. 1–21.

Some Generalizations

The preceding tour through the East European countries should have made evident that there are many significant differences among them in the laws and patterns of abortion. As with Latin America, it is hazardous to speak of the whole region in overly general terms. Still, certain trends and similarities appear, and some broad conclusions are in order. Two central questions come to mind: First, have the East European laws achieved the general goals desired, i.e., a decrease in

TABLE 18

CZECHOSLOVAKIA: REASONS FOR INDUCED ABORTION
SELECTED YEARS: 1960, 1963, 1967 (IN PERCENTS)

	1960	1963	1967
Health	12.7	18.7	20.6*
Advanced age of woman	2.5	3.0	2.4
3 or more living children	45.3	44.8	29.0
Death or disability of husband	—	0.6	0.2
Economic responsibility for support of family	2.0	2.1	1.6
Disruption of family	7.0	5.3	4.6
Unmarried woman	12.5	11.3	14.0
Family financial difficulties	3.8	2.7	7.6
Inadequate housing	8.2	7.3	10.3
Other	5.8	4.2	9.7

* This figure may be too high, since it is reported that many doctors employ this category in order to avoid paying the fee required for abortions on other grounds.

TABLE 19

CZECHOSLOVAKIA: INDUCED ABORTIONS BY MARITAL STATUS
AND NUMBER OF CHILDREN
SELECTED YEARS: 1959, 1963, 1967 (IN PERCENTS)

MARITAL STATUS	1959	1963	1967
Single	10.2	10.5	13.7
Married	84.7	83.2	80.4
Concubine	0.5	0.5	0.5
Widowed	1.2	1.5	1.1
Divorced	3.4	4.3	4.3
NUMBER OF CHILDREN			
0	9.4	9.8	13.3
1	13.0	12.6	19.0
2	29.7	28.8	33.5
3	23.5	26.5	20.2
4	12.2	11.5	7.3
5 or more	12.0	10.8	6.7
Unknown	0.2	—	—

Source: For Tables 18 and 19: Tomáš Frejka and Josef Koubek, "Les Avortements en Tchécoslovaquie," Population et Famille, 16 (1968), pp. 1–21.

illegal abortions (and consequent deaths and injuries), and second, have the new laws resulted in an increase in the freedom of women? Based on the available data and on the opinion of those who have carefully studied these countries (Potts, Mehlan, Tietze, Cernoch,

Novak, Hirschler, for instance), the answer to the first question is yes.
East Germany, during its first period of liberalization, was an exception
but its tumultous postwar social situation and the briefness of the experiment hardly make it representative. The critical word here is "decrease"; in all of the countries there remains some incidence of illegal
abortion. In each, the reason seems to be that there are some women
who, for a variety of motives, do not want to go through any official
process, however certain the success of their efforts if they did so.
(Naturally, illegal abortions in those countries which now have tightened
or restrictive laws are more understandable.)

It is hard to say whether women have more freedom as a result of
the East European laws. No surveys have been made to ascertain the
subjective feelings of women in the light of these laws. Yet the availability of legal abortion does give women a significant option when they
make decisions about going through with pregnancies; they can, legally,
have their pregnancies interrupted with a minimal amount of consultation and interrogation. The persistence of illegal abortions, however,
indicates that some women at any rate do not feel they have perfect
freedom; they dislike or distrust the legal procedures enough to circum-
vent them, even though this circumvention increases the hazards to
their life and health. Thus, if one's norm of perfect female freedom is
the total absence of any laws on abortion or any checks on purely individual choice (without records of any kind), then East European
women have something less than perfect freedom. Moreover, of course,
in most of the countries, the freedom women have is subject to imposed
shifts in population and family-planning policy—specifically, it is subject
to government concern and action over declining birthrates. This surely
introduces an element of contingency in women's freedom, and that, in
turn, introduces much larger issues of human, and female, freedom.

In the light of pressures in the United States for either legal abortion
on request or the repeal of all laws on abortion, it is worth asking
whether there is any inclination in East Europe to move in this direction. Only in Russia and Hungary is abortion on request now available
regardless of indications, though in most of the other countries it is
available for some categories of women. In many, applications are passed
upon by commissions; only rarely is the decision left to one doctor con-
fering alone with a pregnant woman. As for totally removing abortion
from any kind of legal control, there is nothing in any of the published
East European writings to indicate that such a move is wanted or
planned. In fact, there seems a common conviction that some controls
will always remain necessary. One reason, to be sure, is the apparent
governmental desire in some countries to use and adjust abortion (and
contraception) laws as part of official demographic strategies. Still another reason is the continuing worry over the medical effects of induced

abortion on a large scale, particularly among women who have had no previous children, and among women who have repeated abortions (especially characteristic of countries which have tried abortion on demand).

Finally, and most pertinently so far as women's freedom is concerned, there is a widespread conviction that some kind of compulsory consultative procedure is required (however difficult it may be to ensure in practice), even if the woman herself is allowed to make the final choice. The aim is precisely to insure the greatest possible freedom for women. This goal, many believe, cannot be fulfilled unless women (a) are fully advised of the physical hazards of abortion, (b) are given contraceptive advice in order (in the future) to avoid unwanted conceptions, (c) are provided the chance to accept additional financial and social assistance sufficient to support a child, offered to her not just in general but, specifically, when she comes to the moment of choosing for or against abortion, and (d) it is insured that women are making a free choice, uncoerced by their family or friends. In short, the aim is not to hinder but to enhance the woman's freedom and, it is believed, this is best done by means of compulsory and independent counseling services.[95] Put another way, merely to allow a woman to make her own choice in consultation with a private doctor may present more the appearance than the substance of freedom; full freedom comes with knowledge, the absence of coercion, and the availability of feasible options.

During a tour of East Europe in 1967, a Scandinavian investigative group, composed of members of abortion study commissions charged with studying possible changes in Scandinavian laws (see Chapter 6), were apparently impressed with this general approach. It was, in fact, their own investigation of the East European experience and data, combined with their discussions with experts there, which had much to do with a common conclusion that pressure for total abortion on request should be resisted as an undesirable goal. A law, they felt, which would require compulsory counseling, enhanced assistance to women with unwanted pregnancies, and yet, after that, final freedom of choice in favor of an abortion if a woman persisted in her desire for one, would be the most balanced.[96] That many women are known to be coerced by others into seeking abortions was an important factor as well.

Behind this East European thinking lies a dilemma in the experience with permissive laws. On the one hand, there is a strong conviction that women should be able to make their own choice (assuming the necessary counseling beforehand); there is also a strong conviction that illegal abortions are dangerous. On the other hand, though, there is an abortion rate much higher than most medical men and family-planning officials think safe or desirable; too many women, in a word, are choosing abortion. What, then, is to be done to resolve the dilemma?

One method, chosen reluctantly on occasion in some countries as we have seen, is to make the laws or their application stricter. But this immediately raises the specter of an increase in illegal abortions (often immediately confirmed by a suspicious rise in the number of spontaneous abortions and increased hospital admissions for injuries due to admitted illegal abortion). The other method, which seems most satisfactory in theory, is to press an educational campaign against abortion and, at the same time, an educational and assistance campaign in favor of contraception.

Franc Novak of Yugoslavia, summarizing many of the East European worries about high abortion rates, concludes that legislation should take account of the widespread conviction that unwanted pregnancies should not occur, but

> the law should make it possible for women to be healthier, and not for abortionists to get richer. To the health service, the law should give its strong support in order that it may develop the necessary capacities for promoting contraception, which should become everywhere not only free, but even compulsorily stimulated. . . . Contraceptive devices should be improved and made accessible to all people. Preventive medicine everywhere always makes slow progress, so it needs to be made compulsory. . . . Contraception is the preventive par excellence as it fights the greatest epidemic of all times that is always on the increase. This epidemic is mass abortion which threatens an enormous number of women. Not to ban contraception, or even to tolerate it, is not sufficient. Much more is wanted.[97]

Novak's observation about the difficulty of getting women to use contraceptives on a widespread and effective scale has been underlined in the East European countries permitting permissive abortions. Despite the fact that some of the East European laws require that women granted abortions be instructed in the use of contraceptive techniques, and the rest encourage it, the general adoption and successful use of these techniques has been very slow.

An Anglican abortion study, reflecting on East Europe, well states one problem:

> Idealistically it used to be thought—and still it is said—that a widespread knowledge and practice of contraception would reduce or eliminate resort to abortion, as a means of family limitation, by married women. That expectation is now seen to have allowed too little weight to incalculable factors. One was the uncertainty of existing contraceptive methods, either in themselves or in their use. The other was in the attitude of mind which the practice of contraception might foster. . . . The earlier optimism could be re-stated now only if newer contraceptive methods prove themselves to be efficient enough, and acceptable enough, to match the determined attitude of mind. Otherwise, while the attitude of mind prevails and contraception fails, abortion of the married will continue.[98]

Many of the studies I have cited in this section deal with data collected prior to the more widespread use of oral contraceptives, which came into use in East Europe only during the mid 1960s, and even then very slowly. Novak believes that the decrease in the East European birthrate since that time can probably be traced to the greater efficiency of the oral contraceptives. According to E. A. Sadvokasova, the belief in the Soviet Union is that the number of abortions will drop, and the use of contraceptives will increase, as there is a general growth in the national economy, a rise in the general cultural level and greater provision made for the care of mothers and children. In any event, even though the data do not yet suggest that contraceptives are an indubitably effective means of lowering the abortion rate, the East European countries are assuming that in the long run they will be; and no doubt the existence of the anovulatory pills gives this belief a greater credibility now than before they were available.[99] "If criminal abortion becomes a social problem in a country," Nusret H. Fisek has written, "it means that the motivation for using contraceptives and limiting family size is very high." [100]

On the question of the relationship between abortion laws and birthrates, there is a general working assumption in East Europe that the permissive abortion laws led to a decline in the birthrate. K.-H. Mehlan has summarized the East European demographic trends:

> In Bulgaria, Czechoslovakia and Hungary, where fertility was relatively low before the enactment of the abortion law, the number of births decreased immediately and sharply. In the U.S.S.R., Poland, and Yugoslavia, on the other hand, where fertility was relatively high, the decline began later and, except in Poland, was relatively slow. The lowest live-birth rates are recorded in those countries in which the ratio of abortions to births is highest. In Czechoslovakia, the increase in births since 1963 has been associated with the decline in the number of abortions since 1962.[101]

Mehlan's generalizations, which cover a period prior to 1965, now need some updating, but they remain valid in their general thrust. Some caution is needed, however, in immediately deducing that the permissive abortion laws in themselves are the direct cause of the declining birthrates. I have already cited some of Malcolm Potts' strictures on this point. Moreover, during the period after which the liberalized abortion laws were introduced, the East European countries—in the aftermath of Stalinism—all saw a considerable growth in industrial productivity, prosperity and increased industrialization, factors normally taken to lead to a decline in the birthrate. At the same time, there has been some degree of variation between different countries so far as the birthrate decline is concerned. Yugoslavia, after liberalizing its laws in 1960, saw a drop in the birthrate per 1,000 population from 23.5 in 1960 to 21.4 in 1963, not a very significant decline, comparatively speaking. Between 1955 and 1963 the birthrate in the Soviet Union dropped from 25.7 to 21.2, again a drop something less than precipitous. East Germany, by contrast, with continuing restrictive laws, saw only a slight rise in its birthrate between 1954 and 1964, from 16.6 to 17.6. (A contributing factor here, however, was the emigration of large numbers of young women until 1961, when the Berlin Wall prevented East Germans from leaving.)

What seems apparent is that there are many social factors which lead to a decline in the birthrate, and it is not easy to sort out precisely what the specific role of legal abortion is. In a country like Rumania, with a drop in the birthrate from 24.8 in 1954 to 14.3 in 1966, the correlation seems clear, and is readily granted. In other countries, though, the correlations are less certain. András Klinger, analyzing the East European birthrates, has come to a suitably cautious conclusion:

> It can be stated that in spite of identical legal provisions regarding induced abortions, the role of abortions as an instrument of birth control has varied from country to country. This may suggest that abortion is not the basis, but only a measure of birth control, and that within the context of the socio-economic structure, it is the cultural outlook of women which determines their plans for family size. Induced and legalized abortion is only one of the measures to fulfill these changing plans.[102]

Christopher Tietze believes that the permissive laws have been a major cause of the decline in the birthrate of the countries where abortion has been made permissive, except in the Soviet Union.[103]

As discussed in Chapter 2, a continued worry over the medical effects of abortions, even legal abortions, provides one major reason for a widespread desire among East European authorities for a reduction in the abortion rate. A major aspect of this concern stems from the fact of repeated abortions. András Klinger has noted that in the Soviet Union in 1958 and 1959, 16 percent of aborting women had more than one induced abortion within a year. In Hungary, 22 percent of women aborted in April of 1964 also had an abortion in 1963, and the number of aborting women having their third or more abortion increased from 25.5 percent in 1960 to 31.4 percent in 1964. Women who had five or more legal abortions increased from 5.2 percent in 1960 to 7.5 percent in 1964. Though Klinger points out that his data are rather random and have not been standardized for age or duration of marriage, he feels nonetheless that the available data suggest that there is "an increasing tendency among women [who] resort to this method of birth limitation in the first place [to] continue to rely on its use." [104] Franc Novak of Yugoslavia, in discussing the difficulty of getting women to use contraception rather than abortions, has said:

> Why do women not prefer contraception, which is simpler and less un-

pleasant than abortion? In our country, there are no visible obstacles to modern contraception; on the contrary, it is even supported, urged and stimulated. In a socialist society prophylaxis stands in the foreground of medical thinking and acting. It is included in our health service whose duty is to put it into practice. . . . Our propaganda meets with no obstacles. . . . It seems that the greatest obstacle to the spread of contraception lies in liberal permission of artificial abortions. Through widespread abortions a state of mind is created with women that abortion represents the chief means of planned parenthood.[105]

(One must, I think, allow for some exaggeration here about the extent and effectivenss of East European contraception programs.)

Hans Lehfeldt and Christopher Tietze have attempted some broad generalizations from the East European data. First, the legalization of abortion resulted in a sharp increase in the number of legal abortions. Second, illegal abortions have substantially declined, but even in the East European countries have not been completely replaced by legal abortions. Third, the risk to life from an abortion performed by a trained doctor in a hospital on a healthy woman in the first three months of pregnancy is far less than the risk usually associated with full-term pregnancy and childbirth. Fourth, legalization, which has increased the total number of abortions, has also resulted in an increased number of conceptions. Fifth, despite the liberalization of the laws, in "none of the countries of Eastern Europe where interruption of pregnancy has recently been legalized is it considered a desirable method fertility control by responsible leaders of the medical profession. The intention is that abortion be eventually replaced by contraception." Sixth, the lower level of mortality after legal abortion in the East European countries, as compared with Northern Europe, appears to reflect the greater ease with which women can get an early abortion in the East European countries, thus avoiding the dangers of late abortions.[106]

In a study of the demographic effects of abortion, however, Harald Frederiksen and James Brackett are somewhat less convinced that the liberalization of abortion laws drastically reduces the incidence of illegal abortion. Their prime example is East Germany during its brief experiment with liberalization, when there was not only an increase in legal abortions but also an increase in pregnancies, births and illegal abortions.[107] They concede that the situation may have been different in other East European countries which kept their liberal laws in force long after East Germany repealed hers, but they insist that it should not be assumed that previous illegal abortions were simply transferred to the legal sphere after liberalization. Such an assumption, they say, is based on another, that the pregnancy rate in all these countries remained constant before and after the law changed. On the contrary, they point out, using Bulgaria and Hungary as examples, the sharp rise in the total abortion rate after liberalization was accompanied by an equally sharp rise in the total pregnancy rate, which was caused by a less careful and consistent practice of contraception and by the shorter interval between conceptions after abortion than after childbirth.

Two things account for the latter: first, of course, the duration of an aborted pregnancy is shorter than one allowed to go full term—three months, say, compared to nine; second, the period of postpartum amenorrhea is shorter after an abortion—one month, compared with two months after childbirth if the baby is *not* breast-fed, 11 months if he is. plus, in either case, two months of anovulatory cycles. Thus, the inter-conception interval after abortion is approximately nine months (three for pregnancy, one for postpartum amenorrhea, five months of ovulatory exposure), as compared with 18 or 27 months after childbirth, de-pending on breast-feeding (nine months of pregnancy, two or 11 months of amenorrhea, two months of anovulation, five months of exposure). From this it is usually estimated, then, that, in the absence of contraception, it requires two or three abortions to prevent one birth and, with highly effective contraception, 1.1 or 1.2 abortions to prevent one birth.[108]

These general observations are consistent with the detailed data I have already provided on the individual countries. Some final con-clusions can be drawn from the East European experience. It seems clear, first of all, that the introduction of very permissive laws reduces the resultant deaths and injuries from illegal abortions. András Klinger has said:

> The decreasing number of deaths due to abortion clearly shows the impact of legalized abortions on the health of females. In countries where abortions have been legalized, the number of deaths due to abortions has decreased considerably, in spite of the significant increase in the number of registered abortions. Thus, mortality due to abortions has decreased considerably, and only 1 or 2 females a year die in each of these countries as a result of legally performed abortions.[109]

In sum, insofar as the laws are designed to safeguard women from the danger of illegal abortions, they seem quite successful (even if there remains a small residue of illegal abortions).[110] The data are equally strong that the permissive laws of East Europe also greatly increase the number of legal abortions, the number of conceptions, and the number of repeated abortions. Although there is less information than is desirable, there seems a fair amount of testimony that a very per-missive system, if not a total obstacle to the introduction of contra-ceptive practices, is at least an important hindrance. (Malcolm Potts, though, sees no real problem here, taking abortion and contraception to be "complementary" methods of achieving the same end.) [111] There is a strong suggestion that the possibility of simple and readily accessible abortions leads some women to a dependence upon them as a means of birth control. Finally, although not decisively proven, there is a strong likelihood that the introduction of permissive abortion laws has been at least one major variable in a declining East European birthrate since the mid-1950s.

Behind the East European abortion figures lie a host of social and cultural factors of considerable importance: a high and increasing level of industrialization, a long history of declining birthrates (antedating changes in abortion laws), a high level of female participation in the work force (combined with an ideology of female equality and freedom), chronic economic and housing problems, increasing urbanization, changing patterns of sexual behavior, particularly under the influence of the West. Taken together, they help to illuminate the East European configurations. While, historically, East Europe is Christian, the actual power of this ethos at present is uncertain. Undoubtedly, the advent of Communism/Socialism after World War II made some difference, and continues to do so, in the influence of the churches, Protestant, Catholic and Orthodox; coercion, both direct and indirect, has hardly helped their position.

Yet it would probably be a mistake to think that the declining influence of religion under the Communist regimes explains the East European abortion laws and practice; there is more to it than that. For one thing, as noted, the decline in the birthrate began long before the advent of Communism in East Europe; at best, the legalizing of abortion only helped intensify a long-existing trend. For another, the influence of the churches had begun to decline prior to World War II, a factor undoubtedly connected (as in other parts of the world) with increased urbanization and industrialization; again, Communism would seem only to have intensified an existing trend. Finally, as trends in North and South America and in Western Europe should make evident, the fact that a culture can be labeled "Christian" or "religious" in some nominal fashion provides no guarantee of low abortion rates. Potts seems to me absolutely correct when he says: "A large percentage of women will resort to abortion in order to avoid having more children than they desire. They will do this whatever their religious or ethnic background." [112] The more important variables, transcending religion or ideology, would seem to be the extent of industrialization and urbanization and the general level of living conditions. This seems borne out, in the instance of abortion, by the East European figures, not to mention patterns elsewhere in the world.

Japan

Beyond doubt, the most permissive abortion system in the world is in Japan. Whereas Eastern Europe has shown considerable variation and often vacillation in its abortion laws, the Japanese pattern has been much more consistent. Once the laws on abortion were liberalized in 1948, they remained in effect, with only minor modifications, each making the liberalization more comprehensive. Historically, both abortion and infanticide had been common during the Tokugawa regime (1603–1867), but both were outlawed at the end of that period. Abortion next came under the control of the National Eugenic Law of 1940, copied largely, it is said, from the eugenics laws of Nazi Germany. Under this law comparatively few legal abortions—and those mainly on medical grounds—were performed. Just after World War II and in the face of severe economic difficulties, rising population pressures and a concern about an increase in illegal abortions, the Eugenic Protection Law was passed by the Japanese Diet in 1948. The main pressure group behind this law, particularly as it bore on the liberalization of the abortion statutes, was the medical membership of the Diet (national legislature) and the lobbying of various Japanese medical groups.[113] The motive behind the passage of this law is not clear. Ostensibly, its aim was medical: to stem a large number of illegal abortions, with their various maternal injuries; there was also a general desire to give women greater freedom in choosing their family size. However, it is generally agreed that a major purpose was to reduce the birthrate; although the law was talked about primarily in medical terms, the population problem was apparently a major undercurrent in the discussion.[114] From 1947 to 1949 there were some eight million live births, with an annual birthrate of 34 per 1,000 population—and this at a time when Japan's postwar economy was still in a state of chaos.[115]

The 1948 law established liberal indications for induced abortions, and an amendment in 1949 liberalized them further, adding a financial indication. In 1952, another amendment was added, abrogating an earlier requirement that physicians apply to local medical committees for official authorization to perform an abortion. Since 1952, induced abortions have been entirely at the discretion of those physicians specially authorized to perform them. There are about 13,000 doctors so authorized (by the local medical associations of the Japanese prefectures, after a two-year apprenticeship). According to Article 14 of the Eugenic Protection Law, abortions may be performed under the following conditions:

(1) a person or the spouse who has psychosis, mental deficiency, psychopathias, hereditary bodily disease or hereditary malformation; (2) a relative in blood within the fourth degree of consanguinity of a person with a spouse who has hereditary deficiency, hereditary psychopathias, hereditary bodily disease or hereditary malformation; (3) a person or the spouse who is suffering from leprosy; (4) a mother whose health may be seriously affected from the physical or economic viewpoint by continuation of pregnancy or by delivery;

(5) a person who has conceived by being raped by violence or threat or while incapacitated to resist or refuse.[116]

There are two important things to note about the Japanese law and its application. First, at least formally, abortion remains under legal control and, as noted above, indications are specified. Second, despite such control, the decision is left entirely to the physician so that the result, in effect, is abortion on request. It is only necessary for a woman to make an oral declaration that she needs an abortion on the grounds of one of the required indications for her to receive it; the doctors are usually not in a position to check on the reliability and truth of her declarations and apparently make no attempt to do so in any case. The doctors are, however, required to report all abortions to local medical associations, though not the names of the women who had them.[117] The most common technique employed is the D & C, and most of the physicians licensed to perform abortions are gynecologists. The average cost of an abortion is from 10 dollars to 15 dollars, although it is more when hospitalization is involved (in about 50 percent of the cases) or when more complicated techniques are required (e.g., in the later months of pregnancy). However, about 70 percent of the total Japanese population has public-health insurance of one kind or another, and for anyone so covered the cost of an abortion is less than one dollar.[118] It is noteworthy, too, that an abortion may be performed without the knowledge of the spouse.[119] (The law requires the husband's permission but apparently it is not difficult for wives to forge it; in any case, many doctors do not press the point.) According to Muramatsu,

Despite certain legal restrictions on the performance of induced abortion in Japan, there is a wide gap between what is prescribed in the law and what is actually practiced. Under these circumstances, there is an overall belief on the part of the general public that an induced abortion can be procured without difficulty from a skilled medical practitioner for almost any reason and that a failure in the practice of contraception could be liquidated by means of induced abortion, if it occurs at all.[120]

The effect of the 1948 Eugenic Protection Law was striking. In 1949 there were 246,104 registered legal abortions and by 1950 that figure had almost doubled (Table 20). By 1953 the figure had gone over one million for the first time, reaching a peak in 1955, with 1,170,143 abortions reported. The figure remained over the one million mark through 1961, and then began to decline. In 1962 the figure was 985,351, and by 1967 it had gone down to 747,490. These figures, however, represent only legal abortions which were reported. A large number are not reported. As the Japanese Population Problems Research Council has noted:

It is not correct to assume that these official numbers portray the whole picture of induced abortion in this country, i.e., the accuracy of reported numbers is a problem. First, a reported abortion results in a public record of income that may be used for tax purposes. Second, a physician may report his case in a different category, such as abnormal conception, in order to give his client the benefits from health insurance policy. It is likely that a physician's report on induced abortion is inaccurate when illegitimate pregnancy was terminated. Thus, one may reasonably assume that the officially registered numbers under-report the actual incidence.[121]

Different estimates have been made of the actual number of legal abortions. One study, undertaken in 1953, estimated it at 2.3 million, well over the official number.[122] A more recent comment is:

> As one could easily suppose, these numbers do not represent the true incidence of induced abortions actually performed in this country. . . . Results of these estimations are somewhat different from one another, depending on the assumptions and procedures employed, but it may be fairly safe to say that there were about 2 million induced abortions around 1955 when the reported numbers reached a peak and that the numbers declined since then to some 1.4 million in very recent years.[123]

Muramatsu believes that the number of recorded abortions multiplied by 1.6 gives a reasonably accurate total for all induced abortions.

During these years the ratio of reported abortions to the number of live births shifted significantly. In 1949, when there were 246,104 abortions reported, there were 2,696,638 live births (Table 20), a ratio of approximately ten live births for every reported abortion. By 1953, however, there were 1,068,066 reported abortions and 1,868,040 live births. By 1955 the two figures had drawn to their closest point, with 1,170,143 reported abortions and 1,730,692 live births. (Using Muramatsu's 1.6 muliplier for the actual number of abortions, the figures would, of course, be much closer together.) By 1965, the live births were more than double the number of reported abortions, with 843,248 reported abortions and 1,823,697 live births.[124] In addition to shifts in the gross number of abortions, shifts are also obvious in the distribution of abortions. Between 1950 and 1964, women between the ages of twenty-five and thirty-four years of age made up 55 percent of all cases. While there were, in 1950, 17,022 abortions reported for women under the age of twenty, this figure had dropped to 12,217 by 1964 (a trend most likely traceable to a more widespread use of contraceptives by the young). However, the number of induced abortions per 1,000 live births for women under twenty increased from 302 in 1950 to 745 in 1960, indicating a greater tendency to resort to abortion among the young.[125] Thereafter, the figure stabilized for the younger women but continued to increase for the older women (Table 21). One study, undertaken in 1966, found that 52.7 percent of women aged twenty to twenty-four terminated their first pregnancy by induced abortion, 26.7 percent by full-term childbirth, and 15.8 percent by spontaneous abortion.[126] The sharpest increase, though, came in women aged forty or over. In 1950, for women between the ages of forty and forty-nine, there were 59.2 abortions per 1,000 live births. By 1963 there were 1,350 induced abortions per 1,000 live births for women aged forty-five to forty-nine, and 697.2 for women aged forty to forty-four.[127] The chances of a woman over forty ending her pregnancy by abortion were thus much greater than a younger woman's doing so. While there are many stories in Japan of women who have had a large number of repeated abortions (30–40), a 1965 survey of 3,600 married women found that the majority averaged one to two abortions, with relatively few having three or more.[128]

Minoru Muramatsu has estimated that, had there not been a liberalization of the law, the number of births in Japan in 1955 would have been well over the three million mark, rather than the actual figure of 1,730,692 (that is, there would have been anywhere from 1.3 to 1.7 million more births).[129] Taking account of reliable estimates of unreported abortions, Muramatsu estimates that there would have been twice as many live births as the number actually reported.[130] John Y. Takeshita reports that, on the basis of a 1961 study, 41 percent of all married Japanese women would at that time have had at least one induced abortion.[131]

The reasons why women resort to abortions in Japan are not altogether clear, primarily because it is hard to distinguish the true from the reported reasons. Genichi Nozue reports that, in a 1965 national survey of doctors undertaken by the Japan Association for Maternal Welfare, the reasons reported by the doctors were as follows: medical, 26.5 percent; socioeconomic, 63.2 percent; forcible pregnancies, 9.5 percent; fear of fetal abnormality, 0.5 percent; and pregnancy because of rape, 0.3 percent. Under the category of socioeconomic reasons, the husband's illness was cited in 0.8 percent of the cases, housing problems in 2.3 percent, impairing of domestic life in 3.3 percent, too many children in 9.4 percent, and too many young children in 15.7 percent.[132] Muramatsu, however, expresses considerable skepticism about the reasons reported by doctors as to why women resorted to abortion. Pointing to statistics compiled by the Ministry of Health and Welfare for the period 1952–1964, he notes that

a most striking observation in this connection is that the overwhelming majority of induced abortions are performed on the ground of so-called maternal health protection [98 percent to 99 percent]. Throughout the entire period under discussion, nearly 100 percent are done for this reason and the remaining various reasons are negligible. . . . There are strong suspicions that the reasons thus recorded might not necessarily represent the "true reasons" for induced abortion. If one takes this extraordinarily high proportion of health reasons as such, then one wonders why so many Japanese women become ill to the extent that it requires a therapeutic induced abortion, despite the fact that all other conditions relating to maternal health have been improved for the past years [Table 23].[133]

A survey conducted by the Institute of Public Health in 1949–1950 found that

in 17 percent of the cases the abortion was said to have been performed principally for health reasons. Another 17 percent of women said that they had the abortion to allow a longer interval before the birth of their next child. In 50 percent of the cases, economic considerations were the main reasons given for having the abortion; and 13 percent said the reason was that they did not want more children, which in many cases probably was because of the expense of having a larger family.[134]

A later survey, undertaken in the early 1950s, found similar results.[135] From this and other material, Muramatsu concludes that "in reality reasons related to social, economic or psychological conditions are predominant, (at least 50 percent) even today." [136]

Cultural Background

It is widely believed in the West that a characteristic Oriental indifference to life helps to explain the high Japanese abortion rates. This is a dubious stereotype. Rumania and Hungary have also had high abortion rates, and there are many in the West who argue more vociferously for the morality of abortion than do most Japanese. Infanticide, widely practiced in Japan prior to the nineteenth century, declined sharply after the visit of Commodore Perry and the development of the Open Door Policy. Since 1890, incidents of infanticide in Japan have been negligible. It was specifically forbidden by the National Eugenic Law of 1940 and by the Eugenic Protection Law of 1948, and has since remained illegal and little practiced. Japan, then, provides no support for anyone who would automatically couple abortion and infanticide, much less argue that legal abortion opens the way for infanticide. At the same time, the major Oriental religions in Japan, which, in any event, are not strong forces on the contemporary scene, provide no major obstacle to abortion. Shintoism apparently holds that a fetus is not a living person; Japanese Buddhist leaders, reportedly, consider abortion permissible when there are thought to be good reasons (though Japanese Buddhism seems vaguely opposed to abortion, on grounds similar to that of the Western "sanctity of life"); Confucianism seemingly poses no large obstacle to the performance of abortion.

The Buddhist tradition, absorbed in Japan by way of China (which received it from India), accepted many of the premises of Hinduism, most importantly transmigration. Although for Buddhism there is no permanent "self" to be reborn, nevertheless, rebirth does take place. Actually, to be born into human form is an achievement of no small proportions. As the *Anguttaranikayya Sutra* has it: "Few are the beings born again among men; more numerous are those born elsewhere than among men." [137] This, together with the distinctive Buddhist emphasis on compassion (especially in Mahayanna Buddhism), suggests a strong, though implicit, tendency against a practice like abortion. Even to think thoughts which lead to the taking of life produces the gravest obstacle to *moksha* (deliverance from *samsara*, the cycle of rebirth).[138] Furthermore, through overcoming his own sense of ego, the Buddhist monk enters into identity with all other beings. To harm them is to harm himself:

> I will cease to live as self, and will take as myself my fellow-creatures. We love our hands and other limbs, as members of the body; then why not love other living beings, as members of the universe? By constant use man comes to imagine that his body which has no self-being, is a "self"; why then should he not conceive his "self" to lie in his fellow also? [139]

From such attitudes it may be deduced that there is a certain bias in Buddhism against abortion, and indeed, Japanese Buddhists have on occasion condemned abortion—but with little or no direct apparent effect on the great mass of the Japanese people.

The Confucian tradition, also received from China, gained influence in Japan during the Tokugawa regime. In theory Confucianism has a built-in bias against abortion, since the worst tragedy that could occur in a Confucian society is that one's family line be obliterated. According to Mencius, one of the greatest of the Confucian philosophers, "Three things can be called unfilial, and the worst is to have no descendants." [140] It should be pointed out, however, that familial concern was mainly directed from child to parent. It was "old life," not "new life," that was held in special veneration. Innumerable legends and morality tales testify that it is the child who must sacrifice for the parent, not the other way around. For example, there is the famous Chinese tale of the peasant who found himself without sufficient food to keep both his aged mother and his three-year-old child alive. His decision, reluctant but firm, was to bury the child. As he dug a hole for that purpose, however, he struck a metal object. It proved to be a vase of gold, which bore the inscription: "Heaven thus rewards a filial son." [141] Defenders of the Confucian tradition may counter with the pronouncement of the Duke of Chou (whom Confucius looked upon as one of the founders of "The Way") in the *Book of History*: "The Unfilial are worse than thieves and murderers—but not only the unfilial son but the hard-hearted father is condemned as worthy of punishment." [142] In any case, in both

China and Japan, as the widespread practice of female infanticide testifies, it was only the male and not the female child who was prized. The continuation of the family line depended entirely on having sons. (Daughters were absorbed into the families of their husbands.) Thus, the Confucian tradition tends to be ambiguous on the question of abortion: descendants are necessary, but within the family the primary obligation is to one's parents. Moreover, and this may be decisive, when faced with drought, flood or famine, which periodically afflicted the peasants of Japan and China, or at any other time when there were simply too many mouths to feed, neither Buddhism nor Confucianism was strong enough to prevent recourse to pragmatic solutions such as abortion and infanticide.

However, it is worth examining the problem of Japanese attitudes toward abortion a bit more fully, for there are a number of anomalies. On the face of it, there are no major sources of moral opposition to abortion in present-day Japanese life: the traditional Japanese religions, now of little influence, present no strong basis for a moral castigation of the practice; the law sanctions permissive abortions; for centuries, during the Tokugawa regime, abortion was common. "The similarities in family limitation in past and present are striking but so are the differences. The modern limitation of births in the Western world involved primarily the control of conceptions; that in Japan involved primarily the elimination of the product of conception. . . . Abortion and infanticide were difficult adjustments to the imperatives of survival and the values of hierarchical familism. There is little evidence of the ideal of the small family as such." [143]

There are indications that many Japanese women are ambivalent about the morality of abortion, however much they may practice it; and one can by no means assume a psychological indifference toward abortion among Japanese women. The Mainichi survey conducted in 1965, comprising a representative sample of 3,600 married women, noted at the outset that "no one would deny that abortion is brutal in the light of traditional moral values [presumably traditional Japanese moral values] . . . . Those who have ever experienced abortion did not undergo the operation without any moral or psychological conflict." The survey then goes on to document this statement with its own findings: only 18 percent of those who had undergone induced abortion "did not feel anything particular"; 28.1 percent felt they had done "something wrong," while 35.3 percent felt "sorry for the fetus"; 4.3 percent felt a fear of impairing their future fecundity; 6.5 percent gave a variety of other reasons and 7.9 percent did not answer.[144] The survey also noted that, in the 1965 and earlier surveys, a significant number of women would not answer the questions on abortion, reflecting the fact that, even in Japan, "abortion is a subject seldom discussed openly." [145] If abortion on demand is the *de facto* practice in Japan, the psychological attitudes toward it are less than wholly permissive: 49.8 percent of the surveyed women would permit abortion "only when childbearing would endanger the mother's life or health." The survey also found, not surprisingly, that those women who have had abortions were more prone to argue for its legitimacy than those who had not.[146] By no means, then, do Japanese women display a monolithic attitude in favor of abortion.

But the 1965 survey does not provide the only evidence on this point. Another, smaller survey conducted by the Kaseki Eugenics Protection Center in Nagoya in 1964 found that only 8 percent of the married women saw nothing "bad" in abortion; 59 percent believed it to be "very bad." [147] Muramatsu has brought out some of the reasons for the Japanese ambivalence:

> Truly a woman undergoing this experience is not happy about it and often is remorseful after she has gone through it . . . but, at the same time, one has to note that many women are so firmly determined in their decision on family limitation that they do resort to induced abortion, though reluctantly, when they are faced with the choice between the artificial termination of an unwanted pregnancy and the anticipated consequence of having an additional child. . . . In short, induced abortion is by no means a commendable thing; not infrequently pragmatic or realistic considerations outweigh moral or other personal restraints in the ultimate decision on this matter.[148]

There are persistent reports in Japan that a large number of women go to Shinto or Buddhist temples after an abortion to be cleansed by a priest; it is not clear whether the reason for this is a sense of "sin" in a Western sense or, as some say, a reflection of a traditional Japanese repugnance to anything dirty or bloody.[149]

While it is by no means easy to locate all the sources of the Japanese ambivalence, it is worth mentioning some important ingredients in Japanese culture which provide perhaps a glimmer of insight. First, Japan is a group of islands, lacking space for unlimited population expansion; this helps in part to explain a long tradition in favor of family limitation. "*Mabiki*," which literally means "thinning out a row of vegetables," and is used to express the need for population control, is a concept deeply ingrained in Japanese culture. As late as the end of the nineteenth century, unwanted children, particularly girls, were drowned at birth or shortly thereafter—before they had been given a name, which signified acceptance by the family. Hence, there was a Japanese tradition which, though latent after the end of the Tokugawa Shogunate, provided a basis for the Eugenic Protection Law of 1948 and for the rapid acceptance of abortion. "It is impossible," Taueber states, "that the resort to abortion in Japan could have attained its present magnitude without a cultural base in which post-conception limitation of fertility was accepted and practiced." [150] Moreover, the rapid industrialization of Japan during the late nineteenth and early twentieth century introduced still other factors which contribute to a desire for smaller families, and a will to effect that desire. One also should mention a common Japanese expression, often invoked by women in justifying an abortion even though they may not, in theory, fully approve of it. *Shi kata ga nai* can be translated as "There is no other method." In effect, it means that one must often do unpleasant things when no practical alternative exists; what else can one do? Thus, when a woman is faced with an unwanted pregnancy, she is likely to say, in justifying an abortion: "*Shi kata ga nai.*" As Chojiro Kunii, Executive Secretary of the Family Planning Federation of Japan, has suggested, there is a strongly pragmatic, almost rationalistic bent in Japanese culture, which he believes was particularly intensified after the Meiji era [*c.* 1870], but which can be traced back to the Tokugawa Shogunate as well and which helps explain the recourse to abortion and infanticide during that long, often impoverished era.[151]

If some of these considerations help explain the prevalence of abortion, others help make some sense of the frequent expressions of shame or guilt about it. Kunii, for one, is firmly convinced that Japanese women by and large consider abortion shameful; they try to keep their abortions secret and do not readily admit them to others. Muramatsu and Tameyoshi Katagiri, Regional Secretary of the International Planned Parenthood Federation, Westen Pacific Region, share Kunii's opinion.[152] But why do Japanese women feel this way? The concept of *taikyo*, a strong part of traditional Japanese culture, probably has something to do with it. It expresses the belief not only that the fetus can be "taught" by the mother in the womb, but also that the attitude of the whole family toward the fetus will make a difference in the kind of person who is born and develops. Behind this belief is the assumption that the fetus is human life, in some form, open to the kind of influences which make a difference in the development of personality: affection, warmth and acceptance. Moreover, although population control is built into Japanese culture, Ruth Benedict wrote:

A people so truly permissive to their children very likely want babies. The Japanese do. They want them, first of all, as parents do in the United States, because it is a pleasure to love a child. But they want them, too, for reasons which have much less weight in America. Japanese parents need children, not alone for emotional satisfaction, but because they have failed in life if they have not carried on the family line. . . . A woman wants children not only for her emotional satisfaction in them but because it is only as a mother that she gains status. A childless wife has a most insecure position in the family, and even if she is not discarded she can never look forward to being a mother-in-law and exercising authority over her son's marriage and over her son's wife. . . . Japanese women are expected to be good childbearers.[153]

Miss Benedict's book was, of course, referring primarily to prewar Japan, and much of what she says would now be outdated. Still, she highlights some traditional cultural attitudes which have had an impact in the past and probably still do today. The Mainichi survey found that very few women wanted no children, and almost all of those with one child wanted either one or two more. At every stage of parity, the survey concludes, "those who stated 'three' as the ideal number of children hold the largest proportion." [154] While traditional familial attitudes have changed considerably since the end of World War II, they still retain some force. Moreover, while many Japanese women work, there exists no feminist emancipation movement of the kind to be found in the West. The "freedom of women," as an ideological motive for induced abortion, appears to play a very small part in Japanese thinking (as distinguished, say, from East Europe, where female freedom is officially given as one of the major reasons for permissive laws). Finally, although Buddhism as a living force seems exceedingly weak in Japan at present, many believe that its lingering, latent influence may also contribute to the expressed distaste for abortion on the part of many Japanese women.

In any case, there remain many obscurities about Japanese abortion practice and attitudes. A Western observer cannot help feeling a sense of contradiction between the high abortion figures and the common expressions of repugnance toward abortion (borne out by Japanese polls and informed opinion). Although it will not unravel all the obscurities here, it may be helpful to quote Miss Benedict again:

> Occidentals cannot easily credit the ability of the Japanese to swing from one behavior to another without psychic cost. Such extreme possibilities are not included in our experience. Yet in Japanese life the contradictions, as they seem to us, are as deeply based on their view of life as our uniformities are in ours. . . . They see existence as a drama which calls for careful balancing of the claims of one "circle" against another and of one course of procedure against another, each circle and each course of procedure being in itself good.[155]

In addition, as Miss Benedict and others have stressed, Japanese culture is one in which a sense of "shame," a reaction to the attitudes of others, is more important in any moral reckoning than that of "guilt," which has the connotations of transcendent norms of conduct and an internalized moral code.[156] Hence, it may well be that, when a Japanese woman expresses "guilt" over abortion, she is reflecting a sense of failure to meet cultural expectations, which, even to this day, place a high premium on motherhood (as long as it does not result in excessively large families). If one adds to this a latent, not untraditional, moral disapprobation of abortion, an even greater (though still incomplete) understanding is possible.

In a somewhat less speculative vein, a major impetus toward abortion for married women is Japan's chronic housing shortage. It is not only that housing, as such, is in short supply, but also that the available dwellings (mostly of postwar construction) have been systematically designed for the two-child family. Houses or apartments for families with more than two or three children are practically nonexistent in the cities. In addition, by American or European standards, the size of houses and rooms in apartments are exceedingly small. A bedroom in a relatively expensive middle-class home or apartment may measure only seven feet by seven feet. The custom of sleeping on mats, which are rolled up during the day, is not only a matter of tradition, but also of available space; there is no room for a bed. Still other factors are the high level of parental ambition, to better their own lot and that of their children, and the structure of Japanese industrial life. Parents place a premium on small families so that their children can have a good education. Japanese universities are famous for their stiff admission requirements and there is fierce competition to get into the more prestigious ones. Parents are thus prone to begin very early trying to prepare their children for acceptance at a university. They are acutely aware that graduation from a good university is a *sine qua non* for employment in the higher-paying Japanese companies; there is rarely any other entrance route. Once hired, Japanese men usually stay in the same company for life, and laboriously work their way up the rigid hierarchical ladders. Many companies provide housing, invariably designed for the two-child family. In some companies, an excessive number of children is said to be grounds for dismissal and, in any case, there is often no housing other than what the company provides.

The overall picture which emerges is that of a society with many industrial, economic and educational pressures for small families.[157] The absence of effective contraceptives (see below) exacerbates the pressures, leaving abortion as the only apparent alternative for many. Even the tiny Catholic minority, conservative and vigorously opposed to abortion and the present Japanese abortion laws, believes that not much progress in changing the laws can be expected in Japan unless a housing drive is launched and unless Japanese companies change their attitudes toward large families.[158]

Other factors which Japanese observers mention as important in accounting for the high Japanese abortion rate are (a) abortion is permitted by law, an important consideration among a people highly influenced by what the government sanctions; and (b) a widespread public awareness of the dangers of overpopulation, which has the effect of putting popular social pressure on couples to have small families. The exact weight to be given all of these elements is, of course, impossible to determine.

Some Medical and Social Consequences

A little more clarity is possible when one returns to the more prosaic effects of the 1948 Eugenic Protection law. Has it reduced the illegal abortion rate and resultant injuries? What effect has it had on the Japanese birthrate? On the use of contraceptives?

On the first question, no clear answer is available. Despite the argument that one major purpose of the Eugenic Protection Law was a reduction in the number of illegal abortions, none of the available Japanese sources has attempted to establish what the actual or suspected number of illegal abortions was prior to 1948. During the early 1940s and before, it was alleged that there were a fairly large number of induced illegal abortions. Takuma Terao speaks of a "boom in so-called black-market abortions" immediately after the war, but provides no estimates of their number.[159] The Muramatsu volume, however, notes that "a substantial verification on this point is lacking and it is fairly safe to say that abortions were at least uncommon if not absolutely absent." [160] For whatever the reasons—the new abortion law, postwar economic recovery—the number of maternal deaths from all causes declined sharply from 1948 onwards. In 1948 there were 4,437 recorded maternal deaths; by 1955 this figure had dropped to 3,095, and by 1964 to 1,677. Illegal abortion, in any event, is not now considered a problem in Japan. As noted, many legal abortions are probably not reported by doctors, but they still remain "legal"; there is little reason for a woman to seek an illegal abortion, given the privacy of legal abortions and their inexpensiveness. In the absence of any evidence to the contrary and following Muramatsu's conclusion, one may assume that illegal abortion was not a major problem in Japan prior to the 1948 law and is not a problem now. If Muramatsu is correct about the pre-1948 figures, one can surmise that the sudden jump in the number of legal abortions did not represent simply a shift from illegal to legal abortion on the part of most Japanese women. Instead, the 1948 law (and the attendant concern over population growth) may have had the effect of creating a new clientele for abortion. The rapid drop in the birthrate after 1949 (Table 20) would tend to confirm this hypothesis. In this respect, then, the effect of abortion legalization in Japan was different from that in East Europe, where, as Potts has suggested, such a shift from illegal to legal abortion did occur.

The working assumption among Japanese and most other observers is that the 1948 law was directly responsible for the rapid decline in the birthrate. Thomas K. Burch, in an article published in 1955, observes that a common estimate during the early 1950s was that 30 percent of births were prevented by contraception and 70 percent prevented by induced abortion.[161] Yoshio Koya states flatly that "the spectacular decline in the birthrate was mainly due to the rapid increase in induced abortion." [162] Koya believes that the law itself reflected a widespread desire on the part of Japanese women to reduce their family size, so that they were simply taking advantage of a law which they fully supported. Muramatsu is more precise:

First, the precipitous fall in fertility in Japan after the war was, in fact, not a phenomenon abruptly emerging from the end of the war but rather was a continuation of the steady trend of declining birthrate that had been existing since around 1920, although the trend line was considerably disturbed by social confusions due to the war. In other words, the downward trend in fertility actually began around 1920 with the initiation of the modernization and industrialization process and, after passing through irregularities during the war years, it again became operative and acted as the fundamental driving force in the fertility preformance among the people. Second, in creating the basic motivation towards a small-family pattern even before the war and particularly in promoting it after the war, changes in social, economic, cultural and psychological factors along with the general modernization and urbanization of the country played by far the most important role, indeed. Thus, it would seem that the past experiences in Japanese fertility are, in the final analysis, much closer to those of many Western countries with regard to the basic contributing factors, except the time required for the decline was considerably shortened in the case of Japan.[163]

The 1948 law was a major contributing factor in the shortening of the time required for this rapid decline. The decline in the number of abortions after 1955 is apparently due to the rising level of prosperity, which lessened the anxiety of the postwar years, and to a gradually increasing use of contraceptives. Though in recent years there has been some rise in the number of live births (Table 20), the figure still remains well below the 1949 and earlier figures.[164] According to Yoshio Koya,

the evidence suggests that if women cannot avoid pregnancy they will resort to induced abortion. The high incidence of induced abortion therefore seems to reflect on the one hand the permeation of the small-family concept into all segments of Japanese society and on the other, the lack of experience and skill in the use of other techniques for achieving this goal. A decrease in induced abortion therefore rests on widespread education among the people and the effect of the use of contraceptives.[165]

That this may now be happening is indicated in Table 20, though the rapidly rising birthrate in the past few years may also suggest a shift in attitudes.

There appears to be a consensus in Japan, however, that the permissiveness of the abortion laws and accepted abortion practices have made it more difficult to implement the practice of contraception than

JAPAN: POPULATION, BIRTHRATES, ABORTIONS

1949–1968

	POP. (IN MILLIONS)	RATE OF POP. GROWTH	NO. OF BIRTHS	BIRTHRATE PER 1,000 POP.	NO. OF ABORTIONS **	RATIO PER 1,000 LIVE BIRTHS
1949	81.8	2.1	2,696,638	33.0	246,104	91
1950	83.2	1.7	2,337,507	28.1	489,111	209
1951	84.5	1.5	1,137,689	25.3	638,350	299
1952	85.8	1.4	2,005,162	23.4	805,524	402
1953	87.0	1.2	1,868,040	21.5	1,068,066	572
1954	88.2	1.1	1,769,580	20.0	1,143,059	646
1955	89.3	1.1	1,730,692	19.4	1,170,143	676
1956	90.2	1.0	1,665,278	18.4	1,159,288	696
1957	90.9	0.9	1,566,713	17.2	1,122,316	716
1958	91.8	1.0	1,653,469	18.0	1,128,231	682
1959	92.6	0.9	1,626,088	17.5	1,098,853	676
1960	93.4	0.9	1,606,041	17.2	1,063,256	662
1961	94.3	0.9	1,589,521	16.9	1,035,329	651
1962	95.2	0.9	1,618,616	17.0	985,351	609
1963	96.2	0.9	1,659,521	17.3	955,092	576
1964	97.2	0.9	1,716,761	17.7	878,748	512
1965	98.3	0.9	1,823,697	18.5	843,248	463
1966	99.1	1.0	1,359,221*	13.1	808,378	595
1967	100.2	1.1	1,934,958	19.3†	747,490	387
1968	101.1	1.1	—	19.0	757,389	—

Sources: Population, No. of Births, No. of Abortions, Ratio per 1,000 Live Births: *Selected Statistics Concerning Fertility Regulation in Japan.* Hisao Aoki (Tokyo: Institute of Population Problems–Ministry of Health and Welfare, 1967).

Rate of Pop. Growth: *Demographic Yearbook, 1965, 17th Issue* (New York: United Nations, 1966).

Birth rate per 1,000 pop.: *Japan's Experience in Family Planning—Past and Present,* edited by Minoru Muramatsu (Tokyo: Family Planning Federation of Japan, Inc., March 1967). p. 16.

For 1968: *Population and Vital Statistics Report* (New York: United Nations, Oct. 1969).

* Number temporarily depressed as the "Year of the Fiery Horse" is inauspicious for marriages and births.

** On the accuracy of official Japanese abortion statistics, see p. 256.

† *Demographic Yearbook, 1967, 19th issue* (New York: United Nations, 1968).

TABLE 21

JAPAN: ABORTIONS PER 1,000 LIVE BIRTHS BY AGE OF WOMAN
SELECTED YEARS: 1950, 1955, 1960, 1965

	1950	1955	1960	1965
ALL WOMEN	209	676	662	462
15–19	302	574	745	751
20–24	144	387	377	277
25–29		447	408	276
30–34	279	849	928	648
35–39		1,630	2,629	2,012
40–44	592	3,317	5,677	6,971
45–49		7,793	10,513	14,310

Sources: 1950, 1955, 1960: *Summary of Eighth National Survey on Family Planning* (Tokyo: The Population Problems Research Council. The Mainichi Newspapers, Series No. 19, 1965), p. 66.
   1965: *Selected Statistics Concerning Fertility Regulation in Japan.* Hisao Aoki (Tokyo: Institute of Population Problems–Ministry of Health and Welfare, 1967).

TABLE 22

JAPAN: INDUCED ABORTION BY AGE OF WOMAN
1949–1968 (IN PERCENTS)

	UNDER 20	20–24	25–29	30–34	35–39	40–44	44 & OVER	UNKNOWN
1949	1.8	33.3		48.6		16.3		—
1950	3.9	40.5		45.0		10.5		0.1
1951	3.5	43.0		43.6		9.8		—
1952	2.3	43.1		43.9		10.6		0.1
1953	1.6	16.3	16.3	25.4	19.4	9.7	1.1	0.1
1954	1.4	15.8	26.7	26.2	19.2	9.5	1.1	0.1
1955	1.2	15.5	26.4	27.0	19.3	9.4	1.1	0.1
1956	1.2	15.5	27.3	26.8	19.1	8.9	1.0	0.1
1957	1.1	15.5	27.9	26.9	19.0	8.5	1.0	0.1
1958	1.2	15.4	27.9	26.8	19.3	8.2	1.0	0.1
1959	1.3	15.8	28.2	26.7	19.2	7.8	0.9	0.1
1960	1.4	15.9	28.6	26.2	19.3	7.6	0.9	0.1
1961	1.5	16.1	29.0	26.6	18.4	7.3	0.8	0.1
1962	1.5	16.1	29.0	27.2	18.0	7.4	0.8	0.1
1963	1.4	16.1	28.8	27.3	17.8	7.6	0.8	0.1
1964	1.4	16.5	28.2	27.2	17.8	8.0	0.8	0.1
1965	1.6	16.8	27.9	27.3	17.3	8.1	0.8	0.1
1966	1.9	16.8	28.0	27.2	17.4	7.6	0.8	0.2
1967	2.0	16.7	26.7	27.3	18.5	7.7	0.9	0.2
1968	2.1	17.6	26.8	26.7	18.4	7.5	0.8	0.1

Source: *Selected Statistics Concerning Fertility Regulation in Japan.* Hisao Aoki (Tokyo: Institute of Population Problems–Ministry of Health and Welfare, 1967).
   For 1967 and 1968: *Statistical Report of Eugenic Protection* (Tokyo: Division of Statistics, Ministry of Health and Welfare, 1968).

TABLE 23

JAPAN: REASONS FOR INDUCED ABORTION

1952–1966 (IN PERCENTS)

	HEREDITARY IN WOMAN	HEREDITARY IN RELATIVES	LEPROSY	MATERNAL HEALTH	RAPE	UNKNOWN
1952	0.9	0.2		98.6	0.2	0.1
1953	0.4	0.1		99.3	0.1	0.1
1954	0.3	0.1		99.4	0.1	0.1
1955	0.1	0.1	—	99.7	—	0.1
1956	0.1	0.1	—	99.6	0.1	0.1
1957	0.1	0.1	—	99.7	—	—
1958	0.1	0.1	—	99.7	—	0.1
1959	—	0.1	—	99.7	—	0.1
1960	—	0.1	—	99.7	—	0.1
1961	—	0.1	—	99.7	—	0.1
1962	—	0.1	—	99.7	—	0.2
1963	—	0.1	—	99.7	—	0.2
1964	—	0.1	—	99.7	—	0.2
1965	—	0.1	—	99.6	—	0.3
1966	—	0.1	—	99.6	—	0.3

Sources: 1952–1954: *Japan's Experience in Family Planning—Past and Present,* edited by Minoru Muramatsu (Tokyo: Family Planning Federation of Japan, Inc.; March 1967), p. 73.

1965–1966: *Selected Statistics Concerning Fertility Regulation in Japan.* Hisao Aoki (Tokyo: Institute of Population Problems–Ministry of Health and Welfare, 1967).

TABLE 24

JAPAN: PROPORTION OF "CURRENT USERS" OF CONTRACEPTION

AMONG WIVES UNDER 50 YEARS OF AGE

1950–1967

YEAR	PERCENT
1950	19.5
1952	26.6
1955	34.1
1957	39.0
1959	42.7
1961	42.0
1963	44.0
1965	51.9
1967	53.0

Source: *Summary of the Ninth Survey of Family Planning,* (Tokyo: The Population Problems Research Council, The Mainichi Newspapers, 1968), p. 41.

TABLE 25

JAPAN: PERCENTAGE DISTRIBUTION OF CONTRACEPTIVE
METHODS EVER PRACTICED, BY AREA, 1964

	TOTAL	TOKYO METROPOLI- TAN AREA	SIX LARGE CITIES	OTHER CITIES	TOWNS AND VILLAGES
Safe Period	36.9	43.9	29.0	39.4	33.9
Basal Body Temperature	11.6	17.1	9.7	12.4	9.8
Condom	58.9	68.9	56.1	59.2	56.8
Diaphragm	9.7	6.7	7.1	8.9	12.0
Jelly	11.9	8.5	11.6	11.9	12.7
Tablet	7.9	6.1	7.1	8.1	8.3
Intrauterine Ring	6.3	6.7	6.5	6.7	5.8
Withdrawal	5.7	3.0	7.1	5.9	5.9
Douche	1.6	0.6	1.9	1.8	1.5
Others	2.1	1.2	1.9	2.1	2.2
Not specified	2.7	0.6	1.3	2.6	3.6
No answer	3.1	2.4	5.2	2.2	4.0

Source: *Survey of Contraceptive Practice* (Tokyo: Ministry of Health and Welfare, 1964).

might otherwise have been expected. As early as 1951, alarm was being expressed at the rapid rise in abortions and efforts were set afoot to encourage the use of contraception. In October of 1951, the Japanese Cabinet stated that "the number of abortions is increasing. . . . Occasional damage to the mother's health, however, makes the dissemination of the knowledge of contraception desirable to eliminate the bad influence of abortions on the mother's health." [166] Shortly thereafter, the Ministry of Health issued instructions to all prefectures to initiate educational programs on contraception and family planning; at the same time, provisions were made to supply contraceptives to low-income groups. The results of this effort were less successful than had been hoped. Noting that there has been a drop in the number of abortions since 1955, Muramatsu states that it has been less than anticipated and that "it will not be an easy task to achieve a significant reduction in the near future, while certain factors that favor induced abortion continue, such as the inexpensiveness of the operation, the relative ease with which it can be procured, and a human tendency to resort to an *ex post facto* method to 'liquidate' the failure in contraception." [167] He further observes that a new approach to the whole problem is needed: "In view of the fact that abortions have not decreased markedly even after ten years of family planning programs [using traditional methods, however] and that a considerable proportion of the abortions are performed because of failure in contraceptive methods employed, the need for a new approach is particularly great." The Mainichi survey found in 1965 that 38 percent of "current users" of contraceptives would resort to abortion if contraception failed.[168]

The difficulty here seems to be twofold. First, there is a continuing use of ineffective or relatively ineffective methods of contraception (Table 25). By 1969, the IUD still could not be sold in Japan, mainly because of opposition from the medical profession and an apparent hesitation on the part of the government stemming from a concern about a possible labor shortage. The same was true of the anovulatory pill. Concern about possible side effects of both methods is one reason for the reluctance, but another appears to be a fear of further reducing the birthrate (see below). Not surprisingly, then, there continue to be many contraceptive failures, with a large number of women subsequently resorting to abortion. Though the number of contraceptive users rises every year (Table 24), the reduction in abortions has been less than hoped for. In an extensive survey of 1,116 women currently practicing contraception, conducted in the Aichi Prefecture in 1963, some 50.2 percent of the women stated they had "no confidence" in contraceptives as a means of family limitation; only 28.8 percent could report complete success with contraception, while over 40 percent reported two or more failures—and 75.7 percent of those with two living children had experienced induced abortion.[169]

Second, government efforts in pressing contraception have been erratic and poorly financed; since 1965, they have been all but nonexistent. Curiously, although the Eugenic Protection Law made legal abortions available in 1948, contraception was apparently considered a more delicate matter, and the government did not officially encourage it. Only in 1951, with an increased concern about the high abortion rate, did the government officially commend contraception as a preferable means of fertility regulation. Thereafter, the government took a number of steps to press the use of contraceptives, but at no time did it allot a large budget to the program.[170] In 1965, as the result of a continuing low birthrate, a belief that the Japanese population was already well disposed toward contraception and a growing worry about a shortage of young people in the labor force, the government ceased to allocate a specific amount in the budget for family-planning programs, leaving the matter entirely in the hands of village administrators.[171]

Nonetheless, despite the use of inadequate contraceptives and their relative failure to bring the abortion rate down as much as hoped, it does appear that contraception has helped reduce abortions to some extent. Even allowing for a large number of unreported legal abortions, the officially recorded abortion figures have steadily declined. Since there appears to be no special reason to assume a sharp increase in the number of those going unreported, it seems safe to assume there has been an overall decline in the number of abortions. And this decline parallels the increased use of contraception (Tables 20 and 24). Takuma Terao, reflecting on this conjunction of figures, argues that "if the birth-rate falls in spite of the fall of the rate of induced abortion, it may be justifiable to infer that contraception has taken the place of induced abortion." He adds that the sudden and temporary drop in the number of live births in 1966—the "year of the fiery horse," thought inauspicious for marriage and births—a drop not accompanied by any apparent rise in the number of abortions (Table 20), suggests that contraception may have accounted for it.[172] Muramatsu is of the opinion that more young couples will in the future plan their families through contraception "as compared with the past tendency of older couples resorting to induced abortion as an ultimate check on the number of children they desire." [173] The findings of the 1965 Population Problems Research Council Survey tend to bear out this belief, with an increasing number of younger women "currently practicing" contraception.[174]

Whether Muramatsu's guess turns out to be correct or not, there is considerable agreement in Japan that a major part of the difficulty in switching women from abortion to contraception is an habituation to the ease and success of abortion. With abortion as a readily available second line of defense, many women apparently use the available contraceptives in a casual way, if they use them at all. Genichi Nozue cites one study which investigated the use of contraceptives among women who had received an induced abortion. For women who had received abortion on medical and socioeconomic grounds, only 14.4 percent and 11 percent respectively reported that they "always used" contraceptives; 46.6 percent and 45.2 percent respectively reported that they only "some-times used" contraceptives; 30.3 percent and 35.3 percent, respectively reported "no contraceptives used." Since these figures were taken from the 1965 survey of doctors conducted by the Japan Association for Maternal Welfare, one can easily understand why it is felt that the attempt to shift women to a greater, more effective and more systematic use of contraceptives has been a source of disappointment.[175] Yoshio Koya, analyzing the problem, has stated:

> I have been informed that some countries are preparing a law which would legalize induced abortion, or enlarge the conditions under which the operation may be permissible. I don't object to this idea. But one thing I would like to suggest is that, if people at large were once accustomed to induced abortion, it might be extremely difficult to make them come back to the previous repro-ductive behavior.[176]

In support of this position, Muramatsu observes that the tendency in recent years for abortions to be performed earlier in pregnancy "might be taken as an evidence for diminished psychological resistance to induced abortion on the part of women resorting to the operation, as observed by some social scientists." [177]

The number of repeated abortions, even by women who have been given contraceptive information and material, adds further confirmation to these observations. As W. T. Pommerenke and others have noted, the effectiveness of abortion as a method of birth control depends upon a repeated recourse to abortion.[178] He reports that a study of 1,382 women who had an induced abortion between August 1, 1949, and July 31, 1950, found that 49.1 percent again became pregnant and 23 percent had one or more induced abortions before February 1, 1952. Thomas K. Burch, in studying Japanese data during the early 1950s, concluded that "(a) re-conception tends to occur more quickly after induced abortion than after pregnancy terminating in normal delivery; (b) among those who become pregnant subsequent to an induced abortion, there is a marked tendency to have a second operation." [179] Yoshio Koya has reported in some detail the results of an intensive contraception project in three Japanese villages between 1950 and 1957.[180] One year before the project began, the number of induced abortions per 100 wives was 6.3 and the number of induced abortions per 100 pregnancies was 21.9. After five years of concerted contraception guidance, there was a sharp drop in the number of abortions per 100 wives, down to 2.1, as well as an equally sharp drop in the total number of induced abortions, from 138 (preguidance) to 35 (fifth year).

What is noteworthy, therefore, is that the decline in the birth and pregnancy rates was achieved along with a notable decline in induced abortions. . . . The decrease in induced abortions was not easily achieved. . . . It was not until the fourth year of the program that this rate was brought down below the preguidance level, and it took a full five years to achieve any really gratifying results." [181]

Koya then takes up what he considers the "next vital question":

Do people change their attitude of controlling birth when they experience [a] contraception failure? The results of our survey in six districts show a very interesting phenomenon. Our guidance program did not produce any decrease in the number of induced abortions for every 100 pregnancies [preguidance rate: 21.9; fifth year: 33.5], although the number per 100 wives showed a spectacular decrease [preguidance: 6.3; fifth year: 2.1].[182]

For Koya's purposes, which were those of preventing unwanted pregnancies by contraceptive methods, the most significant figure is the reduction in the number of induced abortions per 100 wives; it indicates the effectiveness of a sustained contraception program for the reduction in the overall number of abortions. Yet he adds a further comment:

However, it is noteworthy that once pregnancy has been achieved, whether intentionally or accidentally, its termination either in a live birth or an induced abortion was almost beyond our control. From the increase in induced abortions per 100 pregnancies, it would appear that women preferred the consequences of an induced abortion to the alternative of bringing an unwanted child into the world. Can we blame them for that? Absolutely not, because this line of reasoning reflects the results of our educational activity. This is the reason why I want to suggest that one should be careful enough in treating the law concerning abortion.[183]

A correlation between the use of contraceptives and resort to abortion was also observed in the Mainichi survey, which commented:

> Since abortion is openly permitted and can be resorted to at a relatively low cost, wives may tend to use conventional methods rather than to expose themselves to some new methods. . . . Also, since they depend on conventional contraceptive methods, they have to resort to abortion in order to terminate unwanted pregnancies. This is a vicious cycle.[184]

Sung Bong Hong, in his Korean study, found a related pattern. While aborted women (especially the more educated) usually plan to use contraceptives more effectively in the future, a large number state they will resort once again to abortion if contraception fails.[185] In fact, he notes, his study found "that the proportion intending to resort to induced abortion again is higher among those who have already practiced contraception since their last abortion (55 percent) than among those who have not used a method (41 percent), from which finding the inference can be drawn that the incidence of induced abortion may increase in the proportion of contraceptors."[186] Hong predicts, however, that "with continued contraception the need to resort to induced abortion should diminish as the contraceptors gain experience in the use of their methods."[187]

Thus the findings of the Mainichi survey, Koya and Hong (as well as some Latin-American data) point in a common direction. While the use of contraceptives may reduce the overall number of abortions, an emphasis on the prevention of unwanted pregnancies also has the result of reinforcing an intention not to give birth to an unwanted child under any circumstances; hence, there is a greater likelihood that women experiencing contraceptive failures will resort to abortion than women who have not attempted contraception. When the cultural background of the contraception program includes a prior acceptance of abortion, then this likely outcome of an intensified contraception program would seem to be enhanced. For just this reason, however, one should be hesitant in concluding that, in cultures where a prior acceptance of abortion is not so widespread as in Oriental countries, the results would be similar. It is sometimes said, for instance, that the introduction of a "contraceptive mentality" will inevitably lead to an "abortion mentality." That is conceivable, but the Japanese experience alone cannot be put forward as proof. An acceptance of abortion in Japan (and Korea) preceded an acceptance of contraceptives, thus introducing a significant cultural variable.

While a phrase like "abortion mentality" has a harsh ring and is something less than empirically precise, it is possible to understand its sense. In the Japanese context, an "abortion mentality" can be understood as the development of an abortion habit, i.e., a persistent and repetitious resort to abortion in order to avoid unwanted births. So understood, one avoids the vagueness of a term such as "mentality," putting in its place an empirical observation about the behavior of women intent on avoiding undesired children. And it is a safe empirical observation, borne out by the data so far related, that the introduction of permissive abortion laws in Japan did have the effect of establishing a widespread abortion habit. This is the basis of Koya's warning to other countries thinking of similar programs and the basis, affirmed by Koya and Muramatsu, of the difficulty in gaining a more ready acceptance of contraception when easy abortions are available. They speak, however, within the context of a country where very poor contraceptives are available.

Finally, a word should be said about recent attitudes toward abortion in Japan. On the one hand, it is clear there is a widespread acceptance of and resort to abortion in Japan, even though a steady decline is discernible. On the other hand, there is a continuing concern about the high abortion rates and a desire to see them reduced. In a statement delivered to parliament on February 14, 1967, Prime Minister Sato called for a reduction in the abortion rate and an effort to provide social conditions conducive to the raising of families.[188] Muramatsu states:

> In the past ten years or so, some civil leaders, social critics, religious authorities, government officials and political members in Japan have been concerned about the widespread resort to induced abortion. They have been worried over the general tendency to ask for it so easily and so readily. Campaigns to appeal to the general masses not to seek an abortion have been organized on the ground of its moral unwholesomeness and possible health hazards. Newspapers and women's magazines have joined them from time to time. Some of the opponents have gone further and tried to amend the Eugenic Protection Law so as to place strict regulations on the legal performance of induced abortion.[189]

Muramatsu emphasizes, however, that, while the rising moral pressure is important, women are still likely to have abortions in large numbers until some practical alternatives are offered them, e.g., more living space for young couples and foolproof contraceptives.[190] Genichi Nozue, also noting the rising pressure from various sources to change the law, believes that the majority of Japanese still prefer the present law and, moreover, that any attempt to make it more restrictive would only occasion illegal abortions. At the same time, he believes that young, educated Japanese women are not enthusiastic about the present abortion laws, citing one very small survey of college women which showed that half felt the law should be changed to allow abortion only for medical indications.[191]

The only systematic and sustained opposition to the Japanese abortion law has come from the tiny Catholic minority (about 300,000), plus the 500,000 members of Seicho no Ie, one of the "new religions." Together they have formed the League for Revision of the Eugenic Protection Law. Although its leaders are not optimistic that they can effect a change, they remain encouraged by the ambivalence of many Japanese toward abortion, by the persistence of governmental and medical concern over the high abortion rate, and by the growing worry over labor shortages. In 1968, it was estimated that some 20 out of 700 members of the Japanese Diet favored a change in the law. While that hardly constitutes even a significant minority in the Diet, the persistent concern about abortion figures and the low birthrate keeps the hopes of the league alive.[192] Moreover, those opposed to abortion believe that most Japanese remain relatively ignorant of the extent of legal abortion and of some of the abuses connected with the implementation of the law; hence considerable effort is expended on disseminating data to the public. Two books circulated by those opposed to the Eugenic Protection Law both stress public ignorance of actual abortion practices. One, *This You Have Not Seen,* by a Catholic nurse, stresses the casualness with which abortions are performed in some clinics, the exposure of well-developed, live fetuses aborted late in pregnancy, and the economic dependency of some Japanese doctors on their abortion practice.[193] Another, by a non-Christian journalist, makes many of the same points, but also relates some public reactions of dismay to photographs of aborted fetuses which the author persuaded a Tokyo department store to exhibit. He thus became convinced that most Japanese have no idea of the gestational process or the human appearance of a well-developed fetus.[194]

There is little disposition on the part even of those who support the present law to deny that some abuses do exist; again, though, fear of a resort to illegal abortion has persuaded them that the law should not be changed. From time to time, editorials appear in Japanese papers about the danger of a labor shortage resulting from the low birthrate and about abuses in present observance of the law. One such editorial, in the Tokyo weekly *Asahi Shimbun* (March 7, 1967) and entitled "Japan the Abortion Paradise," complained about Japan's international reputation as a country of easy abortions and particularly about the ease with which foreigners (especially Americans) could obtain them. Less journalistically, Haruo Mizushima called attention at the World Population Conference (1965) to abuses of the Eugenic Protection Law and the hazards of the present low birthrate.[195] The failure of Japanese family planning organizations and the Japanese government to press vigorously for approval of the IUD and anovulatory pill is widely taken to be an important sign of concern about the low birthrate.

For all that, the belief is no less widespread that, after more than 20 years of a permissive law, public opinion would not accept a more restrictive law, even if the government pressed for one (which it is not expected to do). It is thus likely that, because of the absence of effective contraceptives, legal abortions will continue at a high level, even though the present gradual decline is expected to continue. One is then left with an apparent paradox: while the low (though temporarily higher) Japanese birthrate is in great part attributable to abortion, and there is concern about it, no change in the abortion law is likely. The paradox disappears, however, when one realizes that public opinion in Japan would probably not stand for a change in the law, labor shortage or not. By refusing to approve the IUD and the anovulatory pill, however, the government is trying to see to it that no further, more effective, methods of contraception are introduced in Japan; the lack of public pressure for these methods makes this stance possible.

NOTES

1. András Klinger, "Demographic Effects of Abortion Legislation in Some European Socialist Countries," in *Proceedings of the World Population Conference, Belgrade, 1965*, Vol. II (New York: United Nations, 1967), p. 89.
2. Cf. Ruth Roemer, "Abortion Laws: The Approaches of Different Nations," *American Journal of Public Health*, 57 (November 1957), for a more specific categorizing of the East European laws, especially pp. 1909–12.
3. K.-H. Mehlan, "The Socialist Countries of Europe," in Bernard Berelson (ed.), *Family Planning and Population Programs* (Chicago: University of Chicago Press, 1966), pp. 207–08.
4. *Ibid.*
5. M. G. Field, "The Re-Legalization of Abortion in Soviet Russia," *New England Journal of Medicine*, 225 (August 30, 1956), p. 421–27; Lawrence Lader, *Abortion* (Indianapolis: Bobbs-Merrill, 1966), pp. 120ff; H. Kent Geiger, *The Family in Soviet Russia* (Cambridge, Massachusetts: Harvard University Press, 1968), *passim*.
6. Cited in Lader, *op. cit.*, p. 121.
7. Cf. Rudolf Schlesinger, *The Family in the USSR* (London: Routledge and Kegan Paul, 1949).
8. Lader, *op. cit.*, p. 121.
9. Geiger, *op. cit.*, p. 75.
10. *Ibid.*, p. 73.
11. Cf. Carl Müller, "The Dangers of Abortion," *World Medical Journal*, 13 (May-June 1966), especially p. 79, concerning Soviet discussion in the 1920s.
12. Geiger, *op. cit.*, p. 73.
13. *Ibid.*, p. 84.
14. *Ibid.*, pp. 92–93.
15. *Ibid.*, p. 100.
16. *Ibid.*, p. 98.

17. *Ibid.*, p. 106.
18. Klinger, *op. cit.*, p. 90.
19. Mehlan, *op. cit.*, p. 212.
20. K.-H. Mehlan, "Changing Patterns of Abortion in the Socialist Countries of Europe," paper delivered at the International Conference on Abortion, Hot Springs, Virginia, November 17–20, 1968, p. 5.
21. *Ibid.*
22. *Ibid.*
23. Mehlan, "The Socialist Countries of Europe," *op. cit.*, p. 213.
24. For a discussion of Soviet birthrates, see E. A. Sadvokasova, "Birth Control Measures and Their Influence on Population Replacement," in *World Population Conference, Belgrade, 1965, op. cit.*, pp. 111–12.
25. *Ibid.*, p. 113.
26. Geiger, *op. cit.*, pp. 176–78.
27. Mehlan, "Changing Patterns . . . ," *op. cit.*, p 10.
28. Geiger, *op. cit.*, p. 188.
29. V. E. Ovsienko, "Influence of Social and Economic Factors on Demographic Characteristics," World Population Conference, Belgrade, Paper 230; cited by Malcolm Potts, in "Legal Abortion in Eastern Europe," *The Eugenics Review*, 59 (December 1967), p. 236.
30. K.-H. Mehlan, "Combating Illegal Abortion in the Socialist Countries of Europe," *World Medical Journal*, 13 (May-June 1966), p. 86.
31. K.-H. Mehlan, "The Socialist Countries of Europe," *op. cit.*, p. 214.
32. Lader, *op. cit.*, p. 123.
33. See David M. Heer, "Abortion, Contraception and Population Policy in the Soviet Union," *Demography*, 2 (1965), pp. 531–39; David Robert, "Moscow State University," *Survey* (April 1964), pp. 28–29; Lewis S. Feuer, "Problems and Unproblems in Soviet Social Theory," *Slavic Review*, 23 (March 1964), p. 123.
34. See J. Campbell, "Abortion in Russia," *The Eugenics Review*, 57 (September 1965), pp. 107–08.
35. Mehlan, "Changing Patterns . . . ," *op. cit.*, p. 12.
36. Yugoslavia: Laws, Statutes, etc., "Interruption of Pregnancy," *International Digest of Health Legislation*, 12 (1961), p. 619.
37. Potts, *op. cit.*, p. 242.
38. *Ibid.*
39. Quoted by Herak-Szabo and Mojic, "Legal Abortion in Yugoslavia," unpublished paper, Regional Conference of the International Planned Parenthood Federation (IPPF), London, 1964, paper no. 7.
40. Mehlan, "The Socialist Countries of Europe," *op. cit.*, p. 220.
41. Potts, *op. cit.*, p. 245.
42. Károly Miltényi, "Social and Psychological Factors Affecting Fertility in a Legalized Abortion System," World Population Conference, Belgrade, 1965, unpublished paper No. WPC/WP 334, p. 1.
43. András Klinger, "Abortion Programs," *Family Planning and Population Programs, op. cit.*, p. 468.
44. Miltényi, *op. cit.*, p. 3.
45. *Ibid.*, p. 4.
46. Mehlan, "The Socialist Countries of Europe," *op. cit.*, p. 216.
47. Károly Miltényi, "Demographic Significance of Induced Abortion," *Demográfia*, 3–4 (1964), pp. 419–28; cited in Mehlan, *ibid.*
48. Imre Hirschler, "Abortion in Hungary," paper presented to the International Conference on Abortion, Hot Springs, Virginia, November 17–20, 1968.
49. Imre Hirschler, personal communication, April 1969.
50. Hirschler, "Abortion in Hungary," *op. cit.*, p. 3.
51. Mehlan, "Changing Patterns . . . ," *op. cit.*, p. 14.
52. Potts, *op. cit.*, p. 243.
53. Hirschler, "Abortion in Hungary," *op. cit.*, p. 3.

54. Mehlan, "Changing Patterns . . . ," op. cit., p. 10.
55. E. Szabady and A. Klinger, "The Hungarian Fertility and Family Planning Study of 1965–66," Preventive Medicine and Family Planning, IPPF Conference (1966), Excerpta Medica, p. 265.
56. Klinger, "Abortion Programs," op. cit., p. 468.
57. Miltényi, "Social and Psychological Factors . . . ," op. cit., p. 4.
58. C. Tietze and H. Lehfeldt, "Legal Abortion in Eastern Europe," Journal of the American Medical Association, 175 (April 1, 1961), p. 1151.
59. E. Szabady and K. Miltényi, "Abortion in Hungary: Demographic and Health Aspects," unpublished paper, IPPF Conference, London, June 1964. Of course, it must be borne in mind that these words were written in 1964, before effective contraceptives were available (e.g., IUDs and anovulatory pills). One might also doubt, with Potts, that government promotion of contraceptives in the early 1960s was serious and sustained. On the quality of contraceptive practice in Hungary after liberalization of the abortion laws, see also Harald Frederiksen and James W. Brackett, "Demographic Effects of Abortion," Public Health Reports, 83 (December 1968), p. 1003.
60. Imre Hirschler, personal communication, November 1968.
61. Potts, op. cit., p. 245.
62. Anton Cernoch, personal communication, April 1969.
63. Anton Cernoch, however, believes that the drop in legal abortions during that period may not be wholly attributable to the stricter conditions of the law. The years 1963 and 1964, he argues, were a time of "social hope," reflected in the rise in live births. At the same time, though, he points out that there was a rise in the number of illegal abortions during that period as well as a more careful use of contraceptives (from an interview with Dr. Cernoch, Prague, September 1968).
64. Anton Cernoch, "Social and Medical Aspects of Legal Abortion in Czechoslovakia," paper presented to the Second Conference on Fertility and Contraception, State University of New York, Buffalo, October 31–November 1, 1966.
65. Anton Cernoch, "Les autorisations d'interruptions de grossesse en Tchecoslovaquie," Gynaecologica (Basel), 160 (1965), p. 298. Cernoch adds that there was also a considerable drop in the number of fatal cases and of gynecological inflammations; and, he goes on, "examinations of 561,000 terminations of pregnancies performed during that period showed that with improved techniques the mortality could be reduced to one in 40,000 terminations, the traumatic lesions to 0.06% and the gynecological infections to 3.4%" (ibid.).
66. Potts, op. cit., p. 236.
67. M. Vojta, "Současná úloha antikoncepce v řízení lidské reprodukce," Československa Gynekologie, 32 (nos. 3–4, 1967), pp. 161–67.
68. Interview with M. Vojta, Prague, September 1968.
69. Interview with Anton Cernoch, Prague, September 1968.
70. Mehlan, "The Socialist Countries of Europe," op. cit., p. 222.
71. Roemer, op. cit., p. 1910.
72. Ibid., p. 1911.
73. Potts, op. cit., p. 233.
74. Mehlan, "Changing Patterns . . . ," op. cit., p. 2.
75. "Poland," Situation Report (London: International Planned Parenthood Federation, August 1968), p. 2. Mehlan, it should be noted, reported in the mid-1960s that the program is not so effective in practice as in theory, "because many physicians are not interested in contraception and prefer to perform abortions" (Mehlan, "The Socialist Countries of Europe," op. cit., p. 224). At that time, he noted, only 48 percent to 60 percent of all women were actually receiving information.
76. "Poland," Situation Report, op. cit., p. 2.
77. Mehlan, "The Socialist Countries of Europe," op. cit., p. 222.
78. Rumanian Communist Party: Central Committee. "Analiza starii de sanatate a populatiei si masurile privind perfectionarea organizarii retelei sanitare si

imbunatatirea asistentei medicale in Republica Socialist a Romania," *Scinteia,* October 27, 1968.
79. Mehlan, "The Socialist Countries of Europe," *op. cit.,* p. 222.
80. Potts, *op. cit.,* p. 244.
81. Rumania: Laws, Statutes, etc.; "Interruption of Pregnancy," *International Digest of Health Legislation,* 18 (1967), pp. 822–37.
82. Potts, *op. cit.,* p. 233; and Mehlan, "Changing Patterns . . . ," *op. cit.,* p. 3.
83. C. Tietze, "Legal Abortion in Industrialized Countries," paper given at the International Family Planning Conference, Dacca, Pakistan, January 28–February 4, 1969, p. 25.
84. Christopher Tietze, personal communication, April 1969. See also Roland Pressat, "La suppression de l'avortement légal en Roumanie: premiers effets," *Population,* 22 (1967), pp. 1116–18.
85. Bulgaria: Laws, Statutes, etc., "Interruption of Pregnancy," *International Digest of Health Legislation,* 8 (1957), p. 606.
86. "Bulgaria," *Situation Report* (London: IPPF, August 1968), p. 2.
87. Ministerstvo Na Narodnoto Zdrave I Sotsialnite Grizhi. "Instruktsiya no. 188: za reda za izkustveno prek' svaine na bremeniostta i borbata s kriminalniya abort," *D'rzhaven Vestnik,* February 16, 1968. Cited by C. Tietze, "Legal Abortion in Industrialized Countries," *op. cit.* p. 21.
88. K.-H. Mehlan, "Reducing Abortion Rate and Decreasing Fertility by Social Policy in the German Democratic Republic," *World Population Conference, Belgrade, 1965, op. cit.,* pp. 223–24.
89. *Ibid.,* p. 224.
90. *Ibid.* Mehlan adds, however, that if the change in the law in 1947 did not reduce illegal abortions, it did reduce the number of deaths due to them by about two-thirds.
91. *Ibid.,* p. 225.
92. *Ibid.,* p. 224.
93. Potts, *op. cit.,* p. 232.
94. Mehlan, "Changing Patterns . . . ," *op. cit.,* p. 13.
95. I am particularly indebted to A. Cernoch and M. Vojta for spelling out this general theory during an interview in Prague, September 1968.
96. This information was given me by Henrik Hoffmeyer and Magna Nørgaard of the Mother's Aid Center in Copenhagen and by Gunvor Bergström, Executive Secretary of the Swedish working governmental committee on legal abortion since 1965, in Stockholm.
97. Franc Novak, "Abortion in Europe," *Proceedings of the Eighth International Conference of the International Planned Parenthood Federation, Santiago, Chile, April 1967* (London: International Planned Parenthood Federation, 1967), pp. 138–39.
98. *Abortion: An Ethical Discussion* (London: Church Assembly Board for Social Responsibility, 1965), p. 10.
99. E. A. Sadvokasova, *op. cit.,* p. 113.
100. Nusret H. Fisek, "Problems in Starting a Program," in *Family Planning and Population Programs, op. cit.,* p. 297.
101. Mehlan, "The Socialist Countries of Europe," *op. cit.,* p. 212.
102. *Ibid.,* p. 90.
103. C. Tietze, "The Demographic Significance of Legal Abortion in Eastern Europe," *Demography,* 1 (1964), p. 124.
104. Klinger, "Abortion Programs," *op. cit.,* p. 471.
105. Franc Novak, in *Proceedings of the Seventh Conference of the International Planned Parenthood Federation, Singapore, February 1963. Excerpta Medica:* International Congress Series No. 72 (1964), pp. 634–37.
106. Tietze and Lehfeldt, *op. cit.,* pp. 115–54.
107. Harald Frederiksen and James W. Brackett, *op. cit., pp.* 999–1004.
108. *Ibid.,* p. 1004. Also p. 1001, on the frequency of abortion required to prevent one birth (in the absence of contraception), the authors cite D. M. Heer,

"Abortion, Contraception and Population Policy in the Soviet Union," *Demography*, 2 (1965), pp. 531–39, and R. G. Potter, Jr., "Birth Intervals: Structure and Change," *Population Studies*, 16 (November 1963), pp. 155–66.

109. Klinger, *op. cit.*, p. 89.

110. See also Malcolm Potts, *op. cit.*, pp. 240–41, for some detailed data on illegal abortions prior to the change in the laws.

111. *Ibid.*, p. 249.

112. *Ibid.*

113. Minoru Muramatsu (ed.), *Japan's Experience in Family Planning* (Tokyo: Family Planning Federation of Japan, Inc., March, 1967), pp. 67–68.

114. Takuma Terao, "The Impact of Family Planning Programmes on Incidence of Abortion," *Proceedings of the Eighth International Conference of the IPPF, op. cit.*, p. 220.

115. Minoru Muramatsu, *op. cit.*, p. 68; ———, "Policy Measures and Social Changes for Fertility Decline in Japan," *Proceedings of the World Population Conference, Belgrade, 1965, op. cit.*, pp. 96–97; W. T. Pommerenke, "Abortion in Japan," *Obstetrics and Gynecological Survey*, 10 (April 1955), p. 145; Thomas K. Burch, "Induced Abortion in Japan Under Eugenic Protection Law of 1948," *Eugenics Quarterly*, 2 (September 1955), p. 140; Yoshio Koya, "Some Essential Factors for Fertility Control in Japan," World Population Conference, 1965, unpublished paper No. WPC/WP/159, p. 1.

116. Muramatsu, in *Japan's Experience in Family Planning, op. cit.*, p. 68.

117. *Ibid.*, p. 69.

118. *Ibid.*, p. 75.

119. *Ibid.*

120. *Ibid.*, p. 69.

121. *Summary of Eighth National Survey on Family Planning* (Tokyo: The Population Problems Research Council, The Mainichi Newspapers, 1965), p. 65.

122. M. Muramatsu and H. Ogino, "Estimation of the Total Numbers of Induced Abortions as Well as of Sterilization Operations for Females in Japan for Years of 1952 and 1953," *Bulletin of the Institute of Public Health*, 4 (September 1954), pp. 1–2.

123. Muramatsu, in *Japan's Experience in Family Planning, op. cit.*, p. 70.

124. Hisao Aoki, *Selected Statistics Concerning Fertility Regulation in Japan* (Tokyo: Institute of Population Programs–Ministry of Health and Welfare, 1967).

125. *Cf.* Note 37, Chapter 6, for references to youth of abortion patients.

126. Muramatsu, in *Japan's Experience in Family Planning, op. cit.*, p. 78.

127. *Ibid.*, p. 71.

128. *Summary of Eighth National Survey on Family Planning, op. cit.*, p. 71.

129. Minoru Muramatsu, "Effect of Induced Abortion on Reduction of Births in Japan," *Milbank Memorial Fund Quarterly*, 38 (April 1960), p. 153.

130. *Ibid.*

131. John Y. Takeshita, "Birth Control in Some of the Developing Countries of the Far East," in *Proceedings of the World Population Conference, Belgrade, 1965, op. cit.*, p. 170.

132. *Ibid.*, pp. 3–4.

133. Muramatsu, in *Japan's Experience in Family Planning, op. cit.*, p. 73.

134. Yoshio Koya *et al.*, "Preliminary Report of a Survey of Health and Demographic Aspects of Induced Abortion in Japan," *Archives of the Population Association of Japan*, No. 2 (1953), p. 9.

135. Yasuaki Koguchi, "The Prevalence of Induced Abortion in Present-Day Japan," *Report of the Proceedings, The Fifth International Conference on Planned Parenthood*, 1955, Tokyo, pp. 231ff.: both of these references (134 and 135) are cited in *Japan's Experience in Family Planning, op. cit.*, p. 73.

136. Muramatsu, in *Japan's Experience in Family Planning, op. cit.*, p. 73.

137. Hemann Jacobi (trans.), *The Gaina Sutras, The Sacred Books of the East*, Vol. 22 (Oxford: Clarendon Press, 1884), pp. 79–80.

138. Edward Conze (ed.), Buddhist Texts Through the Ages (New York: Harper & Row, 1964), p. 79.

139. E. A. Burtt (ed.), The Teachings of the Compassionate Buddha (New York: New American Library, 1963), p. 140.

140. James R. Ware (trans.), The Sayings of Mencius (New York: New American Library, 1960), p. 105.

141. Arthur H. Smith, Chinese Characteristics (Edinburgh: Oliphant, Anderson, and Ferrar, n. d.), pp. 177–78.

142. H. G. Creel, Confucius and the Chinese Way (New York: Harper & Bros., 1949), p. 125.

143. Irene B. Taeuber, The Population of Japan (Princeton: Princeton University Press, 1958), p. 33. Taueber's discussion of abortion and infanticide, pp. 29 ff. and passim, is extremely valuable; see also George Sansom, Japan: A Short Cultural History (New York: Appleton-Century-Crofts, 1943), p. 216; E. O. Reischauer, Japan Past and Present (New York: Alfred Knopf, 1964), p. 87.

144. Summary of Eighth National Survey on Family Planning, op. cit., pp. 73–74.

145. Ibid., p. 69.

146. Ibid., p. 75.

147. "Survey on the Morality of Abortion," unpublished (Nagoya: Kaseki Eugenics Protection Consultation Center, 1964). I am grateful to Dr. Shiden Inoue of Nagoya for giving me a copy of this survey.

148. Muramatsu, in Japan's Experience in Family Planning, op. cit., pp. 78–79.

149. Cf. Thomas K. Burch, "Patterns of Induced Abortion and Their Socio-Moral Implications in Postwar Japan," Social Compass, 3 (1955), p. 186.

150. See Irene Taeuber, op. cit., p. 278.

151. Interview, Tokyo, September 1968.

152. Interviews, Tokyo, September 1968. Oddly enough, the Catholics I interviewed in Japan said that Japanese women feel no moral pangs about abortion; the non-Christian Japanese vehemently denied this, pointing to some of the surveys I have cited.

153. Ruth Benedict, The Chrysanthemum and the Sword (Rutland, Vermont and Tokyo: Charles E. Tuttle Co., 1968; first published in 1946), pp. 255–56.

154. Summary of Eighth National Survey on Family Planning, op. cit., p. 44.

155. Benedict, op. cit., p. 197.

156. Ibid., pp. 22ff.

157. See Ezra F. Vogel, Japan's New Middle Class (Berkeley: University of California, 1963).

158. Sachiko Seki, "How Japan's Housing Conditions Spawn Abortion," unpublished paper presented at a meeting of the Catholic Population Research Association, Tokyo, April 25, 1964; Shiden Inoue, "Abortion Will Bring Down Death on Japan," Jiyū (June 25, 1965).

159. Takuma Terao, op. cit., p. 220.

160. Muramatsu, in Japan's Experience in Family Planning, op. cit., p. 67.

161. Burch, op. cit., p. 184.

162. Yoshio Koya, op. cit., p. 1.

163. Minoru Muramatsu, "Policy Measures and Social Changes for Fertility Decline in Japan," op. cit., p. 1; Kingsley Davis argues much the same way, particularly denying that the declining Japanese birthrate can be attributed exclusively to abortion. He especially notes that, "as in Europe earlier, the Japanese are postponing marriage. The proportion of girls under 20 who have ever married fell from 17.7 percent in 1920 to 1.8 percent in 1955" (Population," in Louise D. Young [ed.], Population in Perspective [New York: Oxford University Press, 1968], p. 123).

164. Genichi Nozue, "Abortion in the Far East," Proceedings of the Eighth International Conference of the IPPF, op. cit., p. 130.

165. Yoshio Koya, Pioneering in Family Planning (Tokyo: Population Council, New York, and Japan Medical Publishers, 1963), p. 84.

166. Quoted by Minoru Muramatsu, "Policy Measures and Social Changes for Fertility Decline in Japan," *op. cit.,* pp. 2–3.
167. Minoru Muramatsu, "Japan," *Family Planning and Population Programs, op. cit.,* pp. 16–17.
168. *Summary of Eighth National Survey on Family Planning, op. cit.,* p. 63.
169. Unpublished survey conducted by Drs. Tatsuo Kaseki and Hiroshi Tomota of the Committee on the Eugenics Protection Law and read at a meeting of the Mother-Child Hygienic Association, October 25, 1963.
170. Muramatsu, in *Family Planning and Population Programs, op. cit.,* p. 12.
171. *Ibid.,* pp. 13–14.
172. Terao, *op. cit.,* p. 222; "On the Extraordinary Decline in Births in 1966," Tokyo: Division of Health and Welfare Statistics, Ministry of Health and Welfare; no date.
173. Minoru Muramatsu, "Policy Measures and Social Changes for Fertility Decline in Japan," *op. cit.,* p. 3.
174. *Summary of the Eighth National Survey on Family Planning, op. cit.,* p. 56.
175. Nozue, *op. cit.,* p. 131.
176. Yoshio Koya, "Some Essential Factors for Fertility Control in Japan," *op. cit.,* p. 1.
177. Muramatsu, in *Japan's Experience in Family Planning, op. cit.,* p. 74.
178. Pommerenke, *op. cit.,* p. 150; an Indian doctor, Amir Chand, cites the high rate of repeated abortion in Japan as a major reason why India should not resort to liberalized abortion laws as a means of population control, "Legalizing Abortion for Birth Control," *Journal of the Indian Medical Association,* 45 (July 16, 1965), p. 96; *cf.* also another article in the same journal, Rao B. Krishna, "The Impact of Legalization of Induced Abortion: International Experience," *ibid.,* pp. 97–100. See also Chapter 7, pp. 252–53.
179. Burch, *op. cit.,* p. 184.
180. Koya, "Some Essential Factors for Fertility Control in Japan," *op. cit.,* p. 2.
181. *Ibid.,* p. 3.
182. *Ibid.*
183. *Ibid.*
184. *Summary of the Eighth National Survey on Family Planning, op. cit.,* p. 73.
185. Sung Bong Hong, *Induced Abortion in Seoul, Korea* (Seoul: Dong-A Publishing Co., 1966), p. 75.
186. *Ibid.,* p. 76. See Chapter 5, pp. 167–71, for a discussion of a similar pattern in Latin America.
187. *Ibid.*
188. Reported in the Tokyo newspaper *Asahi Shimbum* (English language edition), February 17, 1967.
189. Muramatsu, in *Japan's Experience in Family Planning, op. cit.,* p. 78.
190. *Ibid.,* p. 79.
191. Nozue, *op. cit.,* p. 131.
192. Interview with Shiden Inoue and Father Anthony Zimmerman, S.V.D., of Nagoya, both active in the league.
193. Aiko Nishioka, *This You Have Not Seen* (Kobe: Taiheishobo, 1962).
194. Kazuo Kenmochi, *A Dialogue with the 99% Disappearing Fetuses* (Tokyo: Yomiuri Press, 1966).
195. Haruo Mizushima, "The Reproduction Rate of Population in Japan," *Proceedings of the World Population Conference, Belgrade, 1965, op. cit.,* pp. 251–252.

CHAPTER 8

Patterns and Probabilities:
Social and Legal

꘎꘎꘎

THE THREE PRECEDING chapters, setting forth the rationale and sociomedical consequences of the three leading types of legal codes on abortion, have presented so much data that their very bulk and variety may make them indigestible. One may ask, then, what it all means and what we can learn from it. Specifically, one may ask whether, despite the great diversity of national laws and customs, any worldwide patterns are discernible. Are there any apparent constants throughout the world, constants which seem to transcend particular cultures? One may also ask about probabilities. What would most likely happen if a country moved from one kind of legal code to another? What would the probable consequences be? Apart from satisfying curiosity, empirical information is most useful when it can be put to some use, when it can help us to answer questions.

This chapter, deliberately short, attempts to map out some of the major worldwide patterns and probabilities which *appear* to emerge from the accumulated data of the three preceeding chapters. And *"appear"* is the only word appropriate. There is still much that is not known about the practice of abortion. The full range of possible evidence is not in, and it may never be available. Thus, any attempt to venture opinions on the different aspects of abortion as a global problem is necessarily risky. Moreover, my research may well have overlooked some important data which might have led me to different conclusions. Nonetheless, some generalizations must be hazarded. Ethical judgments cannot be formulated without some idea of the possible social consequences of different lines of action. Laws cannot be framed without some notion of what they are likely to achieve or fail to achieve. Public policies cannot be devised without some sense of the implications and likely outcomes of different kinds of policies. The general patterns and probabilities sketched in this chapter are based on the evidence presented in detail in Chapter 5, 6 and 7, supplemented somewhat by additional data in the notes. The aim here is to see what may be distilled from the data, what conclusions may be drawn about past and present abortion laws and practices, and what directions may be reasonably be predicted for the future. The countries or areas which provide evidence in support of the generalizations presented will be cited in parentheses.

Underlying the myriad data of the last three chapters, specifically the large number of induced abortions throughout the world, in countries of disparate cultures, political and economic systems, is one central fact: many people in many different parts of the world do not want so many children now as their ancestors did. There are any number of reasons for this shift in attitude. Among the most important are the advance of industrialization and technology, with their accompanying social, cultural, economic and often political changes; increasing urbanization, invariably a concomitant of industrialization; improvements in medicine and public health, which have drastically cut death rates generally and infant mortality particularly; and finally, in some areas, a shortage of food because of the population squeeze. These developments, characteristic of modern society, are interwoven in complex patterns that appear in slightly different forms in different parts of the world. But one result is the same: smaller families, fewer children, are desired or believed necessary. When this happens and contraceptives are nonexistent or ineffective, abortions are turned to as a means of birth control. There are an estimated 30 million to 35 million abortions a year, legal and illegal, throughout the world.[1] Whether abortions are legal or illegal depends on government action (which in turn may depend on public pressure of one kind or another), but people who want to limit births will find a way to do so, in conformity with the law or in defiance of it.

Given a desire for small families, or at least a conviction that they are necessary, what general patterns may be discerned in countries governed by the three main types of laws—restrictive, mixed or moderate, and permissive—and what is likely to happen if a country changes from one system to another?

Legal and Illegal Abortions

In countries with restrictive laws, the pattern is clear: there are comparatively few legal abortions but a great many illegal abortions

(United States, Latin America, Western Europe, the Middle East, Africa, India, Taiwan and Korea). In parts of Western Europe (Belgium, France, West Germany and Italy), where the number of illegal abortions allegedly equals the number of live births,[2] the pattern is very like that in the East European nations before they liberalized their laws. But the practice of illegal abortions is not the same in all restrictive countries. In Israel[3] and the other parts of the Middle East (the Arab nations, North Africa, Turkey and Iran),[4] the laws against abortions are strict, but they are not strictly enforced (except, allegedly, in Algeria), with the result that abortions are usually performed under safe medical conditions. This applies, however, only to the wealthy; poor Arabs rarely have abortions. Therefore, while technically illegal, abortions in this area, for those who can afford them, are comparatively free of the dangers and risks associated with illegal (back-street) abortions in other restrictive nations. The same prohibition-in-law, tolerance-in-practice is found in Taiwan[5] and South Korea.[6] In Africa,[7] however, where the laws and many of the attitudes toward abortion derive from colonial times, abortions are not so tolerated; illegal abortions there have the furtive character and medical risks associated with the practice in Western Europe, the United States, India and most parts of Latin America. (Argentina and Uruguay are notable exceptions, with many doctors there willing to ignore the abortion laws, especially for a fee.)

In countries or states with moderate systems there is also a fairly clear pattern: a large number of legal abortions but a continuingly high number of illegal abortions (Sweden and Denmark, especially before 1965, Great Britain after 1967, and the state of California after 1967). Only a permissive interpretation of a moderate law (or even of a permissive law, for that matter) seems able to bring about a large reduction in the number of illegal abortions (Japan and the East European nations).

The pattern in permissive systems is a large number of legal abortions, few illegal abortions (Poland, Hungary, Czechoslovakia, Rumania before 1966 and Bulgaria before 1967). However, unless all legal impediments, *de facto* and *de jure*, are removed (Japan), a residue of illegal abortions will remain (as in East Europe).

A few probabilities may also be noted: a country that moved from a permissive to a more restrictive system might expect an increase in illegal abortions (Czechoslovakia briefly after 1962). Countries changing from a moderate to a permissive system (or a moderate system more permissively interpreted) might expect a sharp increase in the number of legal abortions (Sweden and Denmark after 1965), although not so radical an increase as countries moving from a restrictive to a permissive system (Japan in 1948, East Europe in the mid-1950s). In sum, the more permissive the law, the greater the number of legal abortions, and at least a decline in the illegal; moderate laws will not substantially reduce the number of illegal abortions. And, in a pluralistic society, where disagreement on the morality and social acceptability of abortion will continue even after a restrictive law has been changed, a move to a moderate system is likely to result in an uneven and inequitable application of the new law (California and Maryland after 1967, Great Britain after 1968).

Mortality and Injury

The mortality rate from legal abortions is lowest in the permissive systems—fewer than five per 100,000 in East Europe and Japan as compared to about 40 per 100,000 in Scandinavia. The mortality rate for illegal abortions in underdeveloped nations with restrictive systems (India, Latin America) is high. Crude methods, incompetent abortionists and unsanitary conditions in these areas have made illegal abortions a major cause of maternal deaths. On the other hand, antibiotics have cut into the death rate from illegal abortions in technologically advanced restrictive countries (United States, Great Britain, Western Europe). Even so, deaths and injuries are higher in restrictive systems than in permissive and moderate.

Early abortion, competently performed under proper medical conditions, is less risky than carrying a pregnancy to term, and the new vacuum technique for early abortions is expected to cut down on already low D & C complications. Even under the best of circumstances, interruptions of first pregnancies, especially in teenagers, are liable to result in injuries to the cervix which can make it difficult later to have children. Naturally, this is more traumatic to young women with no children than to women who already have families. There is some evidence, though inconclusive, that the risk of injury increases in repeated abortions, common where abortion is the major or only form of birth control (Eastern Europe, Japan, Latin America). There is little evidence but apparently a strong conviction, especially in Eastern Europe, that the risk also increases in abortions performed within six months of a previous interruption, more likely in a country with little or no legal supervision of abortions (Japan), and in abortions performed late in pregnancy (Denmark, Sweden, Israel).

A country worried about a rising number of legal abortions and tempted to tighten its laws would hazard an increase in illegal abortions, with their attendant unsanitary conditions and resultant deaths and injuries (Czechoslovakia in 1962). A change from a restrictive to a permissive system, assuming a subsequent decline in dangerous illegal abortions and adequate medical personnel to handle the increased volume of legal abortions, would result in a reduction in deaths and injuries from abortion (Czechoslovakia—except during a brief period of strict interpretation of the law—Bulgaria, Hungary, Rumania, Soviet Union, Poland).

A change from a restrictive to a moderate system in a technologically advanced country (Great Britain) would have some effect in reducing the death and injury rate, but probably not much. In developed countries, even illegal abortions have a lower death and injury rate now because of antibiotics. A change from a restrictive to a moderate system in an underdeveloped country probably would have little effect because moderate systems do not substantially decrease illegal abortions which, in poor countries, cause a considerable number of injuries and deaths. Even a change to a permissive system in underdeveloped areas probably would not be entirely successful in reducing deaths and injuries because of the shortage of doctors and hospitals to cope with the increase in legal abortions. In other words, illegal abortions, with all their attendant medical risks in such areas, would doubtless continue for some time.

Public Health

In countries with restrictive laws, the side effects of bungled illegal abortions not only cause deaths and permanent injuries, but also put a heavy burden on public-health services—hospital beds, blood banks, doctors' time. Illegal abortions are a particular drain in underdeveloped areas (India, Latin America), where they preempt a disproportionate share of scarce medical facilities. If a restrictive underdeveloped nation changed to a permissive system, the public-health situation would be improved in the sense that more abortions would be performed safely and quickly, eliminating prolonged and expensive remedial treatment. On the other hand, it is unlikely that the public-health services of backward nations would be adequate to cope with the large numbers of abortions that would be transferred to the hospital or clinic from the back street, once legal restrictions were lifted. It may be argued that doctors and nurses are already "coping," in that they are dealing with the effects of so many bungled, illegal abortions; but they would not necessarily have the gynecological skills to perform abortions properly.

Permissive and moderate systems also result in a public-health problem, although of a subtler kind and neither of the magnitude nor seriousness of that resulting from widespread illegal abortions. In the permissive systems of East Europe and Japan and in the mixed systems of Scandinavia and Great Britain, medical services are adequate but the large number of abortions each year puts an extra strain on them and also diverts attention from other health needs in the population. Repeated abortions and the increasing number of abortions among young and childless women risk damaging sequelae and represent some degree of threat to female health generally.

Abortion and Social and Economic Discrimination

Restrictive abortion laws *de facto* discriminate against the poor (United States, Latin America, Western Europe, Africa, India), by making it difficult or impossible to secure safe abortions cheaply. The social equity of permissive or moderate systems though depends not only on the law itself but also on the medical-insurance benefits, or socialized medicine, and on the cooperation of doctors and hospital administrators, which make safe abortions practically as well as theoretically accessible to all classes. Thus, in Scandinavia, Europe and Japan, even when there is a fee, it is within the means of the poor and middle classes. When a restrictive system is changed to a mixed or permissive system but no change is made in the medical establishment (California), or the welfare facilities are inadequate (California, Colorado, Maryland), or doctors resist the new law (England), the poor may still resort to criminal abortion. A permissive system that becomes restrictive but fails to provide cheap contraceptives and contraceptive education (Rumania in 1967, Soviet Union in 1936) causes more hardship to the poor and ignorant than to the rich and educated. Even when a moderate system is interpreted fairly strictly (Sweden before 1965), those who can afford to travel to a permissive country can get a safe abortion; those who can't must turn to illegal abortion. Permissive systems are fairest in theory; they are only fairest in practice when they can ensure competent medical treatment to all classes at a minimal (or no) cost.

Abortion and Contraception

In some restrictive countries (United States, Western Europe), the use of contraceptives has been widespread for years among the rich and middle classes—traditional methods until the 1960s, pills and IUDs as well as traditional methods since then—but large groups of the poor and others who remain ignorant of contraceptives or are too weakly motivated to use them turn to illegal abortion as a way out of unwanted pregnancies. Should a restrictive system be changed (as in Great Britain), the latter groups would probably have their abortions legally, under better medical conditions, but it is unlikely that the first group would immediately abandon contraception in favor of abortion, although more might resort to abortion in cases of contraceptive failure.

In a change to a permissive system, restrictive countries with little or no tradition of contraception (Latin America, India) and which now have high criminal-abortion rates, probably would follow the pattern of current permissive countries before legalization (Eastern Europe, Japan), where traditional, frequently ineffective contraception was often supplemented by illegal abortion—that is, legal abortions would soar. And once abortion becomes fixed as a major means of family limitation, as in East Europe and Japan, it is not easy either to substitute modern forms of contraception or to maintain careful contraceptive practice. Even if contraception continues, the quality of the practice is likely to deteriorate. The tendency in permissive systems is for women to rely on early, safe, comparatively cheap abortions rather than undergo the trouble, expense and, to some minds, the dangers of contraceptives (though Poland may be an exception here). Aside from these women, there are those who would choose cure rather than prevention under any circumstances; they might not use the perfect contraceptive should it ever be developed.

Even in countries where pills and IUDs are available, accepted and increasingly used (Sweden and Denmark), abortion continues. In short, the desire to control fertility does not mean automatic acceptance of contraception. Instead, it may prompt women to turn to abortion first. Even when the idea of contraception is accepted, abortion is likely to follow as a remedy for contraceptive failure, often high among those unaccustomed to using contraceptives and which, of course, occurs more frequently when contraception is carelessly practiced, frequently the case when abortions are readily available; and of course there is a small failure rate even with pills and IUDs. Since women tend to conceive more rapidly after an abortion than after childbirth, and can conceive more often in a given time period, the lack of contraception or its inefficient use is likely to result in a spiral of increased conceptions, increased abortions, further increases in conceptions, further increases in abortions, and so on, but only a gradual decrease in the number of births.[8]

From the evidence of some attempts, the introduction of contraceptive family planning on a broad scale (Taiwan, Korea, Chile) results, at least initially, not in the decline of induced abortions but in their increase.[9] Experiments in intensive family planning education and assistance, usually in fairly small, controlled, closely supervised groups (Mexico City, San Gregorio section in Santiago, Chile, three Japanese villages), proved more successful in reducing the abortion rate.[10] These experiments are costly in time, money and personnel, however. Although they are instructive as pilot projects, it is unlikely that similar programs could be adopted on a large enough scale greatly to reduce the number of abortions nationally (again, though, Poland may suggest an exception). Most governments interested in population control hope that over the long run contraception education will sink in, contraceptives will be used habitually and more effectively by the majority of fertile couples and, as the incidence of unwanted pregnancies declines, so will the number of abortions (Poland). But the abortion incidence will continue and perhaps rise until practical alternatives are offered, whether foolproof, cheap, effectively promoted and easily available contraceptives, more living space, more food, a more equitable distribution of wealth, employment and opportunities for education, or more child-caring assistance to mothers. Until then, the present pattern is likely to persist: first, those experiencing contraceptive failure will be more apt to resort to abortion than those who have never used contraceptives; second, when the cultural background includes acceptance of abortion, either in the community as a whole or in one of its subcultures, an intensified contraceptive program is likely to result in increased abortion (Chile, Taiwan, Korea). The result would not necessarily be the same where abortion is culturally unacceptable (e.g., Ireland). That is, a contraception habit will not necessarily lead to an abortion habit—though the introduction of a contraception campaign is likely to increase the number of abortions initially—but an abortion habit is liable to persist and even expand as the contraception habit is introduced and developed (Chile, Korea, Taiwan)—at least among some sectors of a population.

Birthrates

In all countries, industrialization, high literacy, the growth of cities, the extension to women of civil rights, education and economic independence, as well as an increase in the number of women working outside the home, have contributed more to declining birthrates than the legalization of abortions. Birthrates declined in the United States and Western Europe even with their restrictive abortion laws (probably through illegal abortion and contraception), and birthrates had started falling in East Europe, Japan and Scandinavia before legalization. Mixed and permissive abortion laws accelerated the trend; they did not create it.

Nevertheless, assuming a strong motivation for family limitation, legalized abortion (with a wide range of indications, freely interpreted) certainly can play a large part in reducing a birthrate (Japan). It has had this effect even when unintended (Soviet Union, Czechoslovakia, Poland, Rumania, Hungary). A combination of criminal abortions and contraception in restrictive countries that are economically and technologically advanced (United States, Great Britain, Western Europe) and in those that are starting to develop or are semideveloped (Argentina,

Uruguay, Chile) also lowers birthrates, but not so rapidly. Should restrictive laws be liberalized in countries with a weak contraceptive tradition (most countries of Latin America, India), the result would likely be a sharp rise in abortions, a sharp rise in the number of pregnancies and a more gradual, eventual decline in the birthrate. (It should be kept in mind, too, that in a country like India, with a huge population and enormous numbers in the reproductive-age group, it would take millions of abortions a year to lower substantially the birthrate.) A switch in countries with a strong contraceptive tradition (United States, Western Europe) would probably not bring about a radical change in the birthrate because the overall number of abortions probably would not increase drastically. A fairly large percentage would merely be shifted from the illegal to the legal sphere. (This assumes that the level of contraceptive practice remains high and that the pregnancy rate does not dramatically increase.) In short, abortions contribute to the decline in birthrates but not so drastically as might seem at first glance.

Countries with permissive laws that change to a restrictive system because of worry about plunging birthrates (Rumania) may expect at least a temporary rise in the birthrate, but only by outlawing the manufacture or import of modern contraceptives and strictly policing criminal abortions. Rumania's experience suggests, however, that the temporary rise will be followed by a decline, because of contraceptives on the black market and an increase in illegal abortions. Other countries, like Czechoslovakia and Japan, that are also worried about falling birthrates hesitate to tighten their permissive laws, anticipating an increase in criminal abortions with no discernible effect on birthrates or population growth.

Generally speaking, as countries become modernized, a declining birthrate may be expected, accomplished mainly through abortion (legal or illegal) if effective contraceptives are not available or made acceptable by intensive education and promotion (Soviet Union before 1955). Abortions may decline as prosperity and the use of contraceptives rises (Japan, Poland), but the birthrate will continue to decline, too (Japan, Poland). That is, an increase in effective contraception may result in a decrease in abortions *and* a decrease in the birthrate. Finally, the most effective voluntary method of reducing a high birthrate would be a combination of a strong contraception program and permissive abortion laws.

Marital Status

In all three systems (except for the restrictive systems of Africa), most of the women having abortions are married. For one thing, married women have more opportunities to become pregnant. Their prime motives in seeking abortion are the number of living children (and in some cultures the number of living sons) and their socioeconomic situation. In recent years there has been an increase in abortions among the young (see Chapter 6, pp. 202–03 and note 37), married and unmarried, and a corresponding change in their motivation. On the one hand, in the West the trend toward younger marriages, which began around the turn of the century, reversing the pattern of earlier centuries, continued and accelerated, with the young couples not always willing or able to assume the responsibilities or childrearing right away. On the other hand, with changing sexual mores, greater freedom and education for women and freer social contacts between the sexes, men and women tend to have sexual experiences at an earlier age, whether married or not, whether intending to be married or not. Some of these young people, married and unmarried, use contraceptives, but not all do, and not all who do use modern methods use them effectively. For many, and increasingly for the unmarried, abortion solves the problem of unwanted pregnancies.

In Czechoslovakia, for example, the percentage of single women having abortions rose from 10.2 in 1959 to 13.7 in 1967; the percentage of married women receiving abortions declined during the same period from 84.7 to 80.4. This was not a dramatic rise or decline but a persistent sign of the changing clientele for abortions. In Denmark, the change has been somewhat more marked: from 20 percent unmarried in 1952 to 29 percent in 1967 and, during the same period, a decline of those married among the total, from 71 percent to 61 percent. The ratio of married to unmarried having abortions in Denmark is still more than two to one, but it had been three to one. The most dramatic change has been in Sweden. Although married women still predominate among those having abortions, their number showed a decline in 1966 over the previous year, for the first time, while the number of single women having abortions had been rising steadily throughout the 1960s until they were within 500 of the married in 1966. If the number of divorced having abortions (which also had been rising in the 1960s) are added for that year, the "single" category is larger than the married (2,286 unmarried plus 723 divorced = 3,009, compared with 2,773 married).

In some areas, notably Scandinavia and the United States, the older generation seems hesitant to encourage young unmarrieds to use contraceptives; to make anovulatory pills or IUDs available to teenagers as a matter of course is still offensive to many older people since it would seem to encourage promiscuity and threaten family and social stability. The occasional resort to abortion, especially for the unmarried, seems to be taken as a lesser threat to traditional mores than a calculated program of prevention which recognizes and tacitly accepts greater sexual freedom among the young.

Because in most countries a certain social stigma is still attached to unwed motherhood, if not to the "illegitimate" child, the unmarried tend to resort to illegal abortions regardless of the system. A change from a restrictive to a moderate system probably would not disrupt this pattern unless there were a corresponding change in social attitudes toward the unmarried mother.

Age

In recent years there seems to have been an increase in abortions among the young and childless in many parts of the world. (See Chapter 6, pp. 202–03 and note 37.) In Sweden there was a steady shift downward in the age groups of those having the most abortions, from thirty to thirty-four in 1960–1963 to twenty to twenty-four in 1964–1966. In 1966, the second highest number was in the fifteen to nineteen age group, whereas in the five preceding years the second highest was in the age group twenty-five to twenty-nine (Chapter 6, Table 9). In Denmark the percentage of those under twenty who applied for abortions rose from 9.6 percent of all applicants in 1951–1952 to 17.9 percent in 1966–1967; the number of applicants under twenty rose from 778 in 1952 to 1,682 in the same period. Thus the percentage of applicants under twenty nearly doubled in 15 years and the numbers of applicants more than doubled. By 1967, those under twenty accounted for the third highest number of applicants in Denmark. The highest number was found in the twenty to twenty-four age group, the second highest in the twenty-five to twenty-nine age group (Chapter 6, Table 11). As in Sweden, this represented a steady shift to abortion among younger women compared with earlier years. In East Europe generally, the highest number of abortions occurs in women from twenty-five to twenty-nine, the second highest from twenty to twenty-four, but the fifteen to nineteen age group is edging higher although not so rapidly as in Scandinavia. In Japan, there has been a drop in the number of abortions among those under twenty (probably due to an increased use of contraceptives) but the ratio of abortions per 100 live births in this age category has risen from 30.2 in 1950 to 75.1 in 1965—a higher ratio than for those in the twenty to twenty-four or twenty-five to twenty-nine age groups. In Czechoslovakia, too, the ratio of abortions per 100 live births from 1958–1966 was higher in the fifteen to nineteen age group than in the next group, twenty to twenty-four.

Older women, especially those over forty, account for only a small percentage of the total abortions (about 7 percent in Japan and Denmark, for example), but their ratio of abortions per 1,000 live births is very high. In Japan there was a sharp increase in this ratio, from 592 in 1950 (for all women over 40) to 6,971 for those forty to forty-four and 14,310 for those forty-five to forty-nine in 1965. This was substantially higher than in Czechoslovakia, for example, but there, too, the ratio exceeded live births: 1,774 for those forty to forty-four, 1,694 for those forty-five to forty-nine. (Note, then, the ratio for the very oldest group, forty-five to forty-nine: twice as high in Japan but slightly lower in Czechoslovakia.) Female equality, employment and education plus the emphasis on small families all contribute to the rise in abortion among young women. Among older women pregnancy is less frequent, but when it occurs, they, too, turn to abortion, even more readily than younger women.

Parity

The number of children a woman has before she turns to abortion varies from culture to culture, according to living conditions, economic and social development, ideal family size and the limits of personal endurance in childbearing. In Mexico a woman may have five or six children before resorting to abortion, in Chile three or four, in Sweden none to two, in Denmark three or four, and in East Europe and Japan one or two. In many countries there has been a marked increase in recent years in abortion among the childless, corresponding to the increase in abortions among the young and unmarried. In Sweden, for example, the greatest number of abortions from 1962 to 1966 occurred in childless women; the second greatest was in those with two previous deliveries. In Czechoslovakia, too, the proportion of those with no children resorting to abortion is rising although government policy discourages it. In Hungary, where the desired family size is about two children and abortion is the main method of birth control, every sixth childless woman terminated her first pregnancy; among those with one child more than half terminated and among those with two children more than three-quarters terminated their next pregnancy.

With modernization proceeding, prolonged education seen as a necessity more than a luxury, female emancipation and employment increasing, city living becoming the norm and the small-family ideal becoming entrenched, by necessity and by choice, childbearing is increasingly postponed or limited, although sexual relations are not. When contraceptives fail or are not used, abortion is used to eliminate an unwanted pregnancy. Thus modernization tends to lead women to have fewer children overall, to have abortions earlier and even before they have had any children at all. Since repeated abortions are necessary if they are to be effective as a method of birth control and because women can conceive more often and tend to conceive sooner after an abortion than after childbirth, it might be expected that a woman would have ten or more abortions by the end of her reproductive life. But that does not seem to be the case. Medical research on the effects of repeated abortions has been scanty, inconclusive and in some cases contradictory, but it may be, as some contend, that they cause involuntary sterility in some women. In that case those women would have fewer abortions by the end of their reproductive life (even though maintaining a small family size) than might otherwise be expected.

However, there has not been sufficient research to make a firm statement one way or the other. It seems more probable that women eventually turn to contraception, however traditional the method. It is possible that the desire both to limit family size and to avoid another abortion impels women to practice contraception more carefully. In Czechoslovakia, for example, figures (in 1967) fall off sharply after the first and second abortions (from 55 percent having their first abortion, to 28 percent having a second, to 10.5 percent having a third and 5.8 percent having a fourth or more. It should be noted, however, that in this series the numbers of past abortions apparently included spontaneous as well as induced abortions). It is assumed that contraception took up the slack—that is, subsequent pregnancies and abortions were avoided by the use of contraception. And, of course, a certain percent of pregnancies end in spontaneous abortion. Finally, as women near the end of their reproductive years some of their menstrual cycles are anovulant, eliminating the possibility of pregnancy.

Education

The education of women influences the abortion rate in a variety of ways, according to the culture of a country and the state of its development. Generally—but not universally—the higher the educational level of women, the greater is the tendency to seek abortion to eliminate unwanted pregnancies either in the absence of contraceptives or to correct contraceptive failure. Education gives women a sense of independence and, by providing more opportunities for employment outside the home, a chance to achieve status outside the home. Education also encourages a rational, more purposive attitude toward fertility. Thus, educated women are more apt to plan their families and to take steps to limit the number of children they will have.

In countries where women have access to higher education (United States, Europe), the long time required to complete an education leads to widespread postponement of childbearing and therefore to an increase in abortion among young, childless and unmarried women, as well as to smaller families among the married, either through contraception or abortion or both. In Scandinavia and the Soviet Union, for example, university women turn to abortion because they want to finish their education before starting a family. In some of the underdeveloped countries of Latin America and other areas, however, a few years of primary schooling is often enough to trigger an interest in fertility control and, given the lack of effective contraceptives, to lead to abortion. Similarly in Taiwan, those with junior high or more education resorted to abortion more than those with no formal education: 17.9 percent as compared with 8.8 percent.[11] In Korea, more than twice as many wives with college education resorted to abortion than did wives without any schooling: 37 percent compared with 17 percent.[12] On all levels, greater education for women is another aspect of the movement for female equality, and all over the world there is a strong correlation between advances in women's freedom and education and a belief in women's right to control their family size, whether by contraception or abortion.

Cities, Towns and Rural Areas

Women who live in cities are more apt to have abortions, and to have more of them, than women who live in small towns or rural areas. This is true in all legal systems and in advanced and underdeveloped countries. The chronic housing shortage in most of the cities of the world, the higher proportion of women working, often of necessity, the paucity of centers to care for the children of working mothers and the impossibility of maintaining the extended family, which could provide mother substitutes, have all made the small family not only an ideal but a necessity for city couples. Large families can be a liability in the city, not only economically but in the time, energy and sheer physical space which parents must provide to raise them.

As an area becomes urbanized, there is an increasing use of abortion. Cities contain a high proportion of the poor who cannot afford to house, feed and educate large families, but they also have a strong representation of the upward-striving middle class with its stress on personal amenities, extensive education and also the strong belief that a child should be wanted and therefore planned for. The huge migrations from country to city have increased abortions. New city dwellers tend to adopt the patterns and mores of their new surroundings which favor small families. In the absence of contraception or in case of contraceptive failure, they turn to abortion. Even women who do not work outside the home (as in Japan) may be driven to abortion by housing and economic pressures. There seems less possibility of making do with an extra, unwanted child in the cities than in the country.

Religion

The great religions of the world have traditionally seen abortion as posing serious moral problems, though they have differed in their solutions. Today, however, in nations as a whole, religion is nowhere a decisive factor in the practice of abortion except to deter passage of more liberal laws (United States, Latin America, Western Europe). The power which organized religions once exercised over whole peoples and the allegiance they commanded have waned almost everywhere. Thus, despite the traditionally Catholic character of many countries in Western Europe, they reportedly have a high rate of criminal abortions. But this "traditional" character is largely a shell in countries like France, for example, where rejection of Christian teachings or indifference to them has been proceeding apace since at least the turn of the twentieth century. Similarly, "traditional" Lutheranism has been no deterrent to abortions in Scandinavia or elsewhere in Europe, nor has Anglicanism or the Protestant communions in Great Britain, nor Orthodoxy in East Europe, nor Islam in the Middle East, nor Hinduism in India, nor Shintoism and Buddhism in Japan, Korea or Taiwan. Even where some religious influence remains, it can rarely withstand the pressures for family limitation which lead women to abortion regardless of their religious beliefs. Thus in Poland, where traditional and conservative Catholicism still has a strong claim on the people's belief and observance, the legal abortion rate is nevertheless high; and the recent decline in abortions seems due more to an increasing emphasis on contraceptives than to the influence of religion. Here and there, of course, one can detect some difference in degree of the resort to abortion according to religious practice (Orthodox Jews in Israel, better educated Catholics in the United States, evangelical Protestants in Mexico and Chile). That is, the more devout and those more informed about their religion's teachings are less apt to seek induced abortion than the indifferent or the uninstructed. But if circumstances press hard, many women will in desperation set aside their religious principles (just as they will disregard the law) and turn to abortion as a practical necessity, however regrettable.[13]

NOTES

1. K.-H. Mehlan, "Die Abortsituation im Weltmaszstab," *Arzt und Familienplanung* (Berlin: VEB Verlag Volk und Gesundheit, 1968), p. 69.
2. See Franc Novak, "Abortion in Europe," *Proceedings of the Eighth International Conference of the International Planned Parenthood Federation, Santiago, Chile, April, 1967* (London: International Planned Parenthood Federation,

1967), pp. 136–37; Ruth Roemer, "Abortion Laws: The Approaches of Different Nations," *American Journal of Public Health,* 57 (November 1967), p. 1918; Ernest Havemann *et al., Birth Control* (New York: Time, Inc., 1967), pp. 101–02; Christopher Tietze, "Abortion in Europe," *American Journal of Public Health,* 57 (November 1967), p. 1923; P. O. Hubinont *et al.,* "Abortion in Western and Southern Europe," paper presented at the International Conference on Abortion, Hot Springs, Virginia, November 17–20, 1968 (Table XVI); Leopold Breitenecker and Rudiger Breitenecker, "Abortion in the German-Speaking Countries of Europe," in David T. Smith (ed.), *Abortion and the Law* (Cleveland: Western Reserve University Press, 1967), pp. 206–23.

Novak lists high annual criminal-abortion figures for Austria (200,000–300,000), Belgium (30,000–200,000), France (400,000–1.2 million, with 800,000 births a year), Italy (650,000–900,000, with 900,000 births a year), and in West Germany, he says, the ratio of criminal abortions to births is 1:1. Roemer says that "the number of criminal abortions in France has been estimated to equal the number of live births." Havemann *et al.* cite a worldwide survey by *Time* correspondents which disclosed that illegal abortion is the chief method of birth control in Spain and Portugal; that in Belgium the number of illegal abortions is variously estimated to be from half, to equal, to twice the number of live births each year (i.e., from 100,000 to 200,000, to 400,000 illegal abortions annually, compared to 200,000 live births); that in West Germany, with one million live births a year, illegal abortions are estimated to range from one million to three million a year; that most women in the slums of Rome have two abortions for every three children they deliver; and finally that in Greece (a doctor interviewed claimed) every married woman in the cities has had at least one illegal abortion. But Tietze enters a cautionary note: "Illegal abortions are thought to be very common in many of these countries. However, certain widely quoted estimates, according to which the number of illegal abortions in some countries is equal to or greater than the number of births, are not supported by tangible evidence." Hubinont's table (which is based, like the rest of his paper, on an extensive questionnaire to European gynecologists) shows a range for the ratio of all abortions to deliveries in several countries, e.g., from 1:1 to 3:1 in Austria; from 1:3 to 1:1 in Belgium; from 1:10 to 1:4 in Britain; from 1:3 to 1.5:1 in France; 1:1 in West Germany; 1:3 in Greece; from 1:6 to 1:1 in Italy, from 1:10 to 1:5 in Switzerland, and so on. But Hubinont, like Tietze, warns the reader to be wary of such figures and says that the estimates he presents should be taken simply as indicative of the general situation. To sum up: most observers agree, as a general proposition, that, despite restrictive laws, abortions are numerous in Western Europe and that a high percentage of them are illegally performed. Beyond that, little can be said with any certitude because of the impossibility of obtaining complete and accurate data.

3. R. Bachi, "Induced Abortions in Israel," paper presented at the International Conference on Abortion, Hot Springs, Virginia, November 17–20, 1968. According to Prof. Bachi, abortion is one of the most popular methods of family limitation in Israel. Interest in birth control is widespread, but the use of modern contraceptives is minimal; primitive methods, especially coitus interruptus, are employed instead. Since such methods often fail, Israeli women frequently resort to abortion; other women use no contraceptives at all but rely on abortion to limit family size. Bachi estimates that the number of abortions each year almost equals the number of live births.

The law against abortion in Israel dates from 1936, during the British Mandate of Palestine; its regulations were extremely rigid, forbidding all abortions except to preserve the woman's life. Two years later, as in England, this was interpreted to allow abortion if the continuation of the pregnancy would make the woman a "physical or mental wreck." The legal situation was further altered in 1952 by a judgment handed down by the District

Court in Haifa, permitting induced abortion on medical grounds if performed skillfully and in good faith by a physician under proper medical conditions (in a hospital, for example). After this judgment, the Attorney General instructed the police not to prosecute abortion complaints (because of lack of public interest) unless the abortion caused the woman's death, was performed without her approval or by someone not a licensed physician or under improper conditions. Because of these instructions, the Israeli abortion law has been only rarely enforced. Growing doubts about the legality of the instructions resulted in their repeal in 1963, but no new instructions were substituted and therefore the law has continued to be unenforced for the most part.

There is a large number of gynecologists in Israel and most of them are willing to perform abortions despite the law. The operations are cheap and are conducted under sanitary conditions, either in a doctor's office or in small clinics. There are few abortions in hospitals, although many women are subsequently hospitalized from the aftereffects of abortions—not so much from immediate complications, such as a perforated uterus, as from generally bad medical sequelae (cervical and intrauterine adhesions, amenorrhea or hypermenorrhea, later ectopic pregnancy or premature births, secondary sterility, insufficiency of the *os uteri*, chronic inflammation of the internal genital organs, etc.). Mortality due to abortions is low, but the kinds of gynecological damage cited appear to be frequent, in part perhaps because of the reportedly high percentage of late abortions.

According to Bachi's article, the results of a Family Planning Survey taken in 1959–1960 by Hebrew University among nearly 3,000 women interviewed in the obstetrical departments of hospitals throughout Israel, along with other surveys conducted at various times, reveal the following data: Jewish women born in Europe or America had much higher rates of induced abortion (20.8 percent) than those of African or Asian origin (4.6 percent). Native-born Israeli Jews were in between (10 percent). Abortions among Muslims and Christians in Israel were low (1.3 percent on the average, including 1.2 percent for Muslims and 2.7 percent for Christians). Among Jewish women of European origin, use of induced abortion frequently starts with the first pregnancy; those born in Israel resort to it after two or three children; those born in Asia and Africa use it when they have three living children, and the Arab women resort to abortion only when they have four or more children. Some other patterns emerged: the abortion rate rises with increasing education and secularization (the stronger the influence of religion, the lower the abortion rate) and with residence in large towns and kibbutzim (the most secluded places, moshavim, have the lowest abortion rate).

Because of the threat of the surrounding Arab nations and their high birthrates, many are now worried about Israel's low natality and high abortion rate. The government is trying to convince people to have more children and is devising schemes to help them socially and economically to do so. In the future the state may try to enforce the law against abortion, but officials realize that extensive education in modern contraceptives will be necessary as well. There seems to be general agreement among Israeli doctors that abortion is medically dangerous (their feelings on this point seem stronger than in most other countries). Their warning that it may permanently impair women's reproductive capacities has alarmed Israeli leaders and influenced them to promote effective contraception instead.

[The foregoing account is based not only on Prof. Bachi's report but also on the author's interview, in Israel in September 1968, with Dr. Renzo Toaff, Director of the Obstetrical and Gynecological Department of the Hakirya Maternity Hospital in Tel Aviv; see also H. S. Halevi and A. Brzezinski, "The Incidence of Abortion Among Jewish Women in Israel," *American Journal of Public Health*, 48 (May 1958), pp. 615–21].

4. I. R. Nazer, "Abortion in the Near East," *Proceedings of the Eighth International Conference of the International Planned Parenthood Federation, San-*

tiago, Chile, April, 1967, op. cit., pp. 104–42; ———, "Abortion in the Near East," paper delivered at the International Conference on Abortion, Hot Springs, Virginia, November 17–20, 1968. In both reports Nazer remarks that the incidence of induced illegal abortion, particularly among married women of the middle and upper classes (who are the only ones who can afford to pay the high fees charged by doctors and hospitals), is increasing, especially in the cities, and it is expected to rise in the towns as well. In the paper delivered at the Hot Springs conference, Nazer concludes that induced abortion is an increasing problem in the Near East, with a widening gap between law and practice.

5. L. P. Chow, T. T. Huang, and M. C. Chang, "Induced Abortion in Taiwan, Republic of China," an unpublished paper, May 1968, p. 3: "Although induced abortion is illegal and the punishment stipulated in the law is severe, it is widely practiced and generally tolerated."

6. Sung Bong Hong, *Induced Abortion in Seoul, Korea* (Seoul: Dong-A Publishing Co., 1966), p. 79. Although the legality of induced abortion in Korea is limited to medical indications, the author notes "a considerable gap between existing law and actual practice." He cites the findings of a recent study which indicated that "one out of three pregnancies is terminated by induced abortion," and further that "women who undergo induced abortion in Korea receive competent medical care [mostly in private clinics by specialists in obstetrics and gynecology] at a reasonable cost [about U.S. $7.60] and with a minimum of medical complications."

7. Cladele Akinla, "Abortion in Africa," paper presented at the International Conference on Abortion, Hot Springs, Virginia, November 17–20, 1968, p. 5. The author notes that in the countries he surveyed—Sierra Leone, Liberia, Ghana, Dahomey and Nigeria in the West, and Ethiopia and Uganda in the East—illegal abortion is widespread, though the exact incidence is unknown. In particular, he reports that injuries and deaths from these abortions are far higher among the poor than among the well-to-do.

8. Harald Frederiksen and James W. Brackett, "Demographic Effects of Abortion," *Public Health Reports,* 53 (December 1968), pp. 1001–03.

9. According to the report by L. P. Chow *et al.* ("Induced Abortion in Taiwan, Republic of China," *op. cit.*), "The island-wide family planning program, involving mainly the Lippes loop, was started in January 1964, and the increased prevalence of induced abortion shown in the 1967 survey suggests that the incidence of induced abortion has increased since the inception of the large-scale family program." A 1965 survey of family planning practice (KAP) as a result of the program showed that 9.5 percent of the women interviewed (all of whom were married and between twenty and forty-four years old) had had at least one induced abortion. A second survey (KAP II) in 1967, which also covered married women between twenty and forty-four years of age, showed an increase to 12.3 percent having had at least one induced abortion. Chow *et al.* say that the results of both surveys undoubtedly underestimated the real incidence of abortion, which, as noted, is illegal in Taiwan but widely tolerated and rarely prosecuted.

It was found that abortion rates were higher among women who had used contraceptives than among those who had not. Presumably the contraceptive users had high motivation for birth control and resorted to abortion when the contraceptives failed. Thus, 3.5 percent of 2,921 women who had *never* used contraceptives had experienced induced abortion, but 24.8 percent of 2,068 who had *ever* used them resorted to abortion. Chow *et al.* say that it is not clear whether the use of contraceptives preceded abortion or abortion promoted the use of contraceptives, but one thing is clear: those who had used contraceptives tended to use more induced abortion. (See also R. G. Potter, R. Freedman and L. P. Chow, "Taiwan's Family Planning Program," *Science,* 160 [May 24, 1968], p. 852: "Of all the pregnancies by women who had terminated use of the IUD, more than 50 percent were aborted.") The family-planning directors expect that as the people learn to use contraceptives more effectively—and they have high hopes for the Lippes loop IUD—accidental pregnancies will be reduced and so will the number of induced abortions.

In Korea, similarly, women will resort to abortion if contraception fails. Sung Bong Hong (*Induced Abortion in Seoul, Korea, op. cit.*, pp. 18–19) says that the increased ratio of induced abortions per 100 pregnancies from 16.6 in 1961 to 31.2 in 1963 "can be attributed to the inception of family planning campaigns as a nation-wide policy in 1961." On the basis of a 1964 survey of 3,204 married women aged twenty to forty-four years, he reports that although 52 percent of the aborted women (805) had not used any contraception between their last abortion and the time of interview, 75 percent indicated that they intended to use some method in future. Further, the proportion intending to have another induced abortion if necessary was higher among the contraceptive users (55 percent) than among those who had not used contraception (41 percent). Here again, as in Taiwan, the hope is that, as contraceptors gain experience, with the IUD in particular, the need to resort to induced abortion should decline.

10. One of the apparently most successful examples of an effort to reduce abortions is the Mexican Abortion Prevention Program, organized by the Department of Preventive Medicine of the Institute for Social Security and conducted in three large gynecological hospitals in Mexico City. (See Chapter 5, pp. 161–62.)

11. L. P. Chow *et al., op. cit.*, p. 13.

12. Sung Bong Hong, *op. cit.*, p. 77.

13. Very little careful research has been done on the influence of religion on the practice of abortion. A number of studies, however, do discuss the effects of religious belief on contraceptive behavior, birthrates and population policies generally. The following are interesting essays in the latter category, although they only indirectly touch upon abortion: John T. Noonan, Jr., "Intellectual and Demographic History," *Daedalus*, 97 (Spring 1969), pp. 463–85; Arthur J. Dyck, "Religious Factors in the Population Problem," *The Religious Situation 1968* (Boston: Beacon Press, 1968), pp. 163–95; "Do Roman Catholic Countries Have the Highest Birth Rates?" *Population Profile* (July 1968), (Washington, D.C.: Population Reference Bureau). More direct consideration of the relationship between abortion and religious attitudes can be found in "Roman Catholic Fertility and Family Planning: A Comparative Review of the Research Literature," *Studies in Family Planning*, No. 34 (October 1968), 27 pp.; Stephen L. Finner and Jerome D. Gamache, "The Relation Between Religious Commitment and Attitudes toward Induced Abortion," *Sociological Analysis*, 30 (Spring 1969), pp. 1–12; Charles F. Westoff, Emily C. Moore, Norman B. Ryder, "The Structure of Attitudes toward Abortion," *Milbank Memorial Fund Quarterly*, 47 (January 1969), No. 1, Part 1, pp. 11–37.

SECTION III

Establishing a
Moral Policy

Introduction

IN THE FIRST two sections I tried to present some of the relevant information bearing on the establishment of an indications and a legal policy. I also tried to show some of the more important implications and social consequences of different kinds of policies.

I stated my belief that both an indications and a legal policy would and should be determined in great part by moral policy: one's moral evaluation of abortion will have a considerable impact on one's evaluation of abortion indications and abortion laws. Up to a point, it is possible to distinguish between the technical issues involved in analyzing abortion indications and the moral issues involved; but soon one is pressed to recognize the importance of a moral policy in shaping a response to the technical data. Without an awareness of the moral issues implicit in establishing good laws, it will be impossible, in the end, to determine what a good law is or should be.

The present section attempts to spell out the issues inherent in formulating a moral policy. Where the first two sections were heavy with data and information, this section is heavy with theory. For it is the working assumption of this book that a comprehensive approach to abortion must not only have data to work with, but must also have some developed theories with which to interpret the data.

Chapter 9 considers the principle of "the sanctity of life," urging that, properly interpreted, it provides the best available foundation for a moral policy. In that chapter the meaning of a "moral policy" is spelled out. In Chapter 10, the question of when human life begins is approached, mainly by attempting to define some of the major underlying philosophical problems which must be considered in any attempt to answer the question. In Chapter 11, the biological data are examined, as well as the different schools of opinion on how that data should be interpreted. Finally, in that chapter, the different schools of opinion are subjected to the tests suggested as crucial in Chapters 9 and 10.

CHAPTER 9

The Sanctity of Life

IF THERE IS EVER TO BE a consensus on the morality of abortion—and a consequent consensus on legal and public policy—it will be necessary to achieve agreement on some fundamental values concerning human life and human choice. Naturally, it may well be that a social consensus cannot be achieved; that happens frequently in pluralistic societies and has been the mark of the abortion dispute to date. Even a liberalization of abortion laws does not insure social peace. As the experience of England and California indicates, for instance, those who remain opposed to the law (whatever it is) can effectively subvert it or at least cause it to malfunction. In that event, it becomes at least imperative that a way be found to establish some limits to the conduct of the disputants. There must be some minimal agreement on the standards of integrity and openness required of all sides, as well as agreement on what would count as reprehensible conduct. A deliberate misrepresentation of evidence, which can arise when "indications" for abortion are presented, or the use of coercion under the guise of "professional judgment," violate truth and curtail human freedom. Unfortunately, the abortion debate prepares the ground for deception on all sides. Those opposed to abortion, particularly on the grounds that it is the taking of human life, may well be tempted to sacrifice other values—truth-telling, open discussion, freedom of choice—for the sake of protecting that life. Those in favor of abortion and convinced that an embryo or fetus is not human life, may be subject to exactly the same temptations. They could, for instance, attempt to overcome a woman's moral scruples against abortion by psychotherapy or a staged "medical" setting which would seek to convince her that the choice was medically "necessary" and thus out of her hands. And on both sides there can be, and often is, that deliberate lying which goes with attempts to evade the law.

In matters of social morality there must exist the possibility of human trust and honesty. With induced abortion as an option, many interests and values interact with and condition each other. The woeful consequences of a total disharmony of perspectives—between physicians and pregnant women, between legislatures and the medical profession, between different religious and ethical communities, between welfare agencies and clients, between husband and wife—are easily, frighteningly imaginable. Moreover, for the sake of everyone concerned, it is helpful if some degree of agreement exists. Each choice is not then wholly bewildering, but clarified by precedents, guidelines and tested procedures. These possibilities, of course, presuppose the chance of a consensus and a recognition of its value.

If, then, some minimal degree of moral consensus is desirable, what is it and on what can it be based? Without some fundamental points of moral agreement, laws cannot be framed, codes enacted, or trust engendered. To a certain degree, sensible men can enact statutes which reflect a pragmatic agreement to abide by certain rules. But even an apparently pragmatic agreement on procedural questions will almost always reflect some latent shared value commitments, viz., that it is good that procedures for settling disputes exist. But in the instance of abortion, more than pragmatic agreement is needed. Even that can't be effectively achieved unless there exists some basis for a moral consensus, one which could provide a moral setting for fruitful discussion, even if it did not point to agreement on specific problems.

Fortunately, in the principle of "the sanctity of life," Western culture (and much of Eastern culture as well) possesses one fundamental basis for an approach to moral consensus; we are not forced to begin from within a vacuum. On the basis of this principle, moral rules have been framed; human rights claimed and defended; and cultural, political and social priorities established.

To be sure, the principle is vague in its wording, erratically affirmed in practice and open to innumerable differences in interpretation. There are some who would reject it altogether. Werner Schöllgen and Joseph Fletcher, for instance, express distaste for the phrase because they believe it implies a crude vitalism, exalting life as such, whatever its quality.[1] The word "sanctity" carries a religious connotation not always congenial to the nonreligious. "Life" does not clearly specify whether all life (as in the Hindu version) or only human life is meant. Nonetheless, the frequency of the use of the principle in ethical discussions, even by the nonreligious, testifies to its continuing utility, at least as a point of departure. There seems, moreover, to be no other widely affirmed principle which presently serves so well. Perhaps a better formulation for the intent of this principle could be found—for instance, "the dignity of human life." But if one's aim is moral consensus, then it is wise to seek not originality of formulation, but as common and widely understood a principle as possible—one which still lives, is still affirmed, still has a deep cultural resonance and can, without drastic revision, be appropriated by a wide variety of groups (even if these groups feel it necessary to state the principle in somewhat different words).

If "the sanctity of life" is, preeminently, our basic Western principle, what does it mean, where did it come from and how can it effectively be utilized in moral decisions and the formation of moral consensus? The purpose of this chapter is to uncover possible grounds for just such a moral consensus. At the same time, I want also to declare and specify my own general orientation. The first task is to clarify the meaning of "the sanctity of life," which will here be taken to mean "the sanctity of *human* life." This clarification can usefully proceed by analyzing some current explanations and justifications of the principle.

Paul Ramsey has effectively detailed a major Christian tradition on the origin of the principle of the "sanctity of life." In a discussion of abortion, he observes:

> One grasps the religious outlook upon the sanctity of human life only if he sees that this life is asserted to be *surrounded* by sanctity that need not be in a man; that the most dignity a man ever possesses is a dignity that is alien to him. . . . A man's dignity is an overflow from God's dealing with him, and not primarily an anticipation of anything he will ever be by himself alone.[2]

Professor Ramsey goes on to say that "the value of a human life is ultimately grounded in the value God is placing on it," and his point here is twofold.[3] First, it is to make clear that, in the religious view, the sanctity of human life is not a function of the worth any human being may attribute to it; this therefore precludes discussion of any "degrees of relative worth" a human being may have or acquire. "Life's primary value," stemming from God, transcends such dangerous distinctions. Second, Ramsey wants to make clear that a man's life "is entirely an ordination, a loan, and a stewardship. His essence is his existence before God and to God, and it is from Him."[4] In this formulation, man must respect his own life and the life of others not only because it is grounded in God, but, equally important, because God has given man life as a value to be held in trust and used according to God's will. "Respect for life," Ramsey writes, "does not mean that a man must live and let live from some iron law of necessity, or even that there is a rational compulsion to do this, or a rational ground for doing so. It is rather that because God has said 'Yes' to life, man's 'yes' should echo His."[5] Ramsey adds that it is not terribly important which specific Christian doctrine one emphasizes to reach this conclusion; any number point in the same direction, whether it be the doctrine of creation, the belief that man is made in the image of God, the doctrine of God's covenantal relationship with His people or that of the doctrine of Redemption.[6]

Like other Protestant theologians, Ramsey makes prominent use of Karl Barth's theology of creation. In emphasizing the "respect" due human life, Barth wants to give the word a deep resonance, indicating that we should stand in awe of that human life which God has granted man: "Respect is man's astonishment, humility and awe at a fact in which he meets something superior—majesty, dignity, holiness, a mystery which compels him to withdraw and keep his distance, to handle it modestly, circumspectly and carefully. . . . In human life he meets something superior." [7] Martin J. Buss and Helmut Thielicke, also Protestant theologians, have argued in a way similar to Ramsey and Barth. Thielicke, in particular, stresses that a theory of "alien dignity" protects human life from being subjected to utilitarian treatment at the hands of other human beings; the measure of human value is not man's "functional proficiency" or "pragmatic utility" but "the sacrificial love which God has invested in him." [8] In Buss' words, "Theologically . . . the worth of man lies in his being addressed by a deity." [9]

On the whole, the traditional Catholic analyses of the origin of life closely parallel the Protestant, emphasizing God as the source and ultimate guarantor of the sanctity of human life. Thus Josef Fuchs, S.J., asserts that "man as such belongs *directly and exclusively to God.*" [10] Norman St. John-Stevas, who has written more extensively on "the sanctity of life" than any other Roman Catholic, has said that "respect for the *lives* of others because of their eternal destiny is the essence of the Christian teaching. Its other aspect is the emphasis on the creatureliness of man. Man is not absolutely master of his own life and body. He has no *dominium* over it, but holds it in trust for God's purposes." [11] This emphasis on God's purposes, man's creatureliness and man's holding of life in trust brings the Catholic and Protestant arguments together at a critical point. Traditional Catholic theories, however, have been far more prone than Protestant ones to stress, through man's discernment of the natural law, the ability of reason to ascertain the source of the sanctity of life. Quite apart from an acceptance of Christian revelation, man, according to some Catholic natural-law arguments, should be able to recognize man's dignity. As Father Gerard P. Kelly has put it, "Only God has the right to take the life of the innocent; hence the direct killing of the innocent, without the authority of God, is always wrong. This truth we know through human nature (natural law) and through divine revelation (the divine positive law)." [12] But even Father Kelly, having asserted that we can understand the sanctity of life and the right to life through the natural law, concedes that it is not altogether easy to prove the point by reason alone: "The reason for this difficulty seems to be that to those who really believe in creation and the supreme dominion of God, the principle is too obvious to need proof; whereas for those who do not believe in creation there is no basis on which to build a proof." [13]

In any event, Catholic thought as much as Protestant has traditionally pushed the sanctity of life back to a divine origin and preservation. Within this basic perspective, however, some nuances are frequently added, mainly of a pragmatic nature. St. John-Stevas adds to his argument that the sanctity of life stems from God the further contentions (a) that it is a fundamental principle which has sustained Western society, the rejection or dilution of which would endanger the whole of human life, and (b) that, in any case, there is no other principle available which would provide a "criterion of the right to life, save that of personal taste." [14] His fully rounded argument for the sanctity of life draws, finally, on many sources: Western law and history, human experience, the Christian doctrine of man and the continuing cultural necessity that such a principle be accepted. [15]

Central to both Catholic and Protestant theology is the principle that God is the Lord of life and death. [16] This is another way of proclaiming that man holds his own life in trust, of asserting that man's ultimate value stems from God and of saying that no man can take it upon himself to place himself in total mastery over the life of another. To confess that God is Lord of life and death is to affirm that man is a creature, owing his existence, his value and his ultimate destiny to God. But, like the related principle of the sanctity of life, it is a principle which conceals some difficulties. One of these is the relationship of God to the moral and physical evils of the world. Christian theodicy has long wrestled with the apparently contradictory beliefs that God is Lord omnipotent and all-loving and yet that his lordship is not responsible for evil. [17] Another difficulty is that both in principle and in practice Christian theology has allowed many occasions when it is permissible for one man to take the life of another, or for the state to take the life or imprison the body of those it considers dangerous to the common good. Such exceptions clearly seem to presuppose that in some sense God is believed to have granted man some degree of control over human life and death, a presupposition shared by Catholic and Protestant theologians and finding some scriptural justification. James M. Gustafson has made a significant comment on Professor Ramsey's analysis of "the sanctity of life": "Paul Ramsey rests his case ultimately on a theological basis; life is sacred because it is valued by God. Good theological point. But, one can ask, what other things does God value in addition to physical life? E.g., qualitative aspects of life, etc." [18] To this point I would add the observation that the Christian community itself, historically, has valued many goods over physical life: the protection of a free conscience, justice, a just peace, the protection of necessary societal values.

The history of Christian ethics and politics would seem to show that it has never been possible to take decisions out of human hands for long. Even before the advent of modern technology, choices had to be made among human lives and human rights. Unjust aggression, for example, raised the question whether God's sanctification of human life forbade taking the life of aggressors; the historical answer (apart from a pacifist minority) was that it did not. Hence were born laws and practices which granted individuals and communities the right to self-defense, whether defense of lives, values or institutions. In other words, it happened that here, as in many other instances, human decisions had to be made. They could not be "left to God." The inherent stability supposedly built into a divine sanctity-of-life principle turned out to be something less than perfect. The present turmoil of Christian ethics is due in great part to a growing awareness that rigid, formalistic ethical codes too often break down in practice, proving themselves inadequate to moral complexity, and all the more so because of the expanded range of possible choices in contemporary life.[19] This awareness has, though, always been incipiently present in even the most rigid Christian codes. None has been able to escape a recognition that even the most transcendental basis of Christian ethics has not been able to obviate the need for some proximate control by human beings of human life; it has been evident that God does not often intervene in human or natural affairs to back up His sanctification of life by a direct, miraculous protection of life.

While it may be perfectly reasonable to suppose—as the Christian tradition has *de facto* supposed—that man has been given some proximate control over human life, it is a supposition which also places upon human shoulders the burden of deciding under what conditions man has the right to such control. But once these decisions have to be made, there is the danger that the principle of God's lordship may be emptied of any meaningful content. For if it is man who must make most of the practical decisions, then what possible meaning could this "lordship" have? This, I believe, has posed a key dilemma for Christian ethics, placing in conflict a commitment to stand back where God's lordship seems to hold sway and a practical realization that man himself must judge when these situations occur. This is a problem to which I will return after some prior questions are considered.

The advantages of the Christian approach to "the sanctity of life" are evident, just as are some of the disadvantages. The main advantage is that the foundation is laid for a theory of human life which locates man's dignity outside the evaluation of other human beings; our ultimate worth is conferred by God, not by men. Thus, in principle, the value of human life is guaranteed beyond the judgment that an erratic human evaluation might accord it, whether in the form of human laws or mores. Another advantage is that the sanctity of human life is given an ultimate grounding: in God, the creator of everything which exists. Man is not forced to create his own worth; God has, from the outset, given him value. The disadvantages, however, are no less prominent. One is that a considerable portion of humanity is not Christian and does not accept this foundation for the sanctity of human life. Hence, it does not readily provide a consensual norm to which all men can have recourse. Another disadvantage is that it leaves unclear the extent of man's intrinsic dignity. It seems to presuppose that, apart from God's conferral of dignity, man in his own right would be something less than valuable. In the theological problematic, of course, all-encompassing in its scope, it makes no sense to talk of man apart from his creator and redeemer; the "natural man" does not exist, but only the divinely created and redeemed man. In part, this helps to solve the problem of an "alien dignity" which would denigrate man's intrinsic worth, but, at the same time, it requires that one accept the full theological framework; that is just what many cannot do. Finally, any way of positioning the problem which forces a flat either/or choice only (either divine sanction or none at all) seems undesirable; some room must be left for the nonbeliever who asserts there is a sanctity in human life even if there is no God. In his *Ethics*, Dietrich Bonhoeffer speaks of a "natural right" to bodily life. More explicitly than most Protestant theologians, he tries to establish a continuum between a secular mode of grounding human rights and a strictly Christian mode. But even Bonhoeffer, who uses a term such as "innate right," sees the guarantee and sources of these rights wholly in God.[20]

Very different from the Christian position are the arguments put forward by the sociologist Edward Shils and P. B. Medawar, a Nobel laureate in medicine and physiology, to justify the sanctity of life. Pointing to what seems an almost instinctive human revulsion at many forms of contrived intervention in human life, Shils believes that it is not possible to trace this revulsion solely to the religious belief that man is a creature of God. On the contrary, he contends that the Christian belief in the sanctity of life has been sustained by a "deeper, protoreligious 'natural metaphysic,'" which also accounts for the respect given human life by those who are neither Christian nor religious.

The chief feature of the protoreligious "natural metaphysic" is the affirmation that life is *sacred*. It is believed to be sacred not because it is a manifestation of a transcendent creator from whom life comes: It is believed to be sacred because it is life. The idea of sacredness is generated by the primordial experience of being alive, of experiencing the elemental sensation of vitality and the elemental fear of its extinction.

In another place he writes that "if life were not viewed as sacred, then nothing else would be sacred," thus echoing from within his own framework the same kind of pragmatic point made by Norman St. John-Stevas from within a very different kind of framework. Finally, Shils says: "The question still remains: Is human life really sacred? I answer that it is, self-evidently. Its sacredness is the most primordial of experiences." [21]

Like the Christian formulation of the principle, Shils' way of putting the matter has both strengths and weaknesses. Its obvious strength is that the sanctity of human life does not require a justification outside of human life (i.e., in a God), thus providing a basis upon which the non-religious can affirm the sanctity of life, something which the Christian formulation does not. It also has the advantage of drawing directly upon a purportedly common human experience, and a very root human experience at that; no divine revelation is is required. Its chief weakness is that it falls afoul of some obvious philosophical rejoinders. The first would be that the mere experiencing of something as valuable is no guarantee that it *is* valuable. People frequently experience things as valuable which later reflection shows to be lacking in value, and it is common for different groups of people to experience different things as valuable. The second rejoinder would be that Shils' case could not be fully established unless we had evidence that all human beings have at all times and under all conditions experienced human life as valuable; it is not easy to see how this could be done. The third rejoinder would be that "the sanctity of human life" is a human concept, one which has been considered appropriate to ascribe to certain elemental human experiences. But this ascription already presupposes the existence of a conceptual and linguistic system which is utilized to describe and evaluate experience. Such a utilization, though, requires making judgments about experience, particularly the judgment that certain experiences are "valuable" or point to "value." But what we decide to call a "value" will be a function of prior ethical decisions.

On all three of these points, Shils' phrase "self-evidently" quoted above opens the way to a host of objections. P. B. Medawar, whose defense of the sanctity of life is similar to but sketchier than that of Shils, rests his case upon "a certain natural sense of the fitness of things, a feeling that is shared by most kind and reasonable people even if we cannot define it in philosophically defensible or legally accountable terms." [22] The same kinds of objections could be leveled at this argument as against Shils' approach, but perhaps even more strongly: it is notorious, for example, that different people and different cultures have very different senses of "the fitness of things"; it is a norm which does not provide a very reliable criterion in resolving ethical dilemmas. The abortion discussion itself has been complicated by variant notions of "the fitness of things." Some people find it perfectly "fitting" that a woman should not run the risk of bearing a deformed child, others that it is perfectly "fitting" that she should. One or the other may be right, but we are not likely to find out until we are able to fashion criteria more decisive than people's personal sense of "the fitness of things."

Now if both a Christian understanding of "the sanctity of life" and an experiential, nonreligious interpretation, such as put forward by Shils and Medawar, are open to serious objections, each also provides the grounds for a critique of the other. One important intent of the Christian understanding is to remove the ultimate source of the sanctity of life from any dependence upon human experience and judgment; this is accomplished by locating the source of the sanctity outside man. Extending Shils' argument, though, could not one say that the precise weakness of this kind of extrinsic grounding is that it requires one to affirm not only the sanctity of human life in itself but the source of that sanctity as well? One must affirm that there is a God and affirm also that this God sanctifies life. Two affirmations are necessary, making it doubly difficult to make *any* affirmation.

Moreover, an affirmation of the sanctity of life which required that one accept a religious view of man's origin would provide a weak base upon which to build a consensus. One then would seem to be saying that there is nothing whatever upon which to ground the sanctity of life save that of religious belief; and that would logically leave the non-believer (who cannot affirm the existence of a God) free to reject the sanctity of life and do so with the (unwitting) logical sanction of the believer. One untoward consequence of the religious believer's position could be to open the way to placing his own right to life in jeopardy, by making the sanctity of his life dependent upon his ability to convince others to accept his own religious beliefs. Beyond his own beliefs, he would have nothing to appeal to in the face of aggressive action by a person denying these beliefs. An intrinsic norm for the sanctity of life, such as that proposed by Shils and Medawar, would seem to avoid such undesirable consequences. For it would, in principle, provide a norm to which all men could have recourse (or could have pointed out to them); one would need only to refer to a (purportedly) universal human experience and not be dependent upon any special religious belief about the nature of man and the source of his dignity. (Precisely such a perception, of course, helps explain the attraction of a natural-law ethics; but the difficulties inherent in moving from human experience to ethical conclusions also help explain resistance to natural-law theories.)

At this point, however, the religious believer could point out the precariousness of such an intrinsic norm. To be effective as norm, it would first have to be shown that all men are in fact or potentially aware of such an elemental experience of the sanctity of life. It would further and even more critically have to be shown that human beings have a moral obligation to heed this experience, that the experience as such carries with it a manifest set of moral duties. The fact that I might re-spect the sanctity of my own life, my own vitality, does not logically entail that I am required to respect the sanctity of anyone else's life. What would be the source of any obligation to respect the life of another? The mere existence of a common human experience could, on the face of it, entail no moral obligations or duties at all. Only the possession of an ethical framework which can be superimposed upon the experience (or at least work in a dialectical relationship with it) could supply these entailments. The strength of the believer's extrinsic norm is that it bypasses these difficulties. It is not dependent upon any par-ticular human experience. It does not have to work through the haz-ardous business of proving that moral duties are inherent in human experience, and it provides an ethical framework in principle binding upon all. At this point, though, all the difficulties inherent in the be-liever's position recur. We are at an impasse and must move to a different level.

Let us then ask: What are the ultimate justifications for the normative principles embodying a valuation of the sanctity of life? [23] The "ultimate justifications," I believe, have to be human experience; that is where we all start and therein we have a common standard of reference. But, as pointed out, human experience does not, by itself, deliver principles; it is always necessary to have some kind of metaphysical or religious sys-tem with which to organize and interpret experience. The most pressing difficulties rarely arise over what experience actually delivers, though these difficulties should not be minimized. There would, for instance, probably not be too much disagreement with Shils' belief that most people prize their own life. The critical problems more often turn on the meaning and implications of different kinds of experience. Thus one is pushed back to one's ultimate metaphysical insights, affirmations and perspectives: what we take human existence, as a whole, to mean and what value we attach to it. The most critical problem of all is what we choose to count as "ultimate" and how we go about justifying our choice.

My own position is that the ultimate justification of normative prin-ciples rests upon their capacity to serve two functions. First, they must show themselves in use to be coherent with our entire reading of the nature of things; they must make sense in terms of our metaphysics. Second, they must seem to be borne out in our lived experience, pro-ducing what we would count as moral progress, sensitivity and order. Now I think it evident that "ultimate justifications" will always, in an important sense, seem circular, if not to ourselves then to others. The logical conundrum here is that it is always necessary to justify any "ultimate justification" as indeed "ultimate." That process inevitably seems to mean the introduction (to satisfy ourselves) or the manifestation (to satisfy others) of an endless series of further, or deeper, pre-suppositions, each in turn requiring a justification of its own. In the end, we are forced as individual persons to break through this circu-larity or infinite regress (in practice if not in theory) by an existential choice. We decide, for motivations both rational and arational, that we can push the issue no further, that we have reached a point of diminish-ing intellectual return. At that stage, we choose our final (or first) starting point, hoping that it will express all that our limited wisdom has been able to achieve.

This is not to suggest that in the final analysis people act arbitrarily or capriciously when they choose a stance toward life. It is only to say that even a reasonable choice, the fruit of thought and experience, can leave in its wake many unsolved theoretical problems. Religious belief is not (in my view) irrational; it represents a genuine and reasonable human option, serving effectively, in this instance, to justify a belief in the sanctity of life. But this does not mean that the choice of a religious starting point solves all philosophical difficulties, about either God or the sanctity of life; far from it, which is why believers are themselves subject to doubts and agonies. To put the shoe on the other foot, anyone with philosophical training can point out the flaws and unresolved prob-lems in the kind of world view and commitment lying behind, say, Shils' and Medawar's justification of the sanctity of life; which again, is not to say that it is unreasonable or unworthy of a rational man's choice. As to which view we decide is *most* reasonable, much will (or should) have to do with the different consequences of adopting one or the other (or some third view not mentioned here).

Hence, a second pertinent question to ask is this: What difference do different kinds of ultimate justifications for the sanctity of life make for practical judgments? We may agree that either an extrinsic or an in-trinsic grounding of that sanctity provides a basis for a meaningful com-mitment to the protection and furtherance of life. But does that neces-sarily mean each will lead to the same kind of concrete decisions in specific cases? To answer this question, we must sort out a number of issues. There is the empirical question whether in fact ultimate moral justifications resting on a religious basis (e.g., Christian or Jewish or Hindu) lead to significantly different moral decisions, practices, and mores than those resting on a nonreligious basis. As one might expect, this question has a long and confusing history. It has been the working assumption of the important Western religious traditions that their principles do or should lead to moral decisions and practices discernibly different from those exhibited by the nonreligious. The difficulties with this assumption, however, are notorious.[24] Pro-fessed believers often act as badly as professed nonbelievers, and pro-fessed nonbelievers often act in ways identical with (and as good as) the way in which believers act. The impact of this observation has, of late, led some believers to wonder whether the possession of an ultimate religious justification for the choices and actions does in fact make any significant difference in the way people actually behave. Anthony Levi and Michael Novak have both argued recently that it does not, or is at least not the most significant variable in determining moral behavior.[25] They are both persuasive on this point, though neither has, in my opinion, taken sufficient account of the possibility that those non-religious men they single out as "good" are so singled out because their behavior happens to coincide with an implicit Judeo-Christian norm. It has, in any event, proved very difficult to show empirically that the moral behavior of the "average" believer can be predicted with accuracy, from a knowledge merely of that believer's professed religious perspective and commitment. This lack of predictability and consistency has provided opponents of religion with much material for the charge of hypocrisy; the same lack has provided religious "prophets" (in the Old Testament sense) with a fertile ground for righteous condemnation of what passes for religion. Religious believers are, at any rate, increasingly willing to concede that nonbelievers are perfectly capable of acting in admirable and moral ways.

Another issue to be sorted out bears on the more specific question of how religious beliefs function to establish moral limits, particularly limits to "man's tampering with human life." The establishment of limits has been one of the most important thrusts of religion, particularly in its Judaic and Christian forms. Traditionally, Protestant and Catholic theologians had little difficulty agreeing that man's life is not entirely in his own hands, either individually or collectively. (The quotations I provided from Karl Barth, Paul Ramsey and Norman St. John-Stevas on stewardship are as "orthodox" as any could be.) The assumption underlying this tendency to set limits directly stems from the fundamental belief in a "transcendent" God, a God who provides and grounds values, norms and laws (just which and how is hotly argued). Man, for his own good, is obliged to recognize them. Correlatively, it has frequently been contended that a society which recognizes those limits stemming from a divine rather than a human source will be a better, more secure society for its inhabitants. It will not then be open to individuals or majorities subjectively and capriciously to make or break the recognized limits.

Two further problems arise here. One is whether such societies have provided more security. This is open to doubt since most mass religious societies have found ways to justify war, capital punishment and other forms of killing. Yet such societies have also possessed an ideal of human limits which (so they believe) generally works for the protection of life. The killing required a moral rationale, not just arbitrary individual

justification. Another problem is whether it is really of the essence of a
religious ethic to be an ethic of limits and boundaries. At present,
Christian ethics is heavily influenced by variant forms of situation ethics
(sometimes called "the new morality"), most of whose proponents
would agree that, whatever Christian ethics is, it is best not thought of
as an ethics of law. More generally, Christian theology is being influenced
by the pervasive idea that perhaps God left man considerably more
freedom to work out his own destiny and values (including control over
life and death) than was granted by traditional theology. Hence, while
it might be possible safely to say that past Christian theology did have
the function of setting firm limits to tampering with human life—or,
more precisely, discerning the limits God Himself had established—this
may not be the case much longer. I welcome this development since, as
indicated, I think the protection actually offered human life in religious
cultures has often been more a promise than an actuality. A sensible
discussion of this question, however, suffers from an important limitation: until very recently in human history, almost all cultures were
"religious" cultures, including Western culture. The advent of pluralistic,
increasingly secular cultures is too recent and still too permeated with
religious elements to make any clear comparison between "religious"
and "secular" cultures.[26]

This much, though, might be said: it still has to be shown that a
culture which depended for its protection of life on a subjective sense
of the "fitness of things" could actually succeed in providing protection,
especially to the weak, the deformed, the old and the unproductive.[27]
But since, as indicated, it is not clear that religious cultures have been
all that successful in providing such protection either, we are again at
an impasse. If there is any striking difference, it might be this: the
traditional Christian religious ethic has concerned itself very specifically
with the establishment of limits; it has been prone, consequently, to
formulate relatively specific prohibitions. The nonreligious ethic has
not shown a similar concern; it is considerably more open-ended, much
vaguer about what exactly it would prohibit. Yet since the trend in
recent Christian ethics is to adopt a like wariness about formulating
specific prohibitions, this difference may be in the process of disappearing. The impasse may thus be said, for the moment, to remain, and
until we possess good studies of the comparative social results of different kinds of ethical codes, and until the future direction of Christian
ethics takes a clearer shape, much will remain vague and speculative.

Now, it is conceivable that some ingenious person could find a way
out of this impasse—conceivable, but not likely—at least not likely in
the sense that his way out would commend itself to all sides in the
debate. The very nature of the debate, which in the end opposes two
fundamentally different world views, precludes the likelihood of a

common theoretical solution, short of the conversion of one side or the other. In one sense, then, we seem to be in the presence of an ill-fated debate, one which appears doomed to go on forever, perennially resistant to the formation of a socially useful moral consensus, prepetually prone to leave the principle of the sanctity of life in a precarious position.

I don't think it is necessary, though, to draw this kind of pessimistic conclusion. For one thing, it is always difficult to ground metaphysically first or ultimate principles, but this difficulty does not necessarily stand in the way of their acceptance and use. In social, political, cultural and medical situations, what counts most in the debate on the sanctity of life is that both sides affirm the principle, on whatever the grounds, and both sides make it their first and fundamental principle. Moreover, it is clear from a variety of human disciplines that their practitioners can often effectively talk and work together without metaphysical agreement on fundamental principles. They can also often work effectively together when their fundamental principles themselves carry no evident intrinsic justification. The problem of induction in the philosophy of science provides a classic instance. Scientific method presupposes that the future will be like the past, that hypotheses confirmed by observed data provide a warrant for making predictions about similar, but unobserved data, that it is legitimate to base expectations about the future behavior of material objects on our present experience with such objects. Yet it has proved exceedingly difficult to demonstrate the philosophical validity of these presuppositions.[28] Nonetheless, the enterprise of science has been able to proceed and progress in the absence of such demonstrations and in the absence of a full philosophical consensus on the ultimate validity of scientific method.

Another way of expressing this general point is by observing that no method or first principle is self-justifying; it is always logically permissible to ask that a methodology be justified in terms other than its own, just as it is equally permissible to ask for a justification of the justification (*ad infinitum*) of a first principle. For all that, by affirming the utility of certain methods and the value of certain first principles, human beings have effectively developed themselves, their knowledge and their behavior. Both Norman St. John-Stevas and Edward Shils, though differing on the source of the sanctity of life, agree on its value as a first principle, and both make use of a similar collateral argument. "If life were not viewed and experienced as sacred, then nothing else would be sacred," Shils writes. "Once exceptions are made [to the principle of the sanctity of life], the whole structure of human rights is undermined," is the way St. John-Stevas puts it. Both are saying, in effect, the same thing: if you want to make anything sacred, if you want any values honored, if you want to be able to defend any rights, then it is necessary to postulate the principle of the sanctity of life (or, presumably, a principle with the same general thrust). There is, of course, a long philosophical debate behind the validity of arguments taking this logical form (especially from Kant's postulates of practical reason forward).[29] Suffice it to say that, if one's concern is to make use of an available ground of practical consensus, effective consensuses have been built on a common acceptance of arguments taking this logical form. Jacques Maritain, though working within a different tradition, has pointed out that it was possible for the United Nations Organization to reach a consensus on a wide variety of human rights despite the most diverse metaphysical groundings for them.[30]

But a further problem arises. Even if there is agreement that "the sanctity of human life" is worth affirming, indeed socially imperative to affirm, it appears to be singularly abstract and ambiguous as a principle. It is possible to derive from this principle a huge variety of often divergent moral rules and duties. Because it is open to human beings to interpret the principle in different ways, the widespread affirmation of the principle does not lead to any unified consensus on what it means or implies. Each of the important words in the principle—"sanctity," "human" and "life"—is itself open to different and divergent definitions. Given so many difficulties, of what conceivable value is such a principle? Are we not perhaps deluding ourselves in trying to hold on to it or in thinking that it can serve as a basis for consensus? Doesn't it raise more problems than it solves?

In "Levels of Moral Discourse," Henry D. Aiken has provided a perceptive justification for the value and utility of an abstract principle of this kind. While summarizing his analysis, I will provide illustrative examples from the abortion controversy (which played no part in his discussion). Aiken distinguishes four "levels" of moral discourse: an expressive-evocative, a moral, an ethical and a postethical level. At the expressive-evocative level, people simply express their personal feelings: "Ugh!" "Hurray!" "Good!" They are expressed in such a way that "they do not solicit agreement or invite a reply." [31] (E.g., "I could never have an abortion—ugh!") The "moral" level is where "serious questions are asked and serious answers given . . . 'What ought I to do in this situation?' 'Is this object that I admire so much, really good?' . . . Here, in short, there now appears a problem of conduct and a problem for appraisal and ultimate decision." [32] ("The patient has contracted rubella—ought she to have an abortion?") Characteristic, however, of our reasoning at the moral level is that we normally operate within the given rules or codes of our community (social, religious or ideological), trying to apply these accepted rules to concrete situations. Yet if this is what people normally do,

occasionally one is obliged to ask whether an action which is prescribed by existing moral rules *really* is right and whether, therefore, one ought to continue to obey them. When pressed in a certain way, the effect of such a question is to throw doubt upon the validity of the rules themselves. And in that case, there is usually no alternative to a fundamental reconsideration of the whole moral code.[33]

("I've always opposed abortion, but when I think of Mrs. Smith's schizophrenia, I really begin to wonder.") It is when we are faced with this alternative, to reconsider our moral code, that we are forced to move to still another level of moral discourse, which Aiken calls the "ethical" level. It is at this level that very general, very abstract and very formal principles (e.g., "the sanctity of life") show their value. It is the function of such principles to place practical questions arising from our use of a rule system,

on a level of impersonality which requires the subordination of personal bias or preference. It is their function to establish a mood in which the particular moral rule or the moral code as a whole is considered impartially . . . without regard to our own inclinations or benefits. . . . A second characteristic effect of this use of ethical terms is their tendency to "frame" or set apart the questions and answers in which they occur from ordinary practical deliberations.[34]

("I shouldn't let Mrs. Smith's particular case sway me here. What values do I think important in situations like this?")

Aiken's response to the objection that ethical principles are "empty" because of their vagueness—and that is a major objection to the principle of "the sanctity of life"—is to point out that their function is "procedural rather than substantive in aim. Their role is not to tell us what to do in particular cases (the function of a moral rule system) but to provide us with standards of relevance or 'reasonableness' when appraisal of lower-order rules is required." [35] In order to perform this kind of function, the principle must be "empty," must be formal. To give it a specific content would be to turn it into a rule; what we need, when we want to test or validate a rule, is not another rule (which could lead to an infinite succession of rules), but a principle for judging all our rules. An "ethical" principle is "not a rule of conduct but a formula for testing rules of conduct. . . . To enrich its content would be *ipso facto* to transform its role and hence to deprive it of its power as a general principle of ethical criticism." [36]

As we have seen, both Shils and St. John-Stevas agree on the need for the principle of the sanctity of life, even though they totally disagree on its source. Now we can see exemplified in their justification of the need a point Aiken makes about Kant's defense of "empty," high-level ethical principles: "What he [Kant] saw with unrivaled clarity, is that moral criticism which is something more than an *ad hoc* expression of individual attitudes is impossible save on the assumption that there are ethical principles which are general in normative appeal." [37] When Shils and St. John-Stevas say that no human rights and no valuation of human life can be established without presupposing "the sanctity of life," they are saying, on this particular problem, no less than what Kant said about all such problems.

It is now possible to see the function of the principle of "the sanctity of life." If one asks, for example, "Is it a good general rule that abortions ought not to be performed?"—to take a rule which has until recently been a part of the Western moral-rule system—one needs a principle which operates at a higher level than the particular rule in order to judge its validity. "The sanctity of life" provides such a principle. Does that particular rule about abortion serve or enhance or exemplify "the sanctity of life"? That is the kind of question we will want to ask about the rule. That is the kind of question the principle is meant to help us answer; it provides a way of testing the rule, giving us a "frame" within which to validate it anew or to invalidate or amend it.

One might object that the principle could not serve as a measure or test of a particular rule if it was, quite literally and totally, empty. Here, Aiken's account of the function of general ethical principles needs some emendation. Instead of saying that these principles are "empty," it might be preferable to say that they are "indeterminate." They convey a broad range of meaning, but not specific, determinate meanings. We know what the principle is trying to express—roughly. We know what the principle would seem to preclude—vaguely. We know, consequently, how to use the principle as a measure of rules—more or less. If asked to specify what the phrase "the sanctity of life" means, we could substitute for the words "the sanctity," words like "the dignity," "the ultimate value," "the worth," "the significance," "the importance" of human life. We would be trying, all the while, to hit upon that phrase or combination of phrases which would make clear what we had in mind when we spoke of the principle or what we take to be the principle, as commonly used, to mean. Naturally, someone could point out that defining the words of the principle in terms of a list of synonyms or near-synonyms is not altogether illuminating, having about it an air of tautologies and circularities. About the only thing one could reply, faced with this kind of resistance, is that one reaches a point, with any word or any phrase or any ultimate principle, where one simply cannot say anything more. The significance of the phrase "the sanctity of life" is that it is trying to say the *most* that can be said about the value of life. It signifies a whole cluster of final meanings, each of which is related to and dependent upon the other to give it sense and significance. In a very real way, then, the principle of the sanctity of life *is* indeterminate and vague, but not meaningless for all that.

It can be used as a way of saying that human life in all of its forms, states and stages is to be affirmed, cherished and respected. It can be defined in terms of a large range of words which themselves have meaning, yet without overdefining the principle (which would make it too determinate to be useful as an ethical principle). When used in its primary function of judging lower-level rules, the principle is employed to interrogate the rules: Do the rules foster respect for human life? Do the rules lead people to protect human life? Do the rules exemplify the awe we aspire to feel in the presence of human life? If the answer is "no," then we would be justified in rejecting, modifying or changing the rules. In the case of abortion, therefore, any rule which did not foster protection of life, an awe toward life, would be unacceptable, whether the rule be "No unwanted child should be born" or "No abortions ought to be performed" or "Some abortions ought to be performed." (I am not, at this point, concerned to judge these rules, only to offer them as examples and to point out the *kind* of questions we should ask in order to choose among them.)

Yet further specificity is required here. If it is the general function of moral rules to guide our conduct at those moments calling for moral decisions—"What ought I to do?"—there is also a multiplicity of rules and a variety of ways in which rules are expressed. The reason for a multiplicity of rules is not hard to locate: there are many different kinds of human acts, human relationships and moral dilemmas. There are acts bearing directly on the life of others, on their property, on their dignity and their welfare. Human beings enter into sexual, defensive, economic, psychological, legal and social relationships. There are moral dilemmas involving a conflict of lives, rights, freedoms, property, demands and desires. No one rule could cover all these situations and no one rule does. Different contexts call for and ordinarily exhibit different sets of rules, even though there may be considerable overlap.

The reason for a variety of ways in which to express rules can be readily seen also. Sometimes rules are expressed in the form of prohibitions—"Thou shalt not." This form of rule statement is meant to draw a line beyond which one may not go; prohibitions set specified limits to conduct. Sometimes rules are expressed in the language of positive obligation—"One ought to do x" or "One must do y." The aim here is to point out a duty or responsibility. A prohibition may be implicit in this form of rule statement, but the emphasis lies in a different direction. Sometimes rules are expressed in the language of rights— "Citizens have a right to their property," or "Human beings have a right to life." This form of rule statement is most characteristic of legal and political discourse, but by no means exclusively so. Moreover, the way a community or an individual expresses its rules will have to do with the goals it has in mind and the effects it hopes to achieve. The language of morals variously takes the form of prohibitions, exhortations, commands and so on.[38]

An important question has been raised by James M. Gustafson about the choice of moral language. He has pointed out that there could be a considerable difference "if the primary language was 'the right to life' rather than the 'sanctity of life.'"[39] His reason for believing that it could is that

> in function "sanctity" often translates out as "value" rather than as "right." Insofar as it does . . . a predisposition has been established which proceeds to calculate various values and to make a judgment which will be based largely on the potential consequences of alternative courses of action. . . . If one speaks of the fetus's "right to life," it is more difficult to justify an abortion than if one speaks of the value of the life of the fetus in relation to a whole host of other values which might be jeopardized to some degree if the fetus is permitted to live. Fetuses have no significant utility value; mothers have a great deal of utility value. Unless one speaks of the intrinsic value of the fetus being equal to the intrinsic value of the mother, each having fundamentally an inalienable right to bodily existence, it becomes easier to find the value considerations which might make the death of the fetus morally viable.[40]

Up to a point, Professor Gustafson is undoubtedly correct. The language of "rights," particularly "inalienable rights," seems to take life or nascent life off the balancing scale altogether, obviating the need for value calculations; strictly taken, "inalienable rights" cannot be the subject of barter. However, it is not at all evident that the language of "rights" is a fundamental, nontranslatable language. Instead, it would seem to presuppose a still more fundamental language of values or to be translatable into such a language. The "right to life," in other words, would seem to presuppose and be a way of articulating a valuation of life. We believe there is a "right to life" because we already believe that life is valuable. If someone asked why human beings have a "right to life," it would be appropriate to answer, "Because human life is of value"; this latter conviction gives substance to the putative "right." More pointedly, not only the abortion debate but many others involving medical ethics show that the language of rights does not obviate the need to make some calculations, i.e., the need to calculate relative rights and to decide how to weigh rights when they seem to meet in head-on conflict. Tactically speaking, and perhaps legally speaking as well, there is much to be said for giving a practical primacy to the language of "rights." But my contention is that, while the psychological impact of an invocation of rights may be stronger than that of an invocation of values, the former is reducible to the latter, which has the more fundamental status. Hence the gain to be had with the language of rights is more psychological than substantive.

When we speak of "the sanctity of life," we are, then, speaking of the most fundamental substratum of values—the value we attach to human life. For some purposes (e.g., legal or psychological), we may choose to express this valuation in the language of rights and devise a rule system to handle those rights. For other purposes, we may choose the language of prohibition or exhortation. The important point is to understand the possible ways that the ethical principle of "the sanctity of life" can be used to test those moral rules bearing on human life, whatever the linguistic mode in which they are expressed. We have already seen that the meaning of "the sanctity of life" is that life is worthy of affirmation, protection and furtherance. As an expression, it is used to affirm the ultimate respect which people believe ought to be accorded to human life. It expresses a willingness to treat human life with consideration, to recognize its dignity, to commit ourselves to its service.

The function of specific rules is to implement and give concreteness to these commitments. In turn, these commitments, as summed up in the principle, will serve to judge the adequacy of the rules. Thus the relationship between particular moral rules and a general ethical principle is reciprocal. The rules give content, on a lower level, to the principle. The principle, on a higher level, is used to judge the rules. The social importance of the acceptance of the principle of "the sanctity of life" is not that it guarantees agreement on what the rules should be (although it establishes a bias in a certain direction) or that recourse to it automatically resolves disputes about rules, but that a common standard exists which people can have recourse to; debate about rules has a framework of meaning, aspiration and intention, vague though it may be.

Another point is important here. When we attempt to distinguish among the different rule systems, it is helpful to see the way in which they are related to each other. The greater the degree of relationship we can see or devise among them, the more we are illuminated about and in a position to give meaning to "the sanctity of life." This is another way the principle provides a framework for discussing rules and rule systems. It leads us to see, it can even force us to see, that when considering the complexity of human life our rules should have a unified relationship with each other. To express the point another way: *our rules should form a coherent system, each rule consistent with and supporting the other, both within particular rule systems and among them, and all, in turn, serving and supporting the ultimate principle of "the sanctity of life."* Rules concerned with medical experimentation should be congruent with rules dealing with the preservation of an individual's bodily life, which should be congruent with rules dealing with fetal life, which should be congruent with rules dealing with the preservation of the species, and so on. This is simply to say that just as moral rules should not be *ad hoc*, unrelated to an overarching ethical principle, neither should they be *ad hoc* in the sense of being unrelated to other rules bearing on the same overarching ethical principle. To use an image: if the ethical principle—"the sanctity of life"—is the father of the family, then all the children (the concrete moral rules) should bear a family resemblance to each other.

When we look more closely at those rules and rule systems bearing on the sanctity of life, their variety is manifest. There are rules dealing with (*a*) the survival and integrity of the human species, (*b*) the integrity of family lineages, (*c*) the integrity of bodily life, (*d*) the integrity of personal choice and self-determination, mental and emotional individuality and (*e*) the integrity of personal bodily individuality.[41] Not one of these areas has escaped the impact of recent medical, scientific, technological and social change. This change, together with the concomitantly increasing scope of moral decisions, has brought traditional rules into question and, beyond that, is forcing us to see whether these old rules still serve "the sanctity of life." If not, then new rules will be needed. A further complication is that we will not be in a position to judge the rules in relationship to the guiding principle unless we also determine their relationship to the empirical data to which they are applied. Rules are meant (either explicitly or implicitly) to exemplify principles; but their application must be in the context of data, whether in the technical sense of scientific information or in the looser sense of concrete human situations. When the data to which the rules have traditionally been applied change, this can mean either of two things: we will have to judge whether existing rules can handle the new data or whether entirely new rules are needed. Recent debates about the continuing relevance of "just war" theories provide an example of this problem. On one side are those who contend that the advent of nuclear weapons renders the traditional rules of just warfare altogether irrelevant; they were not designed to cope with weapons capable of such vast and potentially indiscriminate destruction. On another side are those who believe that the old rules are sufficiently flexible to handle nuclear warfare. A considerable part of this debate, not surprisingly, turns on an analysis of the known data concerning the destructiveness of nuclear weapons. Short of such an analysis there is no way of knowing whether the traditional rules of just warfare are still valid; and short of knowing that there is no way of judging whether these rules still serve a commitment to the sanctity of life.

I now want to survey the leading rule systems subsumed under "the sanctity of life." My aim will be fourfold, in line with the major issues I have discussed: to bring out the latent general direction of the principle itself, to indicate what appear to be the extant Western moral rules, to point to the kinds of technical data bearing on the individual rule systems, noting in the process the implications of different kinds of data, and to show the bearing (where applicable) of the different rule systems on different aspects of the abortion problem. Since the overall purpose of this chapter is to uncover possible grounds for a moral consensus, rather than at the moment to propose new rules, I have to risk that my reading of the extant cultural rules is wrong. Obviously, different subcommunities within Western culture have different rule systems; that is why they argue with each other. And even when they agree on rule systems, they often disagree on the implications of technical data for an application of the rules. Still, I believe it is possible to discern considerable agreement among the different Western moral subcommunities, at least if one remains at a fairly high level of abstraction and generality. There does exist something of a consensus. One test is whether there are any important groups which flatly oppose the cultural rules. In any event, it is open to the reader to supply his own reading of the extant rules in place of mine. The important thing is to elicit an awareness of the logical structure of the relationship between specific rules and the principle of "the sanctity of life," thus laying the basis for fruitful discussion among contending subcommunities.

(a) THE SURVIVAL AND INTEGRITY OF THE HUMAN SPECIES

The most important broad rule here is that the human species ought to work toward its own survival; it is good that human beings exist on earth. Encompassed within this broad rule are a number of other more specific rules: present human beings ought to behave in such a way as to insure as much as possible a viable life for future human beings; nations ought not to act in such a way as to endanger the present and future life of the human species; human beings are responsible for a moral use of natural resources, and so forth. The rules are myriad, and they are invoked, either explicitly or implicitly, when human beings discuss nuclear warfare, radiation exposure, air pollution, ecology, overpopulation, urbanization, the uses of technology and genetic engineering. The working presumption is that "the sanctity of life" requires moral rules designed to aid the survival of collective human life. Existing rules which can be shown to hinder the possibility of continuing human life would then stand under the judgment of the principle and be subject to rejection or modification. Expressed in the language of rights, the rule says that "the human species has the right to exist." *Mutatis mutandis*, a similar rule can be invoked about racial, ethnic and national groups: "nations, races and ethnic groups have the right to exist." This last specification is important, for it is (so far) more common for there to be threats against such groups than against the entire human race. Implicit within this rule system is not only a collective human obligation, but an obligation for individuals as well; each individual has to take account of the rights of the human species.

The possibility of genetic engineering, which could affect the entire human species, illustrates the complexities of judging old rules and forming new ones. On the one hand, there are questions of technical feasibility. To what extent and by what means is it possible to alter the genetic characteristics of human populations? And what are the likely consequences of choosing different means? "Positive eugenics," involving the engineered breeding of a chosen type or types of human being, poses the technical problem of accurately predicting the genetic consequences of different, artificially induced genetic mixes. "Negative eugenics," generally understood to mean either the discouragement or forbiddance of reproduction by carriers of harmful genes, requires (as does positive eugenics) an ability to predict the long-range consequences for human evolution of nonrandom mating patterns. "Euthenics," the alteration of environment to permit genetically abnormal people to live normal lives, poses the scientific question whether in the long run mankind might become so overburdened with genetic abnormalities as to overwhelm the possibilities of a supporting environmental change. Each of these different possible eugenic techniques, then, requires a knowledge of the different likely genetic outcomes.[42] Any judgment made about rules relating to genetic engineering will require a weighing and comparing of possible outcomes.

On the other hand, there are questions concerning the kind of human beings we want now and in the future. Even if one could predict the outcome of different methods of genetic engineering, there still remains the further problem of deciding what characteristics are humanly desirable; and this problem requires some further scientific calculations about the conditions of human life in the future. The rules we judge advantageous should, therefore, reflect a scientifically valid use of data combined with a conscious (and conscientious) reflection upon the kinds of human beings believed desirable. Overriding such considerations, of course, is the question whether we have the right to do this at all.

As a principle, "the sanctity of life" provides no detailed map for wending our way through this maze of problems. But it does tell us this: Whatever our evolving moral rules will be, they must be designed to promote the survival of the human species (including the survival of particular racial, ethnic and national groups). Negatively, the principle tells us that any practice or rule which is oblivious of or harmful to the survival of the human species is to be rejected.

In the framework of the abortion dispute, the moral-rule system concerning the preservation of the species bears on the general category of both "eugenic" and "socioeconomic" indications for abortion (and, conceivably—with a little imagination—"medical" and "psychiatric" indications as well). While no one has as yet suggested that abortion is necessary for the safety of the species, the possibility of genetic discoveries with ominous implications could make that happen in the years to come. Abortion as a means of "negative eugenics" is surely a possibility. A major impetus behind the Eugenic Protection Law of 1948 in Japan was a desire to limit population growth, and East European laws on abortion have for long been in part a function of government population policies (see Chapter 7). The pressure of too little food, too little housing, a high infant-mortality rate and a desire for economic progress are highly significant elements in determining abortion practices and attitudes toward abortion laws. One can say, in any case, that any abortion rule (for or against) which threatens the survival of the species (and entire subcommunities of that species) will be subject to the negative judgment of "the sanctity of life." Similarly, the formation of rules designed to take account of fetal life in the context of the preservation of the species will have to exemplify respect for "the sanctity of life."

(B) THE SURVIVAL AND INTEGRITY OF FAMILY LINEAGES

The central rule in this instance is that individuals and families ought to be left free to propagate their own children, determine their own family size and be allowed to perpetuate their family lineages. Related rules are that neither the state nor other individuals should interfere with private procreative practices; neither the state nor other individuals ought to impose or deny individual parenthood or to tamper with the process of individual procreation. Phrased in the language of rights, the rule might be phrased in terms of "the rights of individual procreation, family planning and the preservation of family lineages." The intent behind these rules is the conviction that "the sanctity of life" requires respect for voluntary procreative choice and family lines. Artificial insemination and inovulation, sterilization and contraception, as well as genetic engineering, all present technical options bearing on this rule and moral options concerning its recognition and implementation. Beyond these options are problems concerning the common good of societies, groups and humanity as a whole, the procreative rights of individuals in different circumstances (e.g., in times of overpopulation, or in areas of famine, or in cases where known and dangerous genetic characteristics would be perpetuated within families). Again, as in category (A) we have problems relevant to the category of "eugenic" indications for abortion. And, again, we can see the meaning of this category for an exemplification of "the sanctity of life": any moral rule which does harm to procreative freedom and family lineages stands under the judgment of "the sanctity of life."

(c) THE INTEGRITY OF BODILY LIFE

The most general rule is that the individual human being ought to be allowed to live and to enjoy the protection of his fellow human beings. In the language of rights, this is to say that there is a fundamental "right to life." Neither the state nor individuals have the right to (unjustly) deprive human beings of their lives, or to permit or create those social, economic, medical or political conditions which would have that effect. This general rule has traditionally encompassed a great range of subsidiary rules, among them rules relating to the conduct of war, capital punishment, social conditions, the prolongation of moribund life, euthanasia and abortion, among other things. The presumption behind these rules is that "the sanctity of life" implies not only the preservation of human life collectively, but also the preservation and protection of individual human life.

As one moves through the detailed rules subsumed under the general rule, a wide range of definitional, technical and social problems presents itself. Abortion poses the question of the protection owed to prenatal life. In particular, it confronts us with the problem of "When does human life begin?" and that question contains within it the need for a definition of "human life," for criteria which would help us decide what is meant by "begin" and for standards to govern behavior toward potential, borderline or incipient life. Biological data are pertinent to the problem of definition and ordinary, scientific and legal uses of language must be consulted in formulating criteria for "begin."

The prolongation of moribund human life also touches on the definitional and linguistic problem. What do we mean by "death," and at what point do we say that a human body ceases being a "human life"? An important technical context of this last problem is the possibility of prolonging many bodily functions indefinitely. Euthanasia forces us to ask whether there is a "right to die," and whether, in cases of excruciating pain or a hopeless prognosis, we could speak of a "right to kill" even manifestly innocent life. Whatever the continuing or developing rules, however, they would be measured by their compatibility with "the sanctity of life": human beings have a right to bodily life; any rule which threatens that right is placed in doubt by the principle. As might be guessed, the general rule here is relevant to the whole gamut of abortion "indications," from the perspective both of fetal life and the life of the woman.

(D) THE INTEGRITY OF PERSONAL CHOICE AND SELF-DETERMINATION, MENTAL AND EMOTIONAL INDIVIDUALITY

The key rule here is that a person ought to be allowed to make for himself those choices which significantly affect his personal fate; people should be free to determine their own lives. Correlatively, individuals ought to be free to be themselves, unimpeded by the mental or emotional manipulation of others. In terms of rights: human beings have the right to self-determination; human beings have the right to their own complement of voluntarily chosen mental and emotional traits. These rules come into play with the possibility of electrical and chemical alterations of consciousness and affectivity, which could well be judged beneficial or harmful to the individual or society or both. One technical question in that instance is that of measuring the short- and long-range effects of such alterations. The impact of the use of hallucogens is a case in point, as is the existence of brain operations, tranquilizers, drugs and electrical treatments which can affect thought and emotions. Political and social coercion of opinion, attitudes and conduct is still another related problem in this category. Whatever the rules here, worked out in relationship to scientific and other forms of knowledge of the effects of different mind- and emotion-altering techniques, they should be formed with an awareness of the general rule that a person has the right to be himself. This rule is an implication of the affirmation that "the sanctity of life" requires respect for personal identity, choice and self-determination.

While this rule does not directly bear on any of the usual abortion "indications," it does have considerable relevance to the claims of those asking for abortion on request. For a key element in this claim is a putative right of women to make their own decision, uncoerced by males or the state, about whether they should have an abortion or not (see Chapter 13). This claim is a form of the "right of self-determination."

(E) THE INTEGRITY OF PERSONAL BODILY INDIVIDUALITY

The overriding rule in this instance is that the individual ought not to have his body, including the organs therein, violated or imposed upon; one should respect the integrity of human bodies, which belong to those whose bodies they are. In the language of rights, there is a "right to bodily inviolability." This rule comes to the fore when the need for medical experimentation arises, when organ transplants seem medically required or advisable and when, as in wartime, society may feel it necessary (e.g., through compulsory military service) to place the body of a citizen in physical jeopardy. The "need for medical experimentation" involves such technical questions as the likely human/ scientific benefits which could accrue from such experimentations, the relative degree of danger involved in different kinds of experimentation, the scientific value of informing or failing to inform experimental subjects of the purpose of the experimentation (e.g., when a new pain-killing drug is being tested, necessitating an experimental and a control group of subjects). Organ transplantation from a healthy to a sick person requires knowledge of the likely effects on both individuals and an attempt to measure the relative physiological and psychological gains and losses to both. The principle of "the sanctity of life" will be violated if the moral rules governing behavior toward human bodies involuntarily threaten the integrity of those bodies. For abortion debates, this rule might be invoked in a case where refusal to grant a woman an abortion could threaten her physical health, or in the case of rape, where an abortion would rid her body of the effect of an earlier violation of her bodily integrity.

Toward a Synthesis

As mentioned before, there is no end to dispute over rules of the kind sketched above. And no doubt it is possible that I have not succeeded in accurately formulating the rules presently recognized—at least those paid lip service to—in Western culture. There are also endless arguments about the way in which rules should be related to empirical data; about the degree to which rules should be understood as fixed absolutes, admitting of no exception; about the rights of individuals and groups to fix their own rules; about the value and relevance of the kind of typology I have offered here (is it really any help, for instance, to distinguish between "ethical principles" and "moral rules"?). Arguments of this kind are to be expected and, in a time of rapidly changing medical technology, burgeoning life sciences and shifting cultural values, they are likely to be made all the more exasperating and bewildering by a knowledge explosion, the fruits of which are erratically, unevenly and often obscurely disseminated and applied.

That much said by way of anticipating objections to my analysis, let me nonetheless proceed to some further observations and a possible way of effecting a synthesis. First, it can be seen that each of the five rule systems I have discerned as overtly or latently operative in Western culture gives some measure of substantive content to "the sanctity of life," but each from a different angle. Thus "the sanctity of life" implies a spectrum of values ranging from the preservation of the species to the inviolability of human bodies, from man in the aggregate (present and future) to man as individual (present and future). The discrete rule systems each serve an aspect of human life: (*a*) species-life; (*b*) familial-lineage-life; (*c*) body-life; (*d*) person-life; and (*e*) body-individuality life. Each aspect of human life, therefore, has an appropriate rule system designed to protect and foster that aspect. Secondly, it can be seen that each of the discrete rule systems overlaps and together form a whole. One cannot talk for long about rules designed to promote the survival of the human species (or nations or groups) without eventually talking about their relationship to rules governing familial lineage; decisions about the latter will influence the framing of the former, and vice versa. Nor can one talk for long about species survival and lineage rules without moving into a discussion of the integrity of personal choice, with all that it implies about the right to procreate one's own family, to make one's own choices and to act in ways affecting the lives of others. These discussions in turn link up with rules governing the right to bodily life in the first instance and to the individual integrity of private bodies in the second. Even further, however, a decision to grant everyone a guaranteed right to be kept alive indefinitely by artificial means could, conceivably, threaten the survival of the species, as could a decision to halt all further medical experimentation on human subjects. Thus, an ill-conceived rule in one area could inadvertently exert a harmful influence on the observance of rules in other areas. Consistency, congruency and unity are necessary for the totality of rules.

Perhaps this is only to state the obvious, but it is worth stating explicitly since most recent attempts to cope with the new problems posed by advancing medical technology and life sciences tend to be dealt with in almost total isolation from each other. Glanville Williams' otherwise fine book *The Sanctity of Life and the Criminal Law* contains one detailed chapter after another on such subjects as abortion, euthanasia, contraception and suicide. But each of these problems is presented as an independent concern.[43] He neither relates them to each other nor, for that matter, ever attempts to spell out the meaning of his usage of "the sanctity of life." There is a large and growing literature on moral problems of life and death, but it is very rare, for instance, to find a discussion of when life begins (pertinent to abortion) related to a discussion of when life ends (pertinent to euthanasia and the artificial prolongation of life). Yet both problems turn on what is meant by "human life," and the illumination we gain in dealing with one of the problems will be useful when we deal with the other. Similarly, there is much to be said for trying to work for some consistent standards regarding the use of empirical data, standards which do not arbitrarily shift from one rule system to another.[44]

If my points can be granted that rule systems do inevitably overlap and that indeed it is helpful to seek out and utilize their connections, it should also be clear that the most difficult moral dilemmas are those which bring the different rules or rule systems in apparent conflict with each other. Rules granting individuals procreative rights can conflict with rules governing the welfare and survival of the species (as in over-populated countries). Rules forbidding abortion can conflict with rules granting women the right not to procreate involuntarily. Rules controlling the (expensive) preservation of moribund individuals can conflict with the rights of the families of those individuals to economic survival. Examples need not be multiplied; they are easily imaginable and very common.

One solution to such conflicts is to rank different rule systems (and their attendant rights and duties) in some kind of hierarchical order. Traditionally, the individual's right to life would seem to have taken precedence over other rights, though this precedence has admitted the exceptions which may be required when, as in wartime, other rights come to the fore. The reason for this precedence, as a general though not absolute ordering, has undoubtedly been the commonsense perception that an essential condition for the exercise of any human rights is the existence of human beings as the subjects of these rights; if one is not alive, all the rest is beside the point. But the ranking of rule systems and rights in a hierarchical order is complicated even in theory and in practice will obviously be conditioned by changing historical circumstances.

Another solution would be, when faced with a moral dilemma, to refuse any ranking of rules and to depend instead upon a testing of the conflicting rules together in the light of the principle of "the sanctity of life." But it is by no means evident that this would actually resolve a dilemma; indeed, almost by definition, a dilemma occurs when two or more rules, each with a strong claim, are in conflict. A direct reliance on the principle would not be helpful. The principle only comes into play in the preliminary formation and final testing of rules. The relationship between rules will have to be worked out at the level of the rules themselves or by recourse to a combination of other pertinent ethical principles—the principles of "least suffering," "lesser evil" and the like. If conflicting rules each serves the sanctity of life, then a choice which gives priority to one over the other could still serve and pass the final test of the principle from one perspective but fail it from another. One of the most overt cases of such a conflict occurs when those who stress fetal rights (as part of the "right to life") collide with those who stress the "right of self-determination"; both evoke rules sanctioned by "the sanctity of life" and thus a choice either way could be said to pass the test of the principle in one of its elements while failing it in another.

Without pretending to offer anything approaching a complete solution to the ordering of rules, some regulative comments are in order which may prove helpful. The first is that it is unlikely that a fixed ordering could be worked out which would be good for all times and in all circumstances. The setting of human life changes, influenced by a wide range of ecological, psychological and economic considerations, to mention only a few. As suggested, the claim of the individual's "right to life" as the preeminent rule seems well founded. Yet it is clearly conceivable that this right and the attendant rules protecting it could come into question (as they have on occasion in the past) if the survival of the species or of a whole people or nation were in danger from over-population, a scarcity of medical facilities or in time of war. At such historical moments, a reordering of the rules could seem compellingly necessary; some hard decisions would be called for. Not only might the rules governing the individual's "right to life" come into difficult times, but also, consequently, all of the rule systems bearing on different aspects of the sanctity of life. A community or a nation could, naturally, decide to abide by some fixed, traditional ranking of the rule systems. It could decide that the right to individual life was so basic that, rather than permit abridgment, it would prefer to risk a communal demise. It might well argue that a communal or national life which placed individual life in constant jeopardy would be a communal life not worth living. Yet it could as a community also come to a different conclusion: that communal survival was worth some restrictions on the individual's right to life. The abandonment of the elderly in earlier Eskimo culture as well as the practice of infanticide in a variety of earlier societies testify to the extreme pressures which can be placed upon communal survival. To see such practices only as an instance of a primitive insensitivity to human life would be to show a lack of imagination about the desperate straits in which a community could find itself. It is surely not inconceivable that equally dire situations could arise once again, calling forth the need to subject even the most central rules to a critical scrutiny.

A second observation is related to the first and is even more important. Throughout this chapter I have used the word "implies" to speak of the relationship which holds between the principle and the rules subsumed under it: the principle "implies" the rules. By use of this concept, I want to posit a weaker relationship between rules and principle than that of logical entailment. If the relationship was one of entailment, then it would be possible to say that the rules could be derived from the principle by a strict logical deduction; or, put differently, that the rules are formal deductive corollaries of the principle. If this kind of relationship held, then one would be forced to say that the different rules are simply part of the very linguistic meaning of the principle. It would be necessary only to understand the meaning of the principle to understand why that meaning entailed the rules. But this kind of relationship would be too strong. For one thing, as we have seen, rules often come in conflict with each other. But if each rule were a simple deductive consequence of the principle, then the principle would be in the position of generating conflicting corollaries; there would be no way at all of resolving the conflicts. For another, the main value of the principle is that its meaning is indeterminate, and this indeterminacy, as we have seen, is what gives it the power to stand in judgment on the rules. To see the principle as entailing specific rules would be to destroy that power; the principle would then already contain the rules as part of its linguistic meaning.

I want to contend that the principle does not and should not function in this fashion and that it is more accurate and wiser to speak of specific rules being implied rather than entailed by the principle. I mean by "implied" here the sense of "suggested by" or "hinted at": the rules *suggested* by the principle or *hinted at* in the principle. Thus one could say that rules are a reasonable derivation from the principle but not strictly entailed by it; or that the rules are suggested by the principle but not strictly deducible from it; or that the rules are compatible with the principle. It might be immediately objected that, if the principle *entails* no rules whatever, but only suggests them, then the principle ends by providing no protection to life at all. Could we not at least say that the "right to life" is entailed by the principle? Or is even this fundamental right left in doubt by the principle? The problem, unfortunately perhaps, is that there often is a conflict between the right to (individual) life and the right to life of the species or of a community. Hence one has to leave room for a resolution of this kind of conflict of rights, and the way I propose to do so is by denying a strict entailment of either the one right or the other. Both are *implied* rights under "the sanctity of life," but not so strictly entailed that one could not give way to the other if circumstances required it. The aim is to avoid irreconcilable conflicts, a situation which would be inevitable if each rule was thought to be strictly entailed by the principle.

What the principle does is to establish a strong bias in favor of firm rules protecting life (in all of its aspects), so that the protective rules are a reasonable reading of the principle. But the rules are not self-evident deductions from a simple inspection of the principle itself. Thus it is eminently reasonable to see the principle implying a rule about the "right to life," but, once we are aware of the possibility of situations arising where this rule might have to be abridged in the interests of survival of the species or survival of a whole people, we would realize that exceptions might have to be made to the rule. To make exceptions to the rule—or, more precisely, to let other rules (e.g., those pertaining to species survival) take precedence—could be, in some circumstances, to act reasonably. If the relationship between principle and rule was one of entailment only, rigidly conceived, then the limits of reasonable moral choice would be preempted from the outset. In addition, once we realize that the different rules can at times conflict, we are further forced to realize that the principle, to be helpful, must leave us some degree of freedom to come to the most reasonable decision we can concerning the relative ordering of the rules. If the principle entailed an irreconcilable set of conflicting rules, or entailed only one ordering of the rules, or entailed only one possible choice in a moral dilemma, our freedom to act reasonably would be seriously restricted. In the end, we have to leave open a way of working through moral dilemmas which does not predetermine our choice at the very outset. My use of the word "implies" in characterizing the relationship between principle and rules is meant to provide that breathing space.

For all these reasons, the relationship between principle and rules should be kept flexible, sensitive to changing human contexts and shifting human needs (communal and individual). The principle of "the sanctity of life" best serves us when it points us in a life-affirming direction, when it leads us to develop life-protective rules, when it instills in us an overwhelming bias in favor of human life. As a test, it functions most fruitfully not when it logically binds us to a fixed set of logical implications, but when it forces us to look at the general trend of our rules and, on occasion, forces us to ask whether the giving of precedence to one rule or another, or the hanging on to one rule in particular, serves the respect we want to accord human life. If the relationship between principle and rules was only one of strict logical implication, then nothing would require us to interrogate either the rules themselves or human experience. Moral decisions would then become solely a matter of explicating the given linguistic meaning of principle and rules, establishing the fixed logical entailments. As a procedure for coming to moral decisions that would seem to me inadmissable.

As we shall see, a major objection worth leveling at a rigidly restrictive moral code on abortion is that it is prone to hold that an absolute prohibition of induced abortion is a logical entailment of an affirmation of "the sanctity of life." The logical route leading to this prohibition is that "the sanctity of life" means and can only mean under all circumstances that bodily life is to be preserved, which in turn is taken to entail a prohibition of the taking of fetal life. No room is left, in this deductive chain, for a recognition of other demands of the principle. An analogous objection can be leveled at those abortion-on-request arguments which hold that a woman's right to self-determination entails her corresponding right to be the sole judge of whether she ought to bear a child once conceived. In this instance, one aspect only of the principle of "the sanctity of life" is considered, to the exclusion of all others. In both instances, it becomes unnecessary (which it should not) to take account of other rules, to consult a wide range of data and to seek a just adjudication of conflicting claims. The bitterest abortion arguments arise precisely when each side presses the claims of one rule to the exclusion of all others.

There is another important aspect of this last problem, particularly as it bears on religious explanations of the source and meaning of "the sanctity of life." Peter Berger has wisely pointed out that "whatever the 'ultimate' merits of religious explanations of the universe at large, their empirical tendency has been to falsify man's consciousness of that part of the universe shaped by his own activity, namely, the socio-cultural world." [45] One way in which a religious explanation of "the sanctity of life" can lead to a falsification of consciousness is when it is taken to mean that man's moral rules are not of his own making but have, somehow, been imposed upon him by God, either by revelation or by being built into his human nature. The weakness in a narrow natural-law philosophy is less its much-condemned legalism than its tendency to act as if God has *disclosed* or imposed upon man a set of inflexible moral rules which man has only to discern and obey. A Christian Biblical fundamentalism shows the same tendencies, substituting the supposed direct deliverances of revelation for the propositions of natural-law theory. The result in either case is falsification of consciousness: laws and rules believed by men of an earlier era to have been reasonable rules of conduct are transmuted by a later generation into set, transcendent codes. As it happens, the fact that in practice rigid codes very often admit of many exceptions and extenuating circumstances testifies to the meliorating impact of experience and the need to resolve conflicts among basic values. "Thou shalt not kill"—unless one kills in a legitimate war, in self-defense, in imposing lawful capital punishment and so on. The first is the rigid rule, the second is the traditionally accepted understanding of that rule. The falsification of consciousness arises when, despite the conceded exceptions, the rules are still treated as "God-given," through either reason or revelation. That even rigid codes have been forced to admit exceptions and complexities should actually make clear that all moral rules are human artifacts. The fiction of divinely imposed rules does justice neither to the moral rules nor to God. Justice is not done to the rules because their character as guides to and exemplars of higher ethical principles rather than rigid entailments of these principles is obscured. Justice is not done to God because it is presupposed that God's moral relationship to man is essentially that of lawgiver, a less than rich relationship.

The way to avoid such a falsification of consciousness is by man's taking full responsibility for his own fate. The principle of "the sanctity of life," even if given a religious grounding, is best implemented by the recognition that it is human beings who must define, form, set, and live those rules designed to protect and foster that sanctity. There are three reasons why this recognition is necessary. First, as suggested in the discussion of the five rules systems, it is evident that man must define the terms which determine and articulate the rules, examine the data and then make use of the data. The result of this complicated process will, inexorably, make the utilized rules *human* rules; it would be inappropriate to call them anything else after so many human judgments have been made in the process of interpreting and using them. To say, for instance, that God forbids the taking of "innocent" life, while conceding —as I think we must—that it is left up to man to define what an "innocent" life is, is to fail to see that the only possible *meaning* this rule could have is the meaning human beings *choose* to give it. I am not using the word "choose" here to suggest arbitrary choices, but rather rational, considered choices. Second, it is an utter abdication of human responsibility to place passively on God's shoulders the care and protection of human life. Human experience together with reflection upon human freedom show that God does not directly enter into the processes of nature and human life, at least not in the sense of immediately intervening in the biological processes of life and death. With rare exceptions, Christian theology has always granted human beings the right to take those steps—scientific, moral and technological—which they believe necessary for their safety, progress and dignity. That it has done so is a tacit recognition that it is man who is responsible for man. I am only proposing that we carry the implication of this perception to its logical conclusion: man is responsible for everything to do with man, including control over life and death. This is the last step that much Christian theology has been slow to take, but it is now imperative. Contraception, abortion, euthanasia, medical experimentation and the prolongation of human life are all problems which fall *totally* within the sphere of human rules and human judgments. To place the solution of these problems "in the hands of God" is to misjudge God's role and to misuse human reason and freedom.

It is often said that man can't "play God" with human life, that certain natural processes must be left entirely to God's providence. The trouble with that kind of moral reasoning is that it fails to see that God Himself does not "play God" as that phrase is usually understood. God does not directly and miraculously intervene in natural processes. He does not "bring" human beings into life or "make" them die, just as he doesn't "make" them sick or "cure" them of illness. The theology behind the excuse that man can't "play God" is a defective theology. Dr. Alan F. Guttmacher has an effective complaint:

> When it comes to many of the social problems of medicine . . . sterilization, therapeutic abortion, donor artificial insemination, and withholding resuscitative techniques to seriously malformed infants in the delivery room—doctors

retreat behind the cliché that they "won't play God." This type of intellectual cowardice, this mental retreat is irrational. . . . Through the nature of his work a doctor is constantly intruding himself into the work of the Deity. Does he wait for God to show his decision by making some outward manifestation before he undertakes a Caesarean section, orders a transfusion, or performs a risk-fraught open-heart operation? [46]

Martin J. Buss's proposal that "it is best to identify God's purposes with man's good as such, rather than with any specific process" is a wise one, for it helps make clear that man is responsible for himself and the world and, at the same time, it is consonant with more recent Catholic natural-law thinking and Protestant responsibility ethics.[47]

My third reason for the recognition of human responsibilities relates to the first two. Perhaps the most vexing problem of medical ethics and the human uses of technology is what can be called "line-drawing." At what point in gestation are we to say that human life "begins" and thus (if we believe that to be the critical question) draw a line against abortion? At what point are we to say that "death" has occurred and thus feel free to transplant an organ or cease artificial organ support or resuscitation? Where do we draw the line in exposing subjects of medical experiments to mental or physical dangers? Even if we have very explicit formal rules, questions of this type are difficult to answer; the rules themselves do not answer them. They are a matter of human judgment, of finding a way to balance all pertinent rules. More than that, the need to draw lines, to set a limit to moral behavior, is a call to establish a moral policy. If we want to know when life "begins" or "ends," biological and other scientific knowledge will provide us with some clues—empirical data on which to base but not exclusively determine a judgment. But the value of this knowledge, its *meaning* for human use by human beings, will be a function of the human goals we want to achieve. Lines, in a word, do not draw themselves and scientific data will not of themselves draw lines for us. Decisions must be made about how we want to use the data, and these decisions will reflect our moral policy.

Defining "Moral Policy"

Let me define a "moral policy" in this context as any culturally, philosophically or religiously chosen, given or accepted way of devising, relating and ordering moral rules. As I have argued, the principle of "the sanctity of life" itself does not entail any set ordering; it only points us in a life-affirming and life-protecting direction. However, this is not to say that given communities or religions do not in fact have certain ways of ordering rules, usually by placing them in some rank precedence. I mean by a "moral policy," then, whatever the accepted method of ordering the rules might be. Different communities might well agree on what the rules are, but might disagree on how they should be ordered or conflicts adjudicated; these disagreements will be expressive of the different moral policies of those communities. Similarly, different communities might fully agree on the scientific data pertaining to a particular moral problem (e.g., the biology of the gestational process), but disagree about how that data should be used and interpreted; again, such disagreements will be reflective of different "moral policies." For instance, a moral-policy decision to extend protection of individual human life to the utmost conceivable limit—giving precedence to the "right to life"—would suggest drawing a line on the beginning of human life very early in the conception process and very late in the dying process. Another moral-policy decision, however, might be one which sought to strike a balance between individual rights and the needs of a community to survive. In that case, the beginning of human life might be designated as taking place relatively late in gestation (making abortion permissible) and death, as occurring relatively early in the dying process (making an early cessation of artificial support permissible).

Each of these policy decisions, which would have different social consequences, presupposes that the scientific data as such are open to different readings and compatible with different moral policies. The data on the gestational process are of comparatively little use to us unless we have a definition of "human life," just as data on the dying process require being set in the context of a definition of what we choose to call "human death." These definitions will also be part of moral-policy decisions; they will influence our interpretation of the data, which, taken alone, would not necessarily demand any particular policy. In saying this, I would still want to stress a point made earlier: just as our rules should be consistent with each other, our standards concerning the use of data should be consistent from one rule system to another. This stricture holds whatever our "moral policy," but our policy will determine the "standards" we choose. A method of using data to solve the abortion problem which was very different from the method used to solve the problem of sustaining moribund life ought to arouse our suspicion. It could suggest that one or the other of the methods, or perhaps both, was arbitrary. A consistent method of using data from one rule system to another provides some degree of protection against capriciousness.

In sum, the way we decide to formulate rules, to order them in relationship to each other, to use data pertinent to them, to draw lines and to define terms will be a function of our overall "moral policy." That moral policies differ is evident, which is the main reason why the same rules, the same terms and the same empirical data are subject to a variety of interpretations. Just what our "moral policy" should be is an obviously important problem, and it is vital to see at the outset that this policy will determine how we handle rules, terms and data. A failure to recognize implicit moral policies lies behind the tendency, all too common in the abortion debate, to think that certain kinds of data, and certain rules require one moral conclusion only. The first task, in judging among different moral conclusions, is to discern what the implicit or latent moral policy is. The second task is to decide among the different policies.

As my own reading of "the sanctity of life" should by now have been made clear, I believe it points us in the direction of a moral policy which seeks to extend rather than to constrict the rules governing the protection of life; and this, in turn, implies a reading of the empirical data consistent with this aim of extension, i.e., a giving of the benefit of ambiguous data to the preservation and protection of life. This is only to say that an affirmation of "the sanctity of life" implies a moral policy favorable to those rules which affirm the protection and preservation of human life, both actual and potential. To say this is not meant to nullify the earlier argument that we will have to decide, in given situations, what our moral policy toward the ordering and balancing of the rules should be.

There is thus a three-stage movement in the formation of moral policies. The first stage is to establish a bias, a general direction. The second stage is to establish a policy toward all rules, which will usually be a policy biased toward either firm or loose rules. The third stage is to establish a policy toward a hierarchical ordering of the rules among themselves. Concerning the first stage, the moral policies might be more or less permanent, or at least very slow to change. Concerning the second and third stages, the exigencies of circumstance may require comparatively more rapid shifts in policy, e.g., an earlier policy of giving precedence to the right to life of individuals might have to give way, in times of starvation, to the giving of precedence to the rights of species or group survival. Either way, however, it must be seen that the decisions will be human decisions, not imposed or entailed divine decisions. And this follows from my contention that it is improper to call them anything but that when it is up to human beings to define the terms, order the rules and interpret the data.

In developing the three reasons why I believe it necessary, indeed unavoidable, for human beings to take total responsibility for human life and death, I want to open the way for a moral consensus—that is, for a "moral policy" toward abortion—which will win as wide an assent as possible. Some further provisos are therefore necessary. By and large, for the sake of achieving a moral consensus, our rules should be as clear as possible. This is particularly important when one person puts his body or life in the hands of another—clarity and a commonly binding consensus help provide the basis for trust and security. Our rules should also be capable of change if circumstances or changing moral evaluations point toward the need for change. At the same time, I think it imperative to avoid any theory of rules which would preclude human beings from establishing absolute, unbreakable rules, at least absolute for a time and under certain specified social conditions.

"Absolute taboos, with their underlying mystique about life," Joseph Fletcher has written, "make a farce of human freedom. All such taboos cut the ground out from under morality because nothing we do lies in the moral order if it is not humanly chosen." [48] One can see what Prof. Fletcher is driving at here, but some qualifications are in order. All "taboos," for one thing, need not spring from a "mystique about life." They could be the result of very rational decisions. For example, a community with a history of medical abuse and malpractice could decide that the dangers of leaving decisions about the prolongation of moribund life in the hands of individual doctors had become so great as to dictate an absolute rule requiring doctors to take every possible step to prolong life, however extraordinary. This kind of rule could, of course, be very cumbersome to observe in many cases, but a community might decide that, for the value of affording patients a greater sense of security when in the hands of doctors, it would be a desirable rule. A "taboo" against genocide, to choose another example, would not appear irrational. Absolute pacificism, while it has not commended itself to most men, is not an insane position. It is simply the conviction that an absolute rule against war—a "taboo," if you will—would be a wise rule, even in cases of legitimate self-defense. The reasoning behind this position is that human experience shows (or, in the eye of the pacifists, shows) that all wars, even just wars, have bad consequences; hence, an absolute refusal to engage in war is required. For another thing, to take Prof. Fletcher's point, if his standard is "human choice," I see no reason why a "human choice" in favor of "absolute taboos" in some circumstances should be ruled out *a priori*. The important consideration, I should think, would be its character as a "human choice," i.e., reasonable, sensitive, imaginative. A "taboo" which displayed this character could be a very wise one (even if open to debate), representing a prudential "moral policy."

Our policy decisions and the consequent moral rules developed together with further procedural rules for ordering and relating the moral rules must take account of the "whole man." By that I mean man from the beginning to the end of his life, as an individual and as a member of a species and a community, as the subject of bodily, affective and intellectual rights. This is only to say that all our rules must be congruent with each other, and our overall policy coherent and orderly.

The final measure of our moral policy and its attendant rules will be the principle of "the sanctity of life." There is no final test of this principle. In affirming it, we go as far as we can in trying to articulate an ultimate ethical norm against which all other norms must be measured. Beyond a commitment to this principle there is only what Prof. Aiken has called the "post-ethical" level of moral discourse. This is the level at which we move out of ethics altogether to choose a world view.[49] Suppose someone asks, "Why ought I to respect the sanctity of life or even suppose there is such a principle?" It is unlikely we could even begin to give him a convincing answer if he did not share with us some common assumptions or commitments about the nature of everything which exists. There comes a point in moral discourse and human reasoning beyond which we cannot go without an infinite regress or without circling back to where we began. At that point, Aiken correctly notes, "Decision is king." [50]

The direction of my own decision and, I trust, of most human beings is to affirm the value of the principle of "the sanctity of life." James Gustafson, though operating from within a Christian framework, has written what I would hope to be acceptable outside of that framework: "Life is to be preserved, the weak and the helpless are to be cared for especially, the moral requisites of trust, hope, love, freedom, justice, and others are to be met so that human life can be meaningful. The bias gives a direction." [51] To choose this principle, understood in this sense, is to choose a moral policy. The policy takes as its starting point *that* principle (rather than another) and then seeks to see what rules are *implied* as part of such a policy. It will then have to decide, in further stages, how absolute the rules ought to be and how they are to be ordered in relationship to each other.

At the end of Section I, "Establishing an 'Indications' Policy," I tried to show that such a policy would and should be a function of one's larger moral policy toward abortion. At the end of Section II, "Establishing a Legal Policy," I tried to show that this policy as well will be a function of a moral policy toward abortion. I have now, in this chapter, tried to indicate how a "moral policy" might be established (and what it includes), making evident in the process that I believe the principle of "the sanctity of life" provides a good point of departure for a moral policy on abortion. It remains, however, to flesh out that policy. This will be done in the following stages. In the next two chapters, I will take up the complex problem of the "beginning" of human life, exploring first (Chapter 10) the philosophical problems involved in trying to determine a "beginning." In Chapter 11, I will set forth and examine the biological data, categorize and discuss the various schools of opinion on when human life begins and, finally, attempt to lay down some general norms concerning the establishment of a moral policy toward nascent human life. Having established what I believe these norms to be, I will then move on to Section IV. My aim there will be, on the basis of all the foregoing chapters, to provide a critique of the traditional conservative Catholic position as well as a critique of proposals for abortion on request as a moral policy. Finally, I will provide my own solution, both moral and legal.

NOTES

1. Werner Schöllgen, *Moral Problems Today*, trans. Edward Quinn (New York: Herder and Herder, 1963), p. 217; and Joseph Fletcher, "The Right to Die," *Atlantic Monthly*, 221 (April 1968), p. 62.
2. Paul Ramsey, "The Morality of Abortion," in *Life or Death: Ethics and Options* (Seattle: University of Washington Press, 1968), p. 71.
3. *Ibid.*, p. 72.
4. *Ibid.*, p. 73.
5. *Ibid.*, p. 76.
6. *Ibid.*, p. 74.
7. Karl Barth, *Church Dogmatics* (Edinburgh: T. and T. Clark, 1961), Vol. III/4, par. 55, p. 355; cited in Ramsey, *ibid.*, p. 75.
8. Helmut Thielicke, *The Ethics of Sex*, trans. John W. Doberstein (New York: Harper and Row, 1964), p. 231.
9. Martin J. Buss, "The Beginning of Life as an Ethical Problem," *The Journal of Religion* (July 1967), p. 249.
10. Josef Fuchs, S.J., *Natural Law*, trans. Helmut Reckter and John A. Dowling (New York: Sheed & Ward, 1965), p. 65; see also David Granfield, *The Abortion Decision* (New York: Doubleday, 1969), p. 126: "God alone has full and perfect dominion over others, the power of life and death."
11. Norman St. John-Stevas, *The Right to Life* (New York: Holt, Rinehart and Winston, 1964), p. 12.
12. Gerard Kelly, *Medico-Moral Problems* (Dublin: Clonmore and Reynolds, 1955), p. 165.
13. *Ibid.*, p. 167.
14. Norman St. John-Stevas, *op. cit.*, p. 17.
15. See especially Norman St. John-Stevas, "Law and the Moral Consensus," in *Life or Death: Ethics and Options, op. cit.*, p. 46.
16. See, for instance, Bernhard Häring, *The Law of Christ* (Westminster, Maryland: Newman Press, 1965), Vol. III, p. 194; David Cairns, *God Up There?* (Philadelphia: Westminster Press, 1967), p. 27.
17. See especially John Hick, *Evil and the Love of God* (New York: Harper & Row, 1966), for the best recent book on the problem of evil.
18. James M. Gustafson, in a review of *Life or Death, op. cit.*, in *Commonweal*, 86 (October 4, 1968), p. 28.
19. For some discussions about this debate see Joseph Fletcher, *Situation Ethics* (Philadelphia: Westminster Press, 1966); Paul Ramsey, *Deeds and Rules in Christian Ethics* (New York: Scribners, 1967); Charles Curran (ed.), *Absolutes in Moral Theology?* (Washington, D.C.: Corpus Books, 1968): James A. Pike, *You and the New Morality* (New York: Harper & Row, 1967); Harvey Cox (ed.), *The Situation Ethics Debate* (Philadelphia: Westminster Press, 1968); Gene H. Outka and Paul Ramsey (eds.), *Norm and Context in Christian Ethics* (New York: Scribners, 1968).
20. Dietrich Bonhoeffer, *Ethics*, trans. Neville Horton Smith (London: SCM Press, 1955), pp. 106ff.

21. Edward Shils, "The Sanctity of Life," in *Life or Death, op. cit.,* pp. 12, 14–15, 18.
22. P. B. Medawar, "Genetic Options: An Examination of Current Fallacies," in *Life or Death, op. cit.,* p. 98.
23. This question was pressed upon me by James M. Gustafson in his comment on my article "The Sanctity of Life" in *The Religious Situation 1969* (Boston: Beacon Press, 1969), p. 347.
24. For a sociological discussion of some of the problems here, see Gerhard Lenski, *The Religious Factor* (New York: Doubleday, 1961); Louis Schneider (ed.), *Religion, Culture and Society* (New York: John Wiley & Sons, 1964).
25. Anthony Levi, *Religion in Practice* (New York: Harper and Row, 1966); Michael Novak, *Belief and Unbelief* (New York: Macmillan Co., 1965).
26. For a sociological discussion of some of the problems here, see Andrew Greeley, "An Exchange of Views," in Daniel Callahan (ed.), *The Secular City Debate* (New York: Macmillan Co., 1966), pp. 101–08; see also Mircea Eliade, *The Sacred and the Profane* (New York: Harper Torchbook, 1961), and Bernard E. Meland, *The Secularization of Modern Cultures* (New York: Oxford University Press, 1966).
27. Philippe Ariès has vividly described how demographic conditions and a high infant-mortality rate contributed to the view, common in the late middle ages, that a child was something less than a human being: "No one thought of keeping a picture of a child if that child had either lived to grow to manhood or had died in infancy. In the first case, childhood was simply an unimportant phase of which there was no longer any need to keep any record; in the second case, that of the dead child, it was thought that the little thing which had disappeared so soon in life was not worthy of remembrance. . . . Nobody thought, as we ordinarily think today, that every child already contained a man's personality. Too many of them died." (Philippe Ariès, *Centuries of Childhood,* trans. by Robert Baldick [New York: Vintage Books, 1965], pp. 38–39.)
28. See, for instance, S. F. Barker, *Induction and Hypothesis* (Ithaca: Cornell University Press, 1957).
29. In Kant's terms, the demands of the moral life require the postulating of "a cause of the whole of nature, itself distinct from nature, which contains the ground of the exact coincidence of happiness with morality." In Immanuel Kant, *Critique of Practical Reason and Other Writings in Moral Philosophy,* trans. L. W. Beck (Chicago: University of Chicago Press, 1949), I, ii, 2, p. 228.
30. Jacques Maritain, *Man and the State* (Chicago: University of Chicago Press, 1951).
31. Henry D. Aiken, "Levels of Moral Discourse," in his *Reason and Conduct* (New York: Alfred A. Knopf, 1962), p. 69.
32. *Ibid.,* p. 70.
33. *Ibid.,* p. 75.
34. *Ibid.,* p. 76.
35. *Ibid.,* p. 82.
36. *Ibid.*
37. *Ibid.*
38. For a still valuable introduction to the problems, see R. M. Hare, *The Language of Morals* (London: Oxford University Press, 1952).
39. In James M. Gustafson, "Comment on 'The Sanctity of Life,' " in *The Religious Situation 1969, op. cit.,* p. 348.
40. *Ibid.*
41. I am here expanding on a list originally suggested by Edward Shils, *op. cit.,* p. 29.
42. For two good surveys and discussions see Frederick Osborn, *The Future of Human Heredity* (New York: Weybright and Talley, 1968), and Kurt Hirschhorn, "Genetics: Re-Doing Man," *Commonweal,* 85 (May 17, 1968), pp. 257–

61. H. L. Muller is the leading exponent of positive eugenics, as in, e.g., "Genetic Progress by Voluntarily Controlled Germinal Choice," in G. Wolstenholme (ed.), *Man and His Future* (Boston: Little, Brown & Co., 1967), pp. 247–62. P. B. Medawar, *op. cit.*, argues against positive genetics and in favor of negative eugenics.

43. Glanville Williams, *The Sanctity of Life and the Criminal Law* (London: Faber and Faber, 1958).

44. See Max L. Stackhouse, "Technical Data and Ethical Norms," *Journal for the Scientific Study of Religion,* 5 (Spring 1966), pp. 191–203.

45. Peter L. Berger, *The Sacred Canopy* (New York: Doubleday, 1967), p. 90.

46. Alan F. Guttmacher, "The United States Medical Profession and Family Planning," in Bernard Berelson *et al.,* (eds), *Family Planning and Population Programs* (Chicago: University of Chicago Press, 1966), p. 458.

47. Martin J. Buss, *op. cit.*, p. 250.

48. Joseph Fletcher, *op. cit.*, p. 63.

49. Henry D. Aiken, *op. cit.*, p. 83.

50. *Ibid.*, p. 87.

51. James M. Gustafson, "A Christian Approach to the Ethics of Abortion," *The Dublin Review,* (Winter 1967–1968), p. 358.

The "Beginning" of Human Life: Philosophical Considerations

THE QUESTION MAY BE PLACED: When does human life begin? But what is being asked when that question is raised? Is a point in time being sought, some moment in gestation where a line is crossed which differentiates the human from the nonhuman? If a point in time is the aim, for what purpose is it sought: to begin a chapter in an embryology textbook, or to fashion a law dealing with the disposal of embryonic or fetal remains, or to solve an abortion problem? The aim we have in mind in placing the question in the first place will have a bearing on the answer we consider appropriate. Then there are further distinctions to be made. If a moment in time could be specified—"at *this* moment human life begins"—does this entail that the life so begun has or gains value at that moment? Or would it be possible to say, on the one hand, that life begins at "x" moment but, on the other, need not be valued until "y" moment? Again, for what purpose are we asking the question "When does human life begin?" Is our purpose descriptive or classificatory? Or is our purpose legal or social or moral? People do not usually ask such questions out of idle curiosity. They ask them because they arise in the context of some particular problem; and that context will normally have much to do with what they count as an appropriate answer. In this book, the context of the question is the problem of abortion; the answer given must be helpful in that context, appropriate to the type of concern at issue.

That is easier said than done. In the setting of abortion problems, no consensus whatever seems to exist on the beginning of human life. There are those who think it begins with conception and those who think it begins later. Among the latter, no consensus exists about when that "later" is. While the differences in opinion are well known, there have been few systematic attempts to investigate these differences, seeking some sociological patterns. The only studies worth citing are those which were undertaken by Andie L. Knutson of the University of California, Berkeley, in the mid-1960s. In a 1965 survey of 76 student public-health workers (56 Americans, 20 from other countries), he found a wide range of opinion. One interviewee believed that human life began before conception; 27, at conception; 2, during the first trimester; 8, during the second to third trimester; 10, at birth; 13, at viable birth; 13, sometime after birth (with no answer being given in two cases).[1] While he found that these differences of opinion cut across all sex and religious lines (with differences within every religious group), some tendencies were discernible:

> As expected, those who employ spiritual or religious definitions [of when life begins] tend to place the beginning of a life earlier than those who employ psychological, sociological, or cultural definitions. Those who refer to the biological growth process tend also to define a human life as beginning at conception or sometime prior to birth.[2]

Women, he found, tended "to believe that a human life begins at an earlier point in development . . . [and] tend to focus their definitions in terms of biological growth processes with greater frequency than men who, on the other hand, were alone in mentioning independence from the mother, personality, or sociocultural definitions."[3] He concludes his study by noting that the wide range of personal beliefs is often not consonant "with the definitions assumed or stated in medical, hospital or legal codes. . . . The situation tends to foster many types of personal and professional conflicts relating to beliefs, values and professional responsibility."[4] A later, more extended survey achieved substantially the same results.[5] However, Knutson, in the later study, also tried to determine the felt relationship between the beginning of human life and the value to be assigned to that life. He found that "the assignment of full value appears to be a variable that is to a good extent independent of definitions of a new human life. Some persons define a new life as human long before they assign full value to it; others assign full value to it before they define it as human."[6]

Though Knutson notes that his samples were very small and, of course, restricted to public-health workers, it seems unlikely that a much larger sample would achieve substantially different results. And one might guess that a survey taken of the general public or of medical and biological specialists would provide few surprises. People differ on the issue; that much even the casual observer can perceive. In any event, philosophically taken, a survey of beliefs and opinions would hardly provide an answer to the question; it would only establish what people *believe* to be the answer (which is, naturally, important for political and legal purposes).

Obviously people bring to the question different backgrounds and different heritages, not to mention their own personal way of looking at the world. In most circumstances, that is enough to account for differences of opinion. But in this case, I believe, something more accounts for the differences. It is simply a very hard question, and there are no self-evident ways of finding an answer. The biological facts may be evident enough, but—I will try to argue—these facts are open to a variety of interpretations, no one of which is undeniably entailed by the facts. When one moves to the even more difficult question of when value should first be assigned to human life, the range of possible interpretations is just as great. Not only do people differ about the answer to the question, they also differ about how they ought to go about looking for an answer. There exist no universally accepted religious or scientific rules for handling a problem *of this kind*. Every answer will presuppose a different way of looking at the world, at least to some degree. Pluralistic societies are noteworthy precisely because their citizens do not share a common way of looking at the world. An agreement on "the facts" by no means ensures an agreement on the meaning and moral implications of the facts.

How ought the question to be approached? It is best approached by stages, in order to bring out the kind of theoretical and methodological problems hidden beneath the bland wording of the question. At each stage a decision must be made, and I will indicate what I take to be a sound decision, but also indicate other possible alternatives. For the most part, however, most of these segmental conclusions will be primarily negative, serving to bracket those conclusions which seem legitimate (within a given range) and those which do not. The first stage raises the problem of choosing a philosophical perspective on biological "facts." The second stage raises the problem of determining where we get our concept of "human" or "human life." The third stage, with these earlier determinations in hand, requires that one look at the particular facts in question, to see how they could or should be interpreted. The fourth stage raises the problem of how we might go about establishing a "moral policy" in light of the (interpreted) facts. At that stage, the problem of assigning a value or values to the interpreted facts must be confronted, for that is the essence of formulating a moral policy.

Philosophical Perspectives

I will begin with a basic philosophical assertion, which can be defended only in part here: Biological data, however great the detail and subtlety of scientific investigation, do not carry with them self-evident interpretations. There are no labels pasted by God or nature on zygotes, primitive streaks or fetuses which say "human" or "nonhuman." Any interpretation of the known facts is going to be a result not only of our particular interests as we go about establishing criteria for interpretation, but also of the kind of language and the type of analytic-conceptual devices we bring to bear to solve the problems we set for ourselves. This is only to say, at the very outset, that a purely "scientific" answer to the question of the beginning of human life is not possible. "Science" itself is a human construct—a set of methods, terms and perspectives—and any use of science to answer one particular question, particularly when the answer has moral implications, will be a human use, that is, a use subject to human definitions, distinctions and decisions. The language of science is a human artifact; the word "life" is a word devised by human beings in order to refer to certain phenomena which can be observed in nature. Scientific method can classify and analyze the phenomena and draw certain "scientific" conclusions (e.g., establish empirical correlations, causal relationships, etc.). But the conclusions it draws will be a result of the humanly devised conceptual schemes used to approach the phenomena in the first place.

As Pierre Duhem put it in a classic statement about the inextricable relationship of the scientific theorist to the data he theorizes about, "It is impossible to leave outside the laboratory door the theory that we wish to test, for without theory it is impossible to regulate a single instrument or interpret a single reading."[7] If this is true, say, of the word "gene," it is all the more true of the word "human." The latter is also a word created by human beings to talk about certain phenomena, which are of interest to that biological species which human beings themselves decided to call "human beings." The problem of specifying a given point in time as critical for the development or emergence of human life is also going to depend on our purposes in looking for such a point. Embryological facts do not shout at us, "Draw a line here!" or "Draw a line there!" Well-developed adults will draw the lines and affix the labels. And they will draw them in different places and affix the labels at different stages, which they do.

There are few scientific arguments about the broad outline of what is going on at different stages of embryological or fetal development. For all that, men who can agree on the biological facts can and do differ when it comes to saying that certain embryological facts *prove* the presence of a "human being." It is neither plausible nor reasonable to (*a*) assume that one group of scientists, theologians or philosophers understands the "facts" better than another (for the "facts" are not all that obscure, open only to "correct" interpretations by a gifted handful); or (*b*) assume that some future scientific discoveries will decisively answer the question about when human life begins; or (*c*) expect that, with enough scientific "objectivity," a consensus on the "meaning" of the facts could be established for the purpose of ethical discourse on abortion or any other moral problem. To ask people simply to "stick to the facts" is naïve. The "facts" must be used and interpreted, and science provides no fixed rules for the interpretation of facts in moral reasoning. Once this is seen—and the point, for all its simplicity, is crucial—it will be evident that people not only have the right but are indeed forced to bring extrascientific values and conceptual systems to bear on the facts. As James M. Gustafson has pointed out, "The *values* of human life have not appeared more clearly because we have a more accurate account of the *facts* of life." [8]

Michael Polanyi and Marjorie Grene have addressed themselves pertinently to some underlying philosophical issues here. In *Personal Knowledge*, Polanyi wrote:

> Our most deeply ingrained convictions are determined by the idiom in which we interpret our experience and in terms of which we erect our articulate systems. Our formally declared beliefs can be held to be true in the last resort only because of our logically anterior acceptance of a particular set of terms, from which all our references to reality are constructed.[9]

In short, the way we interpret reality will depend upon our prior choice of some particular set of terms with which to do the interpreting. Before we can deal with "facts" at all, we need an "idiom," a particular way of going at the facts. Marjorie Grene has pushed the same point a step further: "Even for apples and pop songs, let alone for human lives, criteria do not present themselves on the face of things for which they are criteria, but have to be discovered—or decided?—in the light of some standard, to which we voluntarily submit ourselves as the right standard for judging this particular kind of thing." [10] To this point, Miss Grene adds still another, arguing that "even the least evaluative, most 'factual' judgments depend for the possibility of their existence on some prior evaluative act." [11] This is only to say that what we choose to call a "fact" will be dependent, at root, upon some evaluative system which enables us to distinguish between a "fact" and a "nonfact"; and it goes without saying that this evaluative system will also be a human creation. This is not to deny there is a reality outside of our language and conceptual systems. It is only to affirm that we cannot get at this reality or interpret it without words and concepts and invented methods.

Both Polanyi and Grene share an emphasis, therefore, on prior, anterior acts of evaluation; we approach facts with these evaluations in hand. But what kind of prior evaluative acts ought to be brought to bear on the question of when life begins? Polanyi and Grene do not address themselves to this question (or to the abortion problem), but both provide a useful framework for approaching such a question. The very fact that we ask the question at all—using words like "human" and "life"—

shows that in some sense (to be determined) we already possess, as shown in our use of language, some prior concepts; our words did not appear out of nowhere. When we ask the question about the beginning of human life, therefore, it is to be supposed that we already have some more or less determinate meaning in mind for these words. Our problem is to relate these words—and the corresponding concepts—to the available biological data.

But an acknowledgment seems necessary before we do so. We should recognize that we already know the *outcome* of the human gestational process; we know "where babies come from." It is because we know this process that we are able to work our way back to seek its beginning; our prior anterior knowledge has enabled us to know that, e.g., zygotes found in human females are *human* zygotes (which give place to human embryos, fetuses and neonates). In Polanyi's more formal terms:

> The analysis of the process by which living beings are formed corresponds to the logic of achievement, as illustrated by the manner in which we find out how a machine works. We start from some anterior knowledge of the system's total performance and take the system apart with a view to discovering how each part functions in conjunction with the other parts. The framework of any such analysis is logically fixed by the problem which evoked it. Its contents may be extended indefinitely and it may penetrate thereby even further into the physical and chemical mechanism of morphogenesis; but its meaning will always lie in its bearing on living situations that are true to type, emerging from a mosaic of morphogenetic fields.[12]

In our case, abortion, the "framework" of which Polanyi speaks has been fixed by our anterior knowledge of postnatal human beings. We know generally what a postnatal human being is and our problem is to find the point when it can be said this "human being" came into existence as a human being. But we could not undertake such an analysis in the first place did we not begin with a prior knowledge of what a human being (once born) is.

To talk in this way is to talk holistically and teleologically. It is to say that we cannot answer the question we have set unless we begin our analysis with postnatal human beings and then work backwards into the gestational process, observing the adult-aimed, forward-moving stages of development. Marjorie Grene has sketched the philosophical presuppositions in such an approach:

> What the higher level of organization does is in some sense to *control* the lower. Parts become the parts they are in relation to the whole, organs are organs *as* their function dictates, embryos develop toward their specific norm. . . . True, organic life cannot exist without both levels: wholes without their parts, functions without the mechanisms needed to perform them, or living individuals without the whole development from fertilized eggs which pro-

duced them. But in some sense the higher level provides a principle which orders or determines the lower. In every case the lower level specifies conditions, while the higher gives us principles of organization, ends or reasons. The conditions are indeed necessary, but while it is possible to understand the principle without reference to the detailed conditions, it is *not* possible to understand the conditions *except* as conditions of the whole, the activity, or the endpoint of development on which they bear.[13]

Later she asks: "Can the biologist proceed to describe what it is he is analyzing without referring to structures, uses or achievements? I think not. In other words, teleological discourse has not only a regulative, but at least a *descriptive* function within biological research." [14]

As an alternative to the use of a teleological language, the psychologist Edna Heidbreder employs the concept of *Gestalten*:

> *Gestalten* are found in processes outside the psychological field altogether. In biology, the process of ontogenesis shows striking examples. Here the orderly development of definite organic structures from the primitive germ-layers gives both spatial and temporal *Gestalten* remarkably similar to those found in psychology. They show the same orderly sequence, the same continuity, the same progress toward a given end, the same relation of particular processes to the whole in which they are involved.[15]

To be sure, not all biologists or philosophers are by any means happy with teleological analyses.[16] But this is not the place to argue out all the myriad philosophical and scientific issues involved in the legitimacy of such an analysis, which would take us far afield. Suffice it to say that, in this context, such an analysis appears extremely helpful. It points out the necessity, if we are to understand when human life "begins," of starting from postnatal, developed human life, seeking its origin and those stages of development which lead to an ultimate full human development. To those who distrust this method of procedure it is open to propose an alternative philosophy of biological analysis, suitable to the present problem. The only thing that seems to me wholly unacceptable here is to ignore altogether the need to provide and explicate *some* philosophy of biological analysis. Unfortunately, that need is often ignored in abortion discussions.

The philosophical perspective I am going to employ and urge is teleological. In a word, if we are to make sense of zygotes, embryos and fetuses, we cannot *begin* our analysis with these entities. Prior to investigating them, we must investigate what the phrase "human life" means or can mean; and this means beginning our analysis with fully developed human beings, working back from them to the initiating stages of human development. Whatever "human life" or "human being" means, it is safe to say that these concepts have not come into use by virtue of an analysis of exclusively prenatal life. Instead, they have been developed by an analysis of postnatal developed human life; and it is this analysis which must be employed, explicitly, in trying to answer the question "When does human life begin?" The only warrant for calling a given zygote a "human zygote" is that a prior knowledge exists of the developmental process whereby those zygotes found in pregnant human females give rise eventually to developed "human beings."

In order, then, to answer our question, it is first necessary to examine the concept "human." This means beginning with the concept "human" as it is employed in describing developed human beings. That done, we will be in a position to examine the prenatal biological data, to see how the concept of "human" can or ought to be applied to that data.

The Meaning and Use of "Human"

To ask what the word "human" means is to ask about the nature of man. What is "man" and what is "human nature"? To be "human" means to possess those characteristics we associate with the word "man." The problem of man and human nature is ancient; all religions and seemingly all important philosophies have tried to provide an answer. Of late, a spate of books and symposia have appeared on the topic, a symptom of its renewed importance in an era of social and technological change, and a symptom as well of considerable uncertainty.[17]

For the most part, historical efforts to define the nature of man have taken the form of a search for one overriding characteristic which constitutes man's essence. Boethius' classic definition of a person—"*Persona est substantia individua rationalis naturae*"—reflects his work as a translator of Aristotle and, more broadly, the Greek tradition, which saw in rationality man's essence: man is a rational animal. This tradition was carried through the ages, manifesting itself in medieval philosophy, the Renaissance and into the Enlightenment. Though later philosophies and cultural currents located the essence of man elsewhere—*zoon politicon* (man as social being), *homo faber* (man as producer), man as symbol-maker—the search for an essence has continued down to the present. Thus Stephen Toulmin has written that "the process of intellectual growth is the salient point in all human development—in the development of society, in the development of the individual, in economic development, and in cultural development alike."[18] Nathan Scott has written of man as that being which is "open to the ineffable."[19] Willard Libby has affirmed that "this, to me, is man's place in the physical universe: to be its king through the power he alone possesses: the Principle of Intelligence."[20]

It is unnecessary to multiply examples of efforts to locate an essence of man; they are familiar enough.[21] Historically, they have been closely tied to attempts to distinguish men from animals, a practice which also continues into the present. "Man is unique," Ernst Mayr has written. "He differs from other animals in numerous properties such as speech, tradition, culture, and an enormously extended period of growth and parental care." [22] The great anthropologist A. L. Kroeber wrote:

> Man is an essentially unique animal in that he possesses speech faculty and the faculty of symbolizing, abstracting, or generalizing. Through these two associated faculties he is able to communicate his acquired learning, his knowledge and accomplishments. . . . This special faculty is what was meant when someone called man the "time-binding" animal. He "binds" time by transcending it, through influencing other generations by his actions.[23]

Marjorie Grene argues that men can be distinguished from animals in that the former are capable of thinking, speaking, knowing, achieving and community-making.[24] For George Herbert Mead the difference lies in man's unique ability to use symbols and to distinguish symbols from objects.[25] Ernst Caspari, surveying the evolutionary evidence, has said that "the differences in mental abilities between man and his nearest relatives are very large. It is impossible to enumerate them. . . . Suffice it to point to the increased ability for and dependence on learning in all behavioral activities, the ability to communicate by speech, and the ability to make tools." [26] A. Irving Hallowell has said that "it seems rather to be the manner in which experience is organized that sets the human line apart from other animals." [27]

Again, though, it is not necessary to multiply examples. More important for our purposes are some of the methodological problems. *For the purposes of an abortion discussion*, what kind of an analysis of the concepts "human," "man," "human nature" is needed? Is it imperative that we be able to stake out and define the "essence" of the "human" or will some other kind of description do? If we must, of necessity, work backwards through the gestational process, using as our starting point the developed human being, what *kind* of a concept of "human" are we looking for? This seems to me an extraordinarily difficult question to answer in our context. This much at least can now be said: We need a concept sensitive to the findings of a number of disciplines. Fortunately, there exist a variety of attempts to find usable definitions of "human," attempts which, precisely because they are far removed from abortion polemics, are especially valuable. We can, I think, try to learn something from these efforts; they provide some suggestive hints.

In zoology, attempts to grapple with the "species problem" provide one example. In essence the problem is this: what is a species, what are the criteria for including a being in a given species, and what distinguishes one species from another? At the level of taxonomy, it is a problem of classifying different kinds of living things. At another level, it is the problem of determining the stages in human evolution (when

did "human beings" first appear?). The most helpful discussion of this
problem remains a book edited by Ernst Mayr, *The Species Problem.*[28]
In his own essay, "Species Concepts and Definitions," Mayr notes that
the history of the problem has included all shades of opinion, ranging
from the view that species exist in nature independent of human clas-
sification to the opinion that species are a human invention, without a
clear referent in nature. Among zoologists, two leading schools of
opinion have contended with each other, the typological (using essentially morphological criteria) and the populationist (using essentially
biological-genetic criteria). J. Imbrie distinguishes the two schools in
the following way, according to their leading concepts: "The *typological*
concept defines species as a group of individuals essentially indistin-
guishable from some specimen selected as a standard of reference. The
biological species concept . . . considers the species to be made up of
one or more inbreeding populations."[29] Philosophically put, the typological concept (according to Mayr) is Platonic: it begins with the
assumption that each species manifests an "idea," some common, underlying trait which a given specimen manifests and which is shared by
other specimens of the same species: "The typological species concept
treats species merely as random aggregates of individuals which have
the 'essential properties' of the 'type' of the species."[30]

The problem which Mayr and others discerned is that typological
concepts are "static," having no conceptual place for individual variations:

> The assumptions of population thinking are diametrically opposed to those
> of the typologist. The populationist stresses the uniqueness of everything in
> the organic world. What is true of the human species, that no two individuals
> are alike, is equally true for all other species of animals and plants. . . . For
> the typologist, the type (*eidos*) is real and the variation an illusion, while for
> the populationist the type (average) is an abstraction and only the variation
> is real.[31]

One consequence of an employment of the concept of a "population"
has been the demise of "single-character taxonomy." As Carleton S.
Coon has written: "[The] obsolete concept of single-character taxonomy
has long since been abandoned. Zoologists now base their decisions on
all the characteristics they can identify and measure, characteristics
which together give the animal its essential nature, its (to borrow a
psychological term) *gestalt.*"[32] An alternative to single-character taxonomy is that of a "population" concept, which stresses all the variations
within a species, but particularly genetic variations. It is part of what
George Gaylord Simpson (among others) called the "new systematics,"
a term meant to signal (in the late 1930s and early 1940s) the shift from
a reliance upon morphotype (a single morphological characteristic) to

that of a population, which is concerned with "*all* of its members collectively, with their resemblances and differences." [33]

As part of this argument, J. M. Thoday has stressed the importance of genetic considerations:

Natural populations are of fantastic genetic complexity, and natural environments are also complex. . . . It is becoming more and more clear, the more experiments we do on the genetics of natural populations, that the old idea, itself relating to the biological type concept, that populations are genetically rather uniform, there being by and large one normal or wild-type, along with many abnormalities, each rare, is totally misleading. Normal flies or normal men, comprise an extensive array of different genotypes. . . . So extensive is their variety that we may say without exaggeration that, apart from identical twins, no two individuals are, or ever have been, genetically exactly alike.[34]

"There are," he adds, "as many human natures as men," a proposition which has also been affirmed by T. Dobzhansky: "The nature of man as a species resolves itself into a great multitude of human natures." [35]

At this point, however, we run into an obvious philosophical problem, one familiar to any student of the age-old problem of "universals." If it is impossible, or at least unfruitful zoologically, to use any kind of "single-character" specification of a species, what warrant is there for talking of a "human species" at all? Or, to put it another way, what warrant is there for calling "x population" in nature a "human population"? Can one speak, as Dobzhansky and Thoday do, of "many human natures," each different, without rendering the word "human" meaningless? Not really if one takes the "many" literally, for unless there is some tacit, generalizable understanding of what the word "human" means, some universal signification, then it could not be used to describe more than one organic entity. One could not even use a phrase like "a great multitude of human natures" unless the word "human" was meant to convey something about the multitudes as a particular multitude. They are a multitude of "*human* natures," not a multitude of some other kind of natures. As Marjorie Grene has observed: "We can only make sense of experience through its subsumption under universals, and that such universals act as standards for the evaluation of experience, or rather that we act in submission to these standards as judges of experience: this much in the Platonic account we must admit." [36] George Gaylord Simpson almost, but not quite, saw the philosophical problem:

It is a convenience to a systematist engaged in identification and cataloguing to recognize taxonomic units by the characters common to all their members. Such a procedure is, indeed, virtually necessary in practice, but it is inherited from the old systematics and lends itself to serious philosophical confusion. The characters-in-common may become a morphotype in the mind of the classifier. He tends to think a category is defined by these characters.[37]

What Simpson might have asked himself is why such a procedure is "virtually necessary in practice." For one cannot begin identifying and cataloguing *at all* unless one possesses some notion, however inchoate, of the common characteristics of a population. This is the kind of point Miss Grene is trying to make in attempting to show the futility of a rigidly nominalist approach to biological entities. This is not to argue, though, that a "single-character taxonomy" is again called for; it is only to argue that, in talking about what counts as "human," the term must have some meaning which will cover a "multitude" of instances.

What we can profitably learn from the struggle over the "species problem" is twofold. First, a useful definition of "human" must be one which takes account of the widest possible diversity of instances, an entire "population," and which implies a consequent skepticism toward single-character or essentialistic definitions; second, a recognition that genetic criteria are more serviceable than morphological criteria in distinguishing a species. On the second point, Mayr argues:

> The very fact that a species is a gene pool . . . is responsible for the morphological distinctness of species as a by-product of their biological uniqueness. The empirical observation that a certain amount of morphological difference between two populations is normally correlated with a given amount of genetic difference is undoubtedly correct. Yet, it must be kept in mind at all times that the biological distinctness is primary and the morphological differences secondary.[38]

The significance of this conclusion for a discussion of abortion, and concretely in order to answer our question of when human life begins, is this: when we talk of "human life" we must try to take account of a wide variety of "human characteristics," and we must also, in the process, not fail to take account of the genetic characteristics of human populations and human life. The import of this conclusion will be developed shortly, but first another example is in order, this time drawn from the field of anthropology.

One of the key problems of anthropological theory is that of the relationship between human biological nature and human social culture. As Marvin Harris has written,

> One of the basic requirements of a theory of cultural continuity and change is a description of what used to be called human nature. All cultural items are partially the product of a set of biophysical constants which are shared by most if not all *Homo sapiens*. Correct though it may be that the explanation of differences and similarities cannot be achieved merely by invoking these constants, it is no less improbable that explanations can be achieved without them.[39]

But the problem of finding the exact relationship between the biological and the cultural has proved vexing. On the one hand, there are those who would stress culture as the sole determinant of human behavior, excluding the biological altogether.[40] On the other are those who have seen everything as biologically determined.[41] Others, however, have tried to find a synthesis of biological and cultural determinants. A. Irving Hallowell, for instance, has pointed out that psychoanalytic theory has helped to clarify (though hardly altogether) those "specific differences in personality structure and functioning which can be shown to be related to cultural differences." [42] He quickly adds, though:

> Implicit in these data are indications that universal dynamic processes are involved which are related to the psychobiological nature of modern man as a species. Likewise, capacities are implied which must be related to generic psychological attributes of *Homo sapiens* that have deeper roots in the evolutionary process.[43]

Hallowell's particular concern is that an emphasis on the cultural characteristics of man not be allowed to open an unbridgeable gap between man and the other primates, which he believes would obscure the evolutionary problem.

> One thinks of such characterizations of man as "the rational animal," the "tool-making animal," the "cooking animal," the "laughing animal," the "animal who makes pictures," or *animal symbolicus*. All these characterizations stress man's differences from other living creatures. Like the criteria of culture and speech, they emphasize discontinuity rather than the continuity, which is likewise inherent in the evolutionary process.[44]

His aim is to stress the importance of biological, psychological and cultural interrelationships:

> Although no unanimity of opinion has been reached, hypotheses should emerge in time which will lead to further clarification of the relations between neurological evolution, psychological functioning and cultural adaptation. Of central importance in this complex web of relationships is the distinctive psychological focus in *Homo sapiens*—the capacity for self-objectification which is so intimately linked with the normative orientation of all human societies.[45]

Thus, while "the capacity for self-objectification" is, for Hallowell, the salient feature of *Homo sapiens,* this capacity must be understood in biological as well as cultural terms, with the psychological forming a major connecting link.

Clifford Geertz is another anthropologist who believes that a synthesis of the biological and the cultural is needed, though he comes down much harder on the cultural side than Hallowell:

> Whatever else modern anthropology asserts, it is firm in the conviction that men unmodified by the customs of particular places do not in fact exist, have never existed, and most important, could not in the very nature of the case exist. . . . This circumstance makes the drawing of a line between what is

natural, universal, and constant in man and what is conventional, local, and variable extraordinarily difficult. In fact, it suggests that to draw such a line is to falsify the human situation, or at least to misrender it seriously.[46]

In another article, he brings his position to a fine point:

The apparent fact that the final stages of the biological evolution of man occurred after the initial stages of the growth of culture implies . . . that "basic," "pure," or "unconditioned" human nature, in the sense of the innate constitution of man, is so functionally incomplete as to be unworkable. Tools, hunting, family organization, and later, art, religion, and a primitive form of "science," molded man somatically, and they are therefore necessary not merely to his survival but to his existential realization. It is true that without men there would be no cultural forms. But it is also true that without cultural forms there would be no men.[47]

Geertz contends that anthropological theory, in its attempt to achieve "an exacter image of man," needs unitary systems of analysis, wherein the biological, psychological, sociological and cultural factors can be treated as variables within the systems. At present, he notes, these variables are "sequestered in separate fields of study," making it difficult to develop unitary anthropological systems.[48]

Man [he says] is to be defined neither by his innate capacities alone . . . nor by his actual behavior alone, as much of contemporary social science seeks to do, but rather by the link between them, by the way in which the first is transformed into the second, his generic potentialities focused into his specific performances. It is in man's *career*, in its characteristic course, that we can discern, however dimly, his nature.[49]

As an example of a synthetic statement, illustrating a thrust toward a unitary theory, Geertz writes: "As our central nervous system—and most particularly its crowning curse and glory, the neocortex—grew up in great part in interaction with culture, it is incapable of directing our behavior or organizing our experience without the guidance provided by systems of significant symbols." [50] For Geertz, then, it is culture which enables man to develop his innate capacities. At the same time, his innate capacities themselves have been in part determined by culture— it is a two-way process. Most importantly,

the extreme generality, diffuseness, and variability of man's innate (i.e., genetically programmed) response capacities means that, without the assistance of cultural patterns he would be functionally incomplete . . . a kind of formless monster with neither sense of direction nor power of self-control, a chaos of spasmodic impulses and vague emotions.[51]

It is evident, of course, that I am here using only a few anthropologists to bring out some of the problems. But this is not the place for a survey of anthropology. It is sufficient to say that the problems the cited authors are circling—the relationship between biology (normally thought of as determining what is "innate") and culture (normally thought of as determining what is "conditioned")—have a considerable bearing on our particular problem. For when we ask what "human" means, we should be asking—if we have learned anything from anthropology—about the relationship of biology and culture, recognizing the importance of culture in contributing to the formation of a "human being." The late psychologist Gordon Allport seems to me to have illuminated a related problem. His concern was to show the weaknesses of general (i.e., typological) categories in explaining the human process of "becoming" and individual uniqueness. His way of working out a synthesis of biology, psychology and culture is well expressed in the following lines:

> Each person is an idiom unto himself, an apparent violation of the syntax of the species. An idiom develops in its own peculiar context, and this context must be understood in order to comprehend the idiom. Yet at the same time, idioms are not entirely lawless and arbitrary; indeed they can be known for what they are only by comparing them with the syntax of the species.[52]

In sum, consistent with major thrusts of zoology, anthropology and psychology, any definition of the "human" must take account of the interaction of biological, psychological and cultural factors; all have their place and none is dispensable. In terms of the abortion problem, one can thus say that any definition of "human" in the question set for this chapter will be defective if it ignores the interrelationship of the three mentioned factors. More pointedly, "human" cannot be defined in a genetic way *only,* or a psychological way *only,* or a cultural way *only;* it must be defined in such a way as to take account of all three elements in the "human."

If it is possible to discern in the biological and social sciences a distinct movement in the direction of enriched, comprehensive definitions of man—an antimonotypism—the same trend is discernible in the social sciences and in theology. Some examples must suffice here. The Jewish philosopher Martin Buber, for instance, personified (and personally stimulated) two major elements in contemporary theological anthropology: a stress on the full complexity of the human and on the centrality of human relationships. "A legitimate philosophical anthropology," he wrote, "must know that there is not merely a human species but also peoples, not merely a human soul but also types and characters, not merely a human life but also stages in life." [53] The extent to which this statement echoes a number of the quotations above does not need underscoring. Resistant to any one-dimensional definition of man (for instance, man as a "rational animal"), Buber saw the essence of man in his relationship with other men (which presupposes rationality, affectivity and the power of willing): "The philosophical science of man, which includes anthropology and sociology, must take as its starting-point the consideration of this subject, 'man with man.' If you consider the individual by himself, then you see of man just as much as you see of the moon; only man with man provides a full image." [54] It is man's capacity to enter into relationship which is his distinctive attribute.

A similar point has been made by an English Dominican:

> To discover what it is to be human and to achieve properly human fulfillment account must be taken of man not simply as a biological object, not even simply biologically (which would introduce a whole consideration of his ecology), but in the specifically human dimension in which he enters into communication with others at a human level. That is "natural" to man which constitutes him not merely in isolation, but in relation to the whole world-for-man which he creates around him . . . and in relation to other persons who stand not simply as objects but as other subjects around him. [55]

Ernest Becker, from a nonreligious perspective, has pressed on the social sciences the importance of a cross-disciplinary, unified concept of man:

> In the human sciences man must be seen at all times in the total social-cultural-historical context, precisely because it is this that forms his "self" or his nature. . . . The narrow positivist fallacy has always been that one can somehow know the object in itself, that it exists as a thing in nature and must be isolated and defined. But this is a species of essentialism. . . . We come to know a thing, furthermore, only in terms of its relationships, never in itself. [56]

Finally, one can cite the eminently judicious words of Erich Fromm and Ramon Xirau, in summing up their excellent examination of the historical course of discussions on the nature of man:

> It can be stated that there is a significant consensus among those who have examined the nature of man. It is believed that man has to be looked upon in all his concreteness as a physical being placed in a specific psychical and social world with all the limitations and weaknesses that follow from this aspect of his existence. At the same time he is the only creature in whom life has become aware of itself, who has an ever-increasing awareness of himself and the world around him. [57]

The Importance of "Potentialities"

The stress on comprehensiveness, richness and flexibility in defining the "human," common to all the authors so far cited, stems from one overriding consideration. When human beings are looked at in all their diversity, as individuals or as members of a species, it become extraordinarily difficult to single out one human attribute that can be counted as normative and decisive. Human beings are rational and irrational, individual and communal, biological and cultural. Any single definition, stressing one attribute, invariably fails to catch the full measure of man. If this is true when one tries to develop a concept of the "human" using developed, adult humans as evidence, it becomes all the truer when one begins dealing with the borderline cases or individuals who display some human characteristics but not others.

Hence, it becomes imperative that any attempt to define "human life" take account of "potentialities" or "capacities." To be "human" is not just to display, here and now, the full range of human characteristics. Geertz, one recalls, stressed that the whole career of man must be taken into account in defining him. But that career is especially noteworthy precisely because, at any given moment in life, a human being may be displaying very few human characteristics. Human beings do not always think; sometimes they are asleep, or drugged, or too young to think. Human beings are not always in relationship with others; sometimes they are alone. It is, in fact, quite easy to imagine a great variety of situations where a whole range of human potentialities may not be realized presently. Yet a mere lack of present actualization of human potentiality would not be sufficient warrant for withdrawing the appellative "human" from a being morphologically or genetically human. One way or the other, we are forced to ask, in cases where actualized human characteristics are not displayed, about the potentiality for such characteristics appearing. The zoological concept of a "population" presupposes the use of "potentiality" as part of any criterion of inclusion in a population: the potentiality for interbreeding. An anthropological concept of man, laying a stress on man as culture-maker, will have to take account of the human potentiality for culture-making. And, as Allport has argued, an understanding of the psychological process of "becoming" must likewise make use of concepts of "potentialities" and "capacities."

Most critically for our purposes, any adequate definition of "human life"—to be consistent with both practice and theory in a variety of disciplines—must include a place for three kinds of potentialities, all interrelated: biological, psychological and cultural potentialities. Human cultural potentialities cannot be realized without the actualization of biological potentialities, just as psychological potentialities cannot be realized without the actualization of cultural potentialities. To repeat Geertz, man is to be defined by the way his innate (biological) capacities are transformed through the medium of culture into actual human behavior. The complaint of those anthropologists who oppose an exclusively culture-oriented definition of the human is to be heeded. To ignore the biological base of human culture is to leave little or no room for an explanation of the process by which human beings, ontogenetically or phylogenetically, have been able to develop cultures. Marjorie Grene has succinctly summarized the thought of the zoologist Adolf Portmann on the way biological potentialities are transformed into cultural actualities:

Our unique pattern of development [as human beings] is not an "after-thought" tacked onto a standard embryogenesis. The human attitudes and endowments which we must acquire in infancy are prepared for very early indeed in embryonic growth: thus the first preparation for the upright posture, in the development of the pelvis, occurs in the second month of the foetus's growth. The preparation for the acquisition of speech, moreover, involves glottal structures very strikingly and thoroughly different from those of any other species. And the huge size of our infants relatively to the young of apes —born more "mature" but very much smaller—is probably related, Portmann conjectures, to the immense development of the brain necessary for the achievement of human rationality—a development which begins, again, very early in ontogenesis. In short, the whole biological development of a typical mammal has been rewritten in our case in a new key: the whole structure of the embryo, the whole rhythm of growth, is directed, from first to last, to the emergence of a culture-dwelling animal.[58]

This last passage, with its key word "directed," reintroduces the teleological problem mentioned earlier. My working assumption is that, when we speak of "human life," we must also speak of (*a*) human potentialities, and (*b*) potentialities in a direction, i.e., not random potentialities, but potentialities which, speaking teleologically, can (in Grene's and Portmann's sense) be said to be "directed." This term does not imply a "director," but is only meant to be a way of interpreting the apparent fact that human development shows certain characteristic patterns and directions. These patterns and directions are *toward* rationality, individuality, culture-making, language, human relationships, tool-making and so on. It is the potentiality of certain kinds of organic beings *toward* these characteristics which provides us with a warrant for calling these beings "human." It is because we know the whole human career (in Geertz's terms) and because we know man as a whole (to use Polanyi's terms) that we are justified in talking of human beings in terms of both their actualized realities and their as yet unrealized potentialities. Our knowledge of the former enables us to speak of the latter, and to speak of the latter in teleological language.

It is for essentially the same reasons that one would be justified in speaking of "levels of organization." If human development, ontogenetically, represents the unfolding of potentialities, then it becomes possible to see the process of development as proceeding by and through different stages. A human adult has reached a different level of organization and complexity than a newborn infant. The problem is how the different levels of organization are related to each other; in particular, whether and to what extent a higher, more developed level is dependent upon a lower. The anthropologist Erich Kahler, discussing A. L. Kroeber's attempt to distinguish between the physicochemical and the cultural level in human life, has written:

Existence is a multilevel affair. As a body, I am a natural organization of lower beings, living, moving, changing, growing and decaying beings, namely the *cells*. Any change or disturbance in this organization, or even in the organization of the cells themselves, has the most powerful and serious effects on what we may consider the essence or quintessence of the physical system, the *psyche*. This is, after all, recognized in the psychosomatic theory and in recent psychiatry. The psyche, in turn, has a well-established influence on the *mind*. . . . We must also realize that all influence effective between different levels is a two-way process: it works upward as well as downward. There is a mutual interaction going on between mind, psyche, body, and so forth.[59]

Though differing somewhat in their emphasis, both Kroeber and Kahler are doing nothing more than trying to account for an increased awareness of the unity between the biological, the psychological and the cultural in man; they cannot be explained independently of each other. Marjorie Grene takes another step in the same kind of analysis, adding the note of increasing complexity in the different, higher levels of development: "In proceeding from the recognition of matter to life to persons to responsible persons, we are proceeding up a scale of complexities, each of which entails the earlier levels. Responsible persons are persons, persons are individuals, individuals are physical structures, yet each kind we recognize as also more, and other, than the preceding, or underlying, level." [60] As Polanyi puts it, "In the course of anthropogenesis, individuality develops from beginnings of a purely vegetative character to successive stages of active, perceptive, and eventually responsible, personhood. The phylogenetic emergence is continuous —just as ontogenetic emergence clearly is." [61]

Of course, a biological analysis which speaks in terms of levels and complexities of organization has a long pedigree, going back to Aristotle. But it still remains a serviceable form of analysis; indeed, it is hard to discern an alternative if one wants to know when human life begins. For the very question presupposes that human life can be comprehended in temporal terms—as having a beginning in time and an end in time. There is some reason (as we shall see shortly) for worrying a bit about this presupposition, but no sufficient reason to reject it. And as part of that same presupposition, there is the antecedent knowledge that individual human life does proceed through stages. We do, after all, refer to neonates, infants, children, adolescents, adults and the elderly. Pediatrics, at one end of the human life-span, and geriatrics, at the other, can exist as independent medical disciplines precisely because there exists a body of knowledge concerning human life at the infant and elderly stages. We know what can or ought to be expected at each stage simply because we know something about the different stages, or levels, of human development. Few would be concerned with genetic abnormalities in the early months of gestation were it not known that these ab-normalities have immense consequences for later development. Knowl-edge of this kind can be termed "teleological knowledge": knowing the direction and likely outcome of a biological process.

A summation is in order before moving to the next stage of this dis-cussion. I have argued, in the first stage, that a teleological analysis of the biological data is legitimate, necessary and illuminating as a philo-sophical basis for approaching an answer to the question of when life begins. I have argued, in the second stage, that an important movement in some scientific disciplines concerned with the "human" is that the "human" must be defined not in single-character, or essentialistic, terms but rather in terms of variety and diversity. Moreover, there is con-siderable agreement that an analysis of the "human" must take account, holistically, of the biological, the psychological and the cultural; no one of them can be scanted, at the cost of misunderstanding the others. I have also tried to point out the importance of "potentiality" and "ca-pacity" in analyzing "human life," adding an affirmation of the language of "levels of organization" as helpful in understanding the process whereby the potential is made actual.

At this point, I want to draw some conclusions pertinent to a dis-cussion of when human life begins. First, a negative conclusion: any answer to the question which rests on one human characteristic alone is to be suspect. Second, a positive conclusion: any answer to the ques-tion must take account of "potentiality," and not rest its case exclusively on achieved human characteristics. Third, a negative conclusion: any answer to the question which ignores the biological, genetic basis of human development and individuality is to be rejected. Fourth, another positive conclusion: the best way to analyze human development in its temporal course is to analyze the different stages of development teleo-logically, in terms of their direction and potential ends.

NOTES

1. Andie L. Knutson, "When Does a Human Life Begin? Viewpoints of Public Health Professionals," *American Journal of Public Health,* 57 (December 1967), p. 2167.
2. *Ibid.,* p. 2169.
3. *Ibid.,* pp. 2171–72.
4. *Ibid.,* p. 2175.
5. Andie L. Knutson, "The Definition and Value of a New Human Life," *Social Science and Medicine,* 1 (1967), pp. 7–29.
6. *Ibid.,* p. 26.
7. Pierre Duhem, "Physical Theory and Experiment," in Herbert Feigl and May Brodbeck (eds.), *Readings in the Philosophy of Science* (New York: Appleton-Century-Crofts, 1953), p. 237.
8. James M. Gustafson, "Christian Humanism and the Human Mind," in John D. Roslansky (ed.), *The Human Mind* (New York: North-Holland, 1967), p. 87.

9. Michael Polanyi, *Personal Knowledge* (New York: Harper Torchbooks, 1964), p. 287.
10. Marjorie Grene, *The Knower and the Known* (New York: Basic Books, 1966), p. 158.
11. *Ibid.*, p. 160.
12. Polanyi, *op. cit.*, p. 357.
13. Grene, *op. cit.*, p. 233.
14. *Ibid.*, p. 236.
15. Edna Heidbreder, *Seven Psychologies* (New York: Appleton-Century-Crofts, 1961), p. 355.
16. One of the best philosophical discussions of such analyses remains that of Ernest Nagel, "Teleological Explanations and Teleological Systems," in *Readings in the Philosophy of Science, op. cit.*, pp. 537–58.
17. See especially Erich Fromm and Ramon Xirau (eds.), *The Nature of Man* (New York: Macmillan, 1968); John R. Platt (ed.), *New Views on the Nature of Man* (Chicago: University of Chicago Press, 1965); William Nicholls (ed.), *Conflicting Images of Man* (New York: The Seabury Press, 1966); Paul E. Oehser (ed.), *Knowledge Among Men* (New York: Simon and Schuster, 1966).
18. Stephen E. Toulmin, "Intellectual Values and the Future," in *Knowledge Among Men, op. cit.*, p. 159.
19. Nathan A. Scott, Jr., "The Christian Understanding of Man," in *Conflicting Images of Man, op. cit.*, p. 10.
20. Willard F. Libby, "Man's Place in the Physical Universe," in *New Views on the Nature of Man, op. cit.*, p. 15.
21. See Fromm and Xirau (eds.), *op. cit.*, for a collection of such attempts throughout history.
22. Ernst Mayr, *Animal Species and Evolution* (Cambridge: Harvard University Press, 1963), p. 623.
23. A. L. Kroeber, *Anthropology: Culture Patterns and Processes* (New York. Harcourt, Brace and World, 1963), p. 8.
24. Grene, *op. cit.*, pp. 172ff.
25. George H. Mead, *Mind, Self and Society* (Chicago: University of Chicago Press, Phoenix Books, 1962), pp. 120–22.
26. Ernst Caspari, "Selective Forces in the Evolution of Man," in M. F. Ashley Montagu (ed.), *Culture: Man's Adaptive Dimension* (New York: Oxford University Press, 1968), p. 165.
27. A. Irving Hallowell, "Cranial Capacity and the Human Brain," in *Culture: Man's Adaptive Dimension, op. cit.*, p. 184.
28. Ernst Mayr (ed.), *The Species Problem* (Washington, D.C.: American Association for the Advancement of Science, Publication No. 50, 1957).
29. J. Imbrie, "The Species Problem with Fossil Animals," in *The Species Problem, op. cit.*, p. 126.
30. Mayr, "Species Concepts and Definitions," in *The Species Problem, op. cit.*, p. 13.
31. Mayr, *Animal Species and Evolution, op. cit.*, p. 5.
32. Carleton S. Coon, *The Origin of Races* (New York: Alfred A. Knopf, 1962), p. 13; Polanyi comments that the downfall of taxonomy lay in its dependence upon "the good taxonomist," with a personal ability to recognize affinity to type (*Personal Knowledge, op. cit.*, p. 351).
33. George Gaylord Simpson, *The Major Features of Evolution* (New York: Columbia University Press, 1953), pp. 340–41; see also J. S. Huxley (ed.), *The New Systematics* (Oxford: Clarendon Press, 1940), and Ernst Mayr, *Systematics and the Origin of Species* (New York: Columbia University Press, 1942).
34. J. M. Thoday, "Geneticism and Environmentalism," in J. E. Meade and A. S. Parker (eds.), *Biological Aspects of Social Problems* (Edinburgh: Oliver and Boyd, 1965), p. 101.

35. Thoday, *ibid.*, p. 103, and Theodosius Dobzhansky, *Heredity and the Nature of Man* (New York: Signet Books, 1966), p. 57.
36. Grene, *op. cit.*, p. 169.
37. Simpson, *op. cit.*, p. 341. For a critique of the "population" concept, see W. R. Thompson, "The Status of Species," in Vincent E. Smith (ed.), *Philosophical Problems in Biology* (New York: St. John's University Press, 1966), pp. 67–126.
38. Mayr, "Species Concepts and Definitions," *op. cit.*, p. 13.
39. Marvin Harris, *The Rise of Anthropological Theory* (New York: Thomas Y. Crowell Co., 1968), p. 429.
40. See, for instance, Benson E. Ginsberg and William S. Laughlin, "Human Adaptability and Achievement," in *Culture: Man's Adaptive Dimension, op. cit.,* p. 266, for a critique of such theories.
41. See René Dubos, *So Human an Animal* (New York: Scribner's, 1969), p. 96, for a brief survey of opinions in support of this view.
42. A. Irving Hallowell, "Self, Society, and Culture," in *Culture: Man's Adaptive Dimension, op. cit.,* p. 201.
43. *Ibid.*, pp. 201–02.
44. *Ibid.*, p. 203.
45. *Ibid.*, p. 225.
46. Clifford Geertz, "The Impact of the Concept of Culture on the Concept of Man," in *New Views on the Nature of Man, op. cit.,* p. 96.
47. Clifford Geertz, "The Transition to Humanity," in Sol Tax (ed.), *Horizons of Anthropology* (Chicago: Aldine Publishing Co., 1964), p. 46.
48. Geertz, "The Impact of the Concept of Culture . . . ," *op. cit.,* p. 106.
49. *Ibid.*, p. 116.
50. *Ibid,* p. 112.
51. Clifford Geertz, "Religion as a Cultural System," in Michael Banton (ed.), *Anthropological Approaches to the Study of Religion* (New York: Frederick A. Praeger, 1966), p. 13.
52. Gordon W. Allport, *Becoming* (New Haven: Yale Paperbound, 1967), p. 19.
53. Martin Buber, "What is Man?," in *Between Man and Man,* trans. Ronald Gregor Smith (New York: Macmillan, 1965), p. 123.
54. *Ibid.*, p. 205.
55. Columba Ryan, O.P., The Traditional Concept of Natural Law: An Interpretation," in Illtud Evans (ed.), *Light on the Natural Law* (Baltimore: Helicon Press, 1965), p. 23.
56. Ernest Becker, *The Structure of Evil: An Essay on the Unification of the Science of Man* (New York: George Braziller, 1968), pp. 387–88.
57. Fromm and Xirau (eds.), *op. cit.,* p. 9.
58. Marjorie Grene, *Approaches to a Philosophical Biology* (New York: Basic Books, 1968), p. 48.
59. Erich Kahler, "Culture and Evolution," in *Culture: Man's Adaptive Dimension, op. cit.,* p. 14.
60. Grene, *The Knower and the Known, op. cit.,* p. 217.
61. Polanyi, *op. cit.,* p. 395.

CHAPTER 11

The "Beginning" of Human Life: Interpreting the Biological Data

ALL OF THE FOREGOING has been prelude to a direct examination of the biological data. I have already argued why such a prelude is necessary. The most convenient initial approach to the data is simply to outline what is at present known.[1] Concerning the process of gestation, three basic questions may be asked: What happens morphologically? What happens genetically? What is the biological dynamic of the development of the conceptus?

What Happens Morphologically?

Week 1: About the fourteenth day after the beginning of the menstrual cycle a mature ovum is released from the Graafian follicle. After remaining momentarily in the peritoneal cavity, the ovum then passes into the uterine (Fallopian) tube, thus beginning its movement toward the uterus. If intercourse has taken place within 72 hours (more or less) of release of the mature ovum, the ovum may then encounter the male sperm in the uterine tube. If one of the sperm fertilizes the ovum, the fertilization will probably occur in the upper part of the uterine tube. Once fertilized, the ovum becomes a single-cell zygote. Within a day or so after fertilization the zygote begins the process of cellular cleavage, first a two-cell cleavage, then four, then eight, etc. By the third day, there are an estimated 16 cells. As this cleavage is taking place, the zygote is continuously moving down the uterine tube. The individual cells formed by the ongoing cleavage are called "blastomeres." At the end of about four days, the combined blastomeres form the morula, which is a solid cluster of blastomeres. By the fifth day, this morula has begun to enlarge and become hollowed out. At this point it is called a "blastocyst," and this blastocyst continues to enlarge and hollow out. By about the fifth day, the zygote, now fully in the blastocyst stage, has reached the uterus. By the sixth or seventh day, the zygote has begun the process of implantation into the wall of the uterus. The implantation activity then takes about four more days; by the eleventh day implantation is completed.

Week 2: During the time of gradual implantation, further changes occur in the blastocyst. The most important is the development of an outer layer of cells (trophoblast), which will become part of the placenta, and an inner cell mass (embryoblast), which will become the embryo. The development of the inner-cell mass is first marked by a single layer of cells, which in turn gives way to the appearance of a second layer of cells (endoderm). This latter layer of cells gradually forms the primary yolk sac (still surrounded by the trophoblast). The inner cell mass is, at the same time, taking the form of a bilaminar disc, made up of the cellular layers (formative cells and endoderm). As these layers are maturing, the blastocyst is also forming the amniotic cavity. By the end of the second week, the conceptus—now usually called an "embryo"—consists essentially of the amniotic cavity, the bilaminar embryonic disc and the yolk sac.

Week 3: During the third week, the bilaminar embryonic disc gradually changes, by the process known as "gastrulation," into a trilaminar disc as another cell layer is added. As gastrulation progresses, signaled by the appearance of the "primitive streak," there emerges the intra-embryonic mesoderm which makes its appearance as a (third) layer of cells between the layers of the endoderm and formation cells. As this is happening, the embryonic disc is gradually being elongated, thus establishing the central axis of the embryo. With the formation of the "gastrula" (the three layers), the fundamental body plan is established. The process of "twinning" (for monozygotic—identical—twins) is believed to occur at some point during the second or third week: "It is likely that the splitting of the embryo occurs at the primitive streak stage and involves the separation of formative cells into two lots." [2]

Weeks 4 and 5: During the fourth and fifth week, important stages of cell development and differentiation take place in the initially trilaminar disc. This development is especially pronounced in the area of the primitive streak, where there is developed, among other things, the notochord (serving as the axial skeleton until replaced by vertebrae), cardiogenic mesoderm (which gives rise to the heart), intermediate mesoderm (which gives rise to adrenal cortex, gonads and kidneys), and the neural tube. A precocious cardiovascular system also begins functioning during this period. During the fourth and fifth weeks, the foundation of all the organ systems is established. By the fifth week a face is beginning to make its appearance as well as primitive limb buds. In general, weeks five to eight mark the appearance of those external features which mark the embryo as visibly human. The development of primitive brain vesicles can be discerned also during the fourth and fifth week.

During these first weeks of development, the size of the conceptus is about as follows: zygote (.14mm.); blastocyst: preimplantation (.2mm.), postimplantation (.8mm.); embryo at three weeks (1.5mm.); 32 days (5.0mm.); 56 days (30mm.); from the third month to term, the growth rate is approximately 1.5mm. per day, slowing down near term.

By the sixth week a full complement of organs is present, though still in a primitive stage. By the seventh week, a stimulation of the mouth or nose of the embryo will cause it to flex its neck. By the eighth week— at which point the conceptus is called a "fetus" rather than an "embryo" —there is a discernible electric activity in the brain; it is possible to get an EEG reading. Toes and fingers are by now clearly visible. During the ninth and tenth weeks, a number of reflex activities are noticeable, particularly squinting and swallowing. By the tenth week, spontaneous movement on the part of the fetus is taking place, independent of external stimulation. By the eleventh week, the skeleton of the fetus can be captured by X-ray. By the twelfth week, the brain structure is essentially complete and a fetal electrocardiograph through the pregnant woman can pick up heart activity. Sometime between the thirteenth and sixteenth week, the woman is likely to feel fetal movements: "quickening," as the old phrase has it. Viability is possible sometime between the twenty-sixth and the twenty-eighth week. Birth normally occurs between the thirty-ninth and the fortieth week.

What Happens Genetically?

Let us turn now to the genetic problem. Nearly all human body cells contain 46 chromosomes. The sex cells, sperm and egg, each have 23 chromosomes, the haploid number (i.e., half the number of chromosomes in body cells). Since the 46 body-cell chromosomes are comprised of 23 pairs of chromosomes, the diploid number, the sex cells thus carry one member of each of the 23 pairs. When an egg is fertilized, the resultant zygote (and the ensuing body cells which develop) then has the full complement of 23 pairs, one member from each parent, restoring the normal 46 chromosomes making up body cells. In the zygote (and ensuing body cells) each of the 23 chromosomes from the mother is matched by a similar one from the father; the matched pairs are then replicated in daughter cells by mitosis as the zygote cleaves. The chromosomes, composed primarily of deoxyribonucleic acid (DNA) and proteins, are the carriers of the genes, which transmit the hereditary characteristics of the parents to the fertilized ovum. A single human sex cell, it is estimated, carries at least two million different genes.

The specific location of the genetic information is now generally assumed to be in the chromosomal DNA. This DNA has chemically been broken down into a type of sugar (deoxyribose), a phosphoric acid and four nucleotide bases (adenine, guanine, cytosine and thymine). T. Dobzhansky has suggested that, if we think of the four nucleotide bases as comprising an "alphabet"—A, T, G, C—it is possible to understand why it is possible for them, in different combinations, to give "a virtually infinite variety of genetic 'words' or 'messages.'"[3] The genes, which are sections of the ladder-like DNA molecules, are different because of the different combinations of the "alphabet"; heredity is thus "coded" in the genes, within the chromosomal DNA. The way in which a person receives his genetic makeup, his heredity, is by receiving the genetic "messages" coded in the DNA of the egg cell of the mother and the sperm cell of the father. "Looked at from the standpoint of genetics," Dobzhansky has written, "the development of an individual may be said to represent a translation, or a decoding, of the genetic messages this individual received from his parents."[4] Taking into account the fact that each parent has the potentiality of forming up to 2^{23} kinds of sex cells, the number of possible genetic combinations for any offspring of one set of parents is $2^{23} \times 2^{23} = 2^{46}$; even this figure, Dobzhansky has suggested, is a low estimate.[5] It is thus possible to see why, genetically speaking, Dobzhansky can conclude:

> Every human being has, then, his own nature, individual and nonrepeatable. The nature of man as a species resolves itself into a great multitude of human natures. Everybody is born with a nature that is absolutely new in the universe, that will never appear again (identical twins and other identical multiple births, of course, excepted).[6]

At this point, a further distinction is useful, originally suggested in 1911 by the Danish geneticist W. Johannsen: the difference between an individual's "genotype" and his "phenotype."[7] The "genotype" is the total heredity of the individual (received from the DNA in the chromosomes in the parental sex cells). The "phenotype," in the narrow sense, is the particular appearance presented by the individual; more broadly, it includes all the physiological, psychological, social and cultural characteristics of an individual. The importance of the distinction, however, should not obscure the fact that the genotype and the phenotype exist in interaction with each other and with their environment. While an individual's genotype is established at fertilization, this must not be understood to mean that the genes of the individual are literally the *same* genes originally received from the parents; instead, they are replicated, identical copies of these genes produced by the ongoing mitotic division of the cells (these cells running eventually into the billions). This process of replication of the genes requires the use of material from the cellular environment; genes can make copies of themselves only by using other material. The phenotype is the result of a further interaction, that between the individual's genotype and the different environments in which he lives his life: "My present phenotype, which I am as an organism and as a human being, has been determined by my genotype and by the whole succession of the environments I have encountered in my life." [8]

F. J. Gottlieb has summed up the relevant observational data:

(1) All the thousands of cells of the multicellular organism arise by *mitotic divisions of the zygote,* the single cell resulting from fusion of two gametes (sex cells). These divisions yield genetically identical cells. (2) In a specific and highly predictable, non-random fashion, adjacent genetically identical cells, in the course of development, give rise to morphologically, physiologically, and biochemically distinct cell lineages and thereby to tissues and organs. (3) Within a species, development proceeds in a precise and regular fashion, resulting in individuals having not only the general morphological, physiological, and biochemical features of the species, but also many of the individual peculiarities of their parents.[9]

What Is the Biological Dynamic of the Development of the Conceptus?

A critical concept here is that of "development." What does this term mean when applied to the embryological data? It refers, simply, to that process of change which results in progressive complexity. As James D. Ebert has written, "All development . . . is characterized by progressive change, by progressive increase in level of complexity." [10] The criterion of development is "an orderly sequence of changes—progressive change —resulting in an increase in level of complexity." [11] "Development," then, is an umbrella term referring to what happens in the activity of changing systems where the end product differs from the initial stage. It does not imply that development proceeds by discrete, easily recognizable, stages. It implies only that something is happening—specifically, gradual complexification—and that we can call this "happening" the process of "development."

For our purposes, two questions are important. First, what are the major processes which interact with each other in embryological development? Second, what is the source of embryological development? The first question can be answered by saying that there are four major processes which take place in embryological development: genetic replication, cellular growth, cellular differentiation and histo- and organogenesis.[12] Ebert has provided a representative answer to the second question:

All development rests ultimately on the genes. The fabrication of a macromolecule, the final form of an organ, or the recognition of a homograft (a major criterion for distinguishing between genotypes) must involve a series of interactions beyond the gene, often beyond the individual cell; but eventually it will be necessary to trace the origin of these interactions to the structure of DNA and the control of its functions.[13]

Yet the process of development, as Ebert also stresses, must take account of the fact that the properties of embryos are distinct from the properties of adults. For, as the fertilized ovum and then the embryo develop, cellular growth and differentiation introduce into the developing being different, more complex properties.

The crucial determinant of development is the action of the genes: "Development is synonymous with gene action." [14] As Gottlieb has put it:

The completion of fertilization and the initiation of embryo development is marked by the fusion of the two haploid pronuclei to form a single diploid nucleus. The resulting cell contains an equal genetic contribution from each of its parents and, within its mass of cytoplasm, many additional components from its mother. Initial multicellularity is then accomplished by a number of mitotic divisions.[15]

As Gottlieb writes in another place, "Development, in another sense, is a process without beginning or end. Through this process, each generation is inseparably tied to the preceding and ensuing generations." [16] If we take into account the importance of interaction with environment, it is then possible to see why one can say:

All subsequent patterns, including the final phenotypic patterns, depend upon the initial pattern—the differential function of regions within the pattern and the differential interactions among regions—which lead to further divergence in function. . . . The genes exercise their control of development by means of their products, through a process involving differential function in time.[17]

Gottlieb has provided a useful analogy:

The developmental system can be likened to an industrial complex. Tool makers provide each factory with tools. The nature of the tools and of the raw materials available will determine the parts that any one factory will produce. These parts will, in turn, affect the final product. As the complex becomes larger, the specialization of each factory increases. For efficiency, the rate of production of each factory is controlled by feedback mechanisms, so that all the plants in the complex are temporarily in phase with one another. The genes are the tool makers of cells.[18]

Throughout the process of development, the conceptus is an entity which, while dependent upon the woman for nourishment, is independent as discrete being. It possesses its own genetic dynamism of development and growth, its own organs, circulatory system and metabolic processes. Its genotype and phenotype are distinct from those of the woman. It is its own source of unity, organic coherence and genetically programmed development.

Interpreting the Data

If I have succeeded in sketching the essentials of the developmental process accurately, a question arises: What are we to do with the data once we have it? Put differently, how should we make use of it in answering the question "When does human life begin?" I have already contended that the data do not provide us with a self-evident answer. Our answer will be conditioned by a number of prior steps, particularly our antecedent definition of "human." And I have further contended that (a) any definition of the human should be a rich definition, not a one-character definition, (b) biological-genetic considerations cannot be excluded from a definition, (c) a significant place must be left in any definition for "potentialities" and "capacities," and (d) a teleological perspective on the development process is desirable and illuminating. We now have in hand, therefore, a number of background, conditioning stipulations of a very general kind, as well as the relevant biological-genetic data.

None of it, however, will be of any use unless we return to some basic questions to provide a focus and a direction. We cannot take a single step unless we ask: What problem are we trying to solve? This is not a book on evolution so we are not concerned directly with the problem of when human life began on earth. Our concern is with abortion. The question of when human life begins arises because we want to know whether and under what circumstances the performance of an abortion—the inducing of an abortion—is an act which kills human life. That abortion is an act which kills something—a being of *some* sort— is not in dispute; that is the purpose of abortion techniques. Or, if the word "kills" seems too strong, and we want to speak more euphemistically, one can at least say that induced abortion is an act which stops a specifiable development process: the development of the product of conception, the conceptus. A decision to abort does not arise until after this developmental process has started (or is believed to have started). Has human life *begun* when an abortion is needed or indicated? A response to this particular question will reflect our general convictions about when human life begins, leaving open the possibility that the time when an abortion is indicated or desirable will have much to do

with whether we say human life is present. It is a further possibility
that, while we may say that human life "begins" at "x" point in the
developmental process, we may not feel compelled to say that it is
necessarily to be fully valued or fully protected at that point (but rather
at "y" point).

We are in search, I want to suggest, of two things. First, we need to
know what the pertinent criteria are in determining whether "human
life" is present in the conceptus—at any given stage of development
(since the need to make abortion decisions can arise early or late in
pregnancy). To ask when human life begins is a way of asking about
when human life is first present in a conceptus. To ask whether human
life *has begun* in the instance of a particular pregnancy is to relate
the question of "beginning" to a concrete situation. Second, we need to
know whether a determination that life begins at a given point entails
that it ought to be valued at that point. Hovering next to the second
question is the intimately related problem of the degree to which life,
once begun, should be valued: absolutely, relatively or not at all? If it
is not self-evident how the biological data can help us answer the first
question, it is even less evident how, if at all, it can help us to answer
the second. Indeed, as I will argue toward the end of the chapter, the
second question is patently a "moral policy" question, while the first
is, in part, one of establishing a moral policy but also, in part, one of
establishing (or working with) a philosophical policy designed to help
answer the question of "the beginning."

Concerning both questions, it is possible to discern three basic schools
of opinion: those who believe the pertinent criteria for establishing the
"beginning" are genetic; those who believe they are developmental, by
which I mean that it is the stage of morphological development which
is crucial; finally, those who believe the criteria are social, a consequence
of the political and social decisions people choose to make. I want to
examine each of these three schools, commenting on how they decided
upon their criteria, as well as noting how they go about solving the
problem of the value to be attributed to life once begun. In other
words, I will be interested in both their philosophical and their moral
policy. My critique of these schools will set the stage for my own conclusions. Those whom I have selected as representative of different
bodies of opinion do not, of course, represent the totality of all those
who have written on the problem; they are meant to be representative
of important suggested approaches.

The Genetic School

John T. Noonan, Jr., has put those arguments I would cluster under
the "genetic school" as directly as anyone. "Once conceived," he has

written defending a central Catholic theological tradition on abortion, "the being was recognized as man because he had man's potential. The criterion for humanity, thus, was simple and all-embracing: if you are conceived by human parents, you are human." [19] In another place, he has said:

I myself know only one test for humanity: a being who was conceived by human parents and is potentially capable of human acts is human. By what other test could you prove that an infant of one day was human? . . . In all these states—infancy, insanity, sickness, sleep—a man is not expressing his humanity by thought or rational action. We know he is a man because he came of human flesh and is expected, at some point, to be able to perform a human act, to think a human thought.[20]

In still another place, he has said that "humanity is an attribute which anyone conceived by a man and a woman has. . . . A being with the human genetic code is *Homo sapiens* in potency; and his potential capacity to reason makes him share in the universal characteristic of man." [21] In addition to using a genetic test as what I have called a "philosophical policy," Noonan argues that this kind of a test provides the basis for the best moral position: "Any attempt to limit humanity to exclude some group runs the risk of furnishing authority and precedent for excluding other groups in the name of the consciousness or perception of the controlling group." [22] At stake here is "a refusal to discriminate among human beings on the basis of their varying potentialities." [23]

Paul Ramsey and André Hellegers argue in much the same way, with, however, some important nuances. Ramsey has written:

Indeed, microgenetics seems to have demonstrated what religion never could; and biological science, to have resolved an ancient theological dispute. The human individual comes into existence first as a minute information speck, drawn at random from many other minute informational specks his parents possessed out of the common human gene pool. This took place at the moment of impregnation. . . . Thus it can be said that the individual is whoever he is going to become from the moment of impregnation. Thereafter, his subsequent development may be described as a process of becoming the one he already is. Genetics teaches that we were from the beginning what we essentially still are in every cell and in every human attribute.[24]

Ramsey's developed argument draws also upon what he believes to be the teleological thrust of modern genetics, which teaches that the genetic informational specks are determining what the individual will be; they provide the basis for development.[25] All of this amounts to what Ramsey, in another place, calls "the 'proof' from genotype." [26] Ramsey, however, allows the possibility of one "significant *modification*" of this "proof," though he puts it forward in a somewhat less than enthusiastic way. That is the possibility that one might want to draw a line at the "primitive streak" stage of development or that moment when twinning could occur. To draw the line at that point would be to assure that the being in question constituted a unique "individual human being," a point in question before the possibility of twinning had passed.[27]

André Hellegers, who notes that it has been a criterion of modern science "that a species shall be recognized by its genetic make-up," contends that it is "of the essence . . . whether we are capable of *diagnosing* the presence of a new genetic package. This can only occur after the implantation."[28] Before implantation, he argues, the cells of the fertilized ovum have a "totipotentiality" and are not decisively activated in "the direction of becoming human" until that phase is passed, i.e., at implantation.[29] Both Ramsey and Hellegers, therefore, leave open the possibility that an abortion performed before implantation (as in a projected morning-after pill) would not necessarily count as the taking of individual human life.

The attractions of the genetic argument—the "proof from genotype" —are evident. While both the sperm and the egg are genetically unique, they are not unique in the same way as a fertilized egg. Unless joined, the former will die, while the latter has the capacity to grow and develop as a zygote. Moreover, one can bring to bear the statements of a number of geneticists and embryologists in its support, statements made far removed from abortion disputes. James D. Ebert has asked a question and provided his answer: "When does an individual first deserve this name? In embryonic development, from the very moment the egg is activated."[30] In the instance of Curt Stern: "The first two months, counted from the time of fertilization, represent undoubtedly the most important period in the development of the new human being."[31] Or Bradley M. Patten: "Every one of the higher animals starts life as a single cell—the fertilized ovum. . . . The union of two such sex cells (male germ cell and female germ cell) to form a zygote constitutes the process of fertilization and initiates the life of a new individual."[32] Or Ashley Montagu: "Life begins, not at birth, but at conception, and what happens in the interval between conception and birth is very much more important for our subsequent growth and development than we have, until recently, realized."[33]

I do not cite these statements to show that the argument from genotype is necessarily valid, much less to imply that all its proponents would draw the moral conclusion that abortions ought not to be performed—Ashley Montagu has specifically objected to his statement being so used.[34] I do so only to indicate the reasonableness of the genetic argument. It is an argument which meets a number of the tests stipulated at the end of Chapter 10: it takes the genetic evidence seriously, it leaves a significant place for "potentiality," and it works out of a teleological perspective. Moreover, it offers the possibility of a prudently safe moral policy. For, by using a genetic test for the "human," it excludes the employment of arbitrary norms which, in principle, could establish precedents for using the same norms in nonabortion contexts; it is not an *ad hoc* criterion. Ramsey, for instance, has stressed the necessity of employing a norm which does not erase the possibility of distinguishing between abortion and infanticide; a genetic norm for the "human," which rests heavily on yet-to-be-realized potentialities, does serve that end. And it also serves, as Noonan has stressed, to forestall possibly dangerous discriminations (working from an abortion precedent) among humans on the basis of varying potentialities. It thus appears to represent a happy marriage of sensitivity to biological evidence and a concern to prevent the introduction of modes of reasoning which could have disastrous implications for the protection of human life, in this and other contexts.

It does, however, also have some significant liabilities, which at least weaken its force. Noonan speaks of a "criterion for humanity," but it is useful to ask whether this is exactly what is needed for abortion decisions. Is our concern to protect human life—humanity in the abstract as an attribute of a being—or is it to protect individual human beings? In abortion decisions, which arise case by case in particular pregnancies, it is the life—or purported life (so as not to beg the question) —of an individual human being which is at issue. We are not asking whether a decision to abort is a decision for or against the attribute of "humanity," but whether it is a decision for or against a particular human being. If we were seeking simply a test for "humanity," then both the egg and the sperm separately could pass that test: under proper conditions (i.e., their union), they could pass the test of constituting a being potentially capable of human acts. Noonan, though, does stipulate that the being must be conceived by human parents; that is the starting point he recognizes as the beginning of "humanity." But just what is the potential at this point?

In the primary article already cited, Noonan contends that, once conception has taken place, "there is a sharp shift in probabilities, an immense jump in potentialities. . . . At the point where the conceived being has a better than even chance of developing, he is a man." [35] The trouble is that this formulation represents a *stipulation* about what should be *counted* as "a man," thus begging the question of whether a particular conceived being is, in fact, a man. That a particular conceived being may, *statistically* speaking, have "a better than even chance of developing" does not entail that it will so develop. Because of genetic or other abnormalities, a particular fertilized egg may be destined for spontaneous abortion or to become a hydatidiform mole.[36] The zygote can develop or fail to develop in a number of directions. Under favorable circumstances, it will develop into a human being; but this is not biologically (or statistically) inexorable. The potentiality of a zygote to become a human being need not *necessarily* be fulfilled; that possibility will in any specific case depend upon many other conditions to bring this potentiality to actuality. As George Wald has put it: "All of us had already been screened for essential fitness by the time we were born. To have reached the stage at which we could be born meant that we had already passed many searching tests that many of our contemporary embryos had failed." [37]

All of this is to say that, given any specific fertilized egg, it remains uncertain whether it "is potentially capable of human acts"; only time can tell. That is why it remains uncertain whether a decision to abort a particular fertilized ovum (or embryo, or fetus—though at that point the odds against its being human drop even more sharply) amounts to a decision for or against a particular human being. Implicit in Noonan's approach—which turns out to be based in part on statistical probabilities —is a moral policy. It is the policy of acting *as if* every fertilized ovum will necessarily develop into a being with the attribute of "humanity." It is a policy designed to protect all fertilized ova, presumably on the grounds that the chances of destroying a particular human being in any given abortion are far greater than the chances of killing a being which does not have a human potential. It is not an unreasonable moral policy, but it is important to see that it *is* a moral policy and not a direct extrapolation from the biological data, though compatible with that data. For, as noted earlier, the way a particular fertilized ovum will develop is not just a question of its human genotype, but of the interaction of that genotype with environment to produce a phenotype. Thus the human potential of a genotype is conditioned by its environment; and how it will be conditioned will not be clear until sometime after the process of gestation is under way.

As Thomas Hayes has observed, moreover, simple criteria "such as functioning genes in the production of human proteins" are insufficient to "define a living system as a human being": "such criteria are necessary but not sufficient conditions. Such parameters do not distinguish between systems such as human tissue culture or the placenta and the embryo. Also, many of the biological qualities exist in the sperm and ovum before fertilization." [38] It is not *necessarily* the case, in other words, to use Noonan's formulation, that "a being with the human genetic code is *Homo sapiens* in potency." For we do not know, if one speaks of "*a* being" (my italics), if it does have this potency. All we know is that, as a statistical generality, the class of beings with the human genetic code have this potency; but this does not tell us whether any particular being within this class has it. We can decide to act *as if* each does, but that is to adopt a moral policy, and, as Noonan recognizes, his is a moral policy based on a desire to forestall any discrimination among human beings "on the basis of their varying potentialities." (I will postpone for the moment a discussion of whether it is a sound moral policy in the instance of abortion.)

Paul Ramsey's approach suffers from similar liabilities. First of all, it is misleading to say that "microgenetics seems to have demonstrated" when a human individual first comes into existence; such an assertion assumes that the antecedent philosophical questions concerning the meaning of "human" have been settled, that a methodology for relating a concept like "human" to biological data has been settled upon and so on. But Prof. Ramsey has not in fact established the validity of his assumptions here. David Granfield's otherwise penetrating analysis of the scientific evidence is open to the same criticism, when he concludes: "Science, however, simply presents the fact that human life begins with fertilization and continues until death." [39] Second, it does not seem wholly accurate to say, as Ramsey does, that at the moment of impregnation "the individual is whoever he is going to become" or to speak of his "becoming the one he already is." Who he is, to return to a fundamental biological point, will be determined not just by his genotype, but by the interaction and interrelationship of the genotype with its different environments. We do not know who a being is or what he will become just by knowing that he has a particular genotype. Who this being becomes is not something rigidly set from the genetic beginning, but will be determined by interaction with the environment. That is the whole point of distinguishing between genotype and phenotype; it makes clear that an individual is something other than (though it includes) his genetic potential. Neither Noonan nor Ramsey gives a sufficient place to the importance of development as part of the process of becoming human. Both of their positions seem to amount to saying that a being with a human genotype, prior to the development of an individuated phenotype, is a sufficiently subsistent being to merit the appellation "human." But this seems a doubtful conclusion, unless one has presumed that an exclusively genetic norm is decisive (which requires a philosophical foundation). Far from presuming a rich definition of the "human," Noonan and Ramsey are willing to stake themselves on the narrowest: genetic individuality alone. This willingness seems to reveal the influence of a moral policy, one which would like to prevent the assigning of different values to different individuals according to the degree to which genetic potentiality is actually realized.

The Developmental School

Under the "developmental school" I would group those who hold that, while conception does establish the genetic basis for an individual human being, some degree of development is required before one can legitimately speak of the life of an "individual human being" as at issue in abortion decisions. Within this "school," however, there are differences of opinion on just how much development is required and decisive. The general argument, though, for some kind of development norm has been well put by Thomas L. Hayes:

> [The] first cell of the new individual [the zygote] contains all the genetic information that, during development, will interact with its environment to produce the first human organism. However, this first cell itself cannot be described in either form or function as a complete human individual. It is not a tiny body that only needs to grow in size to become a developed human person. Development does not take place by growth alone but is an intricate process of interaction between genetic material and its environment that produces new form and function in the embryo as development proceeds. Even the genetic material itself may change in form and function. . . . As development proceeds, certain landmarks can be noted in the continuous transition from single cell to complete human individual. Implantation in the wall of the uterus, development of the placenta, movement or quickening and birth are all important events, but none represents a point in development where the biological form and function of the human individual are suddenly added. . . . The attributes of form and function that designate the living system as a human individual are acquired at various times during development in a process that is relatively continuous. The fetus late in development is obviously a living human individual in form and function. The single cell stage, early in development, does not possess many of the attributes of biological form and function that are associated with the human individual.[40]

Hayes then suggests, as a corollary of his reading of the biological evidence, an attendant moral policy: "The human individual develops biologically in a continuous fashion, and it might be worthwhile to consider the possibility that the rights of a human person might develop in the same way." [41] He points out, though, that to proceed in this fashion might require that "an arbitrary point early in pregnancy may have to be defined by theologians at which time the embryo is endowed with the right of existence." [42]

If Hayes sets forth a general theory which might justify the choice of some particular stage of development as critical for the purposes of drawing a line, others have offered more specific suggestions about where such a line might reasonably be drawn. Rudolf Ehrensing has suggested that "the presence of human life does not necessarily mean that a human person is present," resting his distinction between a "human life" and a "human person" on the necessity in the latter of "the existence of a living human brain in some form." [43] Moreover, "it is not the potential for structuring matter in the form of a body, a human brain, that calls for the presence of a human person, but the actual accomplishment, the actual in-corporation of matter." [44] A moral policy is then hypothesized: "If the developing embryo is not yet a human person, then under some circumstances the welfare of actually existing persons *might* supersede the welfare of developing human tissue." [45] Ehrensing does not pinpoint just when, by the use of a brain-development criterion, personhood is actually present, but another author, Roy U. Schenk, arguing in a similar way, does:

> Each human fetus progresses through a continuous series of developmental stages and ultimately passes through [the] level of complexity at which self-awareness becomes possible. It seems reasonable to propose that this is the point at which the fetus changes from a potential to an actual human person. Embryological studies on the developing cerebral cortex suggest that this level of complexity is probably not achieved before the sixth month of development.[46]

Schenk makes evident his suggested moral policy as well: "The arguments against abortion have stressed the dignity and importance of each human person; and if a fetus has not yet become a human person, then it would seem that the other persons involved, and particularly the mother, should become of major importance." [47]

Malcolm Potts, denying that genetic individuality can be taken as a criterion of humanity (for that is a characteristic of, e.g., hydatidiform moles), contends that the whole reproductive process is a continuum, resistant to the drawing of sharp lines between the human and non-human. The high rate of spontaneous abortions in the early weeks of pregnancy, the relatively late development of a functioning nervous system and the whole range of biological differences between an embryo and a developed human being all militate against ascribing human status to an embryo.[48]

> An ethical system founded on biology [he writes] must begin by recognizing that reproduction is a continuum. It can be traced back to the time when the primordial germ cells are first recognizable in the yolk sac endoderm (at about the 20th day after fertilization in man) and it is still incomplete when a grandmother baby-sits for her daughter's children. . . . The simplest and most satisfactory ethic on abortion is to avoid ascribing any legal or theological status to the embryo during the first two weeks of development; beyond this time the embryo becomes increasingly important and at viability (28 weeks) the fetus should have the same rights as a newborn child.[49]

N. J. Berrill, while noting that "the history of the individual begins with the development of the egg following fertilization," contends that not until sometime between the sixth and eighth week of development— when all the organs are present in a rudimentary way—can one say that "the person in the womb is present." [50] Martin J. Buss, arguing that there are achieved levels of organization at different stages in gestation, suggests that the onset of brain waves provides a reasonable dividing line between the sheerly organic and the sociocultural level of organization.[51]

The most obvious strength of the "developmental school" is precisely that it assigns significant weight to the development process. By not resting the full weight of the "human" on genetic characteristics alone, it thus opens into a fuller understanding of the whole range of human attributes. It also has the advantage of taking account of the possibility that any given zygote may fail to develop in a viable direction; it presupposes that further development is necessary to determine whether in fact a human being does exist. Moreover, and perhaps most importantly, it makes a place for some important ethical distinctions. If our aim, in line with an affirmation of the sanctity of human life, is to recognize the dignity of such life, what exactly are we trying to protect? A distinction can be drawn among "life," "human life," "individual human life," "human being" and "person." Genetically, sperm and ova are "life" and, to a considerable extent, "human life." But only when the sperm and the egg are united in the one-cell zygote can one begin to speak of "individual human life." Those whom I have cited as representative of the developmental school are, for the most part, ready to grant that fertilization genetically establishes "individual human life." But they raise the question, both implicitly and explicitly, whether it is that form of human life which is really critical in establishing the basis for abortion decisions. If one believes it wrong to kill all forms of genetically individual human life, then a decision to use the time of conception as critical is coherent and consistent. But the developmental school is asking whether our real concern ought not to be the protection of "human beings" (which implies some state of development beyond the zygote stage) or of "persons" (which implies an even further state of development). Both Ehrensing and Schenk, for instance, deliberately choose to talk in terms of the development of a "person." Such a choice assumes that, for moral purposes, we ought to be comparatively more concerned with human persons than with "human life," particularly when we are looking for a way to resolve abortion dilemmas. And this *kind* of choice represents a moral-policy decision, just as does the decision to require some degree of development as a condition for the granting of full rights.

Ehrensing and Potts both allude to the ongoing discussion of the "moment of death" as providing some helpful guidelines here. Ehrensing notes that the growing acceptance of cessation of brain activity as a legitimate sign of death indicates that brain activity is a crucial index of the presence of a "person." [52] Neither Ehrensing nor Potts fully develops the point, but it is useful to do so. The problem of the "moment of death" has become increasingly important for a variety of reasons. The possibility of heart and other organ transplants means that greater precision is necessary both in defining "death" and in specifying criteria for establishing the occurrence of death, if these organs are to be made available without undue delay (which would result in their deterioration). Yet to make a precipitate decision that "death" has occurred, out of undue haste to obtain an organ, could, of course, endanger life. Increasingly, by means of more sophisticated devices, it is becoming possible to sustain many vital signs of human life, even though there may be doubt that truly human life persists. When is it morally legitimate to cease such artificial support? The answer to that question will depend in considerable part on what the criteria of "death" are to be (and, correlatively, what the criteria of "life" are to be). Biologically, death itself is a complex process, which proceeds by stages, with some biological activities ceasing before others—and the cause of death can have much to do with the particular sequence of cessation.

The desire to find consistent criteria of "death" has led to an increasing emphasis on the status of brain and nervous-system activities as crucial. An *ad hoc* committee of the Harvard Medical School observed the need for a shift of criteria:

> From ancient times down to the recent past it was clear that, when the respiration and heart stopped, the brain would die in a few minutes; so the obvious criterion of no heart beat as synonymous with death was sufficiently accurate. . . . This is no longer valid when modern resuscitative and supportive measures are used. These improved activities can now restore "life" as judged by the ancient standards of persistent respiration and continuing heartbeat. This can be the case even when there is not the remotest possibility of an individual recovering consciousness following massive brain damage.[53]

The committee itself proposed "irreversible coma" as "a new criterion for death." [54] Diagnosis of this state will rest on four points: unreceptivity and unresponsitivity to external stimuli, no movements or breathing, no reflexes and the confirmatory evidence of a flat electroencephalogram. By these signs, "the characteristics of a *permanently* nonfunctioning brain" can be determined.[55] A number of other recent articles have argued on much the same basis.[56]

What becomes clear in these discussions is that, in defining "death," something more is needed than a related definition of "life" which encompasses only a genetic norm. For, a definition of "death" presupposes an implicit correlative definition of "life." Potentialities are present in the latter which are not present in the former. Genetically, a body still circulating blood is in some sense a "human life," if genetic membership in the human species is the norm. Thus if the moral aim is to preserve whatever genetically counts as "individual human life," then an artificially sustained body meets the standard. But if the moral concern is with personhood—thus presupposing an electrically active brain—then, in the absence of brain activity, no "person" is present. As Richard A. Mc-Cormick, S.J., has noted:

> At a certain point along the way [to death] it is legitimate to say that "this person is dead" or "there is here no longer a human person." What is that point? Since organs function but it is the person who lives and dies, the determination of this point involves not merely clinical knowledge, but also a grasp of the meaning of person upon or against which a definition of the absence of personhood can be made.[57]

As I have suggested, however, the decision to talk in terms of "person" rather than "human life" represents a moral-policy decision, one with different consequences for decision-making in the former than in the latter case.

A question, then: If it is legitimate to be concerned with the existence of a "person"—rather than simply "human life"—in the instance of the end of life, is it equally legitimate in the instance of the beginning of life? Such a course has a number of advantages. First, in line with a point made in Chapter 9, our method of interpreting biological data becomes consistent from one problem to the next; a criterion of significant "human life"—i.e., personhood—which can be used to judge both the beginning and end of life is more valuable than one which is an *ad hoc* solution for one end of the time span only. This helps avoid the possibility that we will tailor our reading of the data to suit pre-determined goals. Second, by emphasizing the existence of a "person" rather than a "human life," the hazards of a sheer vitalism—giving a primacy to life as such, whatever its state—are to a considerable degree obviated. Our attention is then focused on that which—in line with a more precise moral policy—we are actually intent on preserving and protecting. If we decide, as our moral policy, that we should be comparatively more concerned with the lives of particular *persons* than with the general class "human life," we have available some norms for decision-making. Third, if we then center on some particularly decisive aspect of personhood—e.g., the existence of brain activity as the basis for all those characteristics which mark off a person from a nonperson—we then have at our disposal a biological norm to aid our decision-making. Fourth, if we grant that an abortion decision is by definition one in which we have to choose among human lives (granting even a zygote some form of "human life"), then we have a way of choosing which would allow us to weigh the different values of different human lives in a nonarbitrary way; we would, to be exact, compare these lives on the scale of "personhood," a scale more nuanced than that provided by a totally genetic norm of "humanity." If a genetic norm of what counts as a human-who-must-be-preserved-at-all-costs is inadequate for decision-making at the death end of the life-span, is it not reasonable to see it as inadequate at the life end? Were we not called upon to act at both ends of the life-span, to make decisions, then we might not feel compelled to adopt a more finely nuanced scale. But such decisions are pressed upon us; otherwise, there would be no need to discuss abortion at all and no need, other than the joy of speculation, of determining when death occurs. A developmental theory of the beginning of life (with its introduction of finer distinctions than the genetic) thus has much to commend it.

Yet it is not without its difficulties. One of these is that it does not give a wide range to the concept of "potentiality." A zygote has, genetically (dependent upon successful development), the potentiality to become a "person." In terms of actualized personhood—presupposing actualized rationality, interaction with others, affectivity, culture-making —an embryo, despite the presence of brain waves, has a long way to go. The brain waves of a fetus do not in themselves actualize the potentiality of personhood; they signify only a more developed stage of potentiality, with only the physiological *basis* of personhood being (primitively) actualized. An embryo which has not reached that stage has, however— statistically—a good chance of reaching that stage. In an individual's history, all the stages of development are necessary; he can't reach the brain-wave stage unless he has passed through the earlier stages, all the way back to the zygote.

An objection to the use of a common criterion of life for both nascent embryos and dying persons might be based on one important distinction. In the case of an "irreversible coma" (signaled by a flat EEG), it is not the coma as such but the irreversibility which is the critical consideration. For with the "death" of the brain (while the rest of the body remains "alive") comes the loss of all potentiality for personhood; its physiological basis is irretrievably lost. In the instance of a zygote or early embryo, however—even before the advent of brain waves—the potentiality for personhood exists. The potentiality for personhood of a zygote is thus obviously greater than that of a moribund adult, however much greater the morphological development of the latter.

Finally, there is the difficulty that, if one chooses to use a development criterion, there are any number of stages other than that of brain development that might be chosen. Implantation, gastrulation, the presence of all organs, completion of the brain structure, "quickening," viability, birth and so on have each been suggested as the dividing line by different commentators in recent history. Why choose one rather than

another? At each point, the being in question is still far more potentiality than actuality. If one concern, as Paul Ramsey has stressed,
should be the use of criteria which will not simultaneously (by logical
extension) also justify infanticide, then development norms pose some
dangers.[58] For a development norm requires some degree of actualization
of potentiality; it is an attempt to move beyond sheer potentiality as a
norm. But, it might be objected, once some actualization is required, it
is open to people to vary their norms on just how much actualization
should count. That so many different developmental points have been
suggested—all the way to birth and beyond—shows how slippery the
choice of a developmental norm can be. Moreover, many of the possible
developmental points—particularly the time of "viability"—are themselves variable, not necessarily exactly the same from one embryo
or fetus to the next and, in the instance of "viability," conditioned by
the state of medical technology.[59] Noonan's concern about any criterion
of the human based on varying potentialities should be recalled here as
well. That so *many* different stages of development have been suggested
as decisive only underscores his point about the hazards of a developmental theory. The thrust of Noonan's concern, I take it, is this: once
the legitimacy of a developmental norm has been admitted *in principle*
in a society, the way is logically open for a misuse of the norm or for a
shifting of the particular required point of development to serve debased
interests or self-interest. The course of safety is to rule out such norms
in the first place. To put the problem in my terms: could we risk a
moral policy which admits the legitimacy of developmental criteria,
even if such criteria do have a legitimate *biological* basis? Before trying
to answer that question, it will be necessary to look at the third important "school."

The Social-Consequences School

Two authors in particular ought to be mentioned here, Glanville
Williams and Garrett Hardin. Williams contends that the real question
is not when "life" begins but when "human life" begins. "Life" is continuous and thus admits of no simple line drawing: "Of course, the ovum
was alive before it was fertilized, and so was the sperm. Both cells,
before they met, had a life history of their own in the bodies of the
respective parents." [60] But "human life" is another matter, and Williams
denies that a "human being" can be said to exist at the moment of
conception. For one thing, there is, he says, no such thing as a "moment
of conception," since conception itself is a process which takes time.
Moreover, since "life" is present before conception as well as after, "the
argument that life begins with conception is just as unbiological as the

old notion that life begins sometime after conception." [61] For another thing, a number of social practices and attitudes indicates that neither zygotes nor embryos are treated as "human beings" (women for instance, do not mourn the loss of spontaneously aborted zygotes as they do the death of a child).[62] However, Williams does say that "the individual . . . has his origin in the fusion of two cells," but then immediately asks rhetorically, "Can it be said, with any degree of reality, that the week- or month-old embryo is an existing human being?" [63] Biologically, the conceptus during the very early stages of pregnancy is not a human being, but "only a potential human being." [64]

The key to his position, in the end, is that the decision to call the conceptus a "human being" (whatever the stage of development) is to be made on the basis of the social consequences of the decision:

> Do you wish to regard the microscopic fertilized ovum as a human being? You can if you want to, and if there were no social consequences of doing so, there might be no reason why you should not. But there are most important social arguments for *not* adopting this language. Moreover, if you look at actual beliefs and behaviour, you will find almost unanimous rejection of it.[65]

Williams' own inclination, he says, is to establish viability as the dividing line (which he thinks would be socially acceptable), with the beginning of "brain waves" as a possible compromise solution.[66]

Garrett Hardin poses the question as follows:

> What does the embryo receive from its parents that might be of value? There are only three possibilities: substance, energy, and information. As for the substance in the fertilized egg, it is not remarkable: merely the sort of thing one might find in any piece of meat, human or animal, and there is very little of it. . . . The energy content of this tiny amount of material is likewise negligible. . . . Clearly, the humanly significant thing that is contributed to the zygote by the parents is the information that 'tells' the fertilized egg how to develop into a human being.[67]

Hardin goes on to say, however, that this "information" is not in itself valuable either: "The zygote, which contains the complete specification of a valuable human being, is not a human being, and is almost valueless. . . . The early stages of an individual fetus have had very little human effort invested in them; they are of little worth." [68] That a zygote is genetically "unique" is "without moral significance. . . . The *expected* potential value of each aborted child is exactly that of the average child born. It is meaningless to say that humanity loses when a *particular* child is not born, or is not conceived." [69] The upshot of Hardin's argument is similar to that of Glanville Williams: "Whether the fetus is or is not a human being is a matter of definition, not fact; and we can define any way we wish. In terms of the human problem involved, it would be unwise to define the fetus as human (hence tactically unwise ever to refer to the fetus as an 'unborn child')." [70] Hardin concludes his argument on this point by observing that no state or nation requires that a dead fetus be treated the same way as a dead person, a point he takes as confirming his view "that we have never regarded it as a human being. Scientific analysis confirms what we have always known." [71]

The strength of Williams' and Hardin's approach is that it is aware of the necessity that developed, adult human beings must finally decide what is to be called "human"; the biological "facts" do not directly dictate a definition of the "human." Their argument also tries to take account of the apparently widespread fact that people do not feel the same way (in the sense of emotional response) about a zygote, embryo or fetus as they do about a born, living child. They are saying, in effect, that arguments which try to establish that a zygote (embryo, fetus) is a "human being" lack emotional credibility to most people. That most nations and states do not require death certificates for early-aborted fetuses or stipulate methods of disposal for them serves to confirm that legal practice reflects common conviction and common attitudes. Moreover, and most significantly, they are aware that our moral policy (though they do not use that term) does have an important and legitimate role in determining *how* we choose to define our terms and how we choose to draw lines; a sharp distinction cannot be drawn between our philosophical and our moral policy. Their contention (if I interpret them correctly) is that, given the conflict of values that arises in abortion dilemmas and the need to take account of the reasons why women want abortions, we should define the "human" in such a way that our chosen definition does not preclude abortion (by making abortion equivalent to the murder of a "human being").

Yet the arguments of this approach are open to serious objection. The most obvious difficulty is that, while both authors cite biological data and discuss them, their final position logically serves to make all biological data irrelevant. For if we can, indeed, define the human "any way we wish," being concerned only with the social consequences of our definition, then there seems no reason why we should feel obliged to consult biological data at all. If we can define "any way we wish," then this is to say no less than that any one definition (as formal definition) is biologically as good as any other; there are no biological norms or guideposts at all. This procedure, therefore, fails to meet the suggested test of any definition of the "human" laid down at the end of Chapter 10: taking biological evidence seriously, making room for such evidence in any definition. Moreover, it fails to meet another test: making a place for the concept of "potentiality" in any definition of the "human." This is particularly apparent in Williams' handling of his own argument. He concedes that, biologically, a fertilized ovum is a "potential human being," but allows that point to carry no weight at all in his argument. Yet inevitably, on his own terms, it must. For even at the time of viability, and surely at the time of the commencement of brain waves, the conceptus is still only a "potential human being": it has not begun to think, to relate to others interpersonally, to take part in the building of culture, and will not for many months to come. It does not meet any of the broadest conditions for being called a "human being." But it does meet the narrow conditions: genetically human individuality from the outset (fertilization) and, after the eighth week, morphologically human characteristics.

What seems evident, however, is that Williams and Hardin, in working from a moral policy designed to permit abortions, want a way of interpreting the data which does not stand in the way of a predetermined moral goal. The definition of "human," in short, is to be tailored to the desired moral policy, in this case the goal of making abortion available to those women who need or want it. But this method of definition, besides being *ad hoc* and thus potentially inconsistent with other definitions of "human" employed in other situations, has some serious, possibly dangerous social implications. If it is possible to define "human" any way we wish in the instance of prenatal life (according to our reading of social consequences), is there any logical reason why we should not be able to do the same thing with postnatal life? There is nothing in principle in the approach of Hardin and Williams to preclude this; indeed, the principle would seem to sanction it. In short, the enunciated principle of defining *as one wishes* provides no philosophical basis for distinguishing between abortion and infanticide. It becomes open, logically (for we are talking here in terms of an enunciated general principle), to define as nonhuman any being whom we find it socially useful to define as nonhuman. Society (or a power group in society) could, by use of this principle, define the chronically ill, the senile, the elderly as nonhuman and thus justify the taking of their life on grounds of the social good to be obtained.

Now, it should be pointed out that Hardin has vigorously rejected this kind of an implication:

> This is, of course, the well-known argument of "the camel's nose"—which says that if we let the camel put his nose in the tent, we will be unable to keep him from forcing his whole body inside. The argument is false. It is *always* possible to draw arbitrary lines *and enforce them*. We have speed laws for automobiles, and we enforce them. In the enforcement, the line becomes somewhat fuzzy—a policeman will not often make an arrest for infringing the law by one mile per hour—but indefinite escalation need not occur.[72]

But Hardin misses the philosophical point. And the point is that, when it is a question of human life, there is a need to act in ways that are *not* arbitrary. A fundamental basis of human freedom and security is that human beings will not be subject to arbitrary, shifting definitions of "human." We may, to be sure, have to draw lines in order to make decisions, but they ought to be drawn in a way consistent with principle; and the principle at stake in this instance is that of avoiding a drawing of lines by means of a norm which could too easily shift as people's desires or interpretation of social consequences shift. Had Hardin argued that while line-drawing is necessary, it must be guided by general principles concerning the way lines are drawn (and then gone on to sketch out those principles), his approach would be less open to criticism. But he provides no clue here, leaving the impression that he has no developed set of principles. Had he (and Williams, also) specified that one can define "human" in any way one wishes *in attempting to arrive at an abortion policy*, less criticism would be merited. That would be an *ad hoc* procedure, which I have contended is undesirable. But what has been done is more serious: a general norm for decision-making has been laid down (do as you wish in the light of social consequences) which can be used in all situations turning on the definition of "human." By logically severing that norm from biological evidence (as in fact has been done) and by resting the entire weight of decision-making and line-drawing on social consequences (which, of course, shift from time to time, as well as being difficult to determine in all their ramifications), mores, wishes and desires become king.

Moreover (though a lesser argument), if it has not seemed sensible for zoologists, anthropologists and psychologists to define "human" any way *they* wish (that is a voluntarist option they have not taken seriously), it is hard to see why it is any more sensible in the instance of prenatal life, much less human life in general. Hardin would have us take seriously actual practice concerning the definition of the "human." The point is a worthy one—but it is clearly not the practice of a variety of disciplines concerned with the "human" to define the term *as they wish;* on the contrary, they all look for some norms which transcend their individual preferences and desires, and, for that matter, those which may, happenstance, be expressed in the mores of particular societies.

Moral Policy: The Critical Issue

In discussing each "school," I have tried to indicate how a moral policy, implicit or explicit, has much to do with the way the data are interpreted. In terms of the data themselves, each school has some unique strengths and sensitivities just as (I believe) each has some liabilities. The genetic school has the asset of being supported by considerable genetic evidence. The developmental school has the asset of bringing to bear a more nuanced set of concepts concerning the different forms and stages of human life; and these concepts have considerable biological support. The social-consequences school has the asset of recognizing the necessity that human beings define the "human," underscoring the point that biological evidence as such does not establish definitions. Each school has its liabilities as well. The genetic school rests so much of its case on potentiality that the importance and role of development in producing a fully developed human being is not given sufficient attention. The developmental school does not seem to give sufficient weight to potentiality. The social-consequences school appears to make biological evidence irrelevant altogether. If it were only a question of taking account of biological evidence, then, there is something to be said for and against each position (which is not to imply that the assets and liabilities are on an equal level). They each represent *a way* of interpreting the data, and not an unreasonable way. Hence, in terms of the data, none can be excluded as a possibility and each has something to commend it (something which the other does not have). In this kind of situation, which is not that of one theory's being right (*totally* right) and the others, wrong (*totally* wrong), other considerations must determine which one ought to be employed. That is where a moral policy makes its appearance.

Each of the schools takes its stand not just on its theory of how the biological data ought best to be interpreted biologically, but also on the moral consequences of adopting one reading rather than another. The social-consequences school does this most explicitly, but the others do so as well. The genetic school believes it best to use the biologically legitimate norm of genetic individuality because that is a norm with good moral consequences: all forms of human life are respected, without discriminating among them on a scale of relative value. The developmental school believes it best to use the biologically legitimate norm of stages of development because that norm will allow some distinctions among human life, distinctions which are morally useful when choices have to be made between lives, as in abortion decisions. The social-consequences school holds that, since the biological evidence leaves us free to draw a line between the human and the nonhuman as we wish, we should avail ourselves of this freedom and define our terms in such a way as to serve our social needs. If it is the case, as I have argued, that the data as such do not entail either a philosophical or a moral conclusion (which will be the result of the anterior philosophical or moral theory we bring to bear on the data), then it is legitimate to allow our moral theory to help us decide how the data might illuminatingly be read. Indeed, this seems to become imperative when we are in the position of having to make an abortion decision; for we then need to interpret the data with a view toward acting, as the outcome of the decision-making process. Thus our moral policy becomes crucial at each stage of the decision-making process: choosing the relevant data, interpreting the data and then deciding how we should act in light of the data.

But there is a point at which our moral policy must be at least tempered by or consistent with the data. We must take account of the widest range of evidence. We must not read the evidence in one situation (e.g., abortion) in a way inconsistent with the manner in which we read it in other situations (e.g., moribund adult life). We must allow a place for the biological evidence in our moral theory; the aim is a biologically informed moral theory. Moreover, our moral policy must be further tempered by the precise moral problem at stake. It has to be a policy which will help us decide not only the generality of cases (the entire class of abortion cases) but specific cases as well. And it must enable us to do so in a way systematically cognizant of and sensitive to *all* the different values and needs that come into conflict in abortion cases. At the same time, our policy should not make use of general moral principles which could, as principles—if used in other than abortion contexts (which they well could be)—have dangerous consequences.

By these tests, which taken together might be called "biomoral," I believe the developmental school has the weightiest assets. It takes account of the biological evidence and allows this evidence to influence its moral policy. It allows the possibility of making abortion decisions sensitive to the greatest range of values at stake. It provides a way of weighing the comparative value of the lives at stake—a distasteful responsibility, but one which it recognizes must be borne. Its major liability, the hazards of introducing a developmental norm into decisions involving life, seems to me bearable, particularly since we are (in abortion cases) called upon to make a decision, to choose one life or the welfare of one life rather than another life. The moral policy of the genetic school is clearly the safest policy, if the kind of safety desired is to forestall all distinctions, and thus all weighing of the comparative value of lives. But by making its central focus the avoidance of all basis for discriminating among lives, it unfortunately lacks the capacity to do nuanced justice to the conflict of values in particular abortion cases. Its moral policy has the effect of lumping all abortion cases together and dealing with them as a class, thus losing sensitivity to particular cases. This places it at a serious disadvantage in relationship to the arguments of the developmental school. The weakest school is that of the social consequentialists, not only because of its failure to take serious account of the biological data—and thus of the need for a biologically grounded and supportable definition of the "human"—but also because its moral policy rests on an ill-defined and potentially very dangerous moral principle: define as you wish. (Yet to say this is not to erase the force of its arguments altogether, for all the schools use a social-consequence test, also.)

The making of points of this sort, however, forces again upon one the basic problem of a moral policy. In Chapter 9 I argued that a moral policy based upon the principle of the sanctity of life was one which implied the formation of rules which have a bias in favor of the protection and preservation of human life. The critical point in forming a moral policy is in deciding how this bias ought to be explicated and implemented in the formation of rules. The genetic school places the weight on the equal rights of all lives to protection from attack, whatever the stage of development of those lives; it represents a fully protectionist policy, giving even an embryo a status of full equality. The developmental school seeks an understanding of the bias which would allow—in cases of conflict—some nonarbitrary means of distinguishing among lives so that decisions can be made, decisions which would not automatically and always have to go against the pregnant woman. While the genetic and developmental school agree that individual human life begins at conception, they disagree about whether full value ought to be assigned at once to the life thus begun. By allowing development to count in the assigning of value, the developmental school thus argues for a moderate policy, one which allows flexibility when hard choices must be made but which does not, in the process, deny that even a zygote is individual human life. The social-consequences school weights the bias almost entirely in favor of the pregnant woman who needs or desires an abortion; her life and welfare are to have the preeminent respect. In its eyes, the social consequences of defining human life in such a way that value is immediately accorded a zygote or embryo are undesirable; better that human life be defined so that it is the woman's life and welfare which are paramount. The actualized life of the pregnant woman becomes far more important than the potential life of the conceptus; there is no real moral dilemma left.

In Chapter 9 (p. 341), I defined a moral policy as "any culturally, philosophically or religiously chosen, given or accepted way of devising, relating and ordering moral rules." I also tried to show that a decision to establish the principle of the sanctity of life as the key principle of a moral policy toward life, while pointing in a life-affirming and life-protecting direction, does not logically entail any set ordering of the rules designed to implement the policy. There must, minimally, be rules to cover each of the leading aspects of life (species-life, body-life, person-life, etc.), and each rule system (as well as every rule within each system) must be compatible with the other rules and rule systems. At the same time, though, the rule system must be flexible enough to allow a shift in the ordering of the rules and the primacy given one set of rules over another. While body-life (the right of the individual to existence) ordinarily takes primacy—as the foundation of all individual rights—circumstances may raise the question whether other kinds of life (e.g., species-life) may not have to be given a precedence (e.g., when the life of a whole group or the human species would be threatened by giving primacy to individual body-life).

Abortion decisions bring into play—at the present historical moment, at least—issues of body-life and person-life. It is an issue of body-life because it raises the question of the right to existence of unborn human life. It is an issue of person-life because it raises the question of the integrity and welfare of pregnant women. In some circumstances (overpopulation to a desperate degree) it could be an issue of species-life. Yet if abortion decisions bring into play all these issues, it is well to recall that, on a case-to-case basis, a decision is called for when a woman wants or believes she needs an abortion. The whole problem of abortion "indications" arises because of these desires or needs. And the whole problem of devising a legal policy arises because in every society there exist women who want or believe they need abortion. The legal question thus becomes whether these desires or needs should be recognized and under what conditions.

Now, it has been my contention throughout this book that both the problem of an "indications policy" and that of a "legal policy" turn, in the end, on the deeper problem of a "moral policy." While it will be necessary later to discuss the necessary distinction between law and morals, there is always some practical relationship between them; moral attitudes and moral positions will have a considerable influence on what the legal problems are taken to be and on possible legal solutions. It is surely no accident that those who believe abortion to be a form of murder, the taking of an innocent human life, are prone to favor restrictive laws; and no accident that those who believe abortion something less than murder tend to favor more permissive laws. Similarly, one's moral policy will to a considerable extent determine one's response to abortion "indications." If one's moral policy is to give all benefit of doubt to the preservation of life (especially body-life)—to refuse on principle to distinguish among lives or to take account of developed actualities— then almost all of the commonly proposed indications will be logically excludable. For with the exception of a pregnancy which poses a direct threat to the physical life of the mother (exceedingly rare)—a strict "medical" indication—none of the other proposed or commonly employed indications posit the existence of one human life in conflict with the existence of another human life. Instead, the conflict is between the life (and specifically the body-life) of the conceptus and the welfare (or person-life) of the pregnant woman. A moral policy designed to preserve *all* human life would thus in principle not be open to any indication other than (perhaps) a strict medical indication; the primacy given the right to body-life places all other considerations on a lower level. Strictly speaking, then, once it is determined (or, more precisely, decided) that the life of the conceptus at whatever the stage of development is human life (or ought to be treated as such) and determined that there is no direct threat to the life of the woman, the problem is solved: no abortion. Under this kind of moral policy, indications other than "medical" become irrelevant (however much sympathy and compassion they may evoke); that is, they have no real bearing on the issue conceived to be at stake: the overriding right of the conceptus to life, a right so primary and powerful as to put all other considerations in the shade.

Indeed, the logic of the genetic school is such that no consideration of "indications" other than the strictly medical is at all necessary. For the only real question at stake for that school is whether the conceptus is to be counted as human life; if the answer is yes, the moral policy of the genetic school renders unnecessary the asking of any further questions (i.e., it becomes beside the point to inquire into a woman's psychological, socioeconomic or legal state, nor is is germane to know whether the fetus itself may be suffering from some form of defect). Since the genetic school has decided that individual human life is present from conception (or at least from implantation) and since it wants to further a moral policy designed to protect all forms of body-life, its systematic refusal to recognize any "indications" other than perhaps the medical represents a consistent working out of the policy. It is likewise consistent when it supports restrictive laws in principle (which it may not always, on legal, political or prudential grounds, do in practice).

I am now in a position to begin completing the "bracketing" process mentioned at the beginning of Chapter 10. By that I meant, not the coming to specific positive solutions, but the exclusion of unacceptable conclusions. While I believe that the moral policies of all the "schools" cited have their strengths (strengths not enjoyed by the others), both the genetic and the social-consequences school seem to me less persuasive than the developmental school, especially in light of all the norms which I have argued should be met by a good moral policy. I use the phrase "less persuasive" deliberately, to indicate that it is a matter of relative assets and liabilities rather than a clear "hurrah" for the developmental school; it is only to say that the latter comes through the least scathed (but not unscathed).

An element in favor of the developmental school is that, on the one hand, it is sufficiently sensitive to the genetic data to accord the status of "human life" even to a zygote. On the other hand, it is sufficiently sensitive to a wide range of values to recognize the possibility of real dilemmas even when they are not so severe as to pit a life against a life. By contrast, the genetic school, in its eagerness to preclude all forms of discriminating judgments, renders itself systematically deaf to the claims of values other than that of the right to life (body-life). To repeat a question put to Paul Ramsey by James M. Gustafson in a somewhat different context (see Chapter 9, p. 311): "What other things does God value in addition to physical life? E.g., qualitative aspects of life, etc." To put this question in nontheistic terms: Granted that physical life, even the life of the zygote, ought to be respected, what else ought to be respected—or what other values also ought to enter into abortion decisions?

The thrust of my argument about the relationship between the principle of the sanctity of life and the various rules implied by that principle was that the principle should not be taken to entail a specific ordering of the rules. But the genetic school does, in effect, posit an entailment: the sanctity of life requires, inflexibly and invariably, that the rule prescribing respect for body-life be given a primacy over all other rules, all other values. But if there are other rules subsumed under the principle of the sanctity of life and if these rules are implied by the principle as well (the rules concerning person-life, for instance), then any satisfactory ordering of the rules must have a place for the values represented by these rules as well. In the instance of the genetic school, the values are not represented (the issue of woman's rights is simply not worried about at all) and the other rules do not come into play. Put another way, by the logic of the genetic school the outcome of any abortion dilemma is *de jure* decided in advance: a pregnant woman is, by definition, a woman carrying human life within her; she may not, therefore, have an abortion.

The social-consequences school suffers from what amounts to a very similar kind of weakness. By making the meaning of "human" a matter of social utility and, in the instance of abortion, denying the title to any early conceptus (and it is not clear that one must say "early"), it also removes any need to make judgments according to individual cases, any need to see different values in conflict with each other. Specifically, by weighting the conflict of values so heavily in favor of the pregnant woman, it succeeds in removing almost all value from the conceptus; thus any real moral dilemma is resolved in advance. The moral problem is defined out of existence in advance by defining "human" in such a way that a conceptus is denied that attribute. Far from seeking to extend the range of protection to human life, it deliberately seeks to narrow it. The consequences for an "indications policy" are evident. Either any "indication" (i.e., any reason) will do however remote any real danger, or no "indications" (i.e., no reasons) at all need be required. If a conceptus has been defined out of the class of "human," then no reason at all need be given for a desire to have an abortion; the issue is removed from the moral sphere altogether. Moreover, no place is left for attributing any value to potential human life; "human" is defined in terms of achieved potentialities.

My own direction is now beginning to emerge, and it will be the task of the fourth and final section to make it more explicit.

NOTES

1. For this sketch, I am drawing upon three books: Frank D. Allan, *Essentials of Human Embryology* (New York: Oxford University Press, 1960); Bradley M. Patten, *Foundations of Embryology* (2nd ed.; New York: McGraw-Hill, 1964); and E. Blechschmidt, *The Stages of Human Development Before Birth* (Philadelphia: W. B. Saunders Co., 1961).

2. B. I. Balinsky, *An Introduction to Embryology* (2nd ed.; Philadelphia: W. B. Saunders Co., 1965), p. 277; *cf.* Frank D. Allan, *op. cit.,* p. 26.

3. Theodosius Dobzhansky, *Heredity and the Nature of Man* (New York: Signet Science Library, 1966), p. 37; *cf.* Royston Clowes, *The Structure of Life* (Baltimore: Penguin Books, 1967), p. 217.

4. Dobzhansky, *op. cit.,* p. 38.

5. *Ibid,* p. 55.

6. *Ibid.,* p. 57.

7. Edmund W. Sinnott, L. C. Dunn, T. Dobzhansky, *Principles of Genetics* (5th ed.; New York: McGraw-Hill, 1958), p. 18; Curt Stern, *Principles of Human Genetics* (2nd ed.; San Francisco: W. H. Freeman Co., 1960), p. 38; T. Dobzhansky, *Heredity and the Nature of Man, op. cit.,* pp. 57ff.

8. Dobzhansky, *Heredity and the Nature of Man, op. cit.,* p. 59.

9. Frederick J. Gottlieb, *Developmental Genetics* (New York: Reinhold Publishing Corp., 1966), p. 4.

10. James D. Ebert, *Interacting Systems in Development* (New York: Holt, Rinehart and Winston, 1965), p. 8.

11. *Ibid.; cf.* C. H. Waddington, *The Nature of Life* (London: George Allen and Unwin, 1963), p. 51.

12. Gottlieb, *op. cit.,* p. 2.

13. Ebert, *op. cit.,* p. 7.

14. John Tyler Bonner, *The Ideas of Biology* (New York: Harper Torchbooks, 1964), p. 7.

15. Gottlieb, *op. cit.,* p. 17.

16. *Ibid.,* p. 108.

17. *Ibid.,* p. 112.

18. *Ibid.;* see Clowes, *op. cit.,* p. 269, for a more complex version of this analogy.

19. John T. Noonan, Jr., "Abortion and the Catholic Church: A Summary History," *Natural Law Forum,* 12 (1967), p. 126. Others who can be included in the genetic school are M. O. Vincent, "Psychiatric Indications for Therapeutic Abortion and Sterilization," in W. O. Spitzer and C. L. Saylor (eds.), *Birth Control and the Christian* (Wheaton, Illinois: Tyndale House, 1969), p. 197, and David Granfield, *The Abortion Decision* (New York: Doubleday, 1969), pp. 15–41.

20. Statement by John T. Noonan, Jr., to the New York State Legislature (during debate on a bill to reform the state's abortion law), Spring 1968, p. 1.

21. Noonan, "Abortion and the Catholic Church . . . ," *op. cit.,* pp. 128–29.

22. *Ibid.,* p. 129.

23. *Ibid.,* p. 126.

24. Paul Ramsey, "The Morality of Abortion," in *Life or Death: Ethics and Options* (Seattle: University of Washington Press, 1968), pp. 61–62.

25. *Ibid.,* p. 69.

26. *Ibid.,* p. 63.

27. *Ibid.*
28. André Hellegers, "A Look at Abortion," *The National Catholic Reporter* (March 1, 1967), p. 4.
29. *Ibid.*
30. Ebert, *op. cit.,* p. 12.
31. Stern, *op. cit.,* p. 38.
32. Patten, *op. cit.,* p. 3.
33. Ashley Montagu, *Life Before Birth* (New York: New American Library, 1964), p. ix.
34. Montagu's comment on this is a perfect illustration of how there can be agreement on the facts and disagreement about their implications: "By this [his statement] I meant that from the moment of conception the organism thus brought into being possesses all the potentialities for humanity in its genes, and for that reason must be considered human . . . but the embryo, fetus and newborn of the human species, in point of fact, do not really become functionally human until humanized in the human socialization process. . . . I have always supported and will continue to support the legalization of abortion" (letter to *The New York Times,* March 3, 1967).
35. Noonan, "Abortion and the Catholic Church . . . ," *op cit.,* p. 129.
36. There appears to be considerable uncertainty on the percentage likely to abort spontaneously. Garrett Hardin ("Blueprints, DNA, and Abortion: A Scientific Analysis," *Medical Opinion and Review,* 3 [February 1967], p. 85) cites the research of Drs. Hertig, Rock and Adams, which estimated that at least 38 percent of all zygotes are spontaneously aborted. Leslie Corsa, however ("Abortion—A World View," in Alan F. Guttmacher [ed.] *The Case for Legalized Abortion Now* [Berkeley: Diablo Press, 1967], p. 126), employs a figure of 20 percent. George Wald ("Determinacy, Individuality, and the Problem of Free Will," in John R. Platt [ed.], *New Views on the Nature of Man* [Chicago: University of Chicago Press, 1965], p. 30) cites a figure of 15 percent, while Langdon Parsons and Sheldon C. Sommers (*Gynecology* [Philadelphia: W. B. Saunders Co., 1962], p. 409) use a figure of 10 percent, and Gregory G. Pincus a figure of 20 percent (*The Control of Fertility* [New York: Academic Press, 1965], p. 197). *Cf.* Parsons and Sommers (*op. cit.,* p. 409), who estimate the following incidences in the outcome of gestation: hydatidiform mole, 1:2,000; ectopic pregnancy, 1:300; spontaneous abortion, 1:10; normal gestation, 9:10. The incidence of hydatidiform mole, though slight, raises the question of whether one can say that a fertilized ovum has the potentiality of becoming a hydatidiform mole. This is the contention of Rudolph Ehrensing ("The IUD: How It Works: Is It Moral?" reprint from *The National Catholic Reporter* [April 20–27, 1966], p. 6). However, it is not clear from the medical literature whether one should think of a hydatidiform mole as a defective ovum or a defective placenta. Strictly taken, a hydatidiform mole is a mole of the chorionic villi. Some researchers speak of the mole as the cause of the death of the fetus (as a result of a lack of vascularization of the chorionic villi), thus implying a distinction between a fetus and a hydatidiform mole (Parsons and Sommers, *op. cit.,* p. 408; C. J. Louis and P. G. Castran, "Some Aspects of Hydatidiform Mole and Choriocarcinoma," *Medical Journal of Australia,* 1 [February 26, 1966], p. 334; Hugh S. Grady, "Hydatidiform Mole and Choriocarcinoma," *Annals New York Academy of Sciences,* 85 [January 9, 1959], p. 565). Others, though, speak of the mole as a "deranged ovum" (James A. Coraceden and Landrum M. Shettles, "Hydatidiform Mole and Choriocarcinoma," *Bulletin of the Sloane Hospital for Women,* 5 [Summer 1959], p. 41). Perhaps the difference in these formulations results from the difficulty, stressed by some researchers, in pinpointing the origin of hydatidiform moles, or from a difference among medical writers in referring to the chorionic villi as part of the embryo. In any case, it does not seem possible to assert, with absolute confidence, that a fertilized egg could develop into a hydatidiform mole. The commonest way of speaking

in the medical literature implies a distinction between a hydatidiform mole and an embryo.

37. Wald, *op. cit.*, p. 30.
38. Personal communication to the author.
39. Granfield, *op. cit.* p. 31.
40. Thomas L. Hayes, "A Biological View," *Commonweal*, 85 (March 17, 1967), pp. 677–78.
41. *Ibid.*, p. 678.
42. *Ibid.*, p. 679.
43. Rudolph Ehrensing, "When Is It Really Abortion?," *The National Catholic Reporter* (May 25, 1966), p. 4.
44. *Ibid.*
45. *Ibid.*
46. Roy U. Schenk, "Let's Think About Abortion," *The Catholic World*, 207 (April 1968), p. 16.
47. *Ibid.*, p. 17.
48. Malcolm Potts, "The Problem of Abortion," in F. J. Ebeling (ed.), *Biology and Ethics* (New York: Academic Press, 1969), p. 77ff.
49. *Ibid.*, p. 75.
50. N. J. Berrill, *The Person in the Womb* (New York: Dodd, Mead & Co., 1968), p. 46.
51. Martin J. Buss, "The Beginning of Human Life as an Ethical Problem," *The Journal of Religion*, (July 1967), pp. 249–50.
52. Ehrensing, *op. cit.*, p. 4; *cf.* Potts, *op. cit.*, p. 79.
53. "A Definition of Irreversible Coma," *Journal of the American Medical Association*, 205 (August 5, 1968), p. 339.
54. *Ibid.*, p. 337.
55. *Ibid.*
56. "Moment of Death, Medico-Legal," *British Medical Journal*, 394 (August 10, 1963), p. 5353; M. Martin Halley and William F. Harvey, "Medical vs. Legal Definitions of Death," *Journal of the American Medical Association*, 204 (May 6, 1968), pp. 423–25; Hannibal Hamlin, "Life or Death by EEG," *Journal of the American Medical Association*, 190 (October 12, 1964), pp. 112–14; V. A. Negovsky, "Some Physiopathologic Regularities in the Process of Dying and Resuscitation," *Circulation*, 23 (March 1961), pp. 452–57; *Decisions About Life and Death* (London: Church Assembly Board for Social Responsibility, 1965), especially pp. 9–12; "The Medical, Moral, and Legal Implications of Recent Medical Advances (A Symposium)," *Villanova Law Review*, 13 (Summer 1968), especially the articles by Elkinton, Berman, and Wassmer; Paul Ramsey has dealt acutely with the subject in "On Updating Procedures for Stating That a Man Has Died," unpublished paper, Lyman Beecher Lectures, Yale University, April 14–17, 1969.
57. Richard A. McCormick, S.J., "Notes on Moral Theology," *Theological Studies*, 29 (December, 1968), pp. 699–700.
58. See, for instance, Joshua Lederberg's way of using a development norm, which leads him to say that "an operationally useful point of divergence of the developing organism would be at approximately the first year of life" in "A Geneticist Looks at Contraception and Abortion," *Annals of Internal Medicine*, 67 (September 1967), Supplement 3, p. 26; for a critique of Lederberg's argument, see Paul Ramsey, "Shall We Clone a Man," paper given at the Institute of Religion, Houston, Texas, March 25, 1968, pp. 45ff.
59. Julian Pleasants, "A Morality of Consequences," *Commonweal*, 86 (June 30, 1967), p. 413.
60. Glanville Williams, "The Legalization of Medical Abortion," *The Eugenics Review*, 56 (April 1964), p. 20.
61. *Ibid.*, p. 21.
62. See particularly Ariès' quote, Chapter 9, note 27.
63. Glanville Williams, *The Sanctity of Life and the Criminal Law* (London: Faber and Faber, 1958), p. 208.

64. Williams, "The Legalization of Medical Abortion," *op. cit.*, p. 21.
65. *Ibid.*
66. Williams, *The Sanctity of Life and the Criminal Law, op. cit.*, pp. 209–10; it must be noted, however, that Williams at the time believed that such waves are not present until the seventh month, whereas more recent evidence would place them as first occurring around the seventh or eighth *week*. See Hamlin, *op. cit.*, p. 113.
67. Garrett Hardin, "Abortion—Or Compulsory Pregnancy?" *Journal of Marriage and the Family*, 30 (May 1968), p. 250; this argument was also presented in an earlier article by Hardin, "Blueprints, DNA, and Abortion . . . ," *op. cit.*, pp. 74–85.
68. Hardin, "Abortion—Or Compulsory Pregnancy?" *op. cit.*, p. 250.
69. *Ibid.*
70. *Ibid.*, pp. 250–51.
71. *Ibid.*, p. 251.
72. Garrett Hardin, "Semantic Aspects of Abortion," *ETC.*, 24 (September 1967), p. 264.

SECTION IV

Implementing a
Moral Policy

Introduction

IN THE FIRST THREE sections of this book, the aim was to locate and analyze some of the leading issues related to the problem of abortion. This meant, in great part, the sorting out of the different purposes, assumptions and consequences which are involved in the formulation of "policy": indications policy, legal policy and moral policy. The premise of Sections I and II was that a "moral policy" will inevitably come into play in evaluating abortion indications and abortion laws. Section III then examined the problem of establishing a moral policy, coming in the process to a number of conclusions. In Chapter 11, I argued that the "developmental school" of opinion on the problem of "the beginning of human life" seemed to me to offer the most persuasive arguments, particularly in terms of the scope of considerations it tried to bring into balance. However, I also noted that none of the other schools could be dismissed out of hand; each has its particular assets.

My expression of a preference for the developmental option signaled, in an explicit way, the general direction of my thinking: toward a middle position, one which avoids some of the liabilities of more stark options and yet which can take account of the valid points they make. It now remains to spell out the details of the foreshadowed "middle" position, by which I mean a position that (*a*) seeks to avoid two one-dimensional moral solutions to the problem, i.e., a denial of abortion under all but the most unusual circumstances or an acceptance of abortion under all but the most unusual circumstances; and (*b*) seeks to establish the moral seriousness of the problem and to spell out some possible legal solutions. My own thinking about abortion as a moral problem was influenced to a considerable degree by a dissatisfaction with the two most polarized views available: the traditional Christian position, exemplified particularly in Roman Catholic theology, and the abortion-on-demand (request) position. As will become clear, it is not the legal policy urged by the latter group which seems to me unsatisfactory, but rather the "moral policy" which underlies some attempts to justify ethically abortion on request.

Both the Roman Catholic position and the abortion-on-request position (particularly in its moral aspect) require some detailed criticism, and that is the purpose of Chapters 12 and 13. In each position, however, there seem to me important elements worth preserving in any attempt to formulate a moderate or middle way. I will indicate what these seem to be. The method thus chosen amounts to undertaking a process of elimination, to see, in the end, what is worth preserving and developing as key ingredients in a (possibly) acceptable abortion policy, both individually and socially. Chapter 14 will try to undertake this constructive task.

CHAPTER 12

The Roman Catholic Position

THE THESIS OF THIS CHAPTER is that the present Roman Catholic teaching on abortion, while commendable in its emphasis on the preservation and protection of human life, is insufficiently nuanced to admit a full integration of all the values at stake in abortion decisions. Like the abortion-on-request position (to be treated in the next chapter), it can be called one-dimensional. That the dimension it chooses to stake itself upon is critically important—the respect due all forms of human life—does not wholly redeem the weakness of a one-dimensional approach. Put in its simplest terms, the Roman Catholic position does not genuinely allow (with the exception of a few clearly medical dilemmas) consideration of the woman's welfare or that of her family to have an integral place in the making of abortion decisions. The welfare of the conceptus takes full precedence (though, as we shall see, this interpretation of the teaching is denied), allowing little more than sympathy for the woman; and it is a sympathy which cannot be translated into one possible action—induced abortion—which might meet her needs. This is not to imply that the sympathy is feigned or tepid. It could be and often is profound and deep, no less strong in its emotional content than in those who, exclusively because of their sympathy, would allow the abortion on that ground.

Critically at stake is the way in which Roman Catholic theology has intellectually conceived and solved the problem. If it is deficient, it is deficient primarily at that level. My objection to the teaching will, in any case, center on Catholic moral theory; for if Catholic teaching on abortion is one-dimensional, it is because its theory is one-dimensional, not because individual Catholics necessarily are. Specifically, it will be the logic of the Catholic teaching which will concern me: the way in which it presently envisions and structures the problem and its solution.

Historical Summary

It is beyond the scope and intent of this chapter to present anything approaching a full history of Roman Catholic teaching on abortion. This has, in any case, been done by others, from whose writings I will here be drawing, presenting the elements in that history which are important to appreciate the structure of the Catholic position.[1]

The historical source of the Catholic teaching on abortion was the conviction of the early Christian community that abortion is incompatible with and forbidden by the fundamental Christian norm of love, a norm which forbade the taking of life. Though the New Testament itself contains no specific reference to abortion (other than a cryptic condemnation of "medicine" in St. Paul's Epistle to the Galatians [5:20]), it appears that the early Christian community took such a condemnation to be implicit in the ethics of Jesus. In the *Didache*, a very early and authoritative source of Christian law (*c.* 80 A.D.), abortion was treated as a grievous sin and ranked in importance with those acts forbidden by the Ten Commandments. Abortion is treated with equal stringency in the *Epistle of Barnabas* (*c.* 138), which said, quite flatly, "You shall not slay the child by abortions." Thereafter, with increasing frequency and in reaction to the more permissive pagan and Roman attitudes, the condemnations of abortion were to proliferate, finding sharp expression in the writings of the Church Fathers, both Eastern and Western. In his *Pedagogus*, Clement of Alexandria (*c.* 150–*c.* 215) attacked abortion on the dual ground that it destroyed what God had created and, in the destruction of the fetus, was an offense to a necessary love of neighbor. Athenagoras, writing to Marcus Aurelius in 177, said that "all who use abortifacients are homicides and will account to God for their abortion as for the killing of men." Clement of Alexandria used equally strong language in 215, stating that abortions "destroy utterly the embryo and, with it, the love of man." In 240, Tertullian wrote that "for us, indeed, as homicide is forbidden, it is not lawful to destroy what is conceived in the womb while the blood is still being formed into a man."

By the fifth century, while the condemnation of abortion continued without diminishment, distinctions were on occasion being drawn between abortion and homicide. Both were adjudged grave sins, but not necessarily exactly the same sin or to be subject to the same ecclesiastical penalty. While theologians of the Eastern Church were apparently the first explicitly to draw a distinction between the "formed" (ensouled) and the "unformed" fetus, there quickly developed a strong tradition against using the distinction to differentiate homicide and abortion. St.

Basil the Great, in his *Three Canonical Letters* (374–375), set the stage for this refusal to make any moral distinctions by saying, "A woman who deliberately destroys a fetus is answerable for murder. And any fine distinction as to its being completely formed or unformed is not admissible among us." In the Latin Church, however, the distinction took hold, particularly in the writings of St. Jerome and St. Augustine, both of whom were to prove pivotal figures in later Christian ethics. There appears, however, no reason to doubt Noonan's judgment:

> By 450 the teaching on abortion East and West had been set out for four centuries with clarity and substantial consistency. There was a distinction accepted by some as to the unformed embryo, some consequent variation in the analysis of the sin, and local differences in the penance necessary to expiate it. . . . The culture had accepted abortion. The Christians, men of the Greco-Roman world and the Gospel, condemned it. . . . The Christian rule was certain.[2]

The importance of the distinction between the "formed" and the "unformed" fetus, Aristotelian in origin, has been both overstressed and understressed. It has been perhaps overstressed by those (both Catholic and non-Catholic) who believe it affords a basis in Catholic theology (potential or actual) for the excusing of early abortions or a considerable reduction in the gravity of the wrong committed. This mistake rests, as Noonan has shown, on a failure to make the necessary distinction between moral law (as conceived in the Catholic tradition) and canonical penalty. That the latter has at times during the history of the Church treated abortion as something less than homicide in the apportioning of ecclesiastical punishment provides no warrant for the conclusion that it was ever treated as less than a grave moral wrong. Yet the distinction has also been perhaps understressed by those (again, Catholic and non-Catholic) who believe that the Catholic tradition has uniformly refused to take any account of the woman's circumstance and uniformly refused to see abortion as anything but homicide.

While a number of Church councils unequivocally condemned abortion between the fifth and twelfth century, the distinction between a "formed" and "unformed" fetus had made its mark. With the publication in 1140 of Gratian's *Decretum*, the first fully systematic attempt to compile ecclesiastical legislation, the distinction was firmly established and operative. In answer to the question of whether those who procure abortions are homicides, Gratian said: "He is not a murderer who brings about abortion before the soul is in the body." Gratian's position was sustained in ensuing commentaries on the *Decretum*. With the *Decretals* of Pope Gregory IX in 1234, formally legislating for the whole Church, the distinction was sustained, though in an ambiguous fashion. The *Decretals* included both the canon *Sicut Ex*, which contained Gratian's use of the distinction, but also another canon, *Si Aliquis*, dating from the tenth century, which had specified that the penalty for homicide was to be applied to contraception and abortion, regardless in the latter case of the stage of fetal development. The implicit contradiction between the two canons was soon taken, by later commentators on the *Decretals*, to mean that, while all abortion is murder and thus gravely sinful, the canonical penalties (especially for clerics involved in abortions) should vary according to the stage of fetal life.

Thereafter, however, the existence of canonical texts legitimating the distinction between the formed and unformed fetus (e.g., *Sicut Ex*) provided the basis for a number of casuistical attempts from the fifteenth through the eighteenth century to justify abortion when it seemed necessary to save the life of the woman. This attempt was strengthened by Thomas Aquinas' earlier efforts to distinguish between the lawful and the unlawful killing of a man. While Aquinas held that it is never lawful to kill the innocent, his acceptance of capital punishment (even, apparently, in the case of a repentant criminal) and of many acts of warfare which would result in the killing of innocents seemed in fact to open the way for the killing of innocents in some circumstances. Thus Noonan could write, after surveying these developments:

> The monks had transmitted the apostolic and patristic prohibition of abortion. The canon law set it out as a universal requirement of Christian behavior. The theologians explored the relation of the law to the theory of ensoulment, but on one basis or another condemned abortion at any point in the existence of the fetus. The prohibition was still absolute. But the basis for weighing the life of the embryo against other values had been laid, and in the next period of development a balance was to be sought.[3]

That period, 1450–1750, saw a number of attempts to strike a balance between the life of the early conceptus and the life of the woman. The Jesuit Thomas Sanchez (1550–1610), for instance, argued that, while there was an absolute prohibition of contraception, there were exceptions to the prohibition of abortion. In particular, if the fetus was not ensouled and the woman would die without an abortion, then abortion was "more probably" lawful, the fetus in this instance being an invader and attacker. The justification was that the intention of the woman was to save her own life, an act which had the double effect of taking the life of the fetus and preserving the life of the woman. But it was the intention of the woman, rather than the *de facto* end result of the act— the killing of the fetus—which was, in Sanchez's view, decisive. As long as there was no "direct intention" to kill, the act could be lawful, a conclusion sustained by the Belgian Jesuit Leonard Lessius and later by St. Alphonsus Liguori. At the same time, direct means for effecting the abortion were excluded; there had also to be an immediate threat to the woman's life.

With these reservations stated, therapeutic abortion to save the mother from immediate danger was permitted; the intention to save her own life must predominate; only some means were permitted. The balance struck by the casuists and now set out by St. Alphonsus treated the embryo's life as less than absolute, but only the value of the mother's life was given greater weight.[4]

However, while there was a tendency among moral theologians to find exceptions to an absolute prohibition of abortion, the papacy moved in a more stringent direction. Pope Sixtus V, in his bull *Effraenatam* (1588), stated that the same penalties, canonical and secular, should apply to abortion as to homicide, regardless of the age of the fetus; no exceptions were cited. In 1591, though, Pope Gregory XVI rescinded all of the penalties specified in *Effraenatam* with the exception of those which had applied to an ensouled fetus. In 1679, Pope Innocent XI's Holy Office condemned as scandalous and in practice dangerous two propositions:

34. It is lawful to procure abortion before ensoulment of the fetus lest a girl, detected as pregnant, be killed or defamed. 35. It seems probable that the fetus (as long as it is in the uterus) lacks a rational soul and begins first to have one when it is born; and consequently it must be said that no abortion is homicide.[5]

This condemnation, however, was not taken as necessarily precluding altogether the line of exception- and balance-seeking which the earlier casuists had explored; it only set some limits to the exploration.

Since the middle of the eighteenth century, however, the papal trend has been toward an increasingly more stringent prohibition of abortion, thus eclipsing the work of the interim casuists and their quest for a balance. Stimulated by a spread of abortion in the nineteenth and early twentieth century, by a gradual scientific rejection of the Aristotelian analysis of gestation (with its 40- to 80-day theory of the development of a rational from a vegetable soul), and by a parallel decline in its theological respectability, the papacy took the lead in condemning abortion at all stages, denying any exceptions and erasing the distinction between a formed (ensouled) and unformed fetus. Pope Pius IX, in his 1869 Constitution *Apostolicae Sedis*, made a sharp change in Church law by eliminating any distinction between a formed and unformed fetus in meting out the penalty of excommunication for abortion. With the promulgation of the new Code of Canon Law in 1917, the whole of the Code was rewritten to remove reference to the lingering 40- to 80-day distinction used in other parts of the earlier Code. The belief that the woman herself was not included in the stipulation of excommunication was specifically scotched by her inclusion among those to be excommunicated. A series of responses from the Holy Office between 1884 and 1902, increasingly decisive in their elimination of exceptions, further signaled the trend.

These shifts culminated in a series of strong, uncompromising twentieth-century papal statements, which have continued down to the present. In his encyclical *Casti Connubii* (1930), Pope Pius XI set the tone and the thrust:

> We must also allude to another very serious crime, Venerable Brethren: that which attacks the life of the offspring while it is yet hidden in the womb of its mother. Some hold this to be permissible, and a matter to be left to the free choice of the mother or father; others hold it to be wrong only in the absence of very grave reasons, or what are called "indications," of the medical, social, or eugenic order. . . . As for the "medical and therapeutic indications," we have already said, Venerable Brethren, how deeply we feel for the mother whose fulfillment of her natural duty involves her in grave danger to health and even to life itself. But can any reason ever avail to excuse the direct killing of the innocent? For this is what is at stake. The infliction of death whether upon mother or upon child is against the commandment of God and the voice of nature: "Thou shalt not kill." The lives of both are equally sacred and no one, not even public authority, can ever have the right to destroy them. It is absurd to invoke against innocent human beings the right of the State to inflict capital punishment, for this is valid only against the guilty. Nor is there any question here of the right of self-defense, even to the shedding of blood, against an unjust assailant, for none could describe as an unjust assailant an innocent child. Nor, finally, does there exist any so-called right of extreme necessity which could extend to the direct killing of an innocent human being.[6]

Pope Pius XII, in a series of allocutions, frequently spoke on the subject. In 1944 he said to the Italian Medical-Biological Union of St. Luke:

> So long as a man commits no crime, his life is untouchable, and therefore every action which tends directly toward its destruction is illicit . . . whether this destruction be the goal intended or only a means to an end, whether this life be embryonic, or in full flower, or already approaching its term. Only God is Lord of the Life of a man who is not guilty of a crime punishable with death.[7]

In 1951, in an allocution to midwives he said that "now even the child, even the unborn child, is a human being in the same degree and by the same title as its mother. Moreover, every human being, even the child in its mother's womb, receives its right to life directly from God, not from its parents, nor from any human society or authority." [8] And in the same year, in an allocution to the Association of Large Families, he said (after making points similar to those above):

> Never and in no case has the Church taught that the life of the child must be preferred to that of the mother. It is erroneous to put the question with this alternative: either the life of the child or that of the mother. No, neither

the life of the mother nor that of the child can be subjected to an act of direct suppression. In the one case as in the other, there can be but one obligation: to make every effort to save the lives of both, of the mother and the child.[9]

Pius XII's successor, John XXIII, carried forward these themes. In *Mater et Magistra* (1961), he wrote that "human life is sacred: from its very inception, the creative action of God is directly operative. By violating His laws, the Divine Majesty is offended, the individuals them- selves and humanity degraded, and likewise the community itself of which they are members is enfeebled." [10] The Second Vatican Council, which Pope John initiated, stated, in the Pastoral Constitution on "The Church in the Modern World," that "whatever is opposed to life itself, such as any type of murder, genocide, abortion, euthanasia, or willful self-destruction . . . all these things and others of their like are infamies indeed. . . . From the moment of its conception life must be guarded with the greatest care, while abortion and infanticide are unspeakable crimes." [11] After the Council, Pope Paul VI, in his encyclical on birth control, *Humanae Vitae* (1968), said that "in conformity with these landmarks in the human and Christian vision of marriage, we must once again declare that the direct interruption of the generative process al- ready begun, and, above all, directly willed and procured abortion, even if for therapeutic reasons, are to be absolutely excluded as licit means of regulating birth." [12]

While the historical trend of these successive statements is clear, at least two exceptions to the prohibition of abortion remain: abortion in the instance of an ectopic pregnancy and in the instance of a cancerous uterus.[13] Both exceptions are justified on the grounds that the "direct" intention of the act which removes the Fallopian tube (in the instance of an ectopic pregnancy) and the act which removes the cancerous uterus is to save the woman; indirectly these acts kill the fetus, but this is not their direct intention. Pope Pius XII approved the rationale for these exceptions when he said in 1951:

Deliberately we have always used the expression "direct attempt on the life of an innocent person," "direct killing." Because if, for example, the saving of the life of the future mother, independently of her pregnant condition, should urgently require a surgical act or other therapeutic treatment which would have as an accessory consequence, in no way desired or intended, but in- evitable, the death of the fetus, such an act could no longer be called a direct attempt on an innocent life. Under these conditions the operation can be lawful, like other similar medical interventions—granted always that a good of high worth is concerned, such as life, and that it is not possible to postpone the operation until after the birth of the child, nor to have recourse to other efficacious remedies.[14]

In Noonan's eyes, these exceptions are taken to prove that the present teaching of the Church is something less than an "absolute valuation of fetal life." [15]

In the case of abortion, Catholic moralists wanted to draw a line so tightly fixed in favor of the fetus that abortion could rarely be justified—justified indeed only when there was an unusual extra circumstance added such as a cancerous uterus or an ectopic pregnancy. The permission of these two exceptions was consistent with the desire to establish a general rule of inviolability for the fetus; they were inconsistent only with an absolute valuation of fetal life.[16]

The Logic of the Present Catholic Position

This brief sketch of the history of the Catholic Church's teaching on abortion has been meant to prepare the way for a more systematic analysis of the logic of the Church's present position.[17] Two points need to be distinguished in talking about the "Church's present position." The first concerns the matter of the *method* of the argument, and the second the *substance* of the argument. In general, as the position is argued in papal statements and manuals of moral theology, the method is deductive. Fundamental general principles are laid down; specific conclusions, applicable to abortion cases, are then drawn. The principles function as axioms, the conclusions, as consequences derived from the axioms. While this style of argumentation is most obvious in the manuals, where it is explicitly used, it is also present in the papal and conciliar statements. It is possible to look upon this method in two ways. Viewed benignly, it represents simply a common method of moral argumentation: general principles are established and specific applications are made. Viewed more critically, it can fall under the kind of charge leveled by the Protestant theologian James M. Gustafson and echoed by many contemporary Catholic moralists about the method of Catholic moral theology. Gustafson has pointed out, perceptively, that Catholic arguments about abortion are (*a*) "arguments made by an *external judge*"; (*b*) "are made on a basically *juridical model*"; (*c*) "largely confine the relevant data to *the physical*"; (*d*) "are limited by concerning themselves almost *exclusively with the physician and the patient* at the time of a particular pregnancy, isolating these two from the multiple relationships and responsibilities each has to and for others over long periods of time"; (*e*) "are *rationalistic*"; and further that (*f*) "the traditional perspective seeks to develop arguments that are based on *natural law*, and thus ought to be persuasive and binding on all men." [18] Yet, while a general characterization of this kind is accurate, not all who argue the Catholic position necessarily argue in this fashion; instead, one can now find commonly employed a variety of styles (which will be indicated in the ensuing discussion).

The substance of the Catholic position can be summed up in the following principles, which are sometimes developed in a theological way, sometimes philosophically and sometimes mixed together: (1) God alone is the Lord of life. (2) Human beings do not have the right to take the lives of other (innocent) human beings. (3) Human life begins at the moment of conception. (4) Abortion, at whatever the stage of development of the conceptus, is the taking of innocent human life. The conclusion follows: Abortion is wrong. The only exception to this conclusion is in the case of an abortion which is the indirect result of an otherwise moral and legitimate medical procedure (e.g., the treatment of an ectopic pregnancy and cancerous uterus).

1. GOD ALONE IS THE LORD OF LIFE

When the Catholic position is argued theologically, this is a key proposition. "Only God is Lord of the Life of a man who is not guilty of a crime punishable with death," Pius XII said on one occasion, and, on another, "Every human being, even the child in its mother's womb, receives its right to life directly from God" (as quoted above). Norman St. John-Stevas, cited on this point in Chapter 9, argues in a similar way, as do other Catholic authors.[19] Variantly, this argument is often couched in terms of the "right to life," especially when the inviolability of human life is approached from a philosophical—natural-law—perspective. Thus Father T. J. O'Donnell contends that the purposeful termination of a pregnancy "contains the moral malice of the violation of man's most fundamental human right—the right to life itself." [20] Other authors, though more rarely, have also seen in abortion the thwarting of the ends of nature, in this instance that of frustrating the good of the species in favor of the good of an individual (the mother).[21]

I have already criticized, in Chapter 9, the use of the principle of God's lordship as a premise in a consideration of the morality of abortion. To recapitulate, it presupposes that God intervenes directly in natural and human affairs as the primary causative agent of life and death. Not only is this theologically dubious, it also has the effect of obscuring the necessity that human beings define terms, make decisions and take responsibility for the direct care of human life. Moreover, to say that God is the ultimate source of the "right to life," which is less objectionable theologically, still does not solve the problem of *how* human beings ought to respect that right or how they are to balance a conflict of rights. Normally speaking, the right to life takes primacy over other rights, since without life no other rights can be exercised. But abortion problems normally arise because other important rights appear to be in conflict with that right; unless a prior and fixed decision has been made to give always and in every circumstance the right to life a primacy over all other human rights, it is not clear how, without begging some important questions, the "right to life" can be invoked as the sole right in question in abortion decisions. (I have already argued in Chapter 9 against a rigid ordering of rights.) But that is the procedure of many Catholic moralists when it comes to abortion.

2. HUMAN BEINGS DO NOT HAVE THE RIGHT TO TAKE THE LIVES OF OTHER (INNOCENT) HUMAN BEINGS

This proposition is consistent both with Christian ethics, in the theological sense, and with Catholic natural-law morality. The word "innocent," though, is crucial here. Traditional Catholic morality has defended the just war, i.e., defensive, limited war waged for the preservation of life or the protection of vital human rights. These wars have been justified even though they result, often enough, in the foreseen taking of innocent life, particularly the life of noncombatants. The justification for thus taking innocent life, however, is governed by the principle of double effect. Thus innocent (noncombatant) life cannot be taken unless, for the strict demands of self-defense, these lives are taken only "indirectly," that is, by an action "designed and intended solely to achieve some other purpose(s) even though death is foreseen as a concomitant effect. Death therefore is not positively willed, but is reluctantly permitted as an unavoidable by-product." [22] Thus, while the proposition concerning the absence of the right of one human being to take the life of another is basic to Catholic morality, when argued both theologically and in terms of natural law, it admits of an important exception in two circumstances: when the life to be taken is *not* innocent human life (as in punishment for capital crimes and in the case of a just defensive war) and when it is "innocent" life but the taking of that life is "indirect."

3. HUMAN LIFE BEGINS AT THE MOMENT OF CONCEPTION

Whereas the first two propositions were general moral principles, this one is a specific proposition about the nature of the life in question in abortion decisions. While (as we will see below) some Catholic moralists are attempting to revive the earlier distinction between the "formed" and the "unformed" fetus, the general trend in recent decades has been to eliminate the distinction and count as human the immediate product of conception.[23] Thus Pius XII: "Even the child, even the unborn child, is a human being in the same degree and by the same title as its mother." These words were consistent with the earlier words of Pope Pius XI,

who had spoken of the conceptus as "an innocent child" and "an innocent human being." In line with phrases of this kind, the Catholic Hospital Association of the United States and Canada has specified as one of
its principles: "14. Every unborn child must be regarded as a human
person, with all the rights of a human person, from the moment of conception." [24] When speaking cautiously, many theologians would say that,
in the absence of a philosophical or scientific demonstration that a conceptus is human, respect for life requires us to treat it as if it were.

It goes without saying that a decision to call a conceptus, whatever
the stage of development, a "human being" or a "human person" presumes certain convictions about the proper way to read biological evidence. While the papal statements do not give the reasoning behind this
decision, it is safe to assume that the ultimate motive behind so reading
the evidence in this fashion is to extend protection to the earliest reaches
of individual human life. It represents a moral policy, one which has
chosen one possible way of reading the data and chosen that way, the
safest way, as the most compatible with the moral aim: the protection
of all innocent life. In addition, in a way consistent with the Catholic
tradition, Catholic authors overwhelmingly tend to make the problem
of the beginning of human life the major, indeed overriding, particular
factual question to be answered in any approach to abortion. Once it is
determined (as the tradition has determined) that the right to life is the
fundamental human right, and that innocent life may not be taken, then
the only remaining question of consequence is whether the conceptus
ought to be considered "human life." As Father Robert Drinan has put
it, "Every discussion of abortion must, in the final analysis, begin and
end with a definition of what one thinks of a human embryo or fetus." [25]
For John T. Noonan, Jr., "the most fundamental question involved in
the long history of thought on abortion is: How do you determine the
humanity of a being?" [26] David Granfield felt that the centrality of the
question warranted beginning his book on abortion with it. For that
matter, whether dealt with in terms of the question of the "moment of
animation" or "ensoulment" or in some other more contemporary form,
it is a question which has traditionally been given primacy. [27] This
characteristic of Catholic argumentation is important because, by so
ordering the priority of the questions to be asked, all other questions are
thrown into a subsidiary position. Actually this makes it exceedingly
difficult, within the Catholic problematic, to try and weigh other values—
the mother's duty toward her children, her psychological state and
freedom, her economic situation—or to raise or answer other kinds of
questions; the first question asked tends to preempt the others. An important aspect of the one-dimensionality of the Catholic position is thus
its tendency to narrow the issues considered legitimate and important
to very few; issues which, it turns out, bear almost exclusively (with the

noted exceptions) on the status of the conceptus. No room is left for the integration of a full range of rights, personal and communal.

4. ABORTION, AT WHATEVER THE STAGE OF DEVELOPMENT OF THE CONCEPTUS, IS THE TAKING OF INNOCENT HUMAN LIFE

Once the question of whether the conceptus from the moment of conception is "human life" has been answered in the affirmative, then it is only a short, indeed tautological step to state that abortion is the taking of innocent human life. While, as Noonan has shown, there have been theologians who have tried to develop the argument that, in some cases, the fetus can be counted as an "aggressor," this line has had scant papal or theological support. The net result is that the act of abortion is, in the end, defined as an act which takes innocent human life, and thus by definition an act to be condemned and proscribed. If one stays within the framework of the Catholic argument, proceeding from premises (1) to (3), then this is a logical deduction and thus unexceptionable. With premise (2) taken as a principle of the natural law and the conceptus judged factually (biologically) to be human, no other conclusion is possible than a condemnation of abortion. As Josef Fuchs, S.J., has argued (exhibiting both the style and the substance of the argument):

> *Any principle of the natural law remains efficacious in every situation that realizes the facts involved by this principle.* For example, it can never happen that the prohibition of a direct destruction of unborn life—a principle of the natural law—could cease to be an absolute demand even in difficult concrete situations, or out of charitable consideration for a mother and her family.[28]

Put in terms of the four propositions above, the structure of the Catholic argument is comparatively simple and straightforward. It rests on no *obscure* arguments (even if they may strike many as fallacious), requires no elaborate steps to carry it off (as, for instance, Catholic natural-law arguments against contraception do) and draws on few idiosyncratic Catholic ways of arguing moral issues (conservative Protestant and Jewish arguments are not that dissimilar). But it seems to me that one cannot fully appreciate the Catholic position (or the vehemence with which it is supported) without observing a number of collateral arguments commonly brought to bear in support of it. Most commonly, it is contended that a justification of abortion has the force of a justification for treating all human beings as expendable and introducing a principle of expediency into human relations. As David Granfield has put it:

> Abortion is forbidden morally because it is an abuse of human power. It is a destruction of a human being by another human being, and as such it strikes at the heart of human dignity. The usurpation of authority which is abortion

is not wrong simply because it kills unborn children, but because it results in the vilification of all men. To give moral justification to abortion is to condemn all men to the level of expendable things. Morally, the fight against abortion is not primarily to protect the human dignity of the unborn, but is above all to safeguard that dignity in all men.[29]

For Father Robert F. Drinan, an acceptance of the American Law Institute's Model Penal Code on abortion would have the consequence of overthrowing a fundamental value of Anglo-Saxon law, the inviolability of human life: "At no time and under no circumstances has Anglo-American law ever sanctioned the destruction of one human being—however useless and unwanted such a person may be—for the purpose of securing or increasing the health or happiness of other individuals." [30] For Thomas J. O'Donnell, doctors who perform therapeutic abortions have adopted a philosophy of "medical expediency" which they are willing to place above any other moral standard.[31] Bernard Häring sees the possibility of a fundamental threat to motherhood: "If it were to become an accepted principle of moral teaching on motherhood to permit a mother whose life was endangered simply to 'sacrifice' the life of her child in order to save her own, motherhood would no longer mean absolute dedication to each and every child." [32] For John T. Noonan, "abortion violates the rational humanist tenet of the equality of human lives." [33] Finally, it is not unfitting to mention that some older manuals of moral theology—still in use in some places—condemned abortion on the added (but theologically dubious) ground that "it deprives the soul of eternal life." [34]

Extrapolations of this kind, which often strike the non-Catholic as red herrings if not bizarre, make considerable logical sense once one realizes that the premises of the Catholic argument have *defined* abortion as the taking of innocent human life. At stake, in the Catholic view, is the principle of the right to life; if the principle is breached in one place, it could well be breached in another—a precedent has been established for violating the principle. One may object (as I will) to the premises, but it is important to see that, once adopted, the conclusions Catholics draw from them are consistent. The practice of envisioning further erosions of respect for life if abortion is accepted is, in the Catholic view, a perfectly legitimate philosophical procedure, a way of trying to chart the consequences of a change in what are taken to be fundamental moral principles. It is a procedure, moreover, used commonly in all forms of moral argumentation and by no means restricted to Catholics; it is only to say, as others say when their own ox is gored, that the social consequences of a change in basic moral principles can be enormously harmful. Given the Catholic premises, it should at least be understandable (even if not acceptable) why many Catholics cannot but view with alarm the prospect of a moral acceptance of abortion. State the case as bluntly as John Marshall has done and it is easy to see social disaster as a consequence of an acceptance of abortion: "Direct abortion . . . is gravely wrong, because it constitutes the direct killing of an innocent human being." [35] It ought to be understandable why Catholics, given their premises, can envision the antiabortion cause as an attempt to hold on to very basic Western values, values by no means exclusively their own but rather the patrimony of the entire culture. A quotation from Father Richard A. McCormick will help to drive the point home: "The question 'What am I doing?' is the first question to be asked about induced abortion. It is all the more urgent because it is precisely the question our society nearly always neglects." [36] The Catholic answer is that the act being performed in abortion is the killing of an innocent human being; once reached, a conclusion of that kind dictates, at the cost of inconsistency and moral irresponsibility, vigorous opposition to abortion.

The Principle of "Double Effect"

Within the framework of traditional Catholic morality, it is exceedingly difficult for a Catholic—even if he would like to do so—to find a way of taking exception to the received teaching. That is no doubt one reason, at least, why very few efforts have been mounted to change the teaching. With the exception of the premise that human life begins at conception (which can at any rate be challenged on biological grounds, where the evidence is open to varying interpretations), the other premises seem either securely fixed by the Christian tradition or represent straightforward deductions from natural-law premises already accepted. If, then, the traditional teaching is to be challenged within a Catholic framework (and, of course, it is simple to challenge it from an entirely different theological or philosophical framework), it must be done by a critical examination of (a) the premises themselves, (b) the validity of the conclusions drawn from the premises and (c) the details and methods of argumentation. As for the premises, a number of objections have already been leveled at the theological belief that the Lordship of God takes the matter of abortion decisions out of human hands, and at the philosophical belief that the right to life necessarily takes precedence over all other rights (Chapter 9). Once that much has been seen and the premises thrown into question (but only that), then the way is open to dispute the conclusion drawn from those premises: that the direct taking of innocent fetal (or embryonic) life is always and necessarily immoral.

One detail in particular of the traditional Catholic argument opens the way for such a disputation: the principle of double effect. As noted, the only exceptions to the absolute prohibition of abortion are in the case of an ectopic pregnancy or a cancerous uterus. In both of those instances, the justification for the exception is that the indicated medical procedure to save the life of the mother (the removal of the tube or of the uterus) has as its direct intention the saving of the life of the mother; the death of the fetus is the foreseen but unintended and indirect result of the lifesaving surgery performed on the mother. By a use of this distinction, then, an abortion can be performed in the specified cases without directly violating the moral law that innocent life cannot be killed. The basis for the principle is the commonsense observation that an action can have both a good and a bad effect or result. As a theological distinction, it was first employed by Thomas Aquinas, who built upon it a justification for the taking of life in self-defense.[37] In essence, the point of the principle is this: an action which has both a good and a bad effect may be performed if the good effect accomplished is greater than the evil effect and if, in addition, at least four other conditions are met: (1) the act must itself be either good or indifferent, or at least not forbidden with a view to preventing just that effect; (2) the evil effect cannot be a means to the good, but must be equally immediate or at least must result from the good effect; (3) the foreseen evil effect must not be intended or approved, merely permitted—for even a good act is vitiated if accompanied by an evil intent; (4) there must be a proportionately serious reason for exercising the cause and allowing the evil effect.[38] The problem of an ectopic pregnancy illustrates what is considered a legitimate use of the principle:

> The removal of a pregnant Fallopian tube containing a non-viable living fetus, even before the external rupture of the tube, can be done in such a way that the consequent death of the fetus will be produced only indirectly. Such an operation will be licitly performed if all the circumstances are such that the necessity for the operation is, in moral estimation, proportionate to the evil effect permitted.[39]

In this instance, the intent of the operation itself is good (as a standard operation to save life); although the fetus is killed, that effect, though foreseen, is not the intention of the operation (thus the death of the fetus is indirectly caused); the evil effect (the death of the fetus) is not the means to the good end (the saving of the life of the woman), but only the indirect result of the means (the tubal removal) necessary to save the life of the woman. Thus the conditions for an application of the principle are met. By contrast a fetal craniotomy to save the life of the woman would not be licit because, in that case, the life of the fetus is taken directly by the act of crushing its skull. The intention is good (saving the life of the woman), but the means employed are evil (directly taking the life of an innocent fetus); hence, fetal craniotomy is forbidden.[40]

Now, it has been contended that, far from being impersonal and legalistic, the principle of double effect represents "an attempt on the part of theologians to free us to do as much as possible, even though indirectly intended evil—in this case, the death of the unborn—results." [41] For Noonan, the making of exceptions on the basis of the principle represents an attempt to achieve a balance: "In Catholic moral theology, as it developed, life even of the innocent was not taken as an absolute. Judgments on acts affecting life issued from a process of weighing. In the weighing, the fetus was always given a greater value than zero, always a value separate and independent from its parents." [42] One feels compelled to comment, however, that the "weighing" in question is decisively one-sided, takes physical life alone as the only value at stake, leaving no real room for even investigating any other considerations which might come into play. It is evident, moreover, that a theology which would countenance the death of both the fetus and the woman (rare in fact, but pertinent in principle) rather than directly take the life of the fetus is one geared heavily to a preoccupation with preserving individuals from sin or crime. Its real interest in the extreme case of letting both woman and fetus die turns out, in effect, not to be the good of the mother (for, hypothetically, a fetal craniotomy would save her life), but the good conscience of those who might but do not act to save her. The basic moral principle of "Do good and avoid evil" is efficaciously rendered into the avoiding of evil alone.

The way in which a conflict of rights between a woman and a fetus is treated is illuminating of the consequences of this style of moral reckoning; for it is at this point that the style most clearly shows itself. Pope Pius XII was cited above in his statement that "neither the life of the mother nor that of the child can be subjected to an act of direct suppression. In the one case as in the other, there can be but one obligation: to make every effort to save the lives of both, of the mother and the child." But it is, of course, precisely the supposition of the hypothesis in those situations (however rare medically) that, unless the fetus is killed, the mother will die also: both lives cannot be saved. The assumption behind this form of reasoning is that there exists a fixed order of rights, before which man must passively stand, whatever the physical consequences of his passivity. A passage from Josef Fuch's book brings this out:

> The difficulty of a conflict of rights can *easily* [my italics] be solved if one understands that there are no heterogeneous orders and demands of the natural law placed side by side without any relation to one another. There exists indeed *an order* of goods and values, of commands and demands through the

very nature of things, so that there can be no true conflict of rights but at most an apparent conflict. The two obligations concerning a pathological birth, to preserve the life of the mother and not to kill the child, only seem to contradict one another. There is in fact no commandment to save the mother at all costs. There is only an obligation to save her in a morally permissible way and such a way is not envisaged in stating this given situation. Consequently only one obligation remains: to save the mother without attempting to kill the child.[43]

What seems apparent here is that, despite acknowledgment of an obligation to the mother, the *primary* obligation is fulfillment of the moral law, which exists independently of the obligations owed to particular human beings. Once the primary obligation has been discharged, fidelity to the moral law, there exist no remaining human obligations; the woman may be allowed to die. One consequence of a morality which centers obligation and responsibility in preservation of the law is to posit a sharp distinction between physical and moral evils. "Two natural deaths," David Granfield has written, "are a lesser evil than one murder. In the conflict of interests between mother and child, the rights of both to live must be preserved. The conflict cannot be resolved morally by the killing of the weaker party without thereby destroying all morality." [44] Even if one assumes that the killing of the child in the instance of a moral conflict would be "murder," one has to ask why this "murder" would be a greater evil than the death of both. Would it not be a moral evil to let the woman die (when she could be saved), and an even greater moral evil if there were others (husband, other children) dependent upon her? To imply that such an evil is only "physical" is to posit a moral helplessness and lack of human responsibility in the face of natural disasters. On the contrary, it seems to me perfectly reasonable to say that what is initially a physical situation (an event in nature) becomes a moral situation when it enters the realm of potential human action. A choice not to act in the face of a physical evil for the sake of saving another becomes—assuming human responsibility—a moral choice.

In a rigid natural-law formulation, the terms of the choice seem dictated by laws supposedly transcendent to the human beings affected by them. In Granfield's instance, the preservation of the "rights of both to life" becomes nothing more than sheer formalism. For, when one or more human beings refuse to save the mother by the "murder" of the fetus, she is being refused by other human beings the *de facto* right to life; her rights are nullified. To say that "all morality" would be destroyed "by the killing of the weaker party" is only possible if one presumes that "morality" consists in observing a moral law regardless of the consequences for individual human beings. The range of human responsibility is thus narrowed to a point where the good conscience of

those who could act and the abstract demands of the law take precedence over every other consideration. It becomes, at this point, virtually
meaningless to speak, as Noonan has done, of the work of the moralists
as one of "the weighing of fetal rights against other human rights." [45]
For the terms allowable in the "weighing" are such as to insure that,
once the fetus has been defined as innocent human life, the "weighing"
entirely favors the fetus. That two exceptions are admitted (and those
medically uncommon) can hardly be said to constitute "balance." And
it goes without saying, of course, that when the only aspects of the
balance even worthy of consideration are those of physical life, then
the whole network of other responsibilities which the mother may have
becomes morally irrelevant.

Seeking a New Moral Methodology

It is hardly surprising that this method of moral argumentation has
come under increasing criticism by Catholic theologians seeking a more
complex form of moral reasoning. This is not the place to present a
history of recent Catholic moral theology, but some leading elements
can be mentioned. First, there is a desire to move away from a moral
logic which simply deduces ethical conclusions from fixed, abstract and
absolute principles. Second, there is a desire to take account of the
full range of human relationships, which means that moral acts are to
be judged not only in terms of the individuals involved (those who make
decisions or those who are proximately affected by decisions) but also
in terms of the entire human community (both proximate and remote).
Third, there is a desire to take account of the multiplicity of possible
effects of moral decisions. Fourth, there is a desire to see human acts in
terms broader than that of their physical meaning.[46]

These desires, which represent an attempt in particular to move beyond the rationalistic, syllogistic method of the manuals of moral theology
employed in the nineteenth and early twentieth century are slowly and
quietly having their impact on the Catholic discussion of abortion, at
least within a small circle of theologians. Father William H. Van der
Marck, O.P., for instance, has complained that the standard Catholic
treatment of abortion takes account of one form of "intersubjectivity"
only:

> So often the material, bodily reality of the action is unthinkingly and wholly
> identified with one single form of intersubjectivity to the total exclusion of all
> others. . . . This narrowness of outlook results partly from the fact that the
> qualification "good" or "bad" is taken to apply directly and without further
> ado to the corporeal act as such, whereas, in fact and in the nature of the case,
> good or bad can be involved only in the *human* act—the act as intersubjec-

tive. . . . That the same material, bodily act may possibly have a *different* intersubjective significance is something that, in principle, lies outside of its field of vision. Abortion is murder; the possibility that a termination of pregnancy could be medically indicated is something that simply cannot be taken into account. . . . In other words, any view of a *different* intersubjectivity or of a *different* human significance in the act is, so to speak, excluded *a priori*.[47]

One can appreciate Father Van der Marck's point by observing the frequency with which a decision in favor of abortion is systematically categorized by Catholic authors as a choice dictated by expediency, self-interest, insensitivity to the sacredness of life, and utilitarianism. It seems rarely to have occurred to them that, say, a mother with living children, concerned for their welfare, could want an abortion (even on grounds less than a threat to life) as a way of being responsive to her obligation to care for those children. To call this motivation "expediency" or "self-interest" would be to play fast and loose with words. This is only to say, in underscoring Father Van der Marck's point, that a morality of abortion which can see only one meaning in the act of abortion (destruction of the innocent) is rendered systematically deaf to many other possible and important meanings. It is also to render impossible in principle the taking into account of other rights which can come into play in the full meaning of the act: person-rights, species-rights, and so on.

A similar line of criticism has been pursued by Father Cornelius J. Van der Poel. Commenting on the tendency of Catholic moralists, first, to base their judgment on the physical aspect of the act of abortion and, second, to separate human acts into independent, atomistic activities, he goes on to say:

A moral judgment is made not so much about a human act *in itself* as a separate entity, but rather the individual human act should be evaluated insofar as it contributes to or destroys the building of this society. This social aspect of man seems to be overlooked or at least too much deemphasized in the application of the principle of double effect.[48]

A recognition of this "social aspect" would lead to the more profound awareness that man does not live as an isolated human being but within a totality of human relationships.

From this point of view [Van der Poel says] it becomes more clear that individual human action, precisely in its *human* aspects, may not be divided into independent parts each with an independent moral value. The means to the end may have in themselves a merely physical effect which may, precisely in its isolated physical condition, seem harmful to a certain aspect of life, but in the totality of the *human* quality of the total action it may be community-building and not destructive. So it is possible that the same physical act and effect may have an entirely different *human* value because of the total environment (if you wish, call it circumstances) in which the act is performed. . . .

We do not say here that the end justifies the means, but what we do say is that the end *determines the human meaning* of the means.[49]

The point being made here can, I think, aptly be illustrated by a reflection on abortion in Latin-American slums (see the data in Chapter 5). The *physical* meaning of an abortion in that context is, of course, the destruction of a conceptus, which for the moment we can, for the sake of argument, assume to be a "human being." But in the case of a mother with too many children and too few material, familial, social or psychological resources to care for them, the full *human* meaning of the act of abortion is preservation of the existing children. One result of the abortion is the death of the fetus, but other results are (or most likely could be) the removal of one more handicap (and serious ones) to the existing family, to an overpopulated society and to the physical and psychological stability of the mother. To say that the only result of *moral* consequence is the death of the fetus (as, in principle, the traditional position does) is to ignore the full setting of the life of the mother, a setting which has a variety of moral components and relationships. In a word, the mother does not exist alone and it would be irresponsible of her to take account only of herself as an isolated human being charged exclusively with the conceptus within her.

Now, of course, it could be said that even those who support the traditional view take account of the full web of human relationships. For, do they not (e.g., Noonan, Granfield, Drinan) speak collaterally of the harm done all human beings by the taking of human life? Is not one of their fears that precisely the precedent of allowing the taking of innocent human life by abortion will pose a threat to the security of all human relationships? "Morally," as Granfield has vividly put it, "liberal abortion fails because it threatens the meaning and value of life, because it destroys equality among men by recourse to a despotic authority, because, in attacking the fetus, it attacks the principle of morality and the foundations of civilized life." [50]

But the problem here is that it has to be demonstrated, not just by deduction but with some empirical evidence, that abortion always and in all circumstances "threatens the meaning and value of life" in areas beyond abortion. As pointed out in Chapters 6 and 7, there is no evidence that societies which have liberal or permissive abortion laws are societies in which the "meaning and value of life" in general are demonstrably more threatened than in societies which do not have such laws. One might well grant that the life of fetuses is more threatened in such societies—although the prevalence and tacit acceptance of illegal abortion in countries with restrictive laws would not seem (in a comparison of legal codes) to make the threat that much the less in the latter. But to say it is thereby proved that all life would be threatened merely begs the question. The reason, I would suggest, why life in general is not necessarily more threatened where abortion is accepted (*de jure* or *de facto*) is because the *moral* meaning of individual abortions can and often does differ from case to case. All share in the common characteristic of taking the life of the fetus, but the individual intentions and the personal, familial and social consequences may be very different, thus altering the full moral meaning from case to case as well, consequently, as its moral meaning for society as a whole. Moreover, of course, the fact that all those who favor abortion do not regard the conceptus as a human being makes it both implausible and unjust to extrapolate from their conduct toward fetuses a general attitude toward what they do consider a human being.[51]

The question may be raised, however, whether taking into account the full human meaning of the act and judging it by that norm (e.g., specified in terms of "community-building") requires us to abandon or is tantamount to abandoning respect for nascent life. There is no reason automatically to draw this conclusion. If the only acceptable norm of respect is that under no circumstances can nascent life be taken, then, to be sure, to take that life would be, by definition, to abandon the respect. If, on the contrary, the norm of respect was that in all circumstances the right to life of the fetus be a serious, indeed primary, element in our moral reckoning, then one could not be said to be showing disrespect. One need only say that the criterion of due respect be that, in ordinary circumstances, the conceptus has the presumptive right to develop and be born; and to hold that, in such ordinary circumstances, this is the prime and overriding right. This norm would exclude the use of wholly self-interested, solipsistic reasons on the part of the mother, at least as a moral norm. It would also require that the moral reasons for abortion be serious reasons, so serious that one could (*a*) legitimately invoke other rights than those of the conceptus, (*b*) honestly say that the circumstances were extraordinary (which need not only mean extraordinary to the woman personally, as a kind of odd, chance set of misfortunes, but extraordinary also in the sense that the life of the very poor or the destitute as a class is abnormal), and (*c*) meaningfully be able to affirm that no other reasonable options are available.

Charles E. Curran has written a passage indicating how he believes abortion can under some circumstances be justified without overthrowing respect for life:

> In discussing the problem of abortion I believe that a Christian theologian must take the conservative position of treating the fetus at least from blastocyst as human life. However, even in the past the teaching of Catholic theologians and the statements of the hierarchical magisterium on abortion seem too restricted. Conflict situations cannot be solved merely by the physical

structure and causality of the act. The human values involved must be carefully considered and weighed. In Catholic theology there is a precedent for
equating other values with life itself. As a Christian, any taking of life must
be seen as a reluctant necessity. However, in the case of abortion there can
arise circumstances in which the abortion is justified for preserving the life of
the mother or for some other important value commensurate with life even
though the action aims at abortion "as a means to the end." One cannot stress
enough the great respect the Christian has for human life. Human life can
never be taken lightly. However, the conflict situation involving abortion
should be solved according to the pattern and model of other conflict situations involving life and not solved merely according to a restricted notion of
direct or indirect based on the physical causality of the action itself.[52]

In my final chapter, I will specify what in my view constitute serious
and responsible reasons for abortion, thus elaborating on the preceding
points. It is sufficient now only to point out that nothing less than a
wholly impersonal calculus of rights, rigidly identified and unalterably
ordered independently of individual human choice, responsibility and
circumstance, could conclude that the taking of fetal life in all circumstances constituted in principle a disrespect for life. Not only does this
define "respect" unilaterally and *a priori* in theory (making it logically
unnecessary even to know the name, circumstances or motivating reasons of a woman who has an abortion to judge her action as disrespectful
of life). It also makes it difficult in practice to imagine how respect for
life and an acceptance of abortion can, as they often do, psychologically
coexist in the same person. It is this latter point, perhaps, which helps
explain why most Catholic treatments of abortion do not dwell at much
length on the "indications" put forward for abortion; if they are considered at all, it is usually to dismiss them under the category of
"expediency" or "self-interest." But this is the not surprising result of a
moral methodology which has worked its principles out in advance of
particular cases and makes the specifities of the cases logically irrelevant.
Even if one assumes that, with those Catholics who uphold the Catholic
tradition in all its rigor, a "human being" exists from the moment of
conception—and thus that the abortion is the killing of a human being—
the one-dimensionality of the position becomes evident. For it is a
position in which in every possible decision save an ectopic pregnancy
or a cancerous uterus the life of one human being (the conceptus)
takes a place of consummate superiority over the life of another human
being.

Noonan's claim, then, that the Catholic position is not one which gives
"an absolute valuation" to "fetal life," but only establishes "a general
rule of inviolability for the fetus," [53] is true so far as a literal meaning
of the word "absolute" is concerned. But the full weight of the "general
rule" is such that, in the ordinary sense of the word (where the great

run of even disastrous pregnancies are concerned), the force of the rule
is absolutist, displaying no "balance" at all. The laudable desire of Pope
Pius XII and the Catholic moralists to grant full rights to woman and
fetus, and to deprive neither of their rights, amounts, then, to a decision
which in actuality gives the fetus the overwhelming advantage; that
it does so in the case of mortal conflict (save for two exceptions) is
evident, but that it does so in all other cases of conflict is no less evident.
If the right to life of the fetus is inviolable, then it follows logically (and
is in fact the case) that all other human rights become endangered by
the need to preserve that one right.

The Catholic theologians so far cited are, however, not the only ones
who have tried recently to work out a fresh Catholic position.[54] Some,
like Curran, Van der Poel and Van der Marck, approach abortion in
the context of a larger attempt to work through a fresh method of
moral reasoning; they question the entire manual tradition, with its
legalistic, syllogistic and rationalistic bias. Others, however—though
there is considerable overlap between the two groups—try to build upon
some elements which had a large place even in that tradition.

Among the former, in addition to those already cited, may be counted
Bishop Francis Simons of Indore, India. In an article called "The
Catholic Church and the New Morality," he proposes that the "good
of mankind" or the "welfare of mankind" is the ultimate basis of the
natural law and the norm by which particular commandments or moral
laws are to be judged. In the instance of abortion, the question to be
asked is whether an adherence to the law against the killing of an unborn child always contributes to mankind's greater good.

No valid reasons can be advanced for permitting abortion only to avoid an
"unwanted" child or to escape shame or inconvenience. In such cases we can
only speak of murder. Respect for human life is necessary for the good of
mankind, and killing can be permitted only for the most serious reasons, when
the greater good of mankind really demands or permits it. When abortion is
performed to avoid almost certain or very probable serious harm to the health
of the mother, its licitness is at least arguable. . . . The greater good of man
is the decisive factor, but it is not always clear what this imposes on us. In
border cases there can be legitimate doubt, leaving us free to do what we
think best, all things considered.[55]

Leonard F. X. Mayhew has urged:

An illogic places the moral discussion of abortion within the context of the
interdiction of murder. It would seem more reasonable to consider it where
experience places the moral choice—within the context of sexual and marital
morality. The act, or better, the moral choice posed by abortion does not arise
abstractly. It is a particular facet of human sexual experience. Its physical and
psychological reality is actualized primarily in terms of the mother and, to a
lesser degree, of the father. This, rather than an unverifiable abstraction,

would seem the proper framework in which to consider both the moral choice and the principle.[56]

Heinz Fleckenstein has argued that, given the present state of turmoil in Catholic theology, the existing principles are no longer fully adequate and can be taken as a general point of view only; this opens the way for a rethinking of abortion dilemmas.[57]

Others, working more closely within the older natural-law tradition, have seen in the traditional doctrine a possible way out. Father Robert H. Springer, S.J., is one example here:

> One may not intend the death of the fetus but only indirectly tolerate this bad effect, the loss of life is to be deplored, and Christian love demands that we seek alternative solutions to the dilemma, etc. But when all is said and done, we have not closed the door to all exceptions. The epistemology of moral science and St. Thomas' well-known doctrine of exceptions to the secondary principles of morality leave the door ajar. There remains the question of official Church teaching on abortion. The requisite historical and ecclesiological study on this aspect of the problem has not been done. When it is done, we should keep in mind that moral truth in these matters is not impervious to reason, is not shrouded in religious mystery to which faith alone can give an adequate answer.[58]

Springer is also among those who believe that new biological knowledge, especially concerning the process of twinning, which may take place some time after conception, requires a reconsideration of the traditional position that human life begins at conception.[59] Two Jesuits, Joseph Donceel and Thomas Wassmer, have pressed the view that the old distinction between "mediate" and "immediate" animation is by no means so dead as generally believed. Arguing that the Church has committed itself to hylomorphism—a human soul can exist only in a human body—Donceel reasons that a belief in immediate animation is incompatible with that more fundamental teaching. For it is not the case that the fertilized ovum is a "human body"—at best, it is a *virtual* human body; but the soul can only animate an actual human body, not a *virtual* body. Therefore, Donceel contends, some degree of bodily organization and development is necessary before the conceptus can receive the rational soul; the completion of brain development might constitute such a point.[60] Father Wassmer, building upon Donceel's conclusion, adds that the theory of mediate animation is at least theologically respectable enough for one to say that a "doubt of fact" exists about the beginning of a human life. And if that is so, he goes on to say,

> In the event of a *doubt of fact* regarding life, it is *never* permitted to follow the less safe course in the pursuit and realization of other human values. If there are and have been situations . . . in which, in the presence of a *doubt of fact regarding life*, the safer course does not always have to be followed, if

human values are at stake, is it conceivable that, granted respectability for the theory of mediate animation, this theory might be followed, even though it is not the safer course?

Father Wassmer's implicit answer to his own question is "yes." [61]

Regardless of whether the attempt to find a way of changing the traditional teaching takes the form of developing a fresh approach to moral problems in general or attempts to build upon some old distinctions, the common element is a desire to find a way of moving beyond the cul-de-sac toward which the traditional argument seems inexorably to move. The traditional argument makes it nearly impossible (save in very isolated situations) to take account of the fullest possible range of values; once staked out, the inviolability of the fetus comes to overshadow or preclude an integral place for the weighing of other values. In my terms, all of the Catholic reform efforts amount to a way of handling abortion decisions in a multi- rather than a one-dimensional way. These efforts, moreover, move beyond an attempt simply to find a better way of resolving cases of mortal conflict between woman and fetus; their direction is to take account also of cases where something other (but not necessarily less important) than the mother's life is at stake. Needless to say, given the tentativeness of the probings and the concentration upon some basic theoretical issues, there do not exist detailed efforts to work out just how the different values at issue ought to be weighed and compared. About the only point which seems agreed upon is that, whatever form the balancing of values may take, they cannot scant the respect due unborn life, whether that life be adjudged fully human or only potentially human. There should be a bias in favor of this life, a presumption against the taking of it, and a sense of obligation that serious reasons be adduced before turning to abortion. The overriding point in these probes would be, then, to avoid two extremes: on the one hand, a formulation of the problem in such a way that the inviolability of nascent life ends by taking practical precedence over every other consideration; and, on the other, a formulation which results in the trivialization of the value of unborn life and giving precedence automatically to the mother (or to other social interests).

Abortion and the Law

While Catholic legal theory has always distinguished between civil and moral law, and has employed the distinction in response to a variety of moral-legal issues (divorce, contraception, Sabbath observance, for example), it is only recently that some theorists have tried to apply it in the instance of abortion legislation and codes. It is not an oversimplification to say that, throughout the Western world and in other parts of the world as well, Catholic bishops, theologians and medical groups have favored highly restrictive abortion laws and have been in the forefront of opposition to liberalization. In the United States, the hierarchy as a whole as well as local hierarchies have been adamant in their opposition to movements designed to change the generally restrictive American state laws. In both England and the United States, Catholic legislators, doctors and lawyers have been vocal in support of tight laws.[62] A representative episcopal statement was that issued on February 1, 1968, in Maryland in opposition to the then pending proposals to change the Maryland abortion law (a law which, despite the statement was changed later that year):

> With the advent of a new proposal for the revision of the Maryland law concerning abortion, we feel compelled to express our grave concern for both the basic moral aspect and the social impact of such action. . . . Only God, as the author of human life, has absolute dominion over it. . . . Our opposition is not based on the assumption that every immoral act should be prohibited by statute. We reaffirm our view that religious freedom requires that government should not impose the tenets of a particular religion upon all whom it governs solely because they are the tenets of a religion. Our opposition is based upon our belief that any law that imperils the right to life of innocent human persons is a social evil. Our civilization, our culture and the traditions of our state and country are directly opposed to such notions.[63]

Three elements in the statement make it representative. First, its theological basis is the dominion of God. Second, it implicitly invokes the natural law in its reference to the "right to life of innocent human persons." Third, it alludes to the Catholic tradition's distinction between law and morals, but justifies its opposition to liberalized laws on the grounds that, in this instance, fundamental rights are at stake, rights which transcend the doctrinal system of Roman Catholicism.

This last point is important, raising a problem not yet touched upon. Non-Catholics have found it difficult to understand why Catholics, who have shown a capacity to accommodate themselves to a pluralistic society on a number of other issues, have been unable to do so on this one. This statement and others like it help explain the reason. The fact that much of the Catholic case against abortion has been argued in terms of the natural law means that it has not been believed that the opposition represents a sectarian theological conclusion, binding only on Church members. Hence, it has not appeared to Catholics to be a case of imposing idiosyncratic Catholic doctrines on non-Catholics. Moreover, the fact that the Catholic case has concluded with the proposition that abortion is the killing of innocent life means that Catholic attitudes toward abortion laws have been predicated on the social dangers of laws which would allow the taking of such life. Hence, "accommodation" has seemed out of the question, for the issue is one (when so construed) which transcends private beliefs, majority vote and medical opinion. The same logic which dictates a strict moral position also, *mutatis mutandis*, has seemed to dictate a strict legal code. Even if many find this logic unpersuasive, it should be possible to understand why a Catholic, for whom it is plausible, could not in conscience feel himself able to make an "accommodation" or to allow the issue to revert solely to the private conscience.

Yet it is instructive to see the direction that some Catholics are now taking on the legal issue. Three positions can be distinguished: total opposition to liberal laws; acceptance of strictly controlled liberal laws as a lesser evil; removal of all criminal sanctions from abortion statutes. The first position has already been adumbrated above; total opposition from a variety of grounds—theological, social, cultural and legal. Legally, the most common argument is that, short of wholly permissive laws or abortion on demand, moderately liberal laws do not work, succeeding neither in meeting the total abortion demand nor in significantly reducing the illegal-abortion rate.[64]

If total opposition still represents the main weight of Catholic thinking (at least at the professional level), the second position is gaining ground, with the experience of English Catholics providing something of a precedent for American Catholics. In *The Right to Life*, an English Catholic member of Parliament, Norman St. John-Stevas, took a strong position against the liberalization of restrictive abortion laws.[65] Later, as liberalization bills successively came before the English parliament, he led the opposition to a change. However, when it became clear that some kind of a reform bill was bound to succeed in being passed, St. John-Stevas, as a leader of the opposition, worked hard to affect the final form of the bill. In his view, this opposition succeeded in its limited aims. In an article in *America* he wrote:

> As a result of our efforts, although we have not defeated it, the bill is greatly improved from its original form. Nothing would have been achieved, however, had we not taken up our position on the middle ground, accepting the need for some measure of abortion law reform but seeking to get a bill that was well drafted and limited in scope. . . . In any case, in a pluralist society, while Catholics are fully entitled to voice their views and work for their implementation, prudence requires that they take into account the prevailing climate of moral opinion in the country. . . . By taking up a middle position as regards the law, Catholics are not abandoning their principles but recognizing facts. Abortion is an evil, but it does take place, and a regulatory law that would allow some abortions to take place under proper medical conditions would not be contrary to the Catholic faith.[66]

In the same issue of *America*, its Jesuit editors in an editorial asked:

> In the light of the English and the American experience, should the Catholic Church in the United States adopt a more flexible attitude and engage actively

in abortion law reform? We think it should. There is, first of all, the hard fact that changes are going to come (and quickly) whether we oppose them or not. While there can be no doubt that we have a grave obligation to bear witness, however unpopular our position, to the sanctity of fetal life, there can also be no doubt that the Church has never believed that everything immoral should be made criminal. This brings us to the second point: Americans have lost sight of the objectives of their anti-abortion laws. Catholics have an important contribution to make to the clarification of those objectives.[67]

The shifts in the thinking of Father Robert Drinan, S.J., Dean of the Boston College Law School, are particularly interesting in this context. In an essay written in 1965, he took an apparently firm position against any change in American abortion laws: "Any change of a substantial kind in America's abortion laws would be a notable departure from that body of Anglo-American law which regulates conduct deemed to constitute a crime against society." [68] But in a February 4, 1967, article, a change in emphasis was apparent. At that point, he suggested a number of compromises which Catholics might make in the face of non-Catholic pressures for change:

> To allow the legal authorization of abortion under any circumstances seems like a basic compromise that Catholics understandably would be reluctant to make. But if the only choice is between a law that would permit abortion only in the rare cases of rape, incest or a predictably defective infant and a law that would legalize abortion generally, the Catholic's election is clear.[69]

At that time, and subsequently, Father Drinan made clear that his *moral* position remain unchanged; his "strategy" bore on the legal issue and his "compromise" was based on the principle of choosing the "lesser evil."

By the fall of 1967, however, Father Drinan had shifted his position again, this time proposing "that the law should withdraw from the area of regulating abortion." [70] He gives three reasons for the value of a "non-law": (1) the unwillingness or inability of public authorities to enforce existing antiabortion laws; (2) "the law's concern for the solidarity and the stability of the family as an institution suggests that the law should not forbid parents to terminate an unplanned and unwanted pregnancy"; (3) the experience of other nations which, Father Drinan believes, shows that the authorization of abortion "for stated medical reasons" has the effect of escalating the number of illegal abortions (by leading people to think that "*any* reason really suffices"). The key to Father Drinan's proposal is, in effect, a lesser-evil argument. Pointing out that the removal of abortion laws could lead to a rise in the number of fetal deaths, he says:

> But the presumed (though) unproven difference in the loss of lives must be weighed against the long-range consequences of inserting into Anglo-

American law, for the first time in its history, a principle justifying the elimination of a life—not in order to save the *life* of another person but rather to preserve or enhance the health or the greater happiness of another person.

In short, a stipulation by the State of conditions for abortion would have the effect of implicitly sanctioning the taking of fetal lives; silence by the law altogether on abortion would not carry either moral approval or disapproval of abortion.[71] Throughout his article, however, Father Drinan emphasizes that his proposal does not signal any shift in his attitude on the morality of abortion: it remains morally wrong in his eyes.

Two comments are in order about Father Drinan's "no law" position. In the first place, it is noteworthy that he chooses to use in the context of the abortion argument some passages from the writings of the late and influential Father John Courtney Murray, S.J., one of the principal architects of the Second Vatican Council's "Declaration on Religious Freedom." The passages from Father Murray that he cited bore on the necessary and traditional Catholic distinction between law and morality.[72] What is interesting here is that Father Drinan was one of the first to make use of that oft-employed distinction in the abortion context. Norman St. John-Stevas, for instance, did not do so, though he has written knowingly and lucidly of the distinction in other contexts.[73] One can only surmise that the logic of the traditional Catholic abortion position has seemed so strong as to be proof against an invocation of the distinction so far as abortion laws are concerned. It was apparently taken to be one case where the social issues at stake seemed so great that the law had to stand guard over principles at once fundamental to morality and public order. Father Drinan's employment of the distinction would seem to imply, then, that abortion cannot *ipso facto* be counted a grave danger to public order and civil safety.

In the second place, the reasons Father Drinan offers in support of a repeal of abortion laws turn out to be of different kinds, carrying different implications. On the one hand, he argues that repeal would be desirable to take the State out of the business of apparently endorsing laws which distinguish among human lives; better no law at all than that eventuality with its dangerous precedents. On the other hand, the other kinds of reasons he offers—the unenforceability of abortion laws, the undesirability of forbidding parents to terminate unplanned and unwanted pregnancies, and the likelihood that a moderate as distinct from a permissive law would result in more illegal abortions—are of a different order altogether. The first point actually bears on an old point of Catholic jurisprudence: an unenforced or unenforceable law is a bad law, likely to bring all law into disrepute. The second point, more contemporary in its origin, suggests the influence of the United States Supreme Court decision of 1965 in the case of *Griswold* v. *Connecticut*, striking down the Connecticut statute prohibiting the use of contraceptives as an infringement of the right to privacy. The third point, based on a calculus of likely consequences, simply invokes the old principle of choosing the lesser evil. It is important not to read more into Father Drinan's arguments than he may have intended. Nevertheless, by granting the presumption of force to these arguments, he has established grounds for a repeal of the abortion laws not logically dependent upon his more general argument that repeal would obviate the danger of the State's judging among human lives. If this latter argument might be called a novel way of dealing with what is, on his hypothesis, an issue concerning basic human rights (and thus of a kind not normally excluded from the interest of civil law), the former arguments are far more standard, however rarely employed by Catholics in favor of a repeal of abortion laws. What is left unclear is whether Father Drinan would grant the former arguments a force independent of his more overarching contention.

The point is not a trivial one. The crux of the conservative Catholic legal position is the belief that, in the instance of abortion, it is not legitimate to employ distinctions normally used even by Catholics in other cases involving the relationship of law and morality. To bring in these traditional distinctions at all is to set the stage for a change in Catholic attitudes toward abortion laws; for the tradition provides ample precedent for a use of these distinctions to tolerate as law or sanctioned practice what might be considered morally offensive, not only to a few but even to a large number. If nothing else, Father Drinan's "no law" position shows how, even though it may be a point of contention, a Catholic could bring to bear some traditional points to lessen his opposition to liberalized laws. In any case, the traditional points are being employed at least by a few in opening up the possibility of a Catholic acceptance of more liberal laws or no laws at all.[74] Even Father David Granfield, at the conclusion of a book which concedes practically nothing to any of the cases for abortion-law reform, thinks it would be permissible "to work for legislative amendments . . . when the enactment of a liberal statute is inevitable [in order to] contain the substantive harm through sensibly chosen procedural safeguards."[75]

Assets and Liabilities

The weight of my criticism of the traditional Catholic position has centered on the fact that it does not allow a sufficient place in its theoretical approach to the consideration and weighing of other values than that of the right to life. It presumes that the right to bodily life of the fetus takes precedence at all times over other rights. In the case of the two exceptions allowed, it is said that they do not infringe the basic principle at stake when two lives (fetus and mother) are in mortal conflict: that the right to life of neither can take precedence over that of the other. The basis of the exceptions is that the killing of the fetus in those cases does not infringe the principle because its life is taken "indirectly." I have argued, however, that the right to life of the fetus, which the tradition claims is not *de jure* an absolute right (pointing to the admitted exceptions as proof of that contention), is *de facto* and for all practical purposes absolute—the exceptions admitted being so rare and medically uncommon as to afford no relief in the great range of abortion dilemmas. Even if it be granted that the conceptus is human life in the full sense of the term—and thus due full protection—the traditional position is still too narrow; at the very least it could be extended so that abortion cases might be handled with some of the flexibility and nuance of principle available in other cases of conflict between lives, or between lives and values (as in Catholic just-war theory). Moreover, of course, if one moves outside of the traditional problematic, employing a developmental rather than a genetic theory of the "beginning of human life" (which, in traditional terms, is the functional equivalent of the distinction between mediate and immediate animation), then the narrowness of the position could be further alleviated. Then it becomes a question of the rights of a human life, not yet a "person," more potential than actual, but still, for all that, *not* a mere nothingness, of no account in the moral reckoning.

The power of the traditional Catholic position is that it takes all human life seriously, even that life which can claim for itself only genetic individuality and unactualized potentiality. It says that whatever the form of moral reasoning employed in coming to abortion decisions, that life must be given a place of equality. It reflects a moral policy which, so to speak, bends over backward in favor of life, at whatever its stage, however doubtful its degree of development, however unknown its future, whatever its origin or circumstances of origin. It has chosen such a moral policy not only because of a respect for the intrinsic value of nascent life, a value independent of the worth attributed to it by others, but also because it believes that a moral policy of respecting all forms of human life provides the best basis for the security and stability of human law, institutions and society. Whatever one may care to say about the legalistic, impersonal, abstract way this basic affirmation was worked out in Catholic moral and medical manuals, it is a position worthy of something more than scoffing or instant dismissal. At the very least, it offers one coherent way of trying to order the issues, options and data; its motivation is honest and its moral seriousness, unquestionable.

If it is a mistaken approach, its error does not lie at the obvious level of logical fallacies or patently false ways of reading biological evidence. It has been worked out over a long enough period of time to avoid gross fallacies; and its reading of the biological evidence, while by no means the only possible one, is at least compatible with that evidence. Its mistake, to the contrary, lies in the totality of its approach, in the stance it has chosen to take toward the entire problem. By choosing to give the right to life a primacy over all other rights, by choosing _that_ value as one with the presumed power to obliterate all _other_ values, it (1) obviates human responsibility and choice, (2) fails to take account of the full range of human rights, relationships and obligations, (3) makes a whole range of data and experience irrelevant to the moral equation, (4) offers no possibility whatever of responding to the needs of women whose crisis is not one of mortal conflict with their fetuses, but whose conflict lies at the no less important level of their duty to self and to others, (5) so defines the issues in advance of particular cases that their particularities are rendered beside the point, and (6) assumes a fixed order of values, rights and obligations, somehow resistant to human choice, history and contexts.

Pope Pius XI, in _Casti Connubii_, said that "it is permissible and even obligatory to take into account the evidence alleged in regard to the social and eugenic 'indications' so long as the legitimate and proper means are used and due limits observed; but to attempt to meet the needs on which it is based by killing of the innocent is an irrational proceeding and contrary to the divine law." [76] The point of my criticism is that the issues have been so defined by the tradition that the obligation admitted by Pius XI becomes a dead letter, impossible of fulfillment, nullified in advance by the logic of the position espoused. Neither desperate poverty, mental illness, crippling physical disease, grave family responsibilities, incapacity for motherhood nor violent impregnation are allowed a place in the Catholic schematization of the problem. Any position which leads to so many exclusions, to so narrow a focus, merits rejection. The good it would accomplish is at the expense of other goods; the price exacted for the protection of fetal life is too high a price. A reading of the "sanctity of life" which establishes fixed moral entailments, rigid hierarchies of values and rights, and a rigid exclusion of experience and social data is an untenable position.

At the same time, however, what the traditional position wants to affirm—that nascent life has value—is an affirmation which should have an integral place in any alternative attempt to work out a richer method of moral decision-making. It is _a_ value, a critical value, a primary value. But it is not the only value at stake. A presumption in its favor is reasonable and desirable, but not so overwhelming a presumption that human beings are trapped by an iron-clad logic, left helpless and passive in the face of genuine moral conflicts, the resolution of which can go in one direction only. As Noonan has written, "The logic of one principle never rules the solution of a complex moral problem." [77] Unfortunately, he has been unable to make plausible his claim that the traditional position does not amount to a one-principle logic. Those Catholic theologians, however few in number still, who seek a multi-principled, multivalued framework for abortion decisions are on firmer ground. They take seriously, in a way the tradition cannot in practice (whatever it may say in principle), the perception that abortion is a complex moral problem. By holding on, however, to the affirmation of the tradition that nascent life is valuable life, they do honor to the tradition; it has said something of perennial importance. But by trying to move beyond the confines of the tradition, they also do honor to human experience, to the complexity of the problem and to the lives of the born as well as the unborn.

NOTES

1. John T. Noonan, Jr., *Contraception* (Cambridge: Harvard University Press, 1965), *passim*; ——, "Abortion and the Catholic Church: A Summary History," *Natural Law Forum*, 12 (1967), pp. 85–131; Roger John Huser, *The Crime of Abortion in Canon Law* (Washington, D.C.: Catholic University Press, 1942); David Granfield, *The Abortion Decision* (New York: Doubleday, 1969), especially pp. 53–72. Cyril Means, Jr., presented a number of criticisms of Noonan's historical account in a paper delivered at the International Conference on Abortion, Hot Springs, Va., Nov. 17–20, 1968.
2. Noonan, "Abortion and the Catholic Church . . . ," *op. cit.*, p. 97.
3. *Ibid.*, p. 104.
4. *Ibid.*, p. 109.
5. Quoted by Noonan, *ibid.*, p. 111.
6. *Acta Apostolicae Sedis*, 22 (1930), p. 562.
7. From *Papal Teachings: The Human Body* (Boston: St. Paul Editions, 1960), p. 60.
8. *Acta Apostolicae Sedis*, 43 (1951), p. 43.
9. *Ibid.*, p. 855.
10. *Acta Apostolicae Sedis*, 53 (1961), p. 401.
11. "The Church in the Modern World," in Walter M. Abbott, S.J. (ed.), *The Documents of Vatican II* (New York: Herder and Herder and Association Press, 1966), pp. 226, 256.
12. *Acta Apostolicae Sedis*, 60 (1968), p. 481.
13. Other possible exceptions, though disputed, arise in the instance of hydramnios (an excess of amniotic fluid) and a diseased placenta. For a discussion of hydramnios, see Thomas J. O'Donnell, S.J., *Morals in Medicine* (2d ed.; Westminster, Maryland: Newman Press, 1959), pp. 183–90. For a discussion about a diseased placenta, see John J. Connery, S.J., "Notes on Moral Theology," *Theological Studies*, 20 (March 1959), p. 604.
14. *Acta Apostolicae Sedis*, 43 (1951), p. 855.
15. Noonan, "Abortion and the Catholic Church . . . ," *op. cit.*, p. 125.
16. *Ibid.*
17. Since the Second Vatican Council, it has become, in many areas, increasingly problematic to speak of "the Church's position" on anything. Broadly taken, "the Church" includes all those who belong to the Roman Catholic community; this is increasingly the sense in which the term is being used within

that community. More narrowly, "the Church" has meant the teaching authority of the Church, which has traditionally been located in the office of the
Pope and the Bishops. To talk, then, of the "Church's position" or "Church
teaching" is ambiguous: it can mean either the convictions of the entire
Roman Catholic community or the formal teachings of the Popes and Bishops.
It is not always the case that they coincide. Pope Paul VI clearly upheld the
traditional position in his condemnation of contraception in *Humanae Vitae*,
but the dispute following that encyclical, the widespread dissent at the popu-
lar, the theological and even the episcopal level make clear that his position
does not necessarily reflect the position of the entire Roman Catholic com-
munity. (See, for instance, Daniel Callahan [ed.], *The Catholic Case for
Contraception* [New York: Macmillan, 1969], and Charles Curran [ed.],
Contraception: Authority and Dissent [New York: Herder and Herder, 1969].
For a more general discussion of the place of authority in contemporary
Catholicism, see Gregory Baum, *The Credibility of the Church Today* [New
York: Herder and Herder, 1968].) Curiously, however, abortion has been one
subject which has not occasioned much controversy within Catholicism since
the Second Vatican Council; the clamor for a change in the hierarchical
teaching on contraception has by no means been matched by a call for a
change on abortion. This means, therefore, that one can, with somewhat more
confidence than in the case of contraception, continue to speak of "the
Church's position," on abortion, meaning in this case the teaching of the Pope
and the Bishops, a teaching which, though it has not gone unquestioned, has
not been vigorously disputed within the Church. In any case, when I speak
of "the Church's position" here, I will mean the position taken by the Popes,
by the Second Vatican Council and by those theologians attempting to make
their own writings consistent with the position of hierarchical authority.

18. James M. Gustafson, "A Christian Approach to the Ethics of Abortion," *The
    Dublin Review*, (Winter 1967–68), pp. 347–350.
19. See, for instance, Bernard Häring, C.ss.R., *The Law of Christ* (Westminster,
    Maryland: Newman Press, 1966), Vol. III, p. 209: "God alone is the author
    of life and death. No physician may pass and execute the sentence of death
    on one who is innocent. . . . If despite all his sincere efforts . . . he is not
    successful, then God Himself has rendered the decision and passed the verdict
    on a human life." Father Charles McFadden, in line with many other Cath-
    olic moralists, argues that only those who are theists can understand this kind
    of point. (*Medical Ethics* [3rd ed.; Philadelphia: F. A. Davis, 1955], p. 165.)
20. T. J. O'Donnell, "Abortion, II (Moral Aspect)," *New Catholic Encyclopedia*
    (New York: McGraw-Hill, 1967), Vol. I, p. 29.
21. I. Aertnys, C. Damen, J. Visser, *Theologiae Moralis* (17th ed.; Turin: Marietti,
    1956), pp. 547–49.
22. R. A. McCormick, "Morality of War," *New Catholic Encyclopedia, op. cit.*, Vol.
    14, p. 805; see Jonathan Bennett, " 'Whatever the Consequences,' " *Analysis*,
    (January, 1966), pp. 83–102.
23. *Cf.* John P. Kenny, O.P., *Principles of Medical Ethics* (Westminster, Maryland:
    Newman Press, 1952), p. 131; Giuseppe Bosio, "Animazione," *Enciclopedia
    Cattolica* (Rome: Città del Vaticano, 1948), columns 1352–54; H. Noldin, A.
    Schmitt, G. Heinzel, *Summa Theologiae Moralis* II (34th ed.; Innsbruck: F.
    Rauch, 1963), p. 313; Rudolph Joseph Gerber, "When Is the Human Soul
    Infused?," *Laval Théologique et Philosophique*, 22 (1966), pp. 234–47.
24. *Ethical and Religious Directives for Catholic Hospitals* (St. Louis: The Catholic
    Hospital Association of the United States and Canada, 1965), p. 4; see also
    Karl Rahner, *Schriften zur Theologie* (Einsiedeln: Benziger Verlag, 1966), p.
    317, where the unborn child is called a "human being."
25. Robert F. Drinan, S.J., "The Inviolability of the Right to Be Born," in David
    T. Smith (ed.), *Abortion and the Law* (Cleveland: Western Reserve Univer-
    sity Press, 1967), p. 107.
26. Noonan, "Abortion and the Catholic Church . . . ," *op. cit.*, p. 125.

27. See David Granfield, "The Abortion Decision (New York: Doubleday, 1969), Chapter 1, "The Scientific Background," pp. 15–41.

28. Josef Fuchs, S.J., Natural Law, trans. H. Reckter and J. A. Dowling (New York: Sheed & Ward, 1965), p. 123. A standard manual of moral theology which argues in the same fashion is E. Genicot, J. Salsmans, A. Gortebecke, J. Beyer, Institutiones Theologiae Moralis I (17th ed.; [Beyer] Louvain: Desclée de Brouwer, 1964), pp. 304–05.

29. Granfield, op. cit., p. 144.

30. Robert F. Drinan, S.J., "The Right of the Foetus to Be Born," The Dublin Review, (Winter 1967–68), p. 377.

31. O'Donnell, Morals in Medicine, op. cit., p. 219.

32. Häring, op. cit., p. 209.

33. Noonan, "Abortion and the Catholic Church . . ." op. cit., p. 131.

34. I. Aertnys, C. Damen and J. Visser, op. cit., p. 547.

35. John Marshall, The Ethics of Medical Practice (London: Darton, Longman & Todd, 1960), p. 103.

36. Richard A. McCormick, S.J., America, 117 (December 9, 1967), p. 717.

37. Summa Theologica, 2–2.64.7.

38. This set of specifications has been taken from H. Noldin, A. Schmitt, and G. Heinzel, Summa Theologiae Moralis I (31st ed.; Innsbruck: F. Rauch, 1956), pp. 84ff.; for an application to abortion decisions, see A. Vermeersch, Theologiae Moralis (4th ed.; Rome: Gregorian University Press, 1947), Vol. 1, pp. 105–07; F. Hürth, De Statibus (Rome: Gregorian University Press, 1946), p. 325; E. Genicot et al., Institutiones Theologiae Moralis I, op. cit., pp. 305–06; "Aborto," in Enciclopedia Cattolica (Rome: Città del Vaticano, 1948). column 107.

39. A. Bouscaren, Ethics of Ectopic Operations (2nd ed.; Milwaukee: Bruce, 1943), pp. 1–2. Bouscaren's book remains the most thorough treatment of the subject of ectopic operations. See also Gerard Kelly, S.J., Medico-Moral Problems (St. Louis: The Catholic Hospital Association, 1958), p. 26; Joseph J. Farraher, S.J., "Notes on Moral Theology," Theological Studies, 22 (December 1961), p. 622; John J. Lynch, S.J., "Ectopic Pregnancy: A Theological Review," Theological Studies, 28 (February 1961), p. 12.

40. See Noldin, Schmitt, Heinzel, op. cit., pp. 340ff.

41. Granfield, op. cit., p. 139.

42. Noonan, "Abortion and the Catholic Church . . . ," op. cit., p. 130.

43. Fuchs, op. cit., p. 131.

44. Granfield, op. cit., p. 143.

45. Noonan, "Abortion and the Catholic Church . . . ," op. cit., p. 130.

46. A good, brief account of these trends can be found in Charles E. Curran, Christian Morality Today (Notre Dame, Indiana: Fides Publishers, 1966).

47. William H. Van der Marck, O.P., Toward a Christian Ethic, trans. Denis J. Barrett (Westminster, Maryland: Newman Press, 1967), pp. 56–57.

48. Cornelius J. Van der Poel, "The Principle of Double Effect," in Charles E. Curran (ed.), Absolutes in Moral Theology (Washington, D.C.: Corpus Books, 1968), p. 192. Charles E. Curran, in the same volume, makes a substantially similar point in "Absolute Norms and Medical Ethics," p. 112.

49. Van der Poel, op. cit., pp. 204–05. An important attempt to refine the principle of double effect has been undertaken by P. Knauer, S.J., "La Détermination du bien et du mal moral par le principe du double effet," Nouvelle Revue Théologique, 87 (April 1965), pp. 356–76. He argues that, while the usual interpretation of the principle requires that in order for an act with a good and an evil effect to be undertaken, there must be a proportionate reason to justify the act, the concept of "proportionate reason" needs to be reinterpreted. His formula is as follows: "That a reason is disproportionate means that, taking the whole reality into account, a man inhibits the full realization of the value he aims at by the very way in which he aspires to it: the act therefore is not proportionate with its own reason. On the other hand there

is a proportionate reason if he really aspires to the maximal realization of the value on the level of its total reality" (pp. 369–70). Whether this formulation would permit abortion in cases other than those usually encompassed by the principle is not clear. The last sentence of the quotation would, however, seem to encompass abortion in those situations where, say, the lives and critical welfare of the mother and her children might depend upon an abortion. The previous sentence, though, might suggest that to aspire to save the life of the mother through the taking of the life of the fetus would be to inhibit the full realization of the value aspired to, e.g., respect for life. Richard A. McCormick, S.J., has criticized Knauer's reformulation especially on the grounds that exclusive reliance on "proportionate reasons" opens the way to the use of any means to attain a good end ("Notes on Moral Theology," *Theological Studies*, 24 [December 1965], pp. 603–08).

50. Granfield, *op. cit.*, p. 146.

51. This is only to say that the "wedge" or the "camel's nose" argument can be invoked only in those situations where the terms and concepts are commensurable and understood in the same way. Paul Ramsey has pertinently distinguished between the "wedge" argument and the "universalizability" argument. In the former, our concern is with the larger consequences of our actions: "Will we influence ourselves to go on to do other things? Will *my* actions have consequences of a large order on the practices of others? Will *this* social practice have consequences on *other* practices? (Paul Ramsey, "Some Terms of Reference for the Abortion Debate," unpublished paper, Harvard Divinity School–Kennedy Foundation International Conference on Abortion, September 1967). In the latter, "it asks, rather, in regard to an individual act, what *would* be the case if everyone in a morally relevant, like situation did X *as I am doing* . . . ? And in regard to a social purpose it asks, what *would* be the case if every possible X were done that fulfills the warrants now invoked to justify a present practice or reform (whether or not there is any causal connection between one practice and another)?" (*Ibid.*) One reason why Catholics seem to assume that a liberalization of abortion laws or attitudes would lead to other undesirable practices is that the reliance of their abortion argument on what are presumed to be general moral principles leads inexorably to the conclusion that a violation of these principles in one case sets the stage for their violation in another case where the same principles come into play. If moral practices X, Y, Z depend on moral principles A and B, then to change the latter would most likely entail a changing of the former. But this will only happen, one would think, if everyone is using these same principles for their moral reasoning in all situations. If not, then the "wedge" argument loses its force or at least (as many Catholics seem to assume) its self-evident quality. By contrast, the "universalizability" argument could be invoked across different moral systems, for it does not depend upon a commensurateness of moral principles and concepts from one person to the next.

52. Charles E. Curran, *A New Look at Christian Morality* (Notre Dame, Indiana: Fides Publishers, 1968), pp. 242–43. Father Curran, in this quote, is alluding to the fact that Catholic theologians, in their treatment of just and unjust killing, have ordinarily allowed just killing in defense of such values as the preservation of vital human rights and material goods. See, for instance, Benedictus H. Merkelbach, O.P., *Summa Theologiae Moralis* II (10th ed.; Bruges: Desclee), p. 350, and Thomas J. Higgins, S.J., *Man as Man* (Milwaukee: Bruce, 1949), p. 249.

53. Noonan, "Abortion and the Catholic Church . . . ," *op. cit.*, pp. 124–25.

54. A comment is in order here. The possibility of citing, as I am doing, a number of theologians who argue for a position different from that of the Pope and the Bishops (and the conservative tradition) should not be taken to imply any massive groundswell of theological opinion in favor of a change in the teaching. For the most part, the move by some in the direction of a change is tentative and probing, surely anything but a crusade on their part. The contrast between the mode of arguing this issue in a change-oriented direction

and that now employed for a change in the Church's teaching on contraception is striking. In the latter case, public statements have been issued in direct dissent from the papal teaching, the literature in favor of change is massive, and the degree of manifested certainty and impassioned conviction, strikingly intense. No such parallel obtains in the case of abortion, where the theological proponents of change are far fewer and the intensity of their efforts, considerably less.

55. Francis Simons, "The Catholic Church and the New Morality," *Cross Currents*, 16 (Fall 1966), pp. 438–39.

56. Leonard F. X. Mayhew, "Abortion: Two Sides and Some Complaints," *The Ecumenist*, 5 (July-August 1967), p. 76.

57. Heinz Fleckenstein, "Christian Remedies for Medical 'Hopelessness,'" *Arzt und Christ* (11th ed.; Salzburg, 1965), pp. 235–45, especially p. 243.

58. Robert H. Springer, S.J., "Notes on Moral Theology," *Theological Studies*, 28 (June 1967), p. 310. "St. Thomas' well-known doctrine," to which Father Springer refers, is illustrated in the following passage from the *Summa Theologica* (1-2, 94.4): "Thus the natural law in its first general principles is the same for all both as to what is right and in their recognition of it. But in relation to details which come as conclusions from those general principles, it is the same for all for the most part (both as to what is right and in their knowledge of it), but may, in some cases, admit of exception as to what is right because of particular circumstances as well as not being known to all." See also Columba Ryan, O.P., "The Traditional Concept of Natural Law: An Interpretation," in Illtud Evans, O.P. (ed.), *Light on the Natural Law* (Baltimore: Helicon Press, 1965), pp. 31ff.; and Peter Chirico, S.S., "Tension, Morality, and Birth Control," *Theological Studies*, 28 (June 1967), especially the following: "It is precisely because of the complexity of every moral act that the Church has not judged and cannot judge the moral value of a given act *in concreto*. All its moral teaching is necessarily concerned with judgments of abstract morality. Thus, the declaration that a given activity is always wrong can only mean that this aspect of human activity is always morally harmful; it cannot mean that every concrete act embodying this aspect is necessarily sinful" (p. 271).

59. Springer, *op. cit.*, p. 333.

60. Joseph Donceel, S.J., "Abortion: Mediate V. Immediate Animation," *Continuum*, 5 (Spring 1967), pp. 167–71.

61. Thomas Wassmer, "Questions About Questions," *Commonweal*, 86 (June 30, 1967), p. 418. For further discussions of the status of the argument about the time of animation, see: Häring, *op. cit.*, p. 206: "The antiquated opinion of Aristotle at best is only slightly probable"; McCormick, *op. cit.*, especially the following passage (p. 718): "If one were to argue in this way [from a theory of mediate animation], he would still face two harrowing tasks: 1) the proof that a doubtfully animated fetus makes lesser claims on us than an animated one; 2) the determination of what values justify the sacrifice of life which is not yet fully human"; H. de Dorlodot, "A Vindication of the Mediate Animation Theory," in E. C. Messenger (ed.), *Theology and Evolution* (London: Sands, 1949), p. 260; Raymond J. Nogar, "Evolution, Human. 2. Philosophical Aspects," in *New Catholic Encyclopedia, op. cit.*, Vol. 5, p. 684 (Nogar believes that animation takes place "probably not before the end of the third month"); an opposite view, also arguing from biological evidence, is J. E. Royce, "Soul, Human, Origin of," in *New Catholic Encyclopedia, op. cit.*, Vol. 13, p. 471. For a discussion of the theological context of the argument, especially as it bears on the debate about "traducianism" and "creationism," see Harry A. Wolfson, *Religious Philosophy* (Cambridge: Harvard University Press, 1961), pp. 86ff.; Karl Rahner and P. Overhage, *Das Problem der Hominisation* (Freiburg: Herder, 1961), p. 79; Karl Rahner and Herbert Vorgrimler, *Theological Dictionary* (New York: Herder and Herder, 1965), pp. 107 and 464. For a discussion of these issues in the context of an attempt to deal with the problem of evolution, see Peter Schoonenberg, *God's World*

in the Making (Techny, Illinois: Divine Word Publications, 1967), especially pp. 21ff.; Robert T. Francoeur, *Perspectives in Evolution* (Baltimore: Helicon, 1965), pp. 237ff., and especially p. 242: "The moment of conception of which the philosophers and theologians speak even today reveals a basic pattern of thought, a dimension, a world vision, rooted in categories and essences. But the moment of conception, like everything else in our evolving world, has proven to be more a process than a simple black-and-white point in time." Francoeur goes on from there to criticize the entire soul-body distinction (pp. 245ff).

62. The Catholic literature, professional, popular and hierarchical, against liberalized laws is voluminous. A good bibliographical source is the *Linacre Quarterly*, the official journal of the National Federation of Catholic Physicians' Guilds. Hardly an issue goes by which does not have something on abortion, exclusively from a conservative stance. A lengthy series in that journal, "Abortion," by Monsignor Paul V. Harrison, which ran during 1967 and 1968, draws together a host of citations. Russell Shaw's *Abortion on Trial* (Dayton, Ohio: Pflaum Press, 1968) is a sustained attempt to show the undesirability of liberal abortion laws, as well as a good source of references for conservative Catholic authors.

63. "Relaxation of Maryland's Abortion Law Opposed by Bishops," a statement issued by Cardinal Lawrence Shehan of Baltimore, Cardinal Patrick O'Boyle of Washington, D.C., and Monsignor Paul J. Taggart, Administrator of the Diocese of Wilmington, Delaware, *Catholic Mind*, 66 (March 1968), pp. 1–2.

64. See especially Robert M. Byrn, "Abortion in Perspective," *Duquesne University Law Review*, 5 (Winter 1966–1967), pp. 125–41; ———, "A Legal View," *Commonweal*, 85 (March 17, 1967), pp. 679–81.

65. Norman St. John-Stevas, *The Right to Life*, (New York: Holt, Rinehart and Winston, 1964).

66. Norman St. John-Stevas, "The English Experience," *America*, 117 (December 9, 1967), p. 709.

67. "The Abortion Question: Life and Law in a Pluralistic Society," *ibid.*, p. 706.

68. Drinan, "The Inviolability of the Right to Be Born," *op. cit.*, p. 122.

69. Robert F. Drinan, S.J., "Strategy on Abortion," *America*, 116 (February 4, 1967), p. 179.

70. Drinan, "The Right of the Fetus to Be Born," *op. cit.*, p. 371.

71. For a sharp Catholic rejoinder to this line of reasoning, see the "open letter" to Father Drinan by Father William C. Hunt, *National Catholic Reporter* (June 19, 1968), p. 6, and Father Drinan's response in the same issue.

72. They are worth citing here: "Therefore the moral aspirations of law are minimal. Law seeks to establish and maintain only that minimum of actualized morality that is necessary for the healthy functioning of the social order. It does not look to what is morally desirable, or attempt to remove every moral taint from the atmosphere of society. It enforces only what is minimally acceptable, and in this sense socially necessary. . . . Is it prudent to undertake the enforcement of this or that ban, in view of the possibility of harmful effects in other areas of social life? Is the instrumentality of coercive law a good means for the eradication of this or that social vice? And, since a means is not a good means if it fails to work in most cases, what are the lessons of experience in the matter?" (John Courtney Murray, S.J., *We Hold These Truths* [New York: Sheed & Ward, 1960], pp. 166–67.)

73. Norman St. John-Stevas, *Life, Death and the Law* (Bloomington: Indiana University Press, 1961), especially Chapter 1, "Law and Morals," pp. 13–49.

74. See especially Thomas A. Wassmer, "The Crucial Question About Abortion," *Catholic World*, 206 (November 1967), p. 61: "Where men of goodwill and ethical integrity disagree, is it always prudential for Catholics to try to impose their 'traditional' answers on other citizens by way of a general civil law? Is it not the best index of a man's love of freedom that he respects the freedom of others, and is ethically perceptive and morally sensitive to the freedom of Catholics? And this responsibility is of course reciprocal"; Donald A. Gian-

nella, "The Difficult Quest for a Truly Humane Abortion Law," *Villanova Law Review,* 13 (Winter 1968), pp. 257–302; Häring, *op. cit.,* p. 210: "The state cannot declare anything lawful which the law of God forbids. However, it may in certain specially critical cases abstain from punishment, particularly if the attitudes and concepts of 'science' are so confused and unclear as they unfortunately are today"; Springer, *op. cit.,* p. 335: "In the last analysis the hard demands of political reality may mean that we will have to support a compromise measure in place of a given abortion bill"; Bernard J. Ransil, *Abortion* (New York: Paulist Press Deus Books, 1969), esp. p. 101: ". . . specific indications for therapeutic abortion should probably not be legislated." The most radical Catholic advocacy of abortion to date is to be found in Giles Milhaven, S.J., "The Abortion Debate: An Epistomological Interpretation," *Theological Studies,* 31 (March 1970) forthcoming.

75. Granfield, *op. cit.,* p. 201. It should be noted that Granfield distinguishes this possibility from the making of "a strategic compromise—the acceptance of a moderate proposal to avoid the enactment of an extreme proposal" (*ibid.*). The latter, he believes, is not acceptable because it would destroy the basis of opposition to abortion "by supplanting the principle of human dignity and equality with the principle of expediency" (*ibid.*).

76. Pius XI, *Casti Connubii, op. cit.,* p. 564.

77. Noonan, "Abortion and the Catholic Church . . . ," *op. cit.,* p. 109.

CHAPTER 13

Abortion on Request and Legal Reform

THE TRADITIONAL ROMAN CATHOLIC position on the morality of abortion has been criticized for its one-dimensionality. The thesis of this chapter is that abortion on request as a *moral* position, at least in some of its more prominent formulations, suffers from a similar weakness. In particular, I have in mind the contention that a "woman's right" to chart her own procreative destiny is the only moral issue at stake in abortion decisions. But just as the "right to life" of the fetus is too narrow a basis in determining the morality of abortion, so, too, the "rights of women" is equally narrow. Both positions try to rest their case on one, and only one, putative right; or one, and only one, putative value. It has been the argument of this book that many rights and many values come into play in abortion decisions and that a moral logic which tries to decide the issue on the basis of only one right or one value is bound to oversimplify and thus obscure the full moral complexity of the problem.

However, one point needs to be made clear at the outset, to obviate the possibility of any confusion as this chapter progresses. A sharp distinction needs to be drawn between abortion on request as a *moral* position and abortion on request as a *legal* position. The weight of my criticism of abortion on request is directed at it insofar as it is put forth as a moral position. As for abortion on request as a legal position—to anticipate a bit—I will argue that it represents good public and legal policy (though, as will be seen, it would best be effected by permissive laws rather than repeal of all laws). To be sure, many of those who favor abortion on request tend to run the moral and the legal issues together so that the distinction is obscured or lost; but it will be honored here. At the same time, abortion on request as a moral position is by no means without its strong points. Just as the "right to life" of the fetus as a moral issue ought not to be dismissed out of hand (but placed in the context of other rights—and preserved in a multivalued position), so also the "rights of women" surely should not be slighted either, and for the same reasons.

Unfortunately, it is not altogether easy to piece together a full-fledged philosophical picture of abortion on request as a moral tenet. Moreover, some authors speak of "abortion on demand" and others of "abortion on request." Most of the writings in its favor are fairly recent in origin; they tend to be short articles rather than books. Rarely is it possible to determine out of which philosophical or ideological tradition they spring. Some who defend the position stress points which other, equally ardent defenders do not. If the asserted conclusions are clear enough, the premises on which they rest are usually considerably less so. This may present no problems for its defenders, but it poses many for one who would try to see just what, in some detail, the position wants to say about the status of fetal life, the relative rights of women, doctors, males and legislators, and how it would attempt to meet different kinds of objections. These observations are not meant by way of rebuttal; they are only to point out the problems inherent in trying to analyze the position fairly and accurately.

These lacunae are probably not surprising. In most places in the West, it was not possible until recently to present an abortion-on-request position to the general public; the mass media and the public seemed open, at most, to pressure in favor of moderate liberalization of abortion laws, nothing very radical. Prior to the last few years, even those who ultimately favored abortion on request as part of the law or repeal of all laws felt it prudent to press only for moderate reform of the law. As Dr. Alan F. Guttmacher wrote in 1967, before he came out in favor of repeal of abortion laws, "I believe that social progress is better made by evolution than revolution. Today, complete abortion license would do great violence to the beliefs and sentiments of most Americans. Therefore, I doubt that the U.S. is as yet ready to legalize abortion on demand." [1] A 1966 survey conducted by the National Opinion Research Center found that, while a majority of the respondents would favor abortion in the case of danger to health, rape or serious danger of fetal defect, only a minority would favor it on account of an excessively large family or because the pregnant woman is unmarried. [2]

In this climate of opinion—similar to that in England and even in the Scandinavian countries—it is hardly astounding that advocates of abortion on demand or abortion on request had little chance to gain a hearing and, even when they did, felt that an effort toward a reform law would be a wiser interim goal. It is only since the mid-1960s that pressure in favor of abortion on request has surfaced, best signaled perhaps by the formation of the National Association for the Repeal of Abortion

Laws in early 1969, under the leadership of Lawrence Lader. In his 1966 study, *Abortion*, Mr. Lader had presented a "strategy" for law reform, though making it clear at the end of his book that the ideal solution would be "complete legalization." [3] In a word, the abortion-on-request position has hardly had the time or chance to mature and be discussed in a full way. This in itself, however, says nothing for or against the position; it simply helps explain the dearth of fully developed arguments and an extensive literature.

It is possible, though, to piece together the leading points in the position. A prototypical statement can be found in Simone de Beauvoir's *The Second Sex*:

> Nothing could be more absurd than the arguments brought forward against the legalization of abortion. . . . Enforced maternity brings into the world wretched infants, whom their parents will be unable to support and who will become the victims of public care or "child martyrs." . . . We must also reckon with . . . masculine sadism. . . . Contraception and legal abortion would permit woman to undertake her maternities in freedom. [4]

These short passages sum up the key points in most abortion-on-request arguments: enforced maternities should not take place; unwanted children should not be brought into the world; male domination is responsible for stringent abortion laws; female freedom is ultimately dependent upon a woman's full and free control of her procreative life. Many of the same points, even more vehemently put, are made by Lawrence Lader:

> The laws that force a woman to bear a child against her will are the sickly heritage of feminine degradation and male supremacy. . . . The neglect of man-made laws to grant the choice of motherhood not only condemns women to the level of brood animals, but disfigures the sanctity of birth itself. By making birth the result of blind impulse and passion, our laws ensure that children may become little more than the automatic reflex of a biological system. . . . The complete legalization of abortion is the one just and inevitable answer to the quest for feminine freedom. All other solutions are compromises. [5]

Also heard is the additional contention that induced abortion should be treated strictly as a medical question. B. James George, Jr., has written:

> If in fact it is the medical profession, or segments of it, that wishes liberalization of abortion laws, so that decisions to perform dilation and curettage or other medical operations can be made as any other medical determination might be, it seems appropriate to make the primary legal context within which those decisions are to be made that of the statutes regulating doctors and hospitals. [6]

Harriet F. Pilpel has made the same point: "Whether or not to have an abortion is a medical question to be decided like all other medical questions by the patient and her doctor." [7]

Now, it is surely the case that induced abortion is a medical *procedure* which must be carried out (for safety) by trained medical personnel. But it is hard to see how one can move from that fact to the conclusion that the problem of abortion itself is only a medical question. Clearly people's values, motivations and situations come into play as well (both on the part of the pregnant woman and on the part of the doctor). To know *how* to perform an abortion is not to answer the question whether an abortion *ought* to be performed; the latter problem transcends the strictly technical aspects of abortion operations. It is considerations of this kind which no doubt explain the reluctance even of many advocates of abortion on request to press this line of argument, preferring to rest their case on the more general principle of woman's rights, the undesirability of unwanted children, and the hazards of underground abortions. Thomas Szasz, for instance, in the context of a strong plea for legalized abortion, has contended:

> Abortion is a moral, not a medical, problem. To be sure, the procedure is surgical; but this makes abortion no more a medical problem than the use of the electric chair makes capital punishment a problem of electrical engineering. . . . The question is not one of medical and psychiatric justification for abortion, but of ethical judgment and social policy. If we truly believe that in a free society the expert should be on tap, not on top—we must place the power to decide when an abortion may be performed (legally) in the hands of the pregnant woman, and not in the hands of the Church, the State, the American Medical Association, or the American Law Institute.[8]

Moreover, as many advocates of abortion on demand realize, to press the case on medical grounds or to talk of the problem as essentially medical leaves the focus of the debate on the exceptional rather than on the common situation. As Alice S. Rossi has pointed out:

> Few women who seek abortions have been exposed to German measles or taken thalidomide and hence fear a deformed fetus; few have serious heart or liver conditions that constitute a threat to their life if they carried the pregnancy to term; fewer still have been raped by a stranger or by their own father. The majority of women who seek abortions do so because they find themselves with unwelcome or unwanted pregnancies; abortion is a last-resort birth-control measure when preventive techniques have failed or have not been used. It is the situation *of not wanting a child* that covers the main rather than the exceptional abortion situation.[9]

The Unwanted Child

The most important moral elements of the abortion-on-request position reduce to two key points: the undesirability of the unwanted child and the right of women to sexual and procreative freedom. Though these two issues are usually argued in tandem, they involve different considerations and a different line of argument. In its most common formulation, the "unwanted child argument" moves in two directions. One concerns that of the interests of the child himself and the other, the interests of society. They can best be examined in that order, but, before doing so, it is well to mention briefly the general problem of what constitutes a suitable or proper environment for childhood development.

Kerstin Höök cites a formulation of those conditions favorable to normal development by D. Blomberg which is as succinct as any:

> To be born in wedlock, to grow up in a steadfast home environment in the company of both parents and under satisfactory economic conditions, to be given an upbringing that does not go to extremes in the direction either of laxity or of severity, and to escape exposure to the influence of asocial or in other respects abnormal behavior on the part of near relations.[10]

Erik H. Erikson's classic attempt to specify the desirable sequential goals of normal development—trust, autonomy, initiative, industry, identity, intimacy, generativity and ego integrity—are no less pertinent, all of them requiring a healthy, secure and stable environment.[11] There is, however, an essential difference between specifying the optimal environment for childhood development and specifying the extent to which a child could be deprived of one or more vital elements and yet still satisfactorily adjust, however minimally. And, of course, one could argue interminably about what a minimal degree of satisfactory adjustment would require. Beyond these theoretical questions, there eventually looms the moral question: Even if it could be known in advance (which might be difficult) that a potential child would suffer some disastrous deprivations, would this entail the conclusion that such a child ought not to exist at all? The first element is a matter of probabilities; and in attempting to spell out the capacity of human beings to surmount even the worst kinds of beginnings, considerable caution would be in order. Who could readily say, given varying individual capacities, that a given conceptus, if born, could not and would not develop into a satisfactory and satisfactorally adjusted human being, if not at first, perhaps eventually? The trouble in trying to even talk this way—using the language of satisfaction and adjustment—is that such words and phrases are value-laden, influenced by cultural differences and resistant to being specified (even if one wanted to—a moral question in itself) in sheerly empirical terms. One could, to be sure, stipulate an empirical meaning and criteria for these terms, but that would hardly settle the problem of whether that *ought* to be the stipulation.

The crux of one moral problem here—abortion for the sake of the child—is whether it is possible to say, in a morally meaningful way, that one ought to abort a potential human being in the interests of that human being. It is difficult to see how. On the actual life prospects of the potential human being, there could at most be offered some statistical generalizations, bearing on the likelihood of happiness, adjustment, economic and social security, loving nurture and so on. But ought one deny a potential human being the *chance* to develop, however slim, on the basis of statistical probabilities? And could these probabilities ever be perfectly formulated, capable of projecting accurately into the distant future (e.g., all the way into the adult years of the potential human being in question)? One might say that no risk ought to be taken, that any hazard is too great. But, then, by what license are we obligated or free to make that decision for the potential human being in question? No one is ever in any position to say whether any given conceptus would, if it could choose (which, of course, it cannot), decide not to live. Nor, as discussed in the chapter on fetal indications, is it possible, either logically or empirically, to project back from existing human beings conclusions about those who do not exist.

If the conceptus is allowed to develop, then it can eventually make its own decision about whether it wants to live or die. It is one thing to say, "If I had the prospects of that kind of life, I would not want to live," but quite another to say, therefore, "My norms (or those of my community) should be applied to the potential life of someone else." Even the slightest acquaintance with individual variations in what people want out of life, what they would settle for and how they order their own priorities of happiness or adjustment would make such a judgment not only morally presumptuous but empirically groundless. In a word, why ought not the potential human being in question be the one to make the ultimate decision about whether he lives or dies? That he cannot *now* make the decision does not entail that someone else should make the decision for him. On the contrary, it entails—if there is any belief in self-determination at all—that the being be allowed to develop and make his own choice.[12]

Dr. H. B. Munson has written:

> Should we not allow fetuses their right to die if there is a strong likelihood of their being handicapped physically or mentally? Perhaps we are not big enough or wise enough to make that decision, but there seems to be solid grounds for allowing the unborn's parents to decide this, since it is they who will be the most encumbered and troubled in caring for the child.[13]

While one could easily grant, under a number of circumstances, a "right to die," it becomes a very strangely exercised right when the being in question has it exercised on its behalf by others. It becomes stranger still when, in Dr. Munson's formulation, the fact that the life in question

will trouble *others* is urged as a grounds for exercising the unborn's
rights: you have a right to die; your living will trouble me; hence, I
will exercise for you your right to die.

Abortion in the interests of society presents a different moral problem.
As Garrett Hardin has written,

> How then does society gain by increasing the number of unwanted children?
> No one has volunteered an answer to this question. . . . If [a woman] is preg-
> nant against her will, does it matter to society whether or not she was careless
> or unskillful in her use of contraception? In any case, she is threatening so-
> ciety with an unwanted child, for which society will pay dearly.[14]

It could be pointed out to Prof. Hardin that no one has attempted to
argue against abortion on the ground that unwanted children are
socially desirable; even those most opposed to abortion do not take
that line. The conservative Protestant, Jewish and Catholic position has
held only that abortion is not a moral means to achieve what might be
good ends. In another place, however, Prof. Hardin has spelled out the
social case for abortion on request:

> Is it good that a woman who does not want a child should bear one? An
> abundant literature in psychology and sociology proves that the unwanted
> child is a social danger. Unwanted children are more likely than others to
> grow up in psychologically unhealthy homes; they are more likely than others
> to become delinquents, and . . . when they become parents they are more
> likely than others to be poor parents themselves and breed another generation
> of unwanted children. This is a vicious circle if ever there was one. This is
> what an engineer would call positive feedback; it is ruinous to the social
> system. . . . In this day of the population explosion, society has no reason to
> encourage the birth of more children; but it has a tremendous interest in
> encouraging the birth of more wanted children.[15]

Alice S. Rossi, discussing the problem of the unmarried woman, has
written that "to withhold the possibility of a safe and socially acceptable
abortion for unmarried women is to start the chain of illegitimacy and
despair that will continue to keep poverty, crime, and poor mental
health high on the list of pressing social problems in the United
States." [16] Lawrence Lader speaks in the same vein: "The right to abortion is the foundation of Society's long struggle to guarantee that every
child comes into this world wanted, loved, and cared for. The right to
abortion, along with all birth-control measures, must establish the
Century of the Wanted Child." [17]

Some questions need to be raised. First of all, there is no reason to
deny the general proposition that the unwanted child starts life in a
highly unfavorable position. Enough is known about the effects of a
harmful childhood environment and the need for parental love to be
able to conclude that being unwanted is a major liability and conducive

to psychopathology in one form or another. But any generalizations here have to be specified by defining the meaning of "wanted," and this none of the authors cited above does. As we saw in Chapter 3, almost all pregnancies are accompanied by some degree of fear, anxiety or apprehension; many women, on first discovering a pregnancy, do not want the child, but later come to accept it readily enough. Others, of course, continue not wanting the child. The question is, what counts as *seriously* not wanting a child and what may be counted as that kind of transitory recoil which will disappear as the pregnancy progresses? In a word, what are the criteria for being "wanted" and "unwanted"? At one extreme would be such a persistent and deep-seated resentment at having a child that a prognosis might reasonably be made that the child would be in extreme hazard of becoming a "battered child," and perhaps a dead child. Somewhere in between would be a child which, while it might not be battered or killed, could be so deprived of affection and care as to develop in an antisocial direction, thus posing hazards to others in later life. Then, more mildly, are those whose nondesire for a child would be amenable to simple therapy and familial or social support. And a distinction has to be drawn between those whose external situation makes them not want a child (poverty, too many other children, being unmarried, etc.) and those whose subjective situation or personal goals (neuroticism or immaturity, on the one hand, or the desire to pursue a career, on the other) leads them not to want a child. This is only to point out that the word "unwanted" can have a number of possible meanings and occur in a number of different social and psychological contexts. It is possible to distinguish between an unwanted pregnancy (one which comes at a bad or undesired time) and an unwanted child (which has more to do with the child-to-be than the pregnancy itself).[18]

One moral problem here is whether, in the first place, one ought to be concerned with these different possible senses of "unwanted." Put differently, if a woman *says* she does not want a child, ought that to be the end of the discussion? Or would it not at least be necessary to inquire into her reasons for *saying* that? A verbal declaration that a woman does not want a child is only *prima facie* evidence that she does not (though an effort to procure an abortion does serve to substantiate her words). Would she still feel the same way and make the same declaration if help and therapy were offered to her? If she does not want the child because of poverty, she might well change her mind if money is proffered her. If it is fear that motivates her desire not to have a child, then counseling and simple therapy might rid her of that fear. If one is genuinely interested in the welfare of the woman, considerations of this kind would seem imperative. Neither in pregnancies nor in other aspects of life are things always the way they seem to be on the surface, and what people say is not always a perfect index to what they really want or desire. It should hardly be necessary to raise points of this kind, but it is surprising that so many of those who press the "unwanted child" argument do not even mention them. This is all the more surprising since that particular argument almost always occurs in the context of a "rights of women" argument. If the goal is perfect freedom for women, then it is hard to see how it could be fulfilled without taking account of the possibility that, given some genuine options (money, therapy, support), many women who *say*, at first, that they do not want a child might well change their minds and feel all the freer for having some real choices presented to them.

A more complicated moral problem is the relationship between "being wanted" and "having value." Perhaps the implication is not intended, but the way the "unwanted child" argument is phrased often seems to imply that *having value* is directly and totally reducible to *being wanted*. In an abortion-decision situation, something already exists —a conceptus. That immediately distinguishes this situation biologically and socially from the situation where no conceptus exists. But does this conceptus have a value in itself or is its value strictly dependent upon whether someone wants it? Garrett Hardin, for one, appears to make the value of the conceptus entirely dependent upon the social value attributed to it by society.[19] In Thomas Szasz's view, abortion is a "crime without victims":

> During the first two to three months of gestation (when most abortions are performed), the embryo cannot live outside the womb. It may therefore be considered part of the woman's body. If so, there ought to be no special laws regulating abortion. Such an operation should be available in the same way as, say, an operation for the beautification of a nose.[20]

There are a number of problems hidden in this last passage. Biologically, it is odd to talk of an embryo as "part of the woman's body"; it is surely *in* her body but by no means part of it the way, for instance, her nose is part of it. The separate genetic constitution of the embryo, its independent circulatory, hormonal and nervous systems all serve clearly to distinguish the mother as organism from that of the conceptus. Dr. Szasz hedges a bit in saying that the embryo "may be considered part of the mother's body." But he does not say why it ought so to be "considered," and the biological evidence is against it. Nor does Dr. Szasz make clear why viability is significant. If the crux of the moral problem is, as he says, what the woman wants to do (and not what anyone else thinks), there is no reason explicit or implicit here why the woman herself or her doctor ought to recognize viability as a point beyond which she could not decide in favor of abortion. A similar problem appears in Garrett Hardin's formulation. Hardin goes to some trouble to show that, in itself, the ingredients making up a fetus—substance, energy, information—are themselves of negligible value and that we can define the fetus as a human being or nonhuman being "any way we wish." [21] He states that it would be "unwise" to define the "early fetus" as a human being. But if the main line of his argument is that women should not be subjected to compulsory pregnancies, what of the woman who decides, relatively late in pregnancy—after, say, the time of viability —that she does not want the child? If the crux of the moral problem is, as he states, whether a woman is to be forced to go throught with a pregnancy against her will—Hardin's main contention—then there seems to be no reason why she should feel constrained not to have a very late fetus aborted. Where the woman's desire has been stipulated as the ultimate criterion for whether an abortion is to be performed, the status of the fetus, human or nonhuman, becomes logically irrelevant. Hardin's argument, in any case, leaves unclear the link between the biological evidence and the role of the woman's desire.

Ambiguities of this kind leave uncertain the question of whether the conceptus derives whatever value it has exclusively and totally from whether it is wanted or not. The implication seems to be that, in itself, the conceptus is of no value; it awaits someone's wanting it—then and only then is it of moral interest or human worth. There are also two further ambiguities. First, is it the case that if the conceptus is not wanted by the mother, then it is an object of disvalue, something which *ought* to be destroyed? Second, if it can be shown, or at least statistically supposed, that an unwanted conceptus poses an eventual "danger to society," then ought not that conceptus to be aborted even if the mother does not want or cannot in conscience abide an abortion? For not wanting a child and wanting an abortion are not the same. Here is where the arguments which try to show that an unwanted child should not be born on the grounds of the danger to society run into potential conflict with arguments designed to show that the choice of the woman is the critical moral value. Which, in the end, is more important, that women be free to choose to give birth to a child they may not want (moral scruples, for instance, keeping them from abortion), or that unwanted children not be born? If the latter, then coercion might seem justified on the logic of the interests of society; the woman's own desire might take second place. If the former, then society is left with no re- course to protect itself but that of persuasion, which may be ineffective.

The questions being raised here and the implications being discerned are in the main *speculative;* proponents of abortion on request have not drawn these implications. The immediate context of the controversy bears on those women who do not want a child and do want an abortion. But unless it be wholly illegitimate to raise questions of this kind— which is only to ask what exactly is at stake in the long as well as the

short run, and what the possible consequences of the position are—
then questions and speculations of this kind are pertinent. And they are
not wholly speculative, since not all women who do not want a child
necessarily want an abortion. What is to be done about such women,
especially if the key premise is that unwanted children pose serious
dangers to society? Those who support the morality of abortion on
request will eventually have to work out these problems; they do not
necessarily undercut the "unwanted child" argument, but they do indicate the need for further refinement.

More immediately, though, the problem of the first-mentioned implication must be considered—that the unwanted conceptus is a conceptus
which either has no value in itself or has a positive disvalue, making it
worthy of destruction. Unfortunately, as mentioned earlier, those who
argue for the morality of abortion on request do not reveal the full
range of their philosophical presuppositions. One is hard-pressed to
know what philosophical tradition they spring from and how they would
defend or explain themselves in the face of a sustained philosophical
interrogation or critique. Since this cannot be determined from the
literature, it would be presumptuous and possibly unfair for a critic to
attribute to them philosophical theories which they may not hold. What
can be said, though, is that those who argue for abortion on request on
the ground that unwanted children ought not to be born, talk in a way
reminiscent of a familiar philosophical theory of value, what has been
called the "interest theory of value." Without meaning to imply that, for
instance, Hardin, Szasz, Lader, or others so far cited necessarily hold
this theory—they are not philosophers and do not talk in this language—
the affinities are nonetheless striking.

The late American philosopher Ralph Barton Perry was the main exponent of the interest theory of value. "That which is an object of
interest," he wrote, "is *eo ipso* invested with value. Any object, whatever
it be, acquires value when any interest, whatever it be, is taken in it." [22]
Put in formal terms, "*x* is valuable = interest is taken in *x*." [23] Perry
himself wanted to avoid an exclusively subjectivist theory of value,
which located the value of an object exclusively in the satisfaction or
fulfillment which it afforded those interested in it; he thus sought to
establish value in the relationship between subject and object, a relationship marked by interest on the part of the subject. Yet he had difficulty in avoiding the subjectivism, saying at one point, for instance,
that "the silence of the desert is without value, until some traveller finds
it lonely and terrifying; the cataract, until some human sensibility finds
it sublime, or until it is harnessed to satisfy human needs." [24] Perry, of
course, said nothing here about abortion, much less about the "value"
of a conceptus (nor anywhere else, so far as I know). But it is possible
to see how his general theory of value could be construed to take ac-

count of the value status of a conceptus: a conceptus is valuable = interest is taken in a conceptus.

This is not the place to go into the interest theory of value, which has now a considerable history and has been subjected to a variety of criticisms or emendations.[25] It is only necessary to point out that serious philosophical problems arise with an interest theory of value and that, if this is the particular theory being implicitly employed, then these problems have to be faced before it can serve to undergird an application to the problem of the unwanted child. Do all of the adherents of abortion on request want to say that a conceptus has no value if it is unwanted? Or that its value is only reduced by being unwanted? If the fetus, and thus potential human being, is not wanted by some (e.g., the mother), but wanted by others (e.g., the father), does the father's wanting it serve to give that fetus any value, or is the mother's not wanting it sufficient to deprive the fetus of all value? Or what if, in an underpopulated country, the society wants (i.e., values) all fetuses because of their potentiality as human beings, but the mothers do not want them? Do the interests of society in that case give the fetus a value quite independently of the mother's interests? Or what if, in an overpopulated country, the society does not want the fetus, but the mother does?

Whose wanting establishes the value or the relative value of the fetus? On the hypothesis that unwanted children are social dangers (or could become such), is this to say that such children thus have no intrinsic value at all, that their value (if any) is totally dependent upon their prospects of becoming socially beneficial? What of a pregnant woman who neither positively wants nor positively does not want a child, that is, a woman who is ambivalent or indifferent? Does her fetus have value or does it not have value? Or imagine the following situation. A pregnant woman who wanted the child is killed in an auto accident but her fetus is delivered alive by a Cesarean (which happens occasionally). Does this fetus continue to have a value when the woman is dead and no longer able to want it? Does its value terminate at the instant of the mother's death? Or would someone else's wanting it (e.g., the father) be sufficient to give it value? And if the latter point is accepted, does this imply, in general, that the father's wanting a child gives that child a value?

This is a long list of questions and an equally long list could be composed by using the language of "rights" rather than "value." One could, for instance, ask whether the abortion-on-request adherents want to say that a fetus has no rights but those which a woman, by virtue of her interests, endows it with? Or whether in the case of a very late fetus (e.g., eight months) that fetus had rights regardless of whether the woman at that point wants it or not? Beyond that, there are a whole series of possible questions which would have to be raised about the range of morally acceptable options if it were assumed that the fetus had neither value nor rights if the woman did not want it.[26] I will not attempt to guess how adherents of the abortion-on-request position would answer questions of this sort; no doubt all would not answer in the same way. But they are questions which need to be answered before it can be assumed that the moral case for abortion on request on the basis of the nonvalue of unwanted children has been put beyond all doubt.

A further philosophical problem suggests itself. It needs to be shown how and in what way the wanting of fetal life metaphysically grounds the value of that life. This is to put the shoe on the other foot. For, if abortion-on-request adherents have yet to show that the nonwanting of a child establishes its nonvalue or disvalue, they have also not shown why the wanting of it establishes its value. It has been argued that an important reason why birthrates do not decline in many overpopulated countries is that people *want* too many children; the premise of that argument is that not only does the wanting of children constitute a social disvalue, but that the wanted children—however much they may be wanted—are themselves a disvalue in an overpopulated country.[27] If, from one perspective, it is possible to say that those who rest abortion on request on an unwanted-child argument have said too little to establish the validity of their position, it is possible, from quite another perspective, to note they have said too much. For they have said or seem to be saying that the value of the child is constituted or engendered by its being wanted. That leaves them open to the objection that no room is left for an integral place to be given other relevant values, i.e., the value, in an overpopulated country, of not having too many wanted children, or the value, in a poor family, of not having too many wanted children.

Women's Rights

In 1945, Stella Brown said that "woman's right to abortion is an absolute right. Abortion should be available for any woman without insolent inquisition or ruinous financial charges, for our bodies are our own." [28] That was a bold statement in those days, and the arguments since that time have, with one or more variations, persisted in pressing just the case laid down there. "The widespread use of abortion," Edwin M. Schur has said, "is striking evidence that millions of American women do want more control over deciding when they shall bear children; our laws against abortion may well serve to further women's subservient social status." [29] Speaking of women's rights, Marya Mannes has said that "this most important one of all has so far been denied us: the right to control what takes place within our own body. This is our citadel, our responsibility, our mental, emotional, and physical being." [30] Alice S. Rossi has written:

> The passage of . . . a reform statute is only one step on the way to the goal of maximum individual freedom for men and women to control their own reproductive lives. Such freedom should include the personal right to undo a contraceptive failure by means of a therapeutic abortion. . . . The only criterion should be whether such an induced abortion is consistent with the individual woman's personal set of moral and religious values, and that is something only she can judge. [31]

For Garrett Hardin, the aim is "to free women from a now needless form of slavery, to make a woman the master of her own body. The emancipation of women is not complete until women are free to avoid the pregnancies they do not want." [32]

A variety of authors have been cited here, not because they make different points, but because they make generally the same one. In essence, the contention is that, if (a) the freedom to control reproduction is granted as a general premise, then this freedom must be extended to voluntary abortion to give it the possibility of a full implementation; and (b) that if one is serious about female emancipation, then it follows that women must be granted full freedom to control their reproductive capacities, a freedom which would be incomplete without the ability to terminate unwanted pregnancies. Behind these dual contentions, which should be distinguished, lie two important cultural revolutions. One of these may be termed the "birth-control revolution," which presumes, at the minimum, the right to control family size and, at the maximum, the right to use whatever means are necessary to prevent the birth of unwanted children. The story of that revolution and its long history need not be gone into here. Of more immediate concern is the relationship between it and the female-emancipation movement.

While there were scattered precursors in the eighteenth century, the drive for female emancipation began accelerating toward the end of the nineteenth century. From the outset it was possible to distinguish two groups within the movement, those whose emphasis lay in the gaining of equal voting and job rights—giving women the same political and legal rights as those enjoyed by men—and those whose thrust was toward sexual and reproductive freedom (in addition to political and legal rights). [33] At the same time, even within the feminist movement there were (and continue to be) disputes about the extent and range of male-female differences. On the one hand, there have been those who claim that the differences are only culturally induced; and, on the other, those who have held out for some irreducible differences transcending anatomy. [34] In recent years, the heavier emphasis has fallen on sexual and reproductive freedom and on the environmental and cultural determinants of male-female differences.

Thus sexual freedom has become a major plank of the militant feminist groups, ranging from the National Organization for Women (NOW), through the Women's Liberation Movement, to WITCH (Women's International Terrorist Conspiracy from Hell). Most pertinently, repeal of all abortion laws has become a key cause for these groups, pressed by petitions, lobbying, demonstrations and picketing.[35] As Mrs. Barbara Sykes Wright, a member of NOW, put it:

> Therefore I, and thousands upon thousands of women like me, believe that any law forbidding an abortion under good medical conditions is immoral and in addition unconstitutional, for it violates her right to control her property—her body—as well as her life, liberty and happiness. . . . The abortion laws must be repealed, in this state, in this country, and all over the world. It is a basic part of universal human rights and particularly basic to the rights of women.[36]

It is difficult to analyze these arguments because so few of the premises are exhibited. One of the rare attempts to develop in a philosophically systematic way the women's-rights argument for abortion has been made by Ti-Grace Atkinson, a professional philosopher. She compares a woman to an artist; both have special capacities, in the former the capacity for reproduction and in the latter the capacity for the creation of works of art (her example is that of a sculptor). Both have the right to exercise or not exercise their capacities. She writes:

> The woman is the artist. The property which distinguishes her as a woman is her reproductive function. She may choose not to exercise her function at all, or she may choose to exercise it. The man may try to give her certain material which would then become her property. She can accept or reject the gift. Once accepting the gift, she can choose to exercise her special capacity on this material or not. It is at this stage that the initial choice is made by the woman whether or not to exercise her reproductive process on the sperm. The method of implementing her choice might be some contraceptive technique. . . . Both the raw material gift and the special reproductive function are properties of the woman. She may decide to permit the one, i.e., the special function, her function, to operate upon her raw material gift . . . [or] the woman may decide to stop the process: the embryo is destroyed. . . . Both her reproductive function and the fetus constitute her property. She may decide at any time during this period that she does not want to exercise this function any longer, at which time she is free not to do so. It is only when the fetus ceases to be the woman's property (her reproductive process ceases at natural terminations) that the choice to exercise or not her reproductive function on that fetus can be interfered with. The fetus ceases to be property when (1) certain minimal criteria are met defining what it is to be a person: the denotative definitive characteristic is existence as a single *separate* man, woman or child, or (2) the woman decides to give the fetus child-status.[37]

The woman, she says, "can arbitrarily give the fetus child-status by naturally and/or voluntarily expelling the fetus from her body, thereby declaring personhood on the fetus."

This is an interesting argument, but not without its problems. First of all, it is not established why or in what sense the fetus can be called the "property" of the woman. It took the contribution of the male, his sperm, to make the fetus possible; his genetic contribution is as constitutive of the fetus as hers is (and without that contribution there would be no fetus at all); moreover, the fetus exists as a separate, though dependent, organic entity. It is simply declared to be her property, on the undefended grounds that she has total freedom to decide whether, once a conceptus exists, to continue exercising her reproductive process or not.

Second, Miss Atkinson's argument that the fetus ceases to be a woman's property when it becomes a person rests on a very odd definition of "person," i.e., "a single *separate* man, woman, or child." But genetically, hormonally and in all organic respects save the source of its nourishment, a fetus and even an embryo is separate from the woman. The only connecting link is the placenta, from which the fetus derives nourishment; a fetus is *in* a woman, but it is genetically and morphologically quite clearly distinguishable from the woman's body. And after viability it can live without the organic assistance of the maternal placenta. To be sure, it is not a "man, woman or child" in the ordinary sense of those words, but it is a single separate being. Yet apparently this last fact is of small consequence, affecting its status as "property" not at all.

Third, Miss Atkinson's way of talking about the conferral of personhood is curious. Since when has it become possible for one person to "confer" personhood on another? In terms of what extant political or legal code is this right given to anyone? Miss Atkinson claims that legislation which interferes "in any way" with a woman's freedom of reproductive self-determination is a violation of her constitutional rights. Yet there is surely no support in the American constitution or legal system for the notion that one human being has the right to declare personhood on another being. Is Miss Atkinson laying down a general norm for the origin of "personhood"—the declaration or decision of other human beings—or a norm applicable in this instance only? She does not say, but her language suggests that it is the woman's decision alone which determines whether a fetus is to be declared a person.

Fourth, Miss Atkinson does not show why the fact of birth somehow makes the child no longer her "property." Whose "property" is it at that point? She tells us *when* it ceases to be her property but not *why* it so ceases. The only explanation she gives is drawn from trying to show an analogy between a fetus and a sculpture. She says that a work of art achieves an "independent, non-property, status" when "(1) the sculptor states that that is his idea of a statue of a person, or (2) the work meets some objective criteria of what it is to be a statue of a person." It is a poor analogy, spoiled by the obvious legal fact that the sculptor retains the right to destroy the statue if he so chooses (presuming he has not sold it) at any time after its completion. It is still his property, to do with as he pleases; that it is a finished, completed statue does not alter in the least his rights of ownership and disposal.

A considerably more serious objection can be leveled at arguments based on "women's rights." A number of writers, as we have seen, claim that the right to abortion is an "absolute right," a subspecies of the claim that women have an absolute right to control their own procreative destiny. Two questions arise here. First, even if one grants that abortion is *a* right, what justification would there be for elevating it to the status of an "absolute right," a phrase entailing that no other conceivable human right could ever take precedence over it? Second, if abortion is a woman's "right," does this entail or require one to say that the fetus has no countervailing rights at all? On the first question, it seems indefensible to call abortion an "absolute right," for that would make all other human rights relating to procreation relative and, for decision purposes, inconsequential. It would presume that no possible interest of society could ever weaken that right or even admit of a genuine conflict of rights. If the traditional Catholic argument ultimately fails because it makes the conceptus' right to life an absolute, the "absolute" right of women to an abortion fails for the same reason. To call any right "absolute" is to establish it as a supreme human right, capable of being abridged under no circumstances. Moreover, if the right to abortion is seen as a corollary of "women's rights," which is itself presumably a subspecies of what earlier (Chapter 9) was specified as a "person-right," i.e., the right to self-determination, is it the case that "women's rights" are absolute? There seems no basis for this assertion, for, to establish a right is not at the same time to establish an absolute right.

Do not "women's rights" have to be set in the framework of the full spectrum of human rights—species-rights, body-rights, etc.—thus subjecting them to the possible claims of other human rights? It is one thing to emancipate women from discrimination and male tyranny; it is quite another to emancipate them from all human claims and obligations toward the rights of others. But to claim or presume an absolute right to abortion or to make "women's rights" absolute is to create a set of rights for women subject to none of the normal limitations of life in human community. It is not the case that all who advocate a woman's right to abortion speak of this as an *absolute* right, but then neither does any of them (so far as I can discern) stress the limitations of those rights.

Apart from the question of whether a woman's right to an abortion is a far superior right to that of any possible right of a fetus to life, some very practical problems arise out of the failure to specify what limitations, if any, there are to women's rights with respect to abortion. If this right is absolute, then that would mean that no doctor could *ever* refuse to do an abortion. For then the woman's right to an abortion would take precedence over any rights he might claim—his rights as a doctor to decide whether, in any given case, an abortion was medically safe and thus to refuse it on the grounds of the danger; his rights as a human being, if he did not feel free in conscience to perform the abortion. The phrase "abortion on demand" often enough used, underscores this problem. If the phrase is taken quite literally, it would seem to mean that a woman could demand an abortion (whatever the grounds, whatever the circumstances, whatever the hazards), and no doctor could refuse to perform it. If a woman's right to an abortion is indeed an *absolute* right, then there is no right he can claim in the face of it. Unfortunately, the phrase "abortion on request" raises some problems as well. For if a woman can only "request" an abortion, then that would seem to imply that she has *no rights* in the matter; for one can hardly speak of "rights" if one has to "request" others to grant them.

Practically speaking, of course, in a permissive legal system or one in which all abortion laws have been repealed, there would be a considerable number of doctors who would be willing to perform an abortion, some no doubt without asking any questions at all. The kind of problem being raised here might not, in practice, arise often. Yet some doctors would not (as the English experience since 1968 shows), and one would have to ask whether it is within their human rights to refuse to perform an abortion where their conscience opposes it. The 1967 English law contained a conscience clause (see Chapter 5, p. 148), but if it is taken literally that a woman has an "absolute right" to an abortion, that clause should not have been in there. For it allows a doctor, in the name of his conscience, to abridge her "absolute right"; her rights become relative if the doctor's rights of conscience are allowed to take precedence. In sum, a serious dilemma arises: a woman's absolute right to an abortion can be exercised only if a doctor is deprived of his medical and human rights.

The position of the father raises similar problems. Garrett Hardin, consistently with others who press the "women's right" argument, says that, in the end,

powerless men are—and it is nature that has made them so. If we give the father a right of veto in abortion decisions, the wife has a very simple reply to her husband: "I'm sorry dear, I wasn't going to tell you this, but you've forced my hand. This is not your child." With such a statement she could always deny her husband's right to decide. Why husbands should demand power in such matters is a fit subject for depth analysis. . . . In terms of public policy, do we want to pass laws which give men the right to compel their wives to be pregnant? Psychologically, such compulsion is akin to rape.[38]

Hardin's point that it would be unwise for a husband to force a wife to go through with a pregnancy she did not want has considerable force; he would be storing up serious troubles for himself and very likely for the child as well. Yet, since it is presumably not immoral for a husband to want a child and within his human rights to father a child, it is not easy to see why he should be deprived of *all* rights in the matter. Dr. Hardin's point that "nature" has made men "powerless" seems to assume that "nature" is the determinant of what is moral or immoral. But it is doubtful, from the way he handles the problem of the beginning of human life—where society is left free to define that beginning as it wishes—that he would want to be bound to a philosophical position where "nature" was determinant of rights and morality.

Let us put the problem in another way. What if a husband demanded that his wife have an abortion? In terms of the "women's right" argument, which would leave the decision solely up to her, he would not have the right to make such a demand. But there are many family situations in which it would be the husband who would have to bear the economic support of the child to which she gives birth. In addition, he might well perceive that, if his wife had another child, that child could place a heavy, perhaps dangerous burden on her physical and psychological resources, on the other children and on him as the one responsible to support the entire family. Since his responsibilities would be heavy in the face of an additional child, could he not in justice claim a say in the matter? This is not wholly a speculative question since it not infrequently happens that husbands want their wives to have abortions that the wives themselves do not want; it is not always women who do not want to have a child. It is a fundamental principle of a free society that those who will be affected by the actions and decisions of others ought to have a voice in the making of those decisions. If a woman ought not, in justice, be forced to have an unwanted child, on what basis is it to be claimed that a father ought to be compelled to stand passively by during his wife's pregnancy, knowing that he will be the one, as much or more than she, to bear the burden of raising and supporting the child? I am by no means suggesting that a husband should have the right to demand his wife have an abortion. Once again, it is a question of pointing out some of the insufficiently explored problems in the abortion-on-request position.

A good number of the kinds of problems I have been posing here will be less pressing, or pressing in a different way, if the "women's right" argument is not expressed in absolutistic terms. They will at least be reduced to the more familiar difficulties of adjudicating relative rights.

a vexing enough problem, but one which has the virtue of trying to weigh the rights of everyone who would be involved in a decision and in its consequences. Moreover, to make the rights of women the sole rights at issue, and to make the crux of this right exclusively a woman's desire, is to preclude the need to examine any other data than the verbal statement of a woman: The traditional Catholic position was criticized for a like weakness. Both positions have a similar logic. The Catholic position says that the only moral question of importance is when human life begins. Once that has been determined (or believed determined), then all other possible questions and considerations become irrelevant. The "woman's right" position proceeds in the same way, the difference being that it locates the critical moral factor in the desire of the woman. Thus in neither position is room left for an integration of other possibly relevant data or for a balancing of rights.

The one-dimensionality of the abortion-on-request position becomes even clearer in some of its formulations, where the aim seems to be that of denying all value whatever to the conceptus. Dr. Szasz has written; "The question is: What is abortion—murder of the fetus, or the removal of a piece of tissue from the woman's body?" Putting the question in these terms, reducing it to a simple black-and-white dichotomy, is, in effect, to say that it is either a very serious moral issue or not a moral issue at all. His own answer is the second of the options he offers. Dr. H. B. Munson argues in a similar way: "After all, one can hardly equate, on the one hand, the taking of life from a breathing, thinking, full-fledged human being, with, on the other hand, the denial of life to a bit of vegetating unborn matter." [39] It should not be necessary to repeat the discussion of Chapters 10 and 11 on the problem of the beginning of human life to see that this is nothing more than to define the moral problem out of consideration.

The potentiality of the conceptus to become a human being and a human person, its early development of a number of human characteristics (human features, brain waves, etc.) should at least suggest (to use no stronger a term) that a conceptus is something more than "a piece of tissue" or "a bit of vegetating unborn matter." Reduced to those terms, every human being alive today is "a piece of tissue," and a child the moment before birth at term "a bit of vegetating unborn matter." This is the semantic equivalent of defining an "automobile" as a "piece of metal" or a "house" as a "pile of wood." No dictionaries define terms in this way. Such definitions tell us nothing whatever about the nature of the being or object in question, nothing about its potentialities, its origins or its value. Fortunately, not many of those who advocate abortion on request take this route of moral argumentation. Malcolm Potts, after a strong argument in favor of the morality of abortion on request, can conclude that "it is sometimes difficult to decide on terminating a pregnancy but the responsibility to refuse a request to induce an abortion is a grave one." [40] Whatever one may think of Dr. Potts' argumentation leading to this conclusion, it represents a serious attempt to argue the issues, to deal with the problems of definitions and consequences; it does not, that is, do away with the moral problem altogether by means of a selective choice of definitions, designed at the outset to preclude the possibility of envisioning induced abortion as a moral problem.

The Legal Question

The passage cited from Dr. Potts' article provides a good introduction to the legal problem. If the moral case for abortion on request is, at best, undeveloped and far from convincing, the legal case is considerably stronger. Whether and to what extent and under what conditions abortion should be legalized can be approached by examining (*a*) the reasons against making abortion illegal and (*b*) the reasons, of a more positive kind, why it ought to be made legal. Initially, I will simply talk in terms of "legalizing abortion," avoiding the expressions "abortion on demand" or "abortion on request," both of which stand in need of some clarification, but only after some prior questions are dealt with.

Roy Lucas has presented the most common arguments against laws which make induced abortions criminal acts:

> Present abortion laws are (1) largely unenforced, (2) uncertain in their scope, (3) at odds with accepted medical standards, (4) discriminatory in effect, and (5) based upon the imposition by criminal sanction of subjective religious values of questionable social merit upon persons who do not subscribe to these values.[41]

These points can be examined one by one. From all available evidence in the United States (and the same can be said of Great Britain, Western Europe and the Scandinavian countries), illegal abortionists and women who turn to them are rarely prosecuted and, both in principle and in practice, exceedingly difficult to prosecute. As David Granfield has noted,

> Abortion is a particularly difficult area to control by legal means. The abortionist and the woman conceal their complicity. The victim dies and disappears before its existence is publicly known. With no complainant and no witnesses, the prosecutor has not even a *prima facie* case. When an offense is reported, if it does not involve an abortion mill or a maternal injury or death, the prosecutor will frequently use his discretion for leniency, as he does in other areas of the criminal law.[42]

Father Granfield, however, notes that the unenforceability of abortion laws is matched in other areas of criminal conduct: obscene and abusive phone calls, and larceny, for instance. Unenforceability as such, he contends, is no reason to remove a law or not to have a law. But his examples are misleading. There is considerable public pressure for enforcement of the laws against stealing and obscene phone calls. There appears no public pressure whatever to enforce the abortion laws; even those who support the present, mainly restrictive laws in the United States have not called for a concerted effort to prosecute abortionists. And, of course, there exist no lobbying groups or pressures to remove from the books the laws against stealing and obscene phone calls. Whatever the results, the police try to enforce the latter laws, and the success of American political candidates who have stressed the need for stricter law enforcement—the "crime in the streets" issue—shows how real this pressure is.

To be sure, restrictive laws undoubtedly influence the attitude of doctors and hospitals. But, as becomes increasingly clear with each succeeding year, the social disapproval of abortion is diminishing, both as reflected in public-opinion polls and in the increased success of reform groups in moving liberalized laws through state legislatures. In the late spring of 1969, a Louis Harris survey for *Time* found that 64 percent of those polled believed that abortion should be left to the parents and their doctor and not be a matter of law; a 60 percent majority of Roman Catholics supposedly agreed.[43]

Father Granfield has also argued that "they [restrictive laws] limit the number and spread of abortions, and they declare the community evaluation of fetal life." [44] Undoubtedly, restrictive laws do limit the number of *legal* abortions and, to judge from the evidence in countries with permissive laws, they help keep down the total number of abortions (both legal and illegal), but the latter to an indeterminate extent.[45] But the political and legal problem is that people now appear to want more legal abortions; thus there no longer exists the will to use restrictive abortion laws for the purpose of limiting abortions.

The point being made here is legal and not moral. Do the people want restrictive laws and do they want such laws enforced? If it is increasingly doubtful whether they want such laws in the first place, it seems beyond all doubt that they do not want restrictive laws enforced where they presently exist. On the point of declaring the community's "evaluation of fetal life," it does not follow that a desire to liberalize abortion laws or to repeal them altogether need bespeak a loss of interest in or devaluation of fetal life. If the moral case for the abortion-on-request position is pressed the way Garrett Hardin and Thomas Szasz, for instance, press it, and if it is on those grounds that the law is changed, then one can well speak of a devaluation of fetal life. But it is also possible to argue the matter in another way, not taking away the value of fetal life but, rather, trying to place this value in relationship to other important values. It does not follow, in other words, that a repeal of abortion laws or the legislation of permissive laws need or should entail in theory a disrespect for fetal life. As I will try to show, it would be possible, by means of the alternatives offered to abortion and by the kind of liberalized law put into effect, to place a high social evaluation on fetal life and yet have abortions available for those women who want them.

Lucas' second point (2), on the uncertainty of presently restrictive laws, is easily sustained when one notes the great variation among American hospitals in the number of induced abortions performed and by the variation among the *de facto* "indications" accepted in the hospitals (see Chapter 5, p. 137). Moreover, the varying acceptance of different indications from one area or hospital to the next, even in states and countries which have adopted moderate laws, suggests that a move from restrictive to moderate laws by no means does away with this problem. Just how far, though, the point about uncertainty can be pressed is not clear. There exists no uncertainty about the fact that presently restrictive laws do not allow a purely social or economic indication, which is not to say that some doctors do not recognize them, much less an absence of all indications save the expressed desire of the woman to have an abortion. The uncertainty occurs within a limited range of medical and psychiatric indications; which is to say the uncertainty is relative and not total.

Lucas' third point (3), that restrictive laws are "at odds with accepted medical standards," begs a number of questions. Doctors appear as divided on the morality and necessity of abortion as the general public, and even the fact that a majority of doctors would like to see the law changed hardly serves to establish an "accepted medical standard." It makes considerable sense to speak of "accepted medical standards" in the instance of a ruptured appendix (remove it) or a massive loss of blood (transfusion), but it is hardly possible to say the same about abortion standards. With the sole exception of a direct threat to the life of a woman, there are no clear "accepted medical standards" in the instance of abortion; doctors vary on what they think best or necessary. In addition, it is hard to see how one could plausibly speak of accepted medical standards in countries or states where the laws are restrictive and the number of legal abortions, comparatively few; that situation hardly presents the possibility of accepted medical standards developing.

The fourth point (4), that restrictive laws are "discriminatory in effect," is well substantiated. Not only is there an evident imbalance between the availability of legal abortions to the affluent and the poor in the United States, this has also been true of every country with restrictive abortion laws (Chapter 5).

The fifth point (5), that restrictive laws are "based upon the imposition by criminal sanction of subjective religious values of questionable social merit upon persons who do not subscribe to those values," is, at best, half-correct and half-misleading. Within a democratic legislative process, it is perfectly within the rights of minority groups to seek the enactment into law of their convictions about what is good or bad for society; and it is surely within their rights to work to keep on the books laws already in effect even if a majority no longer accepts them. Almost every movement of social reform in the United States—the enactment of laws protecting trade unions, the black civil-rights movement, for instance—began as minority movements, often the object of extreme hostility on the part of the majority. The facts that a pressure group is a minority and that its views are not held or actively resisted by the majority (who normally consider minority views "subjective") have nothing to do with their constitutional rights to press those views and seek to have the law reflect them. From a legal point of view, only two points matter: do the minority groups abide by the procedural rules of the legislative process—persuasion and not coercion—and do the courts uphold the constitutionality of the enacted (or, in this case, retained) laws?

When pressure-group activities pass from open persuasion to covert coercion, in the form of political intimidations or suppression of debate, then their conduct becomes reprehensible and the democratic process is debased. Barring that, however, they are within their legal rights. However, Mr. Lucas and others have argued that such laws ought to be considered unconstitutional, particularly in the light of the 1965 Supreme Court decision in the case of *Griswold* v. *Connecticut,* striking down the restrictive Connecticut birth-control statutes.[46]

Also of potential applicability [Mr. Lucas adds] is the constitutional policy of protecting individual liberty from unduly restrictive state legislation. The fourteenth amendment prohibitions against discriminatory or unduly vague laws might also be employed to invalidate state abortion statutes. Within this framework, a constitutional attack can be launched.[47]

The action of the California Supreme Court in the *Belous* case, declaring the old California law unconstitutional, raises the distinct possibility that, at some point in the future, all such laws could be declared unconstitutional. A late 1969 decision in the District of Columbia that declared its abortion statutes unconstitutional is another important sign.

Mr. Lucas's phrase about "subjective religious values of questionable social merit" raises different problems. Unfortunately, he does not explain what the phrase "subjective religious values" means. Does it mean that they are subjective because they are religious, or subjective because they are values? Or is it that they are subjective because religious values are subjective as a particular species of values? In another place, he says, "The state interest in regulating abortion is a subjective judgment of value based upon a belief of religious character, a belief which enacts one particular concept of 'morality.'" [48] But every judgment about abortion will enact "one particular concept of 'morality'"; the contention, on nonreligious grounds, that abortion is a woman's right, is as much a "subjective judgment" as any other and it embodies one particular concept of morality. That it is based on nonreligious grounds hardly serves, *ipso facto*, to elevate it to the realm of an objective value. For that matter, what is the difference between an objective and a subjective judgment of value? Mr. Lucas, in short, has entered a very old philosophical thicket, one which cannot be escaped by assuming that the difference between objectivity and subjectivity is clear. His point, though, that these values are "of questionable social merit," while, of course, also a subjective judgment on his part, seems better taken; one can, at any rate, do as he has done and point out the social hazards of the position.

In this last respect, two of his points are solid and worth holding on to: that the laws are unenforced and that they are *de facto* discriminatory. These two points are in themselves sufficient to make his case; one can then evoke established jurisprudential principles and not be forced to take a more speculative legal route. "Respect for the legal system," Mr. Lucas says in his concluding comments, "is not enhanced by the flagrant violation of strict abortion statutes nor by the discriminatory application of their silent exceptions." [49] This seems to me an unexceptionable statement and reason enough to remove such laws from the books. Some words of Herbert L. Packer can be cited here:

> Our [American] abortion laws present a classic case of the operation of the crime tariff. Given the inelasticity of the demand for abortions, the legal prohibition has the effect of raising the risk and reward for the illegal practitioner and also of depressing the quality of the services offered. This phenomenon will not be relieved to any appreciable extent by the moderate or "therapeutic abortion" approach to law reform. Nor will that approach diminish the fact, nor the general knowledge of the fact, that every year upward of a million illegal and possibly dangerous abortions take place in this country. More seriously, it must be recognized that moderate reform is essentially middle-class reform. It benefits those who are sufficiently well educated, well connected and well financed to take advantage of the liberalized law. Where will the ghetto dweller find a psychiatrist to testify that she runs a grave risk of emotional impairment if she is forced to give birth to her nth baby? [50]

While it is not a "fact" that there are upwards of a million illegal abortions a year, but only an estimate—for no one has any clear idea how many illegal abortions there are a year in the United States (Chapter 5, pp. 135–36)—that statement is otherwise sound.

If there are, then, good reasons for not making abortion illegal (or maintaining strict laws on the books), there are also a number of more positive reasons why it should be made legal. The high toll of injuries and deaths from illegal abortions (especially in underdeveloped countries with restrictive laws but also in developed countries) is one good reason to bring the *de facto* practice of abortion, which no laws have been able to stop, under medical control or supervision. If many women, running at least into the millions throughout the world and into the hundreds of thousands in the United States, are intent on procuring abortions—safe ones if they can but dangerous ones if they cannot—then they had best be provided the opportunity to have safe ones. The evidence presented in Chapters 2 and 7 shows that the death and injury rate from induced abortions is very low in countries with permissive laws; hence, from a medical point of view—assuming abortions will take place whatever the legal system—hospital abortions performed by qualified doctors are the safest kind. But would a permissive legal code be the best legal code from other perspectives?

At this point, having criticized almost every element of the position put forward by Garrett Hardin—its morality, its biology and logic—I think the way he puts his basic question, "Abortion—Or Compulsory Pregnancy?" is valid. For, from a legal point of view, to deny an abortion to a woman who wants one is tantamount to compelling her to go through with her pregnancy. Life in any civilized society, to be sure, requires that people often do what they do not want to do; they are compelled by law and mores. Compulsion, as such, is no objection to a law. It is only objectionable when it can be shown that substantive and avoidable harm is done to the conscience or freedom of choice of individuals, on the one hand, or when it can be shown, on the other, that no substantive harm would be done to the common good by a removal of legal compulsions.

On the first point, the frequency of illegal abortions and public expressions of a desire to change restrictive laws can be taken as *prima facie* evidence that a significant portion of the populace do not believe abortion to be immoral (though undoubtedly many would qualify this belief in any number of ways). Hence, it is reasonable to conclude that many people—and certainly many women—believe that their consciences are being offended by restrictive laws. Many women say just that and, since it is impossible for anyone to climb into the mind of another, no one is in a position to deny such an assertion. Even so, however, something more is needed than a claim that conscience is being violated; up to a point, this is inevitable in any society, however democratic its principles. People are, in the generality of cases, often required to obey laws they do not believe in, pay taxes to support governmental policies they may abhor and abide by what seem to them offensive court and legislative-majority decisions. They have the right to pressure for change in laws and policies; they are not granted the right (at least the legal right) to violate those laws which offend their consciences. What must be shown, then, is not only a violation of private conscience and private freedom to act, but also that laws which restrict private freedoms are either harmful to the common good or are not necessary to preserve the common good. For those who believe that the taking of the life of a conceptus is a form of murder, it is evident enough why they should think a threat is posed to the common good. On their side is the constitutional premise, explicit in the American Bill of Rights, that certain rights are protected, not subject to majority will or majority vote. The right to life is one of them.

Yet, second, even if it can be argued that induced abortion is a form of murder or the taking of the life of a potential human being (already, soon after conception, human in a number of its characteristics), it is still necessary to show that this form of killing—which is *sui generis* in being the killing of prenatal life—does pose a threat to the common good. It is helpful at this point to put the issue in very primitive terms. A woman says she wants an abortion, claiming that she ought to have the right to have one. She may call it murder or we may call it murder (to take the extreme cases), but we are still confronted with the claim being made by the woman. Do we have the right to deny her this abortion or, as citizens, deny the class of women making such claims the right to an abortion? However repugnant her desire may be, it seems to me that we cannot deny it unless two conditions are met: (1) that granting her this right would violate our consciences (and this would apply only to the doctor being asked to perform the abortion), or (2) that it would pose a threat to the peace, security and safety of the whole society—that is, we, as citizens, would be harmed by granting such a right to women.

Now, it goes without saying that the claim being made upon us by the woman (or class of such women) poses a direct threat to the life of the conceptus; it cannot survive if her claim is granted and an abortion is allowed. On that ground, those who believe the taking of fetal life on other than serious and good grounds is morally wrong, ought to take serious moral offense; and it would be within their legal and moral rights to make their convictions known to her (or all those like her). But a conviction that abortion for less than good and serious reasons is morally wrong cannot serve as a rationale to coerce someone else with different convictions unless it can be shown that the actions following upon a recognition of their convictions threaten the whole of society. It does not seem, in the instance of that form of killing we call "induced abortion," that such a threat is present.

There are two ways it could be present. First, it could be present in the danger posed to basic principles of value or legal policy, the violation of which, in one instance, opens the way for other and perhaps more extensive violations. But in this instance it is simply not possible to prove that basic values would be undermined. The uniqueness of the abortion situation—where it is a question of potential human life (increasingly but gradually actualized as it develops)—means that it is all but impossible to extrapolate from attitudes toward fetal life attitudes toward existing human life. Hence, we do not know what, if any, danger would be posed to basic moral principles or fundamental legal rights. In short, it cannot be said how the life of those already living would be harmed by the taking of the life of the unborn. Second, quite apart from the hazard to principle, it has to be shown that the actual practice of abortion has been harmful to the life of the living. As the discussion in Chapters 6 and 7 tried to show, no such harm can either be demonstrated or even—for perhaps we do not need strict demonstration in such cases—be pointed to informally.

The crux of the issue here is that the purported substantive harm must be *shown* and not just asserted. One may *believe* abortion harmful to the public good; one may *predict* the worst; one may *envision* any number of harmful consequences of granting women their claim to an abortion—and history could prove one right. But in the case of a woman, or all women, pressing a claim to an abortion, more than personal fears and prophecies are necessary; evidence must be produced. There is no evidence that permissive abortion laws have proved hazardous to the life of those living in societies with such laws. The danger has not been shown in countries with restrictive laws and it has not been shown even in those countries with some years of experience behind them with permissive laws (the East European countries and Japan). That being the case, we are deprived of any basis other than our private beliefs for asserting that the granting of the woman's claims will do society substantive harm. We may deplore what she wants, try to dissuade her, be personally offended, mourn the loss of the fetus, and be fearful of the worst for the society. But without a factual basis for showing harm to ourselves or to the society, we have no valid reason to deny her legally what she wants. At that point, we should stand aside; the choice is hers and she is the one who will have to live with it.

Norman St. John-Stevas has put as well as anyone the distinction between law and morality, and the conditions necessary to legitimate laws which limit private conduct:

> Law is concerned with the general good of the community, and while this is also the concern of morality, it goes beyond this to consider the individual good. Law enforces only those standards of moral behavior indispensable for community existence; morality has not such pragmatic limitation, but calls for conformity with the idea. . . . Whether behaviour, private or public, strikes at the common good so gravely that it endangers the fabric of society and so should be suppressed by law, is a question of fact, which can only be answered after full consideration of the conditions prevailing in a given society, includ-

ing the rights enjoyed by the individual. . . . Even when conduct has been so classified, it does not follow that the law should necessarily be invoked. It may not be enforceable, or not enforceable equitably or may give rise to greater evils than those it is intended to eradicate. Political prudence, not jurisprudential theory, must, at this stage, be the guide.[51]

Ought it to be held, however, that all abortion laws should be repealed? Or that society, in its formulation of laws, should have no interest in regulating abortion? Or that, in the end, the decision for or against an abortion is purely a private matter, to be placed beyond the legal pale? A distinction can be made between a regulatory and a prohibitory law. The intention of the first can be described as that of insuring that practices of concern and importance to the common good are protected by those checks and safeguards necessary to reflect the interests of society. Laws governing the licensing of doctors, banking and stock-exchange transactions, the licensing of drivers and real-estate dealers and the conduct of public officials fall under this category. Such laws will usually specify illegal conduct and prescribe penalties for failures to meet the provisions of the law. But the main intent of such laws is to insure that the public interest is represented. Prohibitory laws, by contrast, have as their end the forbidding of those forms of conduct believed to represent a danger to the common good—the laws against stealing and murder, for instance.

There are at least three possible reasons why the practice of abortion should be the subject of regulatory rather than prohibitory laws, each turning on the general interests of society. One reason is that society has an interest in its own survival.[52] While it is hardly that case that the world is suffering from the problem of underpopulation (quite the contrary), it is nevertheless true that some countries have, even in recent years, felt endangered by a low birthrate. Rumania and Bulgaria are examples of this, tightening abortion laws to stimulate the birthrate, but to some extent Japan as well—it is that worry, in the latter country, which has apparently been a major reason why the oral contraceptive has not been legalized for birth-control purposes (see Chapter 9, pp. 276–76). Since, as we have seen, a widespread resort to induced abortion can lead to a drop in the birthrate, it would seem a legitimate interest of society to retain for itself some possibility of control of reproduction, at least for that extreme situation when national survival appears at stake. Objections could surely be leveled at an abortion policy which imposes controls by administrative fiat (as in some of the East European countries), but the principle at stake—that private procreative practices have a bearing on the common good—is less assailable. There can be times when, to recur to the language of earlier chapters, species-rights would take precedence over private procreation and family-lineage rights—when the species or an entire community would be endangered either by overpopulation or by underpopulation. Yet, having said that much, a qualification is in order. In most countries the danger of under-population is so remote that it would seem unnecessary to frame laws with that possibility in mind. If and when the problem arises, laws might then be passed to cope with the situation; they do not necessarily always have to be on the books.

Another possible reason for regulatory laws is to see to it that, if abortions are to be performed, they are performed by qualified doctors. If the aim is to make induced abortions safe for women, then it is necessary that there be regulations which help to insure this safety. It might, though, be objected that this end could be accomplished by the normal methods of professional self-regulation, which already, in the form of ethical codes and regulatory procedures, exist within the medi-cal profession. But should that point seem in doubt, some laws might be in order. From another perspective, a stronger case can be made for regulatory laws: to protect doctors from being forced, against their conscience or medical judgment, to perform abortions they do not want to perform. Thus regulatory laws could specify the rights of all parties.

Still another possible reason is that regulatory laws would be in order to see to it that women themselves were provided with the possibility of having alternatives presented to them and were shielded from the coercion of husbands, family and friends. Full freedom could require something more than the right to walk in off the street and demand of a single doctor that he perform an abortion; that meets only part of the problem of freedom. The rest could be met by a voluntary consultation procedure which sought to offer a woman significant options (therapy, financial help, domestic assistance and so on), which sought to protect the woman from coercion or undue pressure on the part of those around her, which sought to get the woman to think seriously about what she is asking (in case she has not), and which, finally, placed at her disposal either the abortion she asks for or the means to facilitate the option she chooses. The fullest possible freedom would be one that (a) allowed a woman herself the final choice after consultation, giving her the abortion if that is what she finally wants, and (b) guaranteed her the right to the kind of assistance she would need to bear the child if that was her final choice.

It is curious that those in the United States who press so vigorously for a repeal of all abortion laws have not heeded the experience of other countries, particularly the Scandinavian and East European countries. Not one has seen fit to repeal all abortion laws, and the reason cannot be ascribed to the pressure of religious groups or excessive scruples about the status of fetal life.

It would seem, therefore, that, all *a priori* considerations of religion and philosophy apart, there are social reasons, connected with the continuance and well-being of the nation, which have induced States to legislate on abortion, not only to forbid the unskilled and physically dangerous practice of it, but also to limit and control the conditions in which it may be done, even in the best possible way, by skilled and authorized medical practitioners.[53]

A desire to limit an excessively large number of repeated abortions or to forestall a primary reliance upon abortion for birth-control purposes rather than contracepton, the limitation of late abortions, a desire to lead women to consider abortion a serious and not a trivial choice and a desire to maximize female freedom are among these "social reasons."

Regulatory laws, properly and equitably administered, would not necessarily infringe any woman's rights. She would be the one to make the final choice, limited only in those exceptional circumstances or on those occasions when the society believed that it had some rights at stake also, some interests of its own to bring to bear. It is precisely the fact that countries with permissive laws have sought to maximize female freedom while still maintaining an expression of interest on the part of society in the conditions, number and equality of induced abortions, which has led them to bring abortion under regulatory codes. Naturally, the imposition of any conditions whatever or the requirement of any procedural process would, if women's rights are taken to be *absolute*, be an infringement of those rights. But however great women's rights may be, it has not been shown that they are or ought to be absolute, independent of the rights of others. As long as induced abortions have any consequences for society, for family life and for the practice of medicine, society has the right to take a legal interest in them. If it cannot be shown that the practice of abortion has harmful moral consequences for society, it can be shown that it does have a number of important social consequences: it can effect the birthrate, the medical practice and time allocation of doctors, the availability of hospital beds, the health and freedom of women, the use and effective use of contraceptives. Private acts with ascertainable public consequences become a matter of legitimate concern to the public and a legitimate subject for legislation. This conclusion suggests the need for permissive laws rather than an absence of all law.

This chapter has tried to take seriously and employ the distinction between law and morality. It has argued that a permissive law, but not repeal of all law, would be the best law. Despite all the possible moral objections to abortion, the social harm of permissive abortion laws has not been shown; there exist, then, no grounds for society to forbid abortions to those women who want them. Society does have the right, however, to pass such legislation as may seem necessary to protect its own interests and to see that the rights of all those involved in or affected by an abortion have a representation. In the final chapter, an effort will be made to sketch what would seem the rudiments of a good law and public policy. At the same time, this chapter has tried to show why the *moral* argument for abortion on request is unpersuasive. Not only is it too narrow in the range of evidence it is able to consider and integrate, it also serves, in too many formulations, to deprive prenatal life of any intrinsic dignity or value, shows a bias exclusively in favor of the woman, and sometimes elevates real but relative values to the status of absolutes. At the same time, though, women should be accorded the right of control over their procreative faculties—as long as the language of "absolute" rights is avoided. That is a right not to be denied them, and any full moral and legal solution must give a significant place to this right.

Throughout the world, most women have abortions for socioeconomic reasons—whether the abortions are legal or illegal. Those countries that have put "socioeconomic indications" in their laws are, in one sense, only taking account of the overwhelming actualities of abortion motivation and practice. But they are also, in another sense, recognizing that not all the reasons why a woman could want an abortion are limited to specifically medical, fetal, psychiatric or humanitarian (e.g., rape) indications. While a major source of pressure in favor of abortion on request has undoubtedly been to spare women of a degrading requirement that they submit themselves to interrogations, investigations and committee judgments in those cases where there are indications of the kind just mentioned, perhaps a more important reason has been to legitimate the wide range of personal motives which can be grouped under "socioeconomic indications." In the nature of the case, those indications are vague and not easy to specify. They may refer to such concrete pressures as poverty, poor housing, an excessive number of existing children, divorce, widowhood and the like. But they may also refer to the inner world of a woman —her goals in life, her perception of the world, her own felt needs. Women have a right to this inner world, and a right to live out its implications as *they* see it in their choices and behavior. To approve a law that permits abortion on request is, in the end, to legitimate that proposition. It is to say that not only are socioeconomic indications valid but also that, in a great majority of cases, only the pregnant woman can judge the validity of her own reasons. At least this is what an abortion-on-request *law* would be saying: in the absence of concrete evidence of the social harm done by abortion, the law cannot presume to judge the validity of a woman's personal motivations; it must step aside.

To be sure, this is to leave a matter of life and death in the hands of the woman herself. That is a grave weight to be borne. It gives the woman the unparalleled power of deciding the fate of an "other": whether that "other" is to live or die, to develop or not to develop. This is, and should always remain, a profoundly serious decision; and the bias should be against the taking of life, however undeveloped that life. The law should allow women the right to decide. For a woman, however, the real moral drama begins when she is in a position to exercise that right. And it is just at that point that one can hope she will not accept an abortion-on-request morality that would deny the conceptus a value. It has a value, a very significant value. It is this value that she should respect and wrestle over, trying to understand its value in relationship to all the other values she wants to recognize. The wrestling should always be hard, whatever her conscience finally decides.

NOTES

1. Alan F. Guttmacher, "Abortion—Yesterday, Today and Tomorrow," in Alan F. Guttmacher (ed.), *The Case for Legalized Abortion Now* (Berkeley: Diablo Press, 1967), pp. 12–13.
2. Alice S. Rossi, "Abortion Laws and Their Victims," *Trans-action* (September–October 1966); from a reprint published by the Association for the Study of Abortion.
3. Lawrence Lader, *Abortion* (Indianapolis: Bobbs-Merrill, 1966), pp. 167ff.
4. Simone de Beauvoir, *The Second Sex*, trans. H. M. Parshley (New York: Bantam Books, 1961), pp. 457, 458, 464.
5. Lader, *op. cit.*, pp. 167–69.
6. B. James George, Jr., "Current Abortion Laws: Proposals and Movements for Reform," in David T. Smith (ed.), *Abortion and the Law* (Cleveland: Western Reserve University Press, 1967), p. 31.
7. Harriet F. Pilpel, "The Abortion Crisis," in *The Case for Legalized Abortion Now*, *op. cit.*, p. 110.
8. Thomas S. Szasz, "The Ethics of Abortion," *Humanist* (September–October 1966), p. 148; cf. Arthur J. Mandy, "Reflections of a Gynecologist," in Harold Rosen (ed.), *Therapeutic Abortion* (New York: The Julian Press, 1954), p. 287.
9. Alice S. Rossi, *op. cit.*
10. D. Blomberg, *Undersokningar Rorande Ungdomsvardsskolornas Klientel. I: Varden vid Ungdomsvardsskolorna* (Stockholm: Statens Offentliga Utredningar, no. 5 bil. 1, 1954, no page reference cited); cited in Kerstin Höök, "Refused Abortion—A Follow-Up Study of 249 Women Whose Applications Were Refused by the National Board of Health in Sweden," *Acta Psychiatrica Scandinavica*, Supplementum 168, 39 (1963).
11. Erik H. Erikson, *Childhood and Society* (2d ed.; New York: W. W. Norton, 1963), pp. 247–74; cf. Selma H. Fraiberg, *The Magic Years* (New York: Scribners, 1959); and Alfred L. Baldwin, *Theories of Child Development* (New York: John Wiley & Sons, 1968).
12. See *Abortion: An Ethical Discussion* (London: Church Assembly Board for Social Responsibility, 1965), pp. 41ff., for a good discussion of some of the issues here.
13. H. B. Munson, "Abortion in Modern Times: Thoughts and Comments," *Renewal* (February 1967), p. 9.
14. Garrett Hardin, "Abortion—Or Compulsory Pregnancy?" *Journal of Marriage and the Family*, 30 (May 1968), p. 249.
15. Garrett Hardin, "Abortion and Human Dignity," in *The Case for Legalized Abortion Now, op. cit.*, pp. 82–83.
16. Alice S. Rossi, *op. cit.*
17. Lader, *op. cit.*, p. 166.
18. Hans Forssman and Inga Thuwe's article, "One Hundred and Twenty Children Born After Application for Therapeutic Abortion Refused," *Acta Psychiatrica Scandinavica*, 48 (1966), pp. 71–88, is to date the only article available which

has specifically studied the problem of the consequences for the children of refused abortions over a long period of time. While the authors found that, in comparison with a control group, the 120 children showed statistically significant rates of social and psychological disturbance, they did not draw the conclusion that this group had proved to be a "danger to society." Instead, they drew the more limited conclusion—all that their evidence would warrant— that such children have to surmount greater social and psychological handicaps than others (p. 87); see also Edward Pohlman, " 'Wanted' and 'Unwanted': Toward Less Ambiguous Definition," *Eugenics Quarterly*, 12 (1965), pp. 19–27.

19. Garrett Hardin, "Abortion—Or Compulsory Pregnancy?" *op. cit.*, pp. 250–51.
20. Thomas S. Szasz, *op. cit.*, p. 148.
21. Hardin, "Abortion—or Compulsory Pregnancy?" *op. cit.*, p. 250.
22. Ralph Barton Perry, *General Theory of Value: Its Meaning and Basic Principles Construed in Terms of Interest* (New York: Longmans, Green, 1926), pp. 115–16.
23. *Ibid.*, p. 116.
24. *Ibid.*, p. 125.
25. See, for instance, Sidney Zink, *The Concepts of Ethics* (New York: St. Martin's Press, 1962), pp. 62ff; Andrew Reck, *Recent American Philosophy* (New York: Pantheon, 1964), pp. 19ff.; DeWitt Parker, "Value as Any Object of Any Interest," *International Journal of Ethics*, 40 (1930), pp. 465–73; E. W. Hall, *What Is Value? An Essay in Philosophical Analysis* (London: Routledge and Kegan Paul, 1952); Henry D. Aiken, *Reason and Conduct* (New York: Alfred Knopf, 1962), pp. 227ff.
26. Ronald Green, in an important attempt to find a fresh way of conceptualizing the abortion morality problem ("Abortion and Promise-Keeping," *Christianity and Crisis*, 27 [May 15, 1967], pp. 109–13), has suggested that the moral category of promise-keeping is more helpful than that of the rights of and duties toward the fetus. "This would," he says, "place the locus of ethical concern not upon an obligation to the life of the fetus but rather upon the act of faith-keeping or promise-keeping occasioned by the sexual act. This position would state that whenever a woman willingly engages in coitus she, in so doing, makes an implicit promise that in the event of conception she will bear and give life to the fruit of her act. This promise exists even in the case of the woman who responsibly uses contraception in an attempt to avoid pregnancy" (*ibid.*, p. 110). He then goes on to point to a number of situations when it could be said that the woman could not fulfill her promise (medical and health indications), or when its fulfillment would damage the recipient of the promise (a fetal indication in the instance of the implicit promise made to a potential child). He then concludes that, since it is the woman who has the primary obligation to keep the promise made, it should be up to her to decide whether to break or keep it; "in essence, in attempting to postulate the legal conditions for abortion, society usurps the women's own ethical responsibilities" (*ibid.*, p. 112). The line of reasoning pursued here is a strong one, but there is a major gap in his argument. Green grants the fetus the status of a potential human being, but he does not show why the fate and future of this potential human being should be exclusively dependent upon the woman's recognition of or willingness to keep a promise. This implies that its value in its own right is determined by the fact of the woman's promise only. The question of the value of the fetus is bypassed without adequate justification.
27. This, for instance, seems to be the general position of Kingsley Davis in "Population Policy: Will Current Programs Succeed?" *Science*, 158 (November 10, 1967), pp. 730–39; and of Judith Blake in "Population Policy for Americans: Is the Government Being Misled?" *Science*, 164 (May 2, 1969), pp. 522–29. Both argue that the need is to make people *want* fewer children (something that availability of contraceptives will not by itself do) and to get them to see that their *wanting* too many is a social disvalue.

28. Review of *The Abortion Problem*, in *Journal of the American Medical Association*, 128 (1945), p. 472.
29. Edwin M. Schur, "Abortion and the Social System," in Edwin M. Schur (ed.), *The Family and the Sexual Revolution* (Bloomington: Indiana University Press, 1964), p. 376.
30. Marya Mannes, "A Woman Views Abortion," in *The Case for Legalized Abortion Now, op. cit.*, p. 59.
31. Alice S. Rossi, "Public Views on Abortion," in *The Case for Legalized Abortion Now, op. cit.*, pp. 31–32.
32. Garrett Hardin, "Abortion and Human Dignity," in *The Case for Legalized Abortion Now, op. cit.*, p. 82.
33. See, for instance, Eileen S. Kraditor (ed.), *Up From the Pedestal: Selected Writings in the History of American Feminism* (Chicago: Quadrangle Books, 1968); and Betty Friedan, *The Feminine Mystique* (New York: W. W. Norton Co., 1963).
34. For a discussion of this dispute, see Sidney Cornelia Callahan, *The Illusion of Eve: Modern Woman's Quest for Identity* (New York: Sheed & Ward, 1965), especially Chapter 1, pp. 13–34.
35. In New York, skits and short plays emphasizing repressive abortion laws have been a prominent part of the work of the New Feminist Repertory. (See Rosalyn Regelson, "Is Motherhood Holy? Not any More," *New York Times* [May 18, 1969], p. D5.) One of the plays produced by the New Feminist Repertory has been described by Miss Regelson: "A short play by Myrna Lamb, 'What Have You Done for Me Lately?,' raises some basic questions about childbearing, abortion and the 'male-invented' doctrine that maternity is the most beautiful thing that can happen to a woman, and is what gives her importance in the world. In the play, a man wakes up to find a uterus has been implanted in him with a foetus in it. He demands that the woman doctor remove it. She refuses, arguing that human life is involved. He points out that his body wasn't meant to bear children. The doctor retorts that many women's bodies are equally unsuited to childbearing. He says the pregnancy will make it impossible for him to go on with his career, and will shatter the pattern of his life, and she replies that many women feel the same way when they discover they are pregnant."
36. Testimony before the Governor's Commission [in New York state] for the Study of Abortion, February 29, 1968; unpublished.
37. Ti-Grace Atkinson, "Philosophical Argument in Support of the Human Right of a Woman to Determine Her Own Reproductive Process," unpublished paper, November 1967.
38. Garrett Hardin, "Abortion—Or Compulsory Pregnancy," *op. cit.*, pp. 247–48.
39. Szasz, *op. cit.*, p. 148; H. B. Munson, *op. cit.*, p. 9.
40. Malcolm Potts, "The Problem of Abortion," in *Biology and Ethics* (New York: Academic Press, 1969), p. 83.
41. Roy Lucas, "Federal Constitutional Limitations on the Enforcement and Administration of State Abortion Statutes," *The North Carolina Law Review*, 46 (June 1968), p. 752; *cf.*, Cyril C. Means, "The Law of New York Concerning Abortion and the Status of the Foetus, 1664–1968: A Case of Cessation of Constitutionality," *New York Law Forum*, 14 (3) [Fall 1968], pp. 411–415.
42. David Granfield, *The Abortion Decision* (New York: Doubleday, 1969), p. 178.
43. "Changing Morality: The Two Americas," *Time* (June 6, 1969), p. 27. These figures are different than the earlier figures compiled by the National Opinion Research Center and reported by Alice S. Rossi, *op. cit.* But the questions in the two surveys were phrased differently, making it doubtful that they can meaningfully be compared.
44. Granfield, *op. cit.*, p. 180.
45. See the discussion of this point in Chapter 8, pp. 285–86.
46. See also Harriet Pilpel, "The Right of Abortion," *Atlantic Monthly*, 223 (June 1968), pp. 68–71.
47. Lucas, *op. cit.*, p. 755.

48. *Ibid.*, p. 777.
49. *Ibid.*, p. 777.
50. Herbert L. Packer, *The Limits of the Criminal Sanction* (Stanford: Stanford University Press, 1968), p. 344.
51. Norman St. John-Stevas, *Life, Death and the Law* (Bloomington: Indiana University Press, 1961), pp. 15 and 39. As mentioned in the previous chapter, he did not invoke this principle in the case of abortion; but it is applicable.
52. I am drawing, in part, here from *Abortion: An Ethical Discussion, op. cit.,* pp. 18ff.
53. *Abortion: An Ethical Discussion, op. cit.,* p. 19.

CHAPTER 14

On Making Abortion Decisions

AT THE BEGINNING of this book, I pointed out the difficulty if not impossibility of a value-free analysis of abortion. The data one chooses to discuss or thinks important to consider, the strategy chosen to organize and deploy it, and the method of analysis used all depend upon the aims and presuppositions, conscious or unconscious, of the person trying to grapple with the problem. One's view of reality, man and society inevitably come into play; and one's personal history, though possible to disguise from others by the choice of an impersonal style, will also have an impact. To think about abortion ought to be an exercise in which one meditates not only on the available empirical evidence or the opinions and convictions of others, but also about oneself. What do I take to be the source of meaning and value in the world? Where have my own ethical principles come from and how well have I thought them through? How have my own personal experiences, perhaps representative, perhaps not, shaped my thinking? How free have I been in my thinking? Am I perhaps a victim of my own history, whether that history is one in which I was shaped at an early age or one in which my present life space—my friends, my circle, my particular subculture—makes the decisive difference? What do I aspire to, both for myself and for my society?

This book has been an attempt to think through the problem of abortion. It has set forth as much of the relevant data as seemed necessary, while trying in the process to cope with some of the leading philosophical difficulties which arise when an attempt is made to read, interpret and use the data. This approach meant a great deal of circling around the problem, probing at it from different angles; an effort has been made not to close possible approaches in advance. At the same time, however, a considerable amount of bracketing has taken place. I have tried to show that the problem is, most fundamentally, a moral problem; what one makes of questions and answers concerning abortion "indications" will be a reflection of a moral stance, whether recognized or not. The laws that one thinks good or bad, wise or unwise, progressive or retrogressive will be a function of what one thinks important or unimportant for society. I have also tried to argue that, for all of its vagueness and the disagreement it engenders, the principle of the sanctity of life is still highly serviceable in trying to develop some moral concepts and attitudes about abortion. As a principle, it is best interpreted as one which establishes a bias toward the protection and furtherance of human life, even nascent, uncertain and undeveloped human life. In trying to deal with the question of when human life "begins," I made the case that much depends upon what is to be made of the concept of "human." I tried to show that a rich, biologically based definition, giving ample room to the importance of teleological direction and unactualized potentiality was most helpful and, at the same time, most consistent with the practice of a number of disciplines concerned with the "human." I concluded, in a somewhat tentative fashion—the only way I believe a discussion of that problem can conclude—that the "developmental school" seemed the most persuasive, but also that the other leading schools, the genetic and the social, had valuable insights to offer, none of which should be entirely cut off.

The final stage of the bracketing process (Chapters 12 and 13) involved trying to show that the moral one-dimensionality of the traditional Catholic and the more recent abortion-on-request positions render them inadequate to illuminate sufficiently the full complexity of the abortion problem. Each, though, makes a fundamental point well worth including in a more comprehensive moral position: that unborn human life, even very early life, ought to be respected and included within the pro-life bias of the principle of the sanctity of life; and that the right of women to procreative self-determination, though not absolute, is a right to be honored and implemented.

If the foregoing chapters have proceeded more by process of winnowing out the weaker options than by promoting the stronger—for the need seemed to be that of bracketing the possibilities and gradually excluding the less promising directions—the need now is for something in the way of more decisive statements. But they can be decisive only up to a point. Abortion decisions need to be made in the light of moral policies, and a "moral policy" is best conceived of as the decision to move in one possible general direction rather than another. A policy points a way, sets some limits and tries to clarify meaningfully the options available within a given range. It does not lay out a moral blueprint, with every eventuality determined in advance, every rule set permanently and every aspect of the problem placed in a clearly labeled pigeonhole. Perhaps some moral problems can be solved in this way. But the problem of abortion cannot. That is, at any rate, my own conclusion. Abortion does not seem to me the kind of moral issue which is just "solved" once and for all; it can only be coped with. On the personal level, there are any number of human situations where abortion decisions will be difficult; a woman, however conscientious, may not know exactly the right thing to do. On the legal level, there are no known legal solutions which are problem-free; they all have some liabilities. A moral policy can help provide some coherence and a sense of direction when concrete decisions, either legal or personal, have to be made. Many cases calling for a decision will pose no special problems—the policy will make the decision relatively simple; but other instances may present greater complexities.

The question of a wise moral policy on abortion arises at three levels, which, while they overlap, are distinguishable. It arises at the legal level, when society as a whole tries to decide what kind of laws, if any, it should have on abortion. It arises at the personal level for those women who want or are drawn to the termination of an unwanted pregnancy. It arises at the more general social level, where, either apart from or in addition to whatever laws there may be, society decides what its general attitude toward abortion will be. At each of these levels, the problem of abortion "indications" arises, not just at the legal level where they are now commonly an issue.

Abortion Laws

There are, in general, four possible solutions to the legal problem of abortion. There can be highly restrictive laws, making legal abortion generally unavailable in all save the most extreme circumstances. There can be moderate laws, which specify a wide range of acceptable indications and a formal procedure to be followed in applying for an abortion. There can be highly permissive laws, which specify a host of indications, so wide as to cover all possible reasons why a woman might not want a child. There can be even more permissive laws, which specify that, while a prescribed process must be followed and some indication chosen, the final decision is to be left to the woman. Finally, it is possible to remove all abortion laws from the books, leaving the ethics of its medical practice in the hands of doctors individually or in the hands of professional bodies, themselves totally free from government interference or supervision.

The worst possible laws on abortion are those which are highly restrictive. They lead to a large number of illegal abortions, hazardous enough in affluent countries, but all the more so in underdeveloped countries. If they succeed in keeping down the overall number of abortions, they do so at too high a price. Unenforced and unenforceable, they bring the law into disrepute. They have proved to be discriminatory. In a pluralistic society, they offend the conscience of many. They take from a woman's hands the possibility of making her own decision, thus restricting her freedom—but in doing so offer no compensatory or justifying gain for the common good. As a means of symbolizing a society's respect for unborn life, they are poor, too widely disregarded and known to be disregarded to give the symbol any real power. Society ought to have a high regard for nascent life, seeking to protect and further it, but restrictive abortion laws have not proved an effective way of exhibiting this regard.

Moderate abortion laws meet some of the solid complaints directed at restrictive codes, but they do not meet enough of them. They have not shown themselves able to effect a significant reduction of illegal abortions. In some areas, they have been difficult to administer equitably, usually as a consequence, in pluralistic societies, of different attitudes and practices among doctors and hospitals, both difficult to change merely by a change in the law. While moderate laws succeed in widening the range of acceptable indications, they still exclude many women who want and one way or the other will get (illegally if necessary) an abortion. While a moderate law, permissively interpreted, as in Sweden since 1965, can overcome many of the problems of such laws, it does so by administrative rather than legislative means. That solution leaves open the possibility of arbitrary actions and policies on the part of those who administer the laws.

It is not difficult to understand why the goal of a repeal of all abortion laws should have a strong appeal, especially in the light of the known liabilities of restrictive and moderate laws. Repeal holds out the promise of freedom for women to make their own choice, the absence of legal control and supervision of the medical profession in the practice of abortion, and an obviating of the possibility of arbitrary or inequitable interpretations of abortion laws. Such a course might also serve notice that it is beyond the competence of the government to distinguish among the kinds and developmental levels of human life, thus leaving biomoral problems in the hands of individuals.

Nonetheless, it is not necessarily evident that the course of repeal would achieve its own ends, in the first place, or fully meet the broad, underlying problem of the causes of abortion, in the second. To the extent that repeal is aimed at extending to the full the scope of female freedom, there is no evidence—for it has not been tried—that it would do anything more than to bring about a minimal freedom, that of asking for and getting an abortion. But maximal freedom—which alone can give full substance to women's rights—could well require more than that. It would require freedom from external coercion to have an abortion, the availability of meaningful alternatives to abortion, time to think over the decision to abort, and helpful counseling about the best course to follow in the instance of an unwanted pregnancy. Moreover, if, as seems the case throughout the world, some of the social causes of abortion—poverty, housing shortages, ignorance or unavailability of effective contraceptives, the social difficulties of illegitimacy and the like—reflect upon society as a whole, then a simple repeal of abortion laws would make no contribution toward an amelioration of these causes; it would be a palliative only. The drawbacks of *laissez-faire* economics and medicine, which has erroneously assumed that maximum freedom is guaranteed by maximum individual choice and noninterference from government, could possibly be repeated in the area of abortion: there could be the appearance of freedom, but not the substance.

However, even if a palliative only, it is one which women should be free to take advantage of. It would give them an option they do not now have, not forcing them to wait for social reforms which may never arrive, at least during their child-bearing years. This would be particularly the case in developing countries.

The most balanced legal codes now in existence are those which are permissive but regulated by law. An ideal law—most closely approximated in some of the East European countries—would meet the following specifications: (1) It would permit abortion on request up to that point where the medical danger of abortion becomes a concern (normally about 12 weeks); thereafter serious reasons would be required and the decision would not wholly be the woman's (though her voice ought to continue, even then, to carry the greatest weight). This specification would meet the woman's right argument to a considerable degree. (2) It would offer—but not require—prior to the abortion, a formal counseling process by at least one trained person other than the doctor who would perform the operation. During it, (a) an attempt would be made to determine whether a woman's expressed wishes reflect her real wishes; (b) information would be provided her about the nature of the medical procedure and any possible medical consequences; (c) alternatives to abortion would be offered to her—if available—whether in the form of financial assistance, psychiatric counseling, the aid of a mother's helper for a sufficient period after birth, marriage counseling if that is the problem, assistance in finding better housing, and so on. This provision would be designed to maximize the options open to women. (3) It would provide for free abortions for all women who desire an abortion, as well as providing free assistance of the kind needed to bear and raise a child if that option is chosen. (4) It would require a contraceptive counseling and assistance process after an abortion was performed. The aim here would be to prevent further abortions.

(5) It would include a "conscience clause" for doctors and nurses, as well as specifying those conditions under which a doctor could, on medical grounds, refuse to perform an abortion. Thus it would seek to protect the medical and human rights of doctors, not forcing them to act against their conscience or their medical judgment. (6) It would require that all abortions be performed by trained medical personnel and be recorded for statistical purposes.

It is not my intention to present a model law. That is a task for lawyers and legislators, to be performed within the setting of particular states or countries. I simply want to suggest what would seem the main ingredients of a good law. Such a law should seek to accomplish a variety of ends. It should seek to give women optimal freedom. It should seek to express the serious concern of society about abortion. It should express society's respect for unborn life. It should try to provide maximum freedom for everyone concerned with abortion decisions: the women who must make the decisions, the doctors who must perform the abortions, and the society which has a stake in the number, kind and quality of legal abortions. By its provision for the offering of alternative solutions to women and by its requirement for postabortion contraception counseling and assistance, it would reflect society's interest in reducing the number of abortions and the need for abortion. It would also indicate that, in the eyes of society, abortion does not represent by any means the ideal way to limit unwanted pregnancies.

The possibility of a state's or a country's enacting such a law (quite apart from its political prospects) would, of course, be conditioned by many medical and economic factors. It would be almost impossible in most underdeveloped countries at present meaningfully to present a full range of alternatives to a woman; such countries do not have the money, the facilities or the trained personnel to make the alternatives available. It is not possible even in most of the developed countries. Even so, however, an established counseling agency, available to those who choose to make use of it, would still remain desirable even in the poorest countries, and the law might at least look forward to and be an instrument of pressure for expanded maternal-aid facilities. Ideally, abortion assistance, advice and operations should be part of a more general medical-welfare program, open to all without cost; that appears to be the *sine qua non* of equitable abortion policies. Ideally also, abortion legislation and practice should be part of a more general maternal-aid program, set within a wide range of educational, assistance and counseling programs, dealing with all aspects of procreation, family planning, prenatal and postnatal maternal and child care.

To state ideals, however, is not the same as confronting social, economic and political realities. The laws would have to be adapted to these realities. In the United States, for instance, it may prove far less difficult in the long run to get abortion laws repealed or declared unconstitutional than to institute adequate medical- and maternal-welfare programs. In the absence of such programs, either a repeal of abortion laws or the enactment of the kind of permissive law suggested here would represent only a minimal gain. The poor would still suffer the effects of *de facto* discrimination, for they would, by and large, have to pay for their own abortions, and pay, moreover, the price which the American medical supply-and-demand economic system would choose to exact.

Prescinding from these problems and assuming that the ideal could be approximated in some places, what could one expect from such a law? One could—following the conclusions in Chapter 8—expect a significant reduction in the number of illegal abortions, a tremendous rise in the number of legal abortions and, most likely, a rise in the total number of all abortions, a rise in the number of young women and married women with few or no children having abortions. For some (perhaps a large number), abortion would become the primary method of birth control, especially among those who have not learned of effective contraceptives or have not learned to use the available ones effectively. For others, experienced in the use of contraceptives, abortion would become a much more widely used method of secondary protection against unwanted pregnancies. The likelihood of an abortion habit's developing among a significant number of women in affluent countries, where contraceptives are available and used, would be much less than in underdeveloped countries. Thus, while there would most likely be a rise in the total number of abortions in any country which moved from a restrictive to a permissive legal code, it would probably be comparatively less in affluent countries.

In countries which, on the one hand, lack adequate medical facilities and personnel, a shift to a permissive law would undoubtedly place a tremendous amount of pressure on existing resources. Countries which, on the other, have potentially sufficient medical facilities but which do not have adequate medical-welfare programs, could expect a considerable amount of confusion, the likelihood of continuing economic discrimination, imbalanced pressures on medical facilities (depending, for instance, on geographic locality, harrassed and overpressured doctors. By granting doctors the right to refuse to perform an abortion—thereby excluding abortion on demand (understood literally)—the possibility of conflict will remain. This possibility, however, will be considerably reduced if (*a*) the law grants a *prima facie* right to the woman to have the abortion she requests (implying the need for a formal and direct refusal rather than circumvention on the part of a dissenting doctor), and (*b*) the woman is left perfectly free to seek another doctor, one willing to do the abortion. As the British experience since 1968 would suggest, though, problems will remain as long as doctors are granted rights. This seems inevitable and unavoidable, the necessary price to be paid for allowing doctors to maintain their own integrity.

The permissive law proposed here would carry its own set of serious problems; it would replace one set of difficulties with another. Yet it represents a way of trying to cope with the even more serious problems of restrictive and moderate codes: illegal abortion, restriction on woman's procreative and sexual freedom, the enforcement problems of restrictive codes. The possibility, in the long run, of reducing the large number of abortions which could be expected under a permissive code would be dependent upon the successful development of even better contraceptives than those now available together with improved programs of sex education and contraception instruction. The success of a few of the smaller, more intensive abortion-prevention programs here and there in the world through the use of contraception leaves room seriously to hope for the development of larger programs, though necessarily assisted by better contraceptives to make them more widely successful, in the future.

The premise of the kind of law suggested here is that of increased individual freedom for everyone who would be involved in an abortion decision, especially the woman herself and the doctor who performs the abortion. Yet as the practice of some East European countries and Japan shows, abortion laws and governmental regulations on abortion have been influenced by demographic concern, either because of a too high or a too low birthrate. Proposals have also been made to liberalize abortion laws as a method of population control.[1] While these proposals want to build upon an existing desire to limit family size—making abortion voluntarily available as an effective method of birth limitation— Kingsley Davis has raised the possibility of a requirment that illegitimate pregnancies be terminated.[2] Extreme wariness would seem in order about these proposals, especially those which look forward to legally coerced abortions. In extreme situations, underpopulation or overpopulation, it may be necessary for countries to look toward radical solutions. Their very existence may be at stake or the prospect of massive starvation may, obviously enough, threaten life in the most drastic way. Nonetheless, enforced abortion would be the least desirable method of meeting the problem.

The very large problem of coercion in family-planning and population-control programs raises issues too large to be discussed here, but a few comments are in order. If a nation decided to manipulate its abortion laws as an instrument of birth limitation, it would seem imperative that this be done by democratic means; it would have to represent the decision of the people and not that of a self-chosen few. The patent danger is that either a political élite, not responsible to the people for their actions, or a technocratic élite, able and willing to disguise their real reasons for wanting abortion laws changed, would directly impose or subtly foist abortion laws or the removal of such laws on the citizenry. A decision to change abortion laws for the sake of population control, with its far-reaching implications for the future of a country, should only, in justice, be one made by the people as a whole with their eyes wide open. If this should be true even in situations where abortion would be used voluntarily, taking advantage of the desire of individuals to limit family size, it would be all the more important in dealing with any proposals for enforced abortion. Indeed, the very notion of the forceful invasion of a woman's body, a coerced operation, is morally, legally and politically repugnant. It is hard to see how any situation, however dire, could make this acceptable: and it would take far more than a majority approval (for there are limits even to majority views) to make such a step justifiable. The overarching moral problem here is what has been referred to as "species-rights" (Chapter 9), which, I have argued, could in some circumstances—the likely extinction of the entire human species or that of a whole people—take precedence over individual rights, perhaps even the individual's right to life. But clearly one is speaking here of a moral problem which goes beyond those which the human species has experience in dealing with; it takes us into an unexplored moral cave (which will remain unexplored here).

Another problem worth considering, of a very different and less obscure kind, is whether the kind of law I have proposed does not render all further public discussion of abortion "indications" superfluous. If it is the woman herself who is to be allowed to make the final decision, regardless of whether others think it a good decision or not, is there any room left for a analysis of "indications"? I believe that discussion and analysis would be as important as ever. The goal of a permissive law should be that of removing the necessity that a woman convince others, who in effect thus sit in judgment upon her, that she ought to be allowed to have an abortion. But this ought not to mean that the medical profession or those who would be in a position to guide and counsel women or the women themselves should cease attempting to inform their own thinking. For instance, the known facts about the potential risk of fetal abnormalities from a variety of possible causes should be made known to a woman considering an abortion; these facts will undoubtedly influence the type of counseling she might receive and her own decision as well. The same thing can be said of medical indications—where the comparative physical risk of continuing a pregnancy would be a critical piece of information—and of social and economic indications as well. A continuing discussion of the problem of "indications," in professional as well as general writings, would thus remain as important as ever. A permissive law would not nullify the need for information and informed professional and private judgment. The only difference is that the discussion would be shifted from the often coercive forum of legal decisions to the healthier one of a desire for greater knowledge and wiser judgments.

Abortion Decisions: Personal Morality

The strength of pluralistic societies lies in the personal freedom they afford individuals. One is free to choose among religious, philosophical, ideological and political creeds; or one can create one's own highly personal, idiosyncratic moral code and view of the universe. Increasingly, the individual is free to ignore the morals, manners and mores of society. The only limitations are upon those actions which seem to present clear and present dangers to the common good, and even there the range of prohibited actions is diminishing as more and more choices are left to personal and private decisions. I have contended that, apart from some regulatory laws, abortion decisions should be left, finally, up to the women themselves. Whatever one may think of the morality of abortion, it cannot be established that it poses a clear and present danger to the common good. Thus society does not have the right decisively to interpose itself between a woman and the abortion she wants. It can only intervene where it can be shown that some of its own interests are at stake *qua* society. Regulatory laws of a minimal kind therefore seem in order, since in a variety of ways already mentioned society will be effected by the number, kind and quality of legal abortions. In short, with a few important stipulations, what I have been urging is tantamount to saying that abortion decisions should be private decisions. It is to accept, in principle, the contention of those who believe that, in a free, pluralistic society, the woman should be allowed to make her own moral choice on abortion and be allowed to implement that choice.

But pluralistic societies also lay a few traps for the unwary. It is not a large psychological step from saying that individuals should be left free to make up their own minds on some crucial moral issues (of which abortion is one) to an adoption of the view that one personal decision is as good as another, that any decision is a good one as long as it is honest or sincere, that a free decision equals a correct decision. However short the psychological step, the logical gap is very large. As absence of cant, hypocrisy and coercion may prepare the way for good personal decisions. But that is only to clean the room, and something must then be put in it. The hazard is that, once cleaned, it will be filled with capriciousness, sentimentality, a thinly disguised conformity to the reigning moral taste, or strongly felt but inadequately analyzed moral opinions. This is a particular danger in affluent pluralistic societies, heavily dominated by popular tastes, communication media and the absence of shared values. Philosophically, the view that all values are equally good and all private moral choices on a par is all but dead; but it still has a strong life at the popular level, where there is a tendency to act as if, once personal freedom is legally and socially achieved, moral questions cease to exist.

A considerable quantity of literature exists in the field of ethics concerned with such problems as subjective and objective values, the meaning and use of ethical principles and moral rules, the role of intentionality. That literature need not be reviewed here. But it is directly to the point to observe that a particular failing of the abortion-on-request literature is that it persistently scants the moral problem of how a woman, if granted the desired legal freedom to make her own decision about abortion, should go about making that decision. Up to a point, this deficiency is understandable. The immediate tactical problem has been to get the laws changed or repealed; that has been the burden of the public struggle, which has concentrated on statutes and legislators rather than on the moral contents and problems of personal decision-making. It is reasonable and legitimate to say that a woman should be left free to make the decision in the light of her own personal values; that is, I believe, the best legal solution. But it leaves totally untouched the question of how, once freedom is achieved, she ought to go about the personal business of forming a coherent, rational, sensitive moral perspective and opinion on abortion. After freedom, what then? Society may have no right to demand that a woman give it good reasons why she should have an abortion before permitting it. But this does not entail that the woman should not, as a morally responsible person, have good reasons to justify her desires or acts in her own eyes.

This is only to say that a solution of the legal problem is not the same as a solution to the moral problem. That the moral struggle is transferred from the public to the private sphere should not be taken to mean that the moral problem has been solved; only its public aspect, under a permissive law or a repeal of all laws, has been dealt with. The personal problem will remain.

Some women will be part of a religious group or ethical tradition which they freely choose and which can offer them something, possibly very much, in the way of helpful moral insight consistent with that tradition. The obvious course in that instance is for them to turn to their tradition to see what it has to offer them on the particular problem of abortion.[3] But what of those who have no tradition to repair to or those who find their tradition wanting on this problem? One way or another, they will have to find some way of developing a set of ethical principles and moral rules to help them act responsibly, to justify their own conduct in their own eyes. To press the problem to a finer point, what ought they to think about as they try to work out their own views on abortion?

Only a few suggestions will be made here, taking the form of arguing for an ethic of personal responsibility which tries, in the process of decision-making, to make itself aware of a number of things. The biological evidence should be considered, just as the problem of methodology must be considered; the philosophical assumptions implicit in different uses of the word "human" need to be considered; a philosophical theory of biological analysis is required; the social consequences of different kinds of analyses and different meaning of the word "human" should be thought through; consistency of meaning and use should be sought to avoid *ad hoc* and arbitrary solutions.

It is my own conviction that the "developmental school" offers the most helpful and illuminating approach to the problem of the beginning of human life, avoiding, on the one hand, a too narrow genetic criterion of human life and, on the other, a too broad and socially dangerous social definition of the "human." Yet the kinds of problems which appear in any attempt to decide upon the beginning of life suggest that no one position can be either proved or disproved from biological evidence alone. It becomes a question of trying to do justice to the evidence while, at the same time, realizing that how the evidence is approached and used will be a function of one's way of looking at reality, one's moral policy, the values and rights one believes need balancing, and the type of questions one thinks need to be asked. At the very least, however, the genetic evidence for the uniqueness of zygotes and embryos (a uniqueness of a different kind than that of the uniqueness of sperm and ova), their potentiality for development into a human person, their early development of human characteristics, their genetic and organic distinctness from the organism of the mother, appear to rule out a treatment even of zygotes, much less the more developed stages of the conceptus, as mere pieces of "tissue," of no human significance or value. The "tissue" theory of the significance of the conceptus can only be made plausible by a systematic disregard of the biological evidence. Moreover, though one may conclude that a conceptus is only potential human life, in the process of continually actualizing its potential through growth and development, a respect for the sanctity of life, with its bias in favor even of undeveloped life, is enough to make the taking of such life a moral problem. There is a choice to be made and it is a moral choice. In the near future, it is likely that some kind of simple, safe abortifacient drug will be developed, which either prevents implantation or destroys the conceptus before it can develop.[4] It will be tempting then to think that the moral dilemma has vanished, but I do not believe it will have.[5]

It is possible to imagine a huge number of situations where a woman could, in good and sensitive conscience, choose abortion as a moral solution to her personal or social difficulties. But, at the very least, the bounds or morality are overstepped when, either through a systematic intellectual negligence or a willful choosing of that moral solution most personally convenient, personal choice is deliberately made easy and problem-free. Yet it seems to me that a pressure in that direction is a growing part of the ethos of technological societies; it is easily possible to find people to reassure us that we need have no scruples about the way we act, whether the issue is war, the suppresion of rebellion and revolution, discrimination against minorities or the use of technological advances. Pluralism makes possible the achieving of freer, more subtle moral thinking; but it is a possibility constantly endangered by cultural pressures which would simplify or dissolve moral doubts and anguish.

The question of abortion "indications" returns at the level of personal choice. I have contended that the advent of permissive laws should not mean a cessation of efforts to explore the problem of "indications." When a woman asks herself, as she ought, whether her reasons for wanting an abortion are sound reasons—which presumes abortion is a serious enough moral issue to warrant the need to provide oneself with good reasons for choosing it—she will be asking herself about justifiable indications. Thus, transposed from the legal to the personal level, the kinds of concerns adumbrated in the earlier chapters on indications remain fully pertinent. It was argued in those chapters that, with the possible exception of exceedingly rare instances of a direct threat to the physical life of the mother, one cannot speak of general categories of abortion indications as *necessitating* an abortion. In a number of circumstances, abortion may be a wise and justifiable solution to a distressed pregnancy. But when the language of necessity is used, the implication is that no other conceivable alternative is available. It may be granted, willingly enough, that some set of practical circumstances in some (possibly very many) concrete cases may indicate that abortion is the only feasible option open. But these cases cannot readily be determined in advance, and, for that reason, it is necessary to say that no formal indication as such (e.g., a psychiatric indication) entails a necessary, predetermined choice in favor of abortion.

The word "indication" remains the best word, suggesting that a number of given circumstances will bring the possibility or desirability of abortion to the fore. But to escalate the concept of an indication into that of a required procedure is to go too far. Abortion is *one* way to solve the problem of an unwanted or hazardous pregnancy (physically, psychologically, economically or socially), but it is rarely the only way, at least in affluent societies (I would be considerably less certain about making the same statement about poor societies). Even in the most extreme cases—rape, incest, psychosis, for instance—alternatives will usually be available and different choices, open. It is not necessarily the end of every woman's chance for a happy, meaningful life to bear an illegitimate child. It is not necessarily the automatic destruction of a family to have a seriously defective child born into it. It is not necessarily the ruination of every family living in overcrowded housing to have still another child. It is not inevitable that every immature woman would become even more so if she bore a child or another child. It is not inevitable that a gravely handicapped child can hope for nothing from life. It is not inevitable that every unwanted child is doomed to misery. It is not written in the essence of things, as a fixed law of human nature, that a woman cannot come to accept, love and be a good mother to a child who was initially unwanted. Nor is it a fixed law that she could not come to cherish a grossly deformed child. Naturally, these are only generalizations. The point is only that human beings are as a rule flexible, capable of doing more than they sometimes think they can, able to surmount serious dangers and challenges, able to grow and mature, able to transform inauspicious beginnings into satisfactory conclusions. Everything in life, even in procreative and family life, is not fixed in advance; the future is never wholly unalterable.

Yet the problem of personal question-asking must be pushed a step farther. The way the questions are answered will be very much determined by a woman's way of looking at herself and at life. A woman who has decided, as a personal moral policy, that nothing should be allowed to stand in the way of her own happiness, goals and self-interest will have no trouble solving the moral problem. For her, an unwanted pregnancy will, by definition, be a pregnancy to be terminated. But only by a Pickwickian use of words could this form of reasoning be called moral. It would preclude any need to consult the opinion of others, any need to examine the validity of one's own viewpoint, any need to, for instance, ask when human life begins, any need to interrogate oneself in any way, intellectually or morally; will and desire would be king.

Assuming, however, that most women would seek a broader ethical horizon than that of their exclusively personal self-interest, what might they think about when faced with an abortion decision? A respect for the sanctity of human life should, I believe, incline them toward a general and strong bias against abortion. Abortion is an act of killing, the violent, direct destruction of potential human life, already in the process of development. That fact should not be disguised, or glossed over by euphemism and circumlocution. It is not the destruction of a human person—for at no stage of its development does the conceptus fulfill the definition of a person, which implies a developed capacity for reasoning, willing, desiring and relating to others—but it is the destruction of an important and valuable form of human life. Its value and its potentiality are not dependent upon the attitude of the woman toward it; it grows by its own biological dynamism and has a genetic and morphological potential distinct from that of the woman. It has its own distinctive and individual future. If contraception and abortion are both seen as forms of birth limitation, they are distinctly different acts; the former precludes the possibility of a conceptus being formed, while the latter stops a conceptus already in existence from developing. The bias implied by the principle of the sanctity of human life is toward the protection of all forms of human life, especially, in ordinary circumstances, the protection of the right to life. That right should be accorded even to doubtful life; its existence should not be wholly dependent upon the personal self-interest of the woman.

Yet she has her own rights as well, and her own set of responsibilities to those around her; that is why she may have to choose abortion. In extreme situations of overpopulation, she may also have a responsibility for the survival of the species or of a people. In many circumstances, then, a decision in favor of abortion—one which overrides the right to life of that potential human being she carries within—can be a responsible moral decision, worthy neither of the condemnation of others nor of self-condemnation. But the bias of the principle of the sanctity of life is against a routine, unthinking employment of abortion; it bends over backwards not to take life and gives the benefit of the doubt to life. It does not seek to diminish the range of responsibility toward life —potential or actual—but to extend it. It does not seek the narrowest definition of life, but the widest and the richest. It is mindful of individual possibility, on the one hand, and of a destructive human tendency, on the other, to exclude from the category of "the human" or deny rights to those beings whose existence is or could prove burdensome to others.

The language used to describe abortion will have an important bearing on the sensitivities and imagination of those women who must make abortion decisions. Abortion can be talked about in the language of medical technology and technique—as, say, "a therapeutic procedure involving the emptying of the uterine contents." That language is neutral, clinical, unemotional. Or abortion can be talked about in the emotive language of relieving woman from suffering, or meeting the need for freedom among women, or saving a nation from a devastating overpopulation. Both kinds of language have their place, for abortion has more than one result and meaning and abortion can legitimately be talked about in more than one way. What is objectionable is a conscious manipulation of language to incite an irrational emotional response, to allay doubts or to mislead the imagination. Particularly misleading is one commonly employed mixture of rhetorical modes by advocates of abortion on request. That is the use of a detached, clinical language to describe the actual operation itself combined with an emotive rhetoric to evoke the personal and social goods which an abortion can bring about. Thus, when every effort is made to suggest that emotion and feeling are perfectly appropriate to describe the social and personal goals of abortion, but that a clinical language only is appropriate when the actual technique and medical objective of an abortion is described, then the moral imagination is being misled.

Any human act can be described in impersonal, technological language, just as any act can be described in emotive language. What is wanted is an equity in the language. It is fair enough and to the point to say that in many circumstances abortion will save a woman's health or her family. It only becomes misleading when the act itself, as distinguished from its therapeutic goal, is talked about in an entirely different way. For, abortion is not just an "emptying of the uterine contents." It is also an act of killing; there will be no abortion unless the conceptus is killed (or its further existence made impossible, which amounts to the same thing). If it is appropriate to evoke the imagination and elicit sympathy for those women in a distressed pregnancy who could be helped by abortion, it is no less appropriate to evoke the imagination about what actually occurs in an abortion "procedure."

Imagination should also come into play at another point. It is often argued by proponents of abortion that there is no need for a woman ever to take any chances in a distressed pregnancy, particularly in the instance of an otherwise healthy woman who, if she has an abortion on one occasion, could simply get pregnant again on another, more auspicious occasion. This might be termed the "replacement theory" of abortion indications: since fetus "x" can be replaced by fetus "y," then there is no reason why a woman should have any scruples about such a replacement. This way of conceiving the choices effectively dissolves them; it becomes important only to know whether a woman can get pregnant again when she wants to. But this strategy can be employed only at the price of convincing oneself that there is no difference whatever among embryos or fetuses, that they all have exactly the same potentiality. But even the sketchiest knowledge of the genetic uniqueness of each conceptus (save in the instance of monozygotic twins), and thus the different genetic potentialities of each, should raise doubts on that point. Yet, having said that, I would not want to deny that the possibility of a further pregnancy could have an important bearing on the moral reasoning of a woman whose present pregnancy was threatening. If, out of a sense of responsibility toward her present children or her present life situation, a woman decided that an abortion was the wisest, most moral course, then the possibility that she could become pregnant later, when these responsibilities would be less pressing, would be a pertinent consideration.

The goal of these remarks is to keep alive in the consciences of women who have an abortion choice a moral tension; and it is to hope that they will be willing to bear the pain and the uncertainty of having to make a moral choice. It is the automatic, unthinking and unimaginative personal solution of abortion questions which women themselves should be extremely wary of, either for or against an abortion. A woman can, with little trouble, find both people and books to reassure her that there is no problem about abortion at all; or people and books to convince her that she would be a moral monster if she chose abortion. A woman can choose in advance the views she will listen to and thus have her predispositions confirmed. Yet a willingness to keep alive a moral tension, and to be wary of precipitous solutions, presupposes two things. First, that the woman herself wants to do what is right, realizing that what is right may not always be that which is most convenient, most easy or most immediately apt to solve a pressing problem. It is simply not the case that what one wants to do, or would like to do, or is predisposed to do is necessarily the right thing to do. A willingness seriously to entertain that moral perception—which, of course, does not in itself imply a decision for or against an abortion—is one sign of moral seriousness.

Second, moral seriousness presupposes one is concerned with the protection and furthering of life. This means that, out of respect for human life, one bends over backwards not to eliminate human life, not to desensitize oneself to the meaning and value of potential life, not to seek definitions of the "human" which serve one's self-interest only. A desire to respect human life in all of its forms means, therefore, that one voluntarily imposes upon oneself a pressure against the taking of life; that one demands of oneself serious reasons for doing so, even in the case of a very early embryo; that one use not only the mind but also the imagination when a decision is being made; that one seeks not to evade the moral issues but to face them; that one searches out the alternatives and conscientiously entertains them before turning to abortion. A bias in favor of the sanctity of human life in all of its forms would include a bias against abortion on the part of women; it would be the last rather than the first choice when unwanted pregnancies occurred. It would be an act to be avoided if at all possible.

A bias of this kind, voluntarily imposed by a woman upon herself, would not trap her; for it is also part of a respect for the dignity of life to leave the way open for an abortion when other reasonable choices are not available. For she also has duties toward herself, her family and her society. There can be good reasons for taking the life even of a very late fetus; once that also is seen and seen as a counterpoise in particular cases to the general bias against the taking of potential life, the way is open to choose abortion. The bias of the moral policy implies the need for moral rules which seek to preserve life. But, as a policy which leaves room for choice—rather than entailing a fixed set of rules —it is open to flexible interpretation when the circumstances point to the wisdom of taking exception to the normal ordering of the rules in particular cases. Yet, in that case, one is not genuinely taking exception to the rules. More accurately, one would be deciding that, for the preservation or furtherance of other values or rights—species-rights, person-rights—a choice in favor of abortion would be serving the sanctity of life. That there would be, in that case, conflict between rights, with one set of rights set aside (reluctantly) to serve another set, goes without saying. A subversion of the principle occurs when it is made out that there is no conflict and thus nothing to decide.

The Social Problem

If it is possible to distinguish sharply between public law and private morality, it would be a mistake to think the problem of abortion has been met when those two realms have been pondered and some general principles achieved. There is still a third realm, the social, where mores and attitudes will have an impact on individual decisions. In terms of law, my argument has gone in the direction of considerable permissiveness, toward abortion on request. In terms of private morality, it has gone in the opposite direction, toward relative strictness. Society should put few obstacles in the way of women who want abortions; in the end, the choice should be theirs. But women themselves should voluntarily put many obstacles in their own path; though again, the choice is theirs to do so or not. A nagging question at this point is whether, in a society with permissive laws, one can expect that most or many women will take the trouble to reason through the moral problem. Would not a change from a restrictive to a permissive law signal women that the moral bias against abortion had been dissipated and that those who want abortions for whatever reason have the support and approval of society in getting them? It is very rare for laws to be changed solely out of a concern for procedural questions of freedom and due process. They are usually changed because of a shift in the thinking or the attitudes of the public toward the substantive issues at stake. Laws are rarely passed, changed or repealed independently of public opinion; on the contrary, the changes they undergo will reflect that opinion to a considerable degree. This will be true of abortion laws as well.

While restrictive abortion laws have been shown to be ineffective and unenforceable, they nevertheless have the effect of applying some degree of social pressure against abortion. A change from restrictive to permissive laws will, then, indeed signal a change in public attitudes and will reduce the social pressure. Every country which has changed its laws in a permissive direction has seen an initial and usually, with few exceptions so far (Poland and Japan), a sustained and continuing rise in the number of legal abortions. Not all of this rise can necessarily be attributed to a shift from the illegal to the legal sector. On the contrary, the "changing clientele" observable in permissive systems points to the addition of new abortion consumers as a result of the change. This would suggest not only the obvious fact of greater access to abortion, but also, and more importantly in the present context, of a greater social acceptance of abortion. Hence, it seems only realistic to say that the introduction of permissive laws will—if the worldwide data tell us anything—increase the total number of abortions; and this will be a direct result of the increased public acceptability which led to the laws' being changed. (Whether this will hold true in societies already using effective contraceptives is not clear; there is as yet no data on the point.) Put in graphic terms, more embryos and fetuses will be killed after a change in the law (though there will be fewer deaths and injuries from abortion). Put in terms of mores, more women will, under a permissive law, make a moral choice in favor of abortion. Given a choice, they will choose not only in terms of their own personal morality but also in terms of what appears to them socially acceptable. Their choice in favor of abortion will be all the easier if it seems to have public support, especially if their personal morality is such as to incline them toward it in the first place. And as we have seen from the experience of the East European countries and Japan, an abortion habit on the part of a large number of women can be expected in a permissive system, a habit not easy to break by means of contraceptive methods of birth control.

In sum, a permissive law and the public attitudes needed to bring it into existence seem anything but conducive to the engendering of a relatively strict personal morality on the part of women drawn to abortion. This is an important dilemma and it should not be skirted. The reason why countries with permissive laws have been uneasy about them is that they have too many abortions. While the reasons, in turn, why they have too many are complex, an important element in the equation is that too many women select abortion who could choose some other means of birth limitation or could take advantage of some of the available social alternatives to abortion.

Yet the experience of the East European and Scandinavian countries in recent years points a way. For, while these countries already have permissive laws or are in the process of writing such laws, they have not hesitated to conduct extensive educational programs against abortion. They have also worked toward the development of effective contraception programs and toward a good social- and maternal-welfare system which tries to make abortion less necessary and appear as a less inevitable choice for women. Abortion is permitted, but it is not promoted or romanticized by the governments. They use every means—though sometimes efficiently and sometimes not—to inform the public that (a) they should try to avoid getting caught in situations where they will need abortions—which means they should use effective contraceptives; (b) there are nonabortion alternatives available to women with unwanted pregnancies; but that (c) all else failing, abortion is available.

That these efforts have not succeeded so far, for the most part, in reducing the number or ratio of abortions does not tell against the wisdom of the programs or the direction of their public policy. Once it has been decided that restrictive laws are not desirable (as having too many bad side effects on women's freedom and health), then there is no choice (assuming a large number of abortions are not desirable either) but that of trying to strike a balance. The balance is between making abortion freely available while at the same time keeping up a steady pressure against its spread, and particularly against the establishment of an abortion habit, which occurs when large numbers of women begin making an habitual choice in favor of abortion as their chosen method of birth limitation, despite the existence of alternative methods.

The aim is obviously not that of keeping women who need abortions from having them; on the contrary, it is to make them available, cheaply and equitably, for those women. The aim is to influence women who do not, or should not in the ordinary course of their lives, need an abortion away from having them—but even then by means of contraception and welfare programs rather than by coercive means. This is to try and strike a balance, and, like all balances, not everything desired is likely to be achieved at the same time or without paying some price. So far, most permissive systems have not shown themselves able to bring down the number of abortions by means of contraception and welfare programs. A repeal of all abortion laws has nowhere been tried; thus its possible effects cannot be gauged. Until very recently, most abortion codes have operated under the serious collateral handicap of either a lack of available effective contraceptives or the difficulty of educating large numbers of women in a very short time to change their birth-limitation practices and attitudes. In that respect, it cannot fairly be said yet that permissive laws have proved a failure in reducing abortion. They have hardly had the time or the means to establish themselves. In any case, given the dual desire for female freedom and a reduction in the number of and need for abortions, it is hard to envision how any wiser balance could be struck. That the best balance one can strike does not work perfectly hardly entails the conclusion that a better one can be found. I do not, anyway, know what it could be.

The test of the seriousness of the will to strike a balance will lie in the efforts made to provide alternatives to abortion. That is the hard part for, while a change to a permissive abortion law can be a difficult enough battle, massive changes in social and welfare programs will strike at the self-interests of many people concerned to maintain a self-advantageous economic individualism. The East European and Scandinavian countries begin with the major advantage of highly organized, well-financed social and medical programs. A structure exists which makes possible abortion prevention and dissuasion efforts. That is not the case in the United States for reasons of political opposition and in most underdeveloped countries for reasons of poverty. While a large number of abortions are surely desired for what could be called "subjective reasons," that is, reasons having more to do with a woman's personal life goals than with external pressures, a large number, the evidence indicates, are for these latter reasons.

A good abortion-prevention program, one which seeks to use persuasive rather than coercive means, requires a number of critical ingredients in the society as a whole. There must be a good program of sexual education, beginning early in the life of a child. Inexpensive, effective contraceptives must be available and their use promoted in the society. Where it is not already done, such as in the United States, these programs must include teenagers and the unmarried generally. There must be ample provisions made for the health and welfare of women who bear illegitimate children, as well as, beyond that, the creation of a social atmosphere which accepts the unwed mother and her child. There must be ample child-care facilities, making it possible for working women to have children, just as their must be ample welfare and housing programs to provide help—and of a kind which enables them to retain their dignity and self-respect—to those families which need it. There must be facilities and trained personnel to care for and train the handicapped, as well as continued and accelerated research on the myriad genetic and other causes of malformation and deformity. Where present laws interfere with these goals they should be changed.

Abortion, to be seen in its full context, must be viewed against the background of the society in which it occurs. Abortion in underdeveloped countries or among the poor in developed countries can hardly be attributed to a lack of morality among the thousands of women who resort to it: only desperation of the most intense kind could lead so many women to take so many extreme risks not to have a child. That tells us more about the social conditions of a country than about the women themselves.[6]

Besides the right of women not to be forced to live under conditions which make abortion their only choice—and that is as much a feminine right as the right to choose an abortion—the promotion of the necessary welfare and health programs would be a way for society to proclaim its respect for unborn life. It would be saying that such life is not to be needlessly, casually, or, by, force of dire circumstance, coercively taken. But this has to be shown by its actions, and not by mere finger-wagging or pious hopes. The restrictive laws in most American states are doubly wrong. They are wrong in refusing women the right to choose an abortion; and they are wrong in being set within a social context which too rarely offers women any real help in finding viable alternatives to abortion. Too many women—especially the poor—can thus choose neither an abortion nor any reasonable alternative to an abortion. They are deprived of their rights at two levels. Those women, particularly the blacks, who look upon white proposals to liberalize abortion laws for their benefit as a suspicious kind of offering are able to see something others miss. An offering of half the loaf of freedom, that freedom which would enable them only to have fewer children, is a half-offer. Robert Coles has cited the moving words of a black mother on the point:

They say no, no—no more kids; the welfare worker she tells you you're "overpopulating" the world, and something has to be done. But right now one of the few times I feel good is when I'm pregnant, and I can feel I'm getting somewhere, at least then I am—because I'm making something grow, and not seeing everything die around me, like all it does in this street, I'll tell you. They want to give me the pill and stop the kids, and I'm willing for the most part; but I wish I could take care of all the kids I could have, and then I'd want plenty of them. Or maybe I wouldn't. I wouldn't have to be pregnant to feel hope about things. I don't know; you can look at it both ways, I guess.[7]

The credibility of advocates of legalized abortion under the banner of female freedom and "the wanted child" is weakened when their zeal for a change in abortion laws is not matched by a comparable zeal to change those social conditions which force many women to choose abortion. An analogous problem often arises with conservative Christian opponents of abortion: they speak vividly of the alternatives conceivably open to a woman but do all too little to press for those reforms which would make the alternatives actually available. They often also unrealistically fall back on the utopian conceivability of such alternatives as a reason not to change presently restrictive laws.

Would the existence of good medical, maternal and social programs serve, in the long run, to bring down the number of abortions (their concrete value) or serve to proclaim society's concern for unborn life (their pedagogic and symbolic value)? It is impossible to answer this question with full certainty, but it is not unrealistic to hope that they will eventually bear fruit. That abortions have been dropping in Japan and Poland, even if they have not begun to drop elsewhere (save in the special cases of Rumania and Bulgaria), is a clue that the trend of abortions in permissive systems is not irreversibly or inevitably upwards. If seemingly odd to the Western mind, the combination of a large number of abortions in Japan and a widespread belief that, in principle, abortion is not a good, may be very healthy; what one is forced by necessity to do ought not be the occasion to set aside the higher theory of one's ideals, which need to be kept alive.

While abortion has been practiced throughout human history, it has increasingly during recent decades taken on the coloration of technological society. This is true not only in the surface sense that the medical techniques of induced abortion have been refined, especially with the introduction of the vacuum aspirator, but also in the deeper sense of participating in a technological ethos. It is of the essence of that ethos that man should control his own destiny, make his own choices and use, rather than be used by, nature. The search for a safe, effective and simple means of birth limitation, whether for the sake of greater freedom of procreative choice among women or for the limitation of population growth, goes on. Induced abortion, used informally and illegally for centuries, is gradually being added to the formal and legal repertoire of population limitation methods. For the most part, it is desperation which has led to this development; when good means are not available, people will turn to otherwise distasteful means. This is hardly a happy situation. The emergence of the discipline of fetology—which seeks to find ways of improving and protecting prenatal life—has paralleled the emergence of a new acceptance of abortion. In one sense, there is a deep conflict here; fetology seeks to further, and abortion, to stop, the development of nascent life. Yet in another sense they seek the same ends: the control of the kind and quality of human life, together with the introduction of choice into a context where only passivity in the face of nature once seemed possible.

It may be counted a social and technological advance that abortion is becoming legally possible and medically safe as a method of procreation control where other methods have failed. But it is at best an advance to be looked upon with ambivalence. A single and faint cheer only is in order. Any method which requires the taking of human life, even though that life be far more potential than actual, falls short of the human aspiration, in mankind's better moments, of dignifying and protecting life. The time for loud cheering will come when, through a still more refined technological development, a method of birth control is discovered which does not require that we make a choice between the life of a conceptus and those other human values and goods we count important. It is possible to settle for and become comfortable with bad choices. It is better to seek good ones.

NOTES

1. See, for instance, Kingsley Davis, "Population Policy: Will Current Programs Succeed?" *Science*, 158 (November 1967), p. 732; Paul R. Ehrlich, *The Population Bomb* (New York: Ballantine Books, 1968), p. 139; Garrett Hardin, "The History and Future of Birth Control," *Perspectives in Biology and Medicine*, 10 (Autumn 1966), pp. 11–17; *cf.* Bernard Berelson, "Beyond Family Planning," *Studies in Family Planning*, no. 38 (February 1969), p. 4.
2. Davis, *op. cit.*, p. 738.
3. I have already cited the Catholic literature extensively. The Protestant theological writings, some of it already discussed in earlier chapters, though less extensive, provide a wealth of material for those who are part of that tradition. See, for instance, Helmut Thielicke, *The Ethics of Sex*, trans. John W. Doberstein (New York: Harper & Row, 1964), pp. 226–47; Dietrich Bonhoeffer, *Ethics*, trans. Neville Horton Smith (London: SCM Press, 1965), pp. 130ff.; Karl Barth, *Church Dogmatics* (Edinburgh: T. & T. Clark, 1961), III/4, pp. 416ff.; Joseph Fletcher, *Situation Ethics* (Philadelphia: Westminster Press, 1966), pp. 37–39 and *passim.*; Paul Ramsey, "The Morality of Abortion," in *Life or Death: Ethics and Options* (Seattle: University of Washington Press, 1968), pp. 60–93. The Jewish legal and theological literature on the problem is extensive. See especially David M. Feldman *Birth Control in Jewish Law* (New York University Press, 1968), pp. 251–94; Immanuel Jakovits, "Jewish Views on Abortion," in David T. Smith (ed.), *Abortion and the Law* (Cleveland: Western Reserve University, 1967), pp. 124–43.
4. The advent of such a drug or pill may not be so close as is generally thought. So far, the discovery of a safe "M-pill" or "A-pill" has eluded researchers in the field. See Lars Engstrom, "Experiences with F 6103, The Swedish 'M-pill,' " paper delivered at the International Conference on Abortion, Hot Springs, Virginia, November 17–20, 1968, in which Dr. Engstrom concludes that it will be some time before an "abortion pill" is available.
5. Garrett Hardin, for instance, would welcome the development of an oral abortifacient, which "taken on the twenty-sixth day of the menstrual cycle, would induce a period before the woman knew whether she was pregnant or not. The ambiguity of her action would protect her against emotional doubt" ("The History and Future of Birth Control," *op. cit.*, p. 17). It is curious morality which implies that ambiguous actions obviate moral problems and are to be sought to reduce "emotional doubt." If human responsibility for one's actions means anything, it ought to mean a willingness not to seek refuge in ambiguity or to run from the possibility of emotional doubt; one should want to know exactly what one is doing and what the consequences of one's actions are.
6. Among those who have put forward some helpful suggestions about the development of social alternatives are David Granfield, *The Abortion Decision* (New York: Doubleday, 1969), pp. 203–23; Jerome M. Kummer and Zad Leavy, "Therapeutic Abortion Law Confusion," *Journal of the American Medical Association*, 195 (January 10, 1966), p. 99; Robert E. Hall, "Abortion in American Hospitals," *American Journal of Public Health*, 57 (November 1967), p. 1936.
7. Robert Coles, "Who's to Be Born?," *The New Republic* (June 10, 1967), p. 12. Coles added his own comment on these words: "Some day, in a world that none of us alive will probably ever see, women like these . . . will find it unnecessary to weigh their lives and desires on those kinds of scales; and indeed all women will have a chance to do justice to the children they choose to bear" (*ibid.*).

Index